PATERNALISTIC INTERVENTION

STUDIES IN MORAL, POLITICAL,
AND LEGAL PHILOSOPHY

General Editor: Marshall Cohen

PATERNALISTIC INTERVENTION

The Moral Bounds
on Benevolence

Donald VanDeVeer

PRINCETON UNIVERSITY PRESS

PRINCETON, NEW JERSEY

170
V24p

Library of Congress Cataloging in Publication Data
will be found on the last printed page of this book
ISBN 0-691-07306-6

Publication of this book has been aided by
the Whitney Darrow Fund of Princeton University Press

This book has been composed in Linotron Palatino

Clothbound editions of Princeton University Press books
are printed on acid-free paper, and binding materials
are chosen for strength and durability

Printed in the United States of America
by Princeton University Press
Princeton, New Jersey

To my daughter, Lisa,
who helped me understand love and hope,
perseverance and patience.

CONTENTS

CONTENTS

CONTENTS

ACKNOWLEDGMENTS

Unlike many academics, I have had the pleasure of associating with critical yet supportive colleagues for all of my professional life. Most of these colleagues are or have been in the Department of Philosophy and Religion at North Carolina State University. For their most helpful comments on larger or smaller portions of my book manuscript, I am indebted to Paul Bredenberg, Robert Hambourger, Barbara Levenbook, Diane Lauver, Richard Nunan, Robert Simon, Maurice Wade, and Mary Anne Warren. I am especially grateful to Tom Regan for his keen responses to large portions of an earlier draft. For his encouragement, friendly provocation, and inexhaustible supply of counterexamples, it would be hard to have a better critic than W. R. Carter. Undoubtedly, the raised eyebrows of L. Carter (to whom I am grateful) also made me rethink my position on occasion. Some improvement in the writing is due to David Auerbach who, like a magician, detected the need for rewriting the manuscript without reading it. In the latter stages of developing and revising the volume, I profited from numerous, lengthy discussions with two pleasant, perceptive, and patient colleagues, Richard Wyatt and Christine Pierce. For these reasons, it is tempting to suggest that blame for the flaws in the book should be spread among this large group, but, not wishing to lose any remaining friends, I refrain from doing so. I believe that leaves only myself as responsible.

Substantial improvements resulted, I believe, from the vigorous, informed, and fair-minded critique of the entire manuscript by Allen Buchanan. It has also been my good fortune to have had the constant support and understanding of Robert Bryan, Head of the Department of Philosophy and Religion at North Carolina State University. His encouragement and consideration have made scholarship more likely in an undergraduate department whose faculty carries a full teaching load. Without a fellowship during 1980 to 1981 from the National Endowment for the Humanities and the concomitant cooperation of North Carolina State University at that time, *Paternalistic Intervention* would not exist.

I hope that the typing of large portions of the manuscript did not occasion the recent retirement of Ruth Boone. She was an enormous help. So also was, and is, Ann Rives—who, no doubt, will survive the horde of both departmental word and idea processors. It is hard to imagine the creation of this book without the expert help of the dynamic Boone-Rives duo. My thanks to each of them.

Sanford Thatcher of Princeton University Press has been a calm, cool and straightforward guide through the tedious months of navigating the choppy seas of publication. Finally, Ann Hirst has been an excellent copyeditor; I am grateful to her as well.

June 1985

PATERNALISTIC INTERVENTION

INTRODUCTION

The vast majority of those reading this sentence are, no doubt, former children. Hence, it should not be difficult to recall those occasions when, as children, we felt "knocked about" or hemmed in by constraints placed on us. Our urge to choose for ourselves, to explore, to experiment, to find our own way, to "do it ourselves," to take responsibility for our own lives was, at times, almost viscerally felt—like the awakening sexual inclination of an adolescent. Yet, to one degree or another, we were domesticated by barriers placed by adults. We were often told that when, and only when, we acquired the magical status of "being an adult" could we fully decide for ourselves and chart our own course—at least within some vaguely characterized moral constraints having to do with treating others decently or fairly. One favored rationale for the constraints to which we were subjected was that "it's wrong to treat others like that." Another, no less important, rationale was that "it's for your own good."

Arriving at adulthood we better understand that there are defensible limits to what we may do or choose, ones based on considerations of treating others fairly or the avoidance of wronging them. At the same time we find that there remains a wide array of other socially imposed constraints on our lives, constraints which are, still, said to be for our own good. Some are a matter of law, some a matter of institutional policy, some generated by the acts of friends or relatives. These paternalistically motivated constraints are morally troublesome. After all, it seemed that as children we were led to believe that on becoming adults we could direct our own lives as we chose, subject to the constraint of avoiding wrongs to others. But the "promise" is only partly fulfilled. Indeed the range of existing social constraints defended on paternalistic grounds is far more extensive (as Chapter 1 elaborates) than one initially might expect. Indeed, some constraints on choice are so customary and widely accepted that we tend not to notice them—as one does not notice neat lawns in affluent neighborhoods if one lives there, or alternatively, stench in the mill-town where one grows up.

Part of the explanation for our acceptance and/or obliviousness to paternalistically based constraints on adults may be that we are more alert to intrusions into our lives which proceed from the ill will of others, for example, that of the rapist, the burglar, the hostile nation, or a manipulative co-worker. The idea that one should run for one's life if another is bent on *doing one harm* is both familiar and natural. Hence, Thoreau's proclamation that if he was sure that ". . . a man was coming to my house with the conscious design of *doing me good*, I should run for my life . . ." (my italics) jolts our settled habits of thought. We are less inclined to engage in close moral scrutiny of acts, practices, laws, or public policies which appear to proceed from beneficent motives, or appear to be aimed at promoting our own good or preventing harm to us. One reason, then, for this investigation is that such scrutiny is much needed and that too little critical attention has been directed toward the acceptability of paternalistic defenses of acts and policies which significantly restrict the liberties of competent adults to direct their own lives.

We may prefer a society in which our neighbors are neither *hostile* nor *indifferent* to our welfare. Hence, we may prefer a society where others have *paternalistic inclinations* toward us (i.e., are inclined to intervene in our lives with the aim of promoting our own good). Fortunately, there are other alternatives, and we can try to identify those forms of paternalistic intervention in the lives of others which seem reasonable and those which do not. The trick, in part, is to figure out what sorts of benevolent-minded interventions are unduly meddlesome and which are not. Although 'paternalism' often has a pejorative ring, there are cases in which we are inclined to believe that paternalistic intervention is all right, for example, when I push you aside as you are about to step into an empty elevator shaft. In other cases our conviction is a contrary one, for example, a governmentally appointed panel of scientists, with the aide of computers, determines whom you shall marry (for your own good, of course). Other cases seem morally perplexing; we are pulled both ways.

In some situations it seems that invasively interfering with the activities of another competent person is to fail to pay due respect to that person as a moral equal. Competent persons are centers of cognition and originators of decisions, decisions affecting the welfare and life-direction of the decision-maker. Here the contrast with nonsentient entities is striking. Surely part of what is involved in the quasi-opaque notion of *treating something as an object* (e.g., a

4

shovel) is that we influence or control its destiny, and in doing so we do not oppose its will, for it has none; nor do we substitute our judgment for it, for it lacks judgment. In contrast, *respecting a person* must involve, in *some* fashion, not undermining that person's decision-making capacities, his decision-process, or rendering the latter impotent to eventuate in chosen outcomes. Further, in some cases, respecting others involves active cooperation with their choices. If we grant the immense attractiveness of recognizing what Ronald Dworkin has described as each person's equal right to concern and respect, difficult questions nevertheless remain about *what constitutes extending concern and respect* to persons.[1] It seems that if we are to care about persons we sometimes ought to disrupt their lives to preserve their well-being or even advance it; that is, recognition of such a right seems to require some paternalistic intervention in their lives. Still, if we are to respect persons as decision-makers (or indeed as particular kinds of decision-makers: as *directors of their own lives*), then we ought not to disrupt their deciding or render it impotent. In short, there is a perplexity about what it is to respect persons, and that perplexity can be conceived, in part, as one about the question: under what conditions, if any, is it permissible to intervene invasively in the lives of competent persons with the aim of promoting their own good? Alternatively, when, if at all, is paternalistic interference with competent persons morally acceptable?

The focus of this study is actually somewhat broader, for in Chapter 7 some initial and limited probings are undertaken with respect to questions of justifiable paternalism toward incompetents. The general structure of the book is as follows. The focus of Chapter 1 is on defining 'paternalism' and setting out fundamental distinctions which are employed to delimit and sort questions to be explored later. An attempt is made to explain the sources of certain confusions over what counts as a paternalistic act, and certain prevailing, or defended, conceptions are critically assessed. Defenses of the permissibility of paternalistic intervention roughly

[1] Ronald Dworkin, *Taking Rights Seriously* (Cambridge, Mass.: Harvard University Press, 1978). Those theoretically uncomfortable with attributions of basic rights might consider the claim that we have a duty to show concern and respect for persons.

Like many others, I have wrestled with the problem of choosing 'him' or 'her' when gender is irrelevant to my point. No doubt I have lost the match. However, I have deliberately varied my examples (employing references to males and females) to emphasize that gender is usually irrelevant and to jolt certain settled ways of thinking. Almost invariably, 'he' can be read 'she or he,' and so on.

fall into two categories: (1) those which appeal to the consent of the subject of proposed intervention, and (2) those which appeal to promoting or preserving the welfare of the subject of proposed intervention; these latter appeals I label "appeals to good promotion." In Chapter 2 I sort and assess appeals to consent; some are accepted as legitimate grounds for paternalistic intervention, and others are found unpersuasive. In Chapter 3 appeals to good promotion are sorted and assessed. By the end of Chapter 3 the basic structure of a theory of autonomy-respecting paternalism will have been set forth.

Nonphilosophers will find the second and third chapters slow going at points, but throughout the book I have made an effort to avoid jargon. I also try to show how the general principles discussed relate to practical questions about how we may treat people—either in relatively private contexts or as a matter of law or public policy. One reason for doing so is my conviction that ethical theorizing is unavoidable if we are to think reasonably about how we may, or ought, to treat other people (hence, many basic questions of law and public policy are questions of ethics) and that, at some point, philosophers who explore ethical issues must attempt to show what implications ethical theory has for specific, practical, questions of public and private practice. In addition, there is a still unfulfilled need for a serious bringing together of the issues between those who, for various reasons, are concerned with important questions about practices and policies and who approach such matters from various disciplines. Few, if any, professionals in a single discipline possess the range of relevant skills and information necessary to address the complexities of formulating ideal practical policy. None can afford to be aloof. Jurisprudents, economists, philosophers, and health-care professionals do not do well who repeat stereotyped accusations about the failings of "other" workers in the intellectual vineyard. None do well who fail to make a good-faith effort to gain some critical understanding (although often this is no easy task) of the expertise of those in other disciplines, and, hence, of the limits and possible distortions of their own. For a start, disciplinary borders must be crossed, boundaries held less sacred, the virtues *and* deficiencies of specialization recognized, cross-disciplinary discussion advanced, and defensiveness reduced.

To facilitate discussion of specific practices and policies, and also to determine the plausibility of the theory developed in the early chapters, Chapter 4 and the following chapters turn to an examination of disputed policy matters. In Chapter 4 the doctrine of informed consent is appraised; further, the implications of the theory developed in the three initial chapters are explored with respect to moral issues about relations between health-care professionals and patients, for example, the permissibility of paternalistic coercion and deception of patients. In Chapter 5 other specific issues and practices are examined in order to test the theory of autonomy-respecting paternalism and to trace its implications regarding paternalistic constraints on voluntary euthanasia, suicide and suicide prevention, prostitution, and irrevocable consent. Chapter 6 focuses on risks and questions concerning both justifiable risk taking and the justifiability of policies aimed at limiting risk generation and exposure to risk. This broad, and somewhat vaguely characterized area, encompasses questions about constraints on private life-style risks to life and health, risks in the workplace, and risks associated with corporate and governmental activities. One important ground for delimiting risks is paternalistic in nature and, hence, such matters are a fit subject for our inquiry. Further, this fact, I believe, has not been sufficiently recognized in existing discussions. The focus of the first six chapters is solely on our dealings with competent, typically adult, persons. The subject matter of Chapter 7 concerns incompetent persons. Since it is roughly assumed that children and incompetents lack a full right to direct their own lives, a right earlier attributed to competent persons, the need for a different sort of theory of paternalism toward such persons is recognized. A quite limited exploration is made of some problems which such a theory must address. In the discussion of paternalism toward incompetents I examine the slippery notion of competence, the question of whether justice requires that we benefit incompetents in certain ways, and how certain leading theories of justice respond to the latter question. In addition, the legal doctrine of substituted judgment is explored since it is one accepted guide to determining how incompetents may and ought to be treated, especially in circumstances where grave choices must be made.

A few comments about the theoretical import of this investigation may be in order. Few persons would disagree with the claim that invasive interferences in the lives of other persons need to be justified. Few would disagree that the *types* of initially plausible grounds which serve such a justificatory purpose are small in number. One way of classifying the leading defenses of the justifiability of invasive interferences with others is to recognize a set of appeals which allege that interference with a subject is justified because doing so will prevent that person from harming and/or wronging others. Such a set of appeals is, broadly, nonpaternalistic. Another set alleges that interference with a subject is justified because doing so will prevent that person from harming and/or wronging himself. Such a set is, broadly, paternalistic. The leading ethical theories—Kant's, utilitarianism, and contractarianism—all allow the relevance of both sorts of grounds. Hence, a thorough assessment of such theories must include an evaluation of the relevance each assigns to paternalistic considerations. I shall argue that both Kant's theory and utilitarianism allow, and perhaps require, invidious paternalistic intervention and, hence, countenance too great a range of paternalistic intervention. Rawls' contractarian theory is more hospitable to the theoretical structure developed here, but it too is in tension with conclusions drawn here, especially with regard to its implication for our dealings with generally incompetent persons.

One hope in developing a theory of paternalism, then, is to set forth a reasoned, systematic, and comparatively "local" theory which can be marshalled to assess the adequacy of more "global" ethical theories, or theories of justice in particular. Analogously, a closely textured map of some piece of the ethical terrain can be used to check the broad-brushed guide provided by a more global map. Conversely, confidence in a more comprehensive map, with its broader perspective, can be used to revise the distortions to which the more local explorer is subject. The possibility of these latter distortions is the peculiar type of risk run by the inquiry undertaken in this study. Fortunately, there is no lack of critics who are ready to locate the limitations, incompleteness, or downright incoherence of proposed guides to large or small segments of the ethical *terra firma*.

Even though the focus of our inquiry is restricted, its aim is, in a number of respects, venturesome; it seeks to identify in an antirelativistic manner rather basic principles as rationally defensible, universal, guides to deciding fundamental questions about the justifiability of intervention with persons on paternalistic grounds. As such it seeks to illuminate further what Ronald Dworkin has described as the "vague but powerful idea of human dignity." More concretely it seeks to identify some representative implications of acceptable paternalistic principles for various specific issues of public policy and private conduct. To the extent that decisions about such matters turn on which basic ethical principles we accept, the importance of rational scrutiny of such principles is rendered more overt than much policy discussion often acknowledges or implies. Further, to the extent that the principles defended here have determinate policy implications, in conjunction with important empirical assumptions, the theory set forth here can achieve the virtue of being more readily refutable. That is, if its practical implications appear unreasonable, the issues can be joined in a more direct, concrete, and fruitful manner than in the case in which a theory is so ethereal that its purported adherents (or opponents) cannot even reach agreement about its implications—a familiar difficulty with disputes about liberalism, conservatism, Marxism, or Christianity, for example. Indeed, one way of achieving some analytical advance beyond the disputes over the large "isms" is to identify and assess explicit and well-defined specific principles and their implications for comparatively specific cases. The inquiry here seeks to do that kind of "second story job" as opposed to elaborating the Ultimate Theory of ethics, or of justice, not to mention any attempt to explore fully the epistemological and metaphysical presuppositions of the theoretical structure set forth here.

Still, an acceptable local map must be compatible with an acceptable global map. I have tried to sketch an acceptable local map. As such it is compatible with certain refinements. But ultimately it rests on a vision of what is involved in respecting autonomous persons, a vision which is incompatible with certain proposals about what we ought to do, or may do, in order to promote human welfare, excellence, aggregate satisfaction, or even the autonomy of competent persons. Deciding whether such a vision is appropriate does not exhaust the domain of moral perplexities, but it is surely an important member of that domain.

O N E

THE NATURE AND SCOPE OF
PATERNALISM

. . . The sole end for which mankind are warranted, individually or collectively, in interfering with the liberty of
action of any of their number, is self-protection. That the
only purpose for which power can be rightfully exercised
over any member of a civilized community, against his will,
is to prevent harm to others. His own good, either physical
or moral, is not a sufficient warrant. He cannot be rightfully
compelled to do or forbear because it will be better for him
to do so, because it will make him happier, because, in the
opinion of others, to do so would be wise or even right.
Those are good reasons for remonstrating with him, or reasoning with him or persuading him, or entreating him, but
not for compelling him or visiting him with any evil in case
he does otherwise.

In the part which merely concern himself, his independence is, of right, absolute. Over himself, over his own
body and mind, the individual is sovereign.
—John Stuart Mill

As if . . . it were a sin to control, or coerce into better
methods, human swine in any way. . . . Ach, Gott im Him-
mel! —Thomas Carlyle

It may perhaps be censured as an impertinent Criticism in
a discourse of this nature, to find fault with words and
names that have obtained in the World: And yet possibly
it may not be amiss to offer new ones when the old are apt
to lead Men into mistakes, as this of *Paternal Power* probably
has done. —John Locke

1.1 Moral Perplexity

It is a significant, although hardly a new or deep, insight that the
ways in which people interact with one another are enormously
diverse. In some cases people cause severe harm to others and/or

infringe the moral or legal rights of others. In many of these latter cases few of us have serious doubts that the actions in question are wrongful, that such acts violate some rather stringent duties we have toward others. For example, consider ordinary homicide, rape, torture, child abuse, or enslavement. About such acts we feel no "moral perplexity"; we sense no "moral dilemma" about what we ourselves should do regarding such acts (that is, we simply ought to refrain from them). On reflection, we may be led to consider whether such acts might be justifiable in very special circumstances, e.g., whether it would be permissible to torture a terrorist to prevent his attempt at massive destruction of a large number of innocent persons. That there *may* be a moral justification for torture in such a case need not distract us from the fact that torturing innocent people, in otherwise ordinary situations, seems an incontrovertible wrong. I am calling attention to the fact that in a considerable variety of cases the appropriate answer to a moral question (e.g., is rape permissible?) strikes us as obvious, as not calling for serious reflection, discussion, or inquiry.

In contrast, it is obvious that there is serious, sharp, and persistent disagreement about the moral permissibility of a wide variety of acts, such as abortion, mercy killing, suicide, civil disobedience, censorship, capital punishment, homosexual activity, experimentation on humans, and implementation of risk-laden policies such as developing nuclear power or genetic experimentation. About such matters "reasonable people of good will" often disagree, and individuals often find it hard to decide what is permissible or obligatory. When confronted with reasons in defense of one view and then its competitors, we may be torn one way and then another. Deciding what is right in many cases seems no easy matter. There are, then, both "easy cases" about which there may be a virtual consensus as well as "hard cases" that perplex us individually and collectively.

Some problems which demand resolution are not important enough to elicit much time or effort to resolve them. We readily flip a coin or cut the cards to determine who should deal. Other matters are too important to resolve casually. Further, there may be good reasons to think that there is a rational decision or view on a certain disputed issue, although discovering it may be no simple task.

Some activities and policies which are the concern of this book fall into this latter category. There is a range of acts which evoke both moral disagreement (disagreement about whether they are permissible or obligatory) and perplexity. The diverse range of acts which are our focus here are often labeled 'paternalistic.' As a provisional characterization, a paternalistic act is one in which one person, A, interferes with another person, S, in order to promote S's own good. The expression 'promoting S's own good' is sometimes construed narrowly to mean only the prevention of harm to S (harm which would presumably occur to S if S were left alone); sometimes 'promoting S's own good' is construed to mean promoting a benefit for S.

Defining 'paternalistic act' as we have calls attention to two notable features about paternalistic acts, features which may make one wonder why there would be any moral perplexity about the acceptability of such acts. First, by definition, if A acts paternalistically he does so with an altruistic motive; he aims at promoting the good of another.[1] Immediately there is a sharp contrast with many acts that seem evidently wrong; in paradigmatic wrongful acts (e.g., murder or rape) the agent either wants his prospective victim to be worse off (and, hence, has malevolent intentions) or is indifferent to his victim's well-being (and, hence, at least has no benevolent intention). Hence, one familiar source of condemnation (the agent was callous or malicious) is simply absent in cases of paternalistic intervention. Second, if the intervention is successful in its aim, the subject of the intervention (henceforth: S) is either benefitted or protected. So, it *seems* that we have "no harm done" and "benevolent intent"; what could be wrong? Brief reflection suggests that we have so far ignored significant aspects of paternalistic actions by virtue of which they are, and ought to be, controversial. Soon we shall examine these in some detail. At this point it is useful to identify a range of examples of paternalistic actions; surveying them will help indicate the *diversity* of cases that are collected under the label 'paternalism' and why there is a *dispute* about what sorts of paternalistic actions are permissible, if any; and if so, on what grounds.

1.2 Examples of Paternalism

In initially pondering examples, it may be useful to consider them imaginatively from two standpoints: (1) that of the subject who is

[1] More carefully, I shall assume that, for A to act paternalistically toward S, A not only *intends* to promote S's good but that A's dominant or sole *motive* is to bring about this end. This point, however, is generally not a crucial one in later discussions. The characterization does exclude, as nonpaternalistic, cases in which A, for

the recipient of the paternalistic interference, and (2) that of an agent who is deciding whether paternalistically to interfere. I shall propose the rejection of both the view that all paternalism is morally acceptable and that none is acceptable. If this point is noncontroversial, the hard task is one of "differentiation" or "discrimination" (in one sense), that is, *which* types of paternalistic intervention are permissible, and why? A start can be made by trying to discriminate morally between the following cases. It should be noted that although the types of acts mentioned *may* not be paternalistically motivated, they *often are* paternalistically *motivated* and/or *defended on paternalistic grounds*, that is, they allegedly benefit the subjects constrained by the act, practice, or policy:

1. Legal requirements that motorcyclists wear helmets.
2. Legal requirements prohibiting self-medication.
3. Legal prohibitions on the possession or use of certain risk-laden drugs.
4. Laws requiring the testing of drugs by the Food and Drug Administration prior to their legalization in the United States.
5. Prohibitions on access to "obscene" materials by minors.
6. Prohibitions on how long a minor may work or on access to certain types of work.
7. Curfews on those below a certain age.
8. Prohibitions on dueling.
9. Prohibitions on gambling.
10. Compulsory education of the young.
11. Restrictions by brokerage firms on which adults may engage in purchasing stocks or commodities.
12. The indoctrination of young children with political or religious doctrines.
13. Attempts to disallow prisoners from volunteering for biomedical experiments.
14. Attempts to disallow minors and retarded persons from

---

example, prevents S from killing himself so that A may keep S as a viable slave—or an object of ransom. Further, although my focus is typically on persons, 'S' should be understood to stand in place of a sentient creature whether or not it is a person.

being subjects of biomedical experiments or organ donations.

15. Attempts to prevent persons sentenced to capital punishment from undergoing it even when they demand it.

16. Legal prohibitions on suicide.

17. Legal prohibitions on voluntary euthanasia.

18. Psychiatrists' pressuring patients into sexual relations to "uncover areas of sexual blocking."

19. Deception of patients by physicians, or other health care personnel, to avoid disturbing the patient or to facilitate their consent to a procedure the physician believes is desirable for the patient.

20. Use of drugs on patients to make them more compliant and receptive to a procedure the physician believes to be in the patient's best interest.

21. Legally required vaccinations.

22. Refusal to accept otherwise deserving applicants to graduate school on the grounds that they would not be happy in the discipline in question.

23. Compulsory participation in systems providing for adequate income on retirement, e.g., Social Security.

24. Required courses at a university.

25. Prohibitions on voluntary self-enslavement.

26. Civil commitment of those judged dangerous to themselves.

27. Involuntary sterilization.

28. Distribution of welfare in kind (e.g., food stamps) rather than in cash.

29. Involuntary blood transfusion of those opposed to it on moral and/or religious grounds.

30. Deception of children "for their benefit," e.g., telling them that a medical procedure "only hurts a little" when that is false, or perpetuating the Santa Claus myth.

31. Fluoridation of water supplies.

32. Prohibitions on purchase of explosives and poisons.

33. Required waiting periods for divorce.

34. Medical disqualification of student athletes from playing sports.

35. Infanticide of radically defective infants.

36. Force feeding "hunger strikers."

37. Punishment to rehabilitate the punished.

38. Labor laws restricting minimum wages, maximum hours, or who may work.

39. The arrest of drunks to prevent their being "rolled."

40. Laws forbidding anyone to induce Indians into contractual arrangements.[2]

The range of examples noted suggests the great diversity of acts which properly *may* be classified as paternalistic. Intuitively, and prior to systematic reflection on the justifiability of paternalistic intervention (and also prior to having a more precise definition of 'paternalistic act'), we may be inclined to regard some of these acts as innocuous and innocent. Others no doubt strike us as entirely unacceptable restrictions on the liberty of persons to decide and act as they wish. There are various distinctions which we may regard as relevant in deciding which forms of paternalism are acceptable or not. For example, we may think that it is important to distinguish between *types of subjects* affected, for example, paternalism toward adults versus paternalism toward children, between older and younger children, between competent and incompetent persons, or between permanently or temporarily incompetent persons. Relatedly we may think that the *form* of "interference" is important, for example whether it involves force, threat, deception, overt lying or withholding information, physical impairment, or killing. If such distinctions are important, and I will insist that distinctions rather like these are, one task before us (we might call it a philosophical one) is to sort out cases. Doing so will help us isolate and distinguish those where we may think paternalism is permissible from those where we judge that it is not. Sorting out cases will make it clear that we need not be committed to crude and implausible generalizations such as, paternalism toward adults is impermissible and paternalism toward minors is permissible.

These remarks suggest a partial strategy for investigating the moral questions about paternalism. If we think that there are certain important distinctions within the broad category of paternalistic

---

[2] The law is part of the 1964 U.S. Code; see Jay Katz, ed. *Experimentation With Human Beings* (New York: Russell Sage Foundation, 1972), p. 549.

15

acts, and wish to demarcate those, a necessary preliminary is to identify with reasonable care what is to count as a 'paternalistic act.' As will become clear, the term is used in philosophical and other literature in more than one way. If we are to ponder the moral perplexities associated with paternalism, a *sine qua non* is to know what we are talking about. Hence, we next consider a number of proposed or supposed definitions of 'paternalism.'

1.3 Defining 'Paternalism'

Our ultimate focus in this study concerns the *justifiability* of paternalistic acts. We want to *evaluate* them. But when is an act correctly *described* as a 'paternalistic act'? The latter is a conceptual issue; the former is an evaluative one. In familiar discussions these two questions often get confused and, as a result, the inquiry or dispute gets muddled. For example, there is a tendency to use and/or define the term 'murder' as meaning "wrongful killing." On *this* definition of 'murder,' once we label an act as murder we have not merely described the act, we have evaluated it or committed ourselves to a certain evaluation. Hence, if an act is properly labeled 'murder' there is, on the above definition, no further moral question about its legitimacy. It is wrong and that is that. Similarly, some persons explicitly or implicitly define 'abortion' as "the murder of an unborn child." If this is an acceptable operative definition, the "morality of abortion" is settled; if an act is an abortion, in the above sense, it is wrong—period. If, however, we believe that significant moral questions are not settled by merely stipulating that words shall be defined in a certain fashion, we ought to be unwilling to proceed in such a fashion. At the very least we must try to be clear about when we are describing or classifying an act in a *morally neutral* manner and when we are *morally evaluating* the act (or type of act) in question.

Uses of nonneutral or "value-laden" terms are, on reflection, not unfamiliar. Consider the typically pejorative connotation of terms such as 'redneck,' 'queer,' 'sissy,' 'nigger,' 'elitist,' 'atheist,' 'bastard,' 'wop,' 'commie,' and 'unchristian'—as used in certain subcultures. Similarly, acts (and attitudes) are often described as 'paternalistic,' wherein not only a certain descriptive claim is made but there is a clear implication that the act is wrongful (or, more weakly, otherwise objectionable). If we wish to avoid begging the moral question (by simply *assuming* or supposing an act is wrong in labeling it 'paternalistic') we need to identify a morally neutral definition of 'paternalistic act,' or 'paternalism.' In fact, there is a variety of neutral definitions which have a certain currency. One may be found in Webster's wherein 'paternalism' is defined as "a relation between the governed and the government, the employed and the employer, etc.; involving care and control suggestive of those followed by a father."[3] But one possible *relation* between the mentioned parties that satisfies the first definition (prior to the semicolon) is 'occupies the same planet as.' However, astronauts aside, there is *that* relation between *any* two humans. Clearly the first Webster's definition does not begin to capture adequately what 'paternalism' means when native speakers of English use the term. If, more charitably, we focus on the second Webster's definition, we get a little closer to the way the term is used today, but not much—for acts are commonly described as paternalistic when the agent and subject of paternalism are not in a father-child relation. However, the emphasis on 'care' suggests that a paternalistic act proceeds from some well-intentioned or benevolent motive, and the emphasis on 'control' suggests that the act may be done against the will of the subject or without his or her consent. We now seem very close to our earlier characterization of a paternalistic act as one in which one party *interferes* with another for the sake of the other's own good. This characterization seems to accord well with widespread usage of 'paternalistic act.'

However, does 'paternalism' refer only to cases in which one party *interferes* with another? And is 'interfere' a value-laden term? If so, our current definition may be nonneutral. Can there not be purely helpful paternalistic acts which do not interfere, constrain, or restrict? What if, in a benevolent moment, I plant some roses near my neighbor's fence in order to please him (even though I myself am indifferent to roses)? Here we have an act which might be classified as paternalistic; it is clearly a case of *influencing* another with an aim to benefit him (for his own good, if one prefers). I shall not much quarrel with those who wish to define 'paternalistic act' in this manner. However, there are two reasons for resisting the temptation. First, the expression in fact seems not to be used so broadly; second, such a definition blurs a plausible line to be drawn between different sorts of altruistic acts, roughly those which are meddlesome or interfere in some sense and those which do not. Planting roses to please my neighbor hardly seems to interfere with his preferences or disrupt his chosen movement toward

---

[3] See *Webster's New Collegiate Dictionary* (1956).

17

achieving his goals. Moreover, when an act is characterized as paternalistic, it is reasonably clear that a more restricted range of cases is the frame of reference, namely, cases when one party *interferes* with another with the aim of promoting his/her own good (or preventing harm from accruing to that other). For now, by 'paternalistic act' this is what I shall mean. In the final analysis the label seems of secondary importance. Rather, what is crucial is that we are clear about the range of acts whose moral assessment is in question. Further, I lay no great stress on the word 'interference,' and occasionally shall use 'constraint,' 'intrusion,' or 'intervention,' interchangeably. A key point, however, is that *some* paternalistic interferences are of a sort which is morally suspect.

The definition of 'interfere' is a slippery matter: not all forms of influence are interferences. To interfere normally is to disrupt a natural or intended process or activity, especially to block or impede a chosen activity of another. Appearing in another's field of vision *normally* does not interfere. Stopping another to ask the time of day does interfere, albeit typically in a minor and innocuous way (but suppose the other is performing brain surgery). 'Interference' commonly suggests an action at cross-purposes with another; doing so is not by definition presumptively wrong. Interference with the immediate aims of another may *facilitate* larger goals of another (cf. saying "your house is on fire"), or it may promote a goal S has chosen earlier and which, in order to achieve, S has requested another cooperative interference (more on this in Chapter 2). As noted before, we *may* act contrary to another's preferences by omitting actions, for example, by withholding information (even though the omission may not divert another's course in the dramatic way associated with the use of force or coercive threat). What normally makes an act one of interference, as our canonical definition of paternalistic behavior' indicates, is, in part, that it is contrary to the operative preference, intention, or disposition of the subject affected.

However, a further emendation is in order. Infants may be said to lack preferences or at least conscious preferences. And preferences of adults may be settled or not. Further, consider a case in which A by suspect means of indoctrination, or even hypnosis, has either generated new preferences in S which S would not otherwise have had or A has modified indeterminate or unsettled preferences in such a manner that S has preferences S would not otherwise have had. As a result A may so influence S as to make S readily comply, perhaps in a servile fashion, with A's desires or aims (possibly, of course, to promote S's own good; possibly not). Less abstractly, suppose A is S's father, S is A's daughter, A believes that it is for his daughter's own good that she not marry before 30 years of age, and A successfully so indoctrinates S from childhood. By the age of 18 S's operative preference is not to marry before 30. Suppose further that, as a result, any efforts by A to turn away prospective suitors from S while she is 18 to 30 are not contrary to S's preferences. Has A paternalistically interfered with S? Note that any turning away of prospective suitors has *never* been against S's preferences, for her preferences since their inception have never been of a contrary nature. Given our characterization of paternalism as involving interference and the latter as acting contrary to the operative preference or disposition of the subject, it seems that we would have to conclude that A did not (in the acts noted) behave paternalistically toward S. But such a result is counterintuitive. To avoid it we can and ought to recognize a broader conception of what it is to interfere with another. The following emendation will not eliminate difficult to settle, borderline, cases, but it will circumvent an undue narrowness in our previous characterization of what constitutes interference. More adequately, then, I shall assume that

A interferes with S's choices or acts if and only if

either 1. A deliberately acts in a manner contrary to S's operative preferences, intention, or disposition—

or 2. A deliberately acts in a manner so as to shape/ modify S's original or existing preferences in ways that bypass S's cognitive capacities to resist, or ways that shape those very capacities—so as to make S's preferences different from what they would have been in the absence of A's actions.[4]

Without dwelling on further complications, this characterization allows what seems intuitively compelling, namely, that certain forms of indoctrination (and certain other manners of preference shaping) count as interference. Further, since at least some interferences of this sort are objectionable, those who mold the behavior of others (with paternalistic or other aims) *by suspect means* of shaping preferences do not escape moral scrutiny just because at some point those so shaped readily, and perhaps in a servile manner,

---

[4] Perhaps another proviso is needed: or interferences with S by anyone other than S. However, I forego qualifying an already tedious formula.

comply with the wishes of an Orwellian Big Brother (or Big Sister, as the case may be). Later influences, in themselves innocuous, may be part of a larger, invidious, pattern of interference. Nevertheless, my primary focus will not be on paternalistic indoctrination, a matter deserving a separate volume, but with paternalistic interventions which override existing preferences or which manipulate a subject's outlook so that the latter's preferences get disregarded—even by the subject himself.

We have not yet answered the question of whether our proposed definition is morally neutral. *If* we define 'interference' as 'wrongful influencing,' we will not have a neutral definition. Although many interferences (e.g., torture) are wrongful and though particular protests such as "you're interfering!" often are understood rightfully as allegations of wrongdoing, there is clearly a non-evaluative meaning of 'interfere' as when we say, for example, "the storm interfered with the parade." So, we must conclude that our preferred definition of 'paternalistic act' as an act in which one party interferes with another with the aim of promoting his or her own good does not logically *entail* any moral evaluation of such an act. Hence, we can identify paternalistic acts prior to investigating the question of moral justification. This point is not unimportant since some writers assume that "interferences" are presumptively wrong.

If an act rightly describable as a paternalistic act need not be wrong or presumptively wrong, what is all the fuss about? The answer lies in the fact that *certain types of interferences* with the lives of others happen to consist in the performance of acts which transgress certain moral rules or principles, e.g., they involve the use of force, coercive threat, or some form of deception. If it were *always* wrong to act in any of these ways, then any case in which paternalistic interference involved such an act would simply be wrong. However, from a wide variety of ethical perspectives such modes of influencing others are *not* always wrong, even if they frequently or usually are. In allowing resort to such tactics in cases of certain wars, punishment, or self-defense, as most theories do, the assumption is made that such acts are not always wrong. Indeed a much weaker assumption is employed, and it is one that I shall make, namely that such acts (and others to be mentioned) are *presumptively wrong*. What does it mean to say that an act is presumptively wrong? Here we shall assume that an act is presumptively wrong if there is some feature of it which is sufficient to deem it unqualifiedly wrong (or wrong when all relevant matters have been considered) in the absence of any other morally relevant considerations. What acts, then, are presumptively wrong? A satisfactory and full answer to this difficult question would require a full-blown (justified) ethical theory. The provision of such a theory here is both beyond my aim and my grasp. Instead I simply shall assume that acts which cause serious harm to individual human beings or infringe their moral rights, if people have such rights, are presumptively wrong. More specifically, we assume further that certain types of acts are in this category, among them the use of force to alter another's choice or action, the use of coercive threats, killing, physically impairing, certain forms of indoctrination and conditioning, and various modes of deception. Such acts, in an important sense, fail to respect persons.[5] The assumption that some acts are presumptively wrong and the assumption that specific types of acts fall into this category are, I believe, modest, widely shared, and not liable to be a source of dispute (except to those skeptical about any and all attempts to distinguish between right and wrong).

On our definition of 'paternalistic act,' a paternalistic act involves interference, but this *in itself* entails no moral presumptions.[6] Nevertheless, many paternalistic practices happen to involve acts which are presumptively wrong. They are not wrong, to emphasize a point, simply because they interfere. Rather, those which are presumptively wrong are so because they invasively interfere by transgressing independently specifiable moral principles, e.g., it is presumptively wrong to kill, coerce, deceive, and so on. Hence, the moral controversy surrounding *certain* paternalistic acts. One question we shall pursue is whether, in particular cases (or particular types of cases) in which a presumptive wrong is done, there are countervailing, morally relevant, considerations by virtue of which paternalistic acts are justified. Another way to argue for the justification of paternalistic interference is to attempt to show that the particular interference is innocuous and involves no presump-

[5] Here I use 'persons' broadly to include all neonatal human beings. For most of this study no attention will be given to fetuses belonging to Homo sapiens or beings outside of our species.

[6] Herbert Morris rightly notes that there is something odd in describing legitimate and solicitous care of children by parents as "paternalistic." This may be the case because "paternalistic' is often used pejoratively and to refer to quite invasive sorts of interferences. It is worth keeping in mind, for the sake of avoiding confusion, the accordion-like quality of 'paternalistic' (and its cognates) as well as the comparatively broader, and neutral, definition we have adopted. See Herbert Morris, "A Paternalistic Theory of Punishment," *American Philosophical Quarterly* 18, No. 4 (October, 1981), p. 263.

tive wrong. So, paternalistic interference may be justifiable if it either involves no presumptive wrong or, if it does, there are sufficient countervailing considerations in the presence of such a wrong (e.g., beneficial consequences). The cases on which we focus generally *do* involve presumptively wrongful forms of influence; so, a central issue to which we shall return concerns what sorts of countervailing considerations, if any, will serve to render acceptable otherwise wrongful intrusions in the lives of other persons.

At this point it may be objected that even if our definition is fine as far as it goes, it does not go far enough for it does not help us decide about certain puzzling cases, for example, omissions "carried out" with paternalistic aims. If I withhold the information from you (that your spouse has died) to prevent you from experiencing distress when you are about to undergo surgery, it is plausible to describe my behavior as paternalistic. Still, have I, in so doing, interfered with you? In contrast, *telling you* the news more aptly might be labeled "interference" with your plans. In the firm belief that my omission is a bit of "paternalism," it is useful to set out a more comprehensive although far more tedious definition—for reasons that will be noted. Thus, I propose that

A's doing or omitting some act X to, or toward, S is paternalistic behavior if and only if
1. A deliberately does (or omits) X

and 2. A believes that his (her) doing (or omitting) X is contrary to S's operative preference, intention, or disposition at the time A does (or omits) X [or when X affects S—or would have affected S if X had been done (or omitted)]

and 3. A does (or omits) X with the primary or sole aim of promoting a benefit for S [a benefit which, A believes, would not accrue to S in the absence of A's doing (or omitting) X] or preventing a harm to S [a harm which, A believes, would accrue to S in the absence of A's doing (or omitting) X].

In the above (final and here canonical) definition 'A' ranges over an individual person or groups; 'S' ranges over individuals (but, possibly, groups as well).[7] Further, I shall use 'interference' or

---

[7] I leave it unargued, but it may be desirable to let 'S' range over all sentient beings (or even all entities such that we can intelligibly speak of what is in their interests). To do so could be understood as construing 'disposition' broadly to

'intervention' broadly so that 'paternalistic behavior' (as defined) "interferes" or "intervenes." To do so is somewhat stipulative since, in ordinary discourse, we tend to restrict 'interference' to cases which block, disrupt, or divert ongoing activities of persons. Thus, ordinarily we may not say that "A interferes with S" if A withholds information from S which would have influenced S to change course if S had been supplied with the information. Hence, if someone resists my broad use of 'interference' to refer to such cases, he simply should read 'paternalistic behavior' in place of 'paternalistic interference.' Context generally will make clear whether our concern is about an instance of paternalistic commissions (commonly referred to as "paternalistic interferences" or "paternalistic interventions") or paternalistic omissions (which are, of course, *deliberate refrainings* and not merely failures to act).

Our canonical definition, it should be noted, (1) closely fits the current and dominant usage of (although not self-conscious definitions of) 'paternalism' in academic discussions, (2) is largely compatible with vague, not too helpful, dictionary characterizations, (3) is morally neutral, (4) is sufficiently comprehensive so as to encompass paternalistically motivated omissions (a theoretical virtue for purposes of ethical inquiry), and (5) provides a basis (cf. 2. in the definition) for distinguishing paternalistic altruistic acts from nonpaternalistic altruistic acts (a distinction worth preserving).[8]

The proposed definition also allows us to classify as 'paternalistic behavior' (and, for the reasons noted, 'paternalistic interference') certain acts to which S has consented. One example, to which we

---

include teleological ends toward which living organisms are "programmed" to move (e.g., growth or reproduction), even if they lack preferences.

[8] It is worth commenting here on the terms 'paternalism' and 'patriarchalism.' The term 'patriarch' in ancient times referred to a male ruler, typically a venerated elder. A community hierarchically organized with such persons having supreme de facto authority is called "patriarchal," or exhibiting "patriarchalism." Such "authorities" control others. Whether for their own good (focus on: results) is a further question. In addition, whether patriarchs exercised control with altruistic aims (focus on: motives) is an open question. There is then, no necessary connection between "acting in a patriarchal fashion" and "acting paternalistically." Both expressions today have a meaning broader than the original ones. Part of the defense of patriarchal social structures is that they (allegedly) benefit those whom they constrain. A similar defense is given of paternalistic acts. Such a defense will be examined later (primarily in Chapter 3).

In contrast, of course, to 'patronize' (in its typical pejorative sense) is to treat another in an offensively condescending manner. For understandable reasons, the ambiguity of 'patronize' between 'give support to' (a nonpejorative sense) and 'treat condescendingly' is parallel to our familiar ambivalence toward paternalism, treatment which often seems "supportive" but at times seems to involve treatment of others as less than equals.

will return later, is the case in which I, believing I may become inebriated at a party, request that you hide my car keys—or otherwise deter me from driving—if I do get drunk and wish to drive. Suppose that I do and you, from paternalistic motives, deter me. Your act will count as paternalistic on the adopted definition. Note that you act against my operative preference or intent at the time of intervening *even though* I earlier consented to your efforts. My prior consent does *not* preclude your acting against my operative preference at the later time. This distinction has sometimes been overlooked or has evoked conceptual vascillation (a point to which we will return in Chapter 2), for example, in my own prior essays.

Rather than restate our lengthy, analytic, definition of 'paternalistic behavior' when a reminder is useful, I will ordinarily employ the loose but brief expression "interference with another for his (or her) own good." However, this short formula should be understood as an abbreviation for our adopted definition.

1.4 Implications of Our Definition

There are a number of other non-equivalent and competing definitions of 'paternalism' or 'paternalistic act' in the literature, and, to promote clarity and a sense of perspective, it is worth observing how our proposed definition differs, partly to alert us to the possibility that claims "about paternalistic acts" may not be about the same range of cases. Clarity is not everything; but neither is it nothing. As we shall argue, a number of well-known alternative conceptions of paternalism are either too broad, too narrow, fail to be morally neutral, or otherwise impede inquiry.

Our account differs from the succinct, albeit casual, one employed by H.L.A. Hart, namely, "the protection of people against themselves."[9] To see why Hart's account differs, imagine a case where A, a jealous husband, in a fit of rage punches his wife into unconsciousness and, hence, inadvertently prevents his already depressed spouse from taking a fatal dose of cyanide. On a literal, and perhaps uncharitable, interpretation of Hart's account this is paternalism; it is not so on ours, for A does *not* aim at promoting his wife's good or preventing harm to her. This seems the right result since a defining feature of 'paternalism' is that the agent have a certain altruistic aim. Hence, certain acts may be "paternalistic in result" even though the act itself would mistakenly be

[9] H.L.A. Hart, *Law, Liberty, and Morality* (New York: Vintage Books, 1966), p. 31.

described as paternalistic. Our account is closer to common and academic deployment of 'paternalism.'

In his pioneering and instructive essay on paternalism, Gerald Dworkin's initial characterization is this:

> By paternalism I shall understand roughly the interference with a person's liberty of action justified by reasons referring exclusively to the welfare, good, happiness, needs, interests or values of the person being coerced.[10]

One objection to this definition of 'paternalism' is that it is non-neutral for it seems to presuppose that such interferences are *justified*. Whether they are is a moral question which Dworkin himself undertakes to investigate, as do we. Presumably his intent was to suggest 'possibly justifiable' or 'allegedly justified' by 'justified.' Our account, by contrast, leaves open the question of justification. Later in his essay he offers, instead, a neutral characterization, "interference with a person for his own good."[11]

Second, the reference to the "person being coerced" in Dworkin's account is infelicitous. Although all cases of coercion are interferences, not all interferences are coercive. The term 'coercion' is sometimas broadly used to include cases involving the use of *force* against the will of another (e.g., you wrestle me to the ground against my will) and sometimes, more naturally, is used to mean the employment of a coercive threat, a threat which generally has the form "if you do X I will not make you worse off than you (now) are, and if you do not do X I will make you worse off than you (now) are." But suppose Jones is an injured, unconscious, Jehovah's Witness and is opposed to blood transfusions. We decide to transfuse her against her will (so far as we understand it) in order to save her life. This seems a clear instance of paternalistic interference. Yet we do not "use force" nor do we employ coercive threats. Hence, it seems at least misleading to think that paternalistic interference must take the form of coercion narrowly or broadly understood.[12]

---

[10] Gerald Dworkin, "Paternalism," in *Morality and the Law*, ed. Richard Wasserstrom (Belmont, Cal.: Wadsworth, 1971), pp. 107–126.

[11] Ibid.

[12] N. Fotion has claimed that "some philosophers have given paternalism a far worse reputation than it deserves by associating it with coercion by definition and in effect confusing it with coercive paternalism." See N. Fotion, "Paternalism," *Ethics* 89, No. 2 (January, 1979), p. 195. What reputation it does deserve is a central question of this inquiry; given its length it is fair to assume that I do not believe that the answer is self-evident. The type of counterexample mentioned is due to

It is also worth noting here that Bernard Gert and Charles Culver define "A is acting paternalistically toward S" partly by "S's good justifies him in acting on S's behalf. . . ."[13] Hence, their characterization is also nonneutral, even though their subsequent theoretical discussion does not seem constrained by literal adherence to such a definition.[14]

Two other features of Dworkin's initial characterization of paternalism deserve comment. First, it is not obvious that we should restrict 'paternalism' to cases in which the interference is always thought to be an "interference with a person's liberty of action." Although the matter may not be a substantive one, some interferences may only misleadingly be described as "interferences with liberty." Suppose I believe that if you commit suicide you will be damned for eternity, that is go to hell—for suicide is a grave sin (let us suppose). To prevent this harm to you I kill you "for your own good." Setting my fate aside, I believe that by saving you from sin you will now enjoy eternal bliss. Have I, thereby, "interfered with your liberty"? Perhaps so, but the case sharply contrasts with others where I deceive you or threaten you (for your own good), cases in which you *remain free* to choose and act in *certain* ways. I do not exactly "restrict your liberty" if I kill you.

However, it seems less than crucial to decide whether an act "restricts liberty." *In the absence* of delineating or recognizing further features about a given act, the fact that it restricts liberty seems neither a sufficient nor a necessary condition for the act's being presumptively wrong (and, hence, morally suspect).[15] Any act in which A influences S can be said to restrict or thwart S's liberty to be free of that influence, for example, if I remind you that the gun you are about to clean is loaded, I have restricted your liberty to be free of such a reminder. Further, if killing you against your will does not "restrict your liberty," restricting liberty is not a necessary condition of acting wrongly. Still, these brief remarks are not in-

---

Bernard Gert and Charles Culver in "Paternalistic Behavior," *Philosophy & Public Affairs* 6, No. 1 (Fall, 1976), p. 46. On whether paternalism always restricts liberty, see Allen Buchanan, "Medical Paternalism," *Philosophy & Public Affairs* 7, No. 4 (Summer, 1978), pp. 370–390.

[13] Bernard Gert and Charles Culver, "The Justification of Paternalism," *Ethics* 89 (January, 1979), p. 199.

[14] Ibid. Also, see their revised account in Chapters 7 and 9 of Charles Culver and Bernard Gert, *Philosophy in Medicine* (New York: Oxford University Press, 1982).

[15] However, an act which "subverts *or* introduces obstacles to the valued (by S) liberties of a competent person, S" does seem presumptively wrong. *This type* of restriction on liberty evades the complaints made above regarding the assumption "restrictions on liberty are presumptively wrong."

tended to deny that many acts which we select for attention by saying that they are "restrictions on liberty" are indeed morally suspect. In any case there is no compelling need to squeeze paternalistic acts under the category of restrictions on liberty. Even if killing or deception cannot be subsumed under such a label, their suspect quality need not go unrecognized; our descriptive moral vocabulary is much richer.

A further point about Dworkin's initial account is that it omits the crucial feature that for an agent's act to be paternalistic the agent must have a certain type of motive. His account, instead, focuses only on the types of reasons which may justify a paternalistic act. But even if we judged the enraged husband's act to be justified, in our prior example, by appeal to "*reasons* referring to the welfare, good, happiness . . . of the person being coerced," it does not follow that *he acted with the aim* of promoting the good of (or preventing harm to) his wife. Hence, there is good reason *not* to classify his act as "paternalistic" even though we might employ our adopted label to say it was "paternalistic in result" or claim that it was justified (if we, improbably, thought so) by the kinds of reasons to which Dworkin alludes. A more substantive point emerges from this recognition, one bearing directly on questions of justification.

Once it is decided that a given act is correctly *labeled* as paternalistic we can distinguish between three types of *attempts* to justify the paternalistic interference; I shall label them (1) *paternalistic* justifications, (2) *nonpaternalistic* justifications, and (3) *mixed* justifications. To emphasize a point, by 'justification' here I mean 'purported justification' (and *not* necessarily a successful justification). By a *paternalistic justification* I mean, to adopt partly Dworkin's terminology, an attempt to justify an act of paternalistic interference by reasons referring exclusively to the *protection or promotion* of the welfare, good, happiness, needs, interests, or values of the subject of interference.[16] That the reasons focus on *protecting or promoting*

---

[16] My labels 'paternalistic justification' and 'nonpaternalistic justification' are stipulative. Strictly, what I label a paternalistic justification is an appeal to what might be called "subject benefitting" (or protecting) considerations. And, strictly, what I label a nonpaternalistic justification is an appeal to what might be called "nonsubject benefitting" (or protecting) considerations. In one sense there is nothing distinctly "paternalistic" about the former appeals since in themselves they make no essential reference to *interfering* with the subject. Thus, they are appeals to certain types of altruistic reasons for judging acts permissible (except in the case in which the nonpaternalistic justification focuses exclusively on benefitting [or protecting] the agent). Given this clarification and recognizing paternalistic justification' and nonpaternalistic justification' as technical labels, no one should be misled.

the welfare . . . of the subject is an important emendation to Dworkin's terminology. If omitted, a purported justification of malicious interference (call it a "malicious justification") by reasons referring exclusively to (the destruction of) the welfare . . . of the subject of interference would count as a *"paternalistic justification."*[17] By a *non-paternalistic justification* I mean an attempt to justify an act of paternalistic interference by reasons referring exclusively to the protection or promotion of the welfare, good, happiness, needs, interests, or values of persons ('persons' here can designate divinities) other than the subject of interference. By a *mixed justification* I mean an attempt to justify an act of paternalistic interference by reasons referring to the protection or promotion of the welfare, good, happiness, needs, interests, or values of the subject of interference and others. In existing discussions of paternalism it has not always been clear (and frequently there is confusion about) what has been meant by the "justification of paternalism." Abstractly considered, it would seem that a paternalistic act, if justified, may be justified on grounds *other than* paternalistic ones. If so, that is one thing that may be meant by 'justified paternalism.' However, in speaking of 'justified paternalism' what may be meant is that paternalistic justifications succeed, and that is indeed another matter. Although our broad concern as moral agents is whether paternalistic interferences are justified on *any* ground, or justified at all, it is clear that many believe that *paternalistic justifications* sometimes provide adequate ground for paternalistic interference. That this is so seems clear from the frequency with which people invoke, as a *justificatory* remark, the familiar point "after all, it was (is) for your own good!"

So far then we have sought to distinguish three questions: (1) *what* is to count as a paternalistic act, (2) *whether* the act is justified, and (3) *what general sorts* of justification may be offered in an attempt to justify the paternalistic act.

1.5 Two Competing Analyses

It is useful further to compare our adopted definition of 'paternalism' with those adopted by others, partly to convey a sense of the confusions which arise because of the lack of consensus about

---

[17] The useful emendation and its insight must be credited to Tom Beauchamp, "On Coercive Justifications for Coercive Genetic Control," in *Biomedical Ethics and the Law*, eds. James Humber and Robert F. Almeder (New York: Plenum Press, 1979), pp. 383–396.

such matters and partly further to vindicate the definition we have adopted here. Aware that his definition is controversial, but not without reasons, Tom Beauchamp "restricts use of the term *paternalism* to cases where the state coercively protects or benefits a person when his contrary choices are informed and voluntary."[18] As may be obvious, we have found no reason to restrict 'paternalism' to actions by the state; if we wish to focus only on state paternalism it is simple enough to speak, for example, of legal paternalism. Second, for reasons already noted, restriction to cases of coercion is misleading; some paternalistically motivated acts can hardly be thought of as coercion, for example, killing someone to relieve him of his misery. The third sort of restriction—to acts contrary to a subject's informed and voluntary choice—is one Beauchamp defends by an argument of interest for more than one reason. Hence, I shall quote a substantial portion of his remarks:

Intervention in cases of nonvoluntary or of uninformed conduct is not paternalism in any interesting sense, because it is not based on a liberty-limiting principle independent of the harm principle. It is important to be clear about this distinction since some interventions are both coercive and justified on what might deceptively appear to be paternalistic grounds. John Stuart Mill believed that a person ignorant of a potential danger which might befall him could justifiably be restrained, so long as the coercion was temporary and only for the purpose of rendering the person informed, in which case he would be free to choose whatever course he wished. Mill regarded this—correctly, I think—as temporary but justified coercion which is not "real infringement" of liberty: "If either a public officer or anyone else saw a person attempting to cross a bridge which had been ascertained to be unsafe, and there were no time to warn him of his danger, they might seize him and turn him back, without any real infringement of his liberty; for liberty consists in doing what one desires, and he does not desire to fall into the river."

It is not a question of protecting a man *against himself* or of interfering with his liberty of action. He is not acting at all in regard to this danger. He needs protection from something which is precisely not himself, not his intended action, not in any remote sense of his own making.[19]

[18] T. Beauchamp, ibid., p. 388.
[19] Ibid. The quote is from John Stuart Mill, *On Liberty* (Indianapolis: Bobbs-Merrill, 1956), p. 117.

Beauchamp is certainly correct in assuming that there is *a sense* in which a person who did not know the bridge was unsafe was not voluntarily performing the act of crossing an unsafe bridge.[20] Further, we might well agree that detaining such a person, at least to warn him of the danger, is permissible. None of this, however, is a reason to draw Mill's conclusion that turning him back is not "any real infringement of his liberty." One can imagine similar cases of constraining (for hours on end) one who is drunk for the same beneficent end, but it is surely a fiction to pretend that there is no real infringement of liberty. Mill, of course, gives an argument for thinking otherwise; in his view liberty consists in doing what one desires. Mill's argument, reconstructed, seems to be:

1. S's liberty to do X is infringed only if S desires to do X

2. S does not desire to do X

So, 3. S's liberty to do X is not infringed.

The argument is valid, but there is no good reason to accept premise (1). If I only want to sit in my chair and read for two hours and have no desire to get up, my liberty is, nevertheless, infringed if, without my consent, you bind me to the chair for that period of time. Being at liberty to perform an act is more appropriately characterized in terms of the absence of constraints or barriers to certain possible courses of action—independently of whether I do or will desire to perform them.

Gerald MacCallum's suggestions about the analysis of freedom are useful here.[21] To say of some agent that he is free is to be committed to the view that there is an absence of some sort of constraint (the presence *or* absence of something) to the agent's

[20] Some sticky issues arise here. One might argue that since the subject, S, does not voluntarily choose to cross an unsafe bridge, and crossing the unsafe bridge is the same act as crossing the bridge, S does not voluntarily choose to cross the bridge. If so, restraining S from doing the latter *does not* restrict his freedom of choice. Conversely, one might argue that since S voluntarily chooses to cross the bridge, and crossing the bridge is the same act as crossing the unsafe bridge, S voluntarily chooses to cross the unsafe bridge. If so, restraining S from doing the latter *does* restrict his freedom of choice. Difficult questions arise here about individuating acts, the identity statement in the above arguments, and whether acts are intended, or voluntarily chosen, only under certain descriptions. Pursuing these problems would take me too far afield. *Even if* we concede that stopping S against his will (suppose he struggles with the restrainer) does not thwart any intention of S to cross an unsafe bridge, it remains true, certain puzzles aside, that the intervener does restrict S's liberty of action.

[21] Gerald MacCallum, Jr., "Negative and Positive Freedom," *The Philosophical Review* 76, No. 3 (July, 1967), pp. 312–334.

performance of a certain act. Hence, I may be unfree to drive if the constraint of *not having* a car is present. I may be free to walk if the constraint of *being* straitjacketed is absent. Analogously, S is, or may be, free to cross the unsafe bridge in the absence of our turning him back and unfree to do so in the presence of that constraint. Some of the features in virtue of which someone may not be free are "external" to and independent of a person's *desire*. I am not free to steer the Queen Mary, and it matters not one iota whether I want to do so or not. Mill's, and perhaps Beauchamp's, succumbing to the belief that "liberty consists in doing what one desires" may derive from the beliefs that since restrictions on liberty often are wrong and that turning back the person about to cross an unsafe bridge is permissible, doing so must not restrict liberty or be any "real infringement of liberty." But this is a misdescription, even if the moral judgment is a reasonable one. In Joel Feinberg's useful terminology, we can foreclose or leave open a person's options whether or not they are paths a person wishes to take.[22] Alternatively, we might paraphrase Sir Isaiah Berlin to emphasize our central point: it is one thing to say that I may be coerced to prevent a state of affairs whose occurrence I do not desire; and another to say that if I do not desire that state of affairs, I am not really being coerced, even though I do not consent to the restrictions of those who interfere, and struggle against them.[23]

Our slight detour takes us back to Beauchamp's reasons for asserting that "intervention in cases of nonvoluntary or of uninformed conduct is not paternalism in any interesting sense" and that turning back the man approaching the unsafe bridge is "not a question of protecting a man against himself." We have argued that constraining the man *does* restrict his liberty. By assumption it is aimed at the man's own good. Why is that not a paternalistic act? Beauchamp's further key assumption is that intervention is paternalistic only if it interferes with a subject who, through his actions, produces harm to himself. Thus, he assumes that it is only

[22] This use of Feinberg's remarks hardly taps his rich discussion of freedom in his essay, "The Interest in Liberty on the Scales," in *Rights, Justice, and the Bounds of Liberty* (Princeton, Princeton University Press, 1980), pp. 30–44.

[23] Berlin's actual remark is "It is one thing to say that I may be coerced for my own good which I am too blind to see; another that if it is for my good, I am not being coerced, for I have willed it, whether I know this or not, and am free even while my poor earthly body and foolish mind bitterly reject it, and struggle against those who seek to impose it, and with the greatest desperation." Isaiah Berlin, "Two Concepts of Liberty," in *Four Essays on Liberty* (London: Oxford University Press, 1969), p. 134.

31

when someone *voluntarily and knowingly subjects himself to certain risks* that interference to prevent him from doing so is paternalistic.[24] Since, it is alleged, the ignorant bridge-crosser does not do so, intervention with him is not paternalistic; or it is not "paternalism in any interesting sense." For reasons I have already elaborated in part, this is an unwarranted conclusion. In general, harm may occur to S in three different types of circumstances: (1) the situation in which it primarily results from S's action, inadvertent or not; (2) the situation in which it primarily results from the action of others, inadvertent or not; and (3) the situation in which it primarily results from an act of nature, for example, an earthquake. In *any* of these circumstances we may try to prevent S's coming to be harmed by interfering with S—by honest persuasion to alter his choices or by a presumptively wrongful act, such as force, coercive threat, or deception. If we do the latter in *any* of these three types of circumstances, against S's will, with the aim of preventing S from being harmed we have an unproblematic instance of paternalism. It is not at all clear why we should attach any special importance to the fact that the harm may occur in a situation like that of (1) as opposed to (2)—or that, within (1), it results from an inadvertent act as opposed to an act which is not—for purposes of classifying the interference as paternalistic or not. The core of paternalism is not just "protecting people against themselves"—their own risky but voluntary and informed choices—but acting, or omitting action, contrary to the operative preference, intention, or disposition of others in order to promote or preserve their own good. Even in cases like (2), in which a harm to S *may* result from a wrongful act of *others*, we *may* act paternalistically toward S to prevent it, for example, when I vigorously push you out of the way of a reckless, drunk motorist. It is important in all this to keep straight the two questions of (1) whether an act is *classifiable* as paternalistic (I have claimed that Beauchamp's restricted use here is unduly narrow), and (2) the *grounds* proffered to defend the justifiability of intervention (these may be paternalistic: to protect or benefit the person with whom we interfere—or nonpaternalistic, e.g., to protect or benefit persons *other* than those with whom we interfere).

In actual situations it may be reasonable to invoke both paternalistic and nonpaternalistic grounds for the permissibility of, say, A's interfering with S's risky activity, that is, A's doing so may

[24] Beauchamp, "On Coercive Justifications," p. 388.

protect S *and* others from harm. Still, it may be true that A interferes with S solely with the aim of protecting S; A is indifferent to the well-being of those other than S. In such a case A's act is paternalistic toward S, but the act may be most reasonably defended on nonpaternalistic grounds and perhaps not so on paternalistic ones. Or A's interfering with S may be motivated solely by the desire to protect those other than S; A is indifferent toward the well-being of S. In such a case A's act is not paternalistic toward S, but the act may be mostly reasonably defended on paternalistic grounds and not on nonpaternalistic ones. Our primary concern in this initial chapter is, of course, to classify and define. We have not yet begun to sort out, or assess, the various principles which are invoked in an attempt to justify paternalistic intervention by appeal to various paternalistic reasons or grounds for interference.

Beauchamp is rightly concerned to distinguish paternalistic principles (he, and others, sometimes speak of "the paternalistic principle," a misleading expression since there are many principles which appeal to paternalistic grounds in an attempt to justify interference) and (his construal of) "the harm principle." His aim in attempting to distinguish "the harm principle" and "the paternalistic principle," is to sort out what he regards as quite distinct appeals, in my own terminology: to paternalistic grounds for interference and to nonpaternalistic grounds. Yet he offers two quite different versions of the harm principle, and one of these versions blurs a defensible distinction between paternalistic and nonpaternalistic appeals. Compare

1. "The harm principle says that coercive interference with a person's liberty is justified if through his actions he produces harm to *other* persons or perhaps public institutions"

and 2. "the harm principle, as I construe it, says that when specific kinds of harm are caused to a person or a group of persons the state is justified in coercively intervening for the purpose of protection. In some cases the liberty of those causing the harms may be limited and in others the liberty of those harmed may be limited (at least temporarily)."[25]

Note that according to version 1. the harm principle is understood to permit interference with, and only with, *the agent* who causes

[25] Ibid., pp. 383 and 386, respectively.

harm to others. The ground for doing so, on this version, concerns solely the well-being of persons other than the agent. Clearly, version 1. includes no elements of paternalism and stands as a distinct liberty-limiting principle (setting aside the question of its plausibility). On version 2. the harm principle is understood to permit interference not only with the agent causing harm (if there is one) but also interference with those who may be harmed. Further, the aim is to protect those who may be harmed. Hence, on this version the state (absent in version 1., but we set that aside) can interfere with both agents and subjects of harm in order to prevent harm to the subjects of harm. This last point should make it clear how version 2. incorporates elements of paternalism and, therefore, fails to achieve Beauchamp's avowed aim of setting forward two quite distinct liberty-limiting principles. Quite apart from analyzing Beauchamp's competing definition of 'paternalism' and his attempt to distinguish paternalistic and nonpaternalistic principles which purport to justify constraints on others, it is important, in our inquiry, to keep such matters straight. I hope to have shown how our account better enables us to do just that.

The analysis of paternalism which I have proposed also differs in important respects from the rather elaborate and well-known account set forward by Bernard Gert and Charles Culver.[26] They set out a complex "full account" of what, by definition, must be involved in paternalistic behavior; I shall later include it, but initially let us focus on their claim that ". . . an essential feature of paternalistic behavior toward a person is the violation of moral rules (or doing that which will require such violations). . . ."[27] They elaborate further by proposing that "violating a moral rule involves doing something that would be morally wrong unless one has an adequate justification for doing it. Thus, killing, causing pain, . . . depriving of . . . opportunity or pleasure are all violations of moral rules."[28] I was at one time more sympathetic with the claim that, for A to act paternalistically toward S, A *must*, in doing so, violate some moral rule. The expression 'paternalistic interference' *seems* redundant, and if 'paternalism' by definition involves *interfering* (as it does in our account), it seems natural to think that some

[26] This account appears in "Paternalistic Behavior," *Philosophy & Public Affairs* 6, No. 1 (Fall, 1976), pp. 45–47 and a similar one in "The Justification of Paternalism," *Ethics* 89 (January, 1979), pp. 199–210.

[27] Gert and Culver, "Paternalistic Behavior," p. 48. This feature is retained in their most recent study, Gert and Culver, *Philosophy in Medicine*, p. 130.

[28] Gert and Culver, "Paternalistic Behavior," p. 51.

moral rule has been abrogated. As we have noted, however, some "interferences" are morally innocuous, for example, interrupting someone to ask the time of day. Similarly, we might interrupt someone by telling her the time of day (so that she will not be late for an appointment). On our account, if she does not want to be reminded, this last is an act of paternalistic interference. However, there is no reason to think that it involves violating a moral rule. If this is correct, we ought to avoid an unduly restrictive analysis of 'paternalism,' for example, that of Gert and Culver, which disallows the classification of such an act as paternalistic. The tendency to be unduly restrictive here, one to which I have succumbed in previous writings, may be due to a fixation on the *morally interesting* subset of cases of paternalism, interesting because controversial and controversial because they involve violating a moral rule or a presumptive duty. Our current account, of course, avoids such undue narrowness. It also provides us with a morally neutral account of paternalism such that correctly to classify an act as 'paternalistic' does not entail that the act is wrong, not even presumptively wrong. Hence, we can avoid "begging the moral question" at the stage of merely classifying an act; the Gert-Culver account, to say the least, encourages one to do otherwise. For further reasons which I later elaborate, their account "loads the dice" even more.

Both the Gert-Culver account and my own, however, confront the similar questions: what violates a moral rule and what violates a presumptive duty? I have sought to answer the latter question, albeit incompletely and with little defense, by enumerating types of acts which I take to violate presumptive duties toward other persons. Gert and Culver also elaborate "the moral rules" by examples: rules against deception, nontrivial deprivations of freedom, opportunity, or pleasure, disabling others, killing, causing physical pain or suffering.[29] Since they allow that such acts are justified in certain cases, they must also regard such rules as nonabsolute and, rather, as rules delineating presumptive duties; hence, their account is, in this respect, similar to the one defended here in that the controversial instances of paternalism are ones which violate presumptive duties.

Their account, like that of Beauchamp, suffers, however, from an overly narrow conception of what constitutes restricting someone's liberty. They offer two cases as examples of paternalistic

[29] Ibid., p. 48.

action which do not restrict a subject's liberty: (1) performing a blood transfusion on an unconscious member of a religious sect who has, previously, expressed opposition to such a procedure, and (2) the secreting away of sleeping pills from a depressed woman who has expressed the desire to kill herself.[30] They prefer to describe the second case as one of 'depriving a person of opportunity' and perhaps the first case as well.[31] Let us focus primarily on the second case. Should we suppose that the latter case is *not* one involving a restriction of liberty and regard it, rather, as one involving a "deprivation of opportunity" instead? Further, is it plausible to claim that there is a moral rule (presumably a legitimate one and not just an arbitrarily concocted one) against depriving persons of opportunities? Both questions require negative answers, but the first question is not interesting unless we show that the second should be answered negatively. It is unreasonable to think that there is an unqualified moral rule against depriving others of opportunities. If there were, it would be wrong, or at least presumptively wrong, to take a job (if you get it I will not), marry Maria Theresa (if you do, I cannot—at least now), win the race, be first in the class, and so on. Surely, there is no moral rule, as such, against depriving others of opportunities. Relatedly, Gert and Culver suggest that there is a moral rule against depriving another of pleasure; this is equally implausible. If you derive pleasure from watching others stand on their heads, burn witches, or engage in self-immolation, that is simply too bad. There is no general duty for others to perform such acts and, hence, no moral rule making it wrong, not even presumptively, for them to deprive you of such pleasures. Whether or not it is all right, in case (2), to hide the sleeping pills from the depressed, possibly suicidal woman is a question I postpone (see Chapter 5), but it is, I believe, a case of restricting liberty. As we have observed, in discussing the views of Beauchamp and J. S. Mill, we can restrict a person's liberties and render them unfree to perform certain types of acts by introducing barriers to such acts, for example, by hiding the sleeping pills. In case (2) one of the depressed woman's options is foreclosed (that of committing suicide and then and there taking those pills). Relatedly, in case (1) the blood tranfusion renders it impossible for the unconscious person to succeed in preserving his or her body

[30] Ibid., pp. 47 and 51.
[31] To avoid a possible confusion, one may agree that case (1) does not involve *coercion*, i.e., coercive threat; it does not follow that it does not involve a *restriction on liberty*.

"untainted from foreign substances." The freedom to pursue such a goal, rightly or wrongly, has been subverted. Even though we may not capture adequately *all* that is morally significant about a case by judging that it involves a "restriction on a subject's liberty," that is not sufficient reason to deny that a case is correctly so described when it does. If it does, it typically violates, I have maintained, one or another of the presumptive duties we *do* have toward competent persons. If that is so, we need not manufacture dubious, alleged, moral rules, such as those just discussed, in order to identify the locus of moral controversy.

Since we have attended only to certain features of the Gert-Culver account, it is worth setting it out in full:

A is acting paternalistically toward S if and only if A's behavior (correctly) indicates that A *believes that*

1. his action is for S's good;

2. he is qualified to act on S's behalf;

3. his action involves violating a moral rule (or will require him to do so) with regard to S;

4. S's good justifies him in acting on S's behalf independently of S's past, present, or immediately forthcoming (free, informed) consent; and

5. S believes (perhaps falsely) that he (S) generally knows what is for his own good.[32]

This account, unlike some, is clear and admirably explicit. One of the striking features about it and one reason for my delaying its full statement until now is that it is inconsistent with the earlier insistence of Gert and Culver that "an essential feature of paternalistic behavior toward a person is the violation of moral rules." As close inspection shows, the full account does not require satisfaction of this condition; rather it requires only that the agent *believes* that his action violates a moral rule. These are different matters indeed. According to the full account, if I believe that I am exorcising your demon (by, for example, placing the remains of cremated snakes near your driveway) and that this is for your own good, and so on, I *am* acting paternalistically. But if, as seems likely, doing so violates no moral rule, then according to their other claim I *am not* acting paternalistically. Conversely, 1. through 5. may be satisfied even if I do not believe that I violate a moral rule when I

---

[32] Gert and Culver, "The Justification of Paternalism," p. 199.

wrongfully offend you; again, whether I act paternalistically or not depends on which account we employ; the two generate contrary results. Let us set aside this difficulty and focus on other aspects of the full account.

It seems unreasonable to insist on feature 3. in the full account. Although many agents who act paternalistically (e.g., by coercing or lying) no doubt take themselves to be "violating a moral rule" in some sense, many examples come to mind which seem paternalistic, and are on our account, but do not satisfy this condition, for example, you tackle another who is about to inadvertently step off a cliff or you fasten the safety belt in your car around your resistant child. It does seem, as we have argued, that a defining feature of paternalism is that the agent aim at promotion of the subject's good; that the agent must have thought about and morally assessed his act does not. To conclude otherwise seems to "project" on to paternalistic agents the worries of a philosopher, or others, who have consciously considered the moral perplexities attaching to interferences with others for their own good.

A similar objection must be made to 2.: that the agent must *believe* that he is qualified to act on S's behalf. Talk of qualifications suggests the necessity of satisfying formal or official requirements for a certain role or status. Gert and Culver seem to mean, however, nothing so strict by 2. They suggest that when a sober person restrains a drunk he must believe that he can ascertain better than the drunk what is for the latter's own good. However, given the fact that anyone invasively interfering with another for his own good will probably believe something of this general sort (otherwise, what would be the point of interfering?), 2. seems likely to be a true but trivial feature of anyone naturally describable as a "paternalistic" agent. However, this construal makes it all the more puzzling why Gert and Culver maintain that "a small child usually can not be said to be acting paternalistically toward his parents."[33] The force of 'usually' is not clear. Surely a small child (*how* small?) can believe on a few or many occasions that she has superior insight as to what is for her parents' own good; compare the cases of illiterate, blind, deaf, and alcoholic parents. In addition, condition 2. seems misleading since it suggests not only that official conditions must be satisfied but also, again, a high degree of self-consciousness or reflectiveness on the part of the intervening agent. In caring for an accident victim one might act impulsively and, I

[33] Gert and Culver, "Paternalistic Behavior," pp. 50–51.

suggest, paternalistically (e.g., drag him off the expressway) without "thinking the thoughts" about one's "qualifications" to do so. Often an agent simply may see a risk (e.g., an onrushing vehicle) that the subject does not. Why must a "belief about qualifications" come into play?

Feature 4. emphasizes possible consent by the subject. As I shall later argue, such a consideration does have a crucial bearing on whether paternalistic intervention is justified. However, why must A *believe* that (promoting) S's good justifies his intervention apart from S's past, present, or immediately forthcoming free and informed consent? Suppose I hold the belief that deceiving an adopted child about his adoptive status is justified *only if* the child "subsequently consents" to the deception and I engage in such an act "for the child's own good."[34] My act seems paradigmatically paternalistic even though, given my moral belief, it does not satisfy 4. In general, it is arbitrary to restrict 'paternalistic behavior' to cases in which the intervening agent happens to hold a specific and disputed view about the conditions under which interfering with others for their own good is justified.

People frequently interfere to aid another or prevent harm to another, simply because they *care* about the well-being of that person, without always taking the broader view required to make some overall moral evaluation of their intervention. One result of restriction 4. is to narrow the extension of 'paternalistic behavior' to an exceedingly small range of cases in a way that is both contrary to ordinary usage of 'paternalism' and theoretically unfruitful.

A similar complaint must be voiced about 5. If the subject must *believe*, in order to be treated paternalistically, that he (S) generally knows what is for his own good, one important implication is that we cannot (logically) act paternalistically toward those who lack this belief, for example, infants, toddlers (probably), at least some retarded persons, and virtually all animals.[35] This result is linguis-

[34] Or consider a case in which an agent coercively interferes for another's good and believes that his act is justified *only if* the subject does give his "consent" *immediately* after the interference.

[35] It is worth noting that the definition of 'paternalism' adopted here also contrasts somewhat with a narrower one adopted by James Childress, namely, ". . . a refusal to acquiesce in a person's wishes, choices, or actions for that person's own benefit." (See James Childress, *Who Should Decide?* (New York: Oxford University Press, 1982), p. vii.) First, 'acquiesce' seems to imply that the intervener is aware of an explicit request by another that the intervener act in a certain fashion. Second, I think it is sensible to speak of acting paternalistically toward some animals (e.g., fencing them in for their own good); it is so on our definition. So the definition adopted here does not restrict subjects of paternalism to persons. Also, on Childress's view if S

tically counterintuitive. When we give a young child a painful injection for his or her own good or fence-in a pet for its own good, these seem clear cases of paternalistic behavior. If the Gert-Culver account, in other respects, constituted a persuasive and compelling analysis of "paternalistic behavior," one might have reasons to revise or reject what I take to be the natural and commonsense description of these matters. However, for the reasons set forward, the account is conceptually flawed in spite of their conscientious aim at careful, systematic, analysis (and their valuable discussion of specific cases, ones which have not been our focus here).

1.6 Types of Justification

So far we have taken some pains (and perhaps caused a few in the process) to distinguish the issue of definition from the issue of justification, to define 'paternalistic act,' to demonstrate the advantages of our account over alternative ones, and to suggest with some care the broad and diverse range of actions that are collected together, under our definition, as being paternalistic. We have further sought to distinguish categorically different types of attempts (paternalistic, nonpaternalistic, and mixed) to justify paternalism. Carefully examining those attempts is the not so easy theoretical task which lies before us. Indeed that examination is the philosophical core of our inquiry, and will be our focus in Chapters 2 and 3. At later stages (Chapters 4, 5, and 6) we will attempt to determine what implications our theory has for various policies and practices, for example in the field of medicine or, more generally, the "therapeutic professions" but with special reference to patient/health-care professional interactions, and for questions concerning efforts to delimit the risks of certain "life-style" activities and other, hardly avoidable, instances of exposure to risks.

To this point we have left ambiguous the important phrase 'moral justification.' I make a modest assumption at this point: that the most fundamental distinction we can make concerning the morality

---

consents to an action by A, A's act is not paternalistic (p. 241); in contrast A's act can be paternalistic on the definition adopted here. As cases of consensually sanctioned interference show, A can interfere with certain of S's operative preferences even if S has consented to such interferences. There is, however, no conflict with Childress's account on this last point if by 'consents' he means only 'currently consents.' On both accounts doing what accords with another's current wishes or choices lacks the element of interference and, even if aimed at another's good, fails to be paternalistic behavior. However, *earlier* manipulation by A of S's preferences or attitudes to generate later compliance may have been paternalistic interference.

of actions is that between those which are morally permissible and those which are not. If an act, X, is morally permissible for A, then A has no duty to refrain from doing X.

Our *central* question in this inquiry is whether certain types of paternalistic acts or particular paternalistic acts are *morally permissible*. Those claiming that a paternalistic act is wrong deny its permissibility. If it can be established that an act is permissible, there is always the further question of whether it is impermissible *not* to do it. If and only if it is true that both an act is permissible and it is impermissible not to do it is there a duty to do it. So, "the" question of the justification of paternalism can be understood as two questions: (1) *whether paternalism is permissible* or (2) *whether paternalism is a duty*. It is possible to resolve the former question without resolving the latter but not conversely, that is, we cannot resolve (2) without resolving (1) (or at least being logically committed to a certain answer to (1)). In either case the question of permissibility is basic and it will be our primary concern.

As we have observed, some paternalistic interferences seem innocuous and involve no presumptively wrongful acts. Others do and stand in need of defense if we are to conclude that they are morally permissible. What sorts of morally relevant countervailing considerations, if present, would serve to justify a presumptively wrong paternalistic interference? The proposed candidates (for a *paternalistic* justification) seem to fall into two broad categories: (1) those which, in some fashion, appeal to actual, predicted, or hypothetical *consent on the part of the subject* of the paternalistic act, or hypothetical consent of a "fully rational person"; and (2) those which do not. The latter typically suppose that the *consequences* of the paternalistic interference (often cashed in terms of resulting happiness, harm prevention, enhanced freedom, retention of autonomy, life-preservation, expanded skills) are so important as to override any presumption against the act in question (be it the use of force, coercive threat, deception, duress, and so on). These latter *consequentialist* approaches are rather suspect today among many professional philosophers since there appears to be a growing consensus that the leading consequentialist theory, utilitarianism (whose central principle is simply that what we ought to do, or what is right, is whatever act will maximize net aggregate utility or satisfaction—at least as much as any alternative act) is inadequate. One major reason for its widespread rejection is that it is believed to sanction (approve) morally abhorrent acts, for example, the sacrifice of the rights or well-being of innocent persons for the

41

sake of promoting aggregate satisfaction (understood as the sum of the net satisfactions of each and all individuals affected by the act). In general, there is a suspicion that all purely consequentialist approaches to moral decision making are inadequate. Whether this is so we leave open here. Given the seemingly problematic nature of appeals to consequences, some philosophers have been attracted to positions which, instead, appeal to consent of the subject as a factor which renders morally permissible interventions which are presumptively wrong. This strategy, on the face of it, is most inviting for a number of reasons.

The moral relevance and significance of consent will be a crucial matter throughout much of our inquiry. We will return to it more than once. One important point to observe here is that from the standpoint of much traditional morality, as well as certain theories of human rights, the existence of a certain type of consent (for now, let us say, genuine, voluntary, reasonably informed consent) on the part of a subject renders morally permissible certain interactions with that subject which would otherwise be wrongful. For example, if I enter your house without your consent, that is typically a wrongful act. Similarly, if A cuts S with a knife, whether A has wronged S is commonly thought to depend on whether S has consented to the cutting. In a standard case of surgery where S consents to the operation, normally the cutting is morally acceptable. In the absence of consent it is wrong, and may count as assault, battery, or mayhem—with legal penalties attached. Such examples are easily multiplied; consent is commonly a countervailing consideration which may render an otherwise wrongful act permissible.

Why is actual consent thought morally relevant in that manner? The answer *may* be couched in the language of rights, either moral or legal. If we think, for example, that persons have a right to bodily integrity and that this claim of right entails a corresponding duty on the part of others to refrain from infringing that right, then the giving of consent by the right holder can be understood as a *waiving* of his right not to have anything done which would undermine his bodily integrity. It is natural to view the cutting by a party to whom consent is given as not infringing any right normally and previously held by the consenting party (and perhaps still held against *other* parties). Such a perspective seems to lie behind the Roman legal maxim, *"volenti non fit injuria"* (to the one who consents no harm is done).[36] Some legally prohibited acts are, of

[36] Here 'harm' is construed as 'injury' or 'wrongful harm.'

course, *defined* so that their "recipients" do not consent, for example, rape. On the "rights model," acts which infringe rights are presumptively wrong. However, if consent by a right holder is given, the relevant right is waived or relinquished, and certain acts which would otherwise infringe the right (and, hence, be wrong) infringe no right (and, *ceteris paribus*, are permissible).[37]

Must we agree that the moral relevance of consent be unpacked in the way that it is on the rights model? Indeed, must we be committed to some sort of rights theory if we concede the moral relevance of certain types of consent? The answer is not obviously affirmative. We may believe that there are insuperable difficulties in identifying rights, the basis for their attribution or, in general, that the most defensible full-blown ethical theory need not include any assumptions about human rights. Rather, we might think that, talk of rights aside, people have certain basic *duties* toward others (which need not correspond to any distinct rights on the part of those others), for example, duties not to kill, not to deceive, not to injure, not to invade bodily integrity, and so on. Further, on such a view, if S consents to A's cutting him, then S *releases* A from his duty not to transgress S's bodily integrity; the duty A normally has toward S is, so to speak, canceled. Hence, A's cutting S is permissible; it infringes *no* duty A has toward S. On both the rights model and the duty model, a moral barrier to a certain type of act is extinguished; the normal presumption against the act is removed.

Thus, from both ethical perspectives consent of the right sort counts and may count decisively in determining moral acceptability.[38] In short, the genuine, voluntary, reasonably informed consent of one person to otherwise presumptively wrongful treatment seems sufficient to justify the act in the absence of other morally relevant factors. Hence, the attractiveness of attempting to defend

[37] Whether there are certain "inalienable" human rights which cannot be waived, forfeited, or otherwise relinquished is a question I explore in "Are Human Rights Inalienable?" *Philosophical Studies* 37 (1980), pp. 165–176, and later in Chapter 5. See also A. John Simmons, "Inalienable Rights and Locke's Treatises," *Philosophy & Public Affairs* 12, No. 3 (Summer, 1983), pp. 195–204, and the references in both essays.

[38] Thus, we need not suppose that 'consent' *must be defined* as "according another a right" to act in a certain way or as "the relinquishing of a right." The former seems to be done by A. John Simmons when he states "When I speak of consenting, then, I mean the consenter's according to another a special right to act within areas where only the consenter is normally free to act." (See A. John Simmons, "Tacit Consent and Political Obligation," *Philosophy & Public Affairs* 5, No. 3 [Spring, 1976], p. 276.) Still, it is reasonable to explain the moral importance of consent in terms of rights; what is not clear is that we must do so.

certain forms of paternalistic interference on the grounds that the subject consents to them.[39]

"Appeals to consent" to justify paternalism take a variety of forms. Some appeal to the existence of *prior* consent by a subject, some to *current* consent, some to predicted *subsequent* consent. Others appeal to some form of *hypothetical* consent, for example what S would have consented to if he were informed, or "fully rational," or conscious, and so on. Related to these appeals to hypothetical consent are invocations of *proxy* consent (especially for children) and, in law, decisions regarding the treatment of incompetents which rely on the "doctrine of substituted judgment." In the following chapter we examine a variety of appeals to consent, appeals which purport to show that certain types of paternalism are morally acceptable.

[39] I explore these issues in more detail in Chapters 3 and 4.

T W O

APPEALS TO CONSENT

For that some should rule and others be ruled is a thing
not only necessary, but expedient; from the hour of their
birth, some are marked out for subjection, others for
rule. —Aristotle

No man is good enough to govern another man without
that other's consent. —Abraham Lincoln

2.1 Consent

Let us call the ultimately complete and rationally justified ethical
theory the Ultimate Theory. Whether it is couched in terms of
certain basic rights or duties, or both, there is good reason to believe
that the Ultimate Theory will allow the moral relevance of a certain
type of consent, that on such a theory consent will serve to justify
or partially justify acts otherwise presumptively wrongful. This
claim is not *entirely* uncontroversial but it is better to postpone
consideration of objections to it to Chapter 3. Even if the Ultimate
Theory allows for the moral relevance of consent, it may assign to
consent only a restricted role, for example, only the consent of
certain persons counts, or only consent given under certain conditions counts. Hence only certain types of consent are "morally
valid," that is, morally relevant to deciding what are permissible
dealings with, or with regard to, the consenting or dissenting party.
Indeed, such a view is implicit in traditional law and morality, and
that is the view that I shall defend here. However, before attempting to characterize "valid consent," a prior question must be answered, namely, what is meant by 'consent'?

The term 'consent' etymologically derives from an expression
meaning 'to feel together' or 'to agree.' It is also defined as 'voluntary concordance with,' 'acquiescence,' or 'approval.' Such lex-
ical characterizations are a step toward clarity, but only a small
step. We need to do a bit of conceptual sorting. In some cases

45

'consent' means only mere *acquiescence* in, or nonresistance toward, an ensuing event, as when one says that an elderly person consents to growing incapacity or to death. In such a case the "consenting" party, while taking a positive attitude toward an event (or, at least, not a negative one), does not *authorize* or *sanction* or *give permission to* anyone to do anything. In contrast, I may be said to "consent" to a labor strike in Poland. Here, the force of 'consent' (at best) seems to be that of 'approve.' Still, I did not sanction or authorize the act; indeed I seem to have no power to do so, nor is it obvious that my opinion ought to count, or to count in any significant manner. My "agreement" does not authorize any act; it does not grant anyone a right to act. The first "acquiescence" sense of 'consent' and the second "agreement" sense of 'consent' may be contrasted with the "authorization" sense of 'consent.' In many cases, for reasons not yet fully discussed, we regard an individual's decision as relevant, and possibly decisive, in deciding what policy may be pursued. It would be one thing, morally, for my physician to come upon me in my sleep and perform an appendectomy without my consent (my decision to permit the act) and another for her to do it after I have given my explicit approval. Even if it is true that I would have consented to the operation had I had the opportunity, in the case imagined I did not. That I *would have* consented had I been asked does not entail that I *did* consent. This simple point will be of some significance when we consider appeals to hypothetical consent as an attempt to justify paternalistic interference.

For S to authorize A to act in some fashion requires, I propose (1) a choice on the part of S to allow A to act, (2) possession by S of a right, a legitimate claim, or legitimate authority to decide whether or not A may act in a given manner, and typically but inessentially, (3) a successful communication of S's choice to A. If this is correct, consent as authorization involves more than S's having a preference, even an all things considered preference by S that A act in the preferred way. The key features are that S choose or have chosen in a certain manner and that S have the legitimate authority or right to decide whether A may act in a given manner. In the clearest cases of consent as authorization (1), (2) *and* (3) will be satisfied. In cases where (1) and (2) are satisfied and (3) is not obviously satisfied there may be good grounds for speaking of "implied consent," but even this involves more than the existence of an approving attitude, or, revealingly I think, a "willingness to consent." Even if Maria Theresa is willing to marry me, she has not necessarily consented to do so, not even "tacitly."

2.2 Valid Consent

Our discussion of 'consent' only attempts to isolate and clarify that sense of 'consent' which is commonly thought to be of greatest moral significance. We need not suppose here that the preferences of others in the absence of consent have *no* weight at all. Even if, however, we restrict our focus to consent which appears to authorize or give permission to another (as I shall), it is not obvious that when anyone chooses to allow another to act in a certain fashion that such admitted consent is morally relevant, or is *sufficient* or *necessary* to justify (render permissible) that to which consent is given.

Among cases in which one party seems to consent to (authorize) an act of another, some "consentings," in contrast to others, seem to have no moral relevance at all. For example, if a four-year-old child declares that he consents to the proposal that his family put their monetary assets into convertible bonds, we either reasonably doubt that this is consent at all or, if that is conceded, that it has any moral weight in deciding the permissibility of so doing. It is doubtful that the child could understand the proposal and/or have made a reasonable (not: fully rational) choice. Similarly, if you give your permission to Z to test a new poisonous gas on you, under the threat that he will otherwise torture you for weeks, it is doubtful that your consent (although under the circumstances, it is voluntary *in one respect*) should count at all toward justifying the proposed experiment. For the consent so to count we assume that it must be more broadly "voluntary." Consider a further case. I hear that the head of the KGB has decided to adopt a child. I think that is nice and (attempt to) send him (?) a telegram granting my approval. What has misfired here? Why is my "consent" not only without causal impact but of no moral relevance?

For consent to count morally, the consenter must have some right or, more weakly, legitimate claim to be able to influence the outcome of a proposed policy. In the case in which it is proposed that S donate an organ for a sibling such a condition seems satisfied by S, in contrast to our KGB example. In the case of the four-year-old, *perhaps* the child's interest in the destiny of the family's assets gives him some legitimate claim (however weak) to influence the dispensation of the assets. For a different reason, his cognitive incapacities, we assign no relevance to his "declaration of consent." These reflections are designed to support the claim that, even among cases of consent (as authorizings), including marginal ones, it is reasonable to recognize a distinction between consent which is morally relevant and consent which is not. What criteria are to be employed here? I propose, as a rough guide, that

S's consent to A's doing X is valid consent if and only if S's consent is

    1.   broadly voluntary,

    2.   the product of reasoned choice,

and 3.   S has a right or a legitimate claim to influence the performance of S by A.

This rough guide seems to embody a great deal of what is presupposed in the way considerations of consent are commonly taken into account and treated in more systematic doctrines, for example, "the" doctrine of informed consent (a matter we shall closely examine in Chapter 4). Some important matters also turn on the construal of key expressions above, 'broadly voluntary' and 'reasoned choice,' but I shall set these aside here.[1] Now that we have an interpretation of the expression 'valid consent,' I shall also, and independently, assume that valid consent is morally relevant to deciding the permissibility of the act to which it is given or from which it is withheld.

An important point of clarification arises here. Once it is agreed that the consent of an individual is valid, there remains the question of *how morally significant* that consent is in deciding on the permissibility of the act to which valid consent is given. To emphasize a point, I distinguish *that* question from the question of whether consent is valid consent. One possible view is that S's valid consent to A's doing X is *necessary* in order for A's action to be morally permissible. Another view is that S's valid consent to A's doing X is both necessary *and* sufficient for the moral permissibility of A's doing X. Further, there are other, more nuanced, possible views which I shall not attempt to enumerate here.

Since some discussions of paternalism attempt to show that it is justified, there is a natural reliance on the principle that if S validly

---

[1] I note that 'reasoned choice' here is understood weakly and not, for example, synonymously with 'fully rational choice.' I shall not pursue the matter, but I would insist that S's having been indoctrinated in certain ways may preclude S's choice from being a reasoned choice.

consents to A's doing X then A's action is permissible (that valid consent is a sufficient condition for the justification of X). This principle, for reasons partly noted earlier (Section 2.1), will seem immensely plausible to some; indeed it is precisely this principle that seems to be supposed in concluding that the surgeon's cutting you is all right (if you consented) but, perhaps, not otherwise.[2]

2.3 Current and Prior Consent

Our immediate concern is whether paternalistic interferences can be justified by appeal to consent, or more specifically by appeal to prior, current, or subsequent consent. Having laid the groundwork, let us focus on the cases of prior and current consent.

Unless otherwise specified, references to 'consent' are to be construed as references to valid consent, but, as noted, so far we have left open just how morally weighty such consent is. The first task is to take note of a special type of problem regarding prior and current consent so that we may set it aside as a rather special case—in order to address more basic ones. In some cases, previous consent seems to be irrevocable. Suppose I sell my car to you and, five years later, come to you and insist that I have changed my mind; I no longer consent to your having the car. You would rightly be perplexed by both my nerve and my assumption that my prior consent is, as we might say, "revocable." In some cases the giving of consent therefore seems to be a *permanent* waiving of and/or transfer of rights. Once permission is given, there are no lingering prerogatives on the part of the consenter to reclaim that over which she once had a certain authority. By contrast, one may sometimes give prior consent but later legitimately withdraw it or, else, discontinue it. I might consent to my neighbor's harvesting my apples to make pies, but years later as a newly enthused pie maker I

---

[2] In passing, however, we note that the law sometimes prohibits certain activities in which the immediately affected subjects may give what appears to be, or is, valid consent, e.g., gambling, prostitution, euthanasia, mayhem, "crimes against nature," dueling, and homosexual practices.

By contrast, the Roman legal maxim 'volenti non fit injuria' (to him who consents no wrong is done) seems to imply that consent may be sufficient to justify the act to which there is consent. Similarly, many who insist on decriminalization of "victimless crimes" seem to hold that valid consent is sufficient for justification—at least if no one, including third parties, is wronged (i.e., the acts are genuinely victimless). Given this last qualification, it may be misleading to say that some hold (simply) that valid consent to an act is sufficient. For further reflection, however, one might consider the special case of those who hold that divine consent (by itself) renders an act permissible.

discontinue permission for his harvesting efforts. The earlier consent may have had a tacit or explicit rider: "until I deem otherwise." Hence, some acts of consent seem to preclude withdrawal of consent; others are revocable or discontinuable.[3] So prior consent does not entail current consent.

However, there are two sorts of cases in which consent plausibly seems to justify otherwise wrongful acts: (1) S *previously* gave *irrevocable* consent to A's doing X, and (2) S *currently consents* to A's doing X. Regarding (1), since the consent is irrevocable, A, even *now, has* permission to do X (*even if* S currently opposes X or wishes that he had never given permission to A to do X). The contrasting cases are those in which S earlier gave permission but discontinued it—and in which S neither gave nor gives permission. Both of the earlier types of cases, (1) and (2), might be described as ones in which there is "currently operative consent," cases in which consent was given and has not been revoked (it would be odd to speak of current consent as "continuous," as if the consenter repeatedly reassessed his decision, minute by minute, and repeatedly concluded "I consent"). Our primary question here concerns whether the presence of S's currently operative consent to A's doing X is sufficient to justify a paternalistic performance of X by A.

As an aside we note a related special problem. If a patient previously consented to predictably painful (e.g., electro-convulsive) therapy, to take place over a period of time, and after the first session wishes to cease participation, what should be done? What is permissible? The answer seems to depend in part on whether the earlier (valid) consent is revocable, and in part on the answer to our larger question, namely, is S's valid consent to A's doing X sufficient (or necessary) to justify X.[4] I turn to the question of sufficiency.

Suppose someone were to propose what I shall dub the *General Consent Principle* (GCP):

If S has given currently operative consent to A to do X, then A's act, X, is permissible.

Let us suppose further that GCP applies only to competent people and, once more, only valid consent is in question. For a variety of

[3] Alternatively, we may prefer to describe certain cases as ones in which the scope of what is consented to is significantly restricted. For example, in the "apple case" the initial consent may be to "harvesting apples until I deem otherwise," and we may judge that *that* limited consent or authorization is not revoked even though, later, I deem otherwise.

[4] Questions about irrevocable consent are explored in Section 5.7. Also, in the principles to be considered 'X' may stand for commissions or omissions.

reasons, GCP is clearly implausible. Suppose S has consented to A's bizarre plan to infect S with a lethal, contagious disease in order to use S as a human weapon to kill large numbers of innocent people (who do *not* consent to such treatment). I shall assume that A's act is not permissible and that S's consent fails to render it permissible. The act, clearly enough, involves serious wrongs to others, to "third parties."[5] Indeed, it seems possible, in any case in which one party consents to the act of another, that the act will involve indefensible wrongs to third parties. Hence, there is good reason not to accept GCP, even if we may rightly believe that valid consent is morally relevant (or decisive in a more restricted domain of cases).

The important point to consider here is that any act, whether paternalistic or not, may involve serious wrongs to third parties. So any act, paternalistic or not, may be impermissible for such reasons, even if the immediate subject of it gives the weightiest and purest consent one wishes. In such cases it is doubtful that the subject's consent, *in itself*, could be sufficient to render the act permissible. There is a way of dealing with this difficulty, one which circumvents very important issues, but which we shall nevertheless employ. If we assume that all morally assessable human actions can, in principle, be divided into two classes: those that are *wrongful to others* and those that are not, then we can formulate another consent principle less obviously open to objections than GCP. Prior to doing so, I note that (1) although we need the Ultimate Theory to determine the boundary between acts wrongful, and acts not wrongful, to others, we can have a quite well-grounded confidence that certain specific acts (e.g., ordinary murder, rape, and torture) go in one class and certain others in the other class; I leave the reader to supply further qualifications, and (2) I set aside for later discussion whether we can, as Immanuel Kant maintained, wrong ourselves (see 3.9).

A more tempting consent principle is the *Restricted Consent Principle* (RCP):

> If 1. S has given currently operative (valid) consent to A
> to do X,

[5] Note that, given certain unlikely facts, such an act may turn out to be impermissible on a classical utilitarian approach; maybe it would maximize total net utility. Also, one can imagine circumstances where such an act is permissible from other theoretical standpoints, e.g., those allowing extreme measures in cases of national self-defense against unjust aggressors.

    2. in S's own estimation A's doing X is likely to promote a benefit for S or prevent a harm to S,

and   3. A's doing X does not wrong those other than A or S,

then A's paternalistic act, X, is permissible.[6]

Recall that for A's act to count as a paternalistic one, a paternalistic interference if one prefers, it must be one at cross purposes to S's prevailing preference at the time of A's act. Otherwise A's act may simply be an instance of nonpaternalistic altruism. Further, RCP is to be understood as presupposing that S is or was competent to consent at the time of doing so and competent with respect to deciding whether A's doing X will promote a benefit or prevent a harm to S (but competence doesn't preclude being mistaken about such a judgment). If RCP is an acceptable principle a certain range of paternalistic acts is justifiable, that is, when A's doing X is paternalistically motivated and (1) through (3) are satisfied. Any acts doing so will be instances of justified paternalism. This is a possible pattern of justification; in Chapters 4, 5, and 6 we shall look more closely at its implications for specific cases (and try to *respond* to the familiar query often addressed to moral philosophers: what is the relevance for such and such a situation?).

The crucial question here, however, remains: is RCP an acceptable principle? I believe that it is. A full defense of RCP is no mean task. First, I shall consider an objection to RCP. Later I shall suggest a more positive reason for accepting the principle.

RCP seems a more tempting principle than GCP because it avoids the difficulty noted, namely, that S's consenting to an act, X, by A does not by itself render A's Xing permissible; after all, such an act may wrong third parties. However, the very qualification in RCP by which it avoids sanctioning such acts suggests a possible objection to RCP. Consider an example. Suppose you are suffering a severe allergic reaction to an insect bite and you are about to go

---

[6] I normally use the expression "acts not wrongful to others," or cognate expressions, rather than "domain of morally permissible acts" because some claim that there are wrongful acts (and, hence, acts not morally permissible) *other than* those which wrong others. For example, it is claimed, on some purely nonconsequentialist approaches, that some acts are intrinsically wrong; relatedly, in Immanuel Kant's view we have duties to ourselves and, hence, can act wrongly even if we wrong no others. We consider the plausibility and implications of these views in Chapter 3 (and Chapter 5), for they suggest bases for arguments against respecting the autonomy of competent persons. In addition, I construe 'others' to include any existing being with moral standing (e.g., some animals) as well as those beings with moral standing which will exist. Finally, 'wrong others' refers to an all things considered judgment, not merely a presumptive wrong to others.

into anaphylactic shock (and possibly die). I know enough about you and about medicine to recognize these facts. Further, the only readily available anti-allergenic drug with which I can inject you is in a locked house of a stingy neighbor, Scrooge. You consent to the injection (indeed, you request it). Still, the only way to obtain it is to break into Scrooge's house and abscond with the drug. It is tempting to think that the complex act, B, of breaking in, taking the drug, and injecting you is an act of permissible paternalism. After all, *your life* is at stake. Still, it seems that if I so act, I wrong Scrooge. Given the "does not wrong others" proviso of RCP, it seems that RCP fails to sanction a *permissible* act. It may seem, therefore, that RCP is defective.

Against this charge several points are worth making. First, RCP is a principle only purporting to delineate when certain paternalistic acts are permissible. In other words, it proposes that when certain conditions are satisfied that is sufficient reason to conclude that a paternalistic act is permissible. For that reason RCP does not imply that B is impermissible. If it did, we would have to agree that it had a counterintuitive implication since, on the face of it, B seems to be the right course of action under the circumstances. It may be replied that even if RCP does not sanction an intuitively wrongful act, it fails to sanction certain intuitively permissible acts. Hence, RCP by itself is too weak. The theory defended here, however, is not confined to RCP, and there is no suggestion that RCP provides a reasonable ground for all legitimate paternalistic acts.

A second and more important point concerns whether, in fact, RCP fails to sanction B because of its no wrongs to others proviso. I propose here that it does not so fail, at least when combined with a reasonable assumption about what constitutes wronging others. It is just here that it is useful to clarify further how the no wrongs to others proviso is to be understood. To do so is to be committed to a certain view about the contours of the Ultimate Theory, a theory whose full articulation, as noted, is beyond my purview here.

As we have developed the example, doing B does seem to "wrong Scrooge." However, the question arises as to whether B only presumptively wrongs Scrooge or whether it is a wrong when all relevant considerations are taken into account. Although I shall offer no full defense of this claim, it is reasonable to think that all things considered, doing B is *not* wrong. Both utilitarian and non-utilitarian theories can yield just this conclusion; further, it is one which, I believe, corresponds to commonsense views about what is permissible in extreme situations. It is worth observing also that "the doctrine of necessity" in Anglo-American law allows the performance of acts in extreme situations which are, otherwise, disallowed; for example, in a storm you may dock your boat on another's private mooring without the consent of the owner. To the extent that the law allows such presumptively legally wrong acts and does not take the stance that the act is wrong but the agent excused (e.g., because of exculpatory factors such as ignorance or insanity), it is natural to regard the law as viewing such acts as permissible (and not merely wrong but excused). Similarly, from a moral standpoint performing B seems a justifiable act and not wrongful to Scrooge.[7] Hence, there need be no wrong to others, I presume, on the Ultimate Theory. The no wrongs to others proviso is to be understood, then, as "no wrongs to others all things considered." Given the assumption that the Ultimate Theory would imply that no third parties are wronged, we conclude that the Restricted Consent Principle sanctions act B and does not leave the moral evaluation of B an open question—as suggested initially by the proposed example.

Another objection to RCP is waiting in the wings. I lead up to it indirectly. In an intriguing and instructive essay, Joel Feinberg, in order to explore the morality of "exploitation," considers a rich diet of examples where subjects consent to acts at least some of which are morally suspect: an expert pool player's accepting a bet over a pool game with a cocky amateur, cooperating with a beggar who wishes that you cut off his arm (since he thinks he can thereby beg more effectively), selling alcohol to alcoholics, making money by writing about those who are desperate (e.g., Gary Gilmore), "ambulance-chasing" by wreckers or physicians, purchasing organs

---

[7] Perhaps other qualifications are necessary, e.g., Scrooge is adequately compensated for any harms done to him in the performance of B. On these matters I have been influenced by Judith Thomson, "Self-Defense and Rights," (The Lindley Lecture, University of Kansas, 1976).

On Thomson's view, an infringement of a right (e.g., Scrooge's) need not be wrong (i.e., a *violation* of Scrooge's right). Perhaps, one wrongs Scrooge if one infringes his right *and* fails to compensate him adequately, but if one infringes his right and adequately compensates Scrooge one has not wronged Scrooge, all things considered. Although I shall not explore the obvious complexities of duties to compensate, we may have a duty not to infringe rights or to do so without adequately compensating for the infringement. If that is correct, an infringement is *not necessarily* wrong (all things considered); still, an infringement triggers the duty to compensate. If the latter duty is omitted, a wrong *is* done or, more vaguely, "a right is violated." None of this commits one, I think, to the wild view that *in general* and without qualification it is all right to go about infringing rights and providing adequate compensation. Identifying the further requisite provisos, however, would take us far afield.

from the very poor (which is usually illegal, but consider the purchase of blood from the very poor), and the hiring of Ann Meyers by a professional "men's" basketball team, the Indiana Pacers.[8] Not all these cases are of a piece, and Feinberg notes relevant differences. One might characterize 'A exploits S' (in a manner similar to Feinberg) in terms of A's doing something to S in order to turn some feature of S (e.g., a character defect such as impulsiveness or cockiness—or a virtue such as generosity) or S's circumstance (e.g., poverty, hunger) to his own (A's) advantage. Some acts falling in this category are both exploitative (in the mentioned sense) but morally innocuous, for example, exploiting your opponent's weak serve in a tennis match. Some are not. It is no simple task to figure out which cases of exploitation are, thus, *wrongfully* exploitative ('exploit,' of course, is often used pejoratively; so construed, begging the moral question is hardly an uncommon practice).

Feinberg focuses on three relevant considerations in sorting cases which fall under the rubric 'exploitation': (1) whether the act harms S's interests, (2) whether S consents to the act, and (3) whether A profits or gains by the act. When (1) and (3) are satisfied but (2) is not, interference is permitted according to the widely accepted *Harm Principle* (roughly: it is permissible coercively to intervene to prevent agents from imposing harms on unconsenting, innocent, persons). For our purposes the more interesting cases are (1) those in which S's interests are harmed, S consents to the act, and A profits or gains from the act; (2) those in which S's interests are harmed, S consents, and A does not profit or gain; and (3) those in which S's interests are not harmed, S consents, and A profits or gains. Giving the cocky amateur pool player his "comeuppance" is an instance of (1); cutting off the beggar's arm *may* be an instance of (2); and purchasing a bodily organ from a desperate poor person may be an instance of (3). Note that in these three cases there may be valid consent (even if not highly prudent) by S. Thus it may appear that RCP sanctions acts falling into these categories. The apparent dilemma is that such acts may be wrong; if so, and if RCP sanctions them as permissible, we must reject RCP.

I shall not explore these matters fully. However, reflection on

---

[8] See the published essay: Joel Feinberg, "NonCoercive Exploitation," in *Paternalism*, ed. Rolf Sartorius (Minneapolis: University of Minnesota Press, 1983), pp. 201–236. My comments are occasioned by a prior version of Feinberg's essay. I have not explored it, but see also Joel Feinberg's *Harm to Others* (New York: Oxford University Press, 1984).

such cases and the limits built into RCP suggests, I propose, that RCP is not undermined by such considerations. RCP does not sanction acts wronging third parties (all things considered) and some exploitative acts will thus not be sanctioned by RCP. Further, in at least some cases of exploitative acts the consenting party is, arguably, not competent or the consent not sufficiently voluntary or reasonably informed. In such cases RCP will not condone the "consented to" act. Still, there may be a residue of actual or possible cases in which RCP seems to sanction wrongful exploitation. In two of the three types of cases mentioned, (1) and (3), A profits or gains. This feature by itself seems no reason to condemn an act; otherwise reciprocal acts between friends, mutually beneficial agreements, or exchanges would stand condemned. A key feature of exploitation as defined here (and similar to Feinberg's construal) is, however, not merely that A gains or profits from his act but that he *intends* to do so by the act, and, presumably, this is the primary or sole motivation in acting. Such a consideration indeed seems to be a defining feature of our ordinary conception of exploitation. This point is not unimportant since RCP sanctions only *paternalistic* acts of a certain sort, i.e., acts which, among other features, are ones in which the agent intends (primarily or solely) to promote a benefit for S or prevent a harm from befalling S. For this reason, strictly speaking, no paternalistic act is correctly describable as exploitative. Thus, RCP sanctions no act of exploitation; hence, no act of wrongful exploitation.

Still, this reply may not demolish all the worries one may have about exploitation. The types of cases noted, (1), (2), and (3), may not be exploitative since none is characterized in terms of the agent's *intention*. That A profits or gains focuses on a *result* of the act, not on A's intention. The deeper worry concerns whether it is all right to perform acts falling into categories (1), (2) or (3), whether or not the agent primarily intends to benefit himself. Still, for any act falling into category (1), (2), or (3) to be *paternalistic and permissible* according to RCP the agent must believe that he, by acting, will benefit S or prevent a harm to S (all things considered). Thus, RCP does not sanction any act in which A has a contrary belief. For this reason RCP will not sanction the expert pool player's "hustling" the amateur, cutting off the beggar's arm if the agent believes that he (the beggar) will be worse off on balance, selling alcohol to an alcoholic if the agent believes the result will be net harm, or buying an organ from a poor person or abetting a suicide if the agent believes that the subject will be worse off on balance.

But what about the hard cases, for example where we judge that the beggar *will* be better off on balance (not just in terms of income) if his arm is cut off? It does not seem inconceivable that there might be such a situation, albeit a highly improbable one. Even if amputating the arm would not be wrongful exploitation, might it not be wrong (and, hence, impermissible) to do so? It is crucial to recall that our question concerns not whether it is a duty to do so, but whether it is permissible. That one found doing so distasteful or repugnant, might be a perfectly good (self-interested) reason to refuse (a refusal, be it noted, which is not paternalistic in motivation). It is not obvious, I suggest, that in the rare case in which one judged that amputating the beggar's arm would make him better off on balance, that doing so would be impermissible. It is worth keeping in mind here the (limited) similarity of this case to cases in which surgeons accede to requests for cosmetic surgery, transexual operations, or even castration (or radical behavioral modification) for those wishing to prevent themselves from continuing a pattern of rape. Again, in considering what RCP sanctions, it is crucial to recall that the subject must be competent, must voluntarily and reasonably choose to authorize another to so act, and that the act wrongs no third parties on balance. It is not obvious that such acts wrong such consenting subjects, that it is impermissible to perform such acts with paternalistic aims, or that such acts demean, degrade, or defile the subjects.

In attempting to show that RCP, in sanctioning a certain range of paternalistic acts, does not entail the permissibility of acts rightly deemed "wrongful exploitation," I have so far chosen the more complicated path since there is a simpler reason for concluding that RCP does not sanction wrongful exploitation in those, noted, cases in which the subject desires and chooses that A perform the act in question. It is just this. In such cases the agent, if he so acts, will *not* be acting at cross-purposes to the current desire of the subject; given our definition of 'paternalistic act' the agent's so acting simply does not count as a "paternalistic act" or "paternalistic interference." Whether or not, then, complying with a subject's prevailing choices or requests is wrongfully exploitative of the subject, doing so fails to be an instance of paternalistic intervention. In contrast, RCP sanctions, as permissible, only paternalistically motivated acts (or omissions) which are contrary to a subject's prevailing preference, acts to which the subject earlier gave valid, unrevoked or unrevocable, consent.

In brief, I conclude that RCP does not sanction acts which are wrongfully exploitative. Hence, RCP is not subverted by such considerations. We have considered several objections to RCP. Its complete defense may require possession of the Ultimate Theory. I now propose that RCP should be accepted because it is grounded in a more basic principle which, I maintain, should be accepted. The more basic principle asserts that competent persons have a right to direct their own lives. That is, however, only a rough description of the alleged right. My succinctly stated claim is that RCP is justified if competent persons have a right to direct their own lives. This is a strong claim and needs further clarification and defense.

We are following the argument where it leads and it may be useful to recall its winding path to this point. Our overriding concern is with the justification of paternalistic actions. Some attempts to justify paternalism appeal to prior consent. I have maintained that the Restricted Consent Principle, if correct, will serve as a key assumption in justifying an important range of paternalistic actions toward S, namely, those in which there is currently operative consent by S toward the act in question. The question arises as to why one should accept RCP. My contention here is that we should accept RCP because it follows from a more basic principle asserting the right of competent persons to direct their own lives, a principle to be stated with greater qualification. This latter principle is a strong one in the sense that it is in conflict with a variety of widely held and competing principles. Indeed, it will play a role not only in deciding the acceptability of justifications (or alleged justifications) *which appeal to consent*; it will play a crucial role in deciding the justifiability of *all* cases of paternalistic interference with competent persons. The defense of the right to direct one's own life is a complex and challenging matter, but also, for the reasons just noted, a crucial one. Here, I shall turn to a more careful statement of the right and offer a partial defense of it. Its further defense will be developed at those points where we examine competing principles (in Chapter 3). Later we shall return to the appeal to prior and current consent, and also examine the appeal to subsequent consent.

2.4 The Right to Direct One's Own Life

Earlier I proposed that consent should be distinguished from mere acquiescence and mere approval, and further that valid consent must satisfy certain conditions, one of which is that the consenting party has a right or legitimate claim to influence the performance of some act, X, or its outcome. It was further assumed that such consent is morally relevant. A further claim is that competent persons (and 'competent person' is deliberately left comparatively unanalyzed to this point) have a right to direct their own lives. The claim is, in part, that people have a right to influence the performance of acts which nontrivially affect the course of their own lives. This right is a right possessed by all competent persons and, further, is an equal right of all competent persons.[9]

One objection to the assumption of such a right might be posed as follows. Suppose I am starving after being shipwrecked along with Friday and Crusoe. Friday proposes killing Crusoe and sharing the remains with me (for culinary purposes). Does Friday have a right to kill Crusoe? May I assist in doing so? Clearly not; but why? One answer is that Crusoe has a right, against me and others, to have a say over the course of his life, including a right to veto the proposal. But what constraints are there on acts which any one of us might engage in to influence acts affecting the course of his life? A large question once more, and it would be nice to possess the Ultimate Theory. Here I suggest that we must recognize, minimally, that there are some constraints, as we commonly assume and as all ethical theories suppose. Some acts wrong others; many, at least, of the remaining alternatives are not wrongful. For it to be plausible to assume that any competent person has a right to direct his or her own life, we must recognize that the domain of acts within which any such person has a right to choose and act is restricted by the fact that other competents also possess this right and, more fully, the domain excludes any acts which involve, all things considered, wrongs to others. I am suggesting, in a familiar fashion, that as difficult as it may be to delineate *precisely* the boundaries of the sphere of permissible actions it is necessary to recognize such a sphere and, therefore, further qualify any proposed right to direct one's own life. A more careful statement of the right is this:

Each competent person has an equal right to direct the course of his or her life by choosing any alternative within the sphere of acts not wronging others.[10]

[9] Since capacities vary among competent persons, why speak of an equal right of all competent persons? A reason for doing so is set out in Chapter 7.

[10] The restricted scope of this right makes this claim of right less vulnerable to the difficulties which immediately arise for less restricted rights claims, e.g., the alleged fundamental human right which A. I. Melden attributes to each person: a

The claim that certain people have this right to direct their own lives is, on reflection, more modest than a variety of claims of right which are familiar enough today. For one thing it is not attributed to animals, fetuses, or even all humans. Second, it is a right to choose within a limited sphere of possibilities (but, I maintain, not so limited as to be trivial or pointless). Because of this latter feature, it cannot be invoked plausibly to justify the killing of Crusoe. Indeed, no objections to the recognition of this right can be posed on the ground that exercise of such a right will foreseeably lead to wronging others (an objection that, plausibly, is made to the claim that each person has a right to control the destiny of his or her own body). Recognition of the right to direct one's own life does not involve *that* sort of counterintuitive implication. Recognizing the right of self-direction views competent persons as arbiters of their own lives, as final authorities over the dispensation of their own efforts and time, and as proper adjudicators of their own contrary wants, and intrapersonal conflicts of interests. It does *not*, however, attribute to competent persons any authority to impose wrongs on others.[11] Rather, competent persons are viewed as sovereigns within the domain of permissible acts and only equal citizens outside that domain; outside that domain persons sometimes must negotiate to determine goals and resolve interpersonal conflicts of interests.

It is worth observing that determining the precise boundaries of the right to direct one's own life involves large and difficult questions. As noted before, to do so would involve ascertaining the Ultimate Theory. Nevertheless, I have maintained that there are a variety of clear cases of wronging others; we need not pretend that we must remain agnostic about all questions concerning wrongs to others simply because we are not certain of the exact nature and details of the Ultimate Theory. A further point of clarification is that I have deliberately formulated relevant principles not in terms of *harming* others but in terms of *wronging* others. There are several reasons for doing so. First, if we are understood to harm others when we, by our acts, make them nontrivially worse off than they would have been in the absence of such acts, we do not necessarily

right to engage in conduct in pursuit of one's interests. See A. I. Melden, *Rights and Persons* (Berkeley: University of California Press, 1977).

[11] Whether 'others' should include human fetuses, or zygotes, or the permanently comatose, I leave open; I do use 'others' to range over human beings and, though the point is inessential here, sentient animals. Hence, I here take no fully determinate position on the question: what sorts of entities possess moral standing.

wrong them. Often, as J. S. Mill noted, successfully competing against others in fair competition harms opponents but does not wrong them. Further, although causing certain direct harms to others may wrong them, we may wrong others by causing certain risks of harm to others even though, in retrospect, "no harm" occurred. Hence, what counts as a wrong to others (and, in turn, shapes the boundaries of the right to direct one's own life) need not be restricted to some subset of harmful acts (wherein 'act harmful to others' is distinguished from 'acts merely imposing a risk of harm to others'). Finally, it is at least not obvious that all wrongful acts are either harmful to others or impose a risk of harm. It is at least initially plausible that, for example, we can wrong others by making public unfair judgments of others which neither cause those others harm nor subject them to a risk of harm. What we ultimately should conclude about these perplexities awaits a more compelling theory about the relation of 'harm' and 'wrong' than currently exists. These succinct remarks may suggest how the right to direct one's own life should be construed, how it needs further elaboration, and also why its recognition is not without substance even though its precise scope must be regarded as indeterminate.

Besides defending the claim that competent persons have this right by calling attention to the fact that it is immune to a whole range of objections (succinctly: that its recognition sanctions evident wrongs to others) which may be brought against various claims of right, we note that recognition of the right explains the importance which is commonly attached to valid consent. As observed earlier, valid consent seems to involve the waiving of a right, a right not to be treated in a certain fashion (which may occur because of a commission *or* omission by others).[12] As a result, others are released from a duty not to infringe that right. An otherwise wrongful act becomes permissible. But one can only intelligibly authorize or give permission with regard to certain activities (recall our example of sending a telegram to the head of the KGB), namely, those whose performance one has a right to influence. Why do we suppose that one's permission is intelligible and significant (indeed, often decisively so) with respect to allowing another to enter one's house, to damage one's tissue (as in surgery), or to spend one's money? The natural answer is that, normally, we recognize a right on the part of the individual in question to determine the

[12] The objection that some rights cannot be waived is considered in some detail in Chapter 5.

dispensation, use, or treatment of those entities. If the right is not waived or forfeited or transferred, it is, at least presumptively, wrong to so act; if waived, then, *ceteris paribus*, such acts are permissible. The importance we assign to valid consent (or its absence) in such cases is reasonable, I contend, if we recognize a right or a legitimate claim of competent persons to direct their own lives within the domain of acts not wrongful to others.

It is worth noting here, then, that suppositions about the relevance and importance of consent play a fundamental role in ordinary moral assessments (moral assessments common, I would claim, to all cultures). To suppose their importance, then, is not to appeal to some special, and perhaps controversial moral point of view. Neither should the asserted importance of valid consent be thought of as an *ad hoc* postulate favored only by those who have some vested interest in defending "the doctrine of informed consent," a doctrine explicitly formulated and emphasized primarily since the outrages publicized at the Nuremberg Trials (the experiments by Nazis on those who dissented). The view posed here is that, on the contrary, the importance of valid consent is part of the "deep structure" of ordinary moral thought and of any reasonably comprehensive and coherent ethical theory which, at its core, requires a modicum of respect for individual persons; further, that if valid consent is important in deciding the permissibility of a certain range of actions, we must recognize the right to direct one's own life.

There is more that could and ought to be said by way of defending the view that competent persons possess such a right. As our inquiry proceeds we will do so as the opportunities arise (especially in Chapter 3). We began this chapter by questioning whether some paternalistic acts are justifiable by appeal to prior or current consent or, upon analysis, by appeal to "currently operative consent." Provisionally assuming that competent persons have the right to direct their own lives we can conclude affirmatively. Schematically, the argument is this:

1. Competent persons have an equal right to direct the course of their lives by choosing any alternative within the sphere of acts not wrongful to others.

Suppose 2. S is a competent person.

So 3. S has an equal right to direct . . . by choosing any alternative . . . not wrongful to others.

Suppose 4. S previously has validly consented that A do X, such consent has not been revoked, A's doing X is contrary to S's current preference or disposition, A's doing X is not wrongful to others than A or S, and in S's own estimation A's doing X is likely to promote a benefit for S or prevent a harm to S.

So, 5. A's paternalistic performance of X is permissible.

In specific cases it will be *crucial* to determine whether it is true of a particular person, S, and act, X, that 2. and 4. obtain. In many cases an important source of controversy will concern *whether or not* X is within the domain of acts wrongful to others (than A or S); compare consenting euthanasia, dueling, gambling, suicide pacts, or prostitution. In Chapter 5 we examine a number of such specific practices. Here our aim is to identify *principled grounds* for determining the justifiability of certain practices. To paraphrase a remark of Kant, moral principles without empirical facts are empty, but acts apart from moral principles are morally indeterminate. Our focus in this and the next chapter is on moral theory and principle.

2.5 What Has Been Justified?

The short answer to this question is: a number of presumptively wrongful acts but less than many believe justified. If the preceding line of argument is correct, there is a not insignificant range of activities in which A acts permissibly toward S, namely, cases where S has given the appropriate sort of consent to A. Such cases may include a variety of otherwise wrongful acts, typically ones which involve "invasive interference"—possibly involving force or deception. This point may strike some as not obvious and, hence, surprising. So it deserves explanation.

Let us consider the case in which you believe that it would be for my own good that I stop smoking. I agree with you that it is a nasty habit, and I agree that it is bad for my health. Further, I do not value the satisfaction of smoking so much that I prefer to continue in spite of the risks to my health. However, I suffer from "weakness of will." I have trouble mustering the appropriate self-discipline. Suppose further that I am a competent person, as are you, and that I validly consent to (and request) your interfering with me in some well-defined fashion whenever I attempt to smoke. For the reasons discussed, *those* efforts of yours to interfere are permissible, and, if you do so in order to promote my own good, are instances of justified paternalism.

There is an objection which might be made to this conclusion.[13] It proceeds as follows. Since I have validly *consented* to certain delimited efforts on your part to prevent me from smoking, then, even if I later resist your attempts to do so, you are not obviously *interfering* with me; after all, you are simply trying to carry out *my* settled resolve. And if there is no interference there is no paternalistic act. Further, if your efforts at restraint do not count as paternalistic acts, then there is no reason to conclude, as we just have, that they are instances of justified paternalism.

I was once persuaded by this argument and persuaded (I conjecture!) because of the impressive difference between the case in which one person restrains another *at the behest* of the latter and with his consent versus more common instances of restraint in which there is no consent on the part of the restrained party. I emphasized the point as follows:

> In some cases a person's settled preference may be that his choices should be restricted under certain circumstances, including those where he foresees that in such a circumstance he may want to perform an act which will be made difficult or impossible if the restrictions obtain (for which he has a settled preference). In such cases an individual may choose to arrange circumstances in such a way that his passing impulses or whims are interfered with. As noted he may do this by self-administering a pharmacological substance or securing the co-operation of another person who shall in, and only in, the appropriate circumstances perform the function of a Preventer (compare securing the cooperation of Enablers, e.g., a therapist or a neighbor, to achieve other goals). *Cooperative interference*, then, must be contrasted with *coercive interference*. In the latter case the settled preferences of a subject of interference are in opposition to the interference; therefore, it is perceived by him as a threat to make him worse off, on balance. In the former case, it is not. There is nothing mysterious about an individual's choosing to secure cooperative interference. He may rightly believe that it is the most effective way to maximize

[13] I proposed and agreed with this objection in "Paternalism and Subsequent Consent," *Canadian Journal of Philosophy* IX, No. 4 (December, 1979), pp. 631–642.

his own satisfaction in the long run, given his own less than perfect ability to exercise self-control in particular types of circumstances.[14]

It now strikes me as preferable to use the label *sanctioned interference* for the case in which S has validly consented to A's interference and *unsanctioned* interference for the case where S has not done so—since cases of interference without consent need not involve *coercive* (use of coercive threat, or force) interference; they *may* involve deception, embarrassment, humiliation, ridicule, or other acts which genuinely interfere. However, even if we rightly recognize a difference between sanctioned and unsanctioned interference, and, hence, for reasons already given, the permissibility of the former and not the latter, sanctioned interference may be justified paternalism.

The temptation to conclude otherwise derives, I believe, from the inclination to think that 'interference' is by definition coercive and that there is coercion if and only if there has been no consent. Although we often speak of "interference" in cases where coercion or other presumptively wrongful acts are performed, it is worth recalling that 'interference' is not such by definition. Again, "the storm interfered with the parade" indicates otherwise; similarly, if I am momentarily stopped on the street by someone requesting the time of day, my activity is disrupted and an interference has occurred, albeit a mild and a morally innocuous one. You may rightly be described, in our prior example, as interfering with me when you attempt to restrain me from smoking (e.g., by plucking a cigarette from my hand); sanctioned interference remains interference, contrary to my earlier inclination to conclude otherwise. Alternatively, even if one is *not* tempted to assume that there is *coercion* if and only if there has been no consent, one may be tempted to think (more generally) that there is *interference* if and only if there is no consent, but, for reasons noted, this is false. So, the objection in question does not succeed.

How much paternalistic interference is justified if the preceding line of argument, one appealing to current consent, is correct? A not insignificant amount it would seem since the appeal to currently operative consent reasonably may be invoked to establish the acceptability of many activities pursued by physicians, nurses, psychologists, psychiatrists, lawyers, parents, friends, and others, such as automobile mechanics—since much activity by such per-

[14] Ibid.

sons falls into the category of action presumptively wrong in the absence of valid consent, for example invasion of privacy, invasion of property rights, offensive remarks, deception, and so on. One qualification should be noted here: although the presence of currently operative consent may justify an otherwise wrongful act by such persons, it is a further question as to whether the act is one of justified paternalism. Since we have defined a 'paternalistic act' in part as one where the agent acts with the aim of promoting another's own good or preventing harm to that other, the politician who promotes a bill which will benefit you *may or may not* act with this *aim*, even if her act has such a *result*. Hence, the act may or may not count as a paternalistic one. Indeed, if we allow that people often act with "mixed motives" or more than one intention it will often be unclear whether a given act is "purely paternalistic," partly so, or not at all. However, when an act appears to be paternalistically motivated our moral question concerns its justifiability, and that practical concern may remain even if an omniscient discerner of motives may confirm, or refute, our classification of it as paternalistic. To acknowledge this prompts us to emphasize that the moral controversy surrounding paternalism concerns justifiability and, in particular, whether there is a peculiar *paternalistic form of justification* (see Chapter 1) for "apparently paternalistic" acts.

To return to our question of how much paternalistic interference is justified by the appeal to currently operative consent, what has not been emphasized to this point is the rather evident fact that a good deal of paternalistic interference (including many of the more controversial cases) cannot be so justified. In a considerable subset of paternalistic acts there is, as a matter of fact, no currently operative consent. Our moral plot thickens, and we now begin to examine such cases. Given the already noted attractions of appeals to prior consent, it is natural to wonder about the permissibility of paternalistic interference on the grounds that the subject's consent will be forthcoming. We, therefore, turn to the appeal to *subsequent* consent.

2.6 *The Appeal to Subsequent Consent*

In making the transition to focusing on some sort of "consent" other than currently operative consent, we should observe a crucial difference. Appeals to currently operative consent look to actual decisions and desires of the subject as a source of justification for interfering acts and, primarily, to cases where these choices or dispositions have been made explicit. To begin to invoke considerations about what the subject *will* consent to, or *would* consent to under certain circumstances even though she *never* has and *does not now* consent, seems like a different kettle of fish. For an agent to make suppositions about such matters requires that the agent formulate judgments other than those actually made by the subject. Doing so seems to involve a certain circumventing of the subject's choices and/or substitution of the agent's choices for that of the subject. In contrast to appeals to currently operative consent, other sorts of appeals to consent (e.g., to subsequent or hypothetical consent) are radically different, or seem so, for they do not give weight to any actual current choice by the subject. For all that, such appeals may take into account the subject's settled preferences and dispositions, be benign, and the best that we can do. We need not jump to conclusions; so, let us investigate the matter.

Especially as children we often hear not only "it was for your own good" but also "you will be glad we did it" or "you will appreciate it later on." And sometimes we are. We may be pleased, later, that we got the penicillin or tetanus shot we vehemently opposed earlier. Imagine other cases. As a college student you are required to take a course in physics or chemistry. Later you are glad that you were so required. Or suppose, due to an accident, you received third degree burns over most of your body; at the time you wished to die and opposed any life-sustaining efforts. Still, they were imposed on you. Later you are positively disposed toward the imposition of such treatment. Such cases may tempt us to think that some cases of paternalistic intervention are justified because the subject, at a time *posterior* to the interference, *consents* to the interference.[15] Hence, we may formulate the *Principle of Subsequent Consent* (PSC):

A's paternalistic interference, X, with S is justified if S will subsequently consent to A's having done X and A's Xing involves no wrong to those other than A or S.[16]

[15] Compare Jonathan Glover's approval of the view that "If someone wants to kill himself, we often think it right to prevent him, on the grounds that he does have a worthwhile life and that *he will later be glad* of our paternalist intervention." See his *Causing Death and Saving Lives* (Harmondsworth, Middx., England: Penguin Books, 1977), p. 79.

[16] This principle is a slight modification of a principle with the same name which I identified in "Paternalism and Restrictions on Liberty," in *And Justice for All*, eds. Tom Regan and Donald VanDeVeer (Totowa, N.J.: Rowman and Littlefield, 1982), pp. 17–41.

We will later discuss the special problems that arise with regard to incompetents; here we ask whether PSC serves to justify paternalistic interference with competent adults. There are serious objections to answering affirmatively.

Unlike appeals to prior (or current) consent, the epistemological position of the potential interferer may be extremely problematic: the appeal to subsequent consent will be invoked, most probably, only in cases where there is no currently operative consent, and the interfering agent must calculate, infer, or conjecture whether it is certain or likely that S will subsequently consent to a certain interference. Whether S will do so depends not only on his current attitudes, preferences, goals, and perceptions of the world but also on what preferences, attitudes, and so on S will have in the future. Further, there is a tendency, one not to be underestimated, for people glibly to assume that constraints they might sanction *given their own current beliefs, preferences, goals, and values* would be acceptable to another, or that over a period of time the other will come to have similar goals and preferences. Without laboring the point, it seems highly doubtful that the conditions which would have to be satisfied in order for such judgments about subsequent consent to be reasonable are commonly satisfied. The problems with reliance on PSC do not, however, end there.

Not only is there the difficulty of predicting the future preferences, goals, and values of S, it is always an open question as to whether S will survive long enough, to a point where S might indeed "consent" to prior interference. By chance S may be struck down by lightning or, more likely, an automobile. If so, no subsequent consent will be forthcoming. Betting on actual consent in the future is a highly risky matter. Indeed the very idea that the permissibility of interference at time t depends on a possible occurrence at t + n, one which fortuitous factors may prevent, makes the morality of interference depend on chance—a curious element in any proposed justification.[17]

Such difficulties are "real world" considerations that confront potential interveners since their knowledge is limited. For the sake of sorting distinct considerations it may be useful to ask whether an omniscient paternalist, unobjectionably, could rely on PSC.[18]

---

[17] Except cases in which parties mutually agree to let an event be randomly determined, e.g., flipping a coin to see who will receive some indivisible good.

[18] I occasionally invoke the idea of an omniscient agent conceptually to separate epistemological problems from others, a device usefully invoked in Donald Regan's "Justification for Paternalism," in *The Limits of Law, Nomos XV* (Chicago: Lieber-Atherton Press, 1974), pp. 189–210.

Further difficulties remain. Consider two cases. First, suppose that you are knocked unconscious by a gang of hoodlums; at a later time you realize that had it not occurred you would have boarded a plane as you had intended, one which exploded and left no survivors. In retrospect you "are glad" that you were knocked out. Consider a second case. Suppose that you are a woman who was raped when she was eighteen. The experience was devastating and the next few years an enormous struggle, psychologically and otherwise. Seventeen years later, at thirty-five, you judge that, in some sense, it was "good" that the rape occurred. This last remark strikes one as incredible. What could be meant? Suppose that, in spite of a difficult life, there is something that has made your life one of deep happiness for over a decade, namely, the loving and joyous relationship which you have experienced with the two daughters born of the trauma at eighteen. You might be able to say that your life is much happier than it would have been if numerous other sequences had occurred; in that sense and in that sense *only* you have a positive attitude toward the *set* of prior events. But none of this supports the view that the rape was consented to, permissible, or not a heinous wrong.

"Consent after the event" surely does not alter the fact that at the time of the interference, as in the cases mentioned, no permission had been given, no right waived, no interferers released from a duty not to interfere. There was no operative consent. It is difficult to understand how subsequent consent is supposed to "reach back in time," perhaps a considerable segment of time, and legitimize the past act. Furthermore, there may be, and I believe there is, something conceptually incoherent about the use of 'subsequent consent' in PSC. It makes sense to speak of Derek's subsequent consent if, for example, Derek now refuses to lend me his food processor but later relents and does so. If I then use it, I have his permission; there is currently (at the time of the borrowing) operative consent. However, the appeal to subsequent consent with which we are concerned involves no such concurrent permission. If there is something to which 'subsequent consent' refers (there may not be, as we have noted) it will be a later "approval" or "positive attitude" toward a prior event. However, this hardly counts as a giving of permission or a relinquishing of a right. Rather it is only belated approval, or, if communicated to the earlier intervener, a declaration of forgiveness or a waiving of any claim to just compensation for a wrong inflicted. Forgiving a wrong, however, or recognizing a beneficial effect of a wrong done, does not obviously alter the fact that a wrong was committed. If, on the other hand, the earlier act was justifiable on some ground, it is not because of consent since one can only *consent* to what is to be done or the continuation of what is being done.[19]

A further point deserves notice. Some instances of "belated approval" are *not independent* of the disputed intervention. In certain cases of brain surgery, indoctrination, or psychotherapy, belated approval may be a byproduct of the intervention itself. This fact renders suspect the permissibility of the intervention since in such cases there may be no respecting of the subject as an independent judge of the acceptability of the proposed intervention. Consent is not forthcoming from the subject independently of non-invasive modes of influence; rather it is, or may be, a byproduct of intervention which goes beyond fair and open attempts to persuade.[20] To regard any resulting belated approval as a sufficient condition for the permissibility of the intervention would sanction abusive acts, for example reducing a subject to a state of abject servility by forcing her to ingest a servility-inducing chemical.

For the reasons given I conclude that the Principle of Subsequent Consent provides no adequate ground for justifying paternalistic interventions.

2.7 The Appeal to Hypothetical Rational Consent

The domain of justified paternalistic interference which we have identified so far seems comparatively narrow for it fails to include paternalism in the absence of operative consent. It is, however, tempting to believe that paternalism is justified in a wider range of cases. For example, consider the proverbial case in which you are about to cross a bridge which, unbeknownst to you, is dangerous and I coercively prevent you. Or suppose you are deaf and blind and about to walk off a cliff (unintentionally) and I stop you by tackling you. Imagine an even more extreme case. A deaf person is about to quaff her Pinot Chardonnay and unbeknownst to her

---

[19] For the above reasons, the moral permissibility of nonpaternalistic or paternalistic social science experiments where unconsenting subjects are deliberately deceived—then "debriefed," and, therefore, said to have consented after the fact when they do not protest—is much in doubt. This is especially true if the only alleged justification appeals to subsequent consent.

[20] Jeffrey Murphy called attention to this problem in "Incompetence and Paternalism," *Archiv für Rechts- und Sozialphilosophie* 60 (1979), pp. 465–486. Similar difficulties were noted by John Rawls in *A Theory of Justice* (Cambridge, Mass.: Belknap Press of Harvard University, 1971), p. 250.

it has been poisoned by her angry lover. As the glass approaches her lips I can stop her only by hurling a handy paperweight at her. I aim for the glass, but, alas, break her arm. If we are inclined to think, as am I, that these are cases of justified paternalism, we need to be able to say why. Various proposals not appealing to actual consent may be entertained here. One proposal appeals to *hypothetical* consent and it deserves our attention.

In the cases mentioned there seems to be a reasonable presumption that the subjects were unaware of the consequences of their actions, that their acts would lead to their becoming nontrivially worse off, and that if they were aware of the likely consequences, they would choose to refrain from engaging in the acts in question. Perhaps due to reflection on cases like this, Gerald Dworkin proposes to identify "situations in which it seems plausible that *fully rational individuals would agree* to have paternalistic restrictions placed on them" (my italics).[21] In this fashion Dworkin seeks to identify an acceptable ground for justifying a certain range of paternalistic acts beyond those involving explicit valid consent. Although Dworkin does not formulate a principle in just this fashion, we may try to capture his basic idea by what I shall label the *Principle of Hypothetical Rational Consent* (PHRC):

A's paternalistic interference, X, with S is justified if:
1. S would consent to A's Xing were S both fully rational and aware of the relevant circumstances, and

2. A's Xing involves no wrong to those other than A or S.[22]

Clause (2) is not Dworkin's, but helps render the principle immune to objections based on possible wrongs to third parties. PHRC, given certain natural assumptions about the subjects in the three cases just mentioned, seems to give us the right result: the interferences are permissible. Should we, then, accept the principle and, hence, conclude that whenever its conditions are satisfied in a particular case the paternalistic act is justified?

One way to test the principle is to try to see if it "proves too much," that is, whether it has other implications about other cases which seem intolerable. Shortly, I shall suggest that it has an un-

---

[21] Dworkin, "Paternalism," p. 129.

[22] I have used the label 'Principle of Hypothetical Rational Consent' in two other essays [in *And Justice for All* and in "Autonomy-Respecting, Paternalism," *Social Theory and Practice* 6, No. 2 (Summer, 1980), pp. 187–207]. The principle referred to here diverges somewhat from those used there. My aim here has been to consider a more tempting variation.

palatable implication, but first a word or two on the notion of "what would be acceptable to a fully rational individual." As Dworkin notes, there is a problem about ascertaining what would be acceptable to a fully rational individual. One might interpret Dworkin's appeal to paternalistic restrictions acceptable to fully rational individuals as meaning that those interferences are permissible which would prevent or deter individuals from acting in a way which is not fully rational, especially in cases where what would count as a fully rational act is rather straightforward. For example, Dworkin assumes that not buckling one's seat belt before driving is (normally) not rational and that in this situation "there is a stronger and more persuasive argument for paternalism." So it is plausible to read his position as proposing the permissibility of paternalistic interferences whenever generally competent adults act in irrationally imprudent ways.

This is how I shall read the Principle of Hypothetical Rational Consent. What I want to suggest is that PHRC allows invasive interferences to a greater degree than might first appear and, indeed, that it is unacceptable since it would fail adequately to respect the autonomy of ordinary, generally competent, persons. Consider an analogy. As a generally competent adult one could play a chess match as best one can or, alternatively, be hooked up to the P-machine, the P-machine being a paternalistically minded computer which prevents one from making any move which is not "fully rational" with respect to the goal of winning the match. So long as one is generally competent and one's intended moves are "substantially voluntary," I presume one would want to *decide for oneself* whether a possible move is prudent, that is, to "play one's own hand." If so, one would not want the imposition by the P-machine of a "forced" avoidance of the consequences of one's own (possibly) less than fully rational decisions, even if the result of such interference would be more prudent or a "socially desirable outcome." One's goal in such a circumstance is not just to win the match but to *play* it.

Perhaps it is now clearer how interference in accord with PHRC could be seriously invasive. We need not be committed to the view that individuals in all cases ought to be left alone to make their own decisions and carry them out, however irrational, when we take the view that people ought to be left alone with regard to certain decisions, even though they would not be made by *fully rational* individuals. The prerogative to choose for oneself, if not of unlimited value, is a distinct value to be weighed against, for example, the desirability of imposing restraints acceptable to a fully rational individual. A precocious child might say, "It is valuable to 'do it myself,' even if the results of so doing are not optimal." As Dworkin himself rightly observes, "to be able to choose is a good that is independent of the wisdom of what is chosen." My point is that the criterion of "those restrictions which would be permissible to fully rational individuals," as construed here, fails to give due weight to that good.[23]

I am suggesting in part that there may be a range of actions that would be chosen by a fully rational person which may only overlap with the range of actions that some actual competent person, S, might choose if he were fully aware of the relevant circumstances. If so, S would not necessarily choose to do, nor consent to have done to him, acts which a fully rational person might choose to do or consent to have done. It seems reasonable to suppose, assuming *some* degree of clarity about the somewhat obscure expression 'fully rational person,' that ordinary competent persons are not always fully rational. If that is correct, a distinction must be made between

1. what a fully rational person, aware of the relevant circumstances, would choose (to do or consent to have done)

2. what S, if S were aware of the relevant circumstances, would choose (to do or consent to have done)

and, for completeness, we may add 3. what S actually chooses to do or consents to have done. Imposing 1. on S may conflict with both 2. and 3., and, hence, interfere with S's right to direct his own life within the domain of acts not wrongful to others. Interfering with S in order to promote goals or values that a *fully rational individual* may have in a circumstance like the one S is in differs significantly from interfering with S to promote goals S would choose were *he* fully aware of the relevant circumstances.

For example, suppose Jones is about to bet a dollar at a casino. He believes his chances of winning a hundred dollars are 1 in 10. Let us suppose, however, that the chances are actually 1 in 10,000. It seems not improbable that a fully rational and well-informed person would choose not to bet the dollar. If a fully rational person would consent to interferences which would prevent him from acting in such an irrationally imprudent manner, then, according to PHRC, intervention with *Jones* is permissible. But not only may

---

[23] In these paragraphs I draw on remarks made in VanDeVeer, "Autonomy-Respecting Paternalism."

actual Jones resist such interference, it may be true that if Jones were fully aware of the relevant circumstances (i.e., that his odds of winning were actually 1 in 10,000) he would still choose to bet (and not consent to other's preventing him from doing so). Whether this is so, it should be observed, can be determined only by empirical data *about Jones*, that is, his preferences, values, aversion or attraction to risk taking, and so on, and not by conjectures about what a fully rational person would do, choose to do, or consent to have done. Further, it is worth observing that the mentioned bet (above) might be maximizing Jones' utility—if he got a sufficient utility payoff from betting (whether or not he wins). This point may be granted. Still, on this view of matters it is possible to postulate a preference ordering on the part of any decision-maker such that, given it, his choice can be understood to maximize utility and, hence, be fully rational—on this criterion of full rationality. So, for example, the person who chooses to try to set a record for the longest time spent in a room filled with poisonous snakes might be maximizing his utility. Therefore, he *may* be acting, on this criterion of full rationality, in a fully rational way.

In short, on this way of spelling out 'full rationality' it is not clear that many, *or any*, acts can confidently be assessed by observers as not fully rational. For this reason the appeal to "what a fully rational person would choose or consent to" is murky. Unless the concept can be invoked, and defended, in such a manner as to be incompatible with actual choices of actual persons, it can provide no basis for critical assessment of such choices. Thus, we cannot determine the implications of PHRC. This last point serves to undermine another response: namely, would not a fully rational person dissent to interventions which would not allow him to make his own choices (cf. The machinations, again, of the P-machine)? If so, might not PHRC *not* have the unduly meddlesome implications which we attributed to it? What must be said here, I believe, is that the concept of a "fully rational person" is too indeterminate to allow an affirmative answer. Even if to be fully rational is to maximize one's utility, what will maximize utility for a particular person will depend, in part at least, on his preferences. These will vary from person to person. Hence, we cannot know, in the absence of some actual preference ranking, "what a fully rational person would choose or consent to."

Further, talk of the "hypothetical consent of a fully rational person" is potentially misleading in one respect. The expression "fully rational person" refers to no actual person; it is a logical construct as is "frictionless plane." There is no consent given by a fully rational individual, that is, no actual giving of permission to constrain Jones provided by a fully rational person. What PHRC proposes in the final analysis is that it is all right to impose on S constraints or goals which may be foreign to those he does or might autonomously and reasonably choose. Hence, PHRC not only sanctions infringement of S's right to direct his own life; also for the reasons previously mentioned, it is unacceptable.

2.8 The Principle of Hypothetical Individualized Consent

Our discussion of PHRC, and our distinction between (1) what a fully rational person, aware of the relevant circumstances, would choose to do or consent to have done, and (2) what S, if S were aware of the relevant circumstances, would choose to do or consent to have done, suggests a different sort of principle of hypothetical consent, one which seems compatible with the ideal of respecting the autonomy of competent persons, and specifically, their right to direct their own lives. I shall label it the *Principle of Hypothetical Individualized Consent* (PHIC):

A's paternalistic interference, X, with S is justified if
1. S would validly consent to A's Xing if (a) S were aware of the relevant circumstances; (b) S's normal capacities for deliberation and choice were not substantially impaired; and

2. A's Xing involves no wrong to those other than A or S.

The point of my less than elegant label for this principle may now be evident; whether PHIC reasonably may be invoked to justify paternalistic interference with some particular person will depend on facts about *that* person, namely, his beliefs, settled preferences, and goals. As such, PHIC requires no conjectures about what a "fully rational person" would choose or consent to have done. It *does* require reasoning about what S would choose under unactualized circumstances; in that respect PHIC does appeal to hypothetical consent but to the hypothetical consent of a particular, actual, *individual* (hence, "individualized consent").

One advantage of this principle is that it does not require us to decide a difficult question, namely, the precise criteria for employing the not entirely transparent concept "fully rational." Another advantage concerns *confirmability in principle*. We might conjecture that under some non-actual circumstance S would consent to our interference, and we may confirm this by asking S, for example, "if you were in a bad automobile accident and needed a blood transfusion to remain alive would you, if you could, consent to being transfused?" S may reply "certainly not; I am a Jehovah's Witness and that is against one of my basic principles." Such a sincere statement on S's part is virtually decisive. I say 'virtually' because it is conceivable, though improbable, that S, for various reasons (say, he "loses" his faith), would not, on having the accident, so choose. However, S's sincere judgment about what he would consent to must carry the day in the absence of compelling considerations to the contrary, and it allows us to say that judgments about what S would consent to are confirmable in principle. Consider another type of confirmation. In an earlier example you are deaf and blind and I tackle you to prevent your walking off a cliff. You did not consent, but you tell me that you *would* have consented to my intervention if you had had the opportunity (your remark might have been different were you intent on suicide).[24] So, judgments of hypothetical individualized consent can be confirmed or disconfirmed, in principle. Of course, in many of the interesting cases, we have neither indications of hypothetical consent by S prior to the fact, nor such indications after the fact. I do not say "giving of consent" for such indications of hypothetical consent are not givings of consent any more than my saying sincerely that "if I were filthy rich, I would give you a thousand dollars" is offering you a thousand dollars.

PHIC yields, I believe, the "right result" in the three examples noted earlier, on the assumption that the three subjects would have consented to the interventions in the manner required by PHIC. As may be obvious, it respects the autonomy of competent persons in that it sanctions only interferences which are compatible with,

---

[24] To clarify further, it is reasonable to believe that a competent individual would consent to my pushing her out of the way of an onrushing vehicle, even in the absence of overt consent. By contrast, it is not reasonable to believe that a typical senior citizen would consent to a law requiring her to have an alarm system and double cylinder dead bolt locks on all doors of her apartment so that she may be kept out of harm's way. Whether a given competent subject would consent to a constraint depends *in part* on *that subject's assessment* of the severity of the burden placed on the subject, the probability of thereby promoting some good for the subject, and the magnitude of the good aimed at. But note how these "consequentialist considerations" are not appealed to directly to justify the constraint; rather, they are here weighed as *evidence* for a claim of hypothetical individualized consent by the competent person, and they are not suggested to be overriding in the absence of the latter.

and indeed facilitate, the achievement of goals held by the subject.[25] In that respect it does not impose alien basic goals or values, although it allows obstruction of specific activities in which a subject is engaged, activities which a subject would avoid if he were aware of the relevant circumstances, for example, the risks or harms to the subject of so acting. For the reasons discussed, I conclude that PHIC does not conflict with respecting the right of competent persons to direct, within limits, the course of their own lives, and that PHIC is an acceptable principle. Hence, we extend our conception of valid consent to include this particular type of hypothetical consent.

Finally, let us consider a somewhat intriguing objection which may be posed to our Principle of Hypothetical Individualized Consent. Suppose that Ronald wants to have sex with Maggie, but Maggie is opposed. Ronald sends to Maggie a note which threatens torture of her sister unless Maggie agrees to go along. The note fails to reach Maggie. Ronald then goes to Maggie's house and rapes her. Further, let us assume that if Maggie had been fully apprized of the relevant circumstances (Ronald's intent and note) she would have consented to sex and relations with Ronald. Suppose also that no others are thereby wronged. Hence, it seems that, according to PHIC, Ronald's presumptively wrong act is permissible. This result is, to say the least, unwelcome. The example, of course, focuses on a presumably *nonpaternalistically* motivated act but, this type of objection is not, thereby, one to be ignored. Similar cases of a paternalistic nature are easily imagined. Suppose, for example, that Ronald believes Maggie is sexually repressed and

[25] In the absence of overt, express, consent, the inferring of hypothetical individual consent, of course, is often a tricky business. In some cases there is excellent reason to speak of, and assume, *tacit consent* on S's part. For example, if S is asked whether he has objections to meeting at the regular time and S remains silent (but is awake, nearby, and so on), we may assume reasonably that S consents. In the case where S enters a public store, we may asume that he tacitly consents to being viewed by others. However, in one legal case in which a Jehovah's Witness voluntarily came to the hospital for her problems, this fact was taken to express a desire on her part to live and, *further*, evidence that she tacitly consented to whatever was necessary to preserve her life, e.g., a blood transfusion. The latter inference is, however, dubious. Vegetarians may, on moral grounds, voluntarily enter a supermarket but it does not follow that this shows tacit consent to the killing of animals for food. For the legal case mentioned, see the Georgetown Hospital Case in Jay Katz, ed., *Experimentation With Human Beings* (New York: Russell Sage Foundation, 1972), pp. 551–552.

I should add that I attach no special importance to the expression 'tacit consent.' If the contrast is with 'explicit consent,' nonverbal indications of consent can be just as explicit as verbal ones; 'tacit consent' above should be understood to refer to explicit but nonverbal consent.

having sex will be for her own good, a rationale occasionally invoked by a few psychologists and psychiatrists.

The defense of PHIC requires showing why PHIC does not sanction Ronald's wrongful act. The main point to recall is that PHIC condones a presumptively wrongful act by an agent, A, toward a subject, S, only if "S would validly consent to A's Xing" under certain conditions, for example, S was aware of the relevant circumstances. However, for the consent in question to be valid it must be voluntary. Just here it is desirable to clarify my use of 'voluntary.' As noted earlier in our analysis of 'coercion,' a coercive threat (roughly) involves one party threatening to make another even worse off than the latter already is, at the time the threat has been made, unless the threatened party complies with a demand by the threatening party. There is *a sense* of 'voluntary' in which you may "voluntarily choose" to turn over your money when faced with the demand, "your money or your life." Similarly, there is a sense in which Maggie might "voluntarily choose" to have sexual relations with Ronald if she had been aware of relevant facts (his threat). However, the required construal of 'voluntary consent' implicit in our notion of valid consent is broader. In short, we have assumed that if S would not choose to do X (or consent to X) in the absence of a coercive threat by some agent, A, then S's so choosing is not a sufficiently voluntary act on S's part. Thus, assuming that Maggie would not choose to have sexual relations with Ronald in the absence of his threat, it is not true that she would *validly* consent to do so if she were aware of the relevant fact of his threat. This point is compatible with our earlier supposition that she, in one sense, would have consented to sexual relations if she had been aware of the threat. The latter consent rightly does not serve to justify Ronald's act since the consent is not voluntary in the relevant manner. This point accords, I believe, with the traditional view that forced, extracted (or otherwise wrongfully induced) consent to an act does not perform the legitimizing function of unforced, freely given consent.[26] The notion of valid consent

[26] In addition, there can be cases in which it is reasonable to think that S would consent to a certain intervention, i.e., cases in which the conditions mentioned in PHIC are satisfied, but in which the harm-preventing intervention can be equally or more efficaciously carried out somewhat later. In such an event there is a moral presumption that one ought to wait so that S may recover his deliberative capacities (suppose S has fainted) and be supplied with relevant information if S lacks it (S's back is injured but the most promising operation carries a 3% chance of permanent paralysis) so that S may decide. In short, PHIC must *not* be construed so as to license reasonably avoidable invasive paternalistic interventions.

employed in both the Restricted Consent Principle and the Principle of Hypothetical Individualized Consent reflects this fact.

Let us attend to a lingering worry which we might still have regarding the plausibility of PHIC. I shall approach it somewhat indirectly. The setting forward of reasonably clear, defensible, criteria for the interpretation and application of The Principle of Hypothetical Individualized Consent is an unfinished task. As noted earlier there are some cases in which it seems straightforward that if a subject, S, had been apprised of some relevant fact, then S would have chosen differently or would have consented to disruption of his activity, for example, if Jones had known that the apple he ate was poisoned he would have consented to our pumping his stomach. As it was, he fought us "tooth and nail." In contrast, there are occasions in which one might appeal to PHIC in a manner which fails to attend to the underlying notion that we must respect the basic personal beliefs and dispositions of others so long as their choices wrong no others. For example, someone might claim that it is permissible paternalism

1. to impose a blood transfusion on a Jehovah's Witness on the ground that if she were aware that there were no God and she were unencumbered, she would have consented to the transfusion

or 2. coercively to require the atheist to attend church on the ground that if he were aware of God's existence, the risk of eternal damnation, and were unencumbered, he would consent to the requirement

or 3. coercively to prohibit Berg, the mountain climber, from climbing the Matterhorn since if Berg were aware of the actual risks of his plan of attack and were unencumbered, Berg would consent to such interference.

Thus, one might think that coercive impositions on the Witness, the atheist, and the mountain climber are all justified according to PHIC. One might be troubled by such results, thinking that if that is so PHIC sanctions too much intrusion into the lives of competent persons—and that PHIC somehow fails to capture the underlying notion that we often must respect the choices of competent persons even when we think they are imprudent ones. Yet if we do not accept PHIC (or the other principles considered) and there is no prior valid consent, it would be wrong to prevent Jones from eating the poisoned apple; that result also seems intolerable.

A key question here is whether PHIC sanctions too much. Some reflection on the appeals mentioned in 1., 2., and 3. may be useful in this regard. What I wish to propose is that when PHIC is appropriately interpreted it would not sanction the sorts of paternalistic intervention in 1. and 2. and probably not in 3. either. First, PHIC sanctions only invasive interferences with a competent subject to which he would validly consent if he were *apprised* of relevant facts and reasonably able to decide what to do. The "appraisal condition," as I construe it, requires only that the subject be aware of the evidence or arguments, possessed by the potential intervener, in favor of claims (relevant to the prudence of the subject's choice or action) contrary to those the subject holds, not that he (the subject) actually accept or agree with them. Thus, the question relevant to permissible intervention is not simply what the subject would choose if he had beliefs he lacks, but what he would choose if his "epistemological decision base" were not deficient in the respect that he lacks data to which the potential intervener has access. Although it may be obvious that the Jehovah's Witness would choose differently if she believed that there were no God, it is not obvious that such a subject would believe such a claim if confronted with the reasons for believing it which are, presumably, possessed by the potential intervener. Hence, it is not obvious that the subject would consent to transfusion if apprised of relevant "facts"—given the above construal of 'appraisal.' Much the same type of thing can be said of the case of the atheist. The guiding notion here, albeit inadequately developed, is that we must respect, within limits, not only others' choices but also their prerogative to assess reasons for revising their own derivative or basic goals. Apparent or actually superior insight on the part of other competent persons does not by itself render permissible invasive intervention to promote good. In the case of the poisonous apple, it is reasonable to infer that a subject would choose not to eat it (in the absence of evidence that the subject has chosen to commit suicide). By contrast, it is far less likely that a committed Jehovah's Witness or a committed atheist, if confronted with contrary claims and their defense, would surrender certain fundamental choice-affecting beliefs. Thus, it is unlikely that such subjects would consent to invasive intervention if apprised of relevant "facts" which they could assess in a rationally unencumbered manner.[27] Commitments to a theistic or atheistic outlook reflect fundamental views on contested matters, the truth or rationality of which is not easily

[27] Once again, "rationally unencumbered manner" is to be construed not as "fully rational" but as "a manner approximating the subject's rational best."

resolvable; such basic beliefs strongly contrast with straightforward, low-level, readily resolvable, empirical claims such as, for example, that the apple is poisoned or the bridge is dangerous. When the intervener has compelling reasons to believe such latter claims, to assume the subject has contrary assumptions, and to believe that the subject will suffer serious harm because of acting on the latter assumptions, then, other things being equal, it is reasonable to infer that the subject would consent to invasive intervention.

Another feature relevant to deciding whether it is reasonable to appeal to PHIC—or perhaps the same feature viewed from another angle—concerns whether or not the beliefs which affect the subject's choice are comparatively central to the subject's conception of his own personal identity. Again, it is one thing to knock down Jones to prevent him from touching an exposed, high voltage, electric powerline and another to impose a transfusion on the Jehovah's Witness. That one ought to touch such powerlines is not likely to be a belief held by Jones. That one ought to avoid transfusions is not only a belief but an important belief in the Witness's conception of how to live her life and is one derivable from her basic, life-defining and life-guiding, views and attitudes. To conjecture about what the Witness would choose if she believed that blood transfusions were permissible is very different from conjecturing about what Jones would choose if he believed the powerline might kill him. For Jones to come to believe that the powerline has such a potential requires no conceptual renting asunder of Jones' personality, no fundamental, imaginative, disfiguration of his outlook on life. By contrast, it is plausible to conclude that conjectures about what the Jehovah's Witness would choose if she believed transfusions were all right are close to incoherence. Rather, it is to query whether some person would choose or consent differently if she were someone else—or a radically different sort of person. But she is not, and questions about what some *particular* individual would consent to if confronted with relevant choice-affecting data are, at the very least, questions about how *that sort* of person would decide—not about what some psychologically stripped individual, similarly situated, and reclothed with quite different basic values and beliefs, would decide.

2.9 Strong and Weak Paternalism

In an instructive essay Joel Feinberg has distinguished between "strong paternalism" and "weak paternalism." His labels refer not to paternalistic practices but to two different principles which purport to say what sort of paternalistic interference is justified. His discussion focuses on legal paternalism, that is, paternalistic interference by the state and is, therefore, more narrowly focused than our inquiry. Nevertheless, the two principles discussed can be construed to apply more broadly in the absence of special moral considerations about the permissibility of allowing the *state* to do what may be permissible for others to do. Feinberg rejects the principle labeled "strong paternalism" and defends what he labels 'weak paternalism." His position is similar to the position so far defended here and deserves comment. To distinguish between his two principles requires clarification of his prior distinction between *fully* and *not fully voluntary assumptions of risk*; on this matter it is worth quoting Feinberg. With a "fully voluntary assumption of risk"

> . . . one shoulders it while fully informed of all relevant facts and contingencies, with one's eyes wide open, so to speak, and in the absence of all coercive pressure of compulsion. There must be calmness and deliberation, no distracting and unsettling emotions, no neurotic compulsion, no misunderstanding. To whatever extent there is impetuousness, clouded judgment (as e.g., from alcohol), or immature or defective facilities of reasoning, to that extent the choice falls short of voluntariness. Voluntariness is then a matter of degree.[28]

If someone is about to do that which it is doubtful a person in his right mind would do, then, in Feinberg's view, it is permissible to interfere ". . . not to evaluate the wisdom or worthiness of a person's choice, but rather to determine whether the choice is really his." Feinberg's position is more fully clarified, then, by his distinction between two principles of paternalism:

> According to the strong version of legal paternalism, the state is justified in protecting a person, against his will, from the harmful consequences of even his fully voluntary choices and undertakings. . . . weak paternalism would permit us to protect him from "nonvoluntary choices," which, being the choices of no one at all, are no less foreign to him.[29]

The *Principle of Weak Paternalism* that Feinberg finds acceptable is not explicitly couched in terms of hypothetical individualized con-

[28] Joel Feinberg, "Legal Paternalism," in *Today's Moral Problems*, ed. Richard Wasserstrom (New York: Macmillan, 1975), p. 38.
[29] Ibid., p. 50.

sent. However, it seems possible to do so. For example, weak paternalism seems equivalent to the view that paternalistic interference is permissible, and only permissible, if *the subject* would consent to the interference if he were making a fully voluntary choice. More importantly here, Feinberg does *not* propose the permissibility of interventions in just those cases where they would be acceptable to a *fully rational* person.

Weak paternalism, then, sanctions only those interferences with Jones' activity when Jones is functioning at something less than *his* (or *her*) rational best.[30] Weak paternalism, at least implicitly,

[30] John Hodson, in an instructive essay, defends a view about legitimate paternalism largely amenable to the outlook argued here. He claims that paternalistic intervention is justified if and only if "(1) there is good evidence that the decisions with respect to which the person is to be coerced are encumbered, and (2) there is good evidence that this person's decisions would be supportive of the paternalistic intervention if they were not encumbered." (See John Hodson, "The Principle of Paternalism," *American Philosophical Quarterly* 14, No. 1 (January, 1977), p. 65.) What counts, on this view, is an encumbrance evidently is a crucial matter. On this point, Hodson proposes that "a person's decisions are encumbered whenever those decisions are made in circumstances which are known to affect decision-making in such a way that the person making the decision comes to believe that the decisions were mistaken or unfortunate" (p. 66). As examples of such circumstances, Hodson mentions ignorance and emotional stress. The worry here is similar to the one noted with regard to Feinberg's weak paternalism. Considerable ignorance is rather common with respect to a large number of consumer purchases. Similarly, choices of careers, mates, divorce, and treatment for injury or disease commonly involve much ignorance and emotional stress. Persons making such decisions often regret them, but to think that invasive paternalistic intervention is thereby legitimate is to be committed to a wide range of, I believe, invidious and unduly meddlesome interventions. It is worth noting that we often regard our past decisions as based on mistaken assumptions or unfortunate *in result*, but do not necessarily *regret* having made just those decisions. What counts as an encumbrance affects our understanding not just of (1) in Hodson's principle but (2) as well. If 'hypothetical unencumbered decision' is understood in a highly rarefied way, it begins to look like an appeal to what a "fully rational person would choose" (cf. PHRC) or to "the rational will" (Hodson's term) rather than an attempt to ascertain what an actual subject would choose under circumstances more favorable to prudent decision-making. However, both Hodson's focus on the hypothetical unencumbered decision of a particular subject and my own stress on what a subject would consent to if apprised of relevant information (cf. PHIC) are empirically focused on the unique basic dispositions and traits of the subject in question. My main reservation about appeal to a hypothetical, unencumbered will of a subject concerns the fact that not all emotional stress and ignorance need be thought of as an encumbrance. Further, some ignorance may be an essential feature of a person's identity. Consider a competent person, L, who is dedicated to finding the Loch Ness "monster." Suppose further that there is no such creature and we justifiably believe as much. Perhaps L's hypothetical unencumbered choice (if he knew that there were no monster) would be that we coercively halt his search. Hodson's principle would sanction invasive paternalistic intervention. This result is troubling when one thinks of the vast range of similar cases in which the principle yields similar implications which Hodson also, I believe, would regard as unduly meddlesome. In brief, there is a problem here concerning whether the appeal to a hypothetical unencumbered decision (with 'unencumbered' interpreted as Hodson proposes) covertly appeals

rejects interferences with the fully voluntary acts of generally competent individuals, and, as noted, a fully voluntary act need not be a fully rational act. Its "let alone" prescription for fully voluntary acts, then, seems to *avoid* sanctioning an overriding of the autonomy of individuals in the way that, as I have argued, the Principle of Hypothetical Rational Consent sanctions.

Another way of seeing the difference between PHRC and Feinberg's weak paternalism is the following. Although in a particular case it may not be plausible to claim that it is in an individual's overall interest to perform an act he decides to perform, it is generally in one's interest not to be prevented from carrying out decisions which one *believes* to be in one's (other) interests—even if one is mistaken in this belief. An omnipotent, omniscient paternalist acting on the Principle of Hypothetical Rational Consent would intervene with one whose fully voluntary acts were imprudent, and a fully rational individual would consent to such interference. It does not seem unlikely that this procedure would result in an intuitively unacceptable, serious, diminishing of one's liberty to make choices, to direct one's own life according to *one's own* lights. For less than fully rational beings there is something of considerable value in having the effective prerogative to decide for themselves and effectively act on their own choices, even though imprudent results are not always avoided. Life is not in *all* respects unlike a game where there is something valuable, translatable perhaps in terms of self-respect, in *playing one's own hand* as best one knows how, rather than being "helped" to avoid mistakes by "benevolent" and controlling fellow persons. Any reasonable principle permitting paternalistic interference must, I think, give strong weight to this consideration.

Feinberg's weak paternalism substantially succeeds in this latter respect. Although Feinberg rightly regards voluntariness as a matter of degree, one may have qualms about the stringency of the conditions which must be satisfied, on his account, before a decision may count as being fully voluntary. In his view the decision must be one that is made (1) when an individual is "fully informed of all relevant facts," (2) "in the absence of all coercive pressure,"

---

to a hypothetical person's decision instead of appealing to a hypothetical decision of an actual competent person. Imaginatively to strip an actual person of certain beliefs and conjecture about "his" choices runs the risk of failing to respect the core of the individual identity of the actual person. Finally, it should not go unnoted that these difficulties are close relatives of those faced by the theory I have proposed as well.

(3) where there are "no distracting and unsettling emotions," (4) "no misunderstanding," (5) "no neurotic compulsion," and so on (see prior quotation). One might ask whether one has *ever* made a decision satisfying all these conditions. Perhaps Feinberg has overstated his case, although we should note that elsewhere he insists that a decision or act must be "substantially nonvoluntary" in order for interference to be permissible.

The worry, perhaps not a serious one, is that weak paternalism seems, as Feinberg explicates it, not so "weak" after all. Why? It is not difficult to imagine many types of decisions which are unlikely to satisfy anything remotely like the mentioned conditions for being fully voluntary (and, indeed, may be substantially nonvoluntary). For example, consider decisions to become a nun, to go to college, to renounce one's citizenship, to marry, to divorce, to engage in civil disobedience, to purchase nuclear accident insurance, to gamble heavily at a casino, to be sterilized, to have a child, to become a living kidney donor, or to consent to psychosurgery. If, as I have claimed, a competent person has a right to direct his own life, then weak paternalism seems correct in prohibiting interference with fully voluntary acts. My reservation is that the principle may be overly interventionist in allowing excessive interference with acts which are *less* than fully voluntary—for many important decisions which persons commonly make are not, in his sense, fully voluntary. To follow a policy of interference based on "weak paternalism" may call for quite invasive intrusions into the decisions of ordinary folk who are acting, more or less, at their rational best under more or less ordinary circumstances. On certain occasions in which we disapprove of another's decision, believing it to be most imprudent, "it's your life" may not only express our disapproval; it may identify a strong (if not always decisive) reason for letting alone when we also believe that the person is doing *his* (her) rational best.

A full assessment of the relation between Feinberg's position and the position defended in this book will not be made partly because the theory developed here has not been set out completely. Two further points, however, are worth mentioning beforehand. First, since we have claimed that competent persons have a right to direct their own lives and we have, so far, detected only two acceptable principles for invasive interference with competent persons (The Restricted Consent Principle and the Principle of Hypothetical Individualized Consent), the theory developed here, omitting details, implicitly accords with Feinberg's rejection of strong paternalism.

Second, and aside from the reservations already noted regarding the acceptance of the principle of weak paternalism, a further observation is in order, but it requires some discussion of the important concept of *competence*. So far we have assumed some minimal degree of clarity about the notion of competence and have made no attempt to set forth reasonably precise criteria for determining who is a competent person and who is not. We have presupposed, even if competence is "a matter of degree," that there are morally relevant differences between persons regarding their range of competence. We have vaguely assumed, although not relied heavily on the point, that infants, young children, the severely senile, the severely retarded, and psychopaths are generally incompetent, and that, in contrast, most persons outside these categories are generally competent. Further, our entire focus to this point has been on the question of the permissibility of paternalistic interference toward generally competent persons. Now I wish to suggest that generally competent persons are on some particular occasions not competent. There is a significant question here, namely, in virtue of what characteristics or conditions can we say that a generally competent person is on a given occasion not competent. I shall not suggest a full answer here, but a plausible general answer is that a generally competent person is *incompetent* whenever the decision-making *capacity* of such a person has become impaired to such a degree as to render impossible, or extremely difficult, the deliberations requisite to making a *prudent* choice. I shall leave this claim largely unanalyzed here (but see Chapter 7). Although people may be said to be impaired (to decide) by lack of information, I shall not regard sheer ignorance as rendering a decision-maker incompetent. I have in mind rather, as sources of incompetence, losses of capacity reasonably to process information. These, roughly, may be of two general types: (1) inabilities to reason in the absence of emotional disturbance, and (2) inabilities to reason because of emotional disturbance. People who are generally competent become (or may become) incompetent for familiar reasons, for example, because of fainting, shock, pain, severe anxiety (as when phobics are in the presence of feared situations, e.g., heights or public places), the use of drugs, alcohol, and so on.

In cases of genuine though temporary incompetence as well as in cases in which a subject though not competent is unknowingly about to do that which promises serious self-harm, PHIC sanctions paternalistic interference with S *only* in that manner to which, it is reasonable to believe, S would consent if he were able. It appears

that Feinberg's principle of weak paternalism would allow paternalistic interference in a similar, though possibly greater, range of
cases. There are two reasons for thinking that weak paternalism
would sanction a wider range of intervention. One we have noted;
Feinberg's conception of what is a "nonvoluntary choice" is comparatively latitudinarian. Second, it seems to sanction protective
intervention just so long as the subject's choice is nonvoluntary,
with no further (stated) constraint on how this may be done; this
point contrasts with PHIC for the following reason. If an injured
subject refused a blood transfusion while confused, terrified, and
drunk, weak paternalism would seem to allow transfusing him
(protection from his harm-laden nonvoluntary choice). By contrast,
the Principle of Hypothetical Individualized Consent would sanction intervention only in a manner to which, it is reasonable to
believe, the subject would consent if unimpaired and relevantly
informed. Thus, if the subject were a Jehovah's Witness, PHIC
would not sanction a transfusion even if the subject's refusal was,
at the time it was issued, a nonvoluntary decision. The central idea
is that although we may be justified in invasively deflecting an
agent away from a self-harming outcome toward which he moves
as a result of a "nonvoluntary choice," we cannot nudge him toward an outcome which is foreign to his own, permissible, basic
ends or goals. If we justifiably can substitute our judgment for that
of the competent person it must be to nudge him back onto a path
compatible with his own goals and values.

2.10 The Theory of Autonomy-Respecting Paternalism

The definitions, distinctions, and principles so far discussed make
it possible to formulate a significant part of a general theory of
paternalism envisioned here. The general theory would consist of
two major parts. The first part includes a statement of principles
(and their defense) purporting to identify what sorts of paternalistic
interventions are permissible toward generally competent persons.
One might label this part: the theory of autonomy-respecting paternalism. The second major part of a general theory consists of a
statement of principles (and their defense) purporting to identify
what sorts of paternalistic interventions are permissible toward
those who are not generally competent persons (restricting our
focus, however, to post-natal human beings). Limited steps toward
it are taken in Chapter 7, on paternalism toward those generally

incompetent. Now I shall state more fully the theory of autonomy-respecting paternalism.

So far I have defended the view that certain principles purporting to justify paternalistic interference are unacceptable, that is, the General Consent Principle, the Principle of Subsequent Consent, the Principle of Hypothetical Rational Consent, and the Principle of Weak Paternalism unless restricted or interpreted so as not to countenance so wide an area of invasive intrusions. By contrast, we have defended two principles as deserving acceptance, the Restricted Consent Principle and the Principle of Hypothetical Individualized Consent. The partial defense of these latter principles consisted in noting their accordance with certain of our pretheoretical convictions about what is permissible and the principles' apparent lack of seriously counterintuitive implications—in contrast to the principles rejected. Further, it has been claimed that generally competent adults have a right to direct their own lives and that this right provides good reason to accept RCP and PHIC and to reject the other principles mentioned. I have not argued that the support provided by the claim that generally competent persons have such a right amounts to the claim's entailment of RCP or PHIC.

RCP and PHIC each purport to state when paternalistic interference is permissible. Each alleges a condition which, if satisfied, is sufficient to conclude that a certain type of paternalistic interference is permissible. Now I state more fully and explicitly the stronger position to be defended:

A's paternalistic interference, X, with a generally competent subject, S, is justified (morally permissible) if and only if

      1. A's doing X involves no presumptive wrong toward S or others

or 2. A's doing X does not wrong those other than A or S

                     and

      either 1. S has given currently operative valid consent to A to do X

        or 2. S would validly consent to A's doing X

                       if

               a) S were aware of the relevant circumstances

            and b) S's normal capacities for deliberation and choice were not impaired.

Call the above the *Principle of Autonomy-Respecting Paternalism* (PARP). PARP is a strong claim purporting to state correctly the necessary *and* sufficient conditions for justified paternalistic interference toward generally competent adults. A more thorough elucidation and defense of PARP involves showing its advantages over, or rebutting, competing principles (a task primarily undertaken in Chapter 3), explaining and defending its implications (our focus in Chapters 4, 5, and 6), and further defense of the right to direct one's own life (Chapter 3). Our consideration of appeals to consent would be incomplete if we did not examine well-known appeals to *proxy consent* and locate the place of such appeals within the framework developed so far. To that task we turn.

2.11 Appeals to Proxy Consent

In various cases in which one party is contemplating the performance of an act affecting a subject, an act which interferes and is presumptively wrong, it is often thought that the consent of some third party suffices to justify the interference with the subject. Such cases are commonly described as involving "proxy consent." Such cases, however, seem to fall into two disparate categories. In cases which we may describe as paradigmatic cases of proxy consent, S has given currently operative consent to a second party, A, to act and/or authorize others to act in a given manner. One standard case of this sort is that in which you consent to your accountant's investing your money in some fashion. You consent to her acting in your behalf. She may act as your *proxy*, and on your behalf consent to certain transactions affecting you. The range of actions within which she may exercise her own discretion may be quite broad ("investing in whatever she thinks is the best investment") or it may be rather narrow ("investing in whichever government, or triple-A rated corporate bonds she thinks are best"). The precise *content* of your consent (what you consent to) is evidently important, at least if our prior argument is on the right track. Such authorizations by S are often, but not always, part of contractual arrangements. Even when part of contractual arrangements, what S consents to may or may not be spelled out in detail. The content of the consent is often left vague, especially when there is either considerable trust by S toward A and/or expectations about A's performance are well established (compare: what physicians, lawyers, plumbers, caterers, or car mechanics are "supposed" to do). The vagueness of the content of consent is a frequent source of dispute, a point to which we shall return in discussing paternalism and health care (in Chapters 4 and 5). What, for example, do you consent to when you consent to a "physical examination"?

The major point to observe here, however, is that there are cases described as cases of proxy consent in which the affected subject has, as a matter of fact, given currently operative valid consent to act in a certain manner. Since valid consent by competent subjects, under certain conditions, justifies the act to which consent is given, there is nothing morally problematic about such cases (once more assuming that the acts consented to involve no wrong to others). By contrast, appeals to proxy consent often suppose that A can act as S's proxy and consent for S when S has *not* consented to any such act on A's part, indeed when S is incapable of giving (valid) consent. I have in mind, for example, cases where S is an infant, a young child, or is severely retarded, a psychopath, or even a comatose person. In such cases it is often said that some other party, T, has given "proxy consent" to a policy or procedure affecting S. What is meant here cannot be that S has validly consented to T's acting on S's behalf. There is not and cannot be any authorizing of T by S in such cases. It is a mistake to think, in acquiring T's consent in such a case, that we have S's consent, as we do in paradigmatic cases of proxy consent. To think otherwise is not just to make a mistaken inference; it is to be disposed to act in ways that may be unjustifiable or disposed to approve such acts.

Of course there may be grounds for believing that T's consent (not understood as deriving from any authorization by S) on its own has some weight in deciding the permissibility of treatment of S. If this is so, it will not be because T is implementing S's right to direct his own life or that T is cooperatively implementing an autonomous choice of S; rather, it will be because T has some right or legitimate claim to influence the treatment of S, possibly because of the existence of a special relation which T bears to S, such as that of being S's parent, guardian, friend, physician, lawyer, counselor, or patient-advocate. Under what conditions does such a party have such a right or legitimate claim? There are tempting and traditional answers to this question; a full exploration is beyond my purview, but some further analysis is provided in Chapters 4, 5, and 7.

A main point here is that when S cannot give valid consent, and authorize others to act on his behalf, perhaps the consent by another is morally relevant to deciding the permissibility of treatment of S; however, such consent, so-called "proxy consent," does not have whatever weight it has derivatively from S's voluntary and knowing choice, as in paradigmatic cases of proxy consent. It is *not a conveying by T of S's consent*. If T's consent has any weight at all, that must derive from some other source. In such cases it would be less misleading, and less dangerous, to speak of "second-party *approval* or permission," rather than "proxy consent."[31]

Hence, in some cases an appeal to proxy consent is not an appeal to the subject's consent *at all*. Consideration of the weight of such second-party approvals is a distinct matter. By contrast, "proxy consent" *may* allude to cases where a subject has sanctioned a second party to act in the subject's behalf. If the subject is competent and his consent is valid, the sanctioning of some assigned person to convey that consent and its conveyance is itself morally unproblematic. Such valid consent by the subject is, to emphasize a point, the *subject's* valid consent even if conveyed by a proxy. In such cases it retains the same decisive weight it would have if conveyed by the subject himself: namely, it serves to render permissible certain subject-affecting acts which would, in its absence, be wrongful.

To avoid a certain conceptual confusion, it is worth recalling a distinction made earlier. If S directly conveys her valid consent to an agent A that A may act in a certain fashion, or indirectly by means of an authorized representative or proxy, such valid consent renders permissible a certain range of acts by A (determined by the content of the consent). Acts within this range will be paternalistic if the agent performs acts (or omissions) contrary to S's immediate aims or purposes at the time of such acts, with the aim of protecting or benefitting S (e.g., putting S's investment funds in bonds even though S at the time prefers to play the commodities market). If acts within the range consented to are not contrary to S's immediate aims or purposes at the time such acts are performed, they will be nonpaternalistic; rather, they will be cooperative and not interfering—and, possibly, altruistic. The last class of acts, then, involves no substitution of A's judgment for that of S.

By contrast, and as noted, in those cases in which A is sometimes (misleadingly) said to give "proxy consent" for S (and S has not authorized A to decide matters or convey S's decision), A does substitute his judgment for S. Whether A permissibly does so, I

---

[31] This desirable policy is recommended, happily, by the National Commission for the Protection of Human Subjects of Biomedical and Behavioral Research. See "Research Involving Children," *Federal Register* 43 (1978), 2087.

leave open here; the more essential point in this section simply is to sort out two quite diverse sorts of cases which are often referred to 'proxy consent.'

2.12 Intervention to Ascertain Competence

I have maintained that prospective paternalistic-minded interveners sometimes justifiably may interfere with a subject in order to ascertain whether the subject is competent. This point deserves further comment since, on one elaboration of this view, it promises to countenance highly invasive policies which appear to be at odds with the autonomy-respecting theory defended. I will not attempt to spell out precisely a necessary and desirable, information-sensitive, proviso on the Principle of Autonomy-Respecting Paternalism. However, it would read something like this: temporary, minimally invasive, presumptively wrong interventions are permissible by A toward S in order to ascertain whether the conditions mentioned in 1. or 2. are satisfied or whether it is reasonable to so believe. Thus, for example, we justifiably may coercively stop a person from eating his meal if, for example, we have reason to think that he is extremely allergic to its ingredients (and, if he eats the food, may go into anaphylactic shock) and that he is unaware of the risk to which he is about to subject himself.

The epistemologically sensitive consideration adduced in favor of the permissibility of interfering as noted earlier, is one Joel Feinberg has put forward. On his view

> . . . there are actions of a kind that create a powerful *pre-sumption* that any given actor, if he were in his right mind, would not choose them. The point of calling this hypothesis a "presumption" is to require that it be completely overridden before legal permission be given to a person, who has already been interfered with to go on as before. . . . The presumption should always be taken as rebuttable in principle; it will be up to [the person] to prove before an official tribunal that he is calm, competent, and free. . . .[32]

The view we have defended shares some similarities with that of Feinberg. Still, there is a need for considerable caution in this con-

[32] Feinberg, "Legal Paternalism," p. 40. On Feinberg's view, and generally on the relation of liberalism to paternalism, see the thoughtful and provocative essay by Alan Soble, "Paternalism, Liberal Theory, and Suicide," *Canadian Journal of Philosophy* XII, No. 2 (June, 1982), pp. 335–352.

text, and Feinberg's position is, arguably, overly permissive with regard to state intervention. Among the class of actions which, generally speaking, no one "in his right mind" would choose, are, for example, suicide, setting one's house on fire, and severing one's own limbs. There are circumstances, nevertheless, in which such acts are not evidently irrational and may be carried out for intelligible reasons. Still, I do not wish to claim that there are no grossly irrational choices, no cases of incompetence, or no cases of extreme mental impairment. Certain types of acts, such as those mentioned, do create a strong presumption that a chooser of them is *unable* to choose prudently. The theory defended here allows that in such cases intervention may be permissible. A relevant proviso, however, is that the prospective act promises serious harm to the agent.

Some types of acts create a presumption that the chooser is not in his right mind but do not hold forth such a prospect of self-harm. For example, someone with a white collar job who spent four hours every day taking showers is, presumptively, disturbed. However, in the absence of distinctly harmful effects on the participant it is not obvious that such a person should be restricted in order to determine his competence. A second reservation about Feinberg's formulation, once it is clear both that an agent is risking nontrivial self-harm *and* that there is a strong presumption that a person in his right mind (and relevantly informed) would probably not act in the intended manner, concerns the burden of proof. It is not obvious that a subject should be regarded as incompetent unless *he can prove* to a tribunal that he is "calm, competent, and free." This point is a theoretically modest, but practically important, one. The essential consideration is that prospective *interveners* be able to establish, at least in the case of adult persons, that their (the interveners') initially plausible presumption of incompetence is not a misguided one. After all, there is a moral presumption against the legitimacy of invasive interference and no compelling reason why adult persons themselves should have to establish their competence when their prospective acts wrong no others. Although I shall not pursue the point, not only should the epistemological burden not be placed on the shoulders of restricted competent subjects, the requirement of *proof* seems overly demanding. When considering state paternalism, reflection on the history of decisions issuing from public tribunals and judges generates reasonable skepticism about what such persons or bodies would count as an acceptable proof of competence. In this regard the history of public adjudication of the literacy of blacks (as a test for voting) in

93

the United States, official decisions regarding retardation (to make decisions about immigration or compulsory sterilization in the first few decades of this century in the United States), and the tendency by Soviet psychiatrists to classify those critical of governmental policy as mentally impaired or even psychopathic—offer little comfort to those who would allow governmental tribunals or officials to decide whether a presumptively incompetent person has satisfactorily proven that he is, nevertheless, in his right mind. Even if decisions by judges or tribunals are unavoidable, the more essential point is that the burden of demonstrating competence should not be on the alleged incompetent.[33]

[33] Feinberg himself, as an apparent second thought, adds that, perhaps, it "is too great a burden" to expect that the party in question prove that he is calm, competent, and free. Feinberg, "Legal Paternalism," p. 40.

T H R E E

APPEALS TO DOING GOOD

If I knew for a certainty that a man was coming to my house with the conscious design of doing me good, I should run for my life.   —Henry David Thoreau

He is the only animal that loves his neighbor as himself, and cuts his throat if his theology isn't straight. He has made a graveyard of the globe in trying his honest best to smooth his brother's path to happiness and heaven.
—Mark Twain

An act of generosity is permissible only if it does not violate anybody's right; if it does, it is morally wrong.
—Immanuel Kant

3.1 Classifying Competing Views on Permissible Paternalism

There was something paradoxical about the saying, heard during the era when the United States was involved in the Vietnam War, that "we had to destroy this village to save it." Analogously, since we regard possession of liberty as something good for persons or part of a person's "own good," there is something paradoxical about one way paternalistic action has been characterized (by others), that is "interference with a person's liberty for his own good." It sounds a bit like "stealing from you to make you wealthier." The paradox, however, is superficial since possession of a modicum of freedom is only one factor in a person's good. Hence, in restricting the liberty of S we may reduce or eliminate one good and yet, in so doing, promote others, for example, health or survival.

Another way of formulating an appeal to good-promotion sounds even *more* paradoxical, that is, it is permissible to interfere with a person's liberty in order to promote (or preserve) his or her liberty. What is being proposed is not conceptually problematic; rather, the claim is that it is all right to interfere with some of a person's liberties to promote (or preserve) a greater range of liberty on balance. Analogously, it is not conceptually problematic to propose amputating a gangrenous leg in order to prevent even greater impairment. We can roughly distinguish, then, two general types of appeals, the appeal to promote *good* and the appeal to promote *liberty*, ones which purport to identify conditions under which paternalistic interference is justifiable.

There is a third, slightly less familiar, and hard to articulate, category of appeals which proffer a ground for legitimate interference, interference which is paternalistic if we allow 'a person's own good' to be construed as 'a person's own moral good.' Having arrived at a certain state of despair in an attempt to locate a familiar and descriptive label for this sort of appeal, I exercise the *de facto* tyrannical right of authors and label it "the appeal to moral-good preservation." The point of the label and the rationale for distinguishing this third category require some explanation. When later in this chapter we examine such views, the unique characteristics of this approach will be made explicit.

I have identified three broad categories of appeals: (1) appeals to good, (2) appeals to liberty, and (3) appeals to moral-good preservation. Principles which fall into these categories are invoked to justify paternalistic interference without appealing to consent on the part of the subject of the interference. Such principles are the focus of this chapter. My aim is to examine all initially tempting efforts to sort permissible from impermissible paternalism. The adequacy of the defense of PARP depends, in part, on whether we exhaustively explore and subvert its competitors. If the approach is on the right track, all its plausible competitors are subsumable in the mentioned categories.

3.2 Appeals to Promoting the Good

The claim that it is all right to intrude into another person's life on the ground that it is for his *own good*, regardless of whether that other consents to such an intrusion, is not easy to assess, in part because of difficulties surrounding the notions of good and a person's good. Some preliminary mapping of distinction is in order to avoid confusion.

We can distinguish two senses of 'right,' as in 'right action,' in which to say an act is right may be to claim (1) the act is merely permissible, or (2) the act is required (ought to be done). As opposed to evaluations of actions, the term 'good' is frequently used to evaluate objects, processes, or states of affairs, for example, a good hammer, good car, good painting, good weather. Use of 'good' in a purely descriptive or empirical fashion (as in using 'good girl' to mean 'virginal') is an exception. The typical, evaluative, use of 'good' may be used to express a moral judgment, as in 'good character' (though not a moral judgment *directly* about actions), or a *nonmoral* (but still evaluative) judgment; for example, compare 'a good car,' 'pleasure is good,' 'the good of health,' 'self-respect is good,' or 'a good income.' When it is said that some act is for S's own good, what is meant by this? The claim may be understood plausibly as the claim that the act promotes some state of affairs for S which is nonmorally good (e.g., S's health or S's happiness). Call the resulting state of affairs promoted 'R.' To maintain, then, that doing X to S is for S's own good may be to suppose that the (aimed at) resulting state of affairs, R, is a (nonmoral) good. But why think R is good? At this point in our sorting of issues different questions arise. We shall not fully settle these issues, but it is important to explore them in order to examine defenses of paternalistic intervention which appeal to promoting the good of a subject.

It is common to distinguish between what is good (nonmorally) as a means, or "instrumentally good," and what is good in itself or "intrinsically good." A wrench may be said to be a good wrench because it is useful to achieve certain purposes we have—and for which the tool was designed. Or an activity may be said to be good because it enables us to achieve some further goal we have. For example, one might not value lifting weights, or running, for its own sake, but as a mere means to some further end. Some things (e.g., running) may be desired both as a means and as an end in themselves. Are some things intrinsically good? If so, what? And what does it mean to say that something is intrinsically good? These are difficult questions.

Some philosophers have held the view that certain statements of the form 'x is good' are analytically true, for example, 'pleasure is good.'[1] Such claims have proved to be controversial, and we are not likely to settle them by appeals to the ordinary use of words such as 'good' or 'pleasure.' What is, perhaps, less controversial is to say that 'x is good' is to recommend doing, experiencing, using, preserving or achieving x. Similarly, claims such as 'good'

---

[1] Henceforth in this chapter, for 'good' read 'intrinsically good' unless the context makes clear that the focus is on 'good' in another sense.

means 'desirable' or 'valuable' seem formal and empty and are, at least, of little help in settling substantive questions such as *'what is valuable?'* Even if we agreed that 'good' means 'valuable' or 'what we ought to value,' we want to know what sorts of things are properly so described. What are the empirical traits of a thing by virtue of which it is correct to say that that thing is good in itself?

We shall survey some of the leading, substantive, and contending candidates for the title "most reasonable answer to our question." To one degree or another I will be concerned with five main questions about each of five conceptions of the good: (1) is the conception a plausible one?, (2) does it allow the possibility that the subject can be mistaken about what constitutes his or her own good?, (3) does the employment of a given conception of the subject's good in conjunction with a "principle of good promotion" have implications about permissible paternalistic intervention which conflict with PARP (the Principle of Autonomy-Respecting Paternalism)?, (4) what are the epistemological difficulties in applying the good-promotion approach?, and (5) why should PARP be considered as the more defensive view against competing good-promotion principles. I should emphasize here that, although I shall suggest why some conceptions of the good seem more defensible than others, I shall not try to settle the question of which is the right one or the most defensible. That is too large a task to undertake here. Further, I shall examine some tempting views but not try to explore all that might be considered. In the final analysis my main concern is with (5) above, and I try to show why the "good-promotion" approach to deciding permissible paternalism, in conjunction with *any* of the conceptions of the good noted (with one possible exception) fails. One conception of the intrinsic good (it is whatever a person rationally desires) is sufficiently alluring, and slippery to analyze, that I pursue it at greater length in a later section—after most of the philosophical cards have been played.

The leading conceptions of the good fall, I believe, into two broad categories: (1) desire-dependent conceptions and (2) desire-independent conceptions. Of equal or greater interest, however, are the diverse conceptions falling within category (1). Consider the broad distinction first. I will label a conception as a *desire-dependent* one if it assumes that whether a state of affairs x is constitutive of S's good depends in some fashion on whether S desired, desires, or will desire that x occur for its own sake (at some time). If a conception of the good assumes that whether x is constitutive of

S's good does not so depend on S's desires, I will label it a *desire-independent* conception.

It is often said that health is good or life is of value (even "infinite value") even if people on rare occasions do not want them or their continuation. Such a view may reflect what I shall call the *Species-Normal Conception* of the good. I roughly characterize this view as follows:

S's getting[2] R is for S's own (intrinsic) good if and only if

S's getting R allows, or involves, S's functioning in a way typical of the species (or a relevant subset of species) to which S belongs.

It is worth noting that, on this view, organisms can have a "good of their own" even if they lack desires. Thus, a certain condition can be for the good of a tree, for example, receiving sunlight. This view is intelligible and familiar. Our concern, however, is with people, and not with plants or animals lacking desires. The Species-Normal Conception roughly identifies what is for a person's own good with his functioning in ways typical of members of Homo sapiens, for example, normal physical growth, mental development, non-impairment, and living a normal life span. Crudely put, life sustaining, pain preventing, and impairment preventing or alleviating measures are, then, for a person's own good—even if the person in question did not, or does not, want them. This view especially is one it is tempting to classify as an objective[3] conception of the good since, to a very considerable extent, what is normal functioning for the species (or a relevant subset, e.g., 50-year-old white females) is "an objective matter."[4]

The Species-Normal Conception is the main example, I shall

---

[2] Let 'getting' cover doing, being in a state of, experiencing, receiving, being the subject of, and so on.

[3] Conceptions of the good are sometimes classified as "objective" or "subjective." These are slippery, potentially misleading, notions. A 'subjective conception' may mean a theory assuming that S's good is solely or partly a function of S's desires. An 'objective conception' may mean one which views the good as not desire-dependent. Or 'subjective' and 'objective' may concern whether ascertaining that some state of affairs is, or involves, the intrinsically good for S is rationally, intersubjectively, decidable. It seems to me that it is not helpful, barring much effort at disambiguating such terms, to invoke "the" subjective/objective classification.

[4] The issue is considerably more complex. Those interested may wish to examine Christopher Boorse's essay, "On the Distinction between Disease and Illness," *Philosophy & Public Affairs* 5, No. 1 (Fall, 1975), pp. 49–68 or his essay "Concepts of Health" in *Border Crossings: New Introductory Essays in Health-Care Ethics*, ed. Donald VanDeVeer and Tom Regan (New York: Random House, forthcoming).

note, of a desire-independent view. From the standpoint of questioning whether one could promote a competent subject's good by intervening, the answer, on this view, is affirmative. Furthermore, it is evidently possible, on this view, for a person to be mistaken about what is for his own good since he may believe his life not to be a good in itself when it is. Thus, on this view, others may know better than S what is for his own good or what is constitutive of his good. Such a view is especially predominant in the thought, I believe, of health-care professionals and in governmental safety-regulators.

Normally, people generally do value or prefer those states or processes which are involved in species-normal functioning. The serious question about this conception, however, is why such states should be thought good *even when* they are not desired by the subject (or even desired not to exist or continue).[5] A person may desire not to function in a species-normal way. For example, S might prefer to be infertile. Is fertility, nevertheless, constitutive of S's good? On a desire-dependent conception, infertility, on the contrary, may be thought constitutive of S's good. But why? Further, it may be said that unless one is alive and healthy one cannot live a satisfying life. However, if a "satisfying life" is the life one prefers, or a life which is happy, it appears that health is rather an indispensable means, at least in most cases, to achieving desire fulfillment or happiness—and one of these may be what actually constitutes intrinsic good. Normally we do "value" (i.e., prefer) species-normal functioning but I know no compelling reason to think that it, in itself, is constitutive of the good. Even if the inference from what is desired to what is desirable is problematic, it is perplexing to maintain that something is intrinsically good *even if* no one desires or desired it, and this seems to be the implication of the Species-Normal Conception. It seems reasonable to think that for something to be intrinsically good for S, S must at least desire (or rationally desire) it while having it. Defenders of the Species-Normal Conception may allege that this only begs the question; I shall not pursue the matter further except to say that such a conception, I think, remains suspect, given the presumption just stated against such a view. If, then, it is unreasonable to think that

[5] In passing I observe that the view of Thomas Aquinas, that being in the presence of God is the ultimate, intrinsic, good seems to be a desire-independent view as well. G. E. Moore's view that 'good' denotes a "non-natural property" which "supervenes" on some things (e.g., beautiful objects—whether or not anyone is there to observe them), seems to be a desire-independent view as well.

species-normal functioning is constitutive of intrinsic good, paternalistic interventions—to promote S's good—may not succeed in so doing even if they successfully promote such functioning.

Let us, then, turn to desire-dependent conceptions. I shall characterize four representative conceptions:

1. *The Antecedent Desire Conception*

    S's getting R is for S's own (intrinsic) good if and only if

    S desires (given the circumstances), prior to his getting R, the getting of R for its own sake.

2. *The Current Desire Conception*[6]

    S's getting R is for S's own (intrinsic) good if and only if

    S desires (given the circumstances) his getting of R for its own sake while getting R.

3. *The Hedonic Conception*

    S's getting R is for S's own (intrinsic) good if and only if

    S experiences satisfaction or pleasure while getting R.

4. *The Rational Desire Conception*

    S's getting R is for S's own (intrinsic) good if and only if

    S would desire his getting of R for its own sake and if, while getting R, S were rational and relevantly informed about R at the time.

Each conception of the good can and should be considered on its own merits. In addition we are concerned here with the implications of each with regard to permissible paternalistic intervention. I shall explore these two matters with respect to the above four conceptions of the good.

First, we should observe that none of the conceptions noted, conceptions of what is nonmorally, intrinsically good, immediately yields implications concerning what actions are permissible or obligatory. What is needed is a supplemental *act-guiding* principle. The relevant one concerning permissible paternalistic intervention I shall label

---

[6] It may be useful to construe 'current' as 'concomitant.'

The Naive Good-Promotion Principle (NGPP):

> If A and S are competent persons and A's paternalistic per-
> formance of X toward S wrongs no others, and A's doing X
> to S will result in R and R is for S's own good,[7] then A's doing
> X is permissible.

Recall that a paternalistic act, on our definition, may be morally
innocuous (e.g., judiciously interrupting the activities of a friend
in order to remind her of her appointment) and, thus, permissible.
Or the paternalistic act toward S may involve a presumptive wrong;
for example, A intentionally may deceive S against S's will. The
interesting cases are the controversial ones and the latter are those
involving presumptive wrongs. For the Naive Good-Promotion
Principle to yield interesting implications (ones competing with the
implications of PARP), it would have to approve some presumptively wrong paternalistic acts. Whether it does depends on which
conception of the good is assumed. Thus neither a conception of
the good by itself nor the Naive Good-Promotion Principle by itself
has determinate implications regarding what interventions, if any,
are permissible.

3.3 Some Desire-Dependent Conceptions

Let us, keeping NGPP in mind, consider the Antecedent Desire
Conception. It implies that X is constitutive of S's good if S wanted
X prior to the getting of X. Ordinarily however, we are often, on
getting it, averse to something which was antecedently desired—
or find out that we desire something on getting it, something to
which we were previously averse. As an example of the former,
one might have had an intense desire to visit the North Pole but,
on getting there, prefer not to be there. The Antecedent Desire
Conception implies that, nevertheless, being there is good. A more
plausible view is that if desire is the important thing, surely it must
be current desire and not antecedent desire; after all, the "truth is
in the tasting."[8]

---

[7] By "R is for S's own good" I mean "involves, or brings about, what constitutes
S's intrinsic good, on balance."

[8] This simple idea casts serious doubt on a point often made in defense of non-
intervention in market transactions (one which seems to presuppose the Antecedent
Desire Conception), namely: that if a transactor, voluntarily, "knowingly," chooses
to trade he must be better off after trading (achieves a net increase in his share of
the good?). Otherwise he would not have traded. It is doubtful, however, that one
should equate "utility increase" with "fulfillment of antecedent desire."

Another difficulty faces any coupling of the Naive Good-Promotion Principle with either the Antecedent Desire or Current Desire Conceptions of the good, as a proposed basis for permissible paternalism. Since paternalistic intervention is contrary to the operative preference of the subject, it is not clear that the paternalistic aim of promoting a good (or preventing a "bad") for the subject can succeed. If the subject did not or does not want the result the intervener seeks to promote, it cannot count as a good of the subject if his desiring it is necessary and sufficient for its constituting his good. For example, if the motorcyclist does not want to wear a helmet, or to be so protected, our requiring her to do so and the imposed protection does not count as being "for her own good."

Strictly, whether the antecedent desire or the current desire conception is invoked can yield different results. If S is averse at time t^1 to being required to wear a helmet at t^1 but comes to prefer it at t^2, then on the current desire conception no good is promoted at t^1 but is at t^2. This, however, is a curious result. If S at t^2 prefers the helmet it is not so clear that we have, at that time, invasive paternalistic restraint, since S's preference is not being overridden.

Nevertheless, a defender of the Current Desire Conception and NGPP may plausibly insist that there is no incoherence. In intervening with S, one is betting that S will prefer the result of the intervention (and, thus, it is constitutive of S's good) even if S is resistant to the intervention. Since S prefers not to be interfered with, the intervention is an intrinsic bad or "harm" for S, but if the good of the result offsets the bad of intervening there may be a net increase in S's good—or a prevention of a diminishment of S's good. This seems reasonable enough. Here I shall note only that these considerations are clues to the epistemological difficulties which such prospective interveners face, that is, the need to be in a position of ascertaining S's preferences, likely preferences, and, probably, the relative intensity of those preferences. If S is intensely averse to paternalistic intervention, the bad of intervening may not be offset by the admittedly good result achieved. A Jehovah's Witness may desire one result of a blood transfusion (health) but be so averse to that sort of intervention that the bad exceeds the good (employing relative intensity of the desires as the criterion of the magnitude of the good and the bad involved). I shall let this approach stand. On the face of things, it seems more defensible than an approach combining NGPP with either the Antecedent Desire Conception or the Species-Normal Conception. We need to consider also the comparative plausibility of the Hedonic Conception

103

and the Rational Desire Conception—in conjunction with NGPP. The full assessment, and critique, will occupy us in this section as well as the one following.

Let us turn to the Hedonic Conception of the good. On both the Current Desire and the Hedonic Conceptions, it is possible for a person to be mistaken at *some* time about what fosters his good. Prior to eating raw fish one might be averse to doing so, or expect no satisfaction or pleasure from doing so. Yet on doing so one might desire it, or one might find it pleasant. So, it is possible that someone else might know better than a subject what will promote his good. On the hedonic view, acquisition of knowledge, health, friendship, or possession of wealth are not good in themselves. They are good if and only if they yield (possibly indirectly) satisfaction or happiness. Charitably, the hedonic view need not construe satisfaction or happiness as only involving pleasurable bodily sensations or twinges. Still, conscious satisfaction is the key element. On this view, a being incapable of such (a tree, an irreversibly comatose person) has no good of its own. Unless getting what one wanted or does want yields satisfaction it involves no intrinsic good for the wanter. The expression 'S enjoys X' seems to entail that 'S wants X' (perhaps, wants X even if not consciously wanting X), but the converse seems false, that is, S may want X but not find it enjoyable. However, if, as is tempting, we define 'S enjoys X' as 'S wants X for its own sake while having X,' the Hedonic Conception may be equivalent to the Current Desire Conception. (I here postpone problems concerning S's wants for certain things, for example, a good reputation for himself after he dies—or a good reputation for himself while alive, even if he is not aware of it.)

One intuitive worry about the Hedonic Conception is that S may enjoy doing what involves damage to his body, for example overeating or using certain forms of drugs. Some would say that doing so is not for S's good (or welfare or benefit). The apparent tension between the hedonic view and a desire-independent conception such as species-normal functioning is alleviated in part by considering what maximizes S's satisfaction over time and recognizing that the enjoyment (a good) involved in drug usage may be offset by a loss of other enjoyments (goods) as a consequence. At least the hedonic view is compatible with the view that one must exercise moderation, and indeed normally foster life and health, in order to optimize or maximize the stream of intrinsic good.[9] But what is

[9] Thus, one who accepts the Hedonic Conception may reject a "hedonistic life-style" as that expression is often understood.

intrinsically good on this view must be the satisfaction involved—
and not health per se or life per se.

My formulation of the Current Desire Conception is a bit vague
due to the leeway involved in interpreting the phrase 'while getting
R.' If we construe 'the getting of what one wants' to be only 'the
fulfillment of one's wants,' then it is clear that the Hedonic Conception does not collapse into the Current Desire Conception.[10] It
is one thing to have one's desire fulfilled (e.g., that there be no
nuclear war in the twenty-second century) and another to receive
felt satisfaction from getting what one desires (e.g., the desire to
make love with someone). The former desire may be fulfilled even
though one is unaware that it is and, thus, receives no felt satisfaction from it. If the hedonic view is correct, mere desire fulfillment
is not constitutive of the good of the desirer (even though *believing*
[truly *or* falsely] that one's desire will be fulfilled may yield satisfaction).[11] A defender of the hedonic view will deny that mere
desire fulfillment is constitutive of the good. A defender of the
desire fulfillment view will, of course, say that that is where the
argument begins, not where it ends. I shall not try to settle this
dispute.

Let us now consider the view that the proper guide to paternalistic intervention is to be found in a pairing of the Hedonic
Conception and the Naive Principle. Roughly, the idea is that it is
all right for A to intervene invasively with S when A, thereby, can
prevent diminishment of, or increase the sum of, satisfactions (or
"utility") for S.[12] Consider a case in which A is contemplating a
paternalistic interference with S in a particular context. Recall that
the Naive Good-Promotion Principle is:

> If A and S are competent persons and A's paternalistic per-
> formance of X toward S wrongs no others, and A's doing X
> to S will result in R and R is for S's own good, then A's doing
> X is permissible.

Let us flexibly allow as well that A may be a collection of competent
persons. Suppose A is a legislature and S is a competent person

---

[10] Contrast John Stuart Mill's remark that ". . . desiring a thing and finding it
pleasant . . . are . . . two parts of the same phenomenon; in strictness of language,
two different models of naming the same psychological fact." J. S. Mill, *Utilitarianism*
(Indianapolis: Bobbs-Merrill, 1957), p. 49.

[11] So we might promote S's good by falsely assuring S that her desire is or will
be fulfilled. For reasons to be elaborated, this is not to condone such a lie.

[12] 'Utility' in the literature is sometimes construed hedonically (as felt satisfaction)
and sometimes as want fulfillment.

who likes to gamble. Suppose, further, that A legally prohibits gambling in order to promote the good (or net utility) of citizens. Will the conditions of the Naive Good-Promotion Principle be satisfied? Will S experience, as a result of the legislative restriction, more pleasure (more good) than if the legislature had refrained from interfering? Even if the Hedonic Conception of the good is correct, the legislature must in practice determine whether or not, as a *matter of fact*, legally restricting S from gambling will promote S's own good (S's satisfaction) on balance. For it to conclude so reasonably, a number of difficulties must be surmounted. One is the widely discussed issue of whether talk of quantities of utility or satisfaction is meaningful; second, if so, is there a rational basis for the legislature to conclude that S will be better off (utilitywise) on being restricted or not? The latter judgment involves what some have described as a problem of making *intra*-personal comparisons of utility (in contrast to the more widely discussed problem of *inter*personal comparisons of utility, e.g., does B's gain [loss] in utility from implementing policy P outweigh C's gain [loss] in utility from P). Indeed, if the legislature contemplates such a question prior to the restriction on gambling, it may need to compare S's current utility level with that which S would obtain if gambling were prohibited (a possible world or world-path just like the pre-restriction one, except that it is one in which the legislature has imposed the restriction). To oversimplify considerably, such a task is hedged about with very thorny problems even if we conclude that it is logically possible.

It may be worth observing here that one strategy often proposed as a means of avoiding second party conjectures about increases or decreases in utility levels (compare: levels of pleasure, etc.) of another person is unavailable here. Defenders of voluntary contractual agreements, including familiar "free market" trades, often suggest that voluntary bilateral transactions are a superior and unproblematic means of distributing goods since no "third" party is required to conjecture as to what distribution will be best, for example, maximize the sum of utilities for those receiving goods—since, it is presumed, each party to a voluntary transaction will trade only if he judges that he will be better off or no worse off, on trading, *in his own estimation*. Since each is left to decide whether a proposed transaction will improve his lot (or, at least, not worsen it), no one else need determine whether the participants will gain or lose. Specifically, if Ivan is a potential participant, no one else need determine whether Ivan will increase his share of the good or decrease it by participating—or compare his pretransaction utility level with his posttransaction utility level. Ivan can make his own judgment and act accordingly (as noted before, this view seems to focus problematically on antecedent desire).

However, in contemplating the case of the legislature's imposing a restriction on S's gambling, S is not free to decide the matter and, typically, will have virtually no opportunity to provide significant input as to whether the proposed restriction will be for his own good or not. Further, even if S's input is acknowledged, the legislature may regard S's conjecture as fallible. After all, it may be claimed, S's judgments about the *future* course of his own utility levels on introduction of the proposed restriction may be mistaken. It may be argued further that it is characteristic of gamblers to be myopic about what will promote their own good, overestimating the satisfactions to be obtained from the thrill of taking risks or the likelihood of winning and underestimating the satisfactions of a life lived with greater moderation and security. If legislatures take this view and yet paternalistically aim to interfere according to the guidelines of the Naive Good-Promotion Principle, they are forced to draw conclusions about the difficult question of whether the restriction will increase, or preserve, S's utility level. Let us allow that the restriction might increase it, but whether it will seems to be dependent in a crucial way on particular, possibly idiosyncratic, traits of S. For example, does S unambivalently delight in gambling or does S regard his habit as a character defect or weakness of will? Is S a lover of risk or does S reluctantly gamble to try to escape gnawing poverty? Or does S gamble to fund a life-saving operation for a sibling? Does S, in general, deeply resent governmental intrusions or does S readily adapt to them? Whether the restriction will actually promote S's good on balance depends on these matters. Since legislatures rarely have access to this sort of data, how could they reasonably draw conclusions about whether the restriction is for S's own good? Legislatures, of course, typically promulgate laws for entire classes of persons, and not one individual, but recognizing this fact only complicates matters for those who claim that legislative interventions into the lives of competent persons are justifiable by appeal to the Naive Good-Promotion Principle, since the task of supporting the requisite empirical claim(s) that a policy will promote someone's good is only magnified.

If the notion of quantities of utility or, more weakly, higher and lower utility levels is conceptually unproblematic (as we have allowed), it is conceivable that correct judgments could be made about whether an intervention will increase another's utility level. As we have observed, however, there are serious epistemological difficulties in obtaining the relevant empirical information necessary to arrive reasonably at such judgments. It is worth observing that an omniscient agent contemplating paternalistic interference would not face this difficulty. This, however, is not a good reason to conclude that such a difficulty is a "merely practical" or a "merely evidential" obstacle to employing the Naive Good-Promotion Principle. In a wide variety of circumstances the difficulty is a decisive reason to refrain from paternalistic interference which *may* be sanctioned by the Naive Good-Promotion Principle for the agent simply will fail to have a justified belief that his intervention will promote the subject's good on balance.

This epistemological gap is especially likely to persist in cases in which the agent and the subject are unacquainted, or in which the agent has little access to facts about the subject's values, attitudes, long-term goals, as well as other psychological traits. For example, possible negative effects of transfusing an unconscious, injured person may seem improbable; belatedly, it may be discovered that the person is a Jehovah's Witness who is horrified by the fact that his blood is now tainted. Similarly, deception of a patient about her terminal cancer may save her from serious depression but may prevent her from getting her affairs in order, or cause worse trauma if deception is belatedly discovered. Unconsented-to sterilization may not promote the subject's own good on balance. Deceptive use of placebos, even if having a temporary beneficial effect, may harm, on balance, by promoting an excessive readiness to pop pills to solve problems. Injections intended to be therapeutic may induce lethal allergic reactions. Guilt-inducing remarks to young children, aimed at curbing bed-wetting, may create a persistent, cramping, sense of shame and a negative self-image. The causal chains leading to an overall diminution in the good of the subject may be direct or indirect, familiar or esoteric. The general point is that, on the approach under consideration, the facts about the effects of an intervention are crucial. They are often hard to come by, and interveners may be ignorant of the relevant empirical data about the subjects of intervention. Recognition of this point provides reason to conclude that, even if there were not other objections to the Naive Good-Promotion Principle, the range of cases in which it can be reasonably invoked is far narrower than might initially appear. It is worth stressing that those difficulties arise for employment of the Good-Promotion Principle whether in conjunction with the Current Desire or Hedonic Conception.

To recognize these epistemological difficulties, however, leaves the door open to the possibility that in some cases, however few in number, invasive paternalistic interference with competent persons is justified when one can in fact promote the subject's own good on balance.

I turn now to a consideration of the Rational Desire Conception of the good. On all the conceptions of the good mentioned, it is possible for a person to make an irrational choice of *means* in pursuit of his good. Our focus here, of course, is not on means but on what *constitutes* a person's good. The more defensible views, so far, seem to be the Current Desire and the Hedonic Conceptions. There are some states of affairs that people seem to want for their own sake, want while getting them, and perhaps enjoy as well— which, however, some would deny to be constitutive of the good of such persons. Possible examples are: occupying a masochistic role, engaging in avoidable, exceedingly risky, activities, being quite passive, being relatively uninformed, or living a hermit-like existence. It may be maintained that although such states of affairs are desired they are not the objects of *rational* desire, and what is constitutive of intrinsic good is whatever is rationally desired for its own sake. On this approach some actual desires are irrational and some absent desires would be rational to have. For our purposes the prior point is of greater interest. If a subject desires a state of affairs for its own sake, the fulfillment of that desire will not be constitutive of his good unless it is a rational desire. Thus, others might promote his good by intervening with some of his actual, perhaps deeply entrenched, desires. The Rational Desire Conception, combined with NGPP, seems inviting since it suggests a principled basis for invasive paternalistic intervention in cases in which we are much tempted to do so—in cases in which competent persons seem to be acting stupidly or recklessly, so as to risk loss of life, health, or their autonomous capacities.

It is clear that the plausibility of this approach rests quite heavily on how 'rational' is to be understood. The concept of rationality is complex and there are a number of competing analyses. Our examination here, at best, can be only an attempt to consider broad possibilities in an effort to appraise one good-promotion approach to the question of permissible paternalism—one which seems to be a competitor to the autonomy-respecting view defended here. My order of discussion at this point will be slightly unnatural. First,

I wish to make a case against acceptance of the fundamental outlook embodied in all good-promotion strategies, as I think they are commonly understood. This case is a central part of the defense of PARP. Then I shall return to a fuller examination of approaches which place great stress on the rationality of the subject's desire and choice. I employ this ordering for three reasons. First, the rational desire approach is difficult to assess fairly but it promises to be a chief competitor to PARP. We should allow it an extensive "run for the money." Second, the apparent conflict between the rational desire approach and PARP is better judged and assessed when the argument for PARP (in particular, its view of what constitutes proper respect for competent persons) is developed more fully than it has been so far. Third, on one possible reading of the rational desire approach the apparent conflict with PARP seems to vanish. Again, whether this is true is better judged when the view I am defending is further clarified.

3.4 The Case for Respecting Competent Persons Instead of Promoting Good

It is of some importance, then, that the more tempting conceptions of the good of persons (the Current Desire, Hedonic, and Rational Desire Conceptions) all allow that a competent subject may be mistaken in some fashion regarding what is for his own good. Thus, all seem to allow for situations in which invasive paternalistic intervention may preserve or promote a subject's good. I have not tried to settle fully the dispute between such theories of the good. In some cases a subject, S, and an intervener, A, will have conflicting conceptions of what is *constitutive* of the intrinsic good of persons, for example, S's good. Suppose that S thinks that (or, perhaps, "acts on" the assumption that) the Current Desire Conception is correct, and A believes the Hedonic Conception is correct. A thinks he can promote (or preserve) S's stream of satisfactions by thwarting S's effort to achieve what S currently desires. Why think the Hedonic Conception is superior to the Current Desire Conception? If it is not, A will not, by invasive intervention, actually promote (or preserve) what is really for S's good. Thus, one worry is whether one who acts on NGPP and a particular, disputed, conception of the good of persons can defend (whether anyone adequately can defend) the particular conception of the good involved. For reasons noted, this seems no unproblematic task. It is, then, one obstacle to all of the variants of the good-promotion approach.

However, suppose A's conception of the intrinsic good is correct and S's explicit or implicit view is mistaken. Why think that A's superior wisdom on this score *not only* renders S's conception *properly criticizable* but also that it is all right for A invasively to "impose his conception" on S by constraining his choice? One answer is that S will (by assumption) be the better off for it. But this answer just seems to beg the question; for our question simply is *why should the fact that S will be better off for it be thought a sufficient reason to impose our judgment.* Some will say, unpersuasively I think, "it just is." Good promoting (or harm preventing) paternalistic principles imply that it is all right to intervene in ways which go beyond fair, rational, persuasion or criticism, or invasive but consented-to intervention. To develop the argument against so doing, consider another case. Suppose that we and S adhere to the same conception of what constitutes S's intrinsic good. We and S might accept the Hedonic Conception, for example. Is it, then, all right invasively to interfere with S to preserve or promote S's own good (as we and S abstractly conceive it; further, assume it is the most defensible conception)? The argument against an affirmative answer is, I believe, a compelling one.

The core of the argument rests on a hitherto set-aside distinction between (1) promoting or preserving what constitutes *S's intrinsic good*, and (2) what facilitates or does not subvert S's realizing *S's conception of the good.* S's conception of the good includes *not only* a conception of what constitutes his intrinsic good but also a conception or judgment about its relative importance in comparison with achieving or promoting the intrinsic good of other subjects. This fact is an important one. Even invasive intervention which in fact will succeed in preserving or promoting S's good can fail to respect S as a competent person. S, as a competent person, will have a conception of the *relative importance of his own good* compared with that of others. S will have other-regarding or, perhaps, "moral" preferences about what he ought to do, or may do, to preserve or promote *what really* is *for his own good*—or what others should do, or may do, to preserve or promote his own good. Just as S will have some conception of which of his "lower-order" desires (e.g., to eat roast duck, to lose weight, to lessen the demand to kill animals) ought to prevail, so he will have some conception of whether his own interests should or should not prevail in cases in which they may conflict with those of others. This outlook will include and reflect rather complex beliefs and judgments about what he, as an independent moral agent, regards as ideals, values, matters of personal integrity, a prerequisite for self-respect, conceptions of those to whom decent treatment is owed, and a vast network of empirical assumptions. In short, his conception of the relative importance of his own good, the extent to which it should be promoted or preserved against that of others, will be a byproduct of a certain idiosyncratic global outlook, including S's conception of what is for his own good. Of course, such an outlook may or may not be highly self-conscious, articulated, well-reasoned, systematic, and so on. Thus, what will maximize or preserve S's good may not coincide with those ends S chooses to promote or have promoted. Certain cases of altruistic suicide (or other altruistic and seriously self-sacrificing acts) are prime examples.[13]

If we are to respect S as an active, autonomous, moral agent with his own conception of the good, we cannot invasively intervene in his choices on the basis of a myopic focus on what constitutes *his own good* even if we happen to possess superior insight on that score (or with regard to means to that end). To allow S to function as an independent moral agent, responsible for his choices and acts, invasive intervention is prohibited except when we have S's valid authorization or there is compelling reason to believe that he would appropriately consent to it. To do otherwise is to treat S as a "good receptacle" or a "utility location," but persons are not just that. They are arbiters of their own well-being, and not merely sentient, computing, devices to be kept in good repair. They both assess their competing lower-order, self-regarding desires, determine which is most urgent, and form moral preferences as to the extent to which their own interests or urgent self-regarding desires should be promoted, cultivated, repressed, or thwarted in cases of conflict with the self-regarding desires and interests of others. They may choose to retard or undermine the advancement of their own good. Unlike computers, they originate, adopt, and revise ultimate ends.

There are some objections to the view I am espousing, ones

---

[13] Consider the case reported (*The Raleigh News and Observer*, August 26, 1983) of a 35-year-old woman with liver cancer who refused treatment which, physicians claimed, could have saved her life. Rather than have an abortion (essential to the treatment) she gave birth to a second child—only to die soon after. It is doubtful that her choice was *for her own good* on most or all of the conceptions of the good we have reviewed. Still, she was allowed to pursue her conception of the good. What it was in this case, is at least readily intelligible by others—and was known by them—but, importantly, this is not always the case.

concerning rationality, to which I shall return in due course. However, it may be useful to clarify one point here to ward off one
source of objection. By a person's conception of the good, I do not
mean his espoused idle dreams, wishes, or merely romantic aspirations of what sort of person he ought to be or how he would
live if only he were a different sort of person. The cliché, "actions
speak louder than words," contains a truth. A person's efforts,
strivings, and actual choices are the key to his conception of the
good. Thus, just because S says "I intend, or hope, to quit smoking"
is not a decisive reason to conclude that we would promote his
conception of the good (his own, perhaps, in this case) by forcing
him to stop. If his operative conception of the good really includes
his quitting and a choice to allow others to intervene invasively,
then we may promote his conception by so doing. This act, however, is in accord with PARP. In short, respecting a person's conception of the good does not include imposing on him what accords
with his passing fancies, those romanticized wishes in which he
had no real investment, and for which he is not willing to undergo
anymore than a nontrivial sacrifice. The goal of "being thinner" is
not part of the glutton's conception of the good unless he takes
steps to avoid gluttony. Consenting to intervention by others is
one possible step.

To treat competent persons as beings with relevant wants and
needs, like ourselves, is an advance over treating them as inanimate
objects, as "mere things" to be used as a natural resource. However, to treat them *as if* they lack what we have and expect to
pursue, namely a conception of the good, is to deny them a certain
moral equality. For if, as paternalistically inclined agents we invasively interfere with nonconsenting competent persons when they
wrong no others, we act on our own conception of the good while
subverting the efforts of others to act in a like manner. If we believe
their vision myopic, their conception defective, as we might and
for good reasons, there is no good reason why we may do more
than engage in fair, open, attempts rationally to dissuade—or to
intervene in ways to which they did not or would not validly
consent. To act in a contrary way is to act as if others are clay to
be sculpted and not, as we regard ourselves, active sculptors of
unique lives.

The allure of good promoting principles, including utilitarianism,
is not easily vanquished.[14] Hence, some further consideration is in

[14] Without making much of the point, I suggest that utilitarianism has a certain
bent in favor of paternalistic intervention. Compare the remark of one utilitarian,

order with regard to the view that respect for competent persons requires the high degree of forbearance which I have defended here. Any theory insisting that we have rather stringent duties toward certain beings will be implausible unless it can be based on some reasonable conception of the sorts of beings owed such duties and also what it is about those beings which provides a basis for those duties in contrast to other sorts of beings to whom the duties are not owed. All plausible theories presuppose some sort of relevant distinctions between what is owed to people, penguins, and plastic trees (for example). A duty to forbear must derive from considerations about the sorts of beings *to whom* the duty is owed. A duty to promote or preserve the good, if there is one, must be derived from considerations about the sorts of beings *to whom* the duty is owed. It is extremely strange to think, for example, that we have a duty *to pleasant mental states* as such, for example, to preserve or promote them.[15] If there is a duty to promote or preserve such states, it must be based on considerations about the set of beings to whom the duty is owed and it must explicate why *that* set of beings is owed that *particular* duty in contrast to other beings or entities. Good-promotion principles, I believe, fail in this task. Among the entities of whom we intelligibly (in *some* sense) can speak of their well-being or lack of well-being are trees, nonhuman animals, and competent persons. Assuming that trees lack desires and are nonsentient but have "needs" (in some sense), trees are mere "needons." Assuming that some non-human animals have needs, also have wants, are sentient, but lack a conception of the good, they are mere "wantons."[16] In both cases, of course, we plausibly can speak of what is for their own good (perhaps, only

Peter Singer, ". . . I accept that the possession of consciousness makes it wrong to cause the conscious being harm, or to make its conscious states less pleasurable than they otherwise would be" (see his "Killing Humans and Killing Animals," *Inquiry* 22, Nos. 1–2 [Summer, 1979], p. 151). If "causing" is construed to include omissions, then we sometimes cause others to experience less pleasure than they otherwise would have by omitting certain paternalistic lies. If lying to another competent person would prevent diminishment of, or enhance, her sum of satisfactions, then, according to the principles Singer seems to endorse, that is what we should do. The implication is troublesome in itself—as is the perplexing assumption that preserving or promoting the sum total of pleasure of existing sentient beings is the desideratum in deciding how to treat persons.

[15] On this point I have benefitted from Tom Regan's suggestive essay, "A Refutation of Utilitarianism," *Canadian Journal of Philosophy* XIII, No. 2 (January, 1983), pp. 141–159.

[16] For a skeptical view on whether any nonhuman animals have desires, see R. G. Frey, *Interests and Rights* (Oxford: Clarendon Press, 1980); for a skeptical review, see my comments in *Canadian Philosophical Reviews* 1, No. 1 (Spring, 1981), pp. 16–19.

the species-normal functioning criterion of the good is feasible with regard to trees). Competent persons, who have their own conception of the good, are not, then, mere wantons or mere needons. They alone have a conscious conception of their own good and a conception of its importance or comparison with that of other beings, permissible or desirable adjudication of conflicts, and so on.[17] They alone are full-blown, autonomous, moral agents. The conception of justifiable limits on paternalistic intervention defended here recognizes and incorporates these relevant distinctions. It appears, with one possible exception, that good-promotion principles do not. The admonitions to preserve, promote, or maximize the good (or utility), of nonconsenting competents fail to take into account adequately, if at all, the distinction between mere wantons, needons, and persons, all of whom, in some sense, have a "good of their own."[18] For reasons already elaborated, these

[17] The position I am defending assigns priority to respecting a subject's right to direct his life over considerations of promoting the good or welfare of *that subject*, and parallels, or is analogous to, a view held by recent critics of utilitarianism who maintain that certain rights of persons take priority over satisfying competing claims based on considerations of promoting the *general welfare*. Just as various forms of utilitarianism too readily permit the sacrifice of the welfare of some for the sake of the many, various consequentialist approaches to the dispute over paternalism too readily allow the bypassing or undermining of the choices of persons in order to promote their welfare. Both views tend to treat competent persons, not as centers of choice and will but, as "utility (or welfare) containers"—whose utility level is to be maximized, increased, or preserved. The apt phrase "utility container" is due to Robert Nozick, *Anarchy, State, and Utopia* (Cambridge, Mass.: Harvard University Press, 1974). Relatedly, just as utilitarianism seems mistakenly to treat a collection of individuals as a superperson some of whose interests rightly can be sacrificed to promote those of others, so good promoting paternalistic principles mistakenly regard individual competent persons as mere collections of interests, some of which (e.g., the interest in directing one's own life) rightly may be sacrificed to promote others. (I here partly rely on some useful phraseology in Rolf Sartorius's "Utilitarianism, Rights, and Duties to Self" [unpublished manuscript], University of Minnesota, Minneapolis, p. 8.) There are, of course, notable differences between the case of sacrificing a welfare interest of one individual to promote those of the many, on the one hand, and sacrificing an interest in liberty of an individual to promote his other interests. In the latter case, successful intervention may provide counterbalancing benefits to the constrained party, but this may not be true in the former nonpaternalistic case. This fact accounts in part, I think, for the seeming innocence of much paternalistic intervention. An act "for your own good" does not obviously use you as a *mere* means, e.g., harm you without compensations. Of course, I have claimed that such "offsetting benefits" are *not* adequate compensation: even adequate compensation for wrongs done do not make it true that no wrong was done.

[18] Three conceptions of "persons" tend to crop up in recent discussions: (1) S is a person if and only if S is a member of Homo sapiens (the genetic sense), (2) S is a person if and only if S has a serious right to life (a moral sense), and (3) S is a person if and only if S is conscious of itself as existing over time, is sentient, and possesses, at least, certain minimal rational capacities (call this the psychological

admonitions fail to incorporate a crucial moral distinction into ethical theory.

The possible exception is the account which conjoins a good-promotion principle with the Rational Desire Theory of the good. Here I will suggest briefly the sort of response to be made, in defense of my view, against such an account. In the next section a fuller examination will be developed. An account resting heavy weight on the notion of rational desire (for our purposes: rational desire for states of affairs which wrong no others), I suggest, can be elaborated in two basic ways.[19] Either it will do so *substantively* by counting as rational only those desires or choices which are for certain specific outcomes (or types of outcomes), or it will explicate rationality *procedurally* so that a desire will count as rational if and only if the desire or choice would occur, or continue, in conjunction with the employment (in a moderately successful way) of certain rational capacities, for example, to classify, to use abstract concepts, to distinguish sound from unsound or valid from invalid arguments, and so on. If rationality is explicated in the former, substantive, way, the theory is likely to proceed from the assumption that we ought to preserve or maximize (or it is permissible to preserve or maximize) rather specific, indeed controversial, choices. But this seems as puzzling as the notion that we ought to preserve or maximize utility as such—instead of, or only incidentally, respecting persons who satisfy the condition of rationality—procedurally understood. Alternatively, if rational desire is explicated in the procedural manner mentioned, then the resulting account, which will insist on forbearance from invasive intervention with "reasonable persons" when they wrong no others, well may be extensionally equivalent in its implications to the account defended here (in somewhat different terminology). This latter rational desire view of the good conjoined with a good-promotion principle fails, then, to offer a competing view. This is the thesis I shall defend, but we shall explore the issue in more detail. Further, it is worth noting, without elaboration here, that such an account is at such great distance from utilitarian approaches that it hardly deserves to be so labeled—for the shift will have been made to respecting persons with a conception of the good as arbiters of their own lives and not just securing certain outcomes for wantons.

sense). Above, I use 'persons' in the last sense. Our typical focus, however, is on persons in this last sense who are also competent and members of Homo sapiens.

[19] We shall explore further the slippery question of how to explicate 'rationality' in the next section.

In this section I have defended the view that competent persons have a right to direct their own lives and that this places important limits on the range of permissible invasive paternalistic intervention. In the next section we further explore the persistently tempting view that concerns about irrationality of choice provide reason to judge a greater range of paternalistic intervention as permissible. In later sections in this chapter the connections of the view defended here to autonomy are elaborated, and other positions competing with the autonomy-respecting view are examined.

3.5 Intervention and Rationality of Desire and Choice

In the preceding sections we noted difficulties in deciding which is the most defensible conception of the good. We also observed the difficulties in ascertaining what, in concrete situations, would promote or safeguard a person's good—given certain conceptions of what constitutes his good. Further, I have defended the view that we must respect a competent person's conception of the good and that merely promoting his own good may fail to do that. It may be claimed, however, that what is constitutive of a person's good is the fulfillment of his rational desires (the Rational Desire Conception) and that promoting (or preserving) that good does respect a person's conception of the good or at least all that we ought to respect, that is, his conception of the good insofar as it is a rational one. This, quite generally, is the view I shall explore here.

Apparently competent people sometimes want bizarre things, seemingly for their own sake, for example, painful experiences, self-destructive activities, even death-promising pursuits. Such cases may make us skeptical of the Current Desire Conception of the good. Sometimes persons derive satisfaction from such activities or states. This fact may make us wary of the Hedonic Conception. Since we often regard these sorts of activities as irrational in some sense, we may think the preferable view is that what is constitutive of a person's intrinsic good is what he rationally desires for its own sake.[20] Why should we defer to a person's irrational

[20] Much of the literature on rational choice, and rational desire, focuses only on the question of the rationality of a choice of means to a given end. Thus, the proposal is widely accepted that rationality consists in choosing that means which will maximize expected net utility in circumstances in which risk can be calculated. This rule, as well as the maximax or maximin rule for situations of uncertainty, takes the end as given. Our concern here with the notion of rational desire and choice is, also and more directly, with whether an end can be judged rational or not, on

desires and choices? Why should we not, rather, promote fulfillment of a person's rational desires? Is this not promoting *his good*
and even that part of his *conception of the good* which deserves
respect?

We have operated on the assumption that we can often readily
distinguish generally competent from generally incompetent persons. If presumptively competent person, S, desires or chooses in
a way that seems irrational, we may have to decide whether S's
choice evinces a temporary or permanent loss of competence, retention of competence (and, hence, rational capacities) but a rationally defective choice, or a possibly idiosyncratic but reasonable
choice. Let us, however, continue to focus on competent parties.
One general concern is whether choices or desires can be rationally
defective and, if so, whether that provides a legitimate ground for
paternalistic intervention.

As noted, the Rational Desire Conception of a person's good,
combined with the Naive Good-Promotion Principle, countenances
certain invasive interventions. Since such a view presupposes some
way to distinguish rational from irrational choices or desires, critics
might seek to undermine such a view by arguing that there is no
way to do so. This, I think, would be a mistake and the wrong way
to defend (for example) the theory espoused here. The distinction,
I assume, is a legitimate one even though precise criteria of rationality are illusive—and difficult cases are not hard to find. Let
us first explore the highly general features of our common concept
of rationality. It is complex; part of it concerns (1) the capacity to
learn, differentially react to data external to the organism, and store
it to a degree, and (2) the capacity to process the data in some
manner (in accord with the canons of correct deductive and inductive inference). Rocks possess neither capacity, and if plants
are said to possess these capacities at all (albeit "unconsciously")
they are judged to possess them so minimally as to fail to embody
traits (1) and (2) as commonly understood. Unexposed film or an
audio recorder in a crude way may register, but does not process,
"information." Some computers exhibit both traits to a degree. We

---

what grounds, and (if so) what follows with regard to permissible paternalistic
intervention with desires or choices which fail to be fully rational, or not rational
at all. If certain choices of acts wrongful to others can be shown to be irrational,
then, in some sense, irrationality of choice may be a legitimate ground for invasive
intervention. However, my concern is whether choices of acts not wrongful to
others, but in some sense irrational, may be prevented or halted by invasive means
and whether their irrationality is a good reason for intervention, by itself or in
conjunction with other factors.

conceive young children as not having reached the "age of reason" because of their lack of developed capacities to process information to a significant degree. Below a certain threshold of ability we regard a being as 'nonrational' or 'irrational,' above that threshold as rational. However, 'rational' in this sense is clearly a range property; it covers a set of beings which are more or less successful at registering, retaining, and processing data in truth-preserving ways.

One could imagine, perhaps, a conscious computer which had capacities (1) and (2). We have, as a dimension of our view of rationality, an idealization, for example, that of a perfectly rational being, with respect to capacities (1) and (2), one which could register and store all information, and never fail to make correct inferences. On these criteria no human is fully rational. Some are not rational at all. So, we are driven to recognize degrees of rationality among the range of rational beings or rational choices. If failure to make a fully rational choice (for now, one resting on true beliefs in all relevant facts and involving no inferential errors) were necessary for legitimate invasive interference with the chooser, no one would be immune. Conversely, if an agent's choice to intervene invasively is unwarranted unless it is a fully rational choice, it is impermissible for any human so to interfere. Or so it would seem.

The only interesting view which might sanction invasive interference would be one defending its legitimacy not merely in the case of failures of full rationality but also for less than fully rational choices (which fall within our postulated range of rational choice). Such choices, of course, are often labeled "irrational." To avoid confusion, let us call them (objectively) "less than fully rational choices."[21] I shall employ this classification[22] of choices:

1. Those fully rational
2. Those less than fully rational   "rational choices"
   (1) Those quite reasonable
   (2) Those seriously unreasonable
3. Those (seriously) irrational   "irrational choices"

Our classification is crude, but it seems correct to distinguish, at one end of a continuum, fully rational choices and, at the other,

[21] Even if, as in one sort of case, the subject made a "subjectively reasonable choice," roughly, that is, a choice well-reasoned given his beliefs.

[22] The above categorization is admittedly vague; it does not provide a way of classifying hard cases. Further, it is somewhat stipulative. Still, there is a little hope for clarification if we simply rest content with the myriad usages, in ordinary talk, of 'reasonable,' and so on.

"unreasonable choices" (though all are "reasoned" choices). The issue to which we shall return concerns whether the fact that a competent subject makes an unreasonable choice provides reason to think that invasive intervention with him is permissible.

It is of some interest that, so far, our imaginary rational computer might be thought of as being entirely indifferent toward different outcomes, that is, in some sense as lacking any desires whatsoever. This point implies that at least part of our concept of rationality (or one sense of the term if one prefers) has no necessary connection with conscious goals, purposes, or desires. Rather, it concerns what we might call the epistemic (and logical) dimensions of rationality, that is, recording or processing data. A choice or a desire (of a derivative as opposed to the brute sort) then may be labeled unreasonable simply because it "arises" from epistemically defective beliefs (e.g., perhaps, a desire to sell the homestead and bet the money on a horse simply because it has the same name as one's first girl/boy friend). The choice is unreasonable even if the result of the choice is happy (conversely, a choice is not shown unreasonable just because it has an unhappy outcome).

We have identified one intelligible ground for classifying a choice or a desire as unreasonable, namely, that it arises, or continues to exist, because of rational capacities exercised in an epistemically defective way (or the non-exercise of such capacities). So far, our characterization of rationality allows the possibility that a being, in a fully rational manner, might choose to maximize his own pain or self-destruction. Is there not, however, some connection between rationality and desire, or rationality and the concepts of harm and benefit? Economists typically characterize rational choice partly in terms of choosing in a self-interested manner. When pressed, they typically deny that they are assuming that rational choice is (necessarily?) self-interested in the sense that a rational chooser always seeks to promote his own self-regarding interests to the exclusion of, or detriment of, others. Rather, a rational choice by S is construed to mean a choice by S which maximizes his utility, one which achieves maximal satisfaction or fulfillment of S's desires (even if they include a desire to sacrifice S's life to save others).

Even this broad interpretation of rational choice seems to suppose that a choice is rational (more or less so) only if it is a choice aimed at promoting a benefit (including: preventing a harm).[23] If

[23] Charles Culver and Bernard Gert, *Philosophy in Medicine* (Oxford: Oxford University Press, 1982), pp. 26–27, 35. I do not fully examine the Gert-Culver view (that a desire is rational only if it is a desire to benefit); those interested would do well to consult the above-mentioned volume.

this is correct, there is a *conative* dimension (concerning what one desires) to rationality or rational choice, in addition to our identified *epistemic* dimensions (concerning what one believes). A more complex conception of an idealized, fully rational being is one which records or knows all data, or all relevant data, makes no mistaken inferences, and also accordingly chooses with the aim of benefitting someone (self or others). From this perspective, our epistemically nondefective computer with purely self-destructive aims (or, perhaps, complete indifference toward outcomes) is not fully rational.[24]

Accepting this tentative view of idealized full rationality, one might judge beings with rational capacities to have chosen irrationally or unreasonably if their choice arises, still putting matters vaguely, because of a failure to acquire data, a failure to process it correctly, or a failure to aim at benefitting someone. We might regard any of these failures as a proper ground for imputing some degree of irrationality or unreasonableness.[25]

Later, we shall return to consider the relevance of epistemically defective choices and desires. Here we should examine the difficulties with the mentioned conative aspect of our broad working concept of rational choice. If, for a desire to be a rational desire, it must be a desire to benefit someone, it is important to consider what could be meant here by 'benefit.' There are, I believe, three basic alternatives, ones suggested by our prior discussions. 'Benefit' (like 'good') may be construed as a desire-dependent notion, either as (1) desire fulfillment as such, or (2) felt satisfaction or contentment. Or it may be construed in a desire-independent fashion, that is, (3) some state of affairs identified (and alleged to be good) independently of anyone's desires. To avoid losing sight of the forest by looking at the trees, one issue concerns whether a desire, to be a rational one, must be a desire to benefit someone (self or others) and, if so, what is meant by 'benefit.' Suppose S desires to starve himself and that such a desire is not epistemically defective, that is, it arises from no false beliefs, but rather "rests on" true beliefs, and is not a result of mistaken inferences. If benefit means only desire fulfillment, then it seems that S's desire or choice does aim at a benefit to someone, namely, fulfillment of his own desire. Hence, on this view, his desire is rational. Thus, invasive paternalistic intervention to *stop* him would not promote his good

[24] If it had self-destructive aims it could choose; if it were completely indifferent it seems doubtful that it could be said to choose.

[25] Or, perhaps, a total lack of rationality in the absence of a desire to benefit someone.

(what he rationally desires—given our current elaboration). In short, this elucidation of rational desire in conjunction with the Naive Good-Promotion Principle is unlikely to countenance intervention beyond what is allowed by PARP—in cases in which there is no epistemic defect.

Suppose 'benefit' is construed in a desire-independent way. For example, as we have noted, it might be claimed that health, growth, or continued life are benefits whether or not someone desires them. For reasons discussed, it is doubtful that desire-independent notions are independently plausible ones. What is desirable must rest somehow on what sentient creatures actually desire. Again, they normally desire to be alive and healthy—as an essential means to fulfilling other wants, or achieving satisfaction. But why think it is more than a normally important precondition or means to what is intrinsically good—couched in terms of want fulfillment or satisfaction. Traditional arguments, I succinctly suggest, fail to tell us. Further, if benefit is construed independently of actual desires, it is not clear why we should view pleasure, life, or health as a benefit rather than pain, death, or illness. That for a desire to be rational it must aim at a benefit, *so understood*, seems an implausible view. Thus, an account of rational desire as involving a desire *so* to benefit seems unreasonable. Thus, the conjunction of such an account of a person's good (as what a person rationally desires) in conjunction with NGPP does not provide a serious competitor to PARP.

Suppose benefit is construed hedonically—either as experiencing satisfaction, or as pain (broadly construed) avoidance.[26] This seems the most plausible construal of benefit. Here I shall suggest only that this view (when coupled with NGPP) is unlikely to have implications divergent from PARP. It is reasonable to believe that virtually all the desires of persons aim at benefitting someone (self or others) in this sense. The desires of both extreme egoists and extreme altruists would seem to satisfy this "must aim to benefit" condition of rationality. In short, the hedonic interpretation of benefit is plausible but weak; it will fail to exclude many desires (*if any*) from being rational. Hence, the correlative construal of rational desire in conjunction with NGPP is unlikely to sanction intervention in cases in which PARP would not. If there are cases in which the desires of persons do not aim to benefit anyone, it is likely that

[26] That is, pain avoidance by means other than the permanent cessation of consciousness, or at the cost of being unable, for substantial periods, to experience satisfaction.

such persons are radically disturbed and, hence, not competent—in which case PARP's standards for non-intervention do not apply.

Our discussion of a conative condition on rational desire may be summarized. If, to be rational, a desire must aim at a benefit for someone, there are three main ways to interpret benefit. One sort is independently implausible (desire-independent conception). Another, the desire fulfillment view, does not itself promise to exclude any desires as irrational (and thus open the door to paternalistic intervention—when NGPP is invoked along with this conception of rational desire). The hedonic conception seems to be a defensible understanding of benefit but, for reasons noted, is unlikely to exclude many (perhaps, not any) desires as irrational and, in brief, in conjunction with NGPP to countenance paternalistic intervention in cases in which PARP would not.

Let us return to the question of how the *epistemic* dimensions of our conception of rationality can be developed, and what sort of correlative case can be made for intervening with irrational choices. I shall assume that our prior discussion of *conative* considerations is correct. So let us restrict our focus to desires (or choices) in which persons do aim to benefit someone. To recall, we have distinguished roughly, on epistemic grounds, several sorts of choices:

1. Those fully rational
2. Those less than fully rational   } "rational choices"
   (1) Those quite reasonable
   (2) Those seriously unreasonable
and 3. Those (seriously) irrational   "irrational choices"

With regard to category 3., we noted that choices based on irrational desires are likely to be choices of those permanently or temporarily incompetent. Thus, either PARP's standard of non-intervention will not apply (the former case) or some interventions by appeal to PHIC (in the latter case) will be permitted. I shall assume that the more disputatious cases lie elsewhere.

It is worth emphasizing initially that the failure of S to be fully rational, or for S to act quite unreasonably, does not in itself seem a legitimate ground for invasive intervention in S's behavior. For two reasons. First, and as noted before, given our characterization of full rationality, no one makes a fully rational choice. Thus, if failure of full rationality were an adequate ground for intervention, no choice would be immune. Such a view is absurd. Second, consider these examples. I may go to a film mistakenly thinking I had not seen it before, purchase a car falsely believing its mileage will be exactly what official estimates indicate, or make a gross strategic error in a bridge game, but such unreasonable choices on my part hardly seem a reason to conclude that others may intervene invasively. After all, little or no harm to me will result (let us suppose) if I go ahead.[27]

Alternatively, and as we have discussed, *even if* S's choice holds out the prospect of serious harm to S, it is possible that it is a rational choice, indeed a highly reasonable choice. For it may not significantly fail to accord with the epistemic canons of rationality and, also, it may involve a desire to benefit someone, for example, to achieve pain relief for S or to save the life of another. In short, it may be a rational choice on S's part to pursue his *concept of the good* even if viewed in a straightforward manner it is not for *S's good* on balance (as in the case of altruistic self-sacrifice).

The type of situation which is more controversial and in which invasive paternalistic intervention is a more tempting option is that in which there is good reason to believe *both* that S's choice is seriously unreasonable *and* that it promises serious harm to S on balance. Let us, then, focus on cases in which S seems to be competent, has chosen to perform some act, X, X wrongs no others, X will cause severe harm to himself, and S neither validly consents to A's prevention of S's doing X nor can it reasonably be inferred that S would consent to such interference if S were apprized of relevant factual information about his doing X. It might be agreed, in general, that it is impermissible for A to prevent S from doing X *simply* on the ground that doing so would prevent S's being significantly harmed on balance. However, a critic might claim, in circumstances such as the above, that if it is true that S's choice to do X is quite unreasonable *and* his doing X would result on balance in serious harm to S, *then* it is permissible for A to intervene invasively to prevent such an outcome. Let us state what I label the *Unreasonable-Harm Prevention Principle* (UPP) more explicitly:

> A's paternalistic interference, X, with S, is justified if:
> 1. S's choice to do Y is seriously unreasonable,
> 2. S's doing Y is likely to make S significantly worse off than if S refrains, and

[27] Thus, Rawls' remark that "[p]aternalistic principles are a protection against our own irrationality" (*A Theory of Justice* [Cambridge, Mass.: Belknap Press of Harvard University, 1971], p. 250) may need qualification if what is meant is that irrationality *by itself* is sufficient reason to intervene paternalistically.

3. A's doing X will prevent S from doing Y,[28] and

4. S is likely to be significantly better off if A does X than if S did Y,

and 5. A's Xing involves no wrong to others.

There is a considerable range of cases in which S's choices promise harm to S, or involve the serious risk of such. The more recalcitrant issues, instead, are (1) whether the choice is unreasonable or (2) how unreasonable is the choice. It is important how 'unreasonable' in UPP is to be understood. If it means only 'is less than fully rational,' UPP would countenance radically counterintuitive results since virtually all choices of competent persons are less than fully rational, including but not restricted to, self-harming ones. UPP would allow people coercively to intervene in the lives of others who, for example, make ordinary investment, career, marital, and other life-style choices which are unreasonable and prospectively risk serious harm. For UPP to have initial plausibility, then, we must construe it as being restricted to seriously unreasonable choices. Even so, the difficult problem remains of identifying relatively noncontroversial criteria for what is to count as "a seriously unreasonable choice."

It is worth emphasizing that the burden of doing so is a burden for defenders of UPP, a principle ostensibly in competition with the view defended here. However, it is only fair to try to determine whether UPP is a tempting competitor of PARP.

In some cases an apparently competent party might choose a seriously self-harming path (e.g., choosing to inflict burns on himself), and we may discover that he "has no reason" in the sense that it is not a means of achieving his concept of the good, or it involves no desire to benefit (broadly construed) himself or anyone else. How this might be determined is a bit problematic, but let us allow the possibility. Such a case is extremely unusual. To emphasize a point noted earlier, such a case would call in question our initial presumption of competence. One conclusion may be that the subject has taken leave of his senses, that is, has ceased to be competent. Possibly he is mentally ill. If so, what is permissible paternalistic intervention stands outside the scope of the Principle of Autonomy-Respecting Paternalism (see Chapter 7 on the treatment of incompetents).

More important here are less extreme cases. In some cases the

---

[28] In the least damaging but effective manner.

chosen path will be seriously self-harming and will be seriously unreasonable in that it involves an evidently false belief or the absence of an evidently true belief about what we may label "an easily confirmable matter." Suppose you have overlooked the need to turn off the main electric switch as you are about to rewire an electric outlet. You will suffer a severe shock if you go ahead. Given your concept of your own good and your rational capacities, it is reasonable to believe that you would consent to intervention to prevent the harm. Thus, the Principle of Hypothetical Individualized Consent allows invasive intervention.

In some cases there may be no evidently false belief whose truth or falsity is an "easily confirmable matter." Consider the following example. Suppose that 30-year-old Brother Francis is a competent person. He believes that it is a serious evil for rats to be used in a standard LD-50 test for the toxicity of a proposed drug. In the test a group of rats is made to ingest the drug to a level at which half of the group die ("lethal dosage to 50%"). Hence, he chooses to volunteer as a subject to circumvent the need for such testing (thinking that if other persons do so as well, this animal testing will not be "necessary"). If we respect his autonomy, he may die at an early age. Although we may think that Brother Francis's concept of the good is rationally defective, namely, highly unreasonable, his alleged deficiencies of rationality may not involve easily confirmable matters, whether about empirical claims or moral assumptions. The relevant claims may be contested matters among competent persons of good will. It is in just such cases that UPP, on one interpretation, implies the permissibility of invasive intervention beyond that which would be sanctioned by PHIC. Hence, this is where the rub occurs.

The reasons for rejecting UPP, I believe, are already at hand. First, if UPP were accepted, the door would be opened to a broad range of quite invasive paternalistic interventions. Many ordinary choices derive in part from beliefs which will count as unreasonable beliefs on any moderately stringent account of what it is to have a reasonable belief. Again, consider common choices regarding marriage, careers, investments, gambling, purchases of products, and so on. Or consider the case in which atheists view the choice of another to become a Christian missionary as one based on an unreasonable belief (that there is a God) and seriously self-harming (since the chooser must take serious risks or forego certain satisfactions). Would not UPP sanction invasive intervention? Then reverse the case; suppose it is an atheist choosing a self-sacrificing life dedicated to spreading the truth of atheism, and Christians view the atheist here in the manner the atheists viewed the Christian in the prior case.[29] The same worries arise over invidious disruption of the prerogative of competent persons to direct their own lives in ways that do not wrong others.

Furthermore, on the interpretation of UPP which sets a stringent standard of rational choice (1. or 2. (1) in our classification) we cannot respect competent persons as independent beings with a capacity to form and revise their own conception of the good, and as our moral equals, and also accept UPP. Fair, open attempts to dissuade other competents allow them to decide for themselves, to remain the locus of decision making, and the final arbiters of important choices. Invasive intervention, permitted by UPP, relegates others to the position of mere wantons, subject to good or harm, but not themselves beings (like us) with their own conceptions of what is reasonable, what are reasonable risks, or how to resolve contested matters. Even if our judgment is rationally superior, this fact does not justify the imposition of our vision on our moral equals.

In brief, I have argued that UPP, construed so as to interpret 'unreasonable' or 'irrational' narrowly (category 3. of our early classification) does not compete with PARP. Alternatively, on a broader or more inclusive (including 2. (1) or 2. (2)), interpretation, it sanctions invasive practices and also seems to presuppose a kind of moral inequality among competent persons, one whose justification is much in doubt. More figuratively, unless our competent brother (or sister) validly consents, would validly consent, or we intervene only to ascertain competence, the right sort of fraternity supposes a basic moral equality and the latter is incompatible with invasive paternalistic intervention. We are not without qualification "our brother's keeper." In the case of Brother Francis, if his choice

---

[29] It is of some interest that there is a parallel between the view defended here [that so long as certain choices are, at least minimally, rational, we ought not to impose (our conception of) what is "fully rational" on competent persons] and John Rawls' view that a just society would assign a status to a person's conception of the good very much like that assigned to religion in the United States. I take it that he means, roughly, that although we may be critical of certain religious outlooks and believe them quite unreasonable, we do not regard that fact, if it is one, as sufficient reason to prohibit religiously based pursuits—so long as others are not wronged (in regard to the latter, compare some religiously based pursuits, e.g., stoning to death unfaithful wives or ritual sacrifice of human beings. Of interest here are Exodus 21:2, 21:15, 17; Deuteronomy 23:19–20, 13:6–10, 20:10–14, 22:20–21, 25:11–12; Leviticus 20:13; 1st Corinthians 14:34–35; and Ephesians 6:5).

is reasoned and voluntary, and wrongs no others, we must not intervene invasively for his own good.

The objection will be raised that, if this is true, we must "idly stand by and let innocent persons foolishly sacrifice their lives," although surely, our objector insists, this is misguided. So, the view set forth here has absurd implications. This objection is tempting, but I do not believe it is compelling. First, let it be granted that we may regard Brother Francis's choice as foolish, and possibly it is. Further, his dying seems tragic (however, see section 8.4). But we need not stand *idly* by since it is permissible to use fair, open, means to dissuade him. It may be reasonable to intervene invasively to determine his competence. However, if he is competent and goes ahead, I do not find it radically counterintuitive that we wrongfully have failed to permit a tragic choice. Brother Francis has his own conception of the good. He is not merely a utility container; as a moral equal he deserves to be the arbiter of his own life. It is not obvious that we have any legitimate ground for imposing our conception of the good on him—in the absence of some authorization to do so by him—when by his action (we have assumed) he wrongs no others. A certain nonmoral good may not have been promoted or preserved, or a certain nonmoral evil (harm) prevented, but our stringent duty of non-intervention (in this case) is based on respect for persons; there is no duty to good or evil *as such*—to regulate its existence or its extent. Contrary views are indeed counterintuitive, for they sanction a benevolent despotism in which other moral equals are to be treated as inferiors, as mere wantons, by self-appointed regulators and overseers of an individual's (or world's) total (or average) utility level. Put in familiar language and by contrast, S can have a right to choose, one which deserves respect, even if S fails to make the "right choice." Some outcomes are in themselves desirable, but it does not follow that we invasively can secure them by subverting the choices of competent persons. This point, of course, is compatible with a different story with regard to legitimate dealings with animals, children, or adult incompetents.

3.6 Dimensions of Autonomy

It has been argued here that competent persons have a (limited) right to direct their own lives, one which is absolute throughout the domain of acts not wrongful to others. Such a right may be described as an autonomy right, and the central principle defended here has understandably been labeled the Principle of Autonomy-Respecting Paternalism. Crudely put, it asserts that presumptively wrongful paternalistic interferences are unjustified, or unqualifiedly wrong, unless certain types of consent by the subject obtain, that these interferences wrongfully undermine or infringe the autonomy of competent persons. So far, comparatively little has been said about the concept of autonomy and cognate notions such as 'exercise of autonomy,' 'surrender of autonomy,' 'moral autonomy,' or how autonomy is related to prudence, competence, or rationality. Although I have claimed that respecting autonomy is an important consideration in delineating and distinguishing permissible from impermissible paternalism, arguments can be marshalled in favor of the permissibility of a greater range of paternalistic interference than that sanctioned by PARP, arguments which appeal not so much to "promoting good" as to either *preserving or enhancing the autonomy* of the subject. Given the value I have attributed to autonomy, such arguments threaten to undermine PARP "on its own ground," and may embody the intensity of a family quarrel. We shall look at such an argument in the next section. Prior to that, some groundwork must be laid by clarifying concepts and examining some other "autonomy focused" arguments which constitute objections to PARP.

The term 'autonomy' derives from a Greek expression meaning self-rule. The core notion is that of an individual who possesses a sufficiently complex set of capacities to process information, reflect, assess alternative courses of action, and choose among them. Possession of such capacities requires a modicum of self-awareness and rationality. The term 'autonomy' is, however, used in different ways and this is likely to be a source of confusion. It is one thing for an individual to possess the *capacities* to live autonomously (to reflect, assess alternatives, and deliberately choose among them) and another to *exercise* those capacities to such a degree as to place a highly personal stamp upon his own life. As opposed to non-autonomous persons, autonomous persons have the requisite capacities for self-direction. The latter may exercise these capacities in a weak manner, that is, some autonomous persons are quite passive and give little consideration and reflective evaluation to their goals. They use little imagination. They readily do, with little or no independent assessment, what others suggest or prescribe, and imitate with little conscious attention to reasons why, or whether, the example of others is desirable or not. They show little resistance to peer pressure or authoritative demands. It is not that they are incapable of *originating* goals, they simply fail to do so; they are like ships that sail without a rudder. Hence, they move in the direction of the prevailing currents. We may describe such individuals as *weakly autonomous* (or speak of 'weak autonomy').

By contrast, other autonomous persons do more than minimally exercise their autonomous capacities. Rather, they are active and reflective in considering alternative courses of action. They do not readily "take another's word for it" or readily accede to the suggestions or prescriptions of others without independently reflecting on the desirability of proposed courses of action. They seek to determine whether there are reasons for choosing or preferences of their own which may support an alternative view. Such persons are said to be "independent-minded," perhaps even stubborn, or ornery. They *live their own lives* in a way that weakly autonomous persons do not. The *latter* are often described as heteronomous, other-directed, or conformist. The former persons I shall call *strongly autonomous*. On my terminology, then, heteronomous persons need not fail to possess the capacity for autonomy; however, they do not exercise it and so are weakly autonomous.[30] To escape or avoid confusions, and for the sake of completeness, it is worth recognizing two other meanings which often attach to sentences of the form 'S is autonomous.' There is a third, loose, usage of 'autonomous,' one recognizable when it is said that a computer, or a robot is autonomous or, possibly, that a weed just grew up autonomously. We sometimes extend the concept to describe entities which function "on their own" in some fashion and are not entirely controlled throughout every segment of their functioning by (at least weakly) autonomous beings. There is also a fourth sense assigned to 'autonomous.' For example, to say that a governmental agency or unit is autonomous is to claim not only that it can function with a certain independence but that it has a certain panoply of rights to function in this way. We can, and should, distinguish this latter, value-laden, use of 'autonomous' from the neutral uses noted earlier, for our examination of paternalism supposes that it is morally controversial as to whether (weakly or strongly) autonomous individuals have a right to exercise their autonomy in certain ways. Hence, earlier and later references to autonomy should be

---

[30] By contrast, Stanley Benn asserts "To be a chooser is not enough for autonomy, for a competent person may still be a slave to convention." (See S. I. Benn, "Freedom, Autonomy, and the Concept of a Person," *Proceedings of the Aristotelian Society* LXXVI (1976), p. 123.) Perhaps the contrast is only terminological; I would agree with Benn's remark if his 'autonomy' meant 'strong autonomy.'

construed as meaning weak or strong autonomy unless otherwise indicated.

It is worth noting that a person may be *cognitively* autonomous but not able to act on his decisions, for example, due to "external" interference. We might describe such a person as lacking *volitional* autonomy.[31] A slave or an inmate of a prison may be said to have his autonomy constrained or thwarted due to his inability to act on certain of his choices. He may be free to cogitate but not free to act overtly. Some acts by others undermine only volitional autonomy; others, for example, "brainwashing," behavior modification, electro-shock treatment, hypnosis, use of aversive drug "therapies" (such as the use of Antabuse with alcoholics), can undermine (at least for a while) the capacity to reflect, consider, and choose.[32] One might add to this list the use of guilt-inducing remarks, humiliating comments, and "double messages" which disorient the cognitive capacities of others. Some interferences, then, present *obstacles to chosen acts* (or potentially chosen acts); others disrupt the *capacity to choose*. The degree, or severity, and permanence of the disruptions vary greatly of course.

Most adult humans are both generally competent and autonomous. Some are neither, for example, the severely retarded, certain psychotics, and those who are comatose. Some children are both generally competent and autonomous. Some are neither, for example, infants and the severely retarded. This last remark demands qualification, however, for some retarded children, although not generally competent, may exhibit a degree of autonomy. And a child not competent to make certain decisions (for example, whether to undergo surgery) may be competent to make others, for example, to choose a flavor of ice cream or to choose her own friends.

Note that we have defined 'autonomy' as involving a set of capacities to choose or to act. Given that, whether a being is autonomous or not is an empirical question to be decided case by case. 'Autonomous' also seems to be a "range property." Competent persons exhibit varying degrees of autonomy. When we describe a person as "very autonomous" we usually mean quite independent-minded, an active thinker or decider, not easily duped

---

[31] I earlier drew this distinction in "Intrusions on Moral Autonomy," *The Personalist* (now: *The Pacific Philosophical Quarterly*) 57, No. 3 (Summer, 1976), pp. 251–265.

[32] For a useful discussion of various behavior control techniques, see Ruth Macklin, *Man, Mind, and Morality: The Ethics of Behavior Control* (Englewood Cliffs, N.J.: Prentice-Hall, 1982).

or seduced, relatively immune to outside influences, and so on. Other persons, as noted, exhibit none of the prerequisites of autonomy. Still others will strike us as "borderline cases." This admitted imprecision about the criteria for deciding who is autonomous, however, seems no more reason to dispense with the concept than it is in the case of 'blue,' 'tall,' or 'sexy.'

Given this conception of autonomy, we are forced to recognize that a person's autonomous choice need not be "intelligent" (though it involves intellect), "wise," "virtuous," "prudent," or "praiseworthy." Claims are made, however, that we ought to strive to be autonomous persons, that autonomy is a value, or an ideal, that we have a stringent duty to *increase* our own autonomy or that of others, or a stringent duty to *preserve* our autonomy or that of others. Having some grasp of what autonomy involves is clearly a prerequisite for understanding and assessing these moral claims, claims which are not all equivalent and which may be easily confused with one another.[33] In Section 3.7 we shall examine arguments which purport to justify a range of paternalistic interventions by appeal to such claims.

If an autonomous person *can* surrender his autonomy, perhaps there are cases where he *ought* to do so. And if there are cases where a *subject* ought to do so, perhaps there are cases where *we ought to infringe* his autonomy, for example, for paternalistic reasons. To assess this line of thought, let us first ask whether a person *can* surrender his autonomy. That is, can a person cause it to be the case that he is unable to function autonomously or cause it to be the case that his capacities for autonomy are diminished? Setting

[33] It is worth noting that some thinkers employ highly restrictive concepts of autonomy. Others conflate 'autonomy' and 'moral autonomy.' All this can lead to considerable confusion. For example, Kant seems to regard a person as autonomous only if he acts "from reason rather than desire." This point is somewhat obscure. It is hard to imagine a case in which a person who is motivated by a desire has no reason for acting. Alternatively, if one must have *certain sorts of reasons* in order to be acting autonomously, then self-directing, purposive, even highly individualistic, persons may not count as acting autonomously, a conceptual result at odds with ordinary notions of autonomy. Further, Kant, and others, often characterize autonomy so as to require that one must, to be autonomous, self-legislate moral rules for oneself which one is willing to universalize (i.e., willing to be followed by all persons). Although such a proposal may be a definitive feature of 'moral autonomy,' it does not seem to be definitive of 'autonomy.' To equate the two terms is most misleading. A final point is that if autonomous beings (and perhaps only they) deserve the highest sort of respect which may be extended, the comparatively narrow extension of 'autonomous persons' on Kant's view, and that of others, may imply an unduly diminished moral standing for those who turn out to be, on such views, non-autonomous.

aside the case of suicide, the answer is clearly affirmative for we can place ourselves in a position where we diminish our volitional or cognitive autonomy, for example by self-enslavement, use of drugs, exercising to exhaustion, choice of psychosurgery, or aversive therapies. The degree of diminution varies of course. There are less dramatic ways in which persons restrict their own autonomy. We have noted them earlier; the prerogative to make certain medical or economic decisions affecting oneself effectively may be placed in the hands of a physician or financial advisor. Such acts are evidently *compatible* with the retention of significant cognitive autonomy and with a diminished but significant range of volitional autonomy. The wisdom, prudence, or moral acceptability of such surrenders remains an open question. To the extent that a person's surrender of autonomy is more thorough and permanent (as, perhaps, in voluntary psychosurgery or self-enslavement) and to the extent that autonomy is regarded as a good or an ideal to which one should aspire, such acts will be morally suspect.

It is clear that autonomous choices are not necessarily prudent choices. The claim that it is all right to interfere with extremely imprudent choices of competent persons to prevent choosers from suffering harm (when they have not consented to constraint) seems to be a variant of the Naive Good-Promotion Principle we have already considered. We have generally construed "good-promotion" or "what is for a person's own good" to be interpretable as meaning either 'making someone better off than he would have been in the absence of interference' (cf. 'promoting good' or 'benefitting') or 'preventing someone from becoming worse off than he would have been in the absence of interference (cf. 'preventing harm'). To claim that it is all right to prevent highly imprudent choices (that is, choices harmful to the chooser) presents us with no new principle and we have already found reasons to reject it. Among *autonomous* choices that one may make are choices to *surrender* a portion of one's autonomy. Such surrenders of autonomy may be imprudent. Once more, if the preceding argument is correct there is no justification for interfering with such unfortunate (if they are) surrenders of autonomy in the absence of appropriate consent. If, as I have maintained, competent persons have a right to direct their own lives, it follows that they have a right to do so by surrendering some or even all of their autonomy in pursuit of their conception of the good, even if such a conception or judgment is from the standpoint of others, and in reality, foolish or self-defeating.

133

3.7 Preventing Versus Not Causing the Loss of Autonomy

By way of objection, it may be claimed that I have been too hasty in dismissing the appeal to autonomy preservation as an adequate ground for paternalistic interference, especially since I have allowed that autonomy is valuable and that competent persons have what reasonably may be described as a fundamental autonomy right, that is, a right to direct their own lives, a right not exercisable unless the right holder possesses autonomy. Hence, the right I have attributed to competent persons would be empty in the absence of the capacity to exercise it. Further, it may be claimed that it is one thing to focus on cases in which a competent person gives up only some, perhaps a minor, portion of his autonomy and another to consider cases where the surrender results in substantial impairment of, or total loss of, autonomy. Here, it may be claimed, the case for paternalistic intervention is stronger. In addition it may be objected that I have overlooked an important distinction. It is one thing for a competent person autonomously to engage in activities risky to some of his welfare interests, and another autonomously to engage in acts promising to terminate his autonomy. Is invasive paternalistic intervention permissible in the latter type of case even if not in the former? To explore the matter, consider this case.

> A young woman, Karla, is, at 19, a promising professional tennis player, having reached the first round at Wimbledon. She "eats, breathes, and sleeps" tennis. Though intense and obsessed by tennis, she is a competent person; tennis is her primary source of satisfaction. But Karla was adopted and when her "real" mother locates her, she wonders whether to tell her that she has an hereditary disease which will physically incapacitate her (Karla) to the extent that her career as a tennis professional will fail in two or three years. A psychiatrist judges that so informing Karla will severely depress her and render her incapable of managing her own affairs, that is, of functioning autonomously, for months or even years.

In this case there are two "harms" to be considered. One is, by assumption, the inevitable harm which will accrue from the debilitating hereditary disease. The other is the depression, disorientation, and possible loss of autonomy Karla is likely to experience if she is informed about her affliction. The paternalistic act under consideration here is not like most of the "interferences" we have discussed thus far for it does not involve a "commission" involving force, threat, or an overt lie; rather it is a matter of omitting the truth, that is, simply not informing Karla. It is reasonable to assume that Karla has a presumptive right to know and/or that Karla's mother has a presumptive duty to disclose such information. Hence, it seems presumptively wrong not to inform Karla; if the omission is paternalistically motivated it is a paternalistic act (commission *or* omission) standing in need of justification. One argument in favor of such paternalism might appeal to the Naive Good-Promotion Principle, but we have found reasons to reject this principle. A different sort of principle, a narrower one, might appeal not to promoting good in the sense of welfare, but simply and only to the *preservation* of autonomy. Such a principle may be called the *Autonomy Preservation Principle* (APP):

> A's paternalistic interference (by act or omission), X, with S is permissible if
> 1. it is necessary to preserve S's autonomy, and
> 2. A's Xing involves no wrong to those other than A or S.

There are several objections to arguments employing this principle. One is similar to that adduced against arguments invoking the Naive Good-Promotion Principle. The principle, APP, is applicable only in cases where it is reasonable to believe that the paternalistic act (or omission) is in fact necessary to preserve the autonomy of S. Potential paternalists assume a heavy burden here, namely, of having to find compelling reasons for so concluding. A great deal could be said at this point about different standards of evidence which may be necessary in order to support the relevant empirical claim adequately. Must there be only a "preponderance of the evidence," or must it be "beyond reasonable doubt" that informing Karla will result in a loss of autonomy? Further judgments also may be necessary and even more difficult: how severe is the loss? for how long a period? is it a reversible loss? Both in the treatment of criminals and those who are or may be subjected to civil commitment, *similar* difficulties are a notorious problem; for judgments are often made as to whether an individual is "likely to be dangerous to himself or others." It is not obvious that the empirical data and theory required reasonably to make such judgments or such predictions are both accessible and available, and controversy persists here among professional psychologists and psychiatrists.

It is also worth observing that in the case of Karla, the empirical task is not simply one of determining whether Karla fits in some familiar "diagnostic" category (e.g., anorexic) but whether she *will* become substantially impaired, with respect to autonomy, if she is treated in a certain manner. Put another way, the question is not whether an already impaired individual (e.g., a "borderline schizophrenic") will react in a certain fashion to some new circumstance, but whether a loss of autonomy will be *induced* in a competent, autonomous person by disclosure of disturbing information. Furthermore, although it might be well established that we can, for example, induce death in a healthy human by an injection of arsenic, we have a less well-developed body of data about how competent persons react to shocking news. Much seems to depend on the "psychological resources" of the individual. Further, data about how normal persons cope with, for example, divorce or death of a spouse, are not obviously useful with regard to the case of Karla. These reasons strongly suggest that the number of cases where one might *reasonably* invoke an argument including APP and relevant empirical assumptions are few and far between. Hence, APP does not "open the door" much, if at all, to concluding that a significant range of cases of justified paternalism exist—beyond those sanctioned by PARP.

In addition to the epistemological difficulties involved in making the assumptions APP requires, there is another objection, one aimed more directly at APP. I shall lead up to it indirectly. So far we have assumed Karla is a competent person. However, it is reasonable to believe that persons who have never exhibited incompetence (since "maturity") may become incompetent as a result of "traumatizing" occurrences, for example, by going into shock or as a result of some other defense mechanism's becoming operative. In specific cases, like that of Karla, there may be much uncertainty as to whether a subject will become incompetent and nonautonomous or will continue to choose and act autonomously, whether prudently or not, in the face of adverse circumstances. Suppose, for a moment, that we were omniscient; hence, we would know whether a subject will retain her autonomy or not. If the subject would become incapable of autonomous functioning on encountering a "traumatic" event (e.g., being told that she has a severe and progressively debilitating disease), then there would be reason to conclude that the subject was not competent after all, despite earlier presumptions. Why think so? My reason is just this: a person who cannot minimally cope with disturbing and perhaps tragic information is either incompetent or only apparently competent—for a plausible necessary condition of correctly classifying a person as competent is that such a person be able to "handle" disturbing events (especially tragic news) without "going mad." A full defense of this not uncontroversial claim requires, I believe, a developed theory of competence. I shall not offer one here nor more than a sketch of one later. An adequate theory would, I believe, support the claim made. So, if we were omniscient we might know that a subject was, indeed, not competent. If that were the case, neither PARP nor APP would be relevant to deciding what treatment is permissible, for, to recall an earlier qualification, the scope of our discussion thus far and the principles adduced are restricted to competent subjects. Attempts to sketch partially a theory for dealing with incompetent individuals (including the apparently competent) we leave to a later point. Of course, we are not omniscient. Nor are professional psychologists and psychiatrists; hence, real-world epistemological problems return to cloud our landscape.

A reasonable approach to deciding about recalcitrant cases like that of Karla, cases in which there is some nontrivial reason to wonder about whether autonomy will be retained, is, I believe, the following. Any theory distinguishing permissible paternalism toward competents versus permissible paternalism toward incompetents requires distinguishing competents from incompetents in order to determine which principles are relevant. That judgment, on such theories (including PARP), is unavoidable. If the weight of the evidence is that a subject is not competent, principles regarding incompetents are relevant. If the weight of the evidence is that a subject is competent, then it is probable that autonomy will not be lost upon experiencing psychologically disturbing events. If so, a principle such as APP lacks application. Given the limited information presented about Karla (excluding the psychologist's assessment of it), it seems clear that there is a strong presumption that Karla is a competent person. If so, and if our arguments for PARP are reasonable, she has a right to direct her own life. This includes the right to cope with her own misfortunes as she pleases, with no interferences other than those sanctioned by PARP. She must be allowed to play her hand even if fate deals her a poor one—not because "suffering is good for you" or "struggle builds character" but because it's her life. The presumptive wrongness of deceiving Karla about a fact crucial to her choices and plans is not overcome, I maintain, by the fact that the considerations mentioned will facilitate retention of her autonomy. Paternalistically shielding competent persons from tragic information out of a concern for autonomy retention, by presumptively wrongful acts, still fails to respect competent persons as independent centers of choice, emotion, and action, as moral equals with their own conception of the good—in contrast to, for example, machines to be kept, *no matter what*, well oiled and in good repair.

A qualifying comment on the appeal to autonomy preservation is in order. If it is reasonable to presume, in the case mentioned, that Karla is competent, then Karla is owed the truth. However, given lingering doubt as to whether Karla really is competent (and whether she will retain autonomy in the fact of tragic news), the choice is not simply between a deceptive omission *or* a blunt truthtelling. It *may* be possible to explore indirectly with Karla whether she would want to be told the truth (immediately) about any grave or debilitating condition she suffers. Compare an exploratory question: how would you feel if some unexpected event were to undermine your goal of having an outstanding athletic career? That is, indirect inquiry might provide further evidence concerning whether paternalistic deception might be justified by appeal to the Principle of Hypothetical Individualized Consent. One sort of response by Karla may make such an appeal appropriate and reasonable; another (e.g., panic at the very *thought* of a debilitating development) might lend support to the view Karla is only apparently competent, in which case she lacks the absolute right to direct her own life. In either case, we find no reason to reject or revise the Principle of Autonomy-Respecting Paternalism. If Karla is not competent, PARP does not apply. If she is, there is no good reason, I have argued, to shield her from the truth owed to her, unless sanctioned by PARP. From this, of course, it does not follow that we can be indifferent as to how and *when* it is disclosed; there are both harsh and gentle ways of doing so. Respect for persons as centers of choice, will, and emotion normally requires the latter mode.

In the absence of explicit evidence to assume the contrary, it is reasonable to presume that competent persons sometimes would consent to another's delay in conveying information to a more opportune moment rather than its being communicated at the earliest possible moment. Normally, a broker may owe her client information about the latter's investment but has no duty to convey it in the middle of the night. A professor must provide information about grades to students but need not make it available within minutes of calculating the grade. In general, *when* information or apparent information must be provided, *if* it is owed, would seem to be a function of whether delaying its revelation would subvert a subject's opportunities to make choices that are, in all probability, important to the latter's pursuit of his conception of the good. Thus, a Presidential adviser normally may delay relaying some information to the President until the next day but, for example, cannot delay conveying the (apparent) fact that enemy missiles have been launched. Such matters seem obvious but serve to emphasize that, even if it is sometimes wrong to withhold information indefinitely, doing so temporarily is compatible with the permissibility of some delay in its disclosure. Doing the latter will often be defensible by appeal to the Principle of Hypothetical Individualized Consent.

It is also worth noting that persons normally want to live *realistic lives*, that is, they want to be able to formulate their conception of the good (including their conception of what is for their own good), or to revise it, on the basis of true beliefs and rather complete information about relevant facts. Few would choose to have others insulate them from such facts with the result that their pursuits rest on an illusion. Although it may be profoundly disheartening to learn that one's spouse loves another, that one's retirement plans are doomed because one has Alzheimer's disease, that one's children will die within five years due to Tay-Sachs disease, who would prefer living, planning, and making commitments on the basis of a false, contrary, view of the present and the future? Who would regard the deception of others to facilitate or preserve such a false conception as not making a mockery of one's life, as importantly subverting one's opportunity to live one's life as an autonomous person—even subject to the risk of a loss of autonomy—as *all* autonomous persons are. Of course, in some cases autonomous persons do prefer not to know things and choose not to be informed in their pursuit of their conception of the good. However, it is one thing validly to consent not to be informed and another to be deprived of information without one's consent—*when* its disclosure is owed by others. This, I note, is a point to which we shall return in Chapter 4.

Although our focus excludes questions about the treatment of normal children who are not yet competent and autonomous but who have the potential to become so, I observe in passing that, in the theory of paternalism being elaborated, the *preservation and enhancement* of the partially developed capacities for autonomy, possessed by such *children*, are quite another matter. It is one thing to constrain the not-yet-autonomous with an eye to *fostering* their autonomy and another to undermine the *existing* autonomous capacities (or their deployment) of developed, competent persons— even when the aim is to preserve or maximize their autonomy. Parents are not only permitted to preserve and foster autonomy in more restrictive ways in their children; they have a duty to do so. The common moral belief that parents must at some point "let their children go" and take a stance of non-interference, that at maturity children are and should be "on their own," lends some intuitive support to the view proposed here: that competent persons must be allowed to lead their own lives and deal with their problems as they individually see fit (with the qualifications frequently noted). The familiar, contrary, meddlesome attitude of parents toward their competent offspring is rightly a source of well-documented resentment. On the view defended here it is often resentment toward unjustified paternalistic intervention.

3.8 The Appeal to Moral-Good Preservation

So far I have defended the position that generally competent persons have a right to direct their own lives, a right absolute throughout the domain of acts not wronging others. Further, I have proposed that respect for this right requires non-interference (except for that to which relevant consent is or would be given) on the part of others, even when it is paternalistically motivated and even when such interference may in reality be for the good (welfare) of the subject, or when it may preserve the subject's autonomy. This partially developed theory of autonomy-respecting paternalism is, as noted, anti-utilitarian in outlook.

It maintains that it is wrong paternalistically to interfere invasively in a certain range of cases, even if the consequences of doing so may be, in some fashion, good promoting or good maximizing on balance. As such, the theory here resembles important aspects of Immanuel Kant's ethical theory. Kant is well known for his claims that we must never treat persons as a mere means, that persons must be viewed as ends-in-themselves, and that persons are morally autonomous beings. On such a view it would seem that we are under a stringent duty not to override the will of others in order to achieve net aggregate good (e.g., happiness). On the Kantian outlook there are, then, rigorous moral constraints on how we may deal with others. Acknowledging that our theory has Kantian elements, it is worth noticing that there is another strain in

140

Kant's thought which might be thought to provide a justification for a greater range of paternalistic interferences than we have allowed. It is on that other strain that I shall focus here. It is present in the following passage:

> But man is not a thing—not something to be used merely as a means: he must always in all his actions be regarded as an end-in-himself. Hence I cannot dispose of man in my person by maiming, spoiling, or killing.[34]

Not only, on Kant's view, is it wrong to treat others as a mere means; one must also treat humanity in oneself as an end-in-itself, never as a mere means. As he explicitly states elsewhere,

> the practical imperative, therefore, is the following: Act so that you treat humanity, whether in your own person or in that of another, always as an end and never as a means only.[35]

Although there is considerable difficulty in unraveling the mere means/end-in-himself distinction, Kant clearly takes his prescription to prohibit certain self-destructive acts, for example, maiming or killing oneself. Elsewhere Kant suggests that it would be wrong for a person to engage in highly risky acts for merely prudential or even frivolous purposes.[36] Not only, in Kant's view, do persons have duties to refrain from killing or spoiling themselves, or engaging in acts risking serious harm to themselves, there are also duties to improve oneself, to avoid sloth.

That we ought to improve ourselves is an initially plausible proposal. However, there are evident puzzles about the notion of having a *duty to oneself*. Normally, if A has a duty to B, then B has a correlative right against A that A perform in some fashion; however, it is not obviously intelligible to say that one has a right against oneself. Relatedly, one can release *another* from a duty by excusing the other, permitting him not to do or perform the duty, or waiving the right. However, the notion of a duty to oneself would seem to suppose that there is a duty from which the *duty holder* could release

[34] Immanuel Kant, *Groundwork of the Metaphysics of Morals*, trans. H. J. Paton (New York: Harper & Row, 1950), p. 97.

[35] Immanuel Kant, *Foundations of the Metaphysics of Morals*, ed. Oskar Piest, trans. Lewis Beck (New York: Liberal Arts Press, 1959), p. 47.

[36] Kant states, ". . . we ought not to risk our life and hazard losing it for interested and private purposes. To do so is not only imprudent but base. It would for instance be wrong to wager a large sum of money that we would swim across some great river. There is no material benefit in life so great that we should regard it as a duty to risk our life for it." See Immanuel Kant, *Lectures on Ethics*, trans. Louis Infield (New York: Harper & Row, 1963), p. 155.

himself (not the right holder as in the normal case) by an act of will; as Marcus Singer notes, a duty from which a duty holder could be released just by an act of will (by the duty holder) seems no duty at all.[37]

These counterarguments, among others, cast suspicion on the claim that we have duties to ourselves. However, for the sake of discussion, I wish here to leave open the question of their success. *Perhaps* it can be shown that we have duties to ourselves. First, I shall consider a line of argument not tied to Kant's; later, we shall examine a more Kantian strategy.

In favor of the view that we have duties to ourselves is, perhaps surprisingly, the consideration that on virtually all ethical theories, not just Kantian ones, we have some duties to *others*. Even if they are only negative duties, performing them will require choice and a modicum of effort. That in turn may necessitate taking care of one's health and capacities. Hence, to carry out our duties toward others (supposing we have *some*) we have a derivative duty to maintain our own capacities to choose and act in various ways. However, does this show that we have duties *to* ourselves? The answer would seem to be negative if we take into account a much noted distinction by H. L. A. Hart.[38] Hart points out that we may, for example, promise B to take care of her cherished paintings when she travels abroad. If we agree to do so, we have a duty *to* B *with regard to* her paintings. The duty is owed to B, not to the paintings. If we have any stringent positive duties to others, all that follows, it may be asserted, is that such duties *to* others require taking care of ourselves, but this is only a duty *regarding* ourselves and not a duty *to* ourselves. A derivative duty of self-care is not a duty *to* oneself; neither the set of paintings nor oneself is the entity to which the duty is owed. Neither need be a bearer of correlative rights.

It may be objected here that even if the earlier argument fails to show that we have duties *to* ourselves, it is enough that we sometimes have *derivative duties regarding ourselves*. That, it may be claimed, is sufficient to show that it is not permissible to abuse, neglect, or despoil ourselves in various ways. If that is correct, it will be wrong to so act, *ceteris paribus*. Hence, it may be claimed that in such cases there is an adequate ground for interference,

[37] See Marcus Singer, "Duties to Oneself," in *Limits of Liberty*, ed. Peter Radcliff (Belmont, Cal.: Wadsworth, 1966), pp. 109–110.
[38] See H. L. A. Hart, "Are There Any Natural Rights?" in *Human Rights*, ed. A. I. Melden (Belmont, Cal.: Wadsworth, 1970), pp. 65–66.

and since it would be interference to promote or preserve the well-being of the subject, or for his own good, we may be tempted to conclude that we have found a reasonable ground for the permissibility of a range of paternalistic interventions, ones not sanctioned by PARP.

This line of thought, initial appearances to the contrary, fails to show that any paternalistically based invasive interference is justified. Let us see why. If there are cases, as there surely are, in which we have duties to others (e.g., to care for our children) then, in the absence of powerful countervailing considerations, it does follow that we have a duty regarding ourselves, namely, to preserve or enhance our capacities to perform such duties toward others. And if we fail to do so, we will wrong others. Analogously, in our earlier example, we would wrong B, *ceteris paribus*, by failing to care for her paintings or by deliberately neglecting our own well-being to such an extent as to make us unable to do so. The key point to be recognized in all this is that the plausible (I do not assume, barring other details, that it is an incontrovertible and decisive ground) ground for interfering with "self-neglecting" individuals provides, at most, a *nonpaternalistic* justification for interference. Interference, on this ground, would not contravene the claims of PARP, for the latter supposes only that competent persons have a right to direct their own lives by choosing among acts (including omissions) which do *not* wrong others. Although a proximate aim in interfering with self-neglecting persons is to promote or preserve their own well-being, the ultimate aim is to prevent or halt a failure in the performance of a duty toward others. The wrong which such interference is aimed at preventing is not a wrong to oneself but a wrong to *others*. Since the ultimate *ground* for interference is not ultimately the good of the subject, we find no new defense of paternalism here—even though we began with our focus "on the subject" and the claim that the subject has duties to himself.

It might be claimed that not only do we have duties *regarding* ourselves *derived* from duties owed to others, we *also* have non-derivative duties to ourselves. This stronger claim seems to have been that of Kant. Let us investigate what follows if such a claim were true. As we shall see, another, purportedly satisfactory, argument for paternalistic interference can be articulated. Suppose that we have an underived duty to ourselves to maintain our own health. It follows that if we fail to perform it, we do what is impermissible and, hence, wrong. At this point we begin to discern the ingredients for an argument purporting to justify paternalism

143

in cases deemed wrong according to the Principle of Autonomy-Respecting Paternalism. Earlier we considered various interpretations of "for your own good" meaning for your own welfare (broadly or narrowly construed), and for your own autonomy preservation (or even maximization). Alternatively, it might be claimed that by "for your own good" what is often meant is "for your own moral good." Further, it may be said that it is for one's own moral good not to do what is wrong. So, apart from promoting nonmoral good or welfare, it may be claimed that there is another, distinct, ground for paternalistic interference, namely, promotion of the moral good of others when they are failing to achieve it, for example, by violating duties they have to themselves. The distinct principle implicit in such reasoning appears to be this:

If S is doing Z (or intent on doing Z) and doing Z will

1. not wrong others

but 2. violate a duty to himself,

then it is permissible for A paternalistically to interfere with S in order to prevent S's doing Z (to preserve S's moral good).

Let us call this principle the *Appeal to Moral-Good Preservation* (AMP). I take it as obvious that AMP is a competitor to PARP. There are at least two sorts of difficulties with AMP. First, there are those noted earlier in this section. The sense of 'duty' in speaking of (underived) duties to oneself is obscure, for it is not clear that there is any correlative right holder. Further, as noted, right holders,[39] for whatever reasons they have, normally can release correlative duty bearers from their duties, but it is not clear what sense is made, if any, in talk of S's releasing S from a duty. Earlier I left open the question of how compelling these objections are. In fact I am inclined to accept them as decisive; nevertheless, a defender of AMP might respond as follows. If 'F has a duty to G' cannot be a meaningful assertion unless 'F' and 'G' refer to different entities, so be it; perhaps, S cannot have a duty to S. Still, there are things persons *ought* to do (e.g., preserve their capacities, etc.), and these have to do with caring for themselves, not others. Even if these "self-regarding oughts" are not *duties*, it is still wrong not to carry them out. Hence, we could revise AMP to get AMP* which is just like AMP except (2) reads: 'violates a self-regarding ought.' So, our objector continues, AMP* avoids the difficulties noted with AMP.

[39] Or, if one prefers, persons to whom duties are owed.

The mysteries about 'duties to self' are thus bypassed and the first type of objection avoided.

Shortly, I shall mention the second type of objection to AMP since I believe that it is also an objection to AMP*. I lead up to that objection indirectly. There are what have been called "prudential oughts," that is, acts that I ought to do because it is in my own interest or, alternatively, to my own advantage. In this category would seem to fall brushing my teeth, exercising to a degree, and so on. Is this the way to understand 'self-regarding oughts,' that is, as prudential directives or prescriptions? If so, as Marcus Singer has proposed, the failure to perform them may be only a "prudential vice."[40] What is not obvious is that one who engages in a prudential vice does what is *morally wrong*. Once more, prudentially I ought to keep my check book straight. Although one of my lesser vices is to fail in this respect, do I thereby commit a moral wrong (assuming that in so behaving I violate no duties toward other beings)? The answer would seem to be negative. If that is correct, interferences with me to prevent me from omitting perfomance of such "self-regarding oughts" do not count as preserving my moral good (preventing me from doing moral wrongs). Hence, the set of interferences permitted by AMP* to preserve my moral good is empty. Indeed, on this interpretation, AMP* seems to reduce to our earlier discussed Naive Good-Promotion (or a good-preservation) Principle.

It may be insisted that I am being quite perverse, or more so than usual, and that I have not been fair, or duly sympathetic, to the ideas of preserving moral good or fulfilling "self-regarding oughts." For example, it may be claimed that there really are certain *moral norms*, not merely prudential directives, which one must strive to satisfy even if, like Robinson Crusoe without Friday, no one else is relevantly affected. It may be claimed that one ought to cultivate one's talents, to develop one's skills, and maintain one's health, even if no one else is wronged by one's failure to do so and even if it were not conducive to one's own welfare. Hence, to fail to do so is not merely a prudential vice (it may be that as well); it is a *moral wrong*. Given this further way of construing what is meant by "self-regarding oughts" (moral oughts regarding self-maintenance and development, if one prefers), then AMP* seems to sidestep the objections previously raised and to provide us with

[40] M. Singer, "Duties to Oneself," p. 110.

a ground for more extensive paternalistic interference than allowed by PARP.

One question here, of course, is whether there are such moral norms. I am not entirely convinced that there are. One might concede that there are attractive ideals which, for various reasons, deserve our consideration and which, unlike others, may be ones toward which we should aspire—apart from prudential reasons. Just as there seem to be morally supererogatory acts toward others (beneficial acts toward others which are permissible and praiseworthy but not required or a matter of duty), so may there be a domain of self-benefitting or harm-avoiding morally "supererogatory" acts toward oneself, that is, acts which we are meritorious to perform but *not* wrong not to perform. If all self-regarding "moral oughts" are like this, then it is not *wrong* not to perform them. Hence, interferences to prevent failures to do so do not preserve our moral good (for they would not prevent *wrong*doing). This may be the truth of the matter; I am not sure. Consider the following reasoning.

Perhaps not all self-regarding moral oughts are like this. Although it may be "beyond the call of duty" to keep oneself in the very best physical condition one can (and not wrong to fail to do so), perhaps we ought not to be servile.[41] Further, this may be a self-regarding ought which is neither a merely prudential one nor "supererogatory"; it is not unreasonable to think that it is wrong to be servile (I do not mean: feign servility). If there are *some* self-regarding oughts such that failure to perform them is wrong, then the prior objection is circumvented. Still, there remains another objection to both AMP and our last construal of AMP*.

If there are such wrongs, we could prevent such wrongdoing (not just "imprudencedoing") by invasively interfering; so, one can promote a subject's moral good in this manner, or so it appears. What precisely is at issue here is a slippery matter, partly because of unclarity about how to answer the question: in what does a person's moral good consist? We might attribute moral good to a person who fulfills all or most of his duties to others. When someone fails in *this* way to achieve some level of moral good, there may well be, and often are, *nonpaternalistic* grounds for interference. But we are not here concerned with *that* source of moral good which a person may or may not achieve. Rather, as we have interpreted

---

[41] Thomas Hill forcefully argues for this point in "Servility and Self-Respect," in *Today's Moral Problems*, ed. Richard Wasserstrom (New York: Macmillan, 1975), pp. 137–151.

the issue, there may be a distinct moral good attributable to persons who perform nonderivative "self-regarding oughts" (Kant speaks of 'self-regarding duties' but, for reasons discussed, we avoid that formulation). Can we by invasive interference bring it about that a person's *moral good* derivable from fulfilling self-regarding oughts is maintained (or increased)?[42] We could threaten or force persons not to be slothful. We could ostracize them for not taking care of their health, or we could deceive or bribe them into doing so (cf. what we do with children, for example, sugar coating vitamin pills or saying "this won't hurt" prior to an injection). Note, once more, that such acts may preserve or enhance the *welfare* of a subject, but our question here is whether we can preserve *moral good* of a sort, by interfering to prevent negligence of self-regarding oughts. It is not clear that, by such interferences, we make subjects virtuous or conscientious about such oughts even if we cause their welfare to be preserved. In general, it seems that a person may maintain or enhance his score of moral good only by *voluntarily and deliberately* carrying out such self-regarding oughts. There is, however, little reason to say that any *moral good* supervenes on a person who is manipulated (by a presumptively wrongful act) into performing such acts. For, in such circumstances, he will act only in *accord* with self-regarding moral oughts but not out of a deliberate choice to do what he ought. The resulting good consequence, if one occurs, does not alter a slothful or self-neglecting disposition. Analogously, in cases affecting third parties, we might prevent the protorapist from raping by forcing him to take anti-androgen treatments, or by castrating him, but his consequent nonviolation of the duty not to rape is hardly a basis for attribution of moral worth or merit. Hence, there seems little reason, if any, to assume that we can succeed, from some paternalistic concern for a person's moral good, in preserving or increasing a person's moral good by presumptively wrong and nonconsensual interferences.[43]

[42] I sometimes switch from talk of preserving moral good to promoting moral good. In many cases objections to appeals to moral good will apply to either an appeal to preservation or promotion. However, the former faces a difficulty that the latter avoids since one way to prevent any diminution in the moral good of a subject (by occurrences of failure to perform self-regarding oughts) would be to interfere with the subject in rather drastic ways, e.g., killing the subject or rendering him comatose. This point also emphasizes the contrast between appeals to moral-good preservation and an appeal to good (as welfare) preservation.

[43] Lest there be confusion, I should note that if a person from weakness of will fails to fulfill self-regarding oughts, PARP allows what I have earlier called "cooperative interference," that is, interference to which the subject previously (voluntarily and knowingly) consented or in which it is true that there is hypothetical

I wish to add here what I hope by now to be a superfluous argument against AMP and the two construals of AMP*. However, it may be a sufficient reason to reject such principles even if the preceding objections fail. If the appeals to moral good were acceptable, the door would be open to an extremely invasive range of intrusions into the lives of competent persons, a result which is radically counter-intuitive. Much of traditional morality assumes, rightly I believe, that it is one thing to recognize a certain mode of life as an ideal one and quite another to constrain persons so as to ensure achievement of these ideals, at least outwardly if not in motive or disposition. If autonomy, tolerance for diversity of views and modes of life, or pluralism are of nontrivial value, it is doubtful that appeals to moral-good preservation or promotion can be accepted. What, however, underlies our assignment of great value to such ideals is, I believe, the view of persons developed earlier. Persons are not mere utility-containers; nor are they mere repositories or exemplars of moral good, entities to be shaped independently of their will and conception of the good into saints or maximally virtuous beings according to our conception of the good or our models of morally good persons. To do otherwise is to suppose what cannot be defended, namely, that we, as interveners, are legitimate moral rulers and that those competent persons who fail to satisfy our ideals are legitimate moral subjects. It need not be denied that some competent persons are higher on the scale of moral goodness than others, that invasive interventions to preserve or promote moral goodness in children often are justifiable, that some invasive interventions with competent persons to prevent self-neglect are defensible on nonpaternalistic grounds, that fair efforts to dissuade or offer therapeutic assistance are permissible toward competents, or that paternalistic and invasive restrictions on competents are all right if they validly consent. However, invasive paternalistic constraints on competents, who do not consent, to preserve their moral good, fails to respect them as our equals with their own capacity for formulating their conception of the good and as responsible agents capable of deciding to what extent they will bend their efforts to achieve it. A more attractive and coherent approach, one which provides a greater unity to com-

---

individualized consent. Hence, if gluttony violates a self-regarding ought and a subject consented to our interfering with his gluttonous propensities (e.g., by our hiding the chocolate chip cookies), our so doing is permissible paternalism. Such a "use" of others is, I think, underemployed. Cooperative interference is not just for repentant alcoholics and drug addicts!

peting views about when interference is acceptable is, I believe, that provided by the Principle of Autonomy-Respecting Paternalism, conjoined ultimately with a suitable theory about acceptable grounds for nonpaternalistic interference (a theory, in part, delineating principles of social justice).

Given the powerful tendency to assume that if another really *ought* to do X it is all right for others to *compel* him to do so, a final comment is in order. It involves examination of a proposal by L. W. Sumner. Its relevance is obvious. Sumner maintains:

> Actions are private in so far as they do not affect the interest or autonomy of any individual except their agent. A moral theory will either contain (or imply) norms for the private sphere or it will not. If it does, it is an *ideal* theory; if it does not, it is a *discretionary* theory. Discretionary theories treat the private sphere as the realm of taste rather than value (and therefore rather than morality). Within the private sphere actions may be rational or irrational, prudent or imprudent—but not moral or immoral. A discretionary theory thus limits the scope of morality to the evaluation of interpersonal activities.[44]

First, let us note an ambiguity regarding the expression, 'private actions.' It can mean (1) those acts of an individual in which others *ought* not interfere, or (2) those acts of an individual which affect only the interests or autonomy of the individual. Sumner's preferred interpretation appears to be (2), but the extension of (2) is far smaller than that of (1). The crucial question is not whether an individual's choice *affects* the interests of others, but whether others *ought not to interfere* with choices which wrong no others. My neighbor's choice to plant garish flowers in his yard may affect my interests; still it seems that I may not interfere with it in presumptively wrong ways. To that extent his act is private in an important sense (1), but *not* because it does not affect my interests. The more important point to which I have been leading concerns whether, as Sumner alleges, moral theories must be *either* ideal *or* discretionary *and not both*. Given the importance of respect for autonomy emphasized in the theory defended here, it would be natural to conclude, if one must, that the theory is discretionary. However, given Sumner's criteria for distinguishing ideal and discretionary theories, it is, I propose, neither. As I have argued, one need *not*

[44] L. W. Sumner, *Abortion and Moral Theory* (Princeton: Princeton University Press, 1982), p. 162.

regard the domain of another's choices or acts with which one must not invasively intervene as coextensive with the domain of "matters of taste" (as opposed to moral evaluation). It is one thing to conclude that S's choice to be gluttonous or self-negligent (when wronging no others thereby) is a matter in which others ought not, in the absence of S's valid consent, interfere. It is another matter to claim that there are no legitimate grounds for morally assessing (and perhaps condemning) S's gluttonous choices (grounds relevant to S's own self-appraisal, as well). It is, however, not unreasonable to claim that S's choice is one he ought not to make or that S would be a better person if he chose differently. S himself may agree. In short, ideals have a place in evaluating acts *within* the "discretionary sphere" if by the latter expression we mean (in contrast to Sumner) that domain of choice and action of a subject in which others *ought* not intervene in presumptively wrong ways in the absence of the subject's valid consent. The main point is that we consistently can recognize an important sense in which there are private or discretionary spheres *without*, at the same time, committing ourselves to the view that there is, therefore, no place for invoking ideals, or making moral assessments, with regard to choices within such domains. Even if we must let alone, we still may have good grounds for remonstration and attempted persuasion. *Ideals do not stop where invasive interference must.* On reflection, this point may seem quite innocuous and familiar; that is how it ought to be. The persistent temptation to act in invidiously paternalistic ways is, in part, the temptation to assume that, on the contrary, when we possess the right ideals about how to conduct life within the "private sphere," we may impose those ideals on other competent persons.

3.9 The Appeal to Reasonable Interference

In a useful and somewhat "dissenting" discussion, Douglas Husak seeks to locate a basis for justified paternalistic intervention which, in a number of respects, resembles the Principle of Hypothetical Individualized Consent.[45] As we shall observe, it holds out the possibility of justifying a greater range of intervention than does PHIC, and for that reason, among others, deserves examination. Further, and contrary to initial appearances, it seems to be a type

---

[45] Douglas N. Husak, "Paternalism and Autonomy," *Philosophy & Public Affairs* 10, No. 1 (Winter, 1981), pp. 27–46.

of appeal to promoting good. Hence, I include discussion of it in this chapter. Husak calls attention to the fact that in law a physician may recover the reasonable value of treatment rendered to an unconscious patient who subsequently refuses to pay, and refuses on the ground that he did not consent, and that consent was not inferable from his behavior. In such cases the law sometimes invokes the notion of "quasi-contract" or "hypothetical consent." The idea here is, roughly, that in some cases it is reasonable to believe that the subject *would have consented had the opportunity to consent been present*. As we have observed elsewhere, and as Husak notes, it is easy to confuse this appeal to hypothetical consent with an appeal to subsequent consent. The latter is subject to serious difficulties (see Section 2.5). Husak seems to extend his sympathy with the legal reliance on the notion of hypothetical consent to an appeal to "reasonably expectable consent." This point, however, needs clarification.

In his view, paternalistic intervention with a child, for example, need not appeal to the claim that the child *in fact* will consent to the intervention. Rather, what is crucial to justifying the intervention is "whether, at the time the act is performed, it is *reasonable to believe* that the child will come to consent" (my italics).[46] It is clear that in many cases it is reasonable to expect, at the time of intervention, future consent even though we may later discover that no consent occurs (again, perhaps due to contingencies such as accidental death of the subject). Since the appeal to *reasonably expectable* consent avoids making the justifiability of intervention a function of unpredictable events, it has an obvious advantage over the appeal to subsequent consent.

It is worth trying to reconstruct more explicitly Husak's emerging argument concerning when paternalistic interference is justified. As noted, he supposes that there are cases in which it is true that

(1) A *reasonably expects* that S will or would consent to A's paternalistic inteference, X, with S's doing Y.

But (1) is compatible, Husak rightly alleges, with

(2) S will not and would not consent to A's paternalistic interference, X, with S's doing Y.

Husak also maintains that

[46] Ibid., p. 34.

(3) If (1) is true, then A's paternalistic interference, X, is justified.

From (1) and (3) we validly can infer that

(4) A's paternalistic interference, X, with S is justified.[47]

So, if the argument inferring (4) from (1) and (3) is acceptable, Husak may have shown that paternalistic interference can be justified even in the absence of not only S's actual or prior consent (this has been left tacit here), but also S's future (or subsequent) consent *and* S's hypothetical consent to A's doing X. Recall again that (1) can be true (we have allowed so far) even if (2) is true. Husak's conclusion is, hence, in tension with the view developed here in its discounting, if not elimination, of the necessity of prior, or hypothetical individualized, consent (to simplify matters somewhat). To emphasize a point, in his view the crucial desideratum is not the subject's actual, forthcoming, or hypothetical consent; rather it is the agent's *reasonable expectation* that there is hypothetical consent or that there will be subsequent consent on the part of the subject (*even if* the former is absent and the latter never comes to pass). As Husak elsewhere claims, the thrust of his view is to *de-emphasize* the importance of respecting autonomy in justifying paternalism and to encourage a return to considering "consequential advantages and disadvantages of particular instances of paternalism."[48]

Let us examine his argument more closely. As we have observed, both (1) and (2) might be true. How is this possible? Clearly A could not be in a position to *know* or have a *justifiable belief* that S will not and would not consent to A's paternalistic intervention if A reasonably expects that S will or would consent to A's intervention. Still, A may have reasons or evidence that warrants our attributing to A a reasonable expectation that S will or would consent. Imagine the situation, for example, wherein A has known S quite well and S has frequently said sincerely that he would welcome a certain type of intervention under certain circumstances, for example, a blood transfusion if he were injured and would suffer or die without one. When an accident to S occurs, A may reasonably believe that S would consent to a blood transfusion if S were able and/or that S will consent if the opportunity arises. And this situation may obtain even though it is the case that S recently became,

[47] Ibid.
[48] Ibid., p. 46.

unbeknownst to A, a Jehovah's Witness and, hence, at the time of the accident is vehemently opposed to undergoing such a transfusion. In this story A has a (subjectively) reasonable belief or expectation, but it happens to be false. Given this state of affairs, is A's paternalistic intervention (for example, in transfusing S) justified? On the theory developed here, the answer is negative because S has not given valid consent to this invasive intervention, and it is false that S hypothetically consents to it; hence, there is no legitimate appeal to principles we have accepted (RCP or PHIC). On Husak's principle, which appeals to the reasonable expectation of subsequent and/or hypothetical consent, the answer is affirmative. There are, however, a number of considerations which militate against accepting the appeal to reasonable expectation.

First, consider that possible case in which A's expectation is, *given his evidence,* reasonable, but nevertheless false. It is not obvious why, in such a case, A's having a reasonable expectation goes any distance *at all* toward *justifying* A's invasive intervention. It is worth recalling that there is a distinction, noted early on, between the question of the *justifiability of the intervention* and the question of the *moral responsibility of the agent* engaging in the intervention. It is plausible that A may not be blameworthy in transfusing S if A had a reasonable belief that S would consent if S had the opportunity to do so, even though, as a matter of fact A's belief to this effect is false. Analogously, if Mat reasonably believes that Nat is assaulting Pat, and Mat coercively interferes with Nat to aide Pat, Mat may be blameless, even though, belatedly, Mat discovers that Nat, a policeman, is legitimately disarming the burglar, Pat. Here we say that the intervention by Mat is wrongful even though Mat may be blameless. In short, in our example, A may be *blameless*; it does not follow that A's paternalistic intervention is *justified*.

Although it does not *follow*, such intervention may be justified. But why think so? It is worth reflecting on the fact that the presence of a reasonable expectation, which Husak stresses, is not just any reasonable expectation but the expectation that S would or will *consent* to the intervention. Hence, it is not obvious, on such a view, that consent is unimportant, that autonomy is discounted, or that, as Husak explicitly proposes, our attention should shift toward weighing consequential advantages or disadvantages (understood in terms of what is for S's own good) of intervening.

In the example we employed, one natural interpretation of what it is for someone to have a reasonable expectation is that the expectation is one based on possession of a preponderance of reasons and/or evidence in favor of a certain view. However, Husak proposes another criterion for attribution of a reasonable expectation. Its effect on the plausibility of his appeal to reasonable expectation is a weighty one. In response to the question: when is it reasonable to believe that a person would consent to an interference?, he claims

> The only sensible answer to this question . . . is that *it is reasonable to believe that a person would consent to whatever interferences are reasonable.* The proper focus, then, is on whether an interference is reasonable—*not* on whether a person would consent to it.

> Once the notion of consent is omitted from the criteria and it becomes evident that the central focus is on the reasonableness of the interference, it is easier to appreciate that the attempt to employ the notion of moral autonomy may not be a serious barrier to the attempt to justify some instances of paternalism.[49] (initial italics are mine)

This passage makes it clearer that Husak is committed to the view that a certain form of argument is adequate to justify (any case of) A's paternalistic interference with S. The reasoning would take this form:

1. A's (prospective) paternalistic interference, X, with S is reasonable.

2. If A's (prospective) paternalistic interference, X, with S is reasonable, then A has a reasonable expectation that S will or would consent to A's doing X.

3. If A has a reasonable expectation that S will or would consent to A's doing X, then A's paternalistic interference, X, is justified.

So 4. A's paternalistic interference, X, is justified.

If this is a fair reconstruction of the argument, then anyone who accepts it is committed to the claim that in any case where A's (prospective) paternalistic interference, X, with S is reasonable, then A's paternalistic interference, X, is justified (that is: if 1., then 4.). This rationale for justifying paternalistic interference evidently places a heavy burden on its defender to specify acceptable criteria for when 1. is true, that is, when A's (prospective) paternalistic interference, X, with S is reasonable.

[49] Ibid., pp. 34–35.

Husak does not, in the essay referred to, attempt to specify when paternalistic interference is reasonable, although he implies that a case by case consideration of prospective benefits and harms ("consequentialist considerations") may be necessary and sufficient. We are left, then, with a serious perplexity. Reasonable interference might be understood as that which satisfied the Naive Good-Promotion Principle, but for reasons stated earlier we have found that principle unacceptable. Similarly, we have found the Autonomy Preservation Principle and the Appeal to Moral-Good Preservation unsatisfactory and, hence, not viable candidates for what counts as "reasonable interference" (or, if accepted, interpretations which make the claim that 1. entails 4. unacceptable). It may be noted that 'reasonable' may be used occasionally as a purely honorific term lacking any descriptive content. With such a use, to say that an act is reasonable is only to say that it is permissible or desirable. Given that use in the aforementioned, reconstructed, argument, the claim that 1. entails 4. simply maintains that "if a paternalistic interference is permissible, then it is permissible" (construing 'justified' as permissible). This latter claim is true and trivial; but it begs our basic question. In the absence, then, of some plausible specification of 'reasonable interference,' the seemingly novel appeal to what it is reasonable for an agent to expect provides no clear and tempting competitor to the principles we have defended so far.

As a final observation it may be worth noting that "reasonable interference" may be understood to mean "whatever interference S reasonably would choose to consent to given S's beliefs and values." On this construal, and simplifying somewhat, the appeal to reasonable expectation simply may be extensionally equivalent in its moral implications to the Principle of Hypothetical Individual Consent. However, Husak's explicit sympathy with attending to "consequential advantages" suggests another reading. We have identified difficulties with a number of alternative possibilities; hence, we must await a delineation of the Appeal to Reasonable Expectation which provides a truly distinct option to the principles defended here and which also escapes the pitfalls we have identified.

3.10 Paternalism, Personal Identity, Successors, and Later Selves

When competent persons are likely to change radically over time a rather special, and perhaps unique, case can be made for pater-

155

nalistic intervention in their lives even if an invasive intrusion is being considered with regard to competent, adult, persons. Consideration of this type of case involves a certain detour, in this section, from the main theoretical course we are pursuing.

Recent discussions of *personal identity* suggest reasons for drawing quite different conclusions from those I have drawn about when it is permissible to interfere with the choices, and in general the lives, of competent persons. It is beyond my purpose fully to explore the metaphysical issues and questions of philosophical psychology to which I allude. Our excursion into the metaphysical forest will be limited to this section. The connection between questions regarding paternalistic interference and personal identity is one we shall approach indirectly.

One morally significant question is: what *counts as a person*? This conceptual question requires an answer if we are to be able to assess the claims that persons are valuable, only persons are valuable, fetuses are not persons, higher animals are not persons, only human beings are persons, and so on. Another question, assuming we can satisfactorily answer the former one, is: just when is personal identity retained over time? If S^1 is a person at time t^1, and S^2 is a person at t^2 (a later time) and S^2 is associated with the same body as was S^1 at t^1 (I set aside here questions about retention of *bodily* identity), are S^1 and S^2 numerically the same person? The commonsense view on this matter is probably that, in a vast range of cases, the answer is affirmative. Just because the person which is associated with my body next week has different desires than I do now does not seem a sufficient reason to conclude that the person occupying my body next week is a numerically different person from me. Normally, the person next week is thought to be numerically the same person even if certain properties (e.g., believes that p) can be attributed to the person next week which are not attributable to the person, me, this week. Analogously, my now undented car is numerically the same car as my dented car next week. On this view bodily continuity over time is taken to be the criterion of retention of personal identity.

By contrast, there is a view, associated with the eighteenth-century Scottish philosopher, David Hume, according to which there is no continuing self or I which persists throughout "my life." Rather "I" at a particular point in time only refers to a complex of desires, beliefs, sensations, and so on. And my "self" throughout my life refers only to a series of such events, a collection of discrete clusters of events each of which instantiates certain types of psychological or physical properties. On this view bodily continuity over time is no guarantee of retention of personal identity over time. Aside from the commonsense view which *tends* to assume that a person associated with the same body at t^2 as was a person at t^1 is numerically the same person, and the Humean view which seems to deny the retention of personal identity over time (or diachronically) in spite of bodily continuity, intermediate views are possible. One such view may be characterized roughly as follows: except for special cases, if S^1 and S^2 are persons associated with the same body at different times, S^1 and S^2 are numerically the same person; however, there are, or may be, exceptional cases, namely, where S^1 and S^2 exhibit radical psychological differences (e.g., in beliefs, desires, memories, self-image, commitments, and so on), and in the latter cases S^1 and S^2 are not numerically the same person. There are important questions here about *how* radical these differences must be to support the view that S^1 and S^2 are not numerically the same person. Also relevant may be the explanation of the generation of these different "personalities." Some philosophers deny that radical psychological differences ever provide adequate reason to speak of "numerically different persons" being associated with the same body. But consider unusual and sometimes hypothetical cases. Some involve the onset of severe amnesia; some the onset of madness, severe senility, brainwashing, or conversion (cf. "born again"). Others are found in science fiction, for example, at t^1 we mutually transplant the brains of Gold and Silver; at t^2 the person associated with Gold's body (call him G^2) has the attitudes, memories, and dispositions of Silver at t^1, and the person associated with Silver's body at t^2 (call him S^2) has the attitudes, memories, and dispositions of Gold at t^1. Are Silver and S^2 numerically the same person? Are Gold and G^2 numerically the same person? The commonsense view, insofar as it relies on bodily continuity as a criterion, would probably say "yes" in both cases. However, it is tempting to believe, on the contrary, that Gold at t^1 is numerically the same person as S^2 and, likewise, for Silver at t^1 and G^2.

Consider some further cases. David Lewis has called attention to the case of Methuselah who is said to have lived over 900 years.[50] Suppose that M^1 is the person associated with Methuselah's body during the first 137 years and M^2 is the person associated with

---

[50] David Lewis, "Survival and Identity," *The Identities of Persons*, ed. Amelie Rorty (Berkeley: University of California Press, 1976), pp. 17–40.

Methuselah's body during the next 137 years. Suppose further that M^2 exhibits virtually none of the sorts of beliefs, desires, or temperament of M^1. Are M^1 and M^2 numerically different persons? These examples are perhaps sufficient to suggest some of the perplexities that arise with questions about the criterion for personhood and the criterion for retention of personal identity. In passing, I note that other perplexities arise with regard to cloning (can we ever rightly say that the same person occupies two different bodies?). Similarly, suppose that scientists could create a duplicate of a person's brain. Let O^1 be the person whose brain is duplicated, and let the body with which O^1 is associated be O^a. Let O^2 denote the person with the duplicated brain and O^b denote the body in which the duplicate brain is implanted. Suppose that the dispositions, attitudes, beliefs, and personality traits of O^1 and O^2 are indistinguishable. Are O^1 and O^2 numerically one person associated with numerically distinct bodies? Further, there are perplexities concerning "fission" cases; is a fertilized human egg a person? A zygote can split into two organisms ("twinning"), each of which may become a distinct person, but, then, does it make sense to say that something which developed into two persons was, prior to that point, a single person? Finally, what shall we make of alleged cases of "multiple personality" (is it conceptually coherent to speak of several persons associated with the same body at one time?).

Fortunately, we need not attempt to unravel all these conceptual knots. However, questions do arise about the legitimacy of intervention and whether there are special grounds for intervening in cases in which a person's choices may significantly affect the well-being, or even the existence, of a not-yet-existent person who may be associated with the body of the potential subject of intervention. Let us explore this admittedly abstract point. An intriguing fact is that ordinary people frequently undergo more or less significant psychological changes as they get older—quite aside from the dramatic discontinuities associated with brainwashing, conversion, senility, or mental breakdown. Often such changes occur quite gradually over time, for example, Jones was an anarchist at 19, a socialist at 22, a liberal at 30, and a conservative at 45; reverse the order if one likes. Other cases come to mind: the meat eater at 20 who is a vegetarian at 30; the male chauvinist at 25 who is a feminist at 35. When people change over time and not just "in one respect" (e.g., political outlook) but in a considerable number of significant respects, there remains a nontrivial question about how to describe such cases and whether such phenomena are morally relevant to deciding how we may treat such persons. Terminology here can be a source of confusion. Suppose that B is a body over time and B^1, B^2, B^3, and so on designate stages of B, and S^1, S^2, and S^3 designate the person(s) associated with B^1, B^2, and B^3 respectively. Suppose, further, that we have a solution to the problem (I defend none) of determining when personal identity is *retained* over time. If so, we could, in principle, decide whether S^3 is numerically the same person as S^1. *If so*, let us here say that S^3 is a "later self" of S^1 or a "future self" of S^1. If S^3 is *not* numerically the same person as S^1, let us say (I *stipulate* once more) that S^3 is a "successor" of S^1. Hence, if S^3 is merely a later self of S^1, S^3 and S^1 are *not* numerically different persons; if S^3 is a successor of S^1, S^3 and S^1 *are* numerically *different* persons, even if, of course, associated with the same body, B, at different times. It is not unreasonable to think that there are, or could be, successor cases, for example, as in the Methuselah case or the brain transplant case. In more ordinary contexts in which S^3 is "quite different" from S^1 it may be hard to decide whether S^3 is only a *later self* of S^1 or, indeed, a *successor* of S^1. For the sake of discussion, at least, let us assume that there are successor cases. What bearing does such an assumption have on questions about permissible interference with competent persons? Some philosophers and jurisprudents have argued that it has a significant bearing.[51]

Consider now those cases in which S^1 and S^3 are persons, both are associated with the same body at different times, and S^3 *is* a successor and not just a later self of S^1. Setting epistemological difficulties aside for the moment, suppose further that we could know that S^1 will be *succeeded* by S^3. Various sorts of examples may be imagined here. There might be a legally required operation on all young males convicted of multiple rapes, a psychosurgical procedure which would ensure that the original person, S^1, will cease to exist and a numerically different, gentler, person, S^3, will come to be associated with the body with which S^1 was previously associated. In such a case we could know, or reasonably believe, that S^1 will have a successor, S^3. Alternatively, we could imagine a case in which a person by herself could decide to bring it about, at 40, that she has a successor, for example, by ingesting a Successor Pill (a "mind-altering" drug of an extreme sort!). Let us focus on the later case, and let us use 'S^1' to denote an appropriate young

[51] See Rolf Sartorius, "Utilitarianism, Rights, and Duties to Self." Also, see Donald Regan, "Paternalism, Freedom, Identity, and Commitment," in *Paternalism*, ed. Rolf Sartorius (Minneapolis: University of Minnesota Press, 1983), pp. 113–138.

woman, and simply assume that she will take the pill and that a successor is, so to speak, on the horizon. Suppose also that S^1 is a competent person knowingly and voluntarily about to engage in a further, highly risky, act (one risky to her bodily health but which does not threaten short-term death), for example, undertake work in a highly radioactive area. Doing so even for a year will subject her to a significant risk of impairment such as gradual and steady bone deterioration over the decades. Assume this involves no harm or wrong to existing others; safeguards for existing others are taken care of and all waive any right to complain, and so on. In addition, S^1 opposes any interference to prevent such deterioration and has never consented to such; nor is there ground to infer hypothetical consent by S^1. May we permissibly interfere?

If our prior argumentation is correct, we cannot legitimately do so on the grounds that we will promote S^1's good, that we will prevent harm from befalling S^1, that S^1 will "subsequently consent," that we will promote S^1's moral good or preserve it, or that a hypothetical fully rational individual would consent to such interference. It is, I have argued, permissible to "interfere" by attempting fairly and honestly to persuade S^1 to desist. But suppose this effort fails. May we act in a presumptively wrong way (use force, coercive threat, or deceit) to stop her? Again, not if our prior argument is correct. However, given our earlier special assumptions here about S^1's having a successor, a new line of defense might be marshalled by a defender of invasive intervention. He might claim that since we have only assumed that S^1's activity will wrong or harm no *existing* others (in bodies other than S's body!) we must consider the effects or possible effects of S^1's choice on S^3. More specifically, it might be claimed that "the harm principle," or what I prefer to call "the wrongful harm principle," sanctions extensive, invasive, interference with persons who are going to wrong, or are wronging others—and not just currently *existing* other persons (or, more generally, beings whose lives or well-being morally counts) but also persons who *will* exist. In the case considered, the young woman, S^1, will have a successor. Assuming that, may we legitimately intervene to protect S^3? After all, S^3 is not numerically the same person as S^1. It may be claimed that since we are *not* intervening in order to protect S^1 nor to "promote S^1's own good," our intervention is *not* paternalistic toward S^1, and it may be defended, instead, on *nonpaternalistic* grounds (to protect or benefit those *other than* the subject of intervention). Further, since we are *not restraining* S^3 (S^3 does not yet exist, but, by assumption, will) for S^3's own good we are not, if we intervene, acting paternalistically toward S^3 either. It seems that our intervention is, as suggested, not paternalistic toward S^1 *or* S^3. The proffered ground for intervention with S^1 focuses on the good of one other than S^1, and the ground is, hence, nonpaternalistic. By contrast, it should be observed that if 'S^3' denoted only a prospective *later self* of S^1, then to interfere with S^1 for the sake of *her* future good, that is, S^3's good (here 'S^3' designates S^1's later self), would be a case of paternalistic interference and subject to the constraints we have earlier defended.

For these reasons I infer that the examination of this general sort of appeal (i.e., that we may constrain S^1 to protect her *successor*) falls within the domain of a theory of nonpaternalistic wrongs to others (or "wrongful harms to others"), a theory which must not only provide grounds for judging which sorts of acts constitute wrongs to others but which must also address the question of when wrongs to others may be obstructed by the use of presumptively wrongful acts (e.g., coercive threat); talk of a "theory of criminal harm" typically alludes to this latter task. There is a slippery point here which bears further comment. A complete theory of wrongs to others would identify at some level of generality both wrongful paternalistic acts *and* wrongful nonpaternalistic acts. Our concern is with the former; we have presupposed that a determination of permissible paternalistic acts by an agent, A, toward S does depend, in part, on whether A or S is acting, or will act, in a way wrongful to others. In that way a theory seeking to determine which paternalistic acts are wrong depends on a theory of nonpaternalistic wrongs to others. Both theories are, in that way, subtheories of a complete theory of wrongs to others for the latter would offer grounds for identifying both paternalistic and nonpaternalistic wrongs.

If the acts of S^1 may wrong S^3 (here: a successor of S^1) and may result in constraints on or impairments of S^3 (e.g., S^1 irreversibly damages her bone structure), the question arises as to whether others may intervene in the life of S^1 to protect S^3. To intervene invasively, I have claimed, would not be a paternalistic act toward S^1 or toward S^3 (again, we do not constrain S^3 by interfering with S^1). Rather, our question about interfering with S^1 to protect S^3 is most closely analogous to *ordinary interpersonal* cases in which we may interfere with C to protect D (where C and D are numerically different *concurrently* existing persons). Hence, it is a question falling within the theory of nonpaternalistic wrongs to others. I hope to have made clear why the question of the permissibility of pro-tecting *successors* of S[1] from S[1]'s choices and acts need not be ad-dressed by a theory attempting to identify legitimate *paternalistic* grounds for interference.

If this reasoning is correct, the result is fortunate in the respect that a theory of paternalism need not deal with a host of peculi-arities which arise in considering S[1]'s relation to her successor S[3]. In passing, I note a few—only to leave the assessment of such features to others. Unlike most ordinary cases of interpersonal relationships in which one party may affect the well-being of an-other, S[1] and S[3] do not exist concurrently.[52] Hence, they cannot bargain or mutually agree about anything. Further, except in ex-treme cases (S[1] submits to brainwashing, chooses a lobotomy, or takes a Successor Pill) S[1] cannot choose to bring about the existence of a successor. This is one respect, along with others, in which the "successor relationship" differs from another interpersonal rela-tionship to which it bears some similarities, namely, parent-child relations. Further, S[1] cannot nurture S[3] in *many* of the ways that parents can look out for the welfare of their offspring. Nor can S[1] and S[3] coexist as can parents and children. Occasionally we have, in order to pursue certain other questions, supposed that S[1] has a successor S[3]. Prior to hindsight, however, there seldom will be reason to believe, of a competent person S[1], that she *will* have a successor; hence, S[1] seldom will have reason to assume this. So, it remains mysterious as to why S[1], or others, ought to care about, plan for, or protect the well-being of a *merely possible* successor.[53] This fact looms so large, I believe, as to make it seriously doubtful as to whether S[1] could have any duty to promote the well-being of, or prevent harm to, such a possible person. If so, how could others, who may be in a worse position epistemologically, be jus-tified in constraining S[1] for the sake of protecting a merely possible successor? Except in fantastic cases, the appeal to such protection, posed as a legitimate ground for interference with S[1], is a matter about which a very high degree of skepticism is in order.

[52] In the case of the young woman, she and her successor cannot concurrently exist. However, there may be "successor cases" of a different sort in which a successor and "predecessor" can concurrently exist, e.g., that in which scientists duplicate a brain, implant it in another body, and there is, so it appears, numerically one person in two bodies—at the same time. This point requires qualification of some later remarks in the above paragraph, but I leave them tacit.

[53] It may be worth noticing that perhaps we *all* have possible successors since anyone, as a result of an accident, may be succeeded by a numerically different person associated with the body formerly associated with the preceding person.

Normally, then, any concern about merely possible successors of S^1 will be very different from more understandable and more reasonable concerns about (1) our children, (2) future generations (a case in which we can be very certain that *some* of the possible future people *will* exist), and (3) concern for later stages of our selves (e.g., *our* future well-being or good).[54] If concern for later stages of our lives is at issue and talk of such is not a reference to successors, we have, I believe, no novel forms of argument for interference; rather we have the more or less familiar rationales for paternalistic interference that we have sought to assess, primarily in this and the prior chapter.

[54] I am, therefore, acknowledging that current persons may act wrongly with regard to future generations (those possible persons who will exist); it is a near certainty that some will exist. By contrast, it is usually unreasonable to believe that a specific person will have, in our technical sense, a successor. If, however, we were momentarily omniscient and knew that S^1 would have a successor, S^3, I am claiming that interference with S^1 to protect his successor, S^3, would not be paternalistic. I leave open whether such interference would be justifiable.

FOUR

THE DOCTRINE OF INFORMED
CONSENT

Consent is not an idle or symbolic act; it is a fundamental
requirement for the protection of the individual's integrity.
—Kaimowitz v. Department of Mental Health[1]

Other courts, though adhering to the fetish of consent,
express or implied, realize that "The law should encourage
self-reliant surgeons to whom patients may safely entrust
their bodies, and not men who may be tempted to shirk
from duty for fear of a law suit."   —Kennedy v. Parrott[2]

4.1 The Therapeutic Professions

Although we might want all social institutions to be structured to
promote human well-being, it is clear that only in some does the
promotion of human good or the prevention of harm occupy an
especially direct and prominent place. In some a great deal is *at
stake*. Hence, how parents raise their children, how people are
educated, and how sick persons are treated are all important matters. We do not expect a physician, nurse, clinical psychologist,
social worker, genetic counselor, dentist, or teacher to operate on
the principle of *caveat emptor* (let the buyer beware), even though
we directly or indirectly purchase their services.[3] We expect them

---

[1] Circuit Court of Wayne County, Michigan (July, 1973). Reprinted in Michael
Shapiro and Roy G. Spece, eds., *Bioethics and the Law* (St. Paul, Minn.: West, 1981),
p. 221.

[2] Supreme Court of North Carolina (1956). Reprinted in D. Sharpe, S. Fiscina,
and M. Head, eds., *Law and Medicine* (St. Paul, Minn: West, 1978), p. 195.

[3] Although I have spoken of the norm of *caveat emptor* as prevailing "in the
marketplace," I do not suggest that there are not legal regulations, regarding a
variety of products and services, requiring sellers to disclose the risks or hazards
of such products or services. Indeed, as Charles Fried has pointed out, courts have
judged that full disclosure is necessary for sellers not only of pharmaceuticals, but
also of cosmetics and automobiles. See Charles Fried, *Medical Experimentation* (Am-
sterdam: North-Holland, 1974), p. 27.

to do well by us and, at least, to "do no harm" on balance. We further expect them not to wrong us. Some professions, especially those aimed at promoting or preserving health, are referred to as therapeutic professions, from the Greek, 'therapeuō,' 'to help.' However, we do not always want to be helped, consent to be helped, or want to be treated in ways that others describe as "helping." In extreme cases we say "with friends like that, who needs enemies?" Questions about paternalistic policies are likely to arise all too frequently in cases in which one party (or more) occupies a therapeutic role and a subject (or patient) is on the receiving end of treatment aimed at helping. The situation displays familiar features: benevolent intentions on the part of the intervener; a subject who may be harmed, or who is at risk of harm, if no intervention occurs; belief on the part of the intervener that he knows best what is for the good of the subject; constraints or pressures of various sorts on the subject to comply (and to subordinate his own judgment to that of the professional); a high degree of trust by the subject; and the absence of a precisely defined contractual agreement between parties as to their mutual expectations (except, typically, for financial arrangements). The domain of health care, of course, includes the treatment of children, fetuses, and noncompetent adults. Our focus, in this chapter, continues to be on paternalism toward generally competent individuals, and, in a few cases, apparently competent persons.

This is not the place to elaborate on the impressive successes, from the standpoint of patients and health care personnel, of medicine, nursing, medical science, or psychological therapies, although they must be acknowledged. Nor is it the place to elaborate on the sincere, well-intended, "good-faith," and even heroic, efforts of professionals in those disciplines, though these too should not be ignored. As noted at the outset of this inquiry, it is one thing to ascertain whether certain acts or policies are morally permissible and another to assign praise or blame to agents. So even if it were true that all professional acts by health-care personnel were sincere and well intentioned, the question of ascertaining the acceptability of such acts would remain. Just as it is possible to do "the right thing for the wrong reasons," so is it possible to do "the wrong thing for the right reasons" (understood here as: with praiseworthy motives). As our prior discussion has indicated, there are perplexities about what is permissible in a broad range of cases. In such "hard cases" we often speak of "moral dilemmas." What is obligatory or permissible is often not obvious or straightforward—in contrast to what moral judgment is to be made, for example, about ordinary rape. The task of identifying permissible paternalistic interventions requires some sorting of cases and assessment of principles, an ongoing task to which health-care professionals and others can contribute. Our aim here, then, is to avoid cynical, aloof, *ad hominem*, or insensitive criticism of the attitudes or motivations of health-care personnel; rather it is to investigate fairly and critically the moral questions about particular, and often common, practices.

The previous chapters develop and defend a theory of paternalism toward competent persons. We shall frequently invoke their results in order to draw conclusions about specific practices. It should go without saying, but unfortunately does not, that it is only in conjunction with specific empirical assumptions (premises) that we can infer specific moral judgments about particular acts or types of act. Most obviously, since our principles, so far, focus only on competent persons it is essential to be sure in a particular case that it involves a competent subject. I have suggested broad criteria of competence; whether they are satisfied by a particular individual may not be easy to decide. Importantly, in considering intervention with a subject's behavior (commissions or omissions), it is crucial to decide whether his actions or omissions wrong others and, if so, whether there is, therefore, a nonpaternalistic ground for intervention. In cases in which paternalistic deception of a patient is being considered, the question arises as to what counts as "deception"? Is withholding medical information always *deception*? If so, is it always wrong? Is the Hippocratic prescription to "do no harm" violated by deceiving a patient? Even when it is "for her own good"? Does prescription of placebos involve deception? Does the cancer-ridden patient who does not overtly inquire about his diagnosis thereby *consent* to the withholding of medical information? Is it unjustified paternalism to *refuse* to euthanize a patient who requests it? Should people be allowed to sell their blood or their bodily parts? To such questions there is no quick and easy answer which can be derived from the theory of paternalism developed here. There *are* some answers, the right answers I believe, but teasing them out requires at least these further steps: (1) satisfactorily solving occasional *conceptual* puzzles, for example, what counts as "deception," (2) correctly ascertaining what the facts are in specific cases (the *empirical* task at which medical scientists, at one level, and professional clinicians, at another, have the greater claim to expertise), and (3) *correctly inferring* what follows from the most defensible principles and empirical judgments issuing from the previously mentioned efforts. These intellectual tasks are demanding but, contrary to popular assumptions, there is no *a priori* reason why ethical inquiry should be simple or easy any more than scientific inquiry should be. The opposing view, of course, continues to be the received opinion in many circles, but it may be diagnosed as intractable myopia, a recalcitrant intellectual "disease."

In this chapter we shall, with an eye on problems concerning paternalism, examine (1) the doctrine of informed consent, and (2) the use of deception in health care.

4.2 Background to the Doctrine

Indirectly I shall lead up to a statement of the doctrine of informed consent; at a later point we shall examine it, some of the arguments for and against it, and the relation of the doctrine to questions regarding paternalistic interference. First, I shall comment on some of the intellectual and cultural factors which may have led to the adoption, legally and institutionally, of more explicit and formal regulations requiring informed consent and disclosure of relevant information to competent subjects in therapeutic and nontherapeutic, broadly medical, settings. Although the onset of the institutionalization of these more explicit requirements may be dated around the 1960s, it would be a mistake to suggest that consent did not play an important role in criminal and civil law in preceding decades or centuries; indeed, its importance can be found in the law of the ancient Roman Empire. A second step toward placing contemporary disputes in perspective involves a brief examination of the relevance of consent in determining whether or not a crime or tort has been committed.

The development of the policy of requiring informed consent on the part of human beings who may be at risk when subjects of medical procedures or, more generally, of certain health-related policies, and the formation of institutionalized methods for monitoring the satisfaction of this requirement marks a noteworthy change in moral outlook and public policy in the United States and other countries where similar developments have occurred. This change is better understood against its cultural and political background. Two elements of the prevailing intellectual and moral climate prior to World War II and the Nuremberg Trials can be characterized, I believe, as (1) *positivistic*, and (2) *organicist*, respectively.

167

A comment first about the dominance of a positivistic intellectual, and academic, view of ethics. In the last few centuries and during the early decades of this century many new "sciences" (for example, physics, chemistry, economics, biology, psychology, sociology) came into being, having sprung forth from the "mother discipline" of philosophy (it is worth recalling that Isaac Newton described himself as a "natural philosopher," that Adam Smith taught moral philosophy, and that J. S. Mill is regarded as one of the fathers of contemporary economics). Some, though not all of philosophizing from the seventeenth to the nineteenth centuries is characterizable as rationalistic and *a priori* in its approach to resolving intellectual problems. Many of the practitioners of the emerging sciences regarded their own concerns as distinct and more limited than the broad concerns of traditional philosophy. Further, they regarded themselves as having identified rather specific and promising methods for making intellectual headway with recalcitrant questions. Thus, they were eager to stand on their own feet and to have their unique domain and distinct modes of inquiry valued and recognized as such. Associations with "armchair philosophizing" (a stereotypical remark seemingly doomed to eternal life) had to be shed. Further, it was clear that questions about morality, about right and wrong, not to mention the esoteric claims of theology or metaphysics, were extremely difficult to resolve by existing "scientific" or empirical methods (for example, observation, collection of data, projecting hypotheses, consequent empirical confirmation or disconfirmation, etc.). Hence, the emerging scientists rested uncomfortably with philosophical bedfellows who were prone to continue to explore metaphysical and ethical questions, much as the *nouveaux riches* seek to rid themselves of traditional garments or other indications of their origins. Not surprisingly, in retrospect, the extreme proposal emerged that the claims of metaphysics, theology, and ethics were not only untested by scientific methods, but that such claims were untestable. If, however, they are untestable, are they at all "cognitively meaningful"? The answer of an emerging group of young scientists, philosophers, and others in Vienna during the 1920s was negative. The central tenet of these Logical Positivists was that a claim is cognitively meaningful if and only if it is empirically verified or, later it was said, verifiable. If ethical claims about right and wrong or about "values" (not just preferences) are not cognitively meaningful, what is their status? After all, people *do* go on making such claims. Various theories were developed throughout the thirties and forties. Such claims were said to be expressions of feeling or taste; perhaps, they were commendations of a sort, or more like commands (for example, 'rape is wrong' means 'I dislike rape' or 'don't rape'). Theories *about* the meaning and function of moral judgments, often described as "metaethical theories," were the central focus of English-speaking ethical philosophy throughout the first half of the twentieth century (*certain* studies of G. E. Moore and Sir David Ross being important exceptions). This generally positivistic outlook was welcomed, consciously or not, by much of the scientific world for it provided a rationale for pursuing a "value-free" science (one devoid of the machinations of seemingly unsolvable and obscurantist issues). If ethical claims are, in the final analysis, profoundly insoluble and subjective (conflicts of private tastes are not amenable to rational solution), so much the worse for moral philosophy and so much the better for a value-free science! The influence of logical positivism is by no means dead. It may remain the prevailing view in the natural and social sciences. A look at almost any introductory scientific text today (especially in the natural sciences, economics, or sociology) would lend support to this claim.[4] Given this positivisitic outlook, the sciences have not been receptive to taking ethical inquiry seriously; nor have the sciences been inclined to *question* (scientifically?, rationally?) the positivist presupposition from which it may be inferred that there is *no need* to examine ethical claims rationally. As such, the positivist assumption has, and continues to be, little more than a dogma, a "leap of faith," something not to be given intellectual scrutiny any more than a good Roman Catholic or Baptist is to

[4] Consider the tendency to "psychologize" issues with an ethical dimension. For example, guilt feelings are often viewed by psychologists as invariably inappropriate, a "hang-up" of some sort. The question of whether there is appropriate guilt is frequently ignored, e.g., for having committed a murder. Or consider the following unqualified claim in an otherwise intriguing sociological study, "Duty is but the mirror image of desire. It is a neurotic rationalization of the individual's own wishes"—in S. Putney and G. Putney, *The Adjusted American: Normal Neuroses in the Individual and Society* (New York: Harper & Row, 1964), p. 149.

Similarly, the current popularity of "assertiveness training," in its *cruder* formulations, tends to encourage moral insensitivity, i.e., lack of charity, an unwillingness to compromise, and a narrow focus on whether one is getting what one wants—as if there were no serious moral questions about pressing for certain advantages or whether one's own preferences should be decisive in matters requiring negotiation. Again, failure to assert oneself glibly is regarded simply as a "hang-up." On this general point, see Claudia Mills, "The Moral Foundations of Assertiveness Training," *Report from the Center for Philosophy & Public Policy* 2, No. 4 (Fall, 1982), pp. 11–14.

puzzle excessively over the doctrines of the Trinity or the Resurrection.

Given this intellectual and moral climate (I do not suggest that it characterized that of "the person on the street"), the emergence of Nazism was not only a practical threat but posed an intellectual problem. For if it is said that Nazism is *evil*, that genocide against the Jews is an horrendous moral *wrong*, or that it would be morally wrong not to resist Hitler, are such claims mere expressions of private feeling? If the Nazi and the anti-Nazi make contrary claims, are these to be understood as expressions of different tastes? If so, is it impossible rationally to establish that killing Jews is wrong? In short, I am suggesting that the prevailing positivistic outlook was disturbed by the idea that there is a rational basis for discriminating among competing moral judgments, a view implicit in the claim that Nazi aims were morally unjustified and countermeasures were not. Shocked by the Nuremberg revelations of the pursuits of Nazi physicians (who, among other things, severed limbs of Jews without anesthesia or their consent), and moved to secure protection for individuals subject to scientific and medical procedures, the doctrine requiring voluntary, informed consent was institutionalized in the United States shortly after Nuremberg. That this development occurred in a hitherto positivistic climate is one reason for regarding it as a notable change—for the doctrine implicitly embodies the notion that moral judgments are not mere "matters of personal opinion" and that how human beings ought to be treated is not a matter to be left to personal (or even "professional") opinion—not even to professional physicians.

The intellectual reassessment provoked by Hitler also caused moral philosophers to question their preoccupation with abstract metaethical questions and their correlative neglect of more specific, and urgent, ethical problems. Not widely known outside of professional philosophy (nor well known within university walls) is the fact that this earlier imbalance has radically altered.[5]

Another background feature, against which the development of

---

[5] Earlier trained philosophers, I conjecture, *tend* to bemoan *the turn to specific, "practical"* moral issues (like those in Chapters 4, 5, or 6 in this book) seeing that as "mere application" of theory or a begging of still important and recalcitrant metaethical questions. Recently trained moral philosophers, I conjecture again, tend to welcome a change of focus from metaethical matters and an opportunity to mine fields left somewhat unexplored by earlier generations. My view is that both concerns are important and merit investigation; what is desirable is both satellite types of maps of the ethical *terra firma*, theories about mapping, and careful surveys of local and uncharted ethical jungles and deserts.

institutionalized protection of human subjects has shown a significant change, is what I shall call, for want of a better term, the *organicist* focus of much public policy in the United States. By this I mean the tendency to evaluate what is desirable political, economic, or health policy by standards which focus on *aggregate benefits*, for example, what promotes "the public interest," the health of the country, national security, scientific knowledge, or maximizes the gross national product. To press the organic metaphor, if the body as a whole has a diseased part, the health of the whole may require sacrificing the diseased part. Analogously, the welfare or rights of certain individuals may be sacrificed to promote net aggregate benefit, perhaps conceived along classical-utilitarian lines as the *sum* of net benefits to individuals producible (or aimed at) by a given policy. This focus on "overall good" tends to encourage the view that individual preferences or choices should not stand in the way of achieving this aggregate goal. To require the voluntary informed consent of competent persons before they are to be subjects of more or less risky medical procedures is to place an important *constraint* on what may be done in order to promote either aggregate goals (e.g., reduction in the incidence of certain diseases) and goals regarding individuals (e.g., what is conceived to be in the patient's best interest). Such a requirement, therefore, legally delimits the range of alternatives employable to achieve therapeutic, nontherapeutic, or mixed ends. The acceptability of the informed consent requirement remains controversial. Many think it is a foolish one, either for ethical-theoretical reasons or because it is costly to implement, or, as some allege, impossible to satisfy in certain cases. In the eyes of some it is an unfortunate byproduct of "unfettered individualism" and a source of cantankerous, self-serving complaints about rights-violations, mounting legal disputes, excessive insurance costs, and growing distrust between patients and health-care professionals. In claiming, then, that institutionalization of the doctrine reflects an important departure in outlook from prior decades of comparatively less restricted medical practice, I do not suggest that the doctrine has received anything like unanimous acceptance or thorough implementation. Except for highly risky procedures, it may be honored more in the breach than in the observance. The recent emphasis on informed consent, however, has antecedents in the not insignificant role that the law has, over a much longer period of time, assigned to the presence or absence of consent in human interactions. To such matters we now turn.

Legal prohibitions of unconsented-to intentional touching, imposition of unconsented-to risks, or nondisclosure of risks to patients who are in institutionalized situations as subjects of therapeutic, non-therapeutic, or mixed procedures have only crystallized and become widespread in the last few decades. References to "the doctrine of informed consent" generally refer to such legal or quasi-legal constraints on institutionalized practices. However, quite apart from recently implemented constraints on subjects in such institutional situations, the law has long assigned an important role to the presence or absence of voluntary consent in its determination of the permissibility of nontrivial interactions between persons. Such is the case both in the domains of tort law and criminal law. Both the concept of a crime and the concept of a tort involve the feature that an individual has been injured or wronged. The purpose of criminal proceedings is to vindicate the interests of the public and punish the wrongdoer; the purpose of a civil action for a tort is the recovery of compensation by the injured party from the wrongdoer.[6] Our concern here is neither with the differences between torts and crimes nor with the appropriateness of awarding damages in tort actions. Rather, it is with the relation of consent and torts. One tort, *battery*, is the intentional, *unpermitted*, contact with another person's body; the contact may extend to a person's clothing or the car in which he is riding.[7] This concern for protection of personal integrity is not limited to cases of physical injury or bodily damage; nor need it be the case that the party affected be aware of the act at its occurrence. Kissing an unconsenting party in her (or his) sleep can be a tort.[8] With the tort of *assault* no contact is necessary; "mental invasion" by frightening or humiliating a person may be sufficient. The effect of consent by a person to such interference with his person or property is that no tort has occurred; as Prosser observes:

> It is a fundamental principle of the common law that *volenti non fit injuria*—to one who is willing no harm is done. The attitude of the courts has not, in general, been one of paternalism. Where no public interest is contravened, they have left the individual to work out his own destiny, and are not

[6] In this section I rely heavily on William Prosser, *Law of Torts*, 4th ed. (St. Paul, Minn.: West, 1971), p. 9 and, generally, Chapters 1, 2, 4, and 5.

[7] Ibid., p. 34.

[8] Ibid., p. 35.

concerned with protecting him from his own folly in permitting others to do him harm.[9]

If Prosser's last claim is understood as an empirical assertion, it is more plausible if its scope is understood to be restricted to white, adult, competent, male citizens in, for example, English-speaking countries. More crucial for our purposes is the fact that, historically, Anglo-American law has generally presumed that valid consent is, with qualifications, a permissibility-making feature and its absence is an impermissibility-making feature, and these suppositions are part of the very definition of numerous torts and crimes. Also of interest here is the traditional view that consent may be present even if not overtly manifested verbally. One who intentionally shows up for a vaccination, in the absence of coercion, or one who enters an athletic contest, will normally be taken to have consented to certain forms of physical contact in spite of later protests to the contrary. Hence, the law traditionally recognized the validity of "tacit" or "implicit" consent. Part of the change in recent decades has been the institutionalization of the requirement that, generally, patients must, if they so choose, *explicitly* consent by word to proposed medical procedures before they are implemented.

As Prosser observes, there is also a tradition, dating from the early years of this century, which allows a physician to operate in emergency cases without obtaining consent, for example, a patient is bleeding to death and his foot must be amputated if his life is to be saved.[10] Prosser rightly objects to labeling such a case as one involving "tacit consent" (assuming there is no behavior by the patient to suggest as much); rather, he proposes that the key supposition is that in such cases the physician is "reasonably entitled to assume that, if the patient were competent and understood the situation, he would consent and therefore to act as if it has been given."[11] This allowance to proceed without express consent in emergency cases is one of several exceptions to the general rule (note its similarity to the Principle of Hypothetical Individualized Consent).

To place the recent emphasis on the doctrine of informed consent further in perspective we should not neglect another tort, namely, *negligence*. The essential elements involved in the tort of negligence are these: (1) a legal duty requiring an agent to conform to a certain

[9] Ibid., p. 101.
[10] Ibid., p. 103.
[11] Ibid.

standard of conduct in order to protect others against unreasonable risks, (2) a failure of the agent to so conform, (3) a close connection between his conduct and the resulting injury, and (4) an actual damage to the interests of another.[12] It commonly has been held that a physician, like other professionals, holds himself out as possessing certain competences or skills, at least those minimally necessary to be a licensed member of her (or his) profession. The standard of care to which he must conform has typically been thought to be whatever standard is customarily recognized and followed by fellow professionals; thus, the courts have been reluctant to impose some "external" standard and have deferred to the norms of the medical profession itself. Hence, if a surgeon saws off the wrong leg or leaves a sponge in the patient after operating, such acts evidently violate "good medical practice." In other cases, whether an act (or omission) is negligent may not be obvious from the standpoint of common sense, and it may be imperative to identify particular standards of care implicit in prevailing medical practice. The view that physicians have a duty to disclose the risks of proposed treatment to the patient prevailed in the earlier decades of this century, but the legal norm for several decades seems to have allowed considerable latitude to "professional medical judgment" in determining what must be disclosed. By about 1960 legal decisions made it increasingly clear that the standards of care included certain norms regarding disclosure; according to Meisel the term "informed consent" did not appear in legal decisions prior to 1957.[13] Since that time we have witnessed the crystallization of a more explicit, more determinate legal standard of adequate disclosure, one which requires medical practitioners to adhere to a more stringent standard than seems to have prevailed in the first half of this century. Performing surgery to which no consent has been given is the tort of battery (except for emergency cases and cases in which the subject lacks competence to consent), but failing adequately to disclose relevant information prior to a medical procedure (which enables informed consent) is, generally, a tort, namely, the tort of negligence.[14] The recent standards requiring voluntary informed consent and disclosure of relevant information render more determinate and more stringent the standard to which

[12] Ibid., p. 143.

[13] Alan Meisel, "The 'Exceptions' to the Informed Consent Doctrine: Striking a Balance Between Competing Values in Medical Decision Making," *Wisconsin Law Review* 413 (1979), p. 420.

[14] Prosser, *Law of Torts*, p. 165.

health-care professionals must conform. As we have noted, these legal and quasi-legal constraints remain controversial, and one might think that they are morally problematic, possibly because they interfere with or impede permissible paternalism or because they impede pursuits morally justifiable on nonpaternalistic grounds. Our primary concern, as we examine the doctrine and the arguments surrounding it, will focus on its relation to questions of paternalism.

4.3 *Elements of the Doctrine*

As far as I am aware, a canonical statement of "the doctrine of informed consent" is not anywhere etched in stone. Sometimes the reference is to the rather complex set of requirements prom-ulgated by the (then) U.S. Department of Health, Education, and Welfare, requirements intended to govern activities funded by DHEW (now: the Department of Health and Human Services) and designed to safeguard "the rights and welfare of subjects at risk." The policy requires the formation of Institutional Review Boards which are to review and approve (or not) proposed activities. It is useful to have before us many of the main elements of this complex set of requirements; the following is an edited version.

> This review shall determine whether these subjects will be placed at risk, and, if risk is involved, whether:
>
> (1) The risks to the subject are so outweighed by the sum of the benefit to the subject and the importance of the knowledge to be gained as to warrant a decision to allow the subject to accept these risks;
>
> (2) The rights and welfare of any such subjects will be ade-quately protected; and
>
> (3) Legally effective informed consent will be obtained by ad-equate and appropriate methods in accordance with the pro-visions of this part.
>
> "Subject at risk" means any individual who may be exposed to the possibility of injury, including physical, psychological, or social injury, as a consequence of participation as a subject in any research, development, or related activity which departs from the application of those established and accepted meth-ods necessary to meet his needs, or which increases the or-

dinary risks of daily life, including the recognized risks inherent in a chosen occupation or field of service.

"Informed consent" means the knowing consent of an individual or his legally authorized representative, so situated as to be able to exercise free power of choice without undue inducement or any element of force, fraud, deceit, duress, or other form of constraint or coercion. The basic elements of information necessary to such consent include:

(1) A fair explanation of the procedures to be followed, and their purposes, including identification of any procedures which are experimental;

(2) A description of any attendant discomforts and risks reasonably to be expected;

(3) A description of any benefits reasonably to be expected;

(4) A disclosure of any appropriate alternative procedures that might be advantageous for the subject;

(5) An offer to answer any inquiries concerning the procedures; and

(6) An instruction that the person is free to withdraw his consent and to discontinue participation in the project or activity at any time without prejudice to the subject.

Any institution proposing to place any subject at risk is obligated to obtain and document legally effective informed consent. No such informed consent, oral or written, obtained under an assurance provided pursuant to this part shall include any exculpatory language through which the subject is made to waive, or to appear to waive, any of his legal rights, including any release of the institution or its agents from liability for negligence.[15]

It is worth observing that the requirement that voluntary informed consent of the subject must exist prior to his becoming the recipient of risky procedures creates a barrier to the performance of nonpaternalistically motivated acts, for example, those of the Nazi physicians who were hardly aiming at the promotion of the good of their Jewish victims. Hence, the requirement deters the performance of certain nonpaternalistically motivated wrongful acts. Closer to our concern is how the doctrine is logically related (not

[15] Reprinted in D. Sharpe *et al.*, *Law and Medicine*, pp. 222–223.

just causally related) to the question of permissible paternalism, and whether the theory here lends support to, or provides a basis for attacking, the consent requirement.

Aside from the aforementioned legally operative requirements promulgated by DHEW, it is possible to identify various *moral* claims that may be made about voluntary, informed consent of a competent person to risk-laden (I set aside *trivial* risks) activities to which he is to be subjected, for example:

1. That A's doing X (an activity involving risks to S) to S, when X wrongs no others, is morally permissible *only if* S validly (voluntarily and knowingly) consented to A's doing X to S. Call this the *Necessity Claim*.

2. That A's doing X to S, when X wrongs no others, is morally permissible *if* S validly consented to A's doing X to S. Call this the *Sufficiency Claim*.

Other claims about the moral relevance of valid consent are: (1) that 1. is false, (2) that 2. is false, (3) that 1. and 2. are both true, (4) that neither 1. nor 2. is true. Deciding on the reasonableness of (1) through (4) requires deciding on the reasonableness of 1. and/or 2.; hence, 1. and 2. are basic as opposed to derivative assertions. Omitting details, it is reasonable to think that the DHEW policy presupposes, or at least may be defended in part by appeal to, the Necessity Claim. By contrast, the DHEW policy does not seem to presuppose the Sufficiency Claim for the policy insists on the satisfaction of other conditions as well; in general, for the context being considered, few would defend the Sufficiency Claim. It is usually insisted that, for example, the procedure, therapeutic or nontherapeutic in aim, must satisfy other conditions as well, for example, involves promise of significant benefit, is not known to be riskier than alternatives promising like benefits, is scientifically well designed, and so on. The primary focus of dispute concerns, for the reasons briefly noted, the Necessity Claim. Although the Necessity Claim focuses on imposition of risks, risks naturally construed in terms of risk of psychological or physical damage to the subject, we earlier have defended a broader view, namely, that (outside of cases where S is wronging others) doing any act which involves a presumptive wrong to S is impermissible in the absence of valid, currently operative, consent (or hypothetical individualized consent) on the part of S. I take it that it is presumptively wrong to subject a person to harm or risk of harm of the sorts

177

noted. However, the category of presumptively wrong acts seems broader than the category of harmful or risky acts. Whether this is so depends on the answer to a difficult question about which I intend to say very little, that is, what counts as "harm" or a "risk of harm." Construed somewhat narrowly, we *may* not harm others, on balance, when we seriously offend them, when we damage the reputation of another, or when we deceive them, or diminish a certain freedom.[16] Hence, as I have construed the notion of a presumptive wrong, it includes a variety of actions which are not easily, or perhaps not appropriately, collected under "harmful acts" or "acts imposing a risk of harm."

If the theory defended here is correct, doing what is presumptively wrong to S (when X wrongs no others and S is capable of giving or withholding informed consent) including the imposition of a risk of serious harm to S, is impermissible in the absence of S's valid consent. Therefore, the Necessity Claim should be accepted.[17] To impose a risk of harm on S for paternalistic reasons, recalling that *therapeutic* procedures share the aim of paternalism (aim at promoting the good of the subject), in the absence of S's valid consent is unjustified paternalism. In short, what I hope to have shown is that, aside from whatever *other* reasons might be given for accepting the Necessity Claim and, relatedly, adopting something like the DHEW policy, a reasonable theory of paternalism lends strong support to so doing. Such a policy must be adopted if we are to avoid unjustified paternalism and, thereby, respect the right of competent persons to direct their own lives.

There are, in addition, utilitarian-type reasons, compelling or not, for adopting the informed consent requirement. Having such

[16] The nature of offensive acts and the morality of constraining them is discussed by Joel Feinberg in "Harmless Immoralities and Offensive Nuisances," and in a reply by Michael Bayles, both in *Issues in Law and Morality*, eds. Norman Care and Thomas Trelogan (Cleveland: Western Reserve University, 1973), pp. 83–140. My own views on this matter are found in "Coercive Restraint of Offensive Action," *Philosophy & Public Affairs* 8, No. 2 (Winter, 1979), pp. 176–193. See also Feinberg's, *Harm to Others* (New York: Oxford University Press, 1984) and the forthcoming volumes in this (Feinberg's) series.

[17] To avoid confusion I emphasize that the context being assumed here is one in which S is a competent person, is either relevantly informed of risks and benefits associated with the proposed treatment or will be, is so situated as to be able to make a reasoned choice to consent or not, and that he can do so in a broadly voluntary manner. So, certain "emergency" situations are excluded as well as cases in which the normally competent subject is severely impaired with respect to decision-making capacities. For these reasons, there is no basis to appeal to the Principle of Hypothetical Individualized Consent. Thus, in such contexts, actual, valid, consent is morally required.

a policy, for example, may promote trust between health-care professional and patient; it may promote self-respect for the patient and enhance his sense of being able to exercise control over his own life (compare the depressing feeling of powerlessness); it may even increase the likelihood of cure. This last claim may be true because patients are more likely to comply with health promoting prescriptions when they can view themselves as having chosen the path to cure or when they can view themselves as co-partners in the healing effort. One might conjecture further about the curative chemical changes in the body which are associated with maintaining or coming to have such a sense of power, control, or self-respect. These matters, I believe, have been researched too little at this point.[18] For our purposes, however, it is worth observing that the question of the health-related *effects* of giving the patient the "final say," or the opportunity to have the "final say" (or "locus of control") is an *empirical* matter. Empirical research may show that, generally, there are such positive effects on the health of such patients. At the same time, it may not. If the theory we have developed here is correct, how the data turn out is not the crucial matter for the theory defended since it is impermissible to impose harms or risks of harms on a subject in the absence of her valid consent, independently of whether "getting informed consent" has therapeutic consequences. For such reasons, the Necessity Claim has, I maintain, adequate theoretical support, and its acceptability does not depend on the contingencies noted, ones which in fact, considered abstractly, are likely *not* to be *invariantly* health enhancing across the domain of *all* (competent) patients.

Even if this line of reasoning is plausible, further issues deserve exploration here. First, we ought not ignore the array of rather specific complaints, and counterarguments, that continue to be marshalled against the Necessity Claim, or more generally and commonly, against the informed consent requirement embodied in the DHEW directive. In addition, it may remain unclear precisely what is permissible and what is not in a variety of particular cases—"hard cases"—where well-informed people of good will disagree or a single such person is pulled both ways about what would be the right thing to do. Examining certain of those cases will make clearer the implications of the theory developed here; it also affords further opportunity reflectively to assess the plausibility of the

[18] See the references in Meisel, "The 'Exceptions' to the Informed Consent Doctrine . . . ," p. 430.

theory against its competitors. If its implications require revision of our intuitions, or pre-analytic moral beliefs, on occasion, that will not be surprising and need not be seriously damaging; for that is a familiar byproduct of acceptable theories. If, however, the theory has *radically* counterintuitive implications in a *wide* array of cases, that provides reason to pause and to revise, or even reject, the theory in favor of some competitor which, on thorough examination, fares better.

4.4 *Against the Necessity of Informed Consent*

Here we shall consider a series of objections to the Necessity Claim; although some of the objections are familiar, others are both less familiar and more ingenuous. Our primary concern is with therapeutic contexts where the aim of treatment is to promote the health, or alleviate the sickness, or injury, of the patient. In a few cases we focus on nontherapeutic contexts in which the aim of the procedure is not the good of the subject but something else, for example, advancing scientific knowledge. Some contexts are, of course, mixed, for example, administering an untested or insufficiently tested drug in order to cure a serious affliction *and* to advance medical knowledge. Many randomized clinical trials fall in the mixed category.

Contrary to the prevailing norms of *caveat emptor* or *caveat auctor*, which prevail in most cases in which customers pay a fee for a service or product, it is generally accepted that the health-care professional's relation to her patient is, in some sense, a *fiduciary* one. A fiduciary relationship is understood to be one in which the patient has a legitimate expectation that the professional look out for, and promote, the patient's interest, and that the professional should exhibit, therefore, a special loyalty to the patient and not pursue activities which may conflict with the interests of the patient. It is generally assumed that such professionals have a duty to supply relevant information to the patient so that the latter may have the opportunity to make a reasonable decision about matters which significantly affect his welfare. This expectation imposes a more demanding standard on the health-care professional than those which prevail (rightly or wrongly) with many sellers of other products or services. In the latter cases it is (often) only expected that the seller engage in no outright falsifications (or fraud); it is not usually expected that the seller will go out of his way to inform the prospective purchaser of all the shortcomings, or risks, associated with the product or service to be purchased. That is, health-care professionals are expected to adhere to a higher standard of disclosure of relevant information. This expectation seems legitimate in view of the typical high degree of importance assignable to health-care treatment and the fact that health-care professionals are sought out by patients partly in order to *find out* things, that is, have their ills diagnosed. *Provision of such relevant information* is typically part of the service for which such professionals are employed. For these reasons it is not only presumptively wrong for such professionals to engage in outright lies but also to withhold information relevant to a patient's *understanding* his condition and having an opportunity to make a reasonable choice among possible courses of treatment. Such a presumption holds when the patient is a competent person. In cases in which the patient is incapable of minimal understanding, no analogously strong presumption exists, for example, in the cases of very young children, fetuses, the comatose, or other incompetents.

I emphasize this rather stringent presumptive duty to disclose relevant information to competent patients for two reasons. First, it is relevant in an obvious way to considering arguments *against* the necessity of informed consent and arguments *against* the claim that health-care personnel ought to disclose information which might facilitate informed consent (or dissent). Second, from paternalistic motives health-care personnel are tempted overtly to lie or withhold relevant information (I shall refer to either as a form of "deception") as a means of achieving what *they* believe is in the patient's interest or "for his own good." After all, employment of other presumptively wrong modes of influencing the patient, such as force, coercive threat, and so on, are likely to be less successful. For this reason a number of arguments and cases to be considered will focus on deceptive practices. Contrary to what these remarks may seem to suggest, I shall later argue that the deception of patients in *certain* restricted cases is a permissible form of paternalism. We turn now to a consideration of arguments against the necessity of informed consent.

One argument deserves only brief consideration. I call it the *Appeal to Customary Practice*. Oppponents of the informed consent requirement sometimes point out that it is not customary in ordinary practice to inform patients of all the details of their diagnosis or how decisions regarding their treatment are made. It is then inferred that the physician (for example) permissibly may refrain from doing so. As stated, this argument is largely irrelevant since

181

it is not necessary to inform patients of *all* the details of their diagnosis or proposed modes of treatment in order for them to have an opportunity to make a reasonable choice about their treatment. Suppose the argument is recast, and it is only claimed that it is not customary in ordinary practice to inform patients of the details of diagnosis or treatment necessary for patients to be able to make a reasonable choice about treatment, and, hence, validly to consent or dissent. Whether or not this claim is true, let us suppose that it is. It remains unclear why it is thought to follow that it is all right to refrain from providing such information. The necessary missing premise is that it is all right to do whatever is customarily done in ordinary practice. When stated explicitly the premise hardly seems tempting; it is a rather bald appeal to tradition. If we were to rely on such appeals we would, at certain periods and places, have to condone slavery, pouring boiling oil on gunshot wounds, clitoridectomy of female infants, burning of brides with insufficient dowries, placing chastity belts on women, burning "witches," and so on—not all medical practices to be sure, but all of which were or are "customary practices" during certain epochs. The argument is so transparently inadequate that I mention it only because it continues to be invoked. It is often proposed in conjunction with other arguments, but it is worth remembering that several bad arguments do not "add up" to a good argument; nor does adding a bad argument to a sound one strengthen the latter.

To avoid misunderstanding, it should be noted that I have not asserted that what is commonly done in ordinary medical practice is of no relevance to any moral questions. Until recent decades the courts have frequently allowed the fact that a health-care professional's doing what was in accord with standard practice to exculpate the professional from a charge of negligence or other form of malpractice. The question of whether an act or omission conformed with prevailing practice has been viewed by the law as important, then, in deciding questions of legal responsibility, and such conformity has been an excusing condition. One reasonably might believe, further, that such a stance is not just legally operative but morally defensible. Standard practice typically will reflect prevailing views about what is scientifically defensible and what is morally permissible. Just as it is not reasonable to expect *every* health-care professional to be at the leading edge of his (or her) discipline in terms of employing the most effective, recently substantiated, therapeutic techniques, it would not be reasonable to expect every such professional to be a moral visionary in terms of having the foresight and courage to deviate radically from pre-vailing assumptions about what is morally acceptable. For example, during an earlier period of even more rampant male chauvinism, we reasonably may judge a certain patriarchal condescension by male physicians toward female patients as *somewhat* excusable (note: not justifiable). In an extremely chauvinistic cultural period we reasonably may view both undue servility in women and pa-triarchal attitudes (or acts) in men as, in part, products of cultural influence. In such a context, individuals are less blameworthy for adopting the common outlook than in periods where the arbitrar-iness of such viewpoints is less hidden from reasonably conscien-tious persons. Perhaps even clearer is the contrast between those who held slaves during a period when the prevailing moral con-sciousness found slavery acceptable (or even a duty, perhaps "com-manded by God") and those who might hold slaves today in a society more enlightened (at least on that point). To regard the former as less culpable or blameworthy (or deserving of punish-ment or owing compensation to those victimized) than the latter, is not to condone or *justify* the practice, and that is a crucial point. Even if conformity to prevailing norms may function, to a point, as an excusing condition, that goes *no* distance toward showing that customary practice is morally permissible. Since our focus is on the permissibility of prevailing practice and not the issue of the excusability of those engaged in it, the argument based on custom-ary practice is unpersuasive even if it is relevant to the latter issue.

In contrast to the appeal to customary practice, many of the grounds adduced for opposing the informed consent requirement and the related duty to disclose relevant information focus, in a variety of ways, on the real or alleged *consequences* of disclosing such information—consequences actually or allegedly harmful to the patient. I turn to these. A more seductive argument, which I shall label the *Erosion of Confidence Argument*, proceeds as follows:[19]

1. It is probable that a very sick patient needs complete con-fidence that his physician has the knowledge to make the best decision regarding his treatment.

2. If the physician reveals a lack of certainty about the best course of treatment, by disclosing risks, probabilities of suc-

---

[19] An argument of this general sort is posed by Thomas Chalmers, "The Ethics of Randomization as a Decision-Making Technique and The Problem of Informed Consent," in *Contemporary Issues in Bioethics*, 1st ed., eds. Tom Beauchamp and Leroy Walters (Belmont, Cal.: Wadsworth, 1978), p. 428.

cess or failure, or alternative modes of treatment, the very sick patient, normally, will not retain complete confidence in the physician.

3. Such a loss of complete confidence may do great harm to the patient.

4. The physician should do nothing to harm the patient.

5. Hence, the physician should not reveal the information (mentioned in 2.) to the patient.

6. Hence, it is permissible for the physician to refrain from revealing such relevant information.

7. Hence, it is permissible for the physician not to carry out his (or her) presumptive duty to disclose relevant information.

8. Hence, in cases like those described above, it is permissible to treat the patient without his informed consent.

I have chosen to reconstruct this line of thought at some length because it involves a number of important assumptions. There are variations on this line of reasoning which crop up with considerable frequency in the literature on biomedical ethics. Some of the variants escape one difficulty only to be ensnared by others. We note initially that even if this argument were entirely unobjectionable it has as its *scope* only the domain of "very sick patients." Hence, the argument would show, at best, only the permissibility of not getting informed consent *from the very sick* and not disclosing relevant information to them. It would leave entirely open the question of what is permissible with regard to those who are *not* "very sick." I have already suggested, however, that there is no presumptive duty to disclose information to those strictly incapable of understanding it. Hence, the argument is of greater interest if we assume that "the very sick" does not include such persons, and construe the argument as one about disclosure to sick but competent persons. Apart from asking whether any of the derived statements or conclusions 5. through 8. do indeed follow from the premises 1. through 4., we may inquire as to the reasonableness of the premises. Contrary to my occasional desire to be charitable, I suggest that only premise 3. is unproblematic, and that is because it is so weak; it does not even insist that the projected loss of confidence will *probably* do great harm to the patient. In any case, let us suppose that 3. is true. With regard to premise 1. it is natural to ask: needs complete confidence for what? It is not obvious that having such confidence is a causally necessary condition for *all* very sick patients to get well. In many cases the crucial factors seem to be skillful surgery or appropriate and effective pharmacological treatment; it is also worth noting that a physician may *deserve* complete confidence on the part of the patient but simply not have it because, for example, the patient is wary or skeptical about young, black, female, oriental, or Hispanic physicians. Complete confidence seems desirable; it is *not* obviously a *prerequisite* to successful treatment. Doubts about the second premise are more serious ones. Again we have an empirical question. Is it in fact true that, normally, sick patients, or "very sick" patients, will lose confidence in a physician who straightforwardly informs the patient of the risks and uncertainties which the physician believes to obtain? Something like this may be probable for patients who are exceedingly naive, that is, those who believe that medical diagnosis and choice of treatment are matters as well understood and rule-governed as the task of repairing a defective flashlight or a flat tire. It is doubtful that in most cases competent patients are unaware of the risks, uncertainties, and lack of knowledge which lead physicians to speak of "the *art* of healing." If patients have at least this minimal degree of awareness, it would seem that they would be more likely to distrust physicians who, by silence or other means, convey the impression that matters are simple or that the physician does not have to cope with uncertainties. Although my point is based only on (overly maligned) "anecdotal" evidence, I am aware of many persons who would quickly flee the examining room of any physician who pretended that all was mechanically clearcut and certain, and treatment was free of risks. It seems clear, contrary to premise 2., that the confidence and trust of many patients in their physician is enhanced when she honestly and openly sets forward the uncertainties, risks, and benefits of the diagnosis or proposed therapeutic procedure. The contrary view seems to suppose that very sick patients are exceedingly naive, skittish, or paranoid, and incapable of putting matters into some reasonably objective perspective. We may concede that this is true of some patients; but that such cases should be taken as a paradigm of all sick patients, or of all very sick patients, lacks credibility.

If our reasoning is correct, the first two premises of the argument are unacceptable (and, hence, the argument as a whole). One may ask, however, what if they are *true of* a minority of very sick patients. Is it permissible to withhold relevant information from *them*?

This question and the limited concession made motivates an examination of the other premises.

Premise 4. embodies the famous prescription of the Hippocratic oath: that the physician should "do no harm" to the patient. Here we come upon a substantive moral claim, one which has played an important role in a variety of arguments in biomedical ethics, such as those concerning voluntary euthanasia. It is worth noting that "do no harm" may be construed in a variety of ways and an assessment of the prescription requires sorting out the different assertions which may be made by the use of "do no harm." In view of the obvious fact that physicians frequently cause pain, tissue-damage, and disability in the course of therapeutic procedures, it is clear that the Hippocratic prescription is *not* plausibly understood to mean "never cause any harmful effects" where pain and impairment are understood as "harmful effects." More plausibly, the prescription is to be understood as "do no harm *on balance*," a directive which does not preclude causing the mentioned effects in the course of promoting the overall physical or psychological well-being of the patient. This is how I shall construe the Hippocratic prescription. The distinction between "harms" and "what is harmful on balance" does not, of course, provide us with an analysis of the elusive concept of harm. It does suggest that premise 4. is plausibly understood to mean that the physician should not do anything which is harmful to the patient on balance, and it may be reasonable to understand this prescription as a prohibition on making the patient worse off on balance. One difficulty here concerns how a projected "loss of complete confidence" in the physician will make the patient worse off. What are the alleged causal links between the loss of confidence and not getting well? Is there a somewhat hidden assumption at this point about the power of positive thinking, and even if it is true (there *is* reason to think so in *some* cases) that having a positive attitude or will plays a causally significant role in recovery, must that involve *complete confidence* in the physician? It is not clear, for reasons mentioned earlier, that it must. But to ask these questions is to assume that the physician should do nothing which may make the patient worse off or, alternatively, make recovery less likely (or even render it impossible). That is, such questions are germane only if we assume that the Hippocratic prescription, as we understand it here, is acceptable.

We have observed that there are difficulties in knowing how a given patient will react to being informed of his diagnosis and to becoming apprised of the various modalities of treatment and their associated risks and benefits. Let us concede that in some cases patients lose confidence in their physicians, that in some cases the diagnosis is extremely disturbing, and that in some cases the result may be a diminished will to recover or a choice not to comply with a recommended mode of treatment which, from the standpoint of medical experts, offers the greatest chance for recovery. To separate out the epistemological from the moral questions, we once again may suppose that our hypothetical physician is omniscient and, hence, knows that the result of disclosure to a particular patient will lead to the dire consequences noted. Must the physician refrain from disclosing the information on the ground that she must do no harm on balance? Here it seems that we must answer negatively. It is the patient's life and the patient's body. If he is a competent person, the patient has the right to make his own choice about the undertaking, including choice of a mode of treatment. Specifically, if the patient is to direct his own life he must not be deceived about discouraging or even tragic news. It is up to him how to chart his own course or play his own, possibly disappointing, hand.

In spite of the seductiveness of the idea that physicians or, for that matter, anyone else, should not do that which would harm others on balance, the principle leads to highly counterintuitive results. In nonmedical contexts there well may be a large number of situations in which competent persons will be disappointed to learn that they are in a most serious predicament. Consider some examples. Jonathan does not know it yet, but he is to be fired in 12 months after working with his company for 25 years. Marie has borne a genetically defective child which will die by 6 or 7 years but whose symptoms will not appear for 2 or 3 years. Oedipus wants to marry Jocasta and, known to us but not to him, Jocasta is his mother. Thaddeus has worked for ten years to formulate a proof of Goldbach's Theorem (that every even number is the sum of two primes) but we know, let us suppose, that Saul accomplished the feat last year but has not published the result. One could go on recalling types of cases in which competent persons would be upset, distraught, or perhaps shattered, by learning the truth. To withhold it in such cases is to allow people to live in an illusory world quite different from the actual one, to allow them to invest their energies in working toward goals which are difficult or impossible to realize. If someone had engendered such false beliefs by overt lying, we no doubt would judge that such a person has made a mockery of the lives of those deceived. Again, to withhold

187

the truth bypasses the cognitive centers of competent persons; in a nontrivial way it renders their powers of reaction, reflection, and choice nonoperative; for such capacities are not allowed to engage important facets of the world as it is. To pursue an analogy, the results of blinding a competent person are similar to shielding such a person from significant personal information (which would, if known, affect a person's substantive choices); in both cases the persons are radically impaired. They cannot accurately perceive the world in which they wish to lead their lives. In some cases, of course, persons who learn the sad truth, in the types of situations recently mentioned, handle it well. In other cases the result is tragic. My claim is that in either type of case people should be allowed to cope as they see fit. To withhold the hard truth in order to prevent harm on balance would be to treat other competent persons as inferiors whose judgment may be bypassed and supplanted by our own. The principle "do nothing which may harm others on balance" sanctions radically counterintuitive acts and policies both in medical contexts and without. When we recall the special fiduciary relation of health-care professionals to their patients and the fact that such professionals are typically employed by patients in order to diagnose and disclose the patient's problem, the case seems even more compelling that there cannot be any unqualified duty on the part of such professionals to "do no harm" on balance. If that is correct, no argument employing the Hippocratic prescription (or our less vulnerable interpretation of it) as an essential premise is acceptable. Hence, we find yet another reason to reject the rationale embodied in the Erosion of Confidence Argument.

At best, the "do no harm" prescription is a plausible rule of thumb. As such, it should be understood as "in the absence of any other morally relevant considerations, one should not do anything which will probably lead to harm on balance." But when a competent person's prerogative to direct the course of his own life will be undermined, there *is* another morally relevant consideration, a consideration which, I have argued, is overriding in the restricted types of circumstances we earlier elaborated.

It may be objected that the fiduciary relationship, although it normally requires disclosure of a patient's diagnosis or prognosis, requires such disclosure only where it is instrumentally valuable to do so, that is, when it is an effective means to helping the patient or, at least preventing harm; otherwise not. Thus, consideration of the norms implicit in the fiduciary role yield no evident support for our stringent presumption in favor of disclosure.

Debating which precise norms are implicit in a fiduciary relationship may be a fruitless task as well as an inessential one. There is no compelling reason to assume that morally defensible practices are to be determined simply by ascertaining socially accepted practices, even long established ones. There are recognized norms in what constitutes being a good physician, a good assassin, a good hangman, or a good astrologist, but there is always a further question as to whether one morally ought to occupy such roles or whether one should do so in such a manner as to conform to the norms traditionally associated with such roles. As we have argued, patients who are competent persons are *persons* with a conception of the good, including their own, and not mere needons, wantons, or properly regarded only as biological organisms to be kept in good repair, or restored to species-normal functioning without regard to their own choices or purposes in directing their own lives. The viewpoint implicit in the "do no harm" maxim fails to give adequate weight to this morally important consideration. As Christopher Boorse has argued, some conditions which must be counted as biologically harmful, or pathological, are desirable from the standpoint of certain individuals, for example, sterility, or low sperm count in those not wanting to procreate.[20] Nondisclosure of information to competent persons fails to allow them an opportunity to pursue the good as they see it, or their own good as they see it (or revise their conception of it), and is not defensible merely on the ground that the health-care professional may preserve or promote health (or species-normal functioning for the relevant group, e.g., young black females) by bypassing the subject's capacities to reason and choose her own course. Later this point will receive further elaboration.

The Erosion of Confidence Argument is one variation on the theme of harm prevention (or good-promotion, as the case may be). Another variation focuses more directly on the alleged fact that when patients are informed of certain relevant facts, such as risks and uncertainties of a treatment modality, or that their treatment will be randomly decided, they may choose not to consent to the proposed treatment.[21] For example, Thomas Chalmers has

[20] Christopher Boorse, "Concepts of Health," in *Border Crossings*, eds. Donald VanDeVeer and Tom Regan (New York: Random House, forthcoming).

[21] Just this sort of rationale for withholding information was invoked by the surgeon (Spence) in Canterbury vs. Spence (Washington, D.C., 1972); he refused

claimed that when the physician wishes to place patients with a life-threatening disease in a randomized clinical trial (wherein the subjects' therapeutic modality will be determined randomly, and either they will receive standard treatment or another promising but insufficiently tested mode of treatment), informing such patients of the randomized choice procedure

> . . . is not in the best interest of the patients because it seems likely that 9 out of 10 would refuse these studies, and therefore the operation, if so informed. If they were in their right senses, they would find a doctor who thought he knew which was the better treatment, or they would conclude that if the differences were so slight that such a trial had to be carried out, they would prefer to take their chances on no operation. Assuming that there is a 50 percent chance that the operation will prove to be effective, then half the patients who were scared out of the operation by having been asked for their informed consent, would have been mistreated.[22]

Again, it might be conceded, for the sake of discussion, that a patient's choice, for example, not to undergo an operation may not be reasonable, or the most reasonable choice to make, if the only goal is to preserve or promote the patient's health. The expression "what is in the patient's best interest" is frequently construed along just these lines, especially by physicians whose preeminent aim is to restore or promote a patient's health. Although a patient may want very much the achievement of that goal, he may judge that the potential benefits are not worth the risks. Judged by some reasonable standard the patient may make an imprudent choice. This rationale for withholding information supposes that it is all right to constrain the choices of competent persons in order to promote their own good, naturally construed here as their health. We have argued that there is no justification for such a principle and its application sanctions, in a large variety of cases, an invidious undermining of the capacity of competent persons to chart their own course.

Physicians who choose to withhold information in such contexts, one must conjecture, myopically focus on the question of how to

---

to inform his patient of the risks of a laminectomy ". . . because it might deter patients from undergoing needed surgery and might produce adverse psychological reactions which could preclude success of the operation." See the discussion in Sharpe, Fiscina, and Head, *Law and Medicine*, p. 198.

[22] Chalmers, "The Ethics of Randomization . . . ," p. 428.

maximize recovery or cure, and tend to equate "what is in the best interest of the patient" with "whatever maximizes chances of recovery." The patient, however, might agree that it is in his best *health-interest* to *choose*, in a voluntary and informed manner, that mode of treatment which will maximize his chances of recovery. He may deny that it is in his best interest to be conned into consenting to a procedure which, in fact, may maximize his chances of recovery. Even though we have denied that it is permissible for the physician to employ presumptively wrongful means to get the patient to "go along" with what, in fact, may be in the patient's best health-interest, we should also not ignore the point that what is in a patient's best *health*-interest cannot be identified, without an arbitrarily expansive definition of 'health,' with what is in a patient's overall interest (not to mention: what would facilitate, or accord with, his conception of the good). What is in a patient's overall interest will include what is in his health-interest, but it also includes interests which a patient has because of goals he has adopted and perhaps also because of loyalties he has toward certain principles. One of a patient's goals may be to consider reflectively and reasonably make his own choices about matters which importantly affect his life. If so, his being allowed to do so and having the opportunity to do so is one of his interests and an important one. Withholding information of the sort we have considered evidently undermines this interest, *even if* it promotes the patient's health-interest and *even if* it is true that the patient, duly informed, may have chosen the course of treatment favored by his physician. Relatedly, a patient may have some particular conviction, one possibly arising from some philosophical or religious outlook, that important choices should never be left to chance—a principle undermined by employing a randomizing procedure to determine his treatment. The common emphasis attached to "doctor knows best" and the reasonable claim that the physician is an expert regarding medical diagnosis and preferable medical treatment tends to obscure the fact that what is in a patient's *overall* interest involves consideration of interests that are not "medical" at all. Nor is the *identification* or *weighting* of such other interests a matter of *medical expertise*. The assumption that the physician knows best, if understood to mean that the physician knows best about what is in a patient's *overall interest*, is a clear example of the "generalization of expertise," the assumption that those who are reliable authorities in their field of professional competence are, therefore, experts about matters falling outside that area of competence.[23] A few analogies may be useful here. An accountant may provide authoritative advice about whether your entering bankruptcy proceedings is in your best *financial* interest; it would be foolish to assume that she knows what is in your overall interest. If you would feel stigmatized, regard yourself as a social outcast, and suffer a substantial loss in self-respect, declaring bankruptcy may be financially prudent but fail to promote your overall interest. Similarly, a genetic counselor may advise against your getting pregnant at 38 (due to the risk of bearing a defective child). Again, her expertise about such matters does not extend to being the best arbiter of what is in your overall interests. That will depend on your goals, beliefs, and attitudes toward risks—matters about which the counselor may be poorly apprised.

In principle, of course, it is possible for a physician, or other professionals, to acquire a great deal of information about your general goals, specific plans, values, and so on. Hence, the medical expert, for example, may be in a better position to ascertain what is in your overall interest than in the absence of such information. Several points are worth noting here. First, it is doubtful that, in practice, acquiring such *highly personal information in sufficient detail* is at all likely even if it is possible in principle. Acquisition of such information would often be difficult due to an understandable reluctance of patients to bare their souls in so thorough a manner. Relatedly, given the demands on physicians and costs to patients, it is unlikely that such time-consuming procedures could become routine. Second, in cases in which the physician may wish to discern a patient's likely reaction to disclosure (e.g., will the patient become suicidally depressed?) and cases in which the physician may earnestly attempt to ascertain what is in the patient's overall interest, and not just his health-interest, the average physician is likely to be less than well qualified to make what Allen Buchanan aptly has called *psychiatric generalizations*.[24] To make reliable inferences about how a patient would react to certain events or, relatedly, to ascertain and weigh all of a patient's interests requires not only *obtaining* much difficult to acquire information, it also requires knowledge of relevant psychiatric or psychological categories, and

---

[23] The quoted expression originates, I believe, with Robert Veatch.

[24] See Allen Buchanan's perceptive essay, "Medical Paternalism", *Philosophy & Public Affairs* 7, No. 4 (Summer, 1978), p. 379. It has been reprinted in M. Cohen, T. Nagel, and T. Scanlon, eds., *Philosophy & Public Affairs Reader: Medicine and Moral Philosophy* (Princeton: Princeton University Press, 1982), pp. 214–234.

sophisticated acquaintance with psychological theories of explanation and prediction. For example, is the patient comparatively rigid and unadaptive, like the sculptor who, on being informed that he could never sculpt again, preferred to die? Is the patient characterizable as phobic? If so, can such phobias be overcome by desensitization techniques? Just as the determination of what is in the patient's best physical health-interest depends on ascertaining relevant physical data (e.g., is the patient allergic to antibiotics, or a hemophiliac?), so determination of overall interest would require *both* acquisition of much psychological data *and* reasonable *processing* of such; doing so frequently would require a level of psychological expertise beyond the reach of most health-care professionals.

There is another, and more general, point about a patient's interests which creates further difficulties for those who wish to defend the claim that health-care professionals may be able to ascertain, in a reasoned manner, what is really in the overall interest of the patient. Much of our discussion here has presupposed that there are matters about which the patient is apprised (roughly, innermost values, attitudes, and goals) which affect what is in the patient's overall interest—and that the health-care professional *might* be able to learn of such factors. But in a case, for example, in which a physician is contemplating nondisclosure of the fact that the patient has Lou Gehrig's disease (amyotrophic bilateral sclerosis), what is in a patient's overall interest may depend in part on the importance to the patient of knowing that he suffers from such a condition. That is, the physician may need to know to what extent the patient values such knowledge. Just here a serious problem arises. Information seems a rather peculiar commodity in that, unlike some other commodities, we frequently *do not know how much we value it until we possess it.* For example, prior to acquiring it one may not value (or value much) knowledge of Greek or Latin but, on acquiring it, one values it a great deal. Much the same can often be said of the information obtained from therapy, tennis lessons, a course in nutrition, and so on. Hence, in the case of the patient with Lou Gehrig's disease it is not the case that the patient already knows how valuable knowledge of his diagnosis is (he does not yet have it) and the only difficulty is for the physician to extract this valuation from the patient. The patient has not yet valued such information; its importance in his network of interests is indeterminate. A dilemma arises. If the physician is to decide whether to disclose the information by first deciding whether it is in the patient's overall interest to have it, he *cannot* ascertain the importance the patient places on such knowledge (by assumption the patient lacks the knowledge at that point). If in order to find out what importance the patient attaches to such knowledge (to determine what is in the patient's overall interest) the physician reveals it, then, of course, the physician cannot, at a later point, decide about disclosure on the basis of fuller information. The disclosure is past history. To put the problem slightly differently, in cases of contemplating disclosure, necessarily the physician can, at best, decide only on the basis of what is in the patient's overall interest *when the patient is ignorant* of a highly relevant and emotionally charged fact. Except for cases in which such ignorance will be permanent, when the patient comes to learn of his condition his values and his network of interests well may change—in which case what was in his overall interest when he was ignorant may radically diverge from, and possibly undermine, what is in his overall interest when he is no longer ignorant. If 'promotion of overall interest' is understood as 'promotion of overall interest in the long run,' as it commonly is, then it seems myopic and unreasonable to regard as decisive what is in a patient's overall interest while he is ignorant of a fact highly relevant to his own hopes and plans. To qualify slightly, this would seem to be the case for the (probable) majority of cases where nondisclosure only *postpones* the time when the patient learns of his plight.

Another attack against the necessity of informed consent appeals to the claim that patients may *lack the capacity to understand* the diagnosis of their condition, the nature of the proposed modes of treatment, or to comprehend the nature of the risks and benefits of the proposed alternatives. If this is true, informed consent is simply not possible, and the correlative insistence that this condition must be satisfied is irrational.[25] What is correct in this line

[25] Eugene Laforet, from another angle, has argued against the very possibility of informed consent in situations involving an experimental element: "If, as the ancients held, an experiment is a question posed to Nature, Nature's answer is presumably unknown prior to the completion of the experiment. Ignorance, then, is an essential element of any experiment. To speak of informed consent under these circumstances would, doubtless, delight the shade of Lewis Carroll. The more important the information to be gained, the less likely it is that there is any precedent; consequently, the less feasible it is that consent can be informed." This argument, I propose, reflects a misunderstanding of the doctrine of informed consent, for that doctrine does not require that patients *know* the outcome, ahead of time, of an experimental procedure. Given Laforet's definition of 'experiment,' an element of ignorance is necessarily involved. But the doctrine of informed consent neither requires the absence of all forms of ignorance nor does it require foreknowledge of outcomes. It does require that patients be provided with relevant available

of argument is that if the patient truly lacks the ability to understand the situation and the alternatives, then informed choice is indeed impossible, and the informed consent requirement cannot be met; thus, it is foolish to demand that it be met. Further, there is undoubtedly a significant range of cases where just this situation obtains, namely, with young children, the comatose, the extremely retarded, and others who are mentally incompetent. Hence, the requirement of informed consent is indefensible for those subjects who are not competent. Decisions about the acceptability of risk-imposition on such parties cannot depend on the acquisition of informed consent. Such a consideration is a major reason for considering the treatment of children and incompetents separately. The relevance, and weight, of choices by proxies, guardians, or relatives I leave open here.

Just as it may be claimed that subjects are incapable of the understanding requisite to making an informed choice, it is often claimed that institutionalized subjects, though capable of such understanding, are not capable of making a substantially or entirely voluntary choice. I have in mind, for example, those competent persons who may live in a prison or who are in subordinate positions in the military. Relatedly, unassertive persons lacking much "ego strength" may be easily intimidated by spouses, bosses, or those in a position of authority, such as their physician, nurse, psychotherapist, professor, pimp, or thesis adviser. In some contexts refusal to "consent" carries a heavy price tag and this may preclude a fully voluntary choice, even in the absence of overt coercive threat. Such factors often provide a compelling reason to conclude that ostensibly voluntary consent is not such at all. Let us note this point, but set it aside here for our current concern is with capacity to understand. Let us suppose, then, that in our current deliberation there is no worry that voluntary choice has been subverted.

Focusing on competent persons who are able to choose freely, the claim that such subjects are incapable of requisite understanding is plausibly made only of a *subset* of such subjects. The stronger claim that no competent person is capable of making an informed

---

information so as to have the opportunity to make an informed choice, but an informed choice is simply one in which the patient is aware of information relevant to making a prudent decision, a subset of existing information; and the latter excludes full knowledge of the actual outcome. For this reason, Laforet's attack on the feasibility of informed consent in the experimental situation must be counted as an attack on a straw man. See Eugene Laforet, "The Fiction of Informed Consent," *Journal of the American Medical Association* 235, No. 15 (April 12, 1976), p. 1583.

choice would (in effect and for example) be tantamount to claiming that to make an informed choice about surgery one would have to be a surgeon, or at least have a modicum of medical training. This claim is so extreme, and so unreasonably stringent, that it deserves no serious consideration. Only some weaker claim about what is required for understanding a diagnosis or prospective treatment can be plausibly posed. If so, the claim that patients lack adequate understanding cannot be made plausibly of all patients. For this reason, any insistence that the informed consent condition cannot be satisfied is reasonable only with regard to a subset of all competent patients. It is evident, then, that the appeal to an inability to understand does not provide a reason for a *wholesale* rejection of the standard. Still, there may be a significant subset of otherwise competent persons who, arguably, lack the requisite ability. It cannot be denied that there are competent but barely literate individuals who are incapable of understanding explanations except when presented in highly simplified fashion; perhaps, some cannot understand sufficiently for informed choosing. One problem that arises here concerns what *counts* as making a particular informed choice. This is, in important part, a context-dependent question about which a great deal cannot be said in the abstract. It is hard to see an alternative to a case by case determination by the clinical practitioner. There are institutionalizable alternatives, however. The determination of possession of capacity to understand and the existence of reasonably informed choice could be made by others than the health-care professional who proposes a certain mode of treatment. These are in part empirical and practical questions. Although the law may require "getting informed consent" to a procedure, from the moral standpoint defended here, informed consent must be provided, if a subject so chooses, only by one capable of it; if a subject is incapable of it, after having access to a sensitive, clear, impartial, and reasonably comprehensive explanation of alternative procedures, risks, and benefits, then it is morally permissible to decide on treatment without it. When the law requires consent of those incapable, it is ill-conceived law. If correct, however, none of this undermines the claim that voluntary informed consent must be present to render morally permissible the imposition of risks on a competent subject.[26] That, of course, has been our central concern.

[26] Excluding those cases in which a subject's noncooperation would wrong others; justice may require the subject's cooperation (cf. criminal punishment), or allow imposition in the absence of consent.

The practical burden of attempting to explain matters necessary for informed consent adequately and fairly is related to another objection to the informed consent requirement, namely, that it is *too costly* to implement such a policy. I wish to give short shrift to this protoargument, not because costs are morally irrelevant but for the following reason. To treat a competent subject, in the absence of his voluntary informed consent, is to treat him as if he were incapable of making a choice. That is, it is to treat him in the same manner as incompetents are treated; his cognitive capacities and his outlook are simply bypassed. Even if the aim in withholding information is benevolent (we'll keep the patient's costs down), doing so contravenes the principle that competent subjects are owed a fair explanation of what is at stake. The subject is not only owed a fair explanation; for reasons mentioned earlier, he has a right to it, unless he has waived it. If the provision of a quite time-consuming explanation (what would be a fair explanation is a function in part of the magnitude of the risks involved) would involve wronging others (because, for example, access to medical care is cut off), then a case may be made for delimiting or, in extreme cases, omitting it. In such cases there would be a nonpaternalistic (and, *possibly*, adequate) ground for deviating from the informed consent requirement. However, standard cases are not of this sort, and the fact that a fair explanation may be more costly to the patient fails to justify omitting it. To appeal to the consideration of reducing or minimizing costs to the patient is an instance of the paternalistic appeal to harm-prevention (or good-promotion), an appeal we have already found wanting. Analogously, you would find it hardly persuasive if a car mechanic unilaterally were to go ahead, without your consent, and perform a "major operation" on your car, without explaining the diagnosis and proposed remedy, on the grounds that "it will cost you too much for me to explain it all."

4.5 *The Contractual Argument for Withholding Relevant Information*

So far we have tended to focus on cases in which a health-care professional, typically a physician, may consider withholding information relevant to the subject's choices and plans in one of two, loosely distinguished, ways. In one type of case a choice has to be made regarding mode of therapy. This is the more familiar and perhaps standard context. The other sort of situation is where the diagnosis is tragic and there is little or nothing which can be done to recover health, for example, should the patient be told that he has an incurable disease. Discussions of the informed consent requirement typically focus on the former type of case for obvious reasons, yet both raise the question of the permissibility of withholding significant information. So far I have argued against the permissibility of doing so in a wide range of familiar cases. There are cases, however, in which it is permissible to do so. These are not rightly thought of as "exceptions to our rule" (and, possibly, arbitrary). Rather they are built-in to our rule, as it were; that is, their permissibility follows from the principles defended here. Since I wish to defend what I label the *Contractual Argument for Withholding Medical Information* against Allen Buchanan's objections to it, let us first consider his clear formulation of the argument.

> The idea is that the physician-patient relationship is contractual and that the terms of this contract are such that the patient authorizes the physician to minimize harm to the patient (or his family) by whatever means he, the physician, deems necessary. Thus if the physician believes that the best way to minimize harm to the patient is to withhold information from him, he may do so without thereby wronging the patient. To wrong the patient the physician would either have to do something he was not authorized to do or fail to do something it was his duty to do and which was in his power to do. But in withholding information from the patient he is doing just what he is authorized to do. So he does the patient no wrong.[27]

Buchanan raises a series of objections against this argument. The first is one that may be brought against the claim that the physician may and ought to treat the patient in whatever way will be "least harmful," even in cases where there is no contractual agreement as described above. So a physician legitimately may withhold diagnostic information if he deems it the least harmful course of action. Buchanan objects that "it is very doubtful that the physician will or even could possess the psychiatric and moral knowledge required for a well-founded judgment about what will be least harmful for the patient."[28] Elsewhere he emphasizes that a physician's judgments about certain matters are problematic—for example, when the judgment is made that a patient is likely to become fearful and develop a despondency which may progress into depressive illness (or culminate in suicide) if certain information is

---

[27] Buchanan, "Medical Paternalism," p. 383.
[28] Ibid.

revealed to him (say he has terminal cancer). Such judgments, in Buchanan's view, as we noted earlier involve *psychiatric generalizations* made typically on the basis of scanty evidence. He claims, further, that *even if* a physician is in a position reliably to predict, he may simply be assuming that suicide "is not a rational choice" for the patient.[29] Buchanan is correct, I believe, in judging that the physician who decides to withhold information on such grounds must make difficult empirical judgments and also difficult evaluative judgments about which alternative will be "least harmful" on balance for the patient. Hence, one might *substantially agree*, as I have earlier agreed in discussing such problems, although two minor reservations are worth noting: (1) such considerations do not show that it is impossible for a conscientious and psychologically sensitive and well-trained physician to make such predictions, and (2) the patient *may* be in no better position than the physician in making such judgments—given the variety of experiences the physician may have had in observing such sequences of events.

More significant, perhaps, is the point that, as the Contract Argument is described, the patient has authorized the physician to minimize harm to the patient by *whatever means the physician deems necessary*. The contract is not and plausibly could not be one in which the physician is authorized to act only on *correct* judgments. It must be an authorization for the physician to act only on the basis of what *he believes to be* a well-founded judgment. If the physician does so, he does not violate the terms of the contract *even if*, as it turns out, his judgment is not well founded. That such judgments are difficult to make or that a physician may have failed to make one would not, *thereby*, show that he has done a wrong to his patient. An unwise judgment is not necessarily an unconscientious, negligent, or reckless one.

A second objection proposed by Buchanan is that not all patients understand their relationship with their physician to be one where they have authorized *him (or her)* to withhold information when deemed necessary to minimize harm.[30] So the physician, it is implied, cannot assume the existence of such a contract with a particular patient unless it is clear that this patient has contracted freely and with full knowledge that he has done so. These points are surely correct. It should be clear, however, that neither supposition

[29] Ibid., p. 379.
[30] Ibid., p. 384.

undermines the Contractual Argument for the latter purports to justify withholding information *only* when there *is* a contractual authorization to do so. Again, one can only advise caution for physicians who may be tempted to assume authorization when there is inadequate reason to make such an assumption. Buchanan's claims may also be taken to urge patients to make explicit agreements with physicians so that there are no false or unfounded assumptions about the reciprocal rights and duties of the contracting parties. Since such matters are often not well defined, the point is well taken. Once more, it does not strike a blow against the Contractual Argument.

Buchanan presses his point further by claiming that if the physician inquires in each case whether the patient wishes to authorize the withholding of certain information "he will defeat the purpose of the authorization by undermining the patient's trust."[31] If correct, this claim shows, not that the Contractual Argument is unsound, but that such contracting is not likely to occur or that there is a reason to avoid forming such contracts. Hence, claims that such a contract was agreed upon ought to be viewed skeptically. The claim that such inquiries do or would undermine the patient's trust is itself, I think, a dubious empirical generalization, although I cannot disprove it. It is not unlikely that a patient, if asked by his physician whether he wishes to have possibly disturbing diagnostic information withheld from him when the physician may judge its revelation harmful to him, would be inclined to judge that his physician is conscientious and principled, that he is a person unwilling to treat a patient in a presumptively wrong manner in the absence of his express consent to such a policy. Such an inquiry well may confirm a patient's hope that his physician respects the patient's right to decide how he shall be treated and will not treat him in a suspect way just because the physician judges it to be "for the patient's own good." That is, the inquiry would support the claim that the physician was *not* inclined toward invidious paternalism.

Buchanan claims, however, that there is yet "a more serious difficulty."[32] He states that even extreme advocates of medical paternalism must agree that there must be some limits on the contractual relationship between patient and physician. In particular, the patient needs to be able to determine whether the physician is

[31] Ibid., p. 387.
[32] Ibid., p. 384.

observing the limitations imposed by the contractual relationship. If the patient authorizes the physician to withhold information, he may deprive himself of the information necessary to determine *whether or not* those limits are being observed. In Buchanan's view such an authorization would show that "(a) one did not view the contract as being conditional or that (b) one did not take seriously the possibility that the conditions of the contract might be violated or that (c) one simply did not care whether the conditions were violated."[33] Thus, Buchanan concludes that it is unreasonable to authorize the physician to withhold information when he (or she) sees fit. There are difficulties with this line of thought. Surely, it cannot be maintained that the patient should do nothing which would make it impossible or difficult to determine whether contractual limits are being observed. If so, the patient would never submit to anesthesia which would, after all, impair his ability to oversee a surgeon's procedure. More importantly, it is possible that a patient might authorize the withholding of information and yet the conditions mentioned in (a), (b), and (c) are not true of the patient. For example, I might want certain information revealed to me and other information not revealed. Recognizing the benefits frequently associated with the "placebo effect" I reasonably may prefer not to be told when a placebo has been prescribed as part of my treatment. Also, I may recognize my penchant for undue anxiety and worry over the fact that certain of my symptoms are suggestive but not conclusive evidence of the presence of some dreaded disease. Hence, I may choose to remain ignorant of such matters until the physician is certain of its presence. Further, if my affairs are in order, I may even prefer to live out my last days falsely hopeful of recovery, even when the physician is certain that I have terminal cancer. These preferences for ignorance with regard to a certain range of information may be made clear to the physician in a contract. With regard to certain matters I may authorize the physician to use his best judgment about whether it will be least harmful to disclose or to withhold information. Ignorance is not always bliss, but an individual may prefer ignorance under certain conditions. The nature of the contract made would obviously depend on one's preferences and one's degree of trust and confidence in the judgment in one's physician.

Thus, whether or not the physician wrongfully withholds information will depend on the nature of the contract. It may authorize

[33] Ibid., p. 385.

and require disclosure of certain information *and also* authorize and require the withholding of other information. An interesting result shows up here. If I contract *not* to be informed of terminal cancer should I have it and the physician later decides that my *not* being informed of this fact is more harmful to me on balance than my being informed and he thus informs me, his *disclosure* would be *paternalistic interference* with my chosen course, with my freedom to choose what information I shall receive. Hence, it is misleading to focus solely on the cases of withholding information, or giving misinformation, from paternalistic motives as actions requiring justification. Disclosing information may also be a paternalistic act and, possibly, an unjustifiable form of paternalism.

Buchanan maintains that "it is unreasonable to authorize the physician to withhold information when he sees fit."[34] If he means "whenever, without qualification," I certainly agree. I have tried to show how it may be reasonable to authorize withholding information on certain matters. Withholding information need not be invidious paternalistic interference, and, indeed, disclosure may be. That depends on the nature of the contract, whether its authorizations are maximally prudent or not.

One further critical point regarding the Contractual Argument has as its target a view previously held by myself. In an earlier assessment of one part of Buchanan's essay I maintained that if the patient validly consents and contracts with the physician for the latter to withhold information under certain circumstances then, in complying with the contractual arrangement, the physician does not interfere with the patient.[35] If that were true, there would be no paternalistic interference. Hence, such a withholding of information would not be an instance of paternalism and not subject to the difficulties standardly associated with paternalistic acts. Nor would the case mentioned be describable as "medical paternalism."

Although my moral conviction remains unchanged, I now think it is more reasonable to describe matters somewhat differently (as noted in Section 2.4). As I have defined 'paternalistic behavior' (see Section 1.3) an agent's commission or omission must be contrary to a subject's operative preference, intention, or disposition to count as paternalistic. Hence, we need to distinguish two sets of cases which I earlier assimilated. If S has not only previously given

[34] Ibid.

[35] The earlier essay of my own is "The Contractual Argument for Withholding Medical Information," *Philosophy & Public Affairs* 9, No. 2 (Winter, 1980), pp. 198–205. It is reprinted in *Medicine and Moral Philosophy*; see Note 24.

valid consent to the physician's withholding certain information but it *also* is not contrary to S's preference or intention that it is withheld when the physician does so, then the physician's doing so is *not* a paternalistic omission. Rather his (or her) doing so is a form of nonpaternalistic cooperation. Consider now a second type of case. Here S, earlier, validly consented to the withholding of the information (and has not revoked such consent) but later wishes to know. In this case, if the physician withholds the information in order to prevent distress to S, his (or her) doing so *is* paternalistic; however, given the Restricted Consent Principle, his (or her) omission is justified paternalistic behavior. The former case does not involve interference; the latter does, but it is a permissible paternalistic intervention.

Since this conclusion is likely to be somewhat controversial, a few further comments are in order. It might be objected that we have spoken of a patient's right to have relevant information disclosed and a correlative duty of the physician to disclose such. Is there not then an inconsistency? The reply, perhaps evident, is that such a right is possessed by the patient unless waived by the patient. This is, I take it, the function of his consenting to the physician's nondisclosure. The physician is, therefore, released from his normal duty to disclose. The term 'deception' like 'paternalistic' tends to imply or presuppose a negative evaluation of an act so labeled. However, on the view defended here there can be justified deception. This conclusion is not, of course, the utilitarian-like claim that deception may be justifiable if overall net utility is promoted; rather the justification is backward looking—to the fact that voluntary informed consent has been given to it. On reflection, the result is intuitively plausible. After all, people often find deception mutually agreeable and something short of a cardinal sin; compare, for example, the deception involved in costume parties, playing poker, disguised gifts at holidays, or closer to our concerns: a pregnant woman's preference to be "deceived" about the sex of the fetus she carries (a fact which may be known from amniocentesis).[36] When contemplating such cases it is worth contrasting "consensual deception" with ordinary deception which typically involves an intention to engender false beliefs in a nonconsenting party. Not all deception, however, is indicative of "cheating" or "dishonesty" (in the sense of being untrustworthy or lacking integrity).

[36] This apt example was supplied by Diane Lauver, R.N., M.S.N.

4.6 A Proposed Modification of the Consent Requirement

We have regarded the Necessity Claim as the core of the Doctrine of Informed Consent; it may be worth recalling that the claim has been defined:

> A's doing X (an activity involving risks to S) to S is morally permissible *only if* S validly (voluntarily and knowingly) consents to A's doing X to S.

We have defended the view that the presence of such consent along with certain other factors (e.g., scientifically supportable proposed therapeutic modes of treatment, and so on) is sufficient to render permissible A's doing X. Further, we have argued that deception can be justified under certain conditions. A similar mode of argument also could justify the use of restraining devices or the use of force; recall our earlier discussions of prior consent; see also the discussion of Odysseus (Section 5.7). Somewhat surprisingly, perhaps, the necessity of informed consent does not create an absolute moral barrier to any and all performances of such actions. On the other hand, its prohibitive implications are nontrivial, and these may also be sufficiently clear by this point. Such normally invasive and normally autonomy-subverting acts are rendered permissible, in part, by the competent subject's valid consent to them; hence, in such an event autonomy is respected and people may chart their own course in pursuit of their own conception of the good.

All of this provides a reason for concluding that a strong case may be made for modifying the *standard legal requirements for informed consent*, modifying them in a direction which would weaken them somewhat. The "weakening" is, from our viewpoint, actually a "strengthening" in the sense of creating a more defensible set of requirements. The modification I shall propose takes a bit of explaining; so, I shall state the proposal somewhat later. The usual focal point in discussing what a subject may consent to is some *specific* proposed mode of therapy, such as a series of injections, radiation therapy, a dietary regime, a surgical operation, and so on. Standard legal requirements, such as those of DHEW, require provision of an explanation of such procedures, their attendant risks and benefits, an explanation of alternatives, their risks and benefits, and an offer to answer questions. The main point is that competent persons must be in a position to make an informed voluntary decision about whether to undergo a specific proposed therapeutic procedure. We can distinguish two sorts of decisions a subject may make. One is whether to undergo treatment T. Let us call such a choice of *specific* mode of therapy a *first-order choice*. Recent legal requirements regarding informed consent place a burden on the health-care professional to provide the information that a *prudent and reasonable person would want to have* in order to make such a decision and not just that amount which "standard practice" provides.[37] Such first-order choices can be distinguished from a *second-order* choice which one might make, namely, deciding to let someone (typically an "expert decider") effectively determine which *first-order* choice to make. It is worth recalling that we often choose to make second-order rather than first-order choices. For example, we direct the mechanic to fix the car, or to fix it if the cost is below a certain sum. We often choose not to be informed about the variety of first-order choices which have to be made, for example, to repair or replace the generator and, if the latter, whether to put in a new or a used one. We may make no voluntary or informed choices about the latter. Rather, we make a voluntary and perhaps informed second-order choice about which mechanic to employ and whether to give him or her a "blank check" ("do whatever is necessary") or some more constrained permission and directive. On reflection it is clear that we make many of our choices at this level. We choose a bus or a restaurant but "leave the driving" (or cooking) to the driver or the chef. I resist the temptation to add further examples.

There are often good reasons for making second-order instead of first-order choices. Most obviously, making well-informed and prudent first-order choices may require a level of expertise which is costly to come by. Few of us can become skilled physicians, accountants, lawyers, mechanics, carpenters, electricians, and so on. It would be "misleading" to describe such cases as ones in which we *forfeit* our autonomy although in one respect we surrender it with respect to directly controlling the first-order decisions to be made. I say "misleading" because the notion of forfeiture of autonomy, or of rights, strongly suggests that one who forfeits ceases to have certain prerogatives as a result of inadvertent or wrongful acts. For example, one may forfeit one's privileges at the

---

[37] See, for example, "Changes in 'Informed Consent' Doctrine," *Medical World News* (February 9, 1973); see also Canterbury v. Spence, U.S. Court of Appeals, District of Columbia Circuit, May 19, 1972. An excerpt is reprinted in Thomas Mappes and Jane Zembaty, eds., *Biomedical Ethics* (New York: McGraw-Hill, 1981), pp. 78–81.

health spa by forgetting to pay one's dues. In contrasting cases of a voluntary, deliberate choice to give up prerogatives we more naturally speak of a *waiving* of rights or a *delegation* of decision-making powers to others. Indeed, one way of *exercising* one's autonomous capacities is to delegate certain powers of choice to others. If we wish to speak of a surrender of autonomy here, it is worth remembering that in such a case there is, or can be, an *autonomous* surrender of autonomy; such a choice may be voluntary, informed, and highly prudent. It need not be a passive and servile "giving in" to some form of intimidation or duress.

Consider now the implications of the distinctions we have drawn. A patient may choose to let his physician decide which therapeutic procedure is to be pursued, to make the requisite first-order choice. He may refuse to learn about or even listen to proffered explanations of the sort the physician legally owes him. Such a choice may or may not be foolish. In any case, the result may be that the physician makes the first-order choice and the patient does not. Hence, the patient does *not* give voluntary, informed consent to the specific therapy undertaken. Rather, if he has given voluntary informed consent, it is consent to the physician's deciding which therapeutic procedure is to be followed. Would such a scenario violate the Necessity Claim? Would it be morally problematic? To consider the first question, it would, I propose, not violate the Necessity Claim for there are risks in letting the physician decide the course of treatment and, by assumption, the patient has given voluntary, informed consent to that policy. Further, there is not anything morally problematic about so doing from the standpoint of the theory I have defended. The physician's deciding *may* be "medical paternalism," but it is permissible. Analogously, in a similar case in which we voluntarily and wittingly delegate powers of choice to an electrician or mechanic, the resulting acts could be described as "electrical paternalism" or "mechanical paternalism." These are curious expressions, to be sure, but recognition of that may help undermine the groundless assumption that so-called medical paternalism is invariably invidious.

The distinctions marked make it clear, then, that a patient may retain what we might call "second-order autonomy" even though relinquishing what may be called "first-order autonomy." Correlatively, the fact that a patient does not give voluntary, informed consent to a first-order choice does not show that he has had his autonomy violated or that his right to direct his own life within the restricted domain has been infringed or otherwise disregarded.

Hence, it is possible both for a patient to retain his (second-order) autonomy and for a health-care professional to respect that autonomy by making first-order decisions within the domain of permissibility created by the competent patient's choice that the professional make such decisions. We are now in a position to draw a more specific conclusion about the standard legal requirement which requires, as commonly understood, that the health-care professional explain the risks and benefits of specific therapies and proceed with one only if the patient gives voluntary, informed consent to that procedure. My proposal is simply that all that is morally required is the presence of such consent to specific procedures *or* voluntary, informed consent to the professional's making the first-order choice. As I have interpreted the Necessity Claim, such a proposed requirement can be construed as compatible with a broad but natural interpretation of the Necessity Claim; in short, "voluntary, informed consent" remains necessary to render permissible the chosen procedure. However, the traditional policy of legally requiring consent to *specific* therapeutic procedures is, from our standpoint, too stringent. The requirement could be weakened without moral compromise.

Consider a further reason in favor of weakening the traditional policy. There are, as we noted, other areas of our lives where we delegate powers to make first-order choices to others. Many such first-order choices have consequences of equal or greater importance than a variety of first-order choices left to health-care professionals. In some cases there is no nontrivial legal requirement that the subject be carefully apprised, by the professional in question, of the risks and benefits of a proposed remedy, for example, by an accountant, architect, or car mechanic. In other cases there are legal requirements, albeit ones less rigorous in nature than those governing patient/health-care professional interaction. There is evidently a certain puzzle about the existence of such disparate policies. Why should we require both provision of detailed explanations of risks and benefits of "remedial" procedures and voluntary, informed consent prior to implementation of such procedures in the field of health care and not require analogously stringent requirements in other cases where competent parties enlist professional aid to deal with matters often of considerable importance to their welfare? One response is that there is a radically significant difference between what is at stake when one is relying on professional help in the case of health care and what is at stake when one is hiring an automobile mechanic. Hence, the two areas are so importantly different that it is reasonable that more stringent legal requirements prevail in the area of health care. This point, however, is not fully persuasive since, with regard to some health problems and their remedies, there is much less at stake than with certain problems not directly bearing on the client's health (cf. management of athlete's foot and investing a large inheritance). If it is conceded that it is often the case that there is as much at stake outside of health-care contexts as there is within, then one of two policies would seem reasonable: either have no legal requisite of first-order consent in the two areas or have equally stringent requirements in both (at least when the interests at risk are comparable). We have argued that voluntary, informed consent at some level is necessary; in its absence, presumptively wrongful acts (e.g., imposing risks of harm) may be paternalistic, and also impermissible. Legally requiring voluntary, informed consent at some level is defensible on the ground that it helps prevent impermissible forms of paternalism (or impermissible nonpaternalistic acts). It is plausible that there be legal requirements for such consent, equally stringent ones, in and out of health-care contexts when there are nontrivial and comparable interests at stake. One alternative is to introduce more stringent requirements outside the health-care domain; in some cases that well may be desirable. Another alternative is to weaken the standard requirement in health care by dropping the insistence on first-order consent within that domain. The greater social and legal tolerance for letting competent persons delegate first-order decision making outside the health-care field is, I believe, the right policy for reasons we have discussed, for example, it allows competent persons to direct their own lives in ways that are reasonable and efficient. To that extent it seems that analogous legal requirements should prevail in health-care contexts of comparable importance.

In some cases what is at stake in medical contexts is life itself or matters of tremendous importance to the patient. When so much is at stake it is hard to imagine a competent person who simply would wish to "leave it up to the physician" and choose to remain substantially uninformed about the first-order choice to be made. Hence, legally requiring that such a patient consent (or dissent) to the specific procedure proposed is likely to impose no burden on the competent patient. As noted earlier, there also may be psychological or other health benefits to the patient when he understands what is to be done, what would be involved in patient-compliance with the proposed regimen, and can regard himself as the final arbiter in decisions about rather specific measures to be taken. For these sorts of reasons, among others, a tempting case can be made for retaining a stringent legal requirement of first-order consent in cases where so much is at stake. For reasons discussed, there is no compelling case to be made for doing so with regard to less important cases. In the latter cases a legal requirement of second-order consent seems sufficient to render the procedure permissible. From a legislative standpoint, ranking cases in order of comparative importance generates some sticky taxonomic problems, but not insurmountable ones. Further, there are benefits to be obtained, benefits of efficiency which, unlike those often gained, are obtainable without infringing the rights of competent persons. Such an alternative has not been adequately explored, and has not, I believe, partly because of confusion and controversy about how to distinguish permissible and impermissible forms of paternalism and different levels of consent.

One conclusion to be drawn is that nondisclosure of information necessary for a competent patient's making a first-order informed choice about treatment *need* not undermine a patient's autonomy. What is morally required (*perhaps* what should be legally required as well) is that such information be provided unless the patient has voluntarily agreed to forego it. This point should not be understood as the claim that a patient must be supplied with relevant information unless he "voluntarily waives his right to informed consent." His right to decide important matters remains; his right to give or withhold second-order consent remains even if he waives his right to make first-order choices. We need not and, I maintain, ought not *compel* the patient to receive and process information relevant to making an informed first-order choice. To do so, for his own good, would constitute unjustified paternalism. This claim does not, however, entail that a physician or others would act wrongly in seeking openly and fairly to persuade a patient *not* to forego his right to receive relevant information or that he would be foolish to delegate the powers of first-order choice to others. Furthermore, a legal requirement which sought to guarantee that there was either first-order or second-order consent may necessitate disclosing a modicum of relevant information to the patient in order to *determine* whether his apparently voluntary second-order choice to delegate the first-order choice to others is actually voluntary and informed. For that second-order choice to be voluntary and informed, the patient must have some grasp of the nature and importance of the decision-making power he is delegating to others.

Beyond making sure of this, pressing further details on the patient against his will seems neither obligatory nor permissible.

A central thrust of much of our recent discussion is in the direction of encouraging appropriate contractual arrangements between patient and health-care providers (as well as in other client-professional arrangements). I have defended the view that appropriate contracting can circumvent impermissible, unilateral, paternalistic decisions and policies, and also secures advantages to patient and professional. Our focus has continued to be only on competent persons who are, in principle, capable of looking out for their own interests as they conceive them. The objection may be raised to the view proposed that, in spite of the restriction to competent parties, the law should not allow the range of contractual freedom which we have defended as morally permissible. In defense of this objection it may be noted that, historically, allowing freedom of contract has often led to a wide range of abuses. For this reason the law has commonly seen fit to (1) place restrictions on who may participate in legally binding contracts, (2) regard certain contracts as legally invalid unless certain conditions regarding their formation are satisfied (e.g., the absence of force, fraud, intimidation, and so on), and (3) regard certain contracts as legally invalid if their "content" included certain types of performances (e.g., to engage in restraint of trade, to conspire to assassinate, and so on). Such restrictions seem designed to prevent wrongful exploitation of one party to a contract by another or to prevent the contracting parties from wronging others. To the extent that minors or the mentally incompetent are disallowed to contract, the primary rationale would appear to be paternalistic. Our restricted focus on contracts between competent persons bypasses worries which we reasonably would entertain about allowing minors or the mentally incompetent to participate in substantive binding contracts; competent persons are at least capable, in principle, of looking out for their own interests in the manner they choose. And we have argued that unconsented-to paternalistic interference (e.g., by legal constraints) with their so doing is unjustified. We have, in addition, insisted on the necessity of voluntary, informed consent of either the first- or second-order variety. This consideration supports the existence of legal constraints [of type (2)] to guarantee that such consent is *given*, and not merely that the patient's signature on a consent form is *gotten*.

There are two further general worries related to the purpose behind the constraints mentioned in (2) above. One concerns the

DOCTRINE OF INFORMED CONSENT

effects of *institutionalization* on competent patients with regard to whether they can freely consent or dissent to proposed modes of treatment, or, alternatively, freely enter contractual arrangements. It is arguable that those who are patients in hospitals or nursing homes, subordinates in military organizations, or inmates in penal institutions (I do not suggest these situations do not exhibit significant differences) are less free or not free at all to refuse participation in therapeutic (or nontherapeutic) procedures proposed or urged by those in authority. Persons in the former categories are, it is claimed, unavoidably intimidated by the power, authority, and/ or expertise of those who manage such institutions. Given this radical inequality, no one in a subordinate position truly could give fully voluntary consent to proposals of "superiors," for they are not free to refuse.[38] Such a view is supported by those empirical investigations which reveal the existence of the widespread use of coercive techniques to generate compliance—especially in the case of prison inmates.[39] The more "total" the institution, the stronger is the empirical presumption that those controlled by it are not free voluntarily to decide whether to undergo a certain procedure. However, it is not *analytically* true that persons in such institutions are unfree. Hence, there is a genuine worry that legal constraints which would disallow or disregard their consent (on the ground that it *could not* be voluntarily given) constitute impermissible paternalism. The nature of appropriate constraints to prevent exploitation and also wrongful paternalism depends in an important way on the specific institutional situation in question. It is my purpose here to identify only the moral considerations relevant to shaping, or morally assessing, legal policy and not to examine specific institutional practices.

Another worry which supports the legal constraints on contracting mentioned in (2) concerns more directly the relationship between the health-care professional and the patient. Even in less all-encompassing institutions or outside such contexts, patients can be under enormous pressure to agree to a proposed procedure. Patients are sometimes weak, weary, and discouraged due to illness

[38] The courts have sometimes concluded that the circumstances of institutionalization are "inherently coercive." For example, see the discussion of Kaimowitz v. Department of Mental Health, Circuit Court of Wayne County, Michigan (July, 1973) found in Fred Cohen, *The Law of Deprivation of Liberty* (St. Paul, Minn.: West, 1980), pp. 543–547.

[39] See Alexander Capron, "Medical Research in Prisons: Should a Moratorium Be Called?," in Beauchamp and Walters, *Contemporary Issues in Bioethics*, 1st ed., pp. 497–501.

211

or injury; reluctant to question the expert; insufficiently assertive to assess alternatives; eager for the reward or "strokes" they may expect from ready agreement; disinclined to speak their minds in a way that may suggest suspicion, distrust, or lack of total confidence in those who may have labored long and hard for their benefit; fearful of disdainful responses by health-care professionals of an authoritarian old-school bent. Some competent persons are unduly acquiescent, if not servile, and legal regulations are unlikely to alter that.[40] Indeed, the occurrence of undue pressure or intimidation originating from the features just noted are most worrisome since legal constraints are not liable effectively to prevent wrongful paternalism, for example, situations in which there is only a facade of voluntary, informed consent. Again, it is not my aim to sketch ways of more effectively securing the opportunity for genuinely voluntary contractual arrangements. I am proposing that overly restrictive legal constraints on contracts can themselves be instances of wrongful paternalism, although too lenient a set of constraints can permit wrongful paternalism by health-care professionals and others. The former prohibits legally effective contracts which are morally permissible; the latter allows legally binding contractual arrangements which are morally impermissible since they only appear to embody valid consent by the subject.

As noted earlier, the law also sees fit to deem invalid contracts which are agreements to perform certain types of acts, for example, engaging in restraint of trade—even if the contract is not defective with regard to (1) who may contract, or (2) the manner in which the agreement comes about. This judgment about the content of contracts initially may not seem relevant to our concerns since the acts which people may not legally contract to perform are typically wrongs to others, and there are, therefore, reasonable nonpaternalistic grounds for prohibiting such contracts (though the contracting itself may fall in the hazy area of "criminal attempts"). However, it is often thought, as we noted in the last chapter, that there are acts wherein people wrong themselves (e.g., suicide), that the act of assisting persons to perform such acts is wrong, and that some acts to which competent persons validly consent are

---

[40] Compare the attitude of one "consenting" patient who said "My philosophy in the Navy was 'yours not to reason why, yours but to do or die.' You will find that people who have been in the service for a long time think that way. That may not be a good outlook, but it is the way I have been raised." From John Fletcher, "Realities of Patient Consent to Medical Research," *Hastings Center Studies* 1, No. 2 (1973), p. 45.

wrong (e.g., voluntary active euthanasia) even if no one beyond those parties is wronged. At least in the last sorts of cases contractual arrangements may be made, and one question is whether they should be legally prohibited. In cases in which there is no plausible nonpaternalistic ground for doing so (I leave open here what sorts of cases these are), we must ask whether there is a legitimate paternalistic ground for doing so or, more realistically, continuing to do so. There are various grounds for constraining the formation of contracts in certain ways. However, if no reasonable complaint can be made regarding the competence of the parties, factors undermining voluntary, informed consent, or wrongs to others, is there any reason to assume that we should not legally permit, for example, mutual suicide pacts, or a contractual arrangement between a patient and physician involving the latter's killing (or allowing to die) the patient under mutually agreed upon conditions? Since questions about the morality of suicide and voluntary euthanasia involve substantive matters themselves, I shall postpone discussion of *contractual* agreements regarding euthanasia to a somewhat later point (in Chapter 5). There we also investigate the morality of suicide prevention and whether a person could ever have a right to be killed—and a physician a correlative duty to do so.

4.7 Balancing Conflicting Interests

Although our almost exclusive focus is on proposed paternalistic grounds for interference with competent persons, we have, from the outset, observed that there are often legitimate nonpaternalistic grounds for interference with or constraint of competent persons. Given the nature of the typically therapeutic contexts of patients, it is natural that arguments purporting to justify overriding or bypassing consent in such contexts will appeal to paternalistic grounds, and, hence, arguments of the sorts we have examined. It is beyond my purpose to investigate all the nonpaternalistic grounds for constraining competent patients in medical contexts. However, it is sometimes thought, and argued, that there is little reason to worry over whether or not this or that paternalistically based defense of interference is justified, since such philosophical fastidiousness about paternalistic strategies of justification can be set aside—set aside because there is a legitimate, familiar, and nonpaternalistic ground for bypassing consent in a variety of cases, namely, one which attends to the interests of others. To take a small step in the direction of placing the dispute over paternalism toward patients in a larger perspective, it is useful briefly to examine this seemingly promising way of rendering practically insignificant the questions we may have over the limits of justifiable paternalism. We shall, therefore, examine one nonpaternalistic strategy purporting to justify certain types of acts, instances of which are often paternalistically motivated and for which, as we have seen, paternalistic justifications are offered.

The type of reasoning to which I allude, one I label *the interests-balancing approach*, involves a decision-making strategy which is inviting to jurisprudents who are comfortable with the familiar mode of resolving the constitutionality of state laws by appealing to the principle that certain important individual interests or rights can be overridden if and only if there is a compelling state interest in doing so. Individual interests which often are at issue in such disputes are the individual's interest in privacy, freedom of thought and expression, and bodily and psychic integrity. Important state interests often recognized are, for example, the interest in maintaining domestic tranquillity, national security, a decent society, or ensuring fair trials. Important constitutional disputes are often resolved by the U.S. Supreme Court's determination that the interest of individuals is not outweighed by competing state interests (e.g., Griswold v. Connecticut, in which a state statute prohibiting the assisting or counseling of persons with regard to the use of contraceptives was ruled unconstitutional) or, conversely, that there is a compelling state interest which outweighs competing individual interests (e.g., Paris Adult Theatre I v. Slaton, in which the Supreme Court ruled constitutional state regulation of access to and use of obscene materials). On the interest-balancing approach, then, it is appropriate and necessary to take into account and weigh relevant interests at stake in a given controversy. It is worth examining the representative line of argument set forward by Alan Meisel, one designed to show that it is sometimes permissible to proceed in the absence of informed consent or, in some cases, even in the presence of dissent.[41] I will set out Meisel's argument in his somewhat informal manner prior to any analysis of it.

Meisel recognizes both "procedural interests" of the individual in deciding about his medical destiny and "substantive interests"

---

[41] Alan Meisel, "The 'Exceptions' to the Informed Consent Doctrine . . . ," pp. 413-488.

of the individual in privacy, bodily integrity, and psychic integrity. As he poses matters

> The purpose of requiring the patient's consent to treatment is to protect his physical and psychical integrity against unwanted invasions, and to permit the patient to act as an autonomous, self-determining being. The duty of disclosure aids in realization of these goals by enabling (though neither assuring nor requiring) the patient to make the decision whether to be treated both on the basis of information about the treatment which is supplied by the doctor and information about other concerns subjective to the patient, to which only he presumably has access.[42]

The mentioned interests of individual patients must, on Meisel's view, be balanced against competing social values, namely, the interests of others, interests he classifies as (1) the interest of family and friends in the individual's health, (2) the interest of society in the health of the individual, and (3) the interest of the health professions. In explaining (1) he notes that "we are pained when we must contemplate a loved one suffering because he has chosen to reject a course of medical treatment which might have offered him relief or because he has chosen to pursue a course of treatment which we believe to be erroneous—possibly because it might prolong a painful terminal illness, or because we believe it inferior to some other form of treatment."[43] With regard to (2), Meisel notes that society often promotes a societal interest "at the expense of individualistic values," for example, by fluoridating public water, allowing deductions for medical care, enforcing a quarantine and motorcycle helmet laws, and allowing involuntary civil commitment and involuntary blood transfusions.[44] Meisel, enraptured by the apparent kindness, permissibility, and desirability of such policies, continues

> This interest is most diametrically opposed to individualism, for in effect the state is saying "we know better than you what is best for you." This interest is not malevolent; quite the contrary, it is highly beneficient. It says to the person about to jump off a bridge that there is hope, that we do care about him, and that life might be better if it were given another

[42] Ibid., pp. 420–421.
[43] Ibid., p. 423.
[44] Ibid., pp. 423, 424.

chance; it says to the psychotic patient who refuses to take an anti-psychotic medication that the medication will make his tormenting hallucinations go away; and it says to the person with a ruptured appendix who faces *certain* death unless operated upon, but who refuses to undergo surgery nonetheless because of the fear of the *minute* risk of death from anesthesia, that his fear of death has dictated the wrong result and that he will be better off with surgery than without.[45]

The third interest, noted by Meisel, is that of the health professionals "whose ethos demands strong adherence to the value of the promotion of health."[46] In this regard, he observes that health-care professionals believe that decisions regarding treatment are *technical* ones; further, since "the patient is often in pain, he has an emotional involvement in the decision-making process which may not be conducive to rational participation"—and, even if not ill, the fact that his well-being is at stake means that "he may not be able to function as an objective, detached decision-maker."[47]

In view of the sorts of competing interests noted, ones that, in Meisel's view, militate against "unfettered individualism," he concludes strongly that

> If there is to be disclosure and participatory decision-making, it must be governed by a standard of medical practice, guided by the doctor's professional training and moral commitment to "do no harm" rather than by a single-minded concern for individualism which is ultimately destructive of the health of the individual himself and possibly the well-being of other persons. It is the responsibility of the physician, on the basis of his education, training, experience, and allegiance to medical professional values, to determine what the patient most needs to ameliorate a particular condition. Once the physician makes this decision, the patient is obliged, for his own good, to cooperate with the physician in accepting treatment.[48]

Meisel's general line of reasoning is widely employed, and, for that reason, deserves examination. In the final analysis and despite its seductiveness, it is, I shall argue, not acceptable. If by saying that some policy, P, is in S's interest we mean that S will be better off if P occurs, and better off in the sense of having needs met *or*

---

[45] Ibid., p. 425.
[46] Ibid., p. 426.
[47] Ibid.
[48] Ibid., p. 429.

desires satisfied, then we may agree that friends or family, society, and health professionals often have an interest in what sort of treatment is extended to a patient or, relatedly, what sort of choice a patient makes regarding treatment. This use of "having an interest" is, of course, quite *broad*, since it allows that one *has an interest* in the destiny of *anything* so long as one has a desire regarding its future states. For example, if I desire that the Pope cut his fingernails then an interest of mine is at stake in regard to decisions affecting the length of the Pope's fingernails. Of course, it may be claimed that if I will not be greatly offended or become distraught by the Pope's failure to cut his fingernails, then my interest is not a weighty one; at best, it is a peripheral interest of mine. It seems reasonable, then, to distinguish roughly between *fundamental* and *peripheral interests* which a person may have—roughly along the lines of how significantly the fulfillment of the interest (or its nonfulfillment) will affect the possessor of the interest. This may depend, in turn, on how highly ranked is the need or desire in an individual's hierarchy of needs or desires.

Given the distinction between fundamental and peripheral interests, it is necessary to ask how weighty are the interests of persons, other than the patient, in a determination of the treatment of the patient—as compared with the interests of the patient. The patient's interests, of course, include not only an interest in psychic and bodily integrity but his not unrelated interest in being able to direct his own life. Consider the interests of family and friends. Such interests may or may not be weighty ones; they often are weighty. However, in some cases families have been known to prefer the demise of a senile, deteriorating relative whose care is financially burdensome. Such an interest may be a weighty one, but this hardly seems a compelling reason to terminate the patient's life. I am calling attention to the fact that even the weighty interests of others do not necessarily constitute a good reason to override the preferences or interests of a third party. One might object that I have focused on a perverse example. Consider, then, a case where another person makes a choice which will cause you serious distress or emotional pain, or would do so if one does not somehow prevent the making of such a choice. We earlier noted the case in which you love another but he (or she) chooses to marry someone else. In this type of situation your interest is indeed weighty, and it is conceivable, we may suppose, that the loved person's choice will bring him (her) less satisfaction than it will cause you dissatisfaction. Is it permissible, then, somehow to sacrifice a basic interest? Should the prerogatives of competent persons to direct their own lives without *wronging* others be constrained in an invasive manner on the ground that their doing so will, in fact, undermine or fail to promote a fundamental interest of others? We must, I maintain, answer negatively. Such a response is reinforced by reflection on further points. In contemplating whether a rapist's act is permissible, should we assign any weight or any nontrivial weight to the fact, if it is one, that the rapist's interests are promoted by his act? As John Rawls has observed, in his critique of utilitarianism, it is a mistake to think that the morality of such interventions is to be decided by assigning moral weight to the various interests of the parties involved.[49] One might concede the point that a person's interest (possibly the rapist's) is fundamental (quite important to the possessor, and "weighty" in that respect) but deny that it is morally weighty, or even morally relevant, in determining whose interest should be allowed to prevail. In the case of potentially stressed, beneficent-minded relatives, their interests may seem less maleficent or not maleficent at all. However, as in the case of your nonmaleficent interest in wanting to marry another, the existence of such a "legitimate interest" seems to deserve little or no moral weight in comparison with the importance of the interest of a competent person in being able to direct his own life in ways that do not wrong others.

In passing, we note that there is an analogous and recalcitrant problem concerning whether to criminalize "offensive actions." Familiar and important problems concern whether to prohibit neo-Nazis from parading the swastika in Jewish communities or allowing other forms of freedom of expression which deeply offend others. It is worth noting here that in some cases people take offense, and their interest in not being offended is undermined, when others act in ways generally deemed permissible and innocuous, for example, those who sincerely believe that plants can suffer pain may be distraught at my wanton pruning of my Japanese maple trees. My basic point is simply that it is too simple to assume that the fact that an act undermines a significant interest of others affords a compelling reason to prohibit the act. If it were, the sphere of autonomy of many persons would become minuscule.[50]

[49] John Rawls, *A Theory of Justice* (Cambridge, Mass.: Belknap Press of Harvard University, 1971), p. 31.
[50] A discussion of this problem may be found in my "Coercive Restraint of Offensive Actions."

Earlier we observed that sometimes persons *do* have stringent duties toward others which would be violated by certain choices they might make, for example, the choice to commit suicide or to refuse a blood transfusion. Here also the interests of others are affected, but the case is quite different from that of the rapist. In some cases we may have a stringent negative or positive duty toward others, one whose fulfillment will promote the interests of others. In other cases our choices and acts significantly affect the, admittedly basic, interests of others, but we may have no duty to act in ways which will promote such interests or not subvert them. It is hardly obvious that friends or family having an interest in a loved one are, therefore, invariably owed a duty by the loved one not to make a choice which would distress them or not "pursue a course of treatment which *we believe* to be erroneous" (my italics). People are not duty bound to lead their lives so as to always please, or promote the interests of, others. In the absence of such duties (which, as noted, may exist in special cases) even important (to their possessors) interests of others may be morally negligible. To think otherwise is to view competent persons as bipedal natural resources and not as autonomous beings who have lives to lead; the former tendency is unfortunately encouraged by the influential theory of classic utilitarianism.

From this standpoint, Meisel's assignation of significant moral weight to the interests of health-care professionals (his third category) is even more bizarre. This is so, first, because the interests of such professionals in the choices and welfare of patients are, in general, likely to be less fundamental than those of friends or family. I take this point to be too obvious to deserve elaboration, conceding the fact that there will be some exceptions to this generalization. Further, if health-care professionals, by virtue of their training or inclination, come to view patients as materials whose welfare they are sculpting and, hence, resist any nonmalleable feature of the materials, that is simply too bad and such medical socialization is morally myopic. It is another instance of a familiar sort of hubris which seems to supervene on persons who have real or alleged expertise and power, whether they are found in health care, academia, politics, or institutions devoted to spiritual pursuits. Meisel claims, unqualifiedly, that health-care professionals *believe* that decisions regarding treatment are *technical* ones. His argument is stronger only if this belief is true, but it is both questionable whether most health professionals actually *hold* this belief and also not obvious that such a belief is true. To suggest that a certain decision about the best, or at least an effective, treatment of a patient is a purely technical one may be to claim, in part, that the efficacy of the chosen treatment is independent of the patient's attitudes, goals, and beliefs. This claim seems evidently false in the case of psychotherapy. Even if we restrict our attention to purely "medical" decisions, whether a treatment will be efficacious often depends on the patient's attitudes and beliefs. For example, the occurrence of a placebo effect depends on the patient's inclination to believe, for example, that she will be helped by a prescribed pill. Whether a male patient's urinary difficulties can be best dealt with by the insertion into his penis of a catheter several times a day depends very much on the patient's tolerance, patience, and cooperativeness toward such a procedure. This last example especially calls attention to the fact that there is a deeper problem about what counts as *the best treatment* (or an effective treatment).

Although there is no doubt at all that decisions about treatment almost invariably involve a "technical" dimension (and, frequently, a most complex one), we must, as noted earlier, make a distinction between

1. *what is the best medical treatment other things being equal*, and
2. *what is best for the patient.*

To emphasize the point, consider an unusual case. Suppose a professional singer, Mario, is suffering from progressive scoliosis which, if left untreated, will result in serious paralysis and severe deformity. The medical decision to be made focuses on how to prevent this awful consequence; technical expertise is evidently crucial in deciding the matter. Mario wants to avoid the mentioned results, but is opposed to undergoing the prescribed treatment: serious surgery which will leave him in a cast and on his back for six months. Should Mario's choice be circumvented? Is it permissible to proceed without his consent? May his consent be "engineered" by means of duress or deception, or on the grounds that the "doctor knows best" about what is for Mario's own good? It is important to note here that, with regard to Mario's scoliosis, the decision as to how best to alleviate that difficulty *is* a technical one and the decision to employ serious surgery may be the best medical treatment, other things being equal. However, when we focus on question 2., "what is best for the patient?," it is not at all obvious, nor does it follow from any of our prior assumptions, that the proposed surgery is the answer to 2. What may best alleviate the scoliosis may not be best for Mario. Let us add some details to our hypothetical and underdescribed case, details which may or may not manifest themselves to the health-care professionals involved. Mario has trained much of his life to participate in a not well-publicized Olympic event and his last genuine opportunity at being successful is nine months away. Mario so values this opportunity that he prefers the risk of increased debilitation by delaying surgery to immediate surgery and loss of opportunity. What is best for Mario, or any autonomous person, is not only a function of objective matters (perhaps technical ones), about which an individual may be mistaken, but also the goals, preferences, and convictions of the individual in question. But these latter factors are matters with which, generally, competent persons are best acquainted in their own cases; further, they are matters about which professionals will typically be partially acquainted. Professionals desirably expert on certain matters are, less desirably, sometimes likely to exclude from their vision at least some of those highly personal psychological variables which enter into a determination of what is best for the patient. To be fair, sensitive health-care professionals will try to take such factors into account, but, for various reasons, such matters may be hidden even from the most discerning. For these reasons, it is a mistake to regard "decisions about treatment" as purely technical ones, as decisions about which *only* technical expertise is relevant or decisive. Such a belief is false; it is also not obvious that health-care professionals generally hold it. Meisel's claim, then, that there are significant interests of health-care professionals which *nontrivially* add to the sum of interests which compete with that of the patient is, in view of the objections noted, a thin reed which will bear little weight. I have not claimed that there are no relevant interests of such professionals to be considered, but Meisel seems to articulate none that is weighty. As we have noted, even if they were weighty to their possessors, it would not follow that such a fact would be an adequate ground for subverting the competent patient's interest in determining his own destiny. Meisel's use of the pejorative "unfettered individualism" rings hollow—as it would if attributed to one who insisted on an individual's right to freedom of thought.

It might be conceded that the interests (1) and (3) mentioned earlier in this section do not constitute a reason to curtail, constrain, delimit, or bypass individual consent, but insisted that the societal interests Meisel mentions in (2) are compelling ones, ones which "outbalance" the patient's interest in self-determination. Again it is worth recalling that on the theory we have defended competent

221

persons only have a right to direct their lives within the sphere of acts not wrongful to others. Hence, if a patient's choice would *wrongfully* subvert, or wrongfully fail to promote, the interests of others, there will be an adequate nonpaternalistic ground for invasively interfering with it (as with the rapist's decision to rape). Although some choices (to do *or* forbear) and consequent acts wrongly subvert or fail to promote the interests of others, some acts subverting or failing to promote the interests of others do so in ways that involve no wrong (recall our examples about choice of mates or succeeding in competition). Hence, in appealing to what could promote or thwart the interests of others, it is crucial to keep in mind such a distinction. This, however, is what Meisel fails to do in his discussion of (1) and (3), and, as we shall observe, more blatantly in (2). As examples of promoting societal interests against choices of particular individuals, he mentions fluoridation of water, laws requiring motorcycle helmets, quarantines, or permitting involuntary blood transfusions. These cases constitute a mixed bag. Some of these policies are, arguably, legitimate on purely nonpaternalistic grounds. For example, in the case of quarantine, possibly diseased individuals would constitute a threat to others if allowed to move about freely, an unprovoked threat of harm to innocent others. It is reasonable to believe that, in this case, protection of the interests of innocent others is a legitimate effort to prevent a wrongful harm. If "unfettered individualism" is construed to mean that individuals should be free without qualification to do what they wish, it is simply a straw man. The example of involuntary blood transfusions, by contrast, is not obviously and universally the type of case in which any important societal interest is promoted. The more obvious interests at stake, other than those of the patient, have already been recognized, and assessed, in categories (1) and (3). Administration of involuntary blood transfusions does not commonly promote public safety, national security, or the maintenance of a decent society. Meisel offers no reason for thinking otherwise; further, simply to assume that there is some sort of societal interest promoted, one which outbalances the individual's interest in directing his own life, is to fail to offer any serious nonpaternalistically based argument for constraining the choice of a competent person. If it is objected that the state does have a compelling interest in promoting the health of its citizens, even by preventing or bypassing the voluntary choices or acts of competent persons *which do not wrong others*, this assertion presupposes that the state has an interest in acting in a manner which is, all things considered, wrongful—for our prior argument has shown such acts to be instances of unjustified paternalism. Meisel does not make this last-mentioned objection. Rather, his strategy is to claim that there are interests, other than those of the individual patient which must be considered. We have conceded that the latter is true only if the other interests are legitimate ones (contrast the rapist's interests), and, even then, the existence of interests important to others does not, without further argument, show that it is permissible to sacrifice the interests of the patient. There are cases in which it is permissible to override the choices of competent persons by deciding to treat them,[51] but we have argued that such cases cannot appeal to residual paternalistic grounds (those other than valid consent); nor is the domain of such cases identifiable by the highly general sort of interest-balancing strategy we have examined. If the latter point is correct, our suspicion of this *sort* of nonpaternalistic strategy invoked should be magnified. If our earlier critique of paternalistic strategies is sound, we also should be wary of appeals to what is in the individual's best interest. In sum, we do well to question vague rationalizations of invasive constraints of autonomous persons which claim that the competent individual's own welfare-interests "outbalance" his own choice *or* that the interests of others "outbalance" his predominantly self-regarding choices.

[51] I have in mind, for example, cases in which administering a truth-serum to a captured spy, or saving her life in order to interrogate her, may be justifiable on nonpaternalistic grounds.

FIVE

DEATH, SEX, ODYSSEUS
AND THE SIRENS

He used to come to my rooms at midnight, and for hours
he would walk backward and forward like a caged tiger.
On arrival, he would announce that when he left my rooms
he would commit suicide. So, in spite of getting sleepy, I
did not like to turn him out. —Bertrand Russell (on
Wittgenstein)

A short death is the last happiness of a human life.
—Pliny The Younger

There are many who proudly call suicide cowardly: let them
try it first, then they can talk. —Johann Nestroy

And men will never see women as equals until there's an
end to prostitution. —Susan Brownmiller

I did not always see the gesture of buying someone as
arrogance because I did not feel that controlled by the customer. I felt I was the boss because I could say no to the
deal.

   I may have hated prostitution but I had the right to do
it. —A prostitute[1]

5.1 Theory and Practice

In the first three chapters our focus was on the concept of paternalism and the identification and assessment of claims regarding
what sorts of paternalistic intervention are permissible. Much of
the theoretical foundation for assessing constraints on specific practices was laid. In the fourth chapter the doctrine of informed consent was analyzed and appraised in the light of theoretical considerations developed earlier. Further, the implications of the doctrine

[1] See Kate Millett, *The Prostitution Papers* (New York: Avon Books, 1973), pp.
53, 77.

and the Theory of Autonomy-Respecting Paternalism were traced with regard to the use of coercion, deception, and withholding information from patients in health-care contexts. Hence, we began to make the transition to the appraisal of familiar, more or less disputed, public and private practices.

In this chapter our focus is more exclusively on the assessment of constraints on practices which are regarded as morally suspect, dangerous to those engaging in the practice, or both. In this vein we shall inquire as to whether invasive constraints on voluntary euthanasia or suicide are permissible; whether persons could ever have a right to be killed; and whether there should be a prohibition on voluntary, knowing engagement in prostitution. Our main concern is to query whether there are legitimate paternalistic grounds for employing presumptively wrong means to prevent competent persons from acting in the ways mentioned, and if so, under what conditions. If there are not, then the primary question is whether there is a compelling nonpaternalistic basis for restrictions on such practices. This latter question is far too complex to explore fully here; nevertheless, a presumptive case is developed such that those who defend such restrictions bear the burden of overcoming the presumptive case to the contrary.

Finally, in Section 5.7 a somewhat narrower issue is explored. We argued earlier that certain paternalistic restraints on competent persons are justifiable if those persons validly consented to the constraints in question. But the valid consent, it was maintained, must be "currently operative," and "currently operative" meant, so it appeared, unrevoked. However, can people revoke their consent whenever they wish? Is valid consent ever irrevocable? Can one who validly consents to a therapeutic regime (e.g., surgery or electro-convulsive therapy) suddenly "back out"—just before the anesthesia, or after one ECT treatment? Alternatively, is it impermissible for the therapist to proceed in such cases if the patient had previously given valid consent?

5.2 Euthanasia of Competent Persons

Euthanizing someone can be a paternalistic act; so also can withholding euthanasia. In each type of case an agent, A, can engage in euthanasia, or refrain from it, with the aim to promote a subject's good. After defining 'euthanasia' and sorting some subcategories, we shall examine, in this and the next section, the morality of euthanasia and the morality of refusals to carry out acts of euthanasia.

Let us restrict our focus solely to human beings, even though it is conceptually unproblematic that some nonhuman animals can be euthanized. I define 'an act of euthanasia' as an act in which one person, A, intentionally kills another individual, S, or intentionally lets S die by discontinuing aid to S, and A does so out of a merciful or benevolent motive toward S (e.g., A believes his act is for S's good or in S's interests).[2] This, partly stipulative, definition has a number of advantages over competing definitions. The etymologically based suggestion that 'euthanasia' (from the Greek *eu*, good or well, and *thanatos*, death) means 'good death' is not very helpful since an assassination, a killing in war, or a killing in self-defense may be judged good on a variety of grounds, but such cases are not commonly counted as cases of euthanasia. Webster's definition, as assessed from the standpoint of current usage, is also unhelpful; it is this: an "act or practice of painlessly putting to death persons suffering from incurable or distressing disease."[3] One major drawback of this definition is its restrictiveness, for the term 'euthanasia' is regularly applied to a wider range of cases which include killings that are not necessarily painless (e.g., shooting a wounded soldier who wishes to die) or cases in which the subject may not have an incurable *disease* (cf. the prior example). Further, the Webster's characterization could include maleficent homicides; it fails to exclude cases of crass motivation. We also note that, arguably, it allows inadvertent acts to count as euthanasia, for example, you kill a person suffering from an incurable disease by forgetting to turn off the gas stove.

It is also linguistically counterintuitive to say that I am euthanizing people as I write this sentence, and doing so simply because I am not now preventing persons from dying whom I could save if I put my energies elsewhere. Not all omissions of aid are intentional; not all cases of letting alone are cases of letting die. One might even say that as I sit down to write I am leaving some to die, but I am not, therefore, "letting them die." This latter point is relevant to the sticky question of how to distinguish cases of killing and letting die, or active and passive euthanasia. I shall not attempt an analysis beyond noting that it is doubtful whether an agent is letting someone die in cases where the agent has no duty

---

[2] This definition is not sufficiently precise to allow ready classification of certain hard cases, but will serve my purposes here.

[3] See *Webster's New Collegiate Dictionary* (1966), 2nd ed.

to make rescue efforts or where the agent expends no effort in order to let someone die. In familiar physician-patient cases of letting die, purposive effort is expended, typically by way of terminating aid, for example, a respirator is cut off, intravenous feeding is withdrawn, or an order to that effect is given. It is sufficient for our purposes to observe that many cases labeled as "passive euthanasia" are like cases of "active euthanasia" in that they (1) involve effort, (2) are acts done with the aim of hastening death or at least where the likelihood of hastening death is foreseen by the agent, and (3) what is done proceeds from a benevolent attitude toward the subject. In *some* pairs of cases there may be no morally relevant difference between killing and letting die, but this does not entail that "there is no morally relevant difference between killing and letting die"—in general.[4]

Of greater importance are the familiar distinctions between voluntary, involuntary, and nonvoluntary euthanasia. As frequently defined (assuming henceforth our prior definition of 'euthanasia'), in the case of voluntary euthanasia the subject consents to euthanasia; in involuntary euthanasia the subject dissents to euthanasia; in nonvoluntary euthanasia *we do not know* whether the subject consents or dissents. These categories are somewhat disparate for two are basic and one is derivative; the taxonomy is rather like that involved in saying that people fall into three categories: those six feet tall or over, those under six feet, and those whose height we do not know. Assuming that at least some people who are euthanized while unconscious dispositionally consent or dissent to being euthanized, euthanasia of them will belong in the voluntary (or involuntary) category *and* the "nonvoluntary category." But we need not be misled by such labels so long as we are clear about the class of cases to which reference is being made when such labels are employed. If a generally competent subject is unconscious (and cannot be "wakened" so that we may discover his will on the matter) and there is no currently operative consent or dissent to his being euthanized, such a person is incompetent with respect to deciding whether to be euthanized. Hence, we may not

[4] Those interested may wish to examine: *Ethical Issues Relating to Life and Death*, ed. John Ladd (New York: Oxford University Press, 1979); *Killing and Letting Die*, ed. Bonnie Steinbock (Englewood Cliffs, N.J.: Prentice-Hall, 1980); Tom Beauchamp and Leroy Walters, *Contemporary Issues in Bioethics*, 2nd ed. (Encino, Cal.: Dickenson, 1982)—especially the essay by James Rachels, "Active and Passive Euthanasia", pp. 313–315; Margaret Pabst Battin, "Euthanasia," in *Border Crossings: New Introductory Essays in Health-Care Ethics*, eds. Donald VanDeVeer and Tom Regan (New York: Random House, forthcoming).

know what would respect his will or how he would exercise his right to direct his own life. The principles we have developed so far, principles delineating permissible and impermissible paternalism toward competent persons, do not provide guidance as to what may be done in such cases, unless there are reasonable grounds for appealing to the subject's hypothetical consent; what is needed is a theory of paternalism toward incompetent persons (one which, of course, must distinguish between important types of cases, e.g., the permanently incompetent versus those temporarily incompetent—barring euthanasia). Let us here restrict our focus to those who are capable of making a reasoned choice with regard to being euthanized, that is, those not incompetent in *that* respect.

Among those capable of expressing their will and who do so by either requesting or refusing euthanasia, there will be some who fail to be generally competent persons. For example, a subject may be a paranoid schizophrenic who is under the delusion that his relatives have set a trap to capture and then torture him; to escape future terrors he prefers to die and, let us suppose, demands to be euthanized while in the hospital. In such a case we have a person who is a "mental incompetent," an "incompetent" in the more usual sense of the word, and not merely a normally competent but temporarily incompetent person. Again, our current principles do not apply. However, it is important to recognize this point. There may be grounds for refusing to accede to a request for euthanasia by such a person, grounds which do not apply in the case of the competent person who makes such a request. Hence, although I shall defend the permissibility of voluntary euthanasia of *competent* persons, such a defense is not tantamount to the *unqualified* claim that "voluntary euthanasia is morally permissible."

An act of euthanasia, as we have defined it, can be a paternalistic act.[5] If a patient is killed or allowed to die solely in order to obtain her organs for transplantation, the act is not paternalistic. If a spouse is poisoned because his mate "cannot bare to see him suffer any longer," the act is, arguably, not paternalistic. Even though euthanasia can be a paternalistic act or practice, the primary question is whether it is ever justified. As with other specific practices, there are appeals to *nonpaternalistic grounds* for allowing or prohibiting paternalistic acts. One might argue that euthanasia ought not

---

[5] It will be if the agent acts contrary to the subject's operative preference or intention and does so with the aim of promoting a good, or preventing a harm.

be impeded, or indeed should be encouraged, on the ground that there are problems of overpopulation—or that euthanasia of those on Social Security should not be discouraged since such persons are a burden to the system. Such arguments are not tempting in view of the fact that if they prove anything, they "prove too much," that is, they would sanction ordinary homicides and, possibly, genocide as well. Related questions might be raised here about the moral limits on cost-benefit analysis as a means of deciding such matters, but I shall forego them. There are adequate nonpaternalistic grounds for killing persons *against their will* in *some* cases, for example, in *certain* cases of self-defense. Our concern here, however, is whether there are permissible instances of paternalistic euthanasia.

Let us sort out relevant types of cases. In one, competent subjects will be able to make a voluntary, reasoned choice as to whether they wish to be euthanized, and there will be no urgent reason for a potential euthanizer to decide hastily whether to accede to such a request or bring about such a result. Hence, the agent would have no reason to conjecture about what the subject *would consent to* if able and aware of facts material to such a choice; in this respect, this case contrasts with those in which the subject is psychologically impaired in nontrivial ways or those cases in which an agent must act hastily to prevent a serious harm if it is to be prevented at all, such as when your friend is inadvertently about to step on a land mine. Thus, in those cases in which the subject is not impaired and there is time to ascertain the subject's choice without letting the serious harm "rush in" (or letting an important benefit to be promoted "escape"), appeal to the Principle of Hypothetical Individualized Consent is out of place; to rationalize invasive intervention by such an appeal, in the context noted, would unjustifiably subvert the competent's right to direct his own life. Further, as is all too obvious, the extreme measure of terminating the life of another makes this context quite special, although not entirely unique, in that terminating life results in a drastic, irreversible, outcome for the subject. An important preliminary point, then, is that we rarely can make a reasonable appeal to PHIC in those cases in which the subject is competent to give or withhold consent to euthanasia.

If the competent subject, however, makes a reasoned, broadly voluntary, choice to be euthanized and authorizes another to perform an act of euthanasia, such an act will not infringe the competent subject's right to direct his own life in ways that wrong no others. Rather, it can facilitate the subject's prerogative to do so. If such an act accords with the subject's current choice it will not be contrary to his operative preference and intention. Hence, it will *fail* to be paternalistic behavior on the part of the euthanizer even if her aim is to prevent a (worse) harm to the subject or to promote a benefit. Rather, such an act, on the view defended here, will count as a form of nonpaternalistic altruism and, given satisfaction of the conditions aforementioned, will be morally permissible.

If the agent, A, were to go ahead against S's wish, and, with paternalistic aims, euthanize the subject, S, A indeed would be acting paternalistically. The more important question is whether A's doing so is permissible paternalistic behavior. Should potential paternalistic agents in such a case accede to the subject's current preference not to die if the subject earlier gave valid consent to be euthanized? Or should they respect the earlier choice (and consent) of the subject to be euthanized? The intuitively natural answer is surely that agents ought to take the former course. But is this because a subject cannot give irrevocable consent at t, to his being treated at some later time t^n in some fashion contrary to his preference at t^n? The answer to this question is, I believe, a negative one (it will be explored further in Section 5.7). Often agents, recognizing their own propensity for weakness of will, giving in to temptation, or the possibility or likelihood of not maintaining what they regard as desirable self-control, grant permission to others to act contrary to their (possible) later preferences in order to achieve some well-considered goal. Recall the examples mentioned earlier in which one authorizes another invasively to interfere at later times when one may be drunk but wants to drive, or when one wishes to deviate from dietary goals adopted in a cooler (or less hungry) moment. In such cases I have claimed that we invasively may interfere at t^n if there is prior valid consent to do so by the subject. But what if the subject claims that he wishes to revoke his consent?

There are, I propose, two types of considerations which are powerful, and probably decisive, reasons to refrain from acting contrary to the subject's choice in the context in which euthanasia (or other acts whose outcomes are devastating to the subject) is being considered. One concerns the *content* of the prior consent. The other concerns how *well-considered* is the subject's preference or choice at t^n. First, a person's expression of consent is often vague, and *what* persons often consent to is to acts under a limited range of prospective circumstances. It is reasonable to think of such consent, typically, as involving tacit riders or provisos such as "barring unforeseen circumstances." For example, if I consent to a friend's spending the holiday at my house and so indicate, it would be excessively tedious for me to add "unless, of course, there is a nuclear war" or "unless I am in a coma at that time." It is unreasonable to regard common, less qualified, indications of consent as commitments and authorizings as of the *no matter what happens* or *no matter what I later prefer* variety. When so much is at stake, as in the contemplation of euthanasia, there is an extraordinarily strong presumption, tantamount to virtual certainty, that a subject at t consenting to euthanasia at t^n is *not* authorizing others to kill him *even if* later at t^n he wishes to live.

The other consideration which should weigh heavily in deciding whether to accede to the subject's preference at t^n or honor his prior request at t concerns whether his preference (or, if one prefers, his "will") is the byproduct of reasoned reflection, a genuine change of mind—and not merely a "giving in" to impulse, fear, ill-considered inclination, or impaired judgment of the sort which the subject in a cooler and more collected period would choose to prevent or avoid by authorizing others to intervene. Assessing a subject's current preference or choice may be difficult, but familiar considerations come into play here. To the extent that the "recent" preference is for a course which is extremely risky, harmful, or ending in death, it is less likely that it is a well-considered change of mind. Further, to the extent that it is made under *circumstances* tending to thwart considered judgment, the new preference is also likely to be one which the subject wished at t to have overridden, for example circumstances which engender fear, severe anxiety, rage, lust, or other impediments to a subject's autonomously directing his life toward well-considered goals. The choice or preference to live, unlike the choice to die or to pursue quite risky courses of action, is, of course, a normal one and not likely to be a byproduct of fear, impulse, a giving in to temptation, or a shortsighted inclination to escape problems. Unlike some preferences it is not the sort, generally, which competents wish to guard against or whose realization they wish to thwart by soliciting interference from others.

For these reasons a subject who chooses at t^n to reconsider his earlier consent to be euthanized should, in virtually all cases, have his way. In short, there is little or no reason to assume that a subject's preference at t^n does not override his earlier, ostensibly unqualified, consent in the context under discussion—or that his earlier consent can reasonably be construed as irrevocable. Thus, paternalistic imposition of *euthanasia* cannot be defended reasonably by appeal to the Principle of Restricted Consent.

If the subject, however, at the time euthanasia is being considered, cannot express a relevant preference, can euthanasia be defended by appeal to the Principle of Restricted Consent (PRC) or the Principle of Hypothetical Individualized Consent (PHIC)? Three sorts of cases within this type of context are worth distinguishing. Since a paternalistic act, by definition, aims at promoting a good of the subject or preventing harm from befalling the subject, consideration of paternalistic euthanasia only arises in extreme contexts—contexts in which dying is reasonably viewed as preventing a worse condition for the subject or acceding to a subject's choice. In the extreme case in which a subject has become irreversibly comatose, I shall assume without here defending the point, that the subject has ceased to exist as a person and that, hence, there is no person to benefit or to protect (or individual which may have contrary preferences or disposition). Thus, one logically cannot act paternalistically toward such an entity.[6] Nonpaternalistic reasons alone are relevant to deciding on termination of the body which continues to function. For this reason termination in such a case is rather misleadingly labeled 'euthanasia' as that term has been defined here (it is not clear how one could act with a *merciful* intent toward an irreversibly comatose individual, or, as noted, against the *subject's* preferences).

Consider next the situation in which, once more, the subject is so disabled as to be unable to express a preference but, in this case, he is not irreversibly comatose. Further, the subject has not previously given valid consent to being euthanized in the type of circumstance which prevails. Again, since paternalistic euthanasia logically must aim, here, at preventing or halting harm, or benefitting the subject as well, the situation must be rare indeed, for example, one in which continuation of the subject's life, with virtual certainty, will be seriously painful on balance. Only in such a situation could one *paternalistically* end a subject's life.

In this type of circumstance, euthanizing S, although (let us assume) not contrary to an expressed preference of S, would be done in the *absence* of a currently expressed preference or disposition to live. Hence, if carried out for S's own good, it would be a paternalistic act (or so I shall construe the situation, although the

---

[6] Or at least no more than one could toward a plant or nonsentient animal.

case is conceptually disputatious). On the theory defended here, the first relevant question to ask is whether euthanasia is defensible by appeal to the Principle of Restricted Consent. Thus, did S previously give valid consent to being euthanized under the sort of circumstance envisioned? If so, and if such consent was expressed with sufficient precision that it is clear that S validly did consent to euthanasia under the prevailing circumstance, then euthanasia is permissible by appeal to PRC.

In the absence of S's having the opportunity and capacity to make a reasoned choice and in the absence of valid prior consent by S, it is then relevant (and only then) to ask whether euthanasia is defensible by appeal to PHIC. Hence it is relevant whether S would choose euthanasia if he were able to do so, functioning at close to his rational best, and relevantly informed. On the view defended here, if the subject's values, attitudes, and prior commitments would support euthanizing S in such a circumstance, it is permissible by appeal to PHIC. If, by contrast, it is reasonable to believe that the subject, hypothetically, would oppose euthanasia and run the risk of a life likely to be painful or seriously impaired on balance, then paternalistic euthanasia is impermissible. It is obvious that it is often difficult to arrive at a rational judgment about what a subject would have chosen, but the position I am defending is that one must attend to those choice-affecting traits of the particular subject to decide such matters and not simply to what is "in his best interest," where the latter expression allows other factors (e.g., whether he will suffer net pain on balance, or not, if he lives) to be decisive and to override the subject's own outlook. In the event that the evidence is so meager as to preclude any reasonable inference as to what the subject would choose, only then is it permissible to fall back on judgments about what "a reasonable person" would choose when confronted with such a difficult choice. Such a standard is appropriate only as a last resort, when deciders or interveners are faced with insurmountable epistemological difficulties to ascertaining what would respect the particular subject's conception of his own good.

In sum, we have focused on the permissibility of euthanizing a generally competent person, S. If S currently chooses to be euthanized, A's doing so will accord with S's currently expressed preference and, hence, does not count as paternalistic euthanasia (to be paternalistic an act must be contrary to a subject's current preference, intention, or disposition, or at least be done in the absence of such). When S is capable of reasoned choice and prefers not to be euthanized, such a preference must generally carry the day even though it may conflict with S's prior valid consent to be euthanized (because such consent can hardly ever be regarded as the "no matter what" variety and a later preference or choice to live cannot plausibly be regarded as a weakness of will which the subject by his earlier consent wished to restrain). I have denied, however, the claim that persons can never give irrevocable consent (see Section 5.7). In those cases in which S cannot express a current preference, due to being impaired (e.g., unconscious), euthanasia may be permissible if there is prior valid consent by S. Again, *paternalistic* euthanasia here is possible only if A believes that he can, by so acting, prevent a worse harm for S; thus, S's prospects must be grave indeed (thus, I am not defending the absurd view that, given valid consent by S, an agent can permissibly euthanize S if S happens to faint or fall asleep!). Next, in those cases in which S cannot express a current preference and there is no prior valid consent to euthanasia under the type of prevailing circumstance, an agent's euthanizing S is permissible if it is reasonable to infer that the subject would consent to such if he were not cognitively impaired and were informed of relevant facts. If the subject would not so consent, it is impermissible. Finally, if no reasonable inference can be made about what the particular subject would, or would not, consent to, then, and only then, is it appropriate to decide on the basis of what "a reasonable person" would choose under the prevailing circumstances. Even here appeal to the notion of a "reasonable person" should not be entirely abstracted from considerations of S's personality, that is, S's values, commitments, dispositions, and long-range goals. In this, ordered, fashion we can and ought to attempt to respect S's right to direct his own life (including the time and manner of dying). The central focus is, therefore, on what S chooses, chose, or would choose within the domain of alternatives involving no wrong to others.

In our prior discussion, often mentioned "slippery slope" arguments have been ignored, and a comment is in order. One form of such arguments maintains that as a matter of empirical fact if we engage in voluntary active euthanasia of competent persons, as a society we shall become increasingly more callous and more insensitive with respect to the value of human life or its preservation. Hence, over time we shall come to condone, possibly legalize, and practice wrongful killings or wrongfully let persons die—even if the sort of euthanasia which has been our focus is, otherwise, morally unobjectionable. I focus on this particular form

234

of slippery slope argument (an empirical as opposed to a conceptual version) because it seems the strongest type of slippery slope counterargument to the position defended here.

One possible response is to deny that there is anything inevitable about the occurrence of such a worrisome course of events. And it is worth observing that, as a society, we *already* sanction some killings (in self-defense or in war) and prohibit others. Thus we are *not* in a position of contemplating the "start-up" of sanctioning some killings and prohibiting or otherwise discouraging others; we already make correlative conceptual, moral, and legal distinctions—in theory and in practice—between permissible and impermissible killings. We already have accepted the challenge of allowing some killings but seeking to avoid their acceptance from "leading to" others. The question, then, is not whether to get on a slippery slope; if there is one, we are already on it. Defenders of such arguments often distort or glibly ignore this point.

The slippery slope advocate may concede this point and also may concede that the worrisome prospect is not inevitable; still, the threat is real and a morally weighty one. These points I would also acknowledge. A crucial matter is how probable it is that callousness (and so on) would be (or has been) induced by allowing active voluntary euthanasia of competent persons. In part we need better data relevant to the crucial empirical assumptions. It *does* seem logically possible that callousness and, ultimately, a correlative increase in the incidence of wrongful killings may result. If there were compelling evidence to this effect, then I should concede that active voluntary euthanasia wronged others albeit indirectly. If so, there might be a compelling nonpaternalistic argument for discouraging or prohibiting active, voluntary euthanasia (and possibly other sorts as well).

I leave the question somewhat open in the absence of the decisive empirical data. However, several considerations lessen the likelihood that a slippery argument will support a broad legal prohibition of euthanasia. There is not space here to elaborate in much detail, but, first, it is not enough to show that others are or will be upset or worse off in certain respects—as a result of the practice—to support the claim that they have been wronged. Again, when A chooses to marry C and not B, B may be distraught; but B has not (evidently) been wronged. When Jones wins a fair race (or gets the government contract), Smith may be worse off but not wronged. Second, whether a practice induces a high degree of callousness seems to depend importantly on *whether* others perceive (or learn of) it, the *extent* to which they do, and the *manner* in which they do. If brutal murders or instances of capital punishment were regularly displayed on the nightly news in a manner suggesting no hint of sadness, tragedy, or moral significance, callousness is more likely to follow—especially, so it would seem, among the young. Such considerations seem persuasive reasons to place restrictions on the time and place of publicly authorized killings and the manner and frequency with which killings are disclosed—at least if there is a genuine worry about the inducement of serious insensitivity, as there seems to be. However, none of these admittedly relevant considerations is sufficient to show that an out and out prohibition on publicly authorized killings is in order, including voluntary, active, euthanasia (acts, we should not forget, commonly requested by those whose continued living seems not worth the cost to them—due to radical impairment or suffering). In short, slippery slope worries are legitimate ones, but they hold out little likelihood of being compelling reasons for a blanket legal prohibition on active, voluntary, euthanasia, of competent persons.

5.3 Voluntary Euthanasia and Alienating Rights

At a number of places we have made the important assumption that competent persons can, by validly consenting to actions of others, render the performance of certain acts permissible which would otherwise be impermissible. The importance of such consent can be thought to rest on the fact that people have certain rights, rights which if respected ensure that a certain sphere of autonomy is not subverted. But if right holders choose to do so, they can let down the moral barriers against the performance of certain acts by others. Hence, the moral relevance of valid consent is that it involves a waiver of rights against others. Once rights are waived, one form of "alienating" a right, others cease to have their former duty to respect such rights, for the former right holder simply lacks those rights which have been waived. Border crossings previously impermissible are now permissible.

There is an objection to this view which threatens to undermine our theory at various locations; it also may be urged against the view that voluntary euthanasia is morally permissible, or that euthanasia can be a permissible paternalistic act. Hence it has both a general and specific importance for our discussion. I have chosen to take it up at this point for reasons which will be evident. It is often claimed, or assumed, that human beings have a right to life, indeed, an *inalienable* right to life. More generally, it is often assumed that human beings have a number of inalienable rights, moral and not merely legal rights. Appeals to "human rights" or "the natural rights of man" typically make such assumptions. Such assumptions are thought to form the basis of an argument whose conclusion is that it is wrong to euthanize persons who request euthanasia. This line of reasoning is both tempting and complex. Hence, I shall develop it somewhat gradually.

Initially, one may doubt whether human beings have any natural rights at all, although conceding the existence of legal rights. Jeremy Bentham, the late eighteenth- and early nineteenth-century British advocate of utilitarian ethics, is well known for his view that talk of rights is "nonsense on stilts," in spite of the considerable importance assigned to the contrary and influential views of Hobbes, Locke, Kant, and Rousseau. Relatedly, in view of the recent appeals to the alleged human rights of blacks, women, Indians, children, and fetuses, it is more fashionable for skeptics to deride talk of rights as itself "fashionable" or by claiming that we must, by parity of reasoning, also assume the existence of rights for turkeys, ticks, trees, or ecosystems. Since the view I wish to examine constitutes an *objection* to our theory, I shall simply suppose that human beings normally have a right to life, that is, concede the point for the sake of inquiry.

There is a prior question about what is *meant* by the expression "right to life." On one interpretation, it is thought to be a *positive* right, that is, a right whose correlative duty on the part of others is to perform *positive* acts, for example, supply the right holder with whatever goods and services are necessary in order to live.[7] That there is such a right is controversial for obvious reasons; respecting it may require radical sacrifices by alleged duty holders, such as donating organs to perfect strangers. On another interpretation 'right to life' is understood as a right not to be killed.[8] On this

[7] I offer skeptical arguments regarding a related, alleged, positive right in my, "A Right to be Saved From Starvation?," *The Personalist* (now: *The Pacific Philosophical Quarterly*) (April, 1979), pp. 216–220.

[8] I deliberately simplify here the question of what is meant by 'right to life.' On Judith Thomson's view it is the right not to be killed *unjustly*; see Judith Thomson, "A Defense of Abortion," *Philosophy & Public Affairs* 1, No. 1 (Fall, 1972), pp. 37–65. On Michael Tooley's view it is a right of a person, a continuing subject of experiences, not to have his (or her) personhood destroyed; on Tooley's view we can infringe your right by psychosurgery which would destroy your identity as a person, even if your body continued to live. See Michael Tooley, "Abortion and Infanticide," *Philosophy & Public Affairs* 2, No. 1 (1971), pp. 47–66.

construal the right to life is a negative right whose correlative duty requires others to forbear from killing the right holder. That people have such a right and that there is such a correlative, negative, duty is far less controversial than the claim that people have a positive right to life. The concession I wish to make, more accurately, is that human beings normally have a negative moral right to life. If so, and on the assumption that it is morally wrong to infringe a right, especially a fundamental human right, then it seems to follow that it is wrong to kill a human being, even a competent person who requests to be euthanized; hence, voluntary euthanasia is wrong.[9]

Against this line of thought it may be claimed that human rights are *alienable*, that is, that although persons normally have such rights, they may by a voluntary act divest themselves of such rights. In some sense persons may lose a previously held right to life. How could this be? One response is that alienation of a right is not a mysterious notion at all, at least when we are speaking of legal rights; for people may cease to have legal rights formerly held. If I sell you my copy of *Crime and Punishment*, my right to it gets transferred to you (assuming it was my property in the first place and not just a possession); hence, I no longer have the right. If you now read that copy, start a fire with it, or wrap fish with it, you infringe no current right of mine. So, persons sometimes cease to have rights, at least legal ones, because they transfer them to others (those who tend to see economics and ethics as exclusive categories might contemplate department stores as places where rights are exchanged). This point, however, is not persuasive in showing that persons can alienate human rights, partly because it is not at all clear how one could be said to *transfer* one's *right to life* to anyone else. In addition, what may be true of legal rights may not be true of moral rights.

There is another strategy designed to show that persons can alienate, and thus lose, their right to life. People sometimes *forfeit* legal rights which they have; for example, Sigmund loses his library privileges by failing to pay his fines. Similarly, drivers lose their right to drive because of traffic violations. It is reasonable to think that persons forfeit certain moral rights as well. If Roe has promised Doe a ride to work at nine in the morning and Doe shows up at ten, Doe forfeits his right to the ride. In contrast to transfers of

---

[9] I note, however, that it is abstractly possible to argue that we may justifiably infringe certain rights.

rights, people are said to forfeit a right without anyone else necessarily acquiring the right; further, we *tend* to restrict 'forfeiture of right' to cases where an agent, by act or omission, does that which is presumptively blameworthy or is, at least, a failure to be responsible in some respect. For example, John Locke spoke of one "having by his fault forfeited his own life by some act that deserves death."[10] Forfeitures may be seriously blameworthy, as with the rapist who forfeits his right to non-interference by others, or comparatively trivial, as in our earlier example of Doe. However, if one forfeits a right only by committing a wrong, this may not aid anyone who wishes to defend voluntary euthanasia by arguing that the right to life is alienated in the case of voluntary euthanasia. To see why, we must further clarify 'alienate.' By 'S alienates a right, R' I understand 'S dispossesses himself of R, inadvertently or not.' Hence, if a right is forfeited or transferred, it is alienated.

If we agree with Locke, at least for the sake of discussion, that a person with a right to life can *forfeit* it, then there are several interesting implications. First, those who believe that persons normally have a right to life can plausibly argue that there is no inconsistency between making *that* assumption and also believing that capital punishment or the killing of wrongdoers in self-defense is justifiable. At least they can point out that such killings need not infringe a right to life of the wrongdoer for, on this view, wrongdoers in certain cases have forfeited their right to life; since they no longer have such a right, killing them cannot infringe it. For our purposes, however, the rub is that persons requesting euthanasia are typically innocent parties; hence, no case can be made that they have alienated, by forfeit, their right to life. Thus, euthanizing them would, so it appears, be wrong since it infringes a right to life. At best, a case could be made that euthanizing serious wrongdoers, those forfeiting their right to life, infringes no right to life. This, of course, is a most restricted range of cases. So much for the forfeiture strategy.

Our frequent talk of waiver of rights suggests, however, another possibility. A waiver of right is a deliberate giving up of the right, typically in blameless fashion, and, hence, a releasing of others from any duties implied by the right of the prior right holder. People can waive legal rights, for example, the right to have an attorney present before being questioned after an arrest, or the

---

[10] John Locke, *The Second Treatise of Government*, ed. Thomas P. Peardon (Indianapolis: Bobbs-Merrill, 1952), p. 15. I here construe 'forfeited his life' to mean 'forfeited his right to life.'

right to silence once informed that they have such a right. Further, it is reasonable to think that persons have some moral rights to privacy in addition to legal rights to privacy, moral rights which can be waived. For example, if you invite someone into your home, you can hardly complain when, on entering, they look at you or listen to your words. The commonsense view accords with the judgment that you have waived certain rights of privacy by the invitation; hence, your visitor does not, by the mentioned behavior, infringe those (limited) rights waived. Hence, it would seem that persons can waive nontrivial moral rights, "human rights" if one prefers. If so, why cannot a competent person waive a more fundamental human right such as the right to life, a right we have supposed human beings normally to possess?

One barrier to answering affirmatively is a claim, indeed an argument, that I believe has been influential since the inception of theories of human rights. As Michael Bayles has recently claimed, "Human rights . . . are inalienable because they belong to people by virtue of their being human. So to lose a human right one must cease to be a human."[11] These remarks reflect the commonly held view that distinctively human rights are natural or status rights; they are rights possessed by their possessors because they are members of a *natural* kind or have the *status* of being members of Homo sapiens—in contrast to the grounds for possessing certain other sorts of rights, that is, the occurrence of *voluntary* acts such as gifts, promises, contracts, or exchanges. What are referred to as "human rights" are, then, natural rights of humans and not "any rights possessed by humans." The assumption that human rights belong to human beings *by virtue* of their being human may naturally be interpreted to entail the following claim, H:

If an entity h is a human being, h has human rights.

The contrapositive of H, then, follows from H, namely,

If an entity h does not have human rights, h is not a human being.

So, if one assumes H, one may infer that "to lose a human right one must cease to be human."[12] For if the rights were alienable by

[11] Michael Bayles, "Limits to a Right to Procreate," in *Ethics and Population*, ed. Michael Bayles (Cambridge, Mass.: Schenkman, 1976), p. 42.

[12] Compare A. I. Melden's view that ". . . if there is a right that one has qua person it is logically impossible for anyone, oneself, or anyone else, to do anything which would deprive one of this moral possession without depriving one of one's status as a person." At the same time, he, paradoxically, claims "any account would

a human possessor and were in fact alienated, that human would not have human rights—a conclusion contrary to the supposition that a human who loses a human right ceases to be a human. If, then, one accepts H, the conclusion that human rights are inalienable inexorably follows. The main reason for accepting H, so far as I can determine, is that it seems to follow from the status claim S:

Any possessor of human rights has them just because it is a human being.

However, it is possible, for reasons I shall mention, to accept S without accepting H, that is, S does not entail H.

The assumption that S entails H confuses, I think, considerations regarding (1) the genesis of a right, and (2) the issue of its retention. Some moral and legal rights which we acquire by voluntary acts may clearly be waived. The genesis of human rights, on the standard view, is not in a prior voluntary act. Hence, I have labeled them 'status rights.' Does *this* feature provide a reason for thinking that they *must be retained*? A crude analogy is useful here. A (natural) citizen under arrest may have a right to hire an attorney 'just because he is a citizen.' Thus, his right may be a status right. Still he may waive that right, but we are not tempted to say that he, therefore, ceases to be a citizen. The status-origin of a right seems no reason to infer that the right cannot be alienated. Why think that it is otherwise with human rights?

The status-genesis of a right does not entail the claim that *so long as* an entity occupies a certain status it must have those rights which, if the entity has them, are possessed just because of occupying the status. Status rights may come with status; they need not invariably remain with the status. This point casts serious doubt on the claim that S (Any possessor of human rights has them just because it is a human being) entails H (If an entity, h, is a human being, h has human rights). So, it seems possible that something could be a human being at time t and not possess human rights at t, even if it is true that at any time at which a human possesses human rights it possesses them just because it is a human being. In short, the status-nature of human rights does not entail the claim that nothing could be a human and lack human rights. If this argument is correct, it shows that a tempting and frequently ad-

---

be in serious error if it attempted to provide a set of necessary and sufficient conditions for the possession of a human right." (See A. I. Melden, *Rights and Persons* (Berkeley: University of California Press, 1977), p. 267.)

duced reason for thinking that human rights are inalienable is not compelling.[13]

There is a further consideration in favor of the view that basic human rights are alienable by waiver. Not only is the right to life commonly believed to be a paradigmatic human right, so also is the right to liberty. Aside from the question of how precisely to analyze 'right to liberty,' it is surely a right to act in a way unhindered by certain constraints which might be imposed by others. Further, if 'right to liberty' denotes a family of more specific rights such as the right to be free from the imposition of certain sorts of harms by others or the right to be free from being under the control of others in certain ways, it is clear that we commonly allow that these specific or concrete rights may be alienated, that is, waived in a wide variety of cases. When I consent to surgery I waive my right not to have certain bodily parts subjected to damage. When I commit myself to a certain vocation I waive my right to be free to use some of my time as my whims might dictate. Such specific rights are alienable. If paradigmatic human rights are simply packages of such alienable rights, it follows that such human rights are alienable, unless it can be shown that there is something like the fallacy of composition here. At the least, the mystery remains as to what features human rights have which would render them inalienable. The preceding arguments support a presumption in favor of the *Alienability Thesis*.[14] Still, there are tempting objections to it which have not yet been considered.

One objection to the Alienability Thesis appeals to the claim that 'no one can take away your human rights.' Perhaps what is meant by this claim is the *Nondeprivability Thesis*, that is, that *no one else* can justifiably separate the possessor of human rights from his rights by a deliberate act. Even if the Nondeprivability Thesis is true, it would be a mistake to infer from that the falsity of the Alienability Thesis. Even if no one else can, by deliberate act, bring it about that the possessor of the right ceases to have it, it does

[13] In the last few paragraphs and throughout most of this section, I draw on my essay, "Are Human Rights Alienable?" *Philosophical Studies* 37 (1980) pp. 165–176.

[14] In a discussion of voluntary euthanasia and the right to life, Joel Feinberg argues that voluntary euthanasia may be justified *even if* the right to life is inalienable. Although I have reservations about Feinberg's reasons for drawing *this* conclusion, one reading of his position suggests that he offers no arguments, nor intends to, against the Alienability Thesis. I infer this because Feinberg allows, in his discussion of a hypothetical spring rite involving the hunting of humans, that the right to life may be waived in a strong sense ('permanently and irrevocably'). See Feinberg, "Voluntary Euthanasia and the Inalienable Right to Life," *Philosophy & Public Affairs* 7, No. 2 (Winter, 1978), pp. 93–123.

not follow that the *possessor* cannot by deliberate act divest himself of the right in question. Hence, the claim that human rights are inalienable finds no support from the Nondeprivability Thesis. The claim that 'no one can take away your human rights,' on the other hand, may be understood to mean that no one justifiably can infringe any human right which you have. This proposal, however, leaves entirely open the question of whether some presumptive possessor may have divested such rights.

Second, it might be claimed that if human rights were alienable certain wildly counterintuitive results follow. For example, if competent adult humans could waive their right to be free or surrender it in exchange for a certain compensation, then, if that were done, there would be no reason to conclude that the enslaving of that human being would be unjustified. Since such enslavement is unjustified, on the view considered, it is more reasonable to conclude that human rights, such as the right to be free, are such that their possessors cannot divest themselves of such rights by voluntary act; hence, they are inalienable.[15] This objection is inconclusive, however, even if one grants that human enslavement is never justified. It is not obvious that an adequate ethical theory which assigns serious weight to considerations of rights must regard such considerations alone as *positively dispositive* with regard to the question of how human beings may justifiably be treated. Even if the right to be free were no longer possessed by Jones, as a result of its being alienated, it does not follow that enslaving Jones would be justified. That it would be justified would require further argument, for it is not obviously wrong that we have duties prohibiting the enslavement of human beings which do not derive from the possession of rights of human beings.

Another objection proposes that I have confused two quite different matters, namely (1) giving up a right (and, therefore, ceasing to have it), and (2) simply not exercising a right (and, therefore, not ceasing to have it). My objector may claim, further, that I have sketched only reasons for thinking that human beings deliberately may choose not to exercise their human rights, but it does not follow from that fact that they are given up and, thus, alienated. Let us consider first the alleged distinction. Suppose a group of us

[15] In a most interesting, though sometimes dense, study Richard Tuck traces disputes in the sixteenth century over whether rights were inalienable and whether self-enslavement was morally permissible; some rights theorists defended slavery *and* absolutism. See Richard Tuck, *Natural Rights Theories* (Cambridge: Cambridge University Press, 1979), Chapter 3.

form an Antidepression Society. Participating members pay dues and acquire a right to be delivered a bouquet of daffodils whenever they choose. If I happily never sink into great gloom, I never exercise my right to receive the daffodils; nevertheless, I retain the right. If the other members abscond with the funds reserved for the agreed purpose such that my right could not be accorded, my right is infringed. By contrast, if I, in an optimistic flush of contentment tell the members that I give up my right to receive a bouquet and they may do as they wish with the funds I have contributed, I waive my right and, hence, no longer have it. Then there is no right of mine to be infringed by another use of my contribution. The alleged distinction between (1) and (2) is, then, a genuine one. What is of more importance is whether cases of apparent alienation of human rights are all actually cases of their non-exercise. There is little reason to think so. It seems intelligible that I might give up my right to be free for ten years in exchange for my contracting myself to a "master" who will spend a large sum for an operation to save my sick child. I thereby become a "slave" for that period, and it is not obvious that I continue to have any right to be free which is infringed by my enslaver, any right to stand on or assert by way of protest. This case of voluntary enslavement contrasts with other imaginable cases. Suppose I were enslaved for a similar period against my preference (to be free); yet, believing I am a 'natural slave' I am too servile to stand on my right to be free. Here it seems appropriate to say that I have such a right, retain it, and yet simply fail to exercise it. A legitimate basis for complaint remains and perhaps a ground for concluding that compensation is necessary for the infringing of a right. These features seem absent in the case of voluntary enslavement, and such a case must, I believe, be classified as one of alienation of rights.

Yet another objection to the Alienability Thesis may be found in the remarks of the author of *Leviathan*. Hobbes believes that 'man's right' to liberty may be "laid aside either by simply renouncing it or by transferring it to another."[16] However, with regard to certain human rights, "the right of resisting them that assault by force to take away his life" or the right not to be imprisoned, he claims that "a man cannot lay down the right."[17] Hobbes proposes that this is so because a man "cannot be understood to aim thereby at any good to himself."[18] Hence, if a man *says* that he renounces

[16] Thomas Hobbes, *Leviathan*, ed. Oscar Piest (New York: Liberal Arts Press, 1958), p. 112.
[17] Ibid.
[18] Ibid.

such rights "he is not to be understood as if he meant it or that it was his will, but that he was ignorant of how such words and actions were to be interpreted."[19] If Hobbes is correct, some human rights are inalienable. Is the argument, however, persuasive? In asserting that one 'cannot' lay down the right, Hobbes is surely not using 'cannot' to indicate logical impossibility as one might in asserting '2 + 2 cannot equal 5.' His assumption may be that no one *ought* to renounce a right unless he believes that doing so is likely to bring about some good to himself. If this is Hobbes's meaning, however, even if his claim is acceptable, it is compatible with the claim that persons *do* renounce rights which they *ought not renounce. Indeed it would seem pointless to propose that one ought* not renounce human rights unless one is *capable* of doing so. And one will be capable of doing so only if the rights in question are alienable. Perhaps Hobbes's claim is rather that as a matter of fact we cannot ascertain or even imagine any 'good for himself' that a man may aim at by declaring that he renounces the mentioned rights. So, there is no reason ever to regard apparent renunciations as genuine, nor would there ever be good reason to do so. On this interpretation, Hobbes's view is similar to the claim that utterances of 'I wish I were dead' are never true (or that the related choice is not rational). The problem with such claims is that there is no reason to think they are *never* true. Likewise, one can imagine a case, for example, where one might prefer to renounce one's right to resist an assailant in order to get the assailant and his cohorts to discontinue the torture of one's family. To the objection that such a case is one where the right bearer does not aim at any *good to himself*, it may be replied that the right bearer may prefer, on balance, the loss of his right and the cessation of torture to, on the other hand, retention of the right and continuation of the torture. He may judge that renouncing the right may best promote what he most prefers among his limited options; in that way he may aim at a "good to himself" or promote his conception of the good. It does not seem difficult to imagine cases where a person would be aiming at such a good by renouncing most fundamental rights.[20] So, Hobbes's supposition, to the contrary, quite simply appears to

---

[19] Ibid.

[20] I am proposing the possibility and potential reasonableness of renouncing a moral right to resist an assailant or a right not to be tortured. Such a proposal is compatible with the claim that such a person may not renounce correlative legal rights and that those rights might be unjustifiably infringed by a torturer. Alternatively, if rights (legal or moral) are not the only morally relevant consideration, it may still be wrong to torture someone.

be, false—and his argument for the inalienability of certain rights unsound.

One upshot of our exploration of the alienability of human rights, including the right to life, is that even if persons do possess a right to life and even if they have that right because they are human beings, they can cease to have it by waiving such rights.[21] Hence, in the case of a competent person who validly consents to be euthanized, indeed requests to be euthanized, euthanizing him does not infringe a right to life; though previously possessing it he no longer does. Hence, euthanizing such a person is not an impermissible act of paternalism *because* of a right infringement.[22] As indicated, it does not follow that others ought to accede to every voluntary, informed request of competent persons. Even if the barrier of rights is let down, it does not follow that we should affect the lives of persons in all the ways which infringe no rights. Nor does it follow that we should not. Even if it is permissible paternalism to euthanize the consenting person, it *may* be permissible to refuse and, perhaps, permissible paternalism to refuse. Analogously, it may be permissible paternalism to tell you that you are late for an appointment or permissible paternalism not to tell you. The question of cooperation is a matter to which we will return at a later point.

Although we have taken human rights seriously in this discussion and suggested that one way of understanding the moral importance of valid consent is that it involves a waiver of rights, the importance of consent need not, I suggest, be wedded to a theory of rights; the importance of consent can be elucidated without mention of rights. Suppose that people simply have a strong presumptive duty not to kill other human beings. This "deep struc-

---

[21] In addition, if further argument would show that it is not humanity *per se* which suffices for certain rights (unless alienated) but rather sentience or rationality, my analysis could easily be accommodated. Whether human rights are only a subset of natural rights of the sentient, or rights of the rational (because they are sentient or because they are rational, as opposed to 'because they are human *per se*'), my basic contention is that those unacquired, basic rights are alienable by their possessors. Or if the rights cannot be alienated *in fact* (I have ignored this consideration to this point), it is because of certain incapacities of the right holder, and not because of the nature of the rights or the basis of their initially being held. For example, a completely paralyzed person, in practice, may not be able to alienate her human right, but this is so because of the paralysis and not because of any feature of the right in question. The right is, thus, alienable, even if its holder is unable to carry out the alienation of it.

[22] Lance Stell, in an instructive discussion, arrives at conclusions regarding consent and alienability of the right to life similar to those drawn here; see Lance Stell, "Duelling and the Right to Life," *Ethics*, 90 (October, 1979), pp. 7–26.

ture" conviction is implicit in common morality and all leading ethical theories. For whatever reason, it may be held that there is no correlative right to life residing in those to whom the duty is owed. Hence, there is, on such a view, no basis to complain that a *right infringement* has occurred when a human being is killed, for example, in the case of voluntary euthanasia. Even if that is a reasonable view of things, it may be true that those *owed* the duty not to kill (call them "objects of duty") can *release* duty holders from their duties by consenting to the nonperformance of such duties toward the consenting parties. Hence, even if we do not analyze the importance of consent in terms of a waiver of rights, we can interpret its importance in terms of release from duties. If we insist that it is only the valid consent of the object of duty which can serve to release others from duty toward that object, the object's choices continue to be of central importance. So, the importance of consent need not be dependent on the existence of a viable theory of rights. Whether a theory assigning importance to release from duties is more than terminologically different from a theory assigning importance to waiver of rights I leave an open question.

We may conjecture that there is an analogue to the thesis of alienable rights in a theory of duty which allows no place for rights. It might be held that we have certain duties toward human beings which *must* be fulfilled quite independently of the wishes or choices of the objects of such duties. For example, one might claim that we ought not to engage in "sadistic sexual practices," of the whips and chains variety, even if a "masochistically oriented" person requests such treatment. This claim does not seem implausible. It might be claimed that such a duty derives from a more general duty not to treat persons in a demeaning fashion or in a way which fosters servility. Hence, on this line of thought there are "unreleasable duties," a doctrine paralleling the doctrine of inalienable rights. Relatedly, it might be claimed that we have an unreleasable duty not to kill innocent persons, a principle paralleling the claim that we ought not to infringe the (alleged) inalienable right to life. What, however, could be said in defense of such claims? One possibility is that acting according to such duties is *for the good* of the object of duty, as when the object's life is preserved. An interesting response. We have already argued that the appeal to good promotion (or welfare promotion) fails to provide adequate grounds for paternalistic intervention.[23] Relatedly it may be claimed

---

[23] That is, which justified non-innocuous paternalistic intervention.

that for a person to cause his own death by his own hand (suicide) or indirectly (by choosing euthanasia) is a wrong even if not a wrong to others; hence, we should not euthanize one who requests it, for we must not contribute to his moral corruption. That is, it is for the requesting person's moral good not to cooperate with the request for euthanasia. If our prior argument is sound, the appeals to welfare preservation (or promotion), to moral-good preservation, or even autonomy preservation are unacceptable and fail to justify paternalistic interference with subjects whose acts wrong no others. So, it is not at all clear that there is an adequate defense of the claim that there are any unreleasable duties toward persons capable of valid consent.[24] I conclude that a strategy appealing to such alleged unreleasable duties fares no better than the appeal to inalienable rights (in particular, the right to life) in an attempt to justify the claim that voluntary euthanasia of innocent competent persons is wrong. More generally, a theory of duties or a theory of rights can and must recognize the moral importance of the presence or absence of valid consent.

5.4 A Right to Be Killed

For the most part, our focus has been on (possibly) paternalistic commissions, such as euthanasia. Some paternalistic behavior, however, consists of paternalistic omissions. A deliberate omitting or refraining from a certain act is paternalistic if the agent refrains out of desire to promote a benefit for, or prevent a harm to, the subject and his omission is contrary to the operative preference of the subject. Although such an omission counts as a kind of intervention or interference (in the somewhat extended sense adopted here), it may be morally innocuous and, thus, not presumptively wrong. If I, for example, refrain from telling you that you, inadvertently, offended your friend by a remark—even though you prefer to be told these sorts of things—my paternalistic behavior

---

[24] There is, however, a trivial sense in which some duties may be said to be unreleasable (not that the duties are trivial). A type of act one might have a duty to omit might be defined such that the type of act is, by definition, one to which a "recipient" does not consent. The duty not to rape is an obvious example. A woman who voluntarily and knowingly consents to intercourse is not raped. There can be consent to intercourse but not to rape. Theft is another example of a criminally prohibited act which is defined as involuntary from the standpoint of the victim. None of this shows that there are unreleasable duties to do or omit acts where the type of act is not defined in such a way as to make it logically impossible for there to be consent to it by the recipient.

(I refrained because I wanted to spare you from excessive self-denigration) does not seem presumptively wrong. We do not owe others the duty to tell them *everything* that they may wish to know. In contrast I have argued (Chapter 4) that some paternalistic omissions are presumptively wrong; if so, they deserve moral scrutiny and assessment.

Suppose that an agent refuses to euthanize a requesting competent subject. Can such an omission be presumptively wrong? Can it be an impermissible paternalistic omission? Correlatively could one ever have a *duty* to kill an innocent, requesting, competent person? That an agent could have such a duty is a most controversial claim; it shall be our initial focus here. Later I will examine the issue of whether a paternalistic refusal to euthanize could be impermissible.

Before we return to the context in which a right to be killed might be said to arise in virtue of a contractual agreement, it is worth noticing that in certain special contexts it is not implausible that a subject may have a right to be killed apart from any contractual agreement, or, if that is too strong, that a subject may have such a strong claim that others normally ought to agree to kill him. I shall elaborate shortly. Killing another innocent is normally wrong because it is against the other's will and the right to life cannot be judged to have been waived. Furthermore, if S wants his own life to end prematurely, that is a goal which S normally may achieve if left to his own devices. In addition, decisions to end life normally are tragic and the role of being terminator of another's life is disturbing and fraught with certain psychological risks for the occupant of the role. Such considerations normally count decisively against the claim that one party has any unacquired duty to kill another innocent. Even when a competent person knowingly and voluntarily requests to be killed, it normally remains true that the subject has alternative means to achieve that end, and others understandably are extremely reluctant to function as terminators of life.

We need to keep in mind both the existence of exceptional circumstances and what may be required by a principle of mutual aid. First, the least controversial but still affirmative claim which may be made regarding the existence of a positive duty to aid others is that we have a duty to perform acts for the benefit of others when those others do not dissent, when the benefit is perceived as one of great importance (or would be under less encumbered circumstances) by the subject and the agent, and the cost (con-

strued broadly) to the agent is small. Even this "minimalist" identification and assertion of a positive duty to help others is viewed
skeptically by some. I shall offer such skeptics no argument except
to note one point.[25] Complying with certain comparatively noncontroversial negative duties sometimes requires expenditure of
effort or even nontrivial risk taking; thus, such features do not
serve as a benchmark for distinguishing what is a duty from what
is not, or positive duties from negative duties.

Supposing that we indeed have the sort of positive duty described above, consider then the existence of exceptional circumstances, ones exceptional beyond the fact we are asked to kill. We
can imagine cases in which competent persons, due to disease,
injury, or other disability, are unable to take their own lives and
want to have others do it—or want their assistance in doing it
themselves. Our focus, of course, is only on cases in which the
subject is competent and voluntarily has made a reasoned choice.
In such cases and where we reasonably can conclude that continued
existence of the subject involves a hopeless prospect such as end-
less deprivation and suffering, the principle of mutual aid supports
the view that we ought to assist such persons in some fashion; in
some cases this may involve euthanasia. However, we should note
that such cases may be quite rare if our only basis for deciding is
the assumption that subjects have a right to whatever they are due
according to the principle of mutual aid. The latter principle only
requires aid when the agent can provide it at little cost. Two factors
may generate a high cost for the agent. One is simply the risks
involved when the form of ending life is legally prohibited with
criminal penalties attached. Such a consideration morally can place
certain acts outside the domain of obligatory mutual aid, even if it
is useless in deciding whether such a law should exist in the first
place. However, aside from the legal status of euthanasia, the
thought, for most persons, of killing another—even at another's
request—is repugnant. This factor again *tends* to exclude euthanasia
from the domain of aid which we ought to provide for others. Still,
there are times when we should aid others even though what is
necessary is repugnant, for example, the amputation of a gangrenous finger when no less painful, less injurious, alternative is
available. For the reasons discussed, it is not implausible to recognize a right to be killed in certain quite special cases, namely

---

[25] For a defense, however, see David Richards, *Sex, Drugs, Death, and the Law*
(Totowa, N. J.: Rowman and Littlefield, 1982), pp. 223–225.

those in which a person may be owed that form of assistance on a reasonable application of the principle of mutual aid. Indeed, if this is not a matter of mere benevolence but of just treatment, the subject has a right to it.

However, one might adopt a more cautious position and still recognize that a person could come to have a right to be killed. The more cautious view would deny that we strictly owe others mutual aid of the sort mentioned (and, hence, others have no natural or unacquired right to it); however, the considerations mentioned (importance to the subject, low cost to the agent, and so on) provide strong reasons for an agent to decide to accede to a request for euthanasia. On this way of thinking the subject has no unacquired right to be killed, but there are good reasons for others to agree to perform the task. This more cautious but weaker view, however, is compatible with the thesis that no one could have a right to be killed. At this point it will be useful to turn to an examination of Peter Williams' defense of that thesis—a defense which, I shall argue, is not successful.

One ground for concluding that someone had a duty to kill an innocent person would be the claim that the innocent had a right to be killed and that he demanded his right.[26] However, if there could not be a duty to kill innocents, then the provocative thesis that under certain conditions innocent persons have a right to be killed is false. In a thoughtful examination of this last claim, Williams has asserted that there *cannot* be such a right; he proposes that an ". . . analysis of the moral force of claims of right demonstrates that we cannot be duty bound to kill innocents."[27] If this view is correct, no one could have *a right* to be killed, even if on occasion it might be morally *permissible* to do so.

After setting forth a plausible and familiar statement of the relation of rights and duties, a distinction between positive and negative rights, and rights and privileges, Williams claims that, in a medical context, for example, before a patient could have *a right* against his physician to be killed the "potential killer must satisfy himself that the killing is preferable to continued life" (for the patient).[28] He continues by proposing that

[26] "Right" here means a claim right which implies that one or more others have a corollary duty to act or forbear in certain ways, as opposed to a mere liberty (right) which has no such corollary duty.

[27] Peter C. Williams, "Rights and the Alleged Right of Innocents to be Killed," *Ethics* 87 (July, 1977), p. 384.

[28] Ibid., p. 392.

As opposed to contexts in which genuine rights exist, one may legitimately refuse to kill another when it seems that the death would be morally worse than continued life. The potential killer need sustain only the burden of proof typical of nonrights contexts. "I don't think it is prudent of you to die," is sufficient reason to excuse the reluctant executioner. The decision doesn't belong to the potential victim in the way characteristic of rights.[29]

The first quoted sentence is noteworthy because it seems to assume that in the situation described we do in fact have a "nonrights context." Merely to assume that we do, however, would beg the question at hand, namely, whether the patient does have a right to be killed. But Williams, in the passage quoted, may be arguing in the following way in support of his claim that this is a "nonrights context":

1. If this were a context in which the patient had a right to be killed, then the fact that the potential killer judged that the patient would be acting imprudently (by choosing to be killed) would *not* be a sufficient reason to conclude that the patient had no right to be killed.
2. But, it is a sufficient reason.
3. Hence, this is not a context in which the patient has a right to be killed.

For the sake of discussion, let us assume that the first premise is correct. My cavil is with the second premise. To assess it, consider another case in which one party has reluctance about performing an act which will provide some good or service for another party (perceived, at least, as a benefit by the second party). It is a case in which the reluctant party's reason for refusal (or temptation to refuse) is based on the judgment that the recipient of the good or service will act imprudently (or imprudently subject himself to certain treatment). If you have a right to be paid three thousand dollars by me since you sold me your solar powered bicycle, should I accord you your right to the money even if I think you are foolish in intending to spend the money on the last pair of shoestrings used by Elvis Presley? In this case, it seems that I must pay you even if I doubt the wisdom of your prospective use of the money. A plausible moral principle here is that *those who hold duties correlative to specific rights of others must, in general, accord those rights even*

[29] Ibid.

252

if in their judgment the upshot of doing so will be an imprudent action by, or an undesirable result for, the right holder. Indeed, such a principle seems presupposed by the first premise of my reconstruction of Williams' argument.

A possible difference between our discussion of the "bicycle case" and the euthanasia case is that the former supposes that a *contractual agreement* has occurred and that the case of a patient's request to be killed supposes that no analogous agreement has been made. If it is assumed that no agreement has been made between the potential killer and the one who requests his own termination, then the case for a right to be killed in such a situation may be quite weak. But the judgment of imprudence made by the potential executioner by itself may justify his decision to *refrain* from putting himself in the position of initially according another a right to be killed. We come, then, to a crucial point. The mentioned euthanasia case focuses on a precontractual or prepromise context in which the patient may *not* have a right to be killed. This focus, however, may divert our attention from possible cases in which a contract *has* been made, whether or not it was one prudent for each party to make. If, for example, physician A explicitly has agreed to administer a lethal dosage to fellow physician S if and when S suffers from serious and irreversible brain damage, then, whether it was prudent for the parties to make such a contract or not, there is a strong presumption that S has a right to be killed under such circumstances and A a correlative duty to kill, notwithstanding A's reluctance to be an executioner. Belated reluctance of the *sort* mentioned on the part of the potential executioner is no reason to assume that no contract was made or that no right to be killed accrued to the patient once a contract was made. The question of whether one ought to commit oneself to be an executioner is distinct from the question of whether a right obtains once an agreement is reached.

We have suggested, then, a possible case in which a contract generates a right to be killed. It may be objected that if such a private "agreement" were reached, it would not necessarily result in any rights or duties. Just as illegal contracts generate no legally binding rights or duties (or, at best, quite limited ones), so a private agreement may not count as a "morally valid" contract. In law, ". . . a bargain may be illegal by reason of the wrongful purpose of one or both parties. . . ."[30] A plausible and analogous moral

---

[30] See Joseph D. Calamari and Joseph M. Perillo, *The Law of Contracts* (St. Paul, Minn.: West, 1970), p. 566.

assumption is that no agreement counts as a *morally valid* contract (one resulting in moral rights and duties for the contracting parties) if the agreement commits either party to performing an act which would be morally wrong. It may be claimed, specifically, that it would be morally wrong for a physician to kill a patient who knowingly and freely consents to be killed. Hence, *even if* the physician *agreed* to do so, the contract, on this view, would not be morally binding and would not result in the patient's having a moral right to be killed.

If there are reasons for thinking that such a contract is not morally valid, it may be that there are reasons for being reluctant to *enter* into such a contract, though not all such reasons need be like those mentioned earlier—namely, that it would be *imprudent* for the patient to choose to die. However, our current question is whether an *existing* agreement would be morally valid. There are cases in which agreements seem neither legally nor morally valid. First, there are familiar cases where the consent of either party is not informed, is "given" under duress, or fraudulently obtained. It is clear, however, that these factors need not be present in a possible agreement of the sort being considered.[31] Second, there are cases in which a contract is for a "wrongful purpose" because performance of the contract would wrong third parties. For example, A may contract with B to assassinate B's rival. Similarly, in a less extreme case a harm to third parties is believed legally to invalidate contracts involving restraint of trade; here A may agree to sell his business to B and agree also to refrain from becoming a competitor to B in a specified area or during a specified interval. The third party interest allegedly violated is the public interest in free competition and avoidance of monopoly.[32] We already have argued that it is reasonable to believe that in certain cases a patient need not cause a wrongful harm to third parties by contracting to be killed, and that a person's death need not thereby result in his failing to perform positive obligations to others.

On the assumptions that no wrong to third parties would occur by the execution (sic) of such a contract between patient and phy-

---

[31] Some would argue that anyone who contracted to be killed *could not* be "in his right mind" and must, therefore, not be competent to contract; so, no morally valid contract results. I assume such a view is false although it *may* be correct that many who choose to die are not competent.

[32] Similarly, agreements to sell a public office or one's vote, to defraud a third party, to relieve a husband's duty to support, or to relieve a wife's duty to have sexual relations with her husband have been held illegal. See Chapter 19, "Illegal Bargains," in Calamari and Perillo, *The Law of Contracts* , pp. 537ff.

sician and that the parties are competent and voluntarily make an agreement, it is necessary to examine two other bases for proposing that such a contract would *not* be morally valid: (1) that it is wrongful because of a conflict with other obligations the physician has undertaken by positive act, and (2) that it is wrongful because the act of killing an innocent, consenting (requesting, and bargaining) competent patient infringes the rights of, or wrongfully harms, the patient. Consider first an obligation a physician may have incurred by a prior positive act. He may have promised another party, for example, the patient's mother, that he would not terminate the patient's life. A later agreement with the patient, therefore, may be morally invalid. Even if this assumption is correct we simply may suppose that such a previously incurred duty, as a contingent fact, may not be present in a given case. The objection may be raised further, that *all* physicians have taken an oath to refrain from killing innocents, quite apart from possible conflicting promises to particular individuals. Williams appeals to just this consideration:

> Another way to see that there is no *duty* to kill in typical euthanasia contexts is that a physician, or another potential killer, may excuse himself by saying "I simply don't do that kind of thing." Professional codes of ethics and personal codes prohibiting killing always justify a refusal to kill innocents.[33]

The claim that there is a duty not to kill innocents on the part of those taking certain professional oaths is not as straightforward as it may appear. Consider the most well known professional oath taken by physicians, the Hippocratic oath. Two key prescriptions in the oath are to "abstain from all intentional wrongdoing and harm" and *not* to "administer a poison to anybody when asked to do so."[34] There may be incompatible prescriptions in the oath. If a patient chooses to die and requests to be killed and, further, does so because he is going to die soon anyway and suffer severe pain in the possible interim, it would appear that *not* honoring his request will *violate* the dictum "do no harm" in two ways. First, his suffering will be perpetuated to no obviously good end. Second,

---

[33] See Williams, "Rights and the Alleged Right of Innocents to be Killed," p. 392. It might be objected that Williams' focus is only on "typical euthanasia contexts" (see last quotation). If the implicit assumption is that such contexts do not involve contracts or agreements of the sort mentioned, his thesis, duly narrowed in scope, is in danger of being trivial even if true. I argue, of course, that if it is understood nontrivially, it is false.

[34] "Oath" in *Hippocrates*, trans. W.H.S. Jonas, Vol. I, Loeb Classical Library (London: William Heinemann, 1948), pp. 299–301.

his (let us assume: competent and reasonable) request and decision is not respected. That is, his prerogative to direct his own life is not given decisive weight. Hence, there is reason to believe that the prescription "do no harm" in fact may *require* that he be killed. If so, in the restricted type of cases indicated, it would be impossible for a physician to obey both the rule not to harm and the rule to withhold poison from those requesting it (construing this latter broadly: do not kill consenting innocents).

It may be objected that surely it *is harming* a patient to kill him. Such a view is extremely tempting since it is commonly correct to say that when an innocent person is killed he has been harmed. Tempting views are, of course, not only seductive but often false. What is meant by 'A harms S'? If by 'A harms S,' one means 'A causes pain to S,' we note that the patient need *not* be harmed if his life is painlessly terminated. If "do no harm" requires alleviating harm (where 'harm' here means 'suffering'), then in certain cases the only way to alleviate harm may be to terminate the patient's life. Suppose that by 'A harms S' is meant 'A makes S worse off,' but on the assumptions mentioned the patient judges that to continue to live is to be worse off. It is not evident that such judgments are always mistaken, and on occasion the physician reasonably may agree. It is worth observing that although dying may indeed be "a harm," it may not be a harm *on balance*. That is, a patient may judge that he is, and he may be, worse off on balance by continuing subjection to intolerable pain, discouragement, and despair than if he dies. The Hippocratic prescription "do no harm" is plausible only if understood as meaning "do no harm *on balance*."[35] If it is understood to prohibit causing *a* harm, it would prohibit all sorts of standard surgical operations, ones which involve "harms" such as pain or tissue damage. Finally, suppose that 'A harms S' means 'A infringes S's right to life.' We have argued previously, however, that a person can waive fundamental human rights such as the right to life. When S competently requests to be killed, he thereby waives any right not to be killed. If so, no right to life is infringed, and no harm occurs on *this* interpretation of 'A harms S.' Killing of innocents *is* typically wrong because it typically *does* wrongfuly harm in one or more of the assignable senses mentioned, but in the case considered it is not obvious that to kill is to harm in any of those senses of 'harm.' Hence, it is not at all obvious that killing in such a case would violate the dictum "do

[35] Recall our earlier discussion in Section 4.4.

no harm." Further, I have stated why the prescription *may* entail, in selected cases and in combination with innocuous empirical assumptions, a duty to kill. So it is not evident that the Hippocratic oath will serve to justify a refusal to kill innocents. It is not clear, then, that physicians who have taken the Hippocratic oath have, for *that* reason, a prior obligation to refrain from killing innocents who so request it. If they do not, then the claim that a physician's contracting to kill *must* be morally invalid, because it conflicts with such a prior duty, fails.

To this point I have ignored, and shall continue to ignore, the questions of whether a physician ought to take such an oath and whether, if he (or she) has, it creates a duty which is always an overriding one. Regarding the second question, it is clear that the ancient oath is not always regarded as so solemnly binding. For example, it also prohibits giving "a pessary to a woman to cause abortion."[36] However, it is not necessary to resolve these matters since even if it could be shown (and we have outlined reasons for thinking the task a *difficult* one) that physicians could never have a duty to kill requesting innocents and, hence, that they cannot *validly* contract to do so, Williams' thesis is not merely that no one could have a right to be killed *by a physician* but rather that no one could have a right to be killed *by anyone*.[37] Since he claims that this is demonstrated by "an analysis of the moral force of claims of right," consideration of other cases is, therefore, in order.

A potential executioner may not have an obligation not to kill innocents *derivable* from a sworn oath. Perhaps it is the case, however, that all moral agents have a duty not to kill requesting innocents. Perhaps it is a duty for reasons other than: having taken an oath and so no actual contract to do so could count as a morally valid one (and, thus, create a right to be killed). If it is defensible that such acts are invariably wrong, then and only then would there be reason to conclude that no contractual right to be killed could arise. It is beyond my purpose to offer further defense of the view that such acts need not be wrong. I will be content to have cast the burden of proof on those who wish to maintain the contrary. For reasons stated earlier it does not appear that certain killings of requesting innocents can be said to be wrong because harm on balance is caused or rights are infringed. Relevant third party interests, as a contingent matter, need not be thwarted. Un-

---

[36] "Oath" in *Hippocrates*, trans. W.H.S. Jonas, pp. 299–301.
[37] Williams, "Rights and the Alleged Right of Innocents to be Killed," p. 394.

less these claims can be undermined or some other basis offered to show that such acts are wrong, there seems to be no barrier to the formation of the requisite morally valid contracts. Hence, if such a contract were made, there would exist a right to be killed.[38] In such an event, as argued earlier, belated reluctance to execute on the part of the party who contracted to do so would fail to show that there is no right to be killed—anymore than belated reluctance on the part of a duty holder to carry out duties respecting rights does in other cases of morally valid contracts.

If the prior argument is correct, in quite special, indeed somewhat rarefied, cases, a competent person might have a moral right to be killed. Granting that right, assuming that the subject has not altered his purpose to be euthanized, would not be an act of paternalistically euthanizing S since doing so would not be contrary to S's operative preference and intent. However, if the party, A, with whom S contracted deliberately were to refrain (from paternalistic motives) from so doing, such a refusal would be a paternalistic omission. On the theory developed here such an omission would be impermissible since it would not be one to which the competent subject validly consented. If the agent, A, belatedly were convinced that S's choice was imprudent or foolish, A, by fair, open, attempts, could seek to persuade S to alter his course and to release A from his acquired obligation. If A fails to dissuade S, it is not clear why one should infer that A permissibly may pater-

[38] I have argued that private contracts may create a right to be killed, but one might argue that the claim there is an obligation to do no harm requires that one ought not omit acts which would meet the serious needs of others and can be done with minimal sacrifice. In such a case, it may be claimed that those who have a serious need to be treated in manner X have a right to be so treated. Indeed, this is the type of assumption currently found in another important context, the problem of obligations to the starving. It occurs, for example, in William Aiken's "The Right to be Saved from Starvation"; I quote "Dire need creates obligations and rights. Starving persons have a moral right against those who are in a position to help them. Their suffering is not simply a harmful by-product of a morally permissible omission on the part of others. It is a wrong committed against them. It is a violation of their moral rights." Analogously, it might be argued that those who find their continued existence intolerable have a need to die, and in special cases to be killed; hence, they have a right to be killed and certain others may have a duty to respond. However, I forego this way of arguing for the existence of a right to be killed because it seems doubtful that entities with a dire need for X have, *thereby*, a right to X or that where it is in the interest of some entity to be treated in a certain manner it has a right to be so treated. I make a similar point in "Defending Animals by Appeal to Rights," in *Animal Rights and Human Obligations*, eds., Tom Regan and Peter Singer (Englewood Cliffs, N. J.: Prentice-Hall, 1976), pp. 224–229. The quotation is from William Aiken's, "The Right to be Saved from Starvation," *World Hunger and Moral Obligation*, eds., William Aiken and Hugh LaFollette (Englewood Cliffs, N.J.: Prentice-Hall, 1977), p. 86.

nalistically refuse to do his duty in this, admittedly extreme, situation.

I have said nothing here about what the law should be with regard to allowing and enforcing such contracts.[39] Such matters introduce further complications. There is, however, a presumption that, if matters are morally as delineated above, then that law should allow such contracts—if wrongs to third parties and other possible abuses can be avoided, and, in general, considerations of justice are not, thereby, subverted. Whether this is possible, or likely, I leave an open question here. The law is often heavy-handed; a certain skepticism is in order with respect to whether the scalpel of the law would be used to separate morally defensible killings from those which are not. Be that as it may, it is useful to reflect on the implications of recognizing the right of competent persons to direct their own lives and the fact that doing so may commit us to some "hard sayings" about what we should do in certain delicate, or indeed, tragic circumstances. Respecting such a right of competent persons unfortunately does not allow us to do all that we believe may be for their own good—or refrain when we believe that an act fails to promote that end. For in the relevant domain, that is for others to decide.

In general, if competent persons wish to end their own lives that is something they can normally do without the aid of others. As noted, however, there are exceptions. Even then the burden on others of performing an act which is in some sense repugnant or offensive may place euthanasia outside the domain of what is required by the duty of mutual aid. Still, if others appropriately contract or promise to provide such assistance, a subject then may have a right to be killed, and belated paternalistic reluctance to carry through may be indefensible. Anyone inclined toward such reluctance would have a self-interested reason to avoid such commitments. Further, for those who "lack the stomach" for it, the

---

[39] I have not been directly concerned with legal rights. In law the consent of one who has been injured may not serve as a defense against criminal prosecution of the one who causes the injury. My comments are relevant to the issue of whether a consenting innocent who is killed in the situations considered should be thought to have been "injured" or to have been "wronged" and to the question of whether the law ought to recognize a right to be killed and a correlative duty in such situations. Some state legislatures have taken steps in this direction by making it legally *permissible* for a physician to withhold or withdraw certain life-perpetuating treatment if the patient explicitly expresses a desire that this should be done under certain conditions (e.g., a 1977 North Carolina law: Ch. 815, S504).

My thoughts and remarks on the issues discussed here have benefitted from the helpful criticisms of a former colleague, Alan Sparer.

cost of doing it (for an agent) may be so great as to preclude any unacquired duty to do it (otherwise derivable from a principle of mutual aid). What has not been very clear historically is whether one should assume that health-care professionals, ostensibly committed to relieving suffering, ever have a duty to end life or could have such a duty. The argument here suggests that they *could* have, but it also supports the view that often they do not because no appropriate promise or contract has occurred and because the principle of mutual aid does not require it when, to put the matter crudely, the performance of such a task is exceedingly burdensome to the agent. It is a mistake to think that euthanasia is always wrong, that people could not have a right to be killed, that one could never have a duty to kill, and also to assume that if euthanasia (of an active sort) of a patient is permissible, particular health-care professionals have a duty to carry it out. The burden for some professionals is too great; it should not be regarded as a duty of all such professionals. Nor should it be thought that all such professionals have a duty to abstain from such acts. There is a middle way.[40]

5.5 Preventing Suicide

One who kills another may have acted paternalistically. Likewise, one who refuses to kill another may have acted paternalistically. With would-be suicides we can, again, assist or refuse. For all that, there can be no "paternalistic suicide," although there can be paternalistic euthanasia. It is commonly thought that suicide prevention (by presumptively wrong means) is both permissible and desirable. Further, the reasons adduced in favor of such a view are typically paternalistic. Hence, suicide prevention is a rather clear example of a type of act thought to constitute justified paternalism—even toward adult strangers. The view to be defended here is that some such interference is unjustifiable, and some is justifiable. On this view there is, again, no reason to be driven toward conclusions of the form that "all acts of type T are wrong" or "all acts of type T are permissible." Let us explore the arguments.

Much ink has been spilt over defining 'suicide.' I shall spill little more and be content with a commonsense, broad-brushed analysis. By an 'act of suicide' I mean an 'act deliberately chosen by a person

[40] An excellent recent essay on euthanasia, one which has influenced my views, is that by Margaret Pabst Battin, "Euthanasia," in *Border Crossings*, eds., Donald VanDeVeer and Tom Regan.

who foresaw that the outcome, almost certainly, would be his own death.'[41] This is a broad characterization and sweeps into its net a large variety of cases.[42] Some are "martyr-type" cases in which an individual chooses to sacrifice his life to save others, for example, the proverbial soldier who jumps on a hand grenade or those who go on an indefinite hunger strike to promote a political cause. The more familiar type of case is not like this and is not "altruistic." Rather, it is typically one in which an agent with prudential motives chooses to avoid the pain, stress, anxiety, or the indignities of his own continued existence. When 'suicide' is mentioned it is usually these latter types of cases to which reference is being made. There is a tendency to assume that in such cases the subject is severely depressed. We may find two quite different sorts of grounds invoked for attributing severe depression. One is simply the fact that the subject wants to take his own life even though we may believe that the circumstances of the subject's life and his potential for "a life worth living" make it unreasonable for the subject to adopt such a despairing outlook. In such contexts a strong case may be made for saying that the subject is psychologically disoriented, disturbed, or victimized by psychological illness. Here there well may be a serious question about whether the party is indeed competent even if, prior to this point, the subject has exhibited little behavior to warrant an attribution of incompetence. In other types of cases the subject's future prospects for a life of net satisfaction seem so dim that there are good grounds for classifying his bleak outlook as a reasonable one. For example, consider the case of a victim with serious (third-degree) burns who assumes that, as a result (technology, of course, affects this), he will have little ability to walk, little or no use of limbs, no sight, will be sexually nonfunctional, and radically disfigured. It may be *possible* for such a person to make the dramatic readjustments (acceptance of severe

[41] It is reasonable to regard a person, Smith, as dead if she permanently has ceased to be sentient and to possess consciousness. Hence, if Smith chooses to bring about such a state, and does, we should, I maintain, regard such an act as an instance of suicide even though the body of Smith continues to function. There is, then, a peculiar but intelligible sense in which someone might be charged with "killing Smith" some time long after Smith committed suicide! This point suggests the desirability of reformulating the law of homicide, but I shall not explore it further.

[42] This broad characterization includes cases in which a subject deliberately takes his own life as a means to a further end even though he prefers (but not on balance) to live—and, also, cases where death is the end. This apparent distinction, however, may be a dubious one for maybe all would-be suicides have a preference to live under better circumstances but, as things are, choose death as a means to an end, e.g., escape from personal difficulties or promoting benefit to others, or both.

limitations, cultivation of new sources of satisfaction) required to live a more or less satisfying life. Nevertheless, it would be unrealistic and unreasonable for such a person *not* to be severely discouraged and pessimistic about his future prospects. Here, *some* sort of depression, at least for a time, seems a natural result of possessing those capacities constitutive of competence. Hence, there are diverse cases and, when necessary, we may restrict our focus to a subset of acts of suicide.

Setting such distinctions aside for a moment, it is clear that the view that suicide is a serious wrong is an ancient one and has not been regularly and vigorously questioned until recent decades. That suicide is wrong has been the prevalent commonsense view and a doctrine widely agreed on by diverse religious traditions. Both suicide and attempted suicide, with few exceptions, have been criminally prohibited.[43] The twentieth-century philosopher, Ludwig Wittgenstein, apparently regarded suicide as one of the clearest examples of a morally wrong act; he said

> If suicide is allowed then everything is allowed. If anything is not allowed then suicide is not allowed. This throws a light on the nature of ethics, for suicide is, so to speak, the elementary sin.[44]

In part, Wittgenstein asserts that if anything is wrong, suicide is. This view is, I believe, unacceptable, but I shall neither argue the point nor here suppose that suicide is not a moral wrong. For the sake of discussion, let us suppose that it is. If so, the question may be asked as to whether it is a wrong to others. It is worth observing that on virtually all ethical theories, there is a powerful presumption that one ought to keep ones promises and carry out contractual agreements (assuming that such promises or agreements are not themselves morally problematic, for example, because of the content of the agreement [cf. an assassination contract] or other factors [e.g., the agreement was fraudulently obtained]). It is reasonable to believe that persons often have duties toward others whose fulfillment requires positive effort; hence, there will be a range of

[43] Lance Stell points out that Texas law, unlike most jurisdictions, has, for most of this century, recognized a right to suicide and also extends a degree of legal immunity to those who aid a suicide; see Stell, "Duelling and the Right to Life," pp. 7–26.

[44] See Ludwig Wittgenstein: *Notebooks, 1914–1916*, ed. G. H. von Wright (Chicago: University of Chicago Press, 1979). The unearthing of this interesting passage must be credited to Jonathan Glover; see his instructive book, *Causing Death and Saving Lives* (Harmondsworth, Middx., England: Penguin Books, 1977), p. 171.

cases in which it is wrong to fail to carry out such duties toward others. There are also natural duties, for example, of parents toward their children, whose nonperformance constitutes a wrong, a wrong toward others. In these types of cases, then, for a duty holder deliberately to take his own life will, foreseeably, prevent him from fulfilling his duties toward others.[45] In such cases suicide is a wrong to others. One typical example would be the suicide of a surviving parent who has infant children who will suffer without his care but not with it.[46]

Is intervention permissible in such cases to *prevent* the suicide? All the leading ethical theories allow the use of force or coercion to prevent wrongful harms to other persons in a wide variety of cases, and there is virtually no disagreement that some degree of intervention is permissible in the type of case mentioned. If it is not already obvious, it should be noted, then, that there are legitimate but *nonpaternalistic* grounds for suicide prevention in selected cases. In such cases the prohibitions on interference with competent persons implied by the Principle of Autonomy-Respecting Paternalism are not challenged. In short, when suicides constitute serious wrongs to others, preventive interference may be permissible for nonpaternalistic reasons. Further, if suicides *always* constitute *wrongs to others*, then we need not trouble ourselves about whether presumptively wrong interventions to prevent suicide can be acts of justified paternalism—for there will be adequate grounds for interfering even though they are not paternalistic.

However, it is doubtful that all suicides constitute wrongs to others. In offering support for this point I shall, however, not be assuming that a suicide which is not a wrong *to others* is not a wrong at all. Shortly, we shall return to this point. There are easily imaginable cases and, I believe, numerous actual ones in which no serious case can be made that a person committing suicide wrongs others. These are cases either of comparatively "alone" individuals, without friends or relatives, who have no stringent duties toward

---

[45] Except, possibly, in cases in which suicide will fulfill a duty to others; I shall not assume that there are such cases.

[46] A qualification is in order. In the extreme case in which a person is so unhappy and despairing of a minimally decent existence, it is not clear that such a person has a stringent duty to remain alive solely to aid others. To do so would be for the would-be suicide to treat himself as a mere natural resource for the "use" or benefit of others. Analogously, persons who choose to lead their own lives normally have no stringent duty to sacrifice their own well-being to a point where their own lives would become absolutely wretched. Compare, for example, the wild claim that one ought to donate one organ or bodily part after another if others can thereby be benefitted. Such a duty to "give of oneself" (sic) is altruism run amok.

specific other persons, or those more social persons who, perhaps atypically, have "paid their debts" and, hence, wrong no others by committing suicide. Objections here to the effect that everyone must remain alive out of gratitude toward all those who have benefitted them or because their continued existence *might* benefit others seem far too thin a branch to bear any weight. Although I have not attempted to unravel the knotty issue of what sort of harms to others count as wrongs, it seems, at the very least, that not all acts which worsen the position of others in some respect (e.g., psychological distress, lost opportunity) are wrong. Doing well on an exam or in a race may in some sense "harm" others; it does not typically *wrong* other participants. As noted before, A's choice to marry B rather than C may "harm" C but typically involves no wrong to C. So, even in cases where S's suicide causes some distress to relatives or friends, that is not, without further argument, a sufficient reason to conclude that S has *wronged* those others. For these reasons I conclude that not all suicides involve a wrong to others.

If this reasoning is correct, the question arises as to whether there is legitimate ground to interfere to prevent suicides which, if successful, would involve no wrong to others. One implication of PARP is, of course, that it is wrong paternalistically to interfere invasively with a competent person, S, to prevent the commission of suicide except in those cases where S has validly consented to such efforts or in which there is good reason to believe that S would so consent if S were more fully aware of what he was doing and the consequences of his action.

This result, for various reasons, will strike some as absurd or even a dangerous conclusion. There are a number of objections which deserve consideration here. One concerns the claim that suicide is a wrong even if not a wrong to others; another that the result of suicide (successful) is catastrophic; another that PARP is irrelevant to deciding about suicide prevention since PARP only concerns dealings with competent persons, and "any person intent on suicide is incompetent."

The last issue raises a question central to the theory we have been developing for rather obvious reasons. I have claimed that different principles apply to our dealings with competent persons as opposed to those who are not. For that reason it is important to say more about the competent/incompetent distinction. Hence, I turn to explore this issue prior to further inquiry as to whether persons intent on suicide must be incompetent. According to Webster's, 'competence' means 'the quality or state of being functionally adequate or having a sufficient knowledge, judgment, skill or strength.'[47] Setting aside the focus on the vague characteristic of "functional adequacy" (one which may be attributable to can openers or hammers), the key features by virtue of which we attribute competence to human beings do concern possession of some knowledge and capacity to make judgments, that is, cognitive and/ or psychological traits enabling a being to make informed choices and to act in the light of those choices seem central to our ordinary notion of a competent person. There is a worry here which we ought not ignore. It may be claimed that competence is a *relativized* notion such that if someone is said to be competent we must always be able to answer the question, if we are to talk sensibly, "competent to do what?" That is, competence is always a capability to perform some particular type of act, for example, play a clarinet, serve a tennis ball, carve a turkey, or do quadratic equations. It may be argued, then, that there is no sensible *generalized* notion of competence, that there are no criteria for determining whether a person "is competent" *simpliciter* (or not). Our objector is certainly correct in insisting that we are often interested in determining whether an individual is competent to perform certain specific acts such as those mentioned. However, we can go some way in filling out the expression 'competent to ——' and, I believe, identify a generalized notion of competence, one which is essential for the theory developed here. The general competence which is of interest is simply: competence to direct one's own life. We can be more specific; it is competence to acquire information, identify alternative courses of action, to employ reason to assess alternatives, to choose among them in such a fashion as to promote what one takes to be the good (which may be what one finds prudent, what one believes to foster the good of others, or what one believes to be right), and to express one's will in action by taking steps toward the achievement of that good. These general capacities require in turn the possession of many more precisely characterizable capabilities, or "competences," for example the ability to understand, foresee, explain, predict, communicate, count, and evaluate in some moderately successful fashion. On reflection, this seems a familiar and natural way to elucidate what is meant by saying of some individual that she is competent, as opposed to incompetent. Some of the specific capacities which are essential to general competence are a

[47] See Webster's *Third International Dictionary* (1966).

matter of degree in the sense that of two generally competent persons one may possess a greater capacity to perform than another, for example, Rex can count rapidly by six (6, 12, 18, etc.) and Tex only slowly by one (1, 2, 3, etc.). If, however, Hex can count only to three, he lacks an important capacity. Lacking that capacity, by itself, or perhaps in conjunction with the absence of other basic capacities, may be sufficient reason to categorize Hex as incompetent (or noncompetent). Clearly, it is often important whether an individual's possession of a trait surpasses a certain threshold (one must not just be able to count but count in moderately complex ways) in order for us correctly to say that he is competent in a certain respect. Further, there may be non-identical *sets* of specific capacities, the possession of which renders the possessor generally competent to direct his own life. Also there will be differing sets of specific incapacities which render persons generally incompetent, for example, some including compulsions, some including serious incapacity to remember, others including pervasive learning disabilities.

Generally competent persons, those who have the capacities to direct their own lives, may, of course, exhibit particular and important incapacities (e.g., be blind, deaf, have paralysis in the legs, or suffer dyslexia) without, thereby, failing to be generally competent. To note this is to recognize that generally competent persons may be incompetent to foster their own conception of the good in certain restricted "areas" of their lives, for example, the deaf person will be unable to react prudently to the ringing fire alarm. In contrast, the generally incompetent person lacks a sufficient array of specific capacities to be able to direct his own life toward his own conception of the good (in certain cases, e.g., of *severe* retardation, the comatose, and so on, the incompetent individual will lack the capacity even to formulate a conception, or to have even minimal awareness, of his own good). Still, he may be quite competent to direct some limited domain or segment of his life, for example, choosing what to wear and dressing himself.

I have sketched what I take to be an initial acceptable analysis of generalized competence and identified what seem to be the general criteria for distinguishing generally competent from generally incompetent persons. Such considerations are important for both theoretical and practical reasons. Since some individuals fail to be generally competent and, hence, lack the capacity to direct their own lives, they, in a wide range of cases, will be unable to give valid consent (a consideration which, according to PARP, is

morally relevant to deciding whether it is permissible to place constraints on persons); further, the reason for recognizing the right
to direct one's own life as a right possessed only by generally
competent persons is clearer. A necessary condition, I believe, of
possessing such a right is that one have the capacities to direct
one's own life. For this reason, incompetent persons lack this
right.[48]

We have taken an extended detour to explicate the competent/
incompetent distinction. One of our aims, in exploring the morality
of suicide prevention in those cases in which it is reasonable to
believe that the suicide would wrong no others, is to determine
whether those who choose to commit suicide *must* be incompetent.

One argument in favor of an affirmative answer would insist
that S's intending to commit suicide is a logically sufficient condition for concluding that S is incompetent, that is, that 'S has
chosen to commit suicide' entails 'S is incompetent.' Put this way,
it is not at all obvious that such an entailment holds. Indeed, S's
having chosen to commit suicide and, hence, intending to do so
seems, on the contrary, a good reason to infer that S has certain
cognitive capacities, that is, has considered alternatives, and made
a choice, a choice which S deems is for the good (it is certainly *not*
a logical prerequisite of competence that competent persons always
choose *what in fact* is for their own good, only that they make a
reasoned choice). It may be objected that the apparent "choice" is
really no choice at all, that the intention to commit suicide may be
a byproduct of inner compulsions or psychological disturbance so
serious as to make consideration of alternatives and reasoned
choice impossible. The judicious thing to say here is that this *may*
be true, but whether it is must be determined, if it can be at all,
by psychological examination of the individuals in question, on a
case by case basis. It is not part of the *concept* of competence, that,
to be competent, one must not choose to commit suicide (or not
choose other self-harms). On the contrary, in particular cases it
seems plausible to conclude that a choice to commit suicide is highly
reasonable. For example, suppose you know that you are about to
be tortured for a long period of time, and then "terminated"; in

[48] Since I concede that incompetents *may* be competent to direct certain limited
segments of their lives, a case can be made for recognizing and respecting a right
to control matters within such segments. That seems to me the right conclusion to
draw and an intuitively plausible claim on its own.

I add also that as I have here explicated 'generally competent person' the term
refers to those who are either weakly autonomous persons (see Section 3.6) or
strongly autonomous persons.

such a case suicide may be the most prudent alternative, for the costs of continued existence may well outweigh the benefits. More crucially, such a choice is not patently irrational or a sign of gross cognitive or emotional incapacity. Hence, I conclude that 'S has chosen to commit suicide' does not *entail* 'S is incompetent.' Even so, it is possible that all or most would-be suicides are, as a matter of *contingent* fact, incompetent. Analogously, it is not definitionally or conceptually true that all bachelors have a (natural) kidney; however, it may be a contingent truth.

Indeed the intention to commit suicide may be *evidence* that the intender is incompetent since it is well established that many would-be suicides turn out to be seriously and chronically depressed or even, for example, schizophrenic. In many such cases it is clear that the psychological disturbance is so severe that the one disturbed lacks, at that time, minimal capacities to reflect on alternatives, realistically assess them, and make a minimally reasonable choice. In such cases we must conclude that the individual is incompetent (even if for some sustained prior period of her life she has been a generally competent person). On the argument developed here, the most general criteria of competence (the logical bases for determining who is to count as competent) are not the proprietary possession of professional psychologists. However, *given* these general criteria, professional psychologists or psychiatrists may be in the best position to decide whether particular individuals are or are not competent. There is a serious danger here, however, since the clinician may allow (not necessarily in conscious fashion) her moral conviction (e.g., suicide is a grave wrong or a sin) to distort her determination of competence in the particular case.

Even though the intent to commit suicide is *a bit* of evidence of serious disturbance and incompetence, it is not decisive by itself—for reasons already noted.[49] In some cases there is a not implausible argument that suicide is not only reasonable; it may be the most rational (in the sense of most prudent) choice one might make. Relatedly, the familiar tendency, for some time, to assume "all criminals are sick" has been shown to be a ludicrous view. One common criterion of rational choice is that a choice is rational if it will maximize the chooser's net expected utility. On this criterion,

---

[49] Some attitudes and some behavior may be both immoral and *also* a sign of illness or disturbance, e.g., hatred of women and/or rape. However, there is a well-documented tendency to confuse the question of immorality with the question of illness. On these matters, see the writings of Thomas Szasz.

as economists have emphasized in the last decade, much crime turns out to be a rational choice—in view of the limited range of options open to some criminals, the large payoffs, and the low probability of getting caught and actually punished.[50] If we make the further, rather weak, assumption that the capacity to make such rational choices (not just, as it were, by accident) is sufficient to infer competence, then many immoral decisions are strong evidence that the chooser is competent. Indeed, rather than assume that "all criminals are sick" it may be more reasonable to assume that *certain* criminals *are* competent, even if morally insensitive.

I have claimed that (1) not all suicides constitute wrongs to others, (2) that it is not analytically true that would-be suicides are incompetent, (3) some would-be suicides are incompetent, and (4) some are not. It is with regard to competent would-be suicides that do not wrong other individuals that PARP generally prohibits (presumptively wrong) interference—in order to prevent the suicide. Earlier, we noted that apart from the appeal to incompetence, some claim that suicide prevention in the type of case just specified is justified in order to prevent the catastrophic result: death. This argument, if fully developed, may deny that intervention is all right to prevent minor harms but that death is a special case—for being alive is a necessary condition of the subject's enjoying any satisfactions whatever, experiencing any welfare, or exercising any freedom at all. At this point what we find, I believe, is either an appeal to good-promotion (couched here in terms of harm prevention or welfare preservation) or, possibly, an appeal to autonomy preservation. We have already examined the appeal to such principles and found them wanting. I shall not, with one qualification, repeat those arguments here.

I have argued that competent persons have a right to direct their own lives, a right absolute throughout its scope. We have found no reason to think that this right does not include having the prerogative to end one's life when doing so wrongs no others. In the special cases noted this may be a prudent decision; alternatively it may not be, but if our argument has been sound, competent persons must be allowed to chart their own course and lead their own lives (within the domain of acts not wronging others). Part of leading one's life is choosing among alternatives, including the choice to continue or terminate one's own existence. We may view

[50] See Gary Becker and William Landes, *Essays in the Economics of Crime and Punishment* (New York: Columbia University Press, 1974).

the actual or intended result as unfortunate or even tragic. That may be so, but in the absence of the appropriate consent to intervention (of the sort described earlier) we must let alone—with two exceptions. If the suicide has not yet occurred, it is not presumptively wrong to try to persuade the would-be suicide to refrain (if we believe that it is the wiser course) but only by honest, sincere, and fair modes of argument (this excludes, e.g., deliberate use of deception, or using arguments one believes to be inadequate in order to seduce a vulnerable subject to change his mind, and other unfair "manipulative" techniques, e.g., unfairly inducing guilt). The other exception was discussed in Section 2.11. Namely, since the intent to commit suicide is a "bit of evidence" for incompetence in the absence of further relevant data, we may be justified in intervening to *find out* whether the person is competent and whether he does not consent to intervention.[51] Such interventions should be the least restrictive ones possible in terms of manner and duration.[52]

A final objection to this view, discussed in Section 3.9, is the claim that suicide by competent persons is wrong, even if not a wrong to others, and apart from the fact that it terminates the autonomy and welfare of the subject. This appeal, once more, seems to invoke one of the principles that we have labeled Appeals to Moral-Good Preservation. In view of the objections noted before, there is no reason to regard such appeals as a source of acceptable

[51] See Joel Feinberg, "Legal Paternalism," reprinted in his *Rights, Justice and the Bounds of Liberty* (Princeton: Princeton University Press, 1980), pp. 110–129.

[52] It is important not to overlook the very general moral question with which we have been concerned, i.e., the permissibility of intervention. Equally important in actual cases are urgent practical questions which we have not emphasized. It is one thing to be faced with a would-be suicide on a ledge of the tenth story of a building; another to be counseling a would-be suicide in an office. Empirical investigations make it clear that not all apparent would-be suicides really intend successfully to kill themselves. *Sometimes* their behavior is a "cry for help," and there *may* be good reason to infer hypothetical individualized consent on the part of the subject to restraint (and, hence, according to PARP, the permissibility of invasive intervention). However, short of commitment to an institution, persons with "suicidal impulses" generally have a continuing opportunity to take their own lives. For this reason, methods of assessing suicidal risk have been developed, and approaches to discourage suicide which respect the subject's powers and autonomy seem preferable (e.g., contractual agreements)—both on moral grounds and in terms of their success in discouraging what are often short-sighted and imprudent decisions. See R. Drye, R. Goulding, and M. Goulding, "No-Suicide Decisions: Patient Monitoring of Suicidal Risk," *American Journal of Psychiatry* 130, No. 2 (February, 1973), pp. 171–174. For an excellent philosophical exploration of the morality of suicide and delineation of relevant empirical data, see Margaret Pabst Battin, *Ethical Issues in Suicide* (Englewood Cliffs, N.J.: Prentice-Hall, 1982).

argument for invasive paternalistic intervention when we confront the matter of suicide prevention. Again, it is crucial to distinguish between the questions of whether an individual ought (prudentially) to commit suicide (or not), whether an individual morally ought to commit suicide (or not), and whether it is all right for others to prevent him from doing so by presumptively wrong means. I have argued that even if it were a moral wrong (though not a wrong to others) to do so, it would be wrong for others to prevent the suicide (except by autonomy-respecting efforts, i.e., open and fair persuasion or more restrictive means sanctioned by consent in the ways already delineated).

5.6 Preventing Commercial Sex

There are many disputed questions about sexual morality. The issues include the propriety of certain sexual acts within the context of marriage; the permissibility of sexual activity outside of marriage; responsible procreation and the treatment of those other than the sexual participants as, for example, in abortion or infanticide. Cutting across these contexts is the important matter of whether or not a "participant" in a two-party sexual act engages knowingly and voluntarily in the act. Rape, by definition, involves an unconsenting party. This paradigmatically wrongful act has as its victims, almost invariably if not necessarily, females—whether children, adults, or the elderly. In recent years it has become more evident how widespread this sort of brutalization of women is, and how predictable rape is in societies where women are myopically viewed as sexual resources, where they have lacked social, political, and economic equality, and where both many women and especially men have viewed rape as a minor peccadillo, as a boys-will-be-boys sowing of wild oats, or have assumed that rapes were really welcomed by their victims (and, hence, not rape at all).[53] It is difficult to step back from this background of insidious, patriarchal, and sexist attitudes and practices, and examine the question of whether *knowing and voluntary prostitution* (I cannot insist too strongly that *not all* prostitution is of this sort) by *competent adult persons* is morally permissible and whether it should be decriminalized. This issue, to emphasize a point, concerns *not* involuntary prostitution but the morality of knowing and voluntary prostitution

[53] An antidote to taking rape casually is: Susan Brownmiller, *Against Our Will* (New York: Simon & Schuster, 1976).

by competent persons; the morality of prohibiting it; and the adequacy of paternalistic grounds for doing so. Investigating the morality of prohibition and placing it in a fuller perspective requires a fuller examination of the nonpaternalistic grounds for interference than we have normally pursued. We shall round out the picture by briefly examining such arguments.

There is a problem of how to define 'prostitution.' The term is sometimes used to mean "devoting oneself to unworthy purposes." A narrower sense is proffered by Webster's: "submission to promiscuous lewdness, especially for hire." The term, of course, is often restricted to activities of women. A less moral question-begging and, hence, more useful definition for our purposes, is "engaging in sexual activities for a monetizable benefit in the absence of emotional commitment." This definition is fuzzy around the edges but will serve our aims. Given this characterization, prostitution is the activity of selling sexual "favors," and the prostitute can be male or female. The purchaser does not "engage in prostitution" (i.e., is not a prostitute), although he or she is "a participant in prostitution" as a customer. I count both buyer and seller as "participants." Questions about the "morality of prostitution" may refer to the activities of the prostitute, the customer, or both. Our primary focus will be on the former. Within our definition prostitution, in principle, can occur between marital partners. The more typical case involves, of course, parties not married to each other. I shall further restrict our focus to cases involving only competent adult persons.

Given the above definition and restrictions of scope, we may inquire whether prostitution between consenting adult persons is morally permissible. A fully adequate discussion of this question is beyond my purposes here. It would thoroughly canvass both allegedly adequate paternalistic and nonpaternalistic grounds for concluding affirmatively or negatively.[54] Related to the moral question, but distinct from it, is the question of whether prostitution should continue to be criminally prohibited, as it is in virtually all parts of the United States (except certain counties in Nevada) or be decriminalized. We shall explore, albeit incompletely, both the

[54] For an extremely thorough, interesting, and cogently argued discussion, see David A. J. Richards, "Commercial Sex and the Rights of the Person: A Moral Argument for the Decriminalization of Prostitution," *University of Pennsylvania Law Review* 127, No. 5 (May, 1979), pp. 1195–1287. More generally, see also *Morality and the Law*, ed. Richard Wasserstrom (Belmont, Cal.: Wadsworth, 1971); Hugo Bedau and Edwin Schur, *Victimless Crimes* (Englewood Cliffs, N.J.: Prentice-Hall, 1974).

moral and the legal questions. On the theory defended here each competent person has the moral right to engage in any act within the domain of acts which do not wrong others. One type of argument against the morality of decriminalizing prostitution is compatible with this principle for it maintains that prostitution does constitute a wrong to nonparticipants. Arguments in defense of this latter thesis are of various sorts; later we shall survey the leading ones. Prior to doing so, let us ask whether there are adequate paternalistic grounds for employing presumptively wrong means to prevent competent persons from participating in prostitution. One naturally might surmise at this stage that our theory supports a negative answer. In view of our prior discussions we need not reiterate the reasons in great detail.

If a competent adult freely and knowingly chooses to engage in prostitution, such a decision may or may not be prudent. The life of a prostitute typically involves benefits and burdens. Some prostitutes, the "call girl" variety, manage to earn an income which places them in the category of the extremely wealthy. Others do poorly. The collateral risks of venereal disease, being assaulted or blackmailed, and so on are too well known to elaborate further. Our question, of course, is not whether to recommend prostitution as a rewarding vocation, but whether it is a morally permissible activity and whether it is permissible to prevent competent adults from voluntarily participating in prostitution. As we have argued, the fact, if it is a fact, that it is not for a competent person's own good (e.g., welfare) to be a prostitute is not a sufficient reason to interfere in a presumptively wrongful manner, for example, by coercion (legal or nonlegal coercion) or force. If participants, *qua* participants, wrong no others (we leave this point open here), a choice of prostitution is a matter for the competent person to decide; if some decide to chart their own course in such a manner, we cannot, on paternalistic grounds interfere (again, excepting the permissible "interference" of fair and open attempts to dissuade or where the subject validly consents to more invasive interventions).

Unlike cases in which a paternalistic-minded agent might use coercion or deception to prevent suicide, the crossing of an unsafe bridge, or self-destructive drug addiction, there is little reason to regard an appeal to autonomy enhancement or preservation as an initially plausible ground for prohibition of prostitution. There is simply not an analogous likelihood of loss of functioning or radical impairment of cognitive-emotional capacities. It may be objected

273

that some prostitutes become bound to the directives of authoritarian pimp protectors and, hence, suffer diminished autonomy. This objection may call attention to a significant fact, but it at least seems misleading. In the cases being considered, competent persons voluntarily choose to engage in prostitution and, possibly, work with a pimp as well. Hence, if they do place themselves in a position in which there are constraints on doing what they wish, this simply can be a voluntary forfeit of autonomy and is not different in kind from the constraints one may accept in voluntary choices of other sorts of less "morally suspect" jobs. Indeed, the pimp *may* act paternalistically toward the prostitute and constrain her for her own good. However, if she voluntarily consents to this, it is, according to our theory, permissible paternalism—analogous to the case in which I hire a bodyguard who places constraints on my activities in order to protect me. In real life, of course, pimps may, and often do, coerce the noncompetent into a life of prostitution and, hence, the choice to be a prostitute may not be voluntary. Even if a competent person voluntarily chooses to become a prostitute and hires a pimp, the latter may constrain her in ways violating their contractual agreement. Such an event is even more likely in view of the fact that prostitution is typically criminalized, and it is unlikely that the state would stand behind such agreements. It is important, however, to keep the question of what wrongs may be done to prostitutes in actual practice distinct from the question of whether constraints on autonomy which may attach to the role of the prostitute are legitimate paternalistic grounds for interference. We have argued that if the constraint, or diminished autonomy, is appropriately self-chosen such grounds are not legitimate since acting on them would subvert the capacity of competent persons to lead their own lives within the permitted domain.

Traditionally a variety of reasons has been posed for concluding that prostitution is morally wrong. Some participants in prostitution intimidate and otherwise take undue advantage of young male and female children in order to press them into the practice of prostitution. It is reasonable to assume in such cases that even when compensation is provided such intimidation seriously wrongs those subject to it. By contrast we have focused on the class of cases, however many or few in number, in which competent adults knowingly and freely enter the practice of prostitution; one of our questions concerns the morality of that practice, and not the morality of other acts that prostitutes may perform. That some participants in prostitution wrong children does not show that prostitution itself is immoral any more than the fact that some parents brutally abuse children shows that "parenting" is wrong. Temporarily setting aside the arguments designed to show that prostitution wrongs nonparticipants, the claims are often made that prostitution is wrong because (1) it involves sexual intercourse for purposes other than procreation, (2) it involves (other) "unnatural" acts, (3) it violates divine commandments, (4) it involves an alienation of one's moral personality, and/or (5) it violates certain duties toward oneself. It is not my aim carefully to assess all these claims, but it is worth noticing that each must confront important objections. With regard to (1), the implicit assumption that any sexual intercourse not aimed at procreation, or in which procreation is not possible or where it has been rendered highly improbable—is wrong—"proves too much."

Such a principle condemns as wrong intercourse of those who are congenitally sterile or no longer fertile even if happily married and otherwise "proper." With regard to (2) there is a well-known difficulty of explicating 'unnatural' in a way which is neither question-begging nor trivial. Some acts, such as skydiving, reading this book, or sculpting are statistically unusual and hence "unnatural" in one sense; this feature, however, hardly provides a ground for moral condemnation. If 'unnatural' is taken to mean 'physiologically or anatomically demanding' then both certain commonly acceptable sexual activities and many innocuous activities (e.g., acrobatics, pole-vaulting, juggling, and ballet) turn out to be unnatural. If 'unnatural' is construed to mean 'not conducive to the survival of the species' and acts having this trait are presumed wrong, once again the argument "proves too much" for much ordinary and innocent activity stands condemned on such assumptions. Defenders of (3) are committed to a controversial set of epistemological suppositions about the existence of God, the possibility of ascertaining the divine will, and the relation of the latter to moral judgments. These are deserving of a separate discussion and we shall set them aside here. It is worth noting, however, that some who maintain that a certain act is "intrinsically wrong" mean that the act is wrong even if it wrongs no human being, a view we have discussed earlier. What occasionally lies behind that claim is that the act in question violates a divine command; hence, even if it wrongs no other human being, it may be thought to wrong a divine being. Thus, the act is thought to be a "wrong to others" more cosmically interpreted. Both (4) and (5) are variants on the previously discussed Kantian theme that one

275

must respect humanity as embodied in *oneself* and others, and there are, thus, moral constraints on how one may treat one's self or one's body. In Kant's view, to "sell" one's body for a profit is to degrade oneself, to allow oneself "to be treated as a thing"; hence, humans are not entitled to sell themselves to satisfy the sexual desires of others.[55] There are circumstances, of course, in which prostitutes are treated in degrading ways against their will, but the same is true of high school teachers, secretaries, janitors, and nurses; so, such a fact hardly shows prostitution to be wrong. Kant no doubt would protest that such a comment is not to the point; rather, his position is that one degrades oneself by *permitting* others to use one in certain ways. Perhaps in his view it is additionally self-demeaning to accept payment for sexual services.

That it is somehow self-demeaning to accept payment for sexual services or indeed to provide such services to some persons only if there is compensation is, on the face of it, a perplexing view. Typically, when one person, A, regularly receives benefits from another, B, and A is unwilling reciprocally to benefit B, there is good reason to judge that B is "being used" or that B is being wrongfully exploited in some sense—unless B knowingly and voluntarily provides the benefit for A. Of course, there is serious doubt that Kant would be less harsh in his condemnation of persons who simply dispensed sexual favors indiscriminately and freely for, in his view, this also would seem to be a case of letting oneself be used. Such judgments are puzzling because one who insists on payment for services rendered seems less (or not) servile, less (or not) used, and possessing more self-respect than the person who freely lets himself be a sexual resource for others. A further objection to Kant's position is the problem of how he could possibly distinguish the case of accepting payment for sexual services from other cases in which it does not seem self-demeaning or impermissible to accept payment for services rendered, for example, the delivery of furniture. It might be objected that furniture delivery is very unlike the delivery of sexual favors. True enough; the latter typically is more personal and intimate, involves mutual self-awareness, and heightened emotions. However, much the same can be said, to varying degrees, about the services involved in nursing and medical care, clinical psychology and psychiatry, and physical

[55] Kant, *Lectures on Ethics*, trans. Louis Infield (New York: Harper & Row, 1963) pp. 119, 165–167.

276

therapy.[56] Such services often involve the absence of normal privacy, touching of "private" areas of the body, and exposure of feelings and attitudes not commonly disclosed. These features, of course, more describe the position of the patient than that of the professional, but it would be a mistake to ignore the mutual involvement which occurs. Importantly, it is not thought self-demeaning for the professional to expect payment for such services. Indeed, persons who provide such services normally cannot survive unless they receive compensation; in short, it is a mark of not respecting such providers and using *them* as a mere means *not* to compensate them.

There is a much-quoted remark of Kant's which deserves serious pondering concerning the issue of how to distribute scarce medical resources or whether we must spare no financial cost in order to prevent the death of an innocent human being, namely, "whatever has a price can be replaced by something else or its equivalent; on the other hand, whatever is above all price, and therefore admits of no equivalent, has a dignity."[57] Regardless of the implications this not so transparent remark has for the recalcitrant question of whether we rationally can place a price on human life, one might conjecture that in Kant's view to attach a *price* to sexual favors is to treat them as impersonal transactions, and to regard the provider as replaceable, not as a particular human being with dignity. No doubt many purchasers of sexual favors have such attitudes toward prostitutes. Still, it does not follow that such attitudes necessarily prevail on the part of the purchaser; nor is it necessarily the case that the seller must take such a dim view of herself or her chosen livelihood. Neither is it the case that the transaction must be impersonal nor true that the provider is not a human being possessing dignity and self-respect. Such conclusions are only reinforced by further reflection on the other occupations mentioned; the fact that

[56] One might also compare the activities of sex surrogates employed to help alleviate "sexual dysfunction." Also, it is worth considering the sexual needs and desires of persons in retirement homes who are unable sexually to satisfy themselves and who, contrary to fact, are treated as asexual beings. Our society, with regard to such persons, tends to acknowledge most important needs, but pretends that sexual desires suddenly vanish at a certain age or refuses to consider the possibility of facilitating the satisfaction of such desires—a curious discounting of one of the basic needs: shelter, nourishment, alleviation of disease or injury, and sexual fulfillment. Whether or not health-care personnel should be regarded as having a duty to accommodate such needs, more closely germane to our exploration in this section is whether it is permissible for them, or others, to do so.

[57] Immanuel Kant, *Foundations of the Metaphysics of Morals*, ed. Oskar Piest, trans. Lewis Beck (New York: Liberal Arts Press, 1959), p. 53.

a price is attached to services has little bearing on whether they are self-demeaning, whether they are unique, or whether there are many or few who could adequately provide what the purchaser wants. Kant's condemnation of "selling" one's body is better described as a "renting," and a renting of one's *services* for finite, indeed, short, periods of time. Put that way, and considering especially the very personal services rendered in the occupations recently mentioned, the point helps subvert the erroneous notion that what the prostitute does is somehow radically different from what certain "high-status" professionals commonly do.

One might object that all of this ignores some important psychological facts. For example, there is reason to believe that many prostitutes in actual practice place themselves in highly vulnerable positions. They often render services to persons stronger than they and are subject to threats and intimidation in the absence of third parties who might intervene to prevent abuses by patrons. Since prostitution is illegal there is likely to be serious reluctance to ask for police intervention even if that were possible. Further, some psychological studies indicate that women with low levels of self-esteem enter prostitution and they are, hence, likely to allow themselves to be used against their will, that is, in ways to which they do not voluntarily consent. In view of such facts, the prostitute does not have the power, authority, or control comparable to that of persons in the other professions mentioned even if, in some respects, the service provided by the prostitute exhibits similarities to those other services. If we concede these points, then we must ask what follows from them. There are risks of abuse or exploitation in many occupations and in many contractual arrangements. Prostitution does not seem unique in this respect; some of the risks arise not from prostitution as such but from the fact that it is criminalized and legal protection is less available. Further, from the fact that people with low self-esteem enter prostitution, it does not follow that this must be the case. Some prostitutes seem to take a certain pride in their work and in the "public service" they perform, even though such a viewpoint is barely imaginable to those who assume its wickedness or focus on the low social status of the profession. But there is no inherent lack of dignity in many low-status occupations which cater to human needs and wants, for example, cleaning cesspools, emptying bedpans, hauling garbage, driving a cab, cleaning houses, or exterminating vermin. If people with low self-esteem or a low estimate of their own skills or talents enter such occupations, they *may* make an imprudent decision, but it is difficult to see how such occupations in themselves are self-demeaning. The fact, if it is one, that persons enter such low-status occupations *because* they have low self-esteem does not entail that such positions *are* self-demeaning any more than the (possible) fact that people with high self-esteem choose to be drug smugglers shows that there is something inherently worthy about the latter enterprise. If it is claimed that prostitution is self-demeaning because it is, in itself, an immoral pursuit, we must note that this claim begs the question in light of our survey of reasons for drawing that conclusion. Hence, to argue that it is immoral because it is self-demeaning and self-demeaning because it is immoral is to offer no reason for thinking that it is self-demeaning or immoral; it is simply to *assume* answers to our questions.

We have considered a number of appeals to show that prostitution is a wrong even if not a wrong to others (postponing a consideration of (3)). Those committed to that view may be forced to respond to the difficulties we have noted or reconsider the widely, but often uncritically, held view that prostitution is a wrong even if not a wrong to others. Such a view, like recent viruses, is resistant to attempts to eliminate it. We need not draw any final conclusions about the view in question; however, as we have previously argued, if the form of prostitution in question wrongs no others and if the prostitute does not validly consent to invasive interference, the Appeal to Moral-Good Preservation (AMP) fails to provide an adequate ground for such interference. If competent persons knowingly and voluntarily choose to engage in acts that are wrongful but do no wrong to others, we cannot justifiably interfere to preserve their moral purity or improve their moral scorecard. The major thesis here is simply that there is no legitimate *paternalistic* ground for presumptively wrongful interventions aimed at preventing competent persons from voluntarily and knowingly engaging in prostitution.

It is beyond my purpose fully to canvass the *nonpaternalistic* grounds for prohibiting prostitution; they primarily fall into six categories and are, I shall argue, all problematic. I shall briefly indicate why in order to emphasize the importance of our prior concern, that is, the investigation of the adequacy of paternalistic grounds for intervention. The categories involve claims (1) that prostitution seriously *offends* nonparticipants, (2) that prostitution fosters and *encourages other crimes*, (3) that it fosters the spread, and hinders the control, of *disease*, (4) that it threatens to undermine an important social institution, the traditional family, (5) that it is

279

not truly voluntary (a vaguely Marxist view), and (6) that it reflects and promotes male chauvinism.

Such claims are invoked in order to argue that the crime of prostitution is *not* in fact what some have claimed it to be, namely, a "victimless crime." Although it may be conceded that competent voluntary participants are not wronged, it is alleged that third parties, in one or more of the direct ways suggested, are wronged, and, hence, victimized. Let us first consider the appeal to offensiveness. It is no doubt true that many people are offended by being approached by prostitutes or purchasers searching for prostitutes, that some are offended by observing such interactions, and that some are offended simply by indirectly learning of the existence of such activities. Offensive actions can, of course, be mildly or seriously offensive, and the degree of offense will vary depending on the particular sensibilities and beliefs of the one offended. Atheists may be offended by public or private prayer or the display of religious symbols. Religious believers may be offended by proposals to remove "In God we trust" from official U.S. currency. Jews may be offended by neo-Nazi marches; neo-Nazis may be offended by Jewish religious symbols. Racists may be offended by the sight of a black holding hands with a white. In a world of nonhomogeneous individuals some offenses are unavoidable; of course, that is no argument against prohibiting some forms of offensive action for the same point may be made of murder. Clearly, any attempt to prohibit activities simply because the bare *knowledge* of them offends others is incompatible with allowing persons to have that modicum of freedom necessary to live their lives in a minimally satisfactory way. A more plausible view is that actions whose *public* performance causes serious offense to others with normal sensibilities should be prohibited or restricted since they cause unprovoked harm to innocent others. Even this more moderate view is subject to serious objections. For instance, it may allow a tyranny of the majority; if a society is predominately racist in outlook such a principle may sanction restricting fundamental liberties of minorities in order to promote the satisfaction of the majority's prejudices. On the face of it, what needs subversion here is not the liberties of minorities to go about their lives in ways allowed by members of the majority but the arbitrary sensibilities and convictions of the latter. The mere fact that a person's act seriously offends another is not, by itself, a sufficient reason coercively to prevent such action.

There are, however, methods of accommodating, to a point, both the interests of those who wish to act in ways which happen to offend others and the desires of others not to be offended. Although few would defend the view that sexual intercourse (or anything more than casual fondling) between a *bona fide* married couple in the shopping mall on Saturday afternoon ought to be permitted, it does not follow that private sexual relations between them ought to be prohibited as well. Morally innocent activities may offend others in such a way as to seriously disrupt or disorient their lives. Hence, in many cases a reasonable ground exists for legally restricting the time and place of such activities. In order to respect the liberties of all parties to live their lives in relatively unhindered ways one solution, therefore, is to delimit seriously offensive actions in the least restrictive manner possible sufficient to avoid or minimize such offenses. The issue is more complex than this (for reasons I have stated elsewhere), but these points may be sufficient to show that the fact that prostitution or its public solicitation is offensive to some is not a compelling reason in favor of employing presumptively wrong means (typically, force or coercive threat) to prevent competent persons from ever voluntarily engaging in such transactions. It *is* a good reason for regulating such activity as to time and place.[58] A similar statement may be made about motorcycle races, political rallies, revival meetings, and solicitation for charities.

The second nonpaternalistic ground for prohibiting voluntary prostitution is that it facilitates and fosters other crimes, for example, violence and theft of patrons, blackmail, illicit payoffs to the police, use of illegal drugs, and enhancement of organizations parasitic on these and other criminal activities.[59] We may concede the fact that such activities are often *associated* with prostitution as a matter of empirical fact. Mere association, however, seems no compelling reason to prohibit the activity itself since criminal involvement is also associated with banking, mail-order selling, athletic events, and trading in stocks and bonds—in short, in any

[58] A more detailed discussion may be found in my "Coercive Restraint of Offensive Actions," *Philosophy & Public Affairs* 8, No. 2 (Winter, 1979), pp. 175–193. As some of my examples may suggest, I do not mean to suppose that the solution to the problem raised by offensive actions is always appropriately resolvable by a simple balancing of interests. In some cases the intense desires of offended parties may be morally negligible and the right of competent persons to direct their own lives may be decisive for it is not always wrong to offend others, even seriously.

[59] David Richards, among others, refers to this alleged fecundity of prostitution as "criminogenesis"; see Richards, "Commercial Sex and the Rights of the Person," p. 1215.

activity where large sums of money can be had and the benefits seem worth the risk of criminal activity to those indifferent to considerations of respecting other people. A further well-recognized point is that much of the criminal activity associated with prostitution occurs *because* prostitution is criminally prohibited. If it were not, there would be no possibility of bribing the police on that score and there would be less blackmail of known participants. Further, criminally inclined organizations (one is tempted to speak of corporations in the crime industry, a business whose prospect is as bullish as computer technology) are naturally drawn to illegal activities in which, because of criminalization, the cost of entry into the market is high and, hence, competitors are few. If prostitution were legalized, competition would increase and, other things being equal, profits would fall. The likely net result would be a less close association between criminal activity and prostitution. Conversely, if there were a powerful drive to study philosophy, which was backed by willingness and ability to pay (alas, there is not) and its teaching were illegal (as some might prefer), it is likely that criminally inclined organizations would discover an untapped niche in the market and pursue it in order to enhance profits. Then, one could imagine a time when the complaint of "crimogenesis" would be directed at the unseemly practice of philosophizing since the haunts of philosophers would no doubt attract other shady characters. As David Richards has noted, if prostitution were not a crime, it would be more publicly visible, participants would more readily complain to the police about associated criminal abuses and, hence, allow the police to cope more effectively with such problems.[60] It is not at all clear, then, that criminal activities associated with prostitution are fostered by prostitution itself rather than by the fact that it is criminally prohibited; if its criminalization fosters other crime, that is a reason for its decriminalization and not for its prohibition.

Venereal disease is currently of epidemic proportions in the United States. Clearly it is a serious problem and no doubt many carriers are participants in prostitution. This by itself might be a reason for regulating prostitution in the form of requiring medical examinations at regular intervals. Such requirements, however, are a far cry from criminal prohibition, and are not different in kind from the sorts of requirements which must be met by persons in other occupations (e.g., nurses, respiratory therapists, dental hy-

[60] Ibid., p. 1216.

gienists, or restaurant employees) who also run the risk of being witting or unwitting carriers of communicable diseases, for example, hepatitis or tuberculosis. This rationale is similar to that for quarantining certain persons; it is, in emergency cases, permissible to employ presumptively wrongful means (e.g., coercive regulations) in order to prevent significant harm to innocent parties who have not consented to the risks. It is also reasonable to believe that the most influential factor in the increase of venereal disease to tragic proportions is not the activities of professional prostitutes, who are likely to be meticulous about their own health care in order to maintain their own livelihood, but rather the increased sexual activity of nonprostitutes, especially the inordinate increase in teenage sexual activity. Teenagers are notoriously either ignorant about precautionary measures, embarrassed to learn, or unwilling to make efforts to acquire information. Some have a propensity toward self-deception, and are reluctant to take precautions because to do so is to acknowledge the full voluntariness and intentionality of (and, hence, responsibility for) their sexual behavior. Some health risks associated with prostitution are risks to the prostitute herself; for example, there is a high degree of cervical cancer among prostitutes. This consideration brings us back to a possible paternalistic ground for interference. Again, the existence of risks, even serious risks, associated with prostitution fails to differentiate voluntary prostitution from other voluntary activities which we think wrong paternalistically to prohibit in order to prevent harm to participants; coal mining with the risks of black-lung disease; textile manufacturing with the risk of brown-lung disease; construction of skyscrapers with the risk of falling; smoking with the risks of cancer; the use of chain saws with the risks of severing limbs (human ones) and loss of hearing. One could go on, but on the theory defended here there is no legitimate paternalistic ground for employing invasive means of interference to promote the good of (or prevent harm to) those who voluntarily and knowingly assume the risks and absorb the costs involved. Again, the paternalistic provision of information or warnings about such risks is not precluded; nor is the institutionalizing of safety or health-aimed procedures to which potential participants voluntarily and knowingly consent, or would if apprized of the relevant facts.

We earlier noted another nonpaternalistic ground for prohibiting voluntary knowing prostitution by competent persons, namely, (4) it threatens to undermine the traditional family. It is impossible here to assess fully this claim and the argument of which it is a part. However, the burden of proof would seem to be on the proponents of the claim. We need to be shown that the availability of prostitution has a seriously erosive effect on such an institution. Further, it would have to be shown that when prostitution seems to be associated with family *breakdowns* that such families had not already contained the seeds of their own destruction; participating in prostitution may be only an expression and not the cause of irretrievable breakdown in a marriage. If it is claimed that the availability of commercial sex discourages the *formation* of traditional families by providing a nonmarital alternative to sexual satisfaction, some skepticism is in order since (1) in any comparatively nonpuritanical society there are similar sexual alternatives quite apart from commercial sex, and (2) studies suggest that primary motives for marriage include a desire for companionship and a desire to raise children, neither of which is successfully achieved in commercial sex. In brief sketch, then, it is doubtful that prostitution significantly erodes the family, an institution which is quite resilient—warts and all. A final point regarding preservation of traditional family life is that those concerned to preserve it as an option, perhaps as a dominant minisocial arrangement, would have a stronger case if, instead, they were to complain of the threat alcoholism poses to stable family life. The evidence suggests that it plays a powerful causal role in destruction of the values of family life even when the family remains legally intact. Furthermore, official statistics fail to show fully the casualties, especially in terms of psychological damage to children and spouses.

There is a vaguely Marxist line of argument deserving our attention as well; it is one which concludes that prostitution is both immoral and, as well, ought to be a crime. It is one which has held an appeal to *some* "radical feminists" (a term that I do not regard as redundant), among others. Since the line of reasoning is often rather inexplicitly presented, we can reconstruct it in various ways. I shall consider one version. Some Marxists, and others, view the existence of prostitution as an inevitable byproduct of capitalism, or perhaps sexist capitalism, in which men have, due to historic property and power relations, exercised dominance over women. Viewing women as property, as less than equal persons and without the same moral standing as men, males have, on this view, exploited women in diverse ways, one paradigmatic example being the perpetuation of (female) prostitution. The sometimes tacit implications of these claims are that prostitution is morally wrong and that it ought not to be decriminalized.

There are a number of difficulties with this loosely put line of thought. We need not press the question of whether, as a matter of empirical fact, capitalism causally brings about or sustains the existence of prostitution. It is worth noting, instead, that the existence of supply and demand, or the practice of contractual exchanges, does not require inequalities of wealth (of the sort commonly associated with capitalist societies, but not only such societies). Still, the fact that men have often controlled wealth does have some explanatory force when we ask why female prostitution is more common than male prostitution. Another explanatory factor, the viewing of women as inferior or as of lesser moral standing, is not obviously a defining feature of capitalism; nor is it confined to capitalist countries. But let us concede that capitalism generates or permits inequalities of wealth and that capitalism, combined with a prevailing sexist norm, tends to generate a significant number of relatively poor women. I set aside the question of the extent to which such an outcome is unique to capitalism; that question is distinct from the central issue with which we are concerned. The existence of poor women, whatever the full explanation of their existence, results, in part, in such women having an incentive to engage in financially rewarding activities, for example, prostitution.

It is worth observing that this "connection" of prostitution to capitalism goes no distance at all toward showing that prostitution is immoral or that it ought to be a criminalized activity—any more than it would show that the incentive to become an electrician, a nurse, or a physician is an incentive toward acting immorally or that such careers should be criminally prohibited. The line of argument we have been considering instead may be directed at a quite different conclusion, namely, that capitalism is corrupt. However *that* argument may proceed, it is reasonable to interpret it as inferring that capitalism is corrupt because (1) capitalism generates an incentive to many women to engage in prostitution, and (2) prostitution is a corrupt activity. Whatever virtues or vices this line of argument possesses, it simply *assumes* the corruption or immorality of prostitution and, therefore, provides no reason to *conclude* the truth of the latter. Thus, it does not address the question of the morality of prostitution or the question of whether prostitution ought to be criminalized because it involves a wrong to women.

A variant line of thought (one focusing on economic considerations) suggests that prostitution is wrong, and ought to be eliminated; it appeals to the claim that poor women (at least) are forced to become prostitutes. If that is true, then the resulting prostitution is not genuinely voluntary—in contrast to our focus on the voluntary, contractual sale of sexual services. It is worth recalling that we should allow that *some* "prostitution" *is* genuinely involuntary, for example, in cases in which women (or men) are captured against their will and by means of personal threat or brute force are made to submit to sexual relations. (Given our definition of 'prostitution,' use of the term here is, of course, dubious.) Such activities, on the view defended here, are both wrong and deserving of criminal status. The focus of the appeal to "economic coercion" is quite different. It is designed to show that prostitution is generally an involuntary act. If that is true, the prostitute generally does not actually give valid consent to acting in that manner; if so, PARP's stringent prohibitions on invasive interventions with the voluntary choices of competent persons would not be applicable. So, it is important to explore the question of whether prostitution is generally voluntary or not.

Consider a case, then, in which a woman, P, is economically deprived because someone, O, has unjustly brought about her deprivation; P then chooses to resort to prostitution. Although P has been wronged, it does not follow that her efforts to escape deprivation are wrongful. Also, it does not follow that her resort to prostitution is involuntary. Against the latter point it may be claimed that she had "no other choice." Clearly this claim is false if understood literally. She has the choice of refraining or not—a hard choice to be sure. Still, it seems that we ought to distinguish the question of whether an act is voluntary from the question of whether it is justifiable. For example, suppose Crusoe can only survive by killing and eating Friday; that is the only available way to escape nutritional deprivation, that is, death by starvation. Suppose Crusoe does so. It is difficult to see why we should regard Crusoe's choice as not voluntary even if we were to concede that he was justified in so acting (I do not propose the latter view).

To return to the case of P, suppose it is conceded that she does have a choice between engaging in prostitution and not doing so. Still, it may be claimed, the alternatives to prostitution may be so burdensome that there is an important sense in which she cannot bring herself to pursue one of them—and, to that extent, her choice of prostitution is involuntary. This reasoning does not seem tempting. In the absence of further reasons to assume that P has some "inner irresistible impulse" to engage in prostitution, it would appear that the case is only one of a reasonable person's making what may be a difficult but voluntary choice. The added feature that she was put in the difficult choice situation by a wrongful act of another does not seem to undermine the claim that the choice is, nevertheless, a voluntary one. This point seems compatible with another (possible) noteworthy feature of the case: P would have chosen differently if it had been the case that her options were less limited. But the latter feature is one that often obtains with regard to any agent in a difficult choice situation. Further, it would be a bizarre result to conclude that most or all decisions in difficult choice situations are involuntary.

That the difficulty of a choice does not undermine voluntariness of the choice seems to be a hard saying. We may be tempted to conclude otherwise because of (1) our reluctance to blame agents for extreme acts (perhaps presumptively wrong acts), and (2) because we assume that an act is not blameworthy if it is involuntary. However, involuntariness is not the only exculpating feature an act can have. Another view of matters is the following. In some circumstances a subject has her range of options affected because an act of another person (*or* an act of nature) attaches heavy "costs" to one or more of the alternatives, that is, prospective burdensome results for the subject if the subject acts (or refrains) in a certain manner. A paradigm instance is that in which a single coercer threatens "your money or your life." In such a circumstance, the one threatened may voluntarily choose to surrender her money to the hoodlum. We rightly refuse to blame the victim as an accomplice in crime (in surrendering her money) *even if* we describe her act as voluntary. A similar tale is to be told if the one being threatened is a bank teller who surrenders the bank's money. In each of these cases the one threatened continues to function as a rational choosing person and her choice affects the outcome. This feature contrasts significantly with those cases where a person contributes nothing to the outcome, for example, when you refuse to submit to a drug injection, but others forcefully administer it to you anyway. In the case in which the teller chooses to turn over the bank's money, such a choice may reflect what the teller most prefers *given the circumstances*. It is, of course, a quite different thing to say that "the teller preferred to dole out the bank's money"—without qualification. Similarly, one who chooses prostitution may prefer to do so *given her circumstances*; that she *prefers other circumstances* does not render her choice involuntary. Analogously, one may choose to undergo radiation treatment; that one would prefer circumstances where that option is unattractive does not render the choice to do so an involuntary one. On reflection, it is clear that when people say they were "forced to do X," the sense of 'forced' often does not preclude voluntariness; still, even if the act is voluntary, that does not preclude the existence of features exculpatory of blame that might attach to the act in the absence of such factors.

One important point I have urged here is simply that most prostitution should, in a straightforward way, be viewed as voluntary—even if it is also true that it is a way of coping with trying circumstances. Indeed, much of what we choose to do has this characteristic. Whether prostitution should be regarded as a *desperate* means of coping depends on other assumptions we make, for example, whether it should be thought of as self-degrading—or inherently wrongful.[61] A second basic point is that we must distinguish the question of the morality of acts which *cause* others to be in difficult circumstances from the question of the morality and voluntariness of acts pursued by those attempting to *cope* with such circumstances. In addition, it should be obvious that the difficult circumstances a person confronts are not *always* traceable to blameworthy acts on the part of moral agents. Some circumstances are tragic *because* of the injustice of others, and some are simply tragic.

It may be objected that aside from focusing on economic considerations, there are distinctly sexist considerations which must not be ignored and that these tip the balance against decriminalizing prostitution.

Apart from the argument that prostitution is wrong and/or ought to be criminalized because it involves some sort of *class* oppression or "economic coercion" of prostitutes, there is, then, a line of reasoning which more distinctly appeals to consideration of *gender*-based oppression. It is found in these remarks by Susan Brownmiller:

> . . . my horror at the idea of legalized prostitution is . . . that it institutionalizes the concept that it is a man's monetary right, if not his divine right, to gain access to the female body, and that sex is a female service that should not be denied the civilized male. Perpetuation of the concept that the "powerful male impulse" must be satisfied with immediacy by a coop-

[61] It is worth recalling how some persons view "blue collar work" as degrading. But 'degrading' seems ambiguous between 'is incompatible with maintaining self-respect and dignity' and 'is viewed as a low-status activity.' Being a shepherd is hardly a "prestigious occupation" in the United States. However, there is no reason to regard it as degrading. For similar reasons, "low-status occupation" is ambiguous.

erative class of women, set aside and expressly licensed for this purpose, is part and parcel of the mass psychology of rape. Indeed, until the day is reached when prostitution is totally eliminated . . . the false perception of sexual access as an adjunct of male power and privilege will continue to fuel the rapist mentality.[62]

Brownmiller's remarks seem to appeal to both paternalistic and nonpaternalistic grounds for prohibiting prostitution. The nonpaternalistic element focuses on the fact, or alleged fact, that the existence of legalized prostitution encourages males to believe that they have some sort of right to gain access to female bodies. The implication is that legalized prostitution would only encourage men to view women in an unjustifiable sexist manner; in turn, the social fostering of this mentality facilitates acts which are indisputably wrong under normal conditions.[63] This line of thought deserves serious reflection and may constitute a form of slippery slope argument. But the reasoning may proceed in two, importantly different ways. One may argue that in no society should prostitution be legalized since doing so would encourage the sort of corrupt attitude mentioned. Alternatively, one may argue, more weakly, that legalization should not occur in an already sexist society in which males are predisposed to interpret such legalization as a sign that "society accepts" male domination of females. Both arguments appeal to a principle rather like this: that it is wrong to legalize a practice which is likely to foster attitudes which in turn are likely to eventuate in indisputably unjustified acts. There are important questions about both (1) this principle and (2) the crucial correlative empirical assumption that is invoked, that is, legalizing prostitution would (or does) have such an effect. It is worth observing that both arguments stress the nonpaternalistic consideration of preventing or halting wrongs that some may inflict on others.

I shall not explore these matters thoroughly, but some comment is in order. Although there is an empirical question about whether legalization of prostitution does or would have the effects mentioned, let us concede that some fostering of less than desirable attitudes does or would occur. The extent of this development and whether it is an inevitable concomitant of legalization are not un-

---

[62] Brownmiller, *Against Our Will*, p. 392.

[63] I say "under normal conditions" only because a reasonable case can be made for the justifiability of acts against which there is a powerful moral presumption (e.g., torture or murder) under certain extreme circumstances, e.g., defensive tactics against an unjust aggressor in war.

important matters. Legalization of flag possession, flag waving, or patriotic celebrations may well promote a kind of jingoistic, xenophobic, or even imperialistic attitude on the part of some of the citizenry. Still, that does not seem a compelling reason to prohibit such activities. Similar points may be made with regard to the potentially invidious effects of allowing athletic or academic competition; some participants develop a myopic, "winning is everything" outlook which facilitates their desensitization and consequent unfair treatment of others. There are a variety of further analogous activities which deserve critical comparison here. A few points may be made briefly. Some activities, such as the moderate consumption of alcohol and the moderate use of certain drugs, seem permissible. Still, excessive use may lead some to wrong others. Should alcohol consumption, therefore, be prohibited? The connection between the practice and the potential wrong is somewhat indirect. When alcohol usage does facilitate the user's wronging others it is usually because the user loses self-control, not because usage has corrupted his attitudes. Legalization of gambling no doubt encourages some to steal or wrongfully squander resources that ought to be used to meet obligations. Should gambling be prohibited? The grounds for a prohibition on gambling by competent persons seem shaky.

Analogously, some activities may "facilitate" (an appropriately vague term to use here) wrongful acts by some against others by directly influencing attitudes and moral viewpoint. The promulgation or encouragement of sexist or racist attitudes by disseminating sexist or racist films or literature well may be a case in point. This is most obvious when we focus on influences on children, a matter, however, which is not our focus here. Relevant to deciding the acceptability of allowing the dissemination of attitude-corrupting materials (by this I mean materials which may influence recipients to wrong others) is the extent to which it can be shown that such dissemination is likely to cause, albeit indirectly, the commission of wrongful acts (cf. the "clear and present danger" test for limiting free speech). One point I shall propose here is that the case for restricting access to, or promulgation of, certain racist, sexist, and other materials encouraging wrongful acts may be comparatively stronger than the case against legalizing gender-neutral prostitution for competent persons as such. For reasons I have noted, sexist attitudes are not a necessary motivation in, or a concomitant to, engaging in prostitution. Fostering sexist and violence-prone attitudes is, by contrast, part and parcel of what occurs in the dissemination of the sort of materials mentioned. What is morally important about "pornographic" material may not be captured by calling attention to its explicit sexual content (e.g., nudity or sexual acts); rather, it may be, when it is present, the tendency to portray wrongful acts approvingly, for example, rape, gratuitous violence, other unjustifiable nonconsensual acts, innocent victims as deserving such treatment—or as possessing inferior or no moral standing. Such modes of influence are less than innocent. However, and in general, the argument that we ought to prohibit *otherwise innocent* activities (which activities are "otherwise innocent" or morally permissible—whether or not desirable—is, of course, no insignificant question) on the ground that allowing them will indirectly foster unacceptable "antisocial" attitudes is by itself a thin reed which will bear little weight. A patriarchal social structure, arguably, will allow female prostitution, but it does not follow that a society which allows voluntary, gender-neutral, prostitution by competents, is patriarchal in attitude or practice.[64]

Several further points deserve mention. As we have defined 'prostitution' here, it is not true by definition that the prostitute is a female. Legalization of prostitution in which *only* females are allowed to be prostitutes would be a practice which would foster sexist attitudes in a way that gender-neutral prostitution would not. We have argued only that there are no legitimate paternalistic grounds for prohibiting prostitution by male or female, competent, persons who knowingly and voluntarily choose to engage in such a practice. If prostitution should be legalized, it should be done on a gender-neutral basis.

A further important point concerns Brownmiller's claim that legalized prostitution (presumably *not* of a gender-neutral sort) "institutionalizes the concept that it is a man's monetary *right*, if not his divine right, to gain access to the female body, and that sex is a female service that should not be denied the civilized male" (my italics). Since we have only argued, in a provisional manner, for

---

[64] Although I have not pressed the point, a number of the arguments in favor of eliminating prostitution by competents, retaining its criminal status, or deeming it immoral also provide reasons for viewing marriage, or many marriages, in a similar fashion, e.g., that some women engage in it because of economic difficulties (thus it is not "truly voluntary"), that it is associated historically with patriarchal power divisions or practices, that in spite of consent it encourages men to regard women as "sex objects," and that getting monetizable compensation for provision of sexual services is somehow degrading or self-demeaning. Or if it were to be insisted that the existence of love or affection makes marriage legitimate but not prostitution, such a point may count in favor of legally prohibiting or terminating a considerable number of marriages.

the legalization of gender-neutral prostitution, it is worth considering a more general point implicit in the quoted remark. Would legalization of gender-neutral prostitution encourage the notion that prospective customers have a *right* (a "monetary right"?) to gain access to a desired sexual partner (male or female)? It is hard to see why. In general, sellers of services (therapists, dentists, physicians, plumbers, and so on) are under no legal duty to supply such services to those who request them. In general, they are free to refuse to make a contractual agreement to provide such services. The legalization of plumbing hardly seems to institutionalize the concept that nonplumbers have a "monetary right" to gain access to the services of plumbers.

There is a deeper point in all this. It concerns the difficult to elaborate Kantian notion of using someone as a mere means. To do something presumptively wrong to another against his (or her) will, arguably, is to treat the other as a mere means and is to exploit that other (in a pejorative sense of 'exploit'). However, it is at least not obvious that we use someone as a mere means, or wrong her (or him), if that person is competent, and knowingly and voluntarily chooses to cooperate with, or be the recipient of, a proposed act. In such cases the subject autonomously chooses to cooperate or not. For this reason it is hard to understand why legalized prostitution, of the restricted sort we have considered, must involve a client's having any right to gain access to the prostitute's body or any right to oppress or dominate her (or him).[65]

At this point a critic might concede that a prospective client has no *right* to a prostitute's cooperation and, hence, there need not be any sort of dubious, superior-inferior, domination in the client-prostitute relationship. That is, the relationship, at least may not exhibit an asymmetrical right of one party to impose his will on the other. Nevertheless, it may be maintained that one ought not sexually cooperate with the willing prostitute. Consider the view posed by Joel Feinberg (regarding voluntary slavery):

> If a weak, foolish, or reckless man freely chooses to harm or risk harm to himself, that is all right, but that is no reason why another should be a party to it, or be permitted to benefit

[65] An important point deserving further investigation, and one which may offer a tempting basis for criticism of much of the theory developed here, concerns whether there is an intelligible and defensible notion of noncoercive exploitation (to put the point crudely). On this, see Joel Feinberg's essay "Noncoercive Exploitation," in *Paternalism*, ed. Rolf Sartorius (Minneapolis: University of Minnesota Press, 1983) pp. 201–236. (Also, recall the discussion in Chapter 2.)

himself at the other's expense. . . . Applied to voluntary slavery, the principle of non-exploitation might say it isn't aimed at preventing one man from being a slave so much as preventing the other from being a slave-owner. . . . To own another human being, as one might own a table or a horse, is to be in a relation to him that is inherently immoral, and therefore properly forbidden by law.[66]

Applying this view to the case of prostitution (though Feinberg, it should be observed, does not), even if a client has no right to a prostitute's services and even if there is no overriding of his (or her) will, it still may be impermissible to purchase a prostitute's services. It may be claimed (though Feinberg does not) that to do so is for the client to take advantage of the willing prostitute, to profit at her (or his) expense, or to involve oneself in a relation that is "inherently immoral." One important question here concerns why we should think that voluntary participation, by competent persons, in prostitution is participation in an "inherently immoral" relation. If to speak of "inherently immoral" acts is to affirm that some acts are inherently immoral but that we cannot identify the wrongmaking feature(s) of such acts we are left with a rather inscrutable, intuitionist, view. Alternatively, we have found reasons to question why it should be thought that the competent, knowing, and voluntary prostitute is "taken advantage of," and why a client profits "at the prostitute's expense" (she [or he] acts freely and receives compensation for services rendered). Thus, even if Feinberg's principle has some force against allowing slavery contracts, it does not obviously provide a basis for concluding that the client-prostitute exchange is inherently, or otherwise, immoral.

Our assessment of the proffered nonpaternalistic grounds for prohibiting voluntary prostitution by competent adults has not canvassed all more or less tempting arguments. Our examination strongly suggests, however, that it is not at all obvious that there are any compelling nonpaternalistic grounds criminally to prohibit knowing and voluntary gender-neutral prostitution by competent persons, although there are plausible reasons (concerning the lessening of offensive action and reducing health risks of nonparticipants) for limited regulation of the activity. If our assessment of such arguments is correct, it is all the more important to weigh the paternalistic arguments sometimes invoked in favor of coercive interference. If our reasoning on that score has been sound, then,

[66] Feinberg, "Legal Paternalism," p. 123.

with the exceptions regarding warnings, fair and open persuasion, or consensual interferences, there is no justification for criminal prohibition: rather it is an impermissible restriction on the liberties of competent persons to chart their own course.[67] To conclude as much is not to praise or recommend prostitution, nor in any substantive way to encourage it; it is to insist on a respect for the liberties of other competent persons who, though we may disapprove of their choices, must direct their own lives as they see fit within the domain of permissible options.

5.7 Irrevocable Consent: The Tale of Odysseus

According to the theory developed earlier it is permissible for agents to engage in presumptively wrong acts toward subjects if those subjects are competent persons and validly consent to the acts in question; a further proviso, of course, is that such proceedings wrong no others. It was maintained that prior valid consent by the subject, at the time of the agent's intervention, must be "currently operative." This qualification implies that if the subject has *withdrawn* or *revoked* her consent, then there is, at the time of the proposed intervention, no currently operative valid consent. In an earlier example, one may have revoked one's consent to a neighbor's harvesting fruit from one's trees. Consent can be ongoing; in at least some cases it can be revoked. Some puzzles arise here. Can consent always be revoked? Is it ever permissible for an agent who previously received valid consent from S to do X to go ahead even though belatedly S resists A's doing X or desires that A not do X? Suppose S validly consents to a therapeutic regimen to be implemented by A, one which takes place over weeks at discrete intervals. Can S be coerced into continuing if he desires not to proceed after the initial treatments? These are practical questions. Adequate answers need to be anchored in some theoretical framework.

[67] We have not rested the case for decriminalizing voluntary prostitution of competents on the "costs" (broadly construed) of criminal prohibitions, but such costs only strengthen the decriminalization argument. As Edwin Schur has noted, such costs include: difficulty of enforcement, the financial burden on taxpayers of doing so, increased price of the service, generation of secondary crimes, the discriminatory manner of enforcement, and the degrading treatment of those arrested; see Edwin Schur, "The Case for Abolition," in Bedau and Schur, *Victimless Crimes*, pp. 8–9.

For further discussion, see Lars O. Ericsson, "Charges Against Prostitution: An Attempt at a Philosophical Assessment," *Ethics* 90 (April, 1980), pp. 335–366, and Alison M. Jaggar, "Prostitution," in *Philosophy of Sex*, ed. Alan Soble (Totowa, N.J.: Littlefield & Adams, 1980), pp. 348–368.

One way of exploring these matters is to consider cases in which people bind themselves, or consent to be bound in some fashion, and, belatedly, desire to be free of those constraints to which they initially committed themselves. Contractual agreements are a case in point, but a useful place to begin is the tale of Odysseus and the Sirens, and the variant tale developed by Donald Regan in his investigation of some of the moral questions which concern us here.[68]

In the *Odyssey*, Odysseus, his crew and ship, will pass near the isle of the Sirens whose seductive song tempts its hearers to abandon ship and swim to the Sirens to gain their knowledge: of all that was, is, or will be. The isle is surrounded by dangerous rocks and those who jump overboard and swim to the isle inevitably will be killed.[69] To avoid this result Odysseus prudently instructs his crew as follows:

> . . . you are to tie me up, tight as a splint, erect along the mast, lashed to the mast, and if I shout and beg to be untied, take more turns of the rope to muffle me.[70]

The crew, with wax placed in their ears by Odysseus, do not hear the Sirens, and row on until the danger is past. Then Odysseus is released.

Regan alters the classic narrative in order to argue that, in his variant tale, keeping Odysseus bound is not justified. In the variant tale the Sirens' song casts no irresistible spell; it is just quite beautiful. Further, a swim to the rocks may result in physical injury but not death. In the variation Odysseus initially decides merely to sail by. Fearful that he will not stick to his decision, he orders himself bound. However, on hearing the song he regards it as more beautiful than he imagined and comes to care more about hearing it close at hand. Further, it is not an unreasonable choice to swim closer in spite of the (now more limited) risk involved. Hence, he changes his mind, wishes to be released, and manages to convey his wishes to his crew. Regan concludes that, in this scenario, the crew ought to release him. Hence, it seems that the earlier valid

---

[68] Donald Regan, "Paternalism, Freedom, Identity, and Commitment," a version of a paper by the same title which later appeared in *Paternalism*, ed. Rolf Sartorius (Minneapolis: University of Minnesota Press, 1983), pp. 113–138.

[69] In contrast to the familiar portrayal of woman as weak, powerless, and in need of paternalistic protection, here we have woman as active, as intellectual temptress; compare Eve's relationship to her "significant other," Adam.

[70] Homer, *The Odyssey*, trans. Robert Fitzgerald (Garden City, N.Y.: Doubleday, 1963), p. 214.

consent of Odysseus (and correlative promise) is not a sufficient condition for the permissibility of the constraint; so Regan concludes. The questions arise as to whether Regan is correct in his inference and, if so, whether that undermines any thesis I have defended. Regan is calling attention to the fact that, at a later time than when consent to interference is given, a subject genuinely may change his mind about what he wants, and that this case must be distinguished from the case in which he has not really *changed his mind* but, due to weakness of will, is succumbing to temptation. To put the point another way, in one case the subject's perception and judgment of what is desirable or prudent is not altered on being tempted, but he cannot resist the temptation. In the other case his assessment of what is desirable or prudent genuinely alters and, even if his powers of self-discipline are not weaker, his resolve has altered; he judges, perhaps rightly, that "the risk is worth it." Regan surely is correct that these are different sorts of cases.

Two points are worth noting. First, from the standpoint of Odysseus' crew, it will be difficult to ascertain which has happened, that is, whether Odysseus merely is giving in to temptation (in which case he should remain bound, for his consent is to be bound so as to *prevent that result*) or he has a reason-based and revised goal, and is not just psychologically unable to keep to his earlier stated resolve. Unless the crew has some reasonable means to determine which explanation is appropriate (there may be such means in unhurried situations), it would seem that they must presume that his former resolution is unrevised. Suppose they somehow come to have a justified belief that Odysseus' plea is not just "giving in" but evidences a revised aim, one which is reason-based and would remain settled even when he is removed from the temptation. Does that undermine our earlier result? The answer, I believe, is negative because on the view we have defended, for restraint to be permissible, there must be *currently operative* consent. In the case in which consent has been given earlier, it must be either revocable but unrevoked or irrevocable.

If Odysseus had earlier said "bind me to the mast and do not release me *no matter what* I say or choose," Odysseus would have sanctioned restraint even if he were to change his mind. In such a case, the crew would do no wrong in restraining him. This result is intuitively plausible for, in (partially) analogous contractual cases, we bind ourselves to certain policies even if, at a later point, we genuinely wish not to be bound, for example, by purchasing a car that turns out to be unsatisfactory from the standpoint of our reason-based revised assessment; normally, we cannot, as a matter of right, demand release from the restraints of the monthly payments. Here, the fact that one is *entitled* to "change one's mind" does not undermine the claim that one is, nevertheless, justifiably constrained. If Odysseus had said "bind me to the mast and do not release me *unless* I genuinely change my mind," this latter consent to restraint is revocable; if the crew could ascertain a relevant change of mind and a revocation of earlier consent, then restraint would be, on the theory I have defended, impermissible. In either case, what is decisive in determining whether restraint is permissible is, at the time of restraint, the presence and nature of currently operative consent. Hence, I conclude that Regan's argument fails to show that valid consent is not a sufficient condition for the moral permissibility of the interference. If this is correct, a matter of principle is settled, although epistemological pitfalls remain for nonomniscient interveners.

It may be objected to the view which I have urged that my car payment analogy is defective and misleading since in that case if one changes one's mind about the wisdom of the purchase the lender will suffer a loss if one defaults, and that this is unlike the position of the crew with regard to Odysseus. So why may the crew go ahead and restrain Odysseus if the crew knew he had changed his mind? They will not lose (let us suppose) if they do not insist on restraining him. Hence, it seems permissible for the crew, if they choose, not to restrain Odysseus. On this point, however, one may agree. The question is not whether it is permissible to restrain him. Even if the former is true, it does not follow that the latter is false. My contention is that the crew acts permissibly in restraining Odysseus if Odysseus, earlier, gave irrevocable consent to restraint—and even if he genuinely has changed his mind. He has, earlier, sanctioned the interference and subjected himself to a liability from which *he* cannot release himself even though he has changed his mind. The crew has the power to release him from that liability, but if they do not (by not untying him) they act permissibly. That they are "licensed" to restrain him does not, however, entail that they would do wrong to give up their license; it may be permissible to untie Odysseus *and* permissible to keep him bound. In the case of the loan company, a genuine change of mind on your part does not render it impermissible for the company to collect even if you are willing to return the car. Typically such companies aim to maximize profits and have an incentive to hold you to your side of the bargain.[71] If they, for whatever reasons, choose to abstain from doing what it is permissible for them to do, that is also permissible. Although your consent, in the loan company case, is irrevocable, the company is free to waive its right to collect and voluntarily to absorb the costs if it so chooses.[72]

For the reasons mentioned there are grounds for denying that the *most recent* choice or preference of a subject *always* should be the decisive factor in determining whether interference is permissible, apart from whether the most recent choice is the most prudent choice. From the standpoint of others, or in reality, the most recent, or the earlier choice, may or may not be the most prudent. Attempts to justify invasive interference which appeal only to promoting the good (or preventing harm) of the competent subject, partly or entirely apart from his choices, are unacceptable, a point we sought to establish in Chapter 3.

A further complication in particular cases in which prior consent is revocable concerns whether or not the most recent choice, for example, Odysseus' revised choice in Regan's variant tale, gives evidence of loss of competence. In Regan's scenario it does not, for Odysseus' revised view is just better informed. However, in some cases an apparent "change of mind" may be indicative of a *loss* of capacity competently to exercise control over one's life. I am not suggesting that this is so just because the most recent choice is imprudent, if it is. A revision of a (revocable) choice about one's (legal) will, for example, might involve disinheriting one's siblings and assigning one's estate to the Roach Protection League, an association whose central tenet is that roaches are reincarnated ances-

---

[71] Contractual agreements are often ones in which both parties seek to improve their own situation. The loan company in my example is not acting paternalistically but pursuing its own advantage. In the variant tale of Odysseus, the crew, if it kept Odysseus bound after his ostensible change of mind, would be paternalistically constraining Odysseus only if they believed that doing so would prevent a harm from befalling him and were thus motivated.

[72] Some acts of consent are "irrevocable," I suggest, in the sense that these grantings of permission cannot be recalled or canceled simply by a choice of the consenting party. Such irrevocable consent can be thought of as a waiver of right which is irreversible by the bearer. The loss of the right, however, need not be permanent. One might consent irrevocably to a visiting dignitary's using one's apartment for a weekend. For whatever reason, one might *wish* to recall one's consent and reacquire the right to the use of one's apartment. Though the consent is, by assumption, irrevocable, one might reacquire the right by purchasing it from the ungracious visitor, or because a gracious one accedes to your request. Some decisions are called "irrevocable" for a quite different reason, namely, that certain *effects* of the decision, or its implementation, are irreversible, e.g., amputation of a limb or certain types of sterilization.

tors. Radically revised "changes of mind" *may be* a byproduct of acquisition of information, increased risk-aversion, diminished risk-aversion, weakness of will, re-ordering of values, *or* mental breakdown. If there is reason to infer loss of competence, the principles developed so far will cease to have direct application for, as noted, they concern only the choices and acts of competent persons. Principles regarding incompetent persons are the focus of Chapter 7. In our discussion of Odysseus we have assumed his competence.

So far I have argued that competent persons *can* bind themselves by certain kinds of agreement. Our primary concern is with what is permissible and not a matter of duty. It is easy to confuse these issues since in the case of Odysseus and in that of the loan company there is not only consent by one party to acts by another, there is a correlative promise to act by the other party. Frequently in such cases, both legally backed and not, the party permitted to act (cf. the crew or the loan company) also has a duty to act. I have maintained that a genuine change of mind by the constrained party (Odysseus or the mortgagee) may not make the imposition of the constraint by the other party impermissible. It, however, can serve to waive any right the party to be constrained has against the other that the constraint must be imposed; hence: the *permissibility* of the loan company's not collecting or the crew's releasing Odysseus when he has had a change of mind (compatible with his retention of competence). As noted before, much depends on the precise *content* of the prior consent. I have claimed that when a competent party, S, consents to a constraint, C, then it is permissible for the recipient of the consent to impose C on S if the consent is irrevocable (e.g., S said: impose C on me no matter what I request in the future) or revocable (e.g., S said: impose C on me unless I later earnestly request otherwise) *but* unrevoked. Giving irrevocable consent may, of course, be *imprudent*, but this by itself does not show that it is impermissible to impose constraints which arise from it. Giving irrevocable consent to constraints while one is calm, reflective, "centered," and at the peak of one's powers may be an effective way of promoting one's conception of the good (which may aim at promoting the good of others as well). Such a strategy may be effective especially in cases in which one has a higher-order desire that one not act on some of one's lower-order desires (e.g., one deeply desires not to give in, or succumb, to one's occasional desire to seek out the Sirens, one's desire to drive while drinking alcohol, one's desire to eat whenever frustrated, one's desire to smoke while writing a book, one's desire to use drugs when pressured by others to do so, and so on), and one reasonably believes that one's self-discipline (resistance to weakness of will) has its limits. Such self-imposed constraints, even if *implemented by others*, allow and facilitate *our* directing our own lives even if they are imposed on us after a genuine change of mind for it is *we* who directed that these constraints exist. Sometimes we choose to circumscribe certain segments of our lives and delimit our alternatives. It is not always possible or feasible to commit ourselves to the least restrictive set of limitations possible; on some occasions we could make things more flexible for ourselves (perhaps, Odysseus, in Regan's variant, should have given revocable consent only), but we neglect to do so.

I do not wish to suggest or imply that we must be "legalistic" in the sense of an overly literal adherence to a subject's actual words in interpreting the content of his consent. For example, suppose you request "please don't let me drive after the party on Saturday; I'll probably be inebriated," and I agree. Such a request is more open-textured than Odysseus' request in the original narrative ("if I shout and beg to be untied, take more turns of the rope to muffle me"). If you are not substantially incapacitated on Saturday night and if you urgently need to drive a long way to have a final moment with a dying parent, it would be insensitively rigid to claim that you gave irrevocable consent to my preventing you from doing so—even though you failed to attach explicitly any "riders" such as "only if I'm quite drunk" or "if there are no urgent reasons for me to drive." Although it is true that *some* circumstances which occur after consent is given are "unforeseeable," only some would seem to be legitimate grounds for a constrained party to insist that he ought to be released from a constraint to which he earlier consented. The circumstance of the dying parent is one such case. In contrast, consider a (nonpaternalistic) example in which I consent that you use my car to go job hunting. When the time comes, I claim that new circumstances, which I did not foresee, have arisen, namely, I now wish to sit in my car and read. Hence, I claim, you no longer have my consent. Aside from the difficult position I put you in, something has gone awry theoretically. In short, some "changes of mind" do not serve to justify the claim that one's prior valid consent is no longer operative.

Much consent to constraint is clearly not of the "no matter what happens" variety; generally, it is revocable. I have claimed, nevertheless, that the existence or not of currently operative consent is morally crucial, and, in selected cases, constraining a person even against his current will or inclination may be justified paternalism for the reasons we have discussed. Sometimes consent is irrevocable, and in such cases it is permissible for others to constrain the consenter against his current desire even if the subject has changed his mind. To apply this conclusion to a practical question raised earlier, patients who validly consent to a therapeutic regimen cannot always complain justifiably that a wrong is done to them if they are coercively made to continue. Respecting the choices of others does not necessarily require our acceding to their *most recent* choices.[73]

[73] The relevance of the Principle of Hypothetical Individualized Consent to our discussion in this section may not be transparent; so a comment is in order. PHIC is relevant only when we do not know the will of the subject or when we have reason to believe that the subject is not aware of all the relevant circumstances that would affect his choice or his consent. In short, it provides a basis for discounting his choices or intentions under certain circumstances. Hence, it *may* sanction a discounting of Odysseus' early choice (in Regan's variant tale) if we rightly think it was made under conditions of significant ignorance. Similarly, it may sanction overriding a revised choice, if we have good reason to believe that the subject under less stressful or better informed circumstances would not choose as he does. These points, oversimplified somewhat, emphasize the fact that what counts decisively, on the theory defended here, is the more or less stable, reasoned, centered, judgment and commitment of the subject. Whether we can ascertain what that is, and whether it is expressed in a current or a prior choice (if exhibited at all), are further matters. Those questions, in turn, are distinguishable from whether valid consent, if we can discern it, is irrevocable. A number of diverse and perplexing cases can arise here, as these points may suggest, but I forego their further pursuit. For a related discussion, see "Can A Subject Consent to a 'Ulysses Contract'?" and Commentary by M. E. and S. M. Winston, by Paul Applebaum, and by Nancy Rhoden, *The Hastings Center Report* 12, No. 4 (August, 1982), pp. 26–28.

SIX

PATERNALISTIC LIMITS ON RISK TAKING

I love hamburgers and chili con carne and hot dogs. And foie gras and sauternes and those small birds known as ortolans. I love banquettes of quail eggs with hollandaise sauce and clambakes with lobsters dipped into so much butter it dribbles down the chin. I like cheesecake and crepes filled with cream sauces and strawberries with creme fraiche. . . .

And if I am abbreviating my stay on this earth for an hour or so, I say only that I have no desire to be a Methuselah, a hundred or more years old and still alive, grace be to something that plugs into an electric outlet.
—Craig Claiborne

The rule is, jam tomorrow and jam yesterday—but never jam today.   —Lewis Carroll

A ship in the harbor is safe, but that is not where a ship ought to be.   —Anonymous

6.1 Risks, Harms, and Wrongs

Understandably, dramatic and extreme acts such as terrorism, torture, euthanasia, suicide, and abortion, among others, grab our attention. In a stark way they press us to make hard decisions and explore recalcitrant issues. By contrast, various other issues promise to fall "between the cracks"; some seem more mundane. For example, may we coercively (e.g., by law) require persons to wear motorcycle helmets while cycling, seat belts while driving, or purchase air bags for cars? Should we prohibit or constrain drug usage, hang gliding, skate boarding, smoking, drinking alcohol, or rock climbing? May we tax citizens to enforce such policies, to warn persons of the attendant risks, or to accumulate information about such risks? Should we, imaginatively, require recorded messages on coffee or cigarette dispensing machines to hector consumers

302

about the prospective risks of their acts? Should we not only coercively prevent our drunken friends from driving but also berate those who are obese because of failure to exercise? In general, what may we do to prevent harm from accruing to others? The diverse activities mentioned largely focus on matters of individual life-style but also on the range of options society makes available to individuals or makes difficult to avoid.[1]

Assessing the broad and diverse array of practices mentioned requires an answer to a number of difficult questions. My primary concern here is captured, albeit crudely, by one such question: What paternalistic attempts to limit risks to others are morally permissible?[2] Vigorously disputed policies concern both those which *impose risks* on others and those which constrain individuals (or organizations) in order to *limit* or minimize *risks* they might otherwise voluntarily assume or to which they might be involuntarily exposed; for example, recall the persistent debates regarding control of pollution, nuclear power, dueling, gambling, coal mining, vaccination, fluoridation, food and drug testing, production of nerve gases, or even the problems that bears pose for tourists in the national parks (or vice versa). Deep disagreement about appropriate "risk management" can be seen to arise from two extreme and contrary convictions. Oversimplified considerably, they are: (1) competent individuals should be left entirely on their own to cope with whatever risks they happen to encounter or to choose whatever levels of risk they wish to assume, and (2) we should strive to create the safest possible society and, hence, should employ whatever governmental measures are necessary to eliminate or minimize risks.

The barriers to thinking clearly about such issues are formidable. Hard questions confront us. What is risk? Is a no-risk society possible? Does the policy of optimizing risk levels grant some a license to generate risks (or, e.g., a "license to pollute")? Are there nonarbitrary criteria for determining "socially acceptable risks"? Do protective-regulative agencies do more harm than good? How should risks be distributed? This list is hardly exhaustive. Indeed, it is impossible to explore all these matters here, and I shall focus

---

[1] An instructive essay, and useful bibliography, on questions regarding governmental efforts to promote health is Dan Wikler's "Persuasion and Coercion for Health," *Milbank Memorial Fund Quarterly* 56, No. 3 (1978), pp. 303–338.

[2] I focus on risks to which others are subject, inadvertently or not, independently of any deliberate effort on our part to cause such risks. Hence, the focus is on what potential interveners may do about independently existing, or prospective, risks to others.

largely on distinctly paternalistic questions about limiting risks to which others may be subject. Prior to narrowing our focus, some stage setting is in order—mainly in order to define terms and identify some relevant distinctions. Indeed, one of the barriers to clear thinking and a more adequate theoretical stance is the current absence of a perspicuous way of sorting the relevant questions and considerations. In the spirit of those who do the initial bush clearing on a jungle expedition, let us try to smooth the path toward a more satisfactory theory of the morality of limiting risks, even though a fully adequate theory eludes our grasp.

'Consumer protection' calls to mind not only competent (usually adult) persons but those who have an impact on market demand. In passing I note that any adequate moral theory about limiting risks would have to consider not only our dealings with consumers, so understood, but all persons, for example, infants, toddlers, the severely retarded, and the mentally ill.[3] *Consumer* protection is, then, only one type of "person protection." As commonly understood, "risk management" has a narrower focus. Our central concern here continues to be with competent persons.

What is meant by 'risk'? To answer this question, it is useful to focus on expressions of the form 'the risk of X to S' where 'X' stands for some possible occurrence affecting an individual(s). As frequently understood, 'the risk of X to S' means 'the product of the probability of X's occurring times a measure of the harmfulness of X to S.' For example, if my being tortured by a being from Pluto constitutes a great harm to me but the probability of its occurrence is virtually nil, the risk to me of such an occurrence is quite small. Conversely, if the probability is high that I shall cut my finger at some time before I die but the resultant harm is small, the risk to me is not significant. Evidently, if it is difficult to measure the probability of X's occurring or the harmfulness of X to S, it will be difficult or impossible to measure the risk of X to S. If what is harmful to S is to be understood solely or entirely as a function of S's preferences after all things have been considered, what we may view as a risk to S may not be so viewed by S. For example, Br'er Rabbit only pretended that his being thrown in the briar patch was a risk to him; Br'er Fox took another view. Analogously, one intending to commit suicide may not view the oncoming train as a

---

[3] Not to mention others who are subject to risk of harm, e.g., sentient nonhuman animals and human fetuses.

risk while she lies on the railroad track.[4] What often counts as a risk seems, at least partially, to be a matter of subjective aims; hence, second-party determination of the existence or degree of risk may be no unproblematic task. Of course, given a certain stability about what people want or what they need in order to pursue their aims, it is not ordinarily unreasonable to *presume* that exposure to disease, injury, or death constitute serious risks to persons. In addition, we note that the fact that people voluntarily choose to engage in certain activities knowing that the activities are "fraught with risks" does not necessarily mean that they view the risky features as in themselves desirable.[5] By contrast, some do; for example, skilled mountain climbers often look with scorn on low-risk climbs.

We do not seem to have a single term analogous to 'risk' for denoting the probability of X times a measure of the benefit to S. The closest expression in use seems to be the "expected utility" of X to S. Roughly, 'risk' typically means 'exposure to harm,' and 'expected utility' 'exposure to benefit.' Hence, it is a bit misleading to speak of the risk of benefit' inhering in X with regard to S.

Is risk itself a harm or type of harm? Here it is preferable to talk of a particular type of risk, for example, the risk of my being run over by a truck. That is a risk I face at times, but it is not obvious that I suffer harm by its mere existence. After all, its mere existence does *not necessarily* cause me physical or psychological damage, property loss, or loss of liberties I value. What if another, without my consent, causes me to be "subjected to" such a risk? He may do so by building a truck or, more likely, by driving his truck recklessly near my person as I cross the street. In the former case it seems incorrect to say he has harmed me. The latter case seems different, but we can reasonably say that I have been *wronged* in such a case without saying, counterintuitively I judge, that I have been harmed. A further qualification, however, is that some impositions of risks cause *fear* of an event, E, and the fear may con-

[4] Compare one reported case of a 49-year-old female patient who, when informed that she had a 1 in 3,000 chance of dying from electro-convulsive therapy, replied, "I hope I am the one." Cited in Loren Roth, Alan Meisel, and Charles Lidz, "Tests of Competency to Consent to Treatment," *American Journal of Psychiatry* 134, No. 3 (March, 1977), p. 282.

[5] At the risk of distracting more somber readers, consider the stance toward risk taking in the limerick: "My doctor has made a prognosis / That intercourse fosters thrombosis / But I'd rather expire / Fulfilling desire / Than abstain and develop neurosis." Reported by Alan Dershowitz, "Toward a Jurisprudence of 'Harm,' " in *The Limits of Law*, eds. J. Roland Pennock and John W. Chapman (New York: Lieber-Atherton, 1974), p. 152.

stitute a harm even if E does not occur, or could not occur. If all that is right, a risk of harm may not itself be a harm, nor is being subjected to a risk *necessarily* a *harm*, although it may be a *wrong*. To stress a point, even if generating risks to others does not harm them, it may wrong them. So, risk generation calls for moral scrutiny *even if* it is not harm generation.

6.2 Limiting Risks: The Case of Motorcycles

In considering the morality of generating, or limiting, risks (these may be risks to oneself, to others, or to both), it is crucial to distinguish the different possible sources of risk to a subject, S. These seem to be exhaustively categorizable by recognizing: (1) risks which S generates, deliberately or inadvertently, (2) risks which others generate, deliberately or inadvertently, and (3) risks generated by natural occurrences. These categories are useful even if fuzzy around the edges. We may recognize some risks as resulting from multiple sources; for example, if S chooses to duel with A, the risks to S arise partly from S's choice and partly from A's actions. The notion, then, of "voluntarily assumed" or "consented-to risks" may cut across our categories.[6] From the point of view defended here, it is morally important whether or not risks are voluntarily assumed or not.

Attempts to minimize or *limit risks* may also be voluntary or not. It is worth observing that attempts to limit risks to some individual, S, may be involuntary from S's standpoint but voluntary from the standpoint of others. For example, if a legislature requires that S refrain from gambling, or forego motorcycling without a helmet, the presumed risk limitation to S may be one not voluntarily chosen by S (or one to which S consents) although the legislature voluntarily creates the risk limitation. Legal requirements to delimit risks to a subject, S, will be a presumptively wrong constraint on S's liberty when S, as a competent person, does not validly consent to the limitation. The *motivation* behind such limitations and the *grounds* proffered in defense of such constraints are, often, paternalistic. Hence, many legal constraints designed to limit risks to subjects by constraining their liberties may be examples of paternalistically based legislation, and their purported justification falls within our domain of inquiry.

[6] Strictly, the quoted expressions are not synonymous; risks in S's mountain climbing may arise from factors in (1) and (3) and be voluntarily assumed even though S does not give consent to anyone else.

As noted in Chapter 1, a given instance of liberty-limiting legislation, one of whose presumed consequences is to limit risks to some group of subjects, *may* be defended (1) solely on paternalistic grounds, (2) solely on nonpaternalistic grounds, or (3) by appeal to both sorts of grounds—aside from whatever sole or primary *motivation* prevailed among those legislating. This consideration is often ignored by those critical of the legislation in question. A case in point, although only one of many possible examples, is the mentioned motorcycle helmet requirement. A typical criticism is that the requirement is "paternalistic," and an example of unwarranted paternalistic interference in the lives of competent persons—another example of Big Brother's unduly invading prerogatives which, by right, ought to remain under the control of competent persons. The question of the justification of such a requirement is not simple, and it deserves our examination since it exemplifies the complexities inherent in assessing a broad range of legislative (and, also, nonlegislative) restrictions aimed at limiting risks to persons.

The motorcycle helmet requirement prevailed in 47 states of the United States in 1975; the three exceptions were Illinois, Utah, and California.[7] After that time 28 states relaxed or repealed such legislation and, possibly as a result, there was a 46 percent increase in deaths nationwide—increasing to 4,850 by 1979. By 1980 only 17 states required helmets for all motorcyclists, 10 had no requirements, and 23 required them for riders under 18 years of age.[8] About half of the accidents involving motorcycles were "caused" by motorists failing to see cyclists at all or in time to avoid collision. About 73 percent of the cyclists' deaths occurred to those not wearing helmets. It is not unreasonable to conjecture, then, that over 3000 premature deaths in a single year might have been avoided and might be avoided by a nationwide prohibition on cycling without a helmet.

On the face of it, our prior argument *seems* to imply that, in spite of the admitted level of tragic results, the prohibition of motorcycle riding without a helmet is not justifiable on paternalistic grounds. The argument for this conclusion would have as a premise that it is impermissible to interfere in a presumptively wrong manner (e.g., by coercive legislation) with the choices or acts of competent

[7] My data are from a University of Southern California study released by the U.S. Transportation Department in 1980 and reported in *The Raleigh Times* (October 13, 1980).
[8] Ibid.

persons if they act in ways not wronging others. As argued in Chapters 2 and 3, the paternalistic appeals to good-promotion or harm prevention, subsequent consent, the hypothetical consent of fully rational persons, moral-good promotion, or autonomy preservation or promotion are unacceptable.

However, there are at least two reasons to pause before concluding that, if the Principle of Autonomy-Respecting Paternalism (PARP) is acceptable, such prohibitive legislation is not justifiable.[9] The first concerns the proviso (2b) in PARP which allows interference with S in those cases in which S would consent to the interference if S were fully apprised of the relevant probable consequences of his intended act. Hence, it is relevant whether, for example, cyclists, are aware of the risks they are taking in riding motorcycles without helmets. A general difficulty arises here concerning perception and determination of risks by subjects who undertake risky activities. Experts sometimes disagree about the risks involved in certain activities. For example, the worldwide flu epidemic in 1918 killed 20,000,000 people; the attempt in 1976 to reduce the risks of an expected flu epidemic in the United States by swine flu vaccination turned out to be misguided.[10] Experts disagreed about the risks involved in *not* developing such a protective program. In addition, public, as opposed to professional, estimation of risk can be shown to be mistaken in certain cases. A sample of members of the League of Women Voters estimated the deaths per year in the United States from automobile accidents to be 28,000; a sample of students estimated 10,000; the actual number for the relevant years was closer to 50,000.[11] More decisively, surveys tend to show that most people regard themselves as *above average* in their ability to avoid automobile or lawn mower accidents, but these beliefs logically cannot all be true any more than most existing people can be taller than the current average height. Some cyclists may underestimate the risks involved in riding without a helmet, but it is *not obvious* that most do. Given the seeming high degree of public awareness of resulting accidents and the fact that the risks are not difficult to discern in this type of case (as they are with the use of intra-uterine devices, using chain saws without ear

[9] For the Principle of Autonomy-Respecting Paternalism (PARP), see Section 2.10.
[10] William Lowrance, "The Nature of Risk," in *Societal Risk Assessment*, eds. Richard Schwing and Walter Albers (New York: Plenum, 1980), p. 7.
[11] Raphael Kaspar, "Perceptions of Risk and Their Effects on Decision-Making," in eds. Schwing and Albers, *Societal Risk Assessment*, p. 74.

plugs, or eating certain foods while taking drugs) it seems unlikely that adult cyclists seriously miscalculate the risks.

With regard to whether PARP allows or prohibits cycling without helmets, a second relevant consideration is whether cyclists are acting within the domain of acts not wronging others. It is surely myopic to focus only on whether the cyclists physically injure others by an accident. Cyclists who are seriously injured often impose nontrivial and unconsented-to costs on others. The cost of medical care is one that cyclists often cannot pay or one for which they have not fully insured themselves. As a result taxpayers have an increased burden when care is publicly funded. Even if there is agreement that justice or benevolence demands providing for those who are *involuntarily* needy or helpless, it does not follow that the public ought to pay to aid those who make themselves needy by knowingly and voluntarily subjecting themselves to avoidable risks which they have no duty to assume. An Australian surgeon, Anthony Moore, has vividly described the result of self-induced sickness and the corollary problem of responsibility:

> Wards, clinics and homes are full of debilitated bodies made wretched by irresponsibility and individual wantonness—ruined by wilful disregard for personal well-being. People who have choked the blood from the heart with cigarettes, and torn the air from their lungs; who have squandered their body through lethargy; who have been digging their own graves with gluttonous gums; whose organs have been eroded with alcohol; whose bones have been splintered by delinquent driving; whose nerves have been snapped on the rack of ambition or anxiety; whose personality has become a plague through drugs; whose kidneys have been gnawed by aspirin; and whose mind has been sludged with sedatives.
>
> The economic cost is huge: an annual Australian health bill of over four thousand million dollars.[12]

Debates about duties to the "truly needy" cannot reasonably ignore the question of whether or not, or to what extent, those in need have voluntarily and knowingly generated their own plight.[13] Still,

[12] Anthony R. Moore, "The Stupidity of Patients," *Journal of Medical Ethics* 5 (1979), p. 207.

[13] Here, as elsewhere, the question of responsibility is often difficult. One who rides a motorcycle without a helmet, and has a serious injury which would have been prevented by use of a helmet, may not act in a fully voluntary manner if doing so is his only means of escaping from a gang of hoodlums. More serious worries arise when one considers whether being subjected to poverty, parental abuse, or

health-care teams confronted with unconscious victims in emergency rooms cannot readily make such determinations. Even when cyclists (or their estates) absorb the financial costs of their care, it may be the case, as we noted in suicide cases, that their resulting incapacitation prevents them from fulfilling nontrivial positive duties they have toward others, for example, caring for their children. In this way prospective cyclists may have duties to abstain from serious and (empirically and morally) avoidable risks, duties derived from positive and serious duties toward others.

But we should not ignore those cases, however many or few, in which it cannot be maintained that the cyclist's impairment will result in an obvious failure on his part to carry out a stringent duty to known others (e.g., to his children). Even if others wind up paying the health-care costs, it may be objected that these costs, nevertheless, are not *imposed* on others. Let us examine this objection.

The question of whether persons in their actions "impose costs on others" is slippery for two reasons. First, there is the question of what is to count as a cost or a harm. Second, if we are in agreement about the prior question, when is a cost *imposed* on others? We need to be clear about when a cost is reasonably avoidable by others. In some cases we may be hit by a cyclist; the same is true of automobiles, but motorcycles are less stable. Of greater interest, some indirect costs are legally unavoidable if aid to uninsured cyclists is publicly required. Since the law can be altered, why say that the requisite taxes to pay for this publicly adopted policy are *imposed*? Analogously, it is questionable whether we should regard the burden of disaster relief as imposed on us if we

---

social discrimination renders some "self-induced sickness or debilitation" involuntary—or, perhaps we should say "not self-induced" at all.

Another, and I think more tempting, view of matters is this. The cyclist who is escaping from hoodlums does act in fully voluntary manner. Still, the risk from which he was escaping was not self-generated but imposed by others. Hence, we may judge that he is not *fully responsible* for the risks he ran (in escaping) even if it is true that his choice of mode of escape was knowing and fully voluntary. Thus, it seems important to distinguish between cases in which a subject is fully responsible for a burden he absorbs (or risk absorbing) and cases in which the subject is not fully responsible. On this view, a subject may not be fully responsible (and should not be held fully responsible) for his final plight even though, in part, it arose as a result of his knowing and fully voluntary choice. This latter view seems closer to the truth. A further relevant factor in gauging responsibility would seem to be whether the risks or burdens a subject chooses to avoid in some fashion are wrongfully generated by moral agents (as in our hoodlum example) or not (e.g., suppose the threat is a tornado). The view we have sketched here is not fully satisfactory and calls for further examination.

publicly authorize the policy. Such considerations may lead one to conclude that many of the costs to others which motorcycle accidents generate are not rightly said to be imposed on the rest of us. But this reasoning seems suspect.

Suppose a significant number of persons choose to play a nondeadly form of Russian roulette. The unfortunate wind up maimed or seriously injured. They cannot pay, and they are not insured for the costs of restorative measures. Do they impose a cost on us if they are cared for by publicly authorized persons? We could revise our laws and health-care policies to omit aid to certain persons, for example those who voluntarily engage in highly imprudent activities when it is "unnecessary" (e.g., not to earn a living, not to escape a catastrophe, and so on). There is something to be said for doing just this since such persons, it is arguable, engage in an invidious, unjust, form of free riding and are blameworthy in contrast to others who without fault come to be in dire need and, as a result, assume serious risks. Or we can continue publicly to authorize aid to such persons, but what can justify this? One sketch of an answer is that in a moderately affluent society justice requires, or a duty to be minimally decent samaritans requires, that we offer aid (up to *some* point) even to those blameworthy persons who "victimize" themselves. If so, there is a moral cost to not doing so (it's not just that we would be upset to see people bleeding to death in the streets, and so on). Analogously, suppose that you regularly send money to meet the basic needs of your destitute uncle. Still, he repeatedly gambles it all away and remains in dire need. You send more money. Does he impose a cost on you by his behavior? The answer, I suggest, is affirmative. Although one could just let the uncle suffer, one cannot do so without (assuming the decent samaritan duty applies here) failing in one's duty. Morally one must (to some point) absorb the cost; it is a *morally incumbent* cost even if an *empirically avoidable* one. A key point is that even if we choose to pay the cost, on the assumption that it is our duty, it does not follow that a cost has not been imposed on us since our burdened choice (surrender the money or violate a duty) is the result (at least in a wide range of cases of motorcycle accidents) of a voluntary, informed choice of others to perform an "unnecessary" act.

More needs to be said about "unnecessary" choices and the extent of duties to aid (or offer aid), but these remarks may be sufficient to capture the case for saying that with regard to many or most ordinary cyclists (and, probably as well, recreational drug users, recreational rock climbers, recreational parachute jumpers, and so on) costs are often imposed on others, and, hence, significant non-paternalistic reasons for restraint may be available, apart from the fact (if it is one) that the byproduct of such restraints may be for the cyclist's own good. However, one should not assume glibly that this type of justification plausibly can be invoked in all the diverse specific cases which may arise even though it is a logically possible one. Here I have tried only to identify the relevant considerations which must be applied in such contexts.

Attention to these complexities shows that there are plausible *non-paternalistic grounds* for regulating or prohibiting motorcycling without helmets. Indeed, in some cases such a practice will wrong others, and, therefore, PARP's prohibitions on certain types of paternalistic interference simply will not apply. Rather, some non-paternalistic principle, formulated along the following lines (I attempt no precise formulation) will apply: a principle permitting third party coercive interference to prevent or halt individuals from engaging in acts which will result, or are likely to result, in wrongful harm to others, whether or not such a wrongful harm is intended by the agents. In short, in this type of case there is a reasonable defense in favor of the view that the legal requirement is justified on nonpaternalistic grounds.[14]

Strictly speaking, this argument for legal prohibition tends not to support the type of all or nothing, "blanket" prohibitions which exist in many states of the U.S. To the extent that certain riders might exhibit exceptional skill in avoiding accidents, avoid nighttime riding or riding under conditions of poor visibility, avoid other inclement conditions, ride in restricted circumstances (e.g., on approved tracks), are well insured, or do not have serious positive duties to others, the case for restraint is weaker; in some cases there may be *no* plausible argument appealing to paternalistic *or* nonpaternalistic grounds for coercive prohibitions. To that extent, legislatures rationally could create more fine-textured sets of laws, laws that could fairly treat relevantly different persons in relevantly different ways. Indeed, there is a presumption in favor of so doing—subject to constraints of workability.[15]

---

[14] Hence, it is too quick to assume that the helmet laws, or prohibitions on swimming at public beaches without a lifeguard, are paternalistically motivated— as Terrance McConnell does in his commendable volume, *Moral Issues in Health Care: An Introduction to Medical Ethics* (Monterey, Cal.: Wadsworth Health Sciences, 1982), p. 63.

[15] It is worth observing that fine textured laws of the sort recommended are not a pipe dream. Just this sort of structure exists for those who are pilots at various

6.3 Limiting Risks to Oneself

So far, our general argument has been that only those presumptively wrong forms of constraints on the activities of competent persons to which they validly consent, or would consent if relevantly informed, are justifiable unless such activities constitute serious wrongs toward innocent others (to emphasize a point, the wrong may be impeding just institutions or practices). This view competes with certain others that will receive our consideration. First, it is worthwhile to note a further implication of autonomy-respecting paternalism which sanctions risk limitation. As our earlier discussion of Odysseus and the Sirens indicated, the view defended here is compatible with the policy of imposing constraints on the risk taking of other persons to which they validly consent even though, posterior to that consent, they may desire to be free of such constraints. Not only may individuals directly impose constraints on themselves (e.g., by placing a time-controlled lock on the refrigerator door); they may "use" consenting others to implement policies of self-restraint to delimit their vulnerability to risk (compare hiring someone to install a "breath analyzer" on one's car which prevents ignition if one's alcohol level is high).

Although impractical in many cases, it is conceivable that governmental, or other institutional, policies could involve *partitioned mechanisms of constraint*, ones which would allow those who wish to delimit certain types of risks for themselves while not constraining those who do not consent to such restraints. For example, some college students may prefer to live in a dorm which requires everyone to be in by midnight on week nights and that all radios, and so on, are turned off by the same time. Others have different preferences. Those who prefer the former arrangement could consent irrevocably (for the year) to living in the "quiet" dorm; others, analogously, could choose a more anarchic arrangment.[16] Those who join "Christmas savings plans" often act similarly, preferring the constraint of having savings withheld regularly to the risk of leaving monthly decisions to themselves (in spite of the opportunity cost of not regularly depositing their money in interest-bearing

---

stages of experience. Some can fly alone; others only with a copilot. Some are restricted to daytime flying, to certain types of planes, and so on.

[16] This example is used in Joel Feinberg, "Legal Paternalism," reprinted in his *Rights, Justice and the Bounds of Liberty* (Princeton: Princeton University Press, 1980), pp. 110–129.

accounts on their own). If a small community (a family, or a town) unanimously consents to place constraints on water usage, again, so long as others are not wronged, such "impositions" of limits or risks are unobjectionable. Or a given alcoholic-prone individual might contract with the only bar in town not to be served liquor during specified periods. The complexities and transaction costs of instituting a consensually agreed upon liquor or cigarette tax make such procedures difficult to implement, but are morally unobjectionable in a way that unconsented-to, presumptively wrong, restraints on risk taking are not. Clearly, one serious objection to many risk-limiting laws, policies, and institutions is that they distribute constraints over both those who consent and those who do not.

6.4 The Role of Government

If there is a presumption against invasively intervening in the lives of competent persons for their own good, there is a presumption against certain governmental activities which have that aim. Still, some governmental activity of this sort seems defensible. We need to investigate further the perplexing problem of identifying grounds for distinguishing legitimate from illegitimate governmental efforts to delimit risks to persons. We have argued, in our discussion of the motorcycle helmet policy, that a strong case can be made in defense of certain governmental restrictions which are *paternalistic in result* (protect those who are constrained) on non-paternalistic grounds (preventing wrongs to nonconsenting "third parties"). Whether this *possible type of defense* can be made successfully for a given governmental policy must be ascertained on a case by case (or sets of similar cases by sets of similar cases) basis. Further, we have observed that those risk-limiting restrictions to which competent persons do or would validly consent can be legitimate forms of paternalistic constraint. But many governmental activities are not evidently defensible on such grounds. We turn to further considerations and arguments which will at least advance the project of trying to formulate a coherent, more perspicuous, theory.

Advocates of minimizing aggregate risk (cf. the goals of a risk-free society, or creating a safe society, one free of unnecessary or unreasonable risks) sometimes ignore the fact that not all risk is undesired or undesirable. Perhaps a more accurate way to pose the point, given our prior analysis of 'risk,' is that reducing the probability of the occurrence of some event or type of event will count as a reduction of risk with regard to some persons but not others. For example, prohibition on a certain drug may count as risk reduction for some (if access to it would increase their probability of being harmed) but not count as a risk reduction for others (indeed, *their* expected utility might increase by legalizing access to the drug). As a case in point it has been claimed that that *bête noire* of drugs, thalidomide, has been shown to have therapeutic effects when used by adult lepers. Still, I do not wish overly to stress the subjective component in what counts as harm and, hence, risk. Although what counts as a risk to a person depends on what constitutes a harm to that person, and the latter in turn depends on possibly idiosyncratic features of that person, it does not follow that we must be extreme relativists about risk (or harm). With rare exception, an increase in the probability of significant pain or death is a risk to virtually anyone.

The more important question is whether competent persons voluntarily and knowingly assume certain risks, consent to their generation by others, or consent to their limitation by others—as opposed to cases where risks or barriers to risk taking are unilaterally imposed by others. This distinction tends to get ignored in proposals to set the average risk for "society" at a certain level. Talk of *"what level of risk society deems acceptable,"* although inevitable, encourages the notion that society is a single person rather than a set of individuals who differ with respect to what they regard as desirable and who differ with respect to consent or dissent. Some goods (e.g., national security) can be construed in terms of limiting risks, and they cannot readily be provided for some without being provided for all; hence, they are called "public goods." Provision of such goods cannot readily be left to individual decision (e.g., to each person to purchase his own preferred amount in the marketplace); hence, such matters are thought to be appropriate matters for governmental determination. Even if this point be granted, questions remain about what goods (including risk reduction) are properly counted as public goods and what governments may do to limit risks when this can be done for some but not all.

Suppose certain empirical disputes were settled, for example, whether private corporations could effectively provide certain goods (e.g., highways or pollution reduction) which individuals or small groups cannot effectively provide for themselves. If so, we could recognize what sorts of benefits count as public goods, that is, goods effectively providable only by governmental entities. Still, the questions would remain as to whether governments *ought* to provide them or whether governments *permissibly* may provide them. Our central concern is with the latter question. Here, once more, considerations of justice cannot be ignored.

It is reasonable to believe, though I shall not defend the point, that some governmental institutions are *just* and that they provide goods which individuals or voluntary groups of individuals cannot effectively provide for themselves by private, voluntary, coordination; national security and the domestic system of criminal justice seem obvious examples. Just institutions, then, will both generate risks and also limit the risks which some individuals prefer to avoid or to undertake, respectively. Compare, for example the risks of having an armed police force, speeding ambulances, being unfairly punished—or alternatively—the limits involved in prohibitions on drugs, driving at high speeds, sky diving, not having a police force, or not having radiation therapy. The large task of identifying certain institutions as just and of defending purportedly correct principles of justice is beyond our scope here. However, some limitations on risk taking are a *not reasonably avoidable byproduct of the functioning of just institutions* and are, for that reason, morally unobjectionable. To the extent that our inquiry here attempts to determine which paternalistic constraints on the choices and acts of persons are permissible and we construe impermissible interventions as instances of injustice, our investigations constitute a partial and limited effort to identify the contours of just institutions. To know their full contours, we need a comprehensive theory of justice, a theory which I neither propose nor possess. We shall return to consider the relevance of justice at a later point.

6.5 Regulatory Agencies

We have assumed that some risks to which individuals are involuntarily subjected are a byproduct of the wrongful acts of others. In such cases, and when such wrongs deserve to be criminally prohibited (itself a question of considerable dispute), governments may legitimately interfere to prevent or penalize the wrong. Most crimes involve (in fact or by definition) acts harmful toward persons who cannot or do not consent to such harms (e.g., rape and theft). Our primary focus, however, is on cases where individuals voluntarily can avoid or assume risks or voluntarily consent to risks involved in their interactions with others.[17] Even if a risk is *vol-*

---

[17] For example: choice of drugs, smoking, alcohol usage, hang gliding, dueling, undergoing surgery, mountain climbing, driving, and so on.

untarily avoidable, the *cost of avoiding it* seems a relevant consideration in deciding who may delimit the risk and how this is to be done. The cost of avoiding some risks is sometimes quite low, for example, for those without a burning desire to do so, foregoing rock climbing is no serious sacrifice. The cost of avoiding some risks can be quite high. For example, not driving on American highways or not using prescription or over-the-counter drugs are, for most, paths which involve considerable deprivation. Hence, although the risks involved in engaging in such activities are not trivial, it is not quite correct to say that individuals are "entirely free" to avoid them. It is worth noting at this point that a social component plays a role in the kinds of choice which are, from an individual's standpoint, given.

Whether governments or private corporations build, maintain, and control highways (cf. drugs), the cost of using them (including the risks) or not using them is determined in large part by factors over which particular individuals have little if any influence. For example, consider the ways in which highways are designed. This lack of control by particular individuals over societal-environmental arrangements is, to a large extent, unavoidable—whether or not prevailing arrangements are desirable. In the case in which governments provide an option, such as highways, they do not merely function so as to protect consumers from alternatives provided by *other persons or businesses* (as when the Food and Drug Administration oversees drug testing and sanctions certain drugs as marketable); rather, to emphasize a point, they determine a broad range of options. Since highway usage is a virtual necessity for everyone and the cost of not using them considerable, governments would appear to have a duty to make them as safe as financial resources allow—(within the range of just alternatives). In the event that some roads are comparatively unsafe (and resources do not allow improvements) it is reasonable to insist that information as to their safety be provided. In this case governmental limitation of risk and/ or provision of information about degree of risk need not involve any presumptive wrong to competent persons. There is an important difference between *fostering risk taking or avoidance with one's eyes wide open*, and *unilaterally foreclosing risks*. Hence, such an information-providing policy is defensible on legitimate paternalistic grounds.[18]

[18] I have made some assumptions here: that the government is legitimate, that its involvement in highway creation and control is justifiable on some grounds; hence, I have set aside certain anarchist and extreme libertarian objections. I also assume that the accumulation and distribution of the information must be done

Governments often function as third parties which, with protective aims, intervene to delimit the risks faced by citizens who are subjected to risks as a result of the acts of others (other individuals, organizations, or Mother Nature). As noted, not all competent citizens voluntarily consent to some of the government's wholesale risk limiting efforts in its function as third party protectors. I assume here that some contested governmental activity, which in fact limits risks, is not a part of the functioning of just governmental institutions. Some is rather beneficently oriented (whether or not it is misguided). Few would deny that national security or protection from and punishment of domestic crime is a legitimate and just governmental function and one that should not be left to the market mechanism. By contrast, governmental efforts to regulate or control environmental pollution, risky foods and drugs, handguns, or activities such as suicide, voluntary euthanasia, motorcycling, and factory safety are a subject of dispute; from the standpoint defended here, and for other reasons, the justifiability of the government's paternalistic role in these cases is in question.

The arguments in favor of, and against, governmental protective intervention (typically in the form of agencies whose function is to delimit risks to which citizens may be subjected or to which they may be allowed access) are far too complex to explore thoroughly here. Still, we shall canvass some of the arguments for and against this sort of governmental regulation. Some claim that it is simply *impossible* for governmental policies to lower risk levels. It is said, for example, that when regulation results in safer vehicles, drivers simply drive more aggressively; presumably, they have less to fear from collisions when their vehicles are equipped with collapsible steering wheels, energy-absorbing bumpers or front ends, and safety belts. Similar evidence, and reasoning, is invoked with regard to governmental attempts to decrease the high mortality levels involved in the use of small airplanes. On this view, governmental protective efforts are futile, and, thus, lack justification. They involve costs to taxpayers and vehicle purchasers but, it seems, no benefits in the form of increased safety. This argument, however, is unpersuasive. First, users of safer vehicles do derive increased benefits. Those who can drive faster at no increased level of risk benefit by saving time. Further, in situations in which that is not

justly. I offer no full-blown theory, of course, as to how to distinguish just from unjust distribution of such benefits.

possible or not chosen, there *is* an increase in the safety level. In addition, although some drivers in safer vehicles may voluntarily adjust their driving habits to maintain their preferred risk level, there is little reason to believe that all drivers do so. A final objection to the "futility argument" is that there are many cases in which there is no effective way for citizens to circumvent governmental attempts at risk reduction. If certain available risky drugs are prohibited there is no ready way, in many cases, for citizens to continue usage of those drugs (I focus on nonrecreational drugs for which there is no significant extra-legal market). Or in the case in which regulations make train or airplane travel safer, train users have no ready way of maintaining their prior level of risk traveling by train, nor is there any obvious incentive for them to do so (except for the rare "riskophile").

A second sort of appeal to futility maintains that regulatory agencies, whose ostensible purpose is to protect citizens, are simply not effective in practice—an argument often set forward by many economists and "limited-government" conservatives, for example, Milton Friedman. The argument is not without substance. It calls attention to the fact that, despite the ostensibly paternal and good-willed intentions of protectors, regulatory agencies (such as the FDA, CAB, FTC, and so on) gradually lose public support; the benefits to any one consumer are seen to be small and, hence, individuals are likely to turn their critical attention to political matters that affect them more directly, such as whether their children will be bussed to school or whether a home for the retarded will be placed in their neighborhood. By contrast, those with the most intense interest in the regulatory activity, namely, *those to be constrained*, expend great effort to influence such agencies; gradually such agencies are "captured" by such interest groups. The vigorous consumer advocate, Ralph Nader, has noted that "nobody seriously challenges the fact that regulatory agencies have made an accommodation with the businesses they are supposed to regulate. . . ."[19] For example, the Civil Aeronautics Board for a long period restricted competition in California and kept airplane fares artificially high, and the Interstate Commerce Commission has restricted competition with similar effect—sometimes inefficiently preventing shippers from hauling freight from Los Angeles to Boston unless they go by way of New Orleans, or even requiring trucks to make

[19] From an interview with Ralph Nader originally published in *Playboy* (October, 1968); cited in Dwight Lee and Robert McNown, *Economics in Our Time* (Chicago: Science Research Associates, 1975), p. 75.

return trips empty.[20] Against this appeal to the ineffectiveness, or downright harmfulness, of regulatory agencies, it may be observed that no one wishes to defend ineffective or stupid regulation, but these sad tales do not demonstrate that effective regulation is impossible— only that it is *difficult*. Similarly, one might call attention to corrupt or ineffective police departments or parents; that by itself is not a compelling reason to infer that we should eliminate such institutions. Comparatively effective, efficient, regulation is not an impossibility; still, the facts call for greater oversight and skepticism as to the effectiveness of such institutions than defenders of welfare-state liberalism commonly exhibit.[21]

6.6 Overview and Residual Difficulties

We have allowed that much governmental limitation on risk generation or risk assumption can, in principle, be justifiable on non-paternalistic grounds, that is, to prevent or halt the wrongful passing on of risks by some to unconsenting others. The motorcycle helmet regulation seems a case in point. The door is open to a similar justification for governmental restraints on environmental pollution toward which competent "recipients" do not validly consent. The precise form of efficient and effective regulation is, of course, a much-disputed matter. If we take into account beings other than existing competent adults who may suffer harm from unconsented-to risk generation by others—namely, beings such as fetuses, young children, the senile, the severely retarded, sentient animals, and future generations of human beings—it is clear that constraint of acts wrongfully imposing such risks is justifiable, on nonpaternalistic grounds, in a broad range of cases. The beings just mentioned cannot validly consent or dissent to risk generation

---

[20] Ibid., pp. 80-81.

[21] Conversely, liberals are more sensitive to, and cognizant of, the defects of state and local efforts to secure civil rights and civil liberties than those ideologically opposed to a powerful "interventionist," federal government.

Another reason to be skeptical about the effectiveness of regulatory agencies concerns one psychological "side effect," namely, the tendency encouraged in the citizenry to believe, with regard to the existence, publicizing, or limiting of risks, that the government reliably protects the citizenry, that an ethereal "they" know what they are doing. Hence, individuals, it is inferred, need not make first-order judgments about what is prudent. One striking example is the naive and gullible assumption made by citizens of Nevada and Utah in the early 1950s—persons who readily "bought" federal government propaganda that nuclear testing in those states presented no serious risks to those near testing areas. Here the government did not warn of risks; rather, it generated risks *and* disguised the fact by issuing systematic "disinformation."

by others. Our central concern, however, is with existing competent adults and with the question of what constraints can justifiably be placed on them in order to limit their exposure to harm. We have allowed that presumptively wrong constraints for this purpose count as acts of permissible paternalism (1) when their subjects validly consent to such constraints and others are not thereby wronged, or (2) when the interferences are not presumptively wrong (again, compare fair, open, attempts to persuade). For this reason there seems no objection to the government's provision of information in an attempt to specify the degree of risk attached to especially risky activities, such as smoking, drug usage, driving small cars, and so on. There are questions here about whether tax funds should be expended to develop and publicize such information, and, if so, the manner and extent of so doing. I shall set these issues aside and presume that some such efforts are justifiable—in view of the inordinate difficulties and costs individuals or small groups of citizens would have in privately securing such information.

A further reason, in favor of limited regulation is that, corporate advertising to the contrary, competition between corporations, and their self-interest in maintaining a good reputation, do not invariably prevent them from marketing shoddy and/or high-risk products or services whose risks are not readily evident to competent persons. Various examples come to mind here. One is the tragedy associated with thalidomide, a drug marketed as a sedative. The extremely harmful effects of working around and producing asbestos have only become publicly evident decades after initial exposure. More recently, a half-million Americans have had their homes insulated with urea-formaldehyde, a substance whose fumes pose a nontrivial health hazard. The Consumer Products Safety Commission banned its use in building insulation in 1982 after a four-year investigation—against heavy resistance from industry. Corporate self-interest in maintaining a good reputation sometimes conflicts with and is subordinated to corporate self-interest in survival or profit maximization, a point which devotees of the "good reputation argument" tend to overlook. Similarly, "fly-by-night" businesses have little self-interest in maintaining a good long-term reputation.[22]

---

[22] It is worth emphasizing that if, as is often *thought* proper, corporations or economic agents are to aim at net profit maximization, it is simply a matter of *contingent* fact whether maintaining a good reputation is instrumental to achieving that end. In some cases the cost of doing so may exceed the benefits which can be

The rationale for governmental efforts to provide information regarding risks, so that competent persons may choose voluntarily and knowingly to purchase (or not) risk-laden products or services, does not obviously sanction more invasive governmental efforts to limit risks (e.g., prohibiting products). Providing information allows competents to direct their own lives along more, or less, risky paths. Protecting persons from risks wrongfully *imposed* by others also enables such persons to choose their own preferred risk levels, as opposed to being thrust in directions not of their own choosing. We still lack, however, a principled basis for assessing the acceptability of some governmental regulatory activity designed to limit or eliminate certain risks, risks which cannot be justified by the fact: (1) that those competents affected voluntarily consent to limitations, or would consent if aware of the relevant circumstances, such as the risks and benefits involved, (2) that the activity fairly and openly seeks to warn those subject to risks, (3) that the activity aims at protecting innocents from wrongful risk generation by others, or (4) that the activity is not a reasonably avoidable by-product of the functioning of evidently just (and, hence, nonoptional) institutions.[23] When such justifications are unavailable and a governmental body exercises its coercive powers to prohibit the use by competent persons of certain risky products or services, it acts in a presumptively wrong manner. The burden remains, I submit, on those who claim that such efforts are morally justified. But there are further attempts to meet this burden which we have yet to explore.

It may be argued that governmental efforts to reduce risk are justified when they prevent competent persons from undertaking risky activities due to such person's having *false* beliefs. To examine this claim, consider the controversy over laetrile, an alleged cure for cancer. In 1981 the Food and Drug Administration made public a study which judged laetrile worthless as a cancer cure, a result contrary to the ardent hopes and beliefs of many afflicted with cancer. If our prior assumptions are acceptable, the governmental effort to ascertain laetrile's usefulness is unobjectionable. The data help competent persons decide for themselves whether to use it.

---

obtained thereby. The *principle* that corporations should maximize their profits will *require*, in some cases, that little or no effort is made to secure or maintain a good reputation (e.g., by avoiding sale of risky products or by refraining from deceptive advertising).

[23] Except that a just institution may be "optional" in that it may be replaceable by another equally just institution.

It is worth noting that although the available evidence shows that laetrile is worthless in curing cancer (except perhaps for any benefit it may have as a placebo), it also *seems* to be a pharmacologically harmless substance. Should its use be prohibited by law? The claim that it is too risky to allow competent persons to use it would have to appeal not to physiologically harmful effects but, perhaps, the risk of persons' wasting money on it or nourishing illusory hopes for cure. These latter considerations, however, hardly seem sufficient reasons to disrupt coercively the choices of competent persons to direct their own lives. So long as competent persons are aware of the results of scientific studies—so that their choices do not reflect ignorance of relevant data—a paternalistic prohibition of laetrile seems unjustified.[24]

It may be objected that we should not allow competent persons to make serious choices on the basis of *evidently* false or irrational beliefs (recall our discussion in Section 3.5). This is a tempting notion, but we should be wary of the policies to which such a principle commits us. Many religious believers (and atheists as well) would no doubt judge that when the leadership of the Jehovah's Witnesses, in the 1960s, predicted the end of the world in 1975, many followers of the sect had a false belief (or an evidently irrational belief) and, hence, should have been prevented from acting on it—as many did, namely: by dropping out of school, selling their homes, cancelling marriage plans and trips to their physicians.[25] Less dramatically, atheists might insist that no one should be allowed to become a priest or nun, given the falsity of theistic belief; to do so is to make sacrifices for an illusion. Conversely, religious believers might claim that atheists should be disallowed from certain pursuits which are based on the assumption that there is no God, another "misdirected effort." Each group tends to underestimate the extent to which its own beliefs and practices offend the other. In short, the view that we may coercively prohibit nonconsenting competent persons from acting on the basis of what some of us may take to be evidently false, or quite irrational, beliefs is incompatible with respecting the right of competent persons to direct their own lives.[26] It is hard to see how we can respect

[24] The FDA not only requires that studies and tests show a drug to be *harmless* but also that it be an *effective cure* for designated ills.

[25] See the report in *Newsweek* (July 20, 1981).

[26] Exceptions to this claim exist when it is clear that the operative beliefs are a result of invidious indoctrination, but I forego exploring such matters here. Questions about "deprogramming" those who have been converted to religious, or other, outlooks by suspect means (duress, deception, etc.) require just such an inquiry.

such persons without forbearing from coercive disruptions even of what we may believe to be the height of foolishness. As discussed in Chapter 2, this conclusion is contrary to those policies that would be dictated by the principle that it is all right to impose those restraints on persons "which would be consented to by a *fully rational person.*" Further, although coercive intervention might promote the good or prevent harm, on balance, for competent persons, we have earlier concluded that such an appeal is unacceptable.

Our critic might object that, nevertheless, anyone who holds beliefs which are evidently false from the standpoint of most rational persons, is, therefore, incompetent. If so, on grounds defended here, such a person lacks a full right to direct his own life within the domain of acts wronging no others. The main difficulty with this objection is that, although holding some beliefs which, in fact, may be quite unreasonable is *evidence* of mental incompetence, it is not, by itself, a *logically sufficient* basis for inferring such incompetence. Otherwise we would have to draw most dubious conclusions, for example, that, historically, a wildly large number of scientists were mentally incompetent (e.g., those who rejected the germ theory of disease, who believed the earth is flat, who believed the earth was the center of the universe, or who believed that mental capacities are a simple function of skull sizes and shapes).

A different line of argument suggests that much governmentally

---

Some converts may be victims of wrongful indoctrination and, as a result, have made only apparently competent choices or judgments. Such a worry arises, I believe, not only with respect to certain publicized sects but also those recipients of drawn-out, "socially acceptable," orthodox religious or secular indoctrination as children. There is a near conspiracy of silence about such matters.

I note that *persistence* in holding *some* false beliefs in the face of strong reasons to the contrary is evidence (perhaps meager) that the subject is, in fact, mentally incompetent. But compare the fact that we can rather decisively demonstrate that a subject who believes he can fly (without a plane) cannot fly; we cannot, now, demonstrate to an obstinate believer that the world will not end in 2990. There is more to explore here, but I shall leave it for another time.

I shall not explore the matter, but in 1983 some spokespersons for the American Medical Association proposed a ban on professional boxing, a ban they thought justifiable on paternalistic grounds. Such a ban is suspect on the view defended here unless (1) there is a plausible appeal to a legitimate ground for paternalistic intervention, e.g., the Principle of Hypothetical Individualized Consent (an appeal plausible only if it could be shown that professional boxers are not reasonably aware of the risks they run)—or (2) it could be shown that professional boxing wrongfully harms nonparticipants (e.g., by promoting insensitivity to violence or recklessly imposing risks on, say, members of the boxer's family). As in other cases, a detailed examination of specific facts is relevant; my mention of the case is only to sketch what seem to be the important moral questions to ask and, hence, why certain facts are relevant.

imposed limitation on risks is justified, beyond that which we have explicitly allowed, without contravening the principles defended here. For example, it may be claimed that we must recognize that competent persons who have not explicitly consented to regulatory activities have *tacitly* consented to them, that is those who choose to live in the United States tacitly consent to the outcomes of majoritarian decision-making bodies (whose representatives are elected by the citizenry) which are constrained, in turn, by constitutional guarantees of certain fundamental rights of citizens. Hence, in electing representatives to make sweeping and difficult policy decisions and laws, citizens waive or forfeit any right to disobey. If citizens believe that their liberties are unduly restricted by governmental policies designed to limit risks, morally they can only pursue legally sanctioned channels to try to alter such policies. The troubles with this argument are not unfamiliar. For one, it "proves" too much; it would also sanction policies of invidious discrimination if sanctioned by legislative bodies and if not deemed unconstitutional (as was characteristic in prior decades). Further, the argument offers a *derivative* answer. Although citizens may be obligated to "bend" to some extent before laws and policies which they disapprove, our question concerns what principles an ideal legislature ought to employ in deciding what are legitimate limitations on voluntary risk taking by citizens. And *this* question is not answered by proposing that citizens ought to acquiesce, since they have tacitly consented to do so, in whatever risk limiting constraints are democratically and fairly generated by legitimate governments.

Another argument in favor of the acceptability of governmental determination of risk levels for those who have not expressly consented in any direct fashion is one which Richard and Val Routley have labeled *the Doubling Argument*.[27] It deserves mention here since it appears to be a relative of the appeal to tacit consent. In this case, the focus is on an escalation of risk. Those favoring the development and use of nuclear power call attention to a certain level of background radiation in the environment of most citizens. The latter arises from natural sources and practices generally regarded as acceptable, for example, radiation generated from medical or dental practices or research. Call the background level B. It is then claimed that the increased radiation generated by nuclear power

[27] See Richard and Val Routley, "Nuclear Power—Some Ethical and Social Dimensions," in *And Justice for All*, eds. Tom Regan and Donald VanDeVeer (Totowa, N.J.: Rowman and Littlefield, 1982), p. 127.

plants *is equal to* or *does not exceed* B. Thus, pro-nuclear advocates, it is claimed, only propose to generate a level of radiation corresponding to what is, it is alleged, socially acceptable (that is, B). The implied conclusion is that if we accept level B we should accept an equivalent amount of risk from nuclear power plants.

There are serious difficulties with this rationale. First, there is a gap between claiming that a policy is accepted and that it is acceptable (it *ought* to be accepted) as reflection on certain facts makes clear (e.g., that, at times, the United States, among other nations, has widely accepted outrageous racist practices). Second, passive acquiescence to a policy is not decisive evidence for the existence of tacit consent. Third, defenders of the argument are not recommending no more risk but, in fact, the acceptability of *doubling* the radiation level. But consider the fact that a consumer who finds the selling price of an automobile acceptable at Y amount hardly entails that he is willing to buy at twice the price, or 2Y. An automobile dealer who employed an analogue of the Doubling Argument would not be taken seriously. So even if, in the nuclear power case, there was tacit consent to being subjected to risk B it does not follow that citizens tacitly consent to its being doubled.

Tacit consent, rightly understood, is a form of genuine consent, for example, if one deliberately does not dissent when another says "then, we agree to meet at noon?" Silence or failure to protest, of course, need not be voluntary, informed, or deliberate. We may wonder whether, in the absence of express protest to governmental risk limiting (or risk generating) policies aimed at promoting the good of (or preventing harm to) the citizenry, it can reasonably be inferred that citizens do consent to the policies. Much can and has been said on this topic. It is worth observing, briefly, that much depends on whether the citizenry has an effective opportunity to voice dissent or consent—and whether they have been supplied with relevant information. Secret governmental decision making and secret implementation of policy clearly erodes any appeal to the tacit consent of the citizenry. Further, when officials make little effort to publicize decisions or their basis and, at the same time, maintain that if citizens were apprised of the relevant information they would voluntarily and knowingly consent to a proposed or operative policy, such officials make a dubious appeal to the legitimate Principle of Hypothetical Individualized Consent (PHIC). Earlier (in Chapter 2) it was argued that invasive intervention in the lives of competent persons is permissible if there is currently operative express consent by such subjects of intervention (the

Restricted Consent Principle). It was argued, further, that, in the absence of current or prior express consent, it is sometimes reasonable to infer that subjects would consent to invasive intervention if apprised of relevant information. However, the perhaps unduly implicit proviso in our discussion of PHIC was that consideration of possible hypothetical consent is appropriate only in cases in which the cost of ascertaining express consent or dissent is too great.[28] A case in point is the bridge-crossing example in which, in our version, there was no non-invasive way of preventing the prospective harm which also allowed a means of ascertaining consent. In short, the upshot is that governments which deliberately bypass reasonable opportunities to ascertain consent or dissent of the citizenry and glibly appeal to hypothetical consent of the citizens undermine the rights of competent citizens to direct their own lives.[29] It is somewhat characteristic of (possibly) benevolent-minded tyrannies or patriarchal forms of government to do just that—whether they be antidemocratic forms of socialism or capitalism. Perhaps more often the rationale "after all, it's for their own good" is invoked, an appeal we have found wanting whether invoked to defend paternalistic government or private paternalistic intervention (involving presumptive wrong acts) toward competent persons.

6.7 Cost-Benefit Analysis and Optimal Risk

To this point we have not considered a most influential proposal as to how to determine what limits on risk taking should be, or should not be, legislatively enacted. I have in mind the view that we, or legislatures, should do whatever will maximize net aggregate good. On one version this is the principle of utility. In the version with which I am concerned here it is associated with what is commonly called "cost-benefit" (or risk-benefit) analysis. Many risks to persons (e.g., from pollution or vehicular accidents) also are a byproduct of activities which generate benefits, for example, the risks and benefits of the use of herbicides or the production of steel. Since the production or attainment of most important benefits also generates certain risks, it is foolish to advocate a zero-risk, or a zero-pollution, society. Rather, it is claimed that we must aim for an *optimal* level of risks, and the criterion for optimality is often

---

[28] I here leave open the question of the criteria for the cost being "too great."
[29] Some emergency situations are cases in which consideration of hypothetical consent is not out of place.

proposed to be: *whatever maximizes net aggregate benefit* (the surplus of benefits over costs). Whatever levels of risk are inherent in policies aimed at this goal, or required by such a goal, are claimed, therefore, to be optimal and acceptable. The precise relation between these broad assumptions and, on the other hand, concerns about whether risks are consented to or not, or their relation to those cases of risk generation commonly assumed to be wrong (e.g., burglary, robbery, arson, and so on), are left unclear. I set this question aside temporarily. Perhaps cost-benefit assumptions are thought to be appropriate only to setting policy in domains where existing or proposed levels of risk generation are not unanimously consented to by those affected or where the risks are not rightly associated with criminalized harms.

In any case, if the question is whether to impose restraints to limit the risks involved in the production and use of some good, this approach at least requires: (1) identification of all the generated costs and all the generated benefits of various proposed sets of constraints, and (2) a determination of which set of constraints (including none—as well as total prohibition) will maximize benefits minus costs.[30] A typical case in point would involve an industrial activity such as steel production at coal-powered plants. Suppose, however, that the activity generates a number of airborne pollutants which both damage crops and cause respiratory problems for humans. The benefits of the activity are commonly construed by defenders of cost-benefit analysis, in the final estimate, in terms of preference satisfaction, and the costs are ultimately analyzed in terms of preference dissatisfaction.[31] When there is a well-established market for the goods involved, market prices are taken as the appropriate measure of the magnitude of the benefits. Correlatively, the damage to crops, and to humans, may be measured in terms of the costs of insurance, the drop in value of the crops produced, the wages foregone from lost days at work, the costs of medical care to cope with respiratory problems, and so on.

[30] Condition (1) needs to be weakened somehow since acquiring such information itself involves costs. How a cost-benefit approach should factor in the costs of doing cost-benefit analysis is not clear. There may be a reasonable way of stating the necessary constraint, but I do not know what it is. Some sort of second-order cost-benefit analysis *seems* in order; the threat of a further regress is present.

[31] 'Preference satisfaction' in modern economic theory is commonly construed to refer to preference fulfillment and not necessarily pleasant feelings associated with perceived fulfillment of preferences; similarly for preference dissatisfaction. It is worth noticing here that the notion of an *economic good* is not as theoretically simple as one might think.

This characterization is exceedingly sketchy but will suffice for our purposes here.

Such a cost-benefit calculus is reminiscent of utilitarian approaches to ethical decision making. However, the former approach *seems* to avoid the problem of some person's (or agency's) estimating the net utility or net disutility which results from instituting a given policy. For, it is claimed, each person can decide for himself whether he prefers to purchase steel, work for the steel mill at a given wage, purchase medical care or not, and so on. That is, each can decide for himself whether such acts make him better off or worse off (will increase or decrease his utility); hence, difficulties in calculating *interpersonal* utilities are avoided.

In spite of its attraction and its influence, there are a number of difficulties with such an approach. It is beyond my purpose to explore them thoroughly here; still, some are worth noting. First, many beings whose welfare is morally relevant cannot cast their dollar vote in the economic or political marketplace so as to reveal their preference for or against the consequences of the policy in question. Sentient animals may suffer from pollution, but any costs to them will not show up as a cost by *their* purchase of medical care. Whether any funds are expended for this purpose will depend on whether the animals which suffer or die, or might be protected at some cost, enter into the "utility function" of *those willing and able to pay* such costs. Some will be unmoved by this point because they suppose that the well-being of sentient animals is not in itself of any moral weight. Since such a supposition seems evidently false, I shall set the dispute to one side.[32] A similar point may be made about those generations of human beings who do not exist now but *will* exist; their interests, or damage to their interests, will get represented in the marketplace only if existing persons are willing and able to pay to avoid harming the interests of future generations.[33] That such *indirect* representation of preferences and/

[32] Those unfamiliar with the recent reassessment of the moral status of animals might wish to investigate: Peter Singer, *Animal Liberation* (New York: Avon Books, 1975); Tom Regan and Peter Singer, eds., *Animal Rights and Human Obligations* (Englewood Cliffs, N.J.: Prentice-Hall, 1976); R. G. Frey, *Interests and Rights* (Oxford: Oxford University Press, 1980); Peter Singer, *Practical Ethics* (Cambridge: Cambridge University Press, 1979), and Vol. 22, Nos. 1–2 of *Inquiry* (solely about the treatment of animals and containing a bibliography); Tom Regan, *All That Dwell Therein* (Berkeley: University of California Press, 1982); Tom Regan, *The Case for Animal Rights* (Berkeley: University of California Press, 1983).

[33] For an instructive, introductory, discussion of questions regarding "future generations," see Mary Ann Warren, "Future Generations," in *And Justice for All*, eds. Regan and VanDeVeer, pp. 139–168. More extensive discussions can be found in

or interests is likely to result in a fair weighting may be viewed with a certain skepticism for reasons noted earlier.[34] These points, however, are only the tip of a theoretical iceberg. Among relevant other parties who are themselves not able to cast a dollar vote in the marketplace are many of the world's children (over a billion people are under age 15), many of the world's incompetents, many of the world's illiterates, others who are severely incapacitated— as well as those who, although willing, are unable to do so because of extreme poverty. It is not far-fetched to assume that a third or a fourth of the world's existing human population cannot directly manifest its preferences in an economic market system where only "dollar votes" count.

Further, it is not clear that all the nontrivial costs to those who may suffer from certain forms of pollution, and who can cast such votes, will get manifested in market transactions. In most modern nations people can spend rather readily to alleviate depression, loneliness, feelings of isolation, and illness; still, the overt manifestation of such human ills in the marketplace is contingent on the existence of markets for certain kinds of goods or services, for example, psychiatrists, therapists, antidepressants, and so on. In the absence of such markets, or well-developed markets, or the awareness of such goods and services, such burdens are likely to go uncounted on a willingness and ability to pay approach. Some who are depressed from loss of work do not purchase therapeutic services because of persisting stereotypes about "mental illness" or "the sorts of persons who need therapy." In addition, harms to individuals, as noted earlier, do not always show up immediately; many who are victimized do not or cannot know whether the policy in question is "costly" to them. The cases of asbestosis or radiation-induced cancers are obvious examples.

In addition to measuring morbidity levels, deep difficulties are

---

Brian Barry and R. I. Sikora, eds., *Obligations to Future Generations* (Philadelphia: Temple University Press, 1978). Further, consider the problem of estimating the long-term costs of nuclear power; according to Richard and Val Routley, the 50 or more nuclear reactors now functioning will each produce nuclear wastes 1000 times more than that produced by the Hiroshima bomb and the return to safe levels of radioactivity takes over one million years. See Richard and Val Routley, "Nuclear Power: Some Ethical and Social Dimensions," in *And Justice for All*, eds. Regan and VanDeVeer, pp. 116–138. The Routleys' essay systematically and vigorously challenges various economic and cost-benefit assumptions invoked to justify serious and unconsented-to risk generation. Another important source is Ernest Partridge, ed., *Responsibilities to Future Generations* (Buffalo, N.Y.: Prometheus Books, 1980).

[34] Some policies benefitting existing persons will, however, fortuitously benefit future generations as well.

also involved in any attempt to assign some monetary value to the loss of lives which may result from risk-generating policies. The frequently espoused notion that the value of a life is equivalent to the foregone income of that person leads to radically counterintuitive results. On such a view, the value of a young executive's life may be five times that of a young waitress. Consider a recent actual case. An economic index used by the federal government (to determine in part how much should be spent on life-saving efforts or devices) placed a value of $328,475 on a 34-year-old white woman and a value of $235 on an 85-year-old black woman.[35] And what shall we say about children who do not have any income or established future career? Or if it is said that such a calculus does not apply to children, what non-arbitrary criteria are to be used to decide on this or other exclusions? Another proposed measure, equating the value of a life with what an individual is willing and able to pay to insure himself against premature loss of his life is similarly troublesome. The very poor person will be able to pay less than the wealthy person; that the former, therefore, values his life less, or is of less value, than the latter is an inference seductive only to the wealthy. To stress a point, what people are *willing* to pay to avoid premature death or a heightened risk of such is partly a function of what they are *able* to pay.[36] Even if we know what people are willing to pay we would not necessarily have an accurate gauge of what value people place on *their own lives*; hence, *other* parties cannot assume the reliability of such individual-determined indications. To the extent that governments or courts engage in such conjectures in determining, for example, whether cotton mills must limit dust exposure to prevent byssinosis (or "brown-lung" disease), they rely on dubious assumptions.

If, as I have mentioned, it is empirically impossible and/or conceptually problematic to identify and measure *all* the relevant costs and benefits of various proposed policies, then cost-benefit analysis fosters a dangerously comfortable illusion and encourages policy

[35] According to a *Washington Post* release (April, 1980).

[36] In a recent essay, "The Value of Life," Michael Bayles explores some of the difficulties in assigning value to life, primarily through the concept of quality adjusted life years. Bayles suggests ways of meeting some of the objections I have noted (e.g., modifying the willingness and ability to pay criterion to avoid the objection based on differences in wealth), but also insists on certain constraints in the employment of cost-benefit analysis. See Michael Bayles, "The Value of Life," in *Border Crossings: New Introductory Essays in Health-Care Ethics*, eds. Donald VanDeVeer and Tom Regan (New York: Random House, forthcoming).

331

makers to engage in a pseudoscientific assessment of alternatives.[37] Analogously, no one would seriously maintain that one could rightly determine whether a corporation is, or is not, "in the black" if one could only identify *some* of its assets and *some* of its liabilities.

As a final point I note that *even if it were possible* to ascertain all the relevant costs and benefits of competing policies, the (sometimes tacit) assumption that we ought to implement the one which maximizes benefits over costs is also subject to objections based on considerations regarding *fair distribution* of risks over the affected populations. The policy which maximizes benefits over costs may involve a complete subversion of the interests of some; this is a point to which we shall return in discussing utilitarianism (in Chapter 7). There is a gap between the not unreasonable assumption that once we have decided on some *permissible and desirable social goal* we ought to identify, as best we can, the most cost-effective *means* of achieving that goal and the highly questionable assumption which *equates* permissible and desirable social goals with whatever policy maximizes benefits over costs.[38]

Defenders of cost-benefit analysis who see it as an appropriate means to determine social goals tend, I submit, to focus on *outcomes* of broad policies and only on outcomes in terms of the amount of nonmoral good or nonmoral harm they involve—to the exclusion, or undue discounting of, independent moral constraints on what may be done to promote such goods or prevent such harms. For example, we can be disturbed by the number of premature deaths in the United States and the fact that the rate of such deaths in this country is far higher than one might reasonably expect in an affluent, technologically advanced, nation with an elaborate, so-

[37] Hence, it is refreshing to see the candid remark of an economist and a political economist, Nancy and Robert Dorfman, regarding the attempt to use cost-benefit analysis to measure (in this case) the benefits of a proposed policy: "One goes through the list of good things that may be expected to result from the measure, and, by *hook or crook*, estimates the value of the good things and adds them up" (my italics). See Robert and Nancy Dorfman, eds., *Economics of the Environment* (New York: W. W. Norton, 1972), p. xxix.

[38] On this point, see Michael Baram's instructive essay, "Cost-Benefit Analysis: An Inadequate Basis for Health, Safety, and Environmental Regulatory Decision-Making," in *Contemporary Issues in Bioethics*, 2nd ed., eds. Tom Beauchamp and Leroy Walters (Belmont, Cal.: Wadsworth, 1982), pp. 470–475. For another critique and, also, a defense of cost-benefit analysis, see respectively Alasdair MacIntyre, "Utilitarianism and Cost-Benefit Analysis" and Tom Beauchamp, "Utilitarianism and Cost-Benefit Analysis: A Reply to MacIntyre," in *Ethical Theory and Business*, eds. Tom Beauchamp and Norman Bowie (Englewood Cliffs, N.J.: Prentice-Hall, 1979), pp. 266–282.

phisticated system of health care.[39] It has become clear, especially in recent decades, that much of this premature death is due to "life-style" factors, such as overeating, poor diet, lack of exercise, smoking, alcohol usage, and so on. We may agree that premature death is the greatest, or one of the greatest, calamities that can befall an individual. As such, it is a great cost, and will (somehow!) count heavily in any attempted cost-benefit approach to determining public policy, for example, public health measures. There is a not unimportant dispute over whether behaviors which increase the risk of premature death are voluntary or, if so, to what extent. Unless one subscribes to the rather incredible view that no such behavior is voluntary, one must assume, for a start, that much premature death (as well as avoidable morbidity, impairment, and other "costs"), although in some sense tragic, is the byproduct of knowing, voluntary choices of competent persons. (Which and *how* much is an important matter, but I do not pursue that point here.) If the position we have defended is correct, that competent persons have a right to direct their own lives in ways not wronging others, then much which is regarded as a social cost is a *morally permissible cost* and, in one sense, desirable. I do not suggest that premature death or avoidable morbidity is desirable in itself or typically desirable as a means to an end; rather, it is a predictable byproduct of treating competent persons as autonomous beings who have the limited right to pursue their own conception of the good. Hence, *certain misfortunes*, although not a cause for celebration, are acceptable. The "cost" of reducing *them* is often morally intolerable, for we would have to place invidious paternalistic constraints on unconsenting, competent, persons who, as a matter of right, have their own lives to lead.

Consider an analogy. We may be disturbed by the high incidence of divorce. Much of it involves, we may surmise, net pain on balance. Although some divorce may result from *prudent* and morally permissible choices on the part of both parties, much may involve *imprudent* but morally permissible choices by both parties. If we are bewitched only by the large numbers, the incidence of divorce, and routinely assume that they reflect only social costs, we may be tempted to place invasive constraints on competent persons in order to reduce or prevent this sort of aggregate out-

[39] We may define 'premature death' as 'death prior to age 65,' as does Dan Beauchamp in his suggestive essay "Public Health and Individual Liberty" in *Contemporary Issues in Bioethics*, eds. Beauchamp and Walters, pp. 442–451. This procedure, however, needs qualification, e.g., for Down's syndrome persons.

come. The attractions of cost-benefit analysis invite us down this path. But out of respect for the autonomy of competent persons to make decisions which influence such outcomes, we must conclude, with a certain sadness, that "avoidable," even tragic, outcomes must, to a point, be accepted. Just as the production of weighty benefits by certain means may not suffice to justify the use of those means (see the criticism of utilitarianism in Chapter 7), so the elimination of certain weighty harms by certain means may not justify the use of those means. Certain paths to the production of social benefits and to the elimination of social harms are morally blocked; morally speaking, for some otherwise desirable goals, we can't get there from here.

A final point should be mentioned concerning the ethical thrust of cost-benefit analysis. If one regards as acceptable the principle of implementing whatever policies will maximize benefits over costs, another principle will have a certain allure in attempting to decide what sorts of restraints may or should be imposed in order to delimit risks. In brief, it is: place legal liabilities on the least-cost avoider. This formulation calls for some explanation. In some circumstances, a harm is likely to result from the prospective interaction of two (or more) parties, a harm which, in principle, is avoidable if one party deliberately acts (or refrains) in some fashion. One party may be better advantaged to avoid the harm, that is, with less effort (cost, or risk). A case in point where such asymmetries exist is avoidance of automobile accidents.[40] If the goal is to maximize benefits minus costs, it would seem that the party who can avoid or prevent a serious harm by absorbing the least cost (less than that which would be incurred by the other party if she were to do so) should be encumbered, that is, should have a duty to do so. The principle attributing such a duty to the least-cost avoider is exemplified in one of the nautical "rules of the road" which, normally, prescribes the right of way to sailboats when they are on a collision course with small motor-powered boats. Such a principle to resolve conflict of interest is not implausible. It seems a way of effectively reducing net aggregate costs and, thus, maximizing benefits minus costs.

However, there is a gap between assuming the plausibility of such a rule in certain limited (and not easy to define cases) and concluding that the rule is a plausible way of initially assigning

[40] Another typical type of case concerns the conflict of interests which may be associated with pollution.

rights or employing it to resolve all conflict of interest cases. There is much more to be said on this matter, but for our purposes here I shall only note one difficulty with the least-cost avoidance principle. Suppose my neighbor has a swimming pool and derives immense pleasure from swimming in the buff on Sunday mornings. In contrast I derive mild pleasure from sitting outside and reading the morning paper. Suppose further that at such times I could, at no great cost, avoid viewing his rather unattractive acrobatics by remaining inside. Do I have a duty, as the least-cost avoider, to do so? It is not obvious that I do even if doing so would maximize aggregate benefits minus costs. Readers may wish to imagine a more intriguing or disputatious variant in which my neighbor wishes to perform eccentric sexual acts instead of swimming. Or analogously, suppose my neighbor wishes to raise swine, derives great satisfaction from doing so, and I, at a lesser cost than is involved in his refraining from so doing, can avoid any unpleasant scenes or odors by going out of my way to avoid them. Must I do so? There are, as many have noted, ways of negotiating contractual agreements here, ones which might maximize net aggregate benefit. However, it is another thing entirely to insist that, *apart* from any such contractual resolution by the parties involved, the courts or legislatures initially *should* allocate rights and duties in such a manner as to maximize net aggregate benefits, for example, by encumbering the least-cost avoider.[41] Such a solution ignores, I suggest, important considerations about initially possessed equal rights. The maximizing focus of cost-benefit analysis again allows for, and may require, indefensible, unjustly inegalitarian resolutions of conflicts of interests.

6.8 The General Position

It may be useful to review the general position which has emerged to this point. There is a strong presumption against invasively interfering (e.g., by coercion, force, or fraud) with the choices and acts of persons competent to make those choices or engage in such

---

[41] On these matters, see Richard Posner, *Economic Analysis of the Law* (Boston: Little, Brown, 1972); R. Coase, "The Problem of Social Cost," *Journal of Law and Economics* 3, No. 1 (1960), pp. 1–44; C. Edwin Baker, "The Ideology of the Economic Analysis of Law," *Philosophy & Public Affairs* 5, No. 1 (Fall, 1975), pp. 3–48; Lawrence Tribe, "Policy Science: Analysis or Ideology," *Philosophy & Public Affairs* 2, No. 1 (Fall, 1972) pp. 66–113; various essays in *The Hofstra Law Review*, Vol. 8, especially No. 3 (Spring, 1980), and J. Coleman and J. Murphy, *Introduction to the Philosophy of Law* (Totowa, N.J.: Rowman and Allenheld, 1984).

acts—so long as their choices and acts wrong no others. Some risks to persons derive from the wrongful acts of others, and the use of certain presumptively wrongful means to stop or prevent many such acts is justifiable on familiar grounds (the precise formulation of the grounds is not, of course, uncontroversial). The central feature of many such acts is that they involve unconsented-to serious harm to innocent persons capable of giving or withholding valid consent. For this reason, placing invasive limits on risk creation can in some cases be justified on nonpaternalistic grounds. Further, a range of restraints aimed at limiting risks to subjects can be justified when competent subjects voluntarily and knowingly consent to such restraints. Compare our discussion of students who voluntarily choose to live in a "quiet" dorm. We have also allowed that when the government is legitimately the only creator of certain alternatives, such as highways, it can and ought to make them as risk-free as resources allow, *within some constraints requiring it justly to obtain and employ its resources*, and/or reveal the degree of risk involved in their use so that users may voluntarily assume or avoid existing risks. Similarly, both the generation of certain risks and limitations on risk taking which arise, and reasonably cannot be avoided by the functioning of just institutions, are permissible. We have also allowed, though not explored to this point, the legitimacy of more restrictive restraints toward those who are not capable of making prudent decisions regarding personal risk taking, for example, many children, the retarded, the senile, or the generally competent who are temporarily incompetent. Our principles also allow a range of invasive but limited interference in order to *ascertain* competence on the part of those who choose to perform certain risky activities. PARP's proviso regarding hypothetical consent also allows invasive interference in those (epistemologically slippery) cases in which it is reasonable to believe that competent nonconsenting, or even dissenting, persons *would consent* to our interference if they were fairly and openly confronted with the reasons or evidence against those beliefs which function as part of their rationale for proceeding in some intended fashion or for dissenting to certain proposals (but note (4) below). Early on we also argued that some "interferences" are, in themselves, morally innocuous, that is, fair and open attempts to persuade (or possibly, a simple reminder, e.g., "that's poison ivy"); thus, many governmental and private efforts to provide information are unobjectionable.

Negatively, we have argued: (1) that the mentioned arguments

336

against having regulatory agencies—which claim that risk regulation inevitably fails (due to consumer readjustments) or that such agencies are often captured by those risk generators it is designed to restrain—are indecisive reasons to reject such institutions; (2) that the argument that presumptively wrongful intervention to promote good or prevent harm to competent persons is all right since the conviction that subjects hold evidently false beliefs is a dubious rationale for risk-limiting interventions; (3) that the claim that whatever policies are decided by elected representatives in a majoritarian, constitutional democracy are all right fails to address our basic questions; (4) that defending governmental or private risk-setting policies by appeal to hypothetical consent is out of place when there is a reasonable opportunity to ascertain actual consent or dissent and also avoid the prospective harm; (5) that the norm of maximizing net aggregate benefit rests on various dubious suppositions, and, hence, is, *by itself*, an inappropriate basis for determining permissible or desirable levels of risk.[42] We have attempted to identify and show (6) that certain grounds for interfering with seemingly voluntary risk taking on the part of competent persons are unjustifiable, for example, the various paternalistic grounds we rejected earlier and also the appeal to cost-benefit analysis which, even if not paternalistic in motivation, sanctions certain invidious restraints which are "paternalistic in result." By contrast, we identified certain legitimate paternalistic grounds for limiting risks and maintained (7) that risk-limiting (as well as risk-generating) governmental acts which are a not reasonably avoidable aspect of the functioning of just institutions are permissible and perhaps obligatory. This last claim places serious weight on determining what are just policies and just institutions. In short, it suggests that a fuller answer to our perplexities about governmental setting of risk levels depends on a theory of justice.

One limitation of our inquiry is that it does not seek to set out such a theory, although the conclusions drawn so far are not neutral as to what sort of theory of justice is acceptable. Indeed, if a defense

---

[42] I do *not* mean to imply that a *suitably constrained* use of the tools of cost-benefit analysis is useless or irrelevant to moral decision making. The problem, as I see it, is to determine what the morally permissible options are (or those which are matters of duty) and cautiously to employ more refined cost-benefit methods and assumptions to achieve cost-effectiveness. Cost-benefit considerations also will be relevant to deciding on permissible or desirable goals, but I am claiming that maximizing social benefits over social costs is not itself a morally acceptable goal. This, on one reading, commits me to the rejection of most if not all forms of utilitarianism: some, albeit limited, defense of this stance occurs in Chapter 7.

of some particular theory of justice requires that the theory be in "reflective equilibrium" with our considered moral judgments about the types of questions we have explored, then an adequate theory, I propose, must be compatible with the basic claims which have been set forth here, in the absence of compelling reasons to the contrary.

6.9 A Rawlsian Approach to Limiting Risks

It is instructive to explore briefly the question of whether one current influential theory of justice can help us in our quest to ascertain what are justifiable limits on risk taking. The theory is that found in John Rawls' *A Theory of Justice*. Here I shall provide only a bare thumbnail sketch of Rawls' heuristic device for identifying principles of justice. Later (in Section 7.8) the core of his theory is discussed in somewhat more detail. After sketching Rawls' view, I then examine one recent attempt, by Dan Beauchamp, to elaborate such an approach in order to identify what are permissible constraints on risk-generating, or risk-assuming, activities—in particular, those likely to result in premature death.

The basic questions of justice are: what are permissible and/or obligatory ways in which benefits or burdens may be, or must be, distributed across a population of beings with moral standing, that is, beings whose welfare is morally relevant (and has positive weight) in itself? For our purposes here, persons are the relevant population. The basic goods to be distributed (or which *get* distributed in one fashion or another) on Rawls' view include liberty and opportunity, wealth and income, and other bases of self-respect. To discern what principles govern a just distribution of such goods, Rawls proposes that we imaginatively enter into a hypothetical contractual situation, the "original position," in which we are to reach mutual agreement as to the principles dispositive of such distributions of goods. However, we are to imaginatively place ourselves behind a "veil of ignorance" in which we are each ignorant of the race, gender, social role, and generation into which we are born; we are not to attend to, or "know," our plan of life or particular attitudes or preferences. We are to be rational, capable of possessing a conception of the good, and concerned to design principles of social interaction (including basic institutions, e.g., form of government, a constitution, or economic system) which will promote our several advantages. Neither are we to be initially committed to particular moral principles or ideologies. Stripped of these accoutrements of actual persons, we are not able to bargain for policies or principles arbitrarily favoring our own (individuating) interests. We are not to know what such interests will be (when the veil of ignorance is removed) beyond what anyone else in the original position knows—roughly, that each will want to carry out his (or her) own life plan, or realize some conception of the good, and have the wherewithal and opportunity to do so. Since none can, or is in a position to, press a case for arbitrary policies favoring himself (or herself), any principles agreed to will be, Rawls alleges, fair or just. The basic principles of justice *are simply whatever principles would be agreed to* by such rational, impartial participants in this special hypothetical situation. I will not here elaborate further on Rawls' seductive and sophisticated reasoning as to what principles would receive unanimous agreement (see Section 7.8). Perhaps such participants would agree on principles designed to delimit risks, both those generated by others and to which there is not consent by the subjects of risk, as well as those which might be voluntarily assumed.

With the core of Rawls' theory before us let us examine its possible implications for our concern with the boundaries of legitimate limitations on risk taking. To do so, we will examine the attempt to apply Rawls' position set forth by Dan Beauchamp.[43] Prior to looking at Beauchamp's positive proposal, let us consider those rationales for limiting risks which he finds untenable. Relying on the inquiries of Gerald Dworkin and Joel Feinberg (see our earlier discussion in Chapter 2) he notes that there is a consensus against strong paternalism (that the state can permissibly interfere with the *fully voluntary* acts of competent persons in order to promote their own good) and some tendency to accept weak paternalism (that the state can permissibly interfere with the liberty of *substantially nonvoluntary* acts of competent persons in order to promote their own good). Beauchamp usefully observes that some advocate such "minimal restrictions" on choice as (1) altering the conditions of availability of harmful substances, (2) deterring risky behavior by mild punishment, for example, fines for smoking in public, (3) "symbolizing the posture of government toward the behavior" (presumably: official condemnation of it), and (4) "influencing the context of messages in the mass media" (presumably: constraints on program content and advertising), and that defenders of these

---

[43] Dan Beauchamp, "Public Health and Individual Liberty," in *Contemporary Issues in Bioethics* eds. Beauchamp and Walters, pp. 442–451.

restraints believe that there is no serious problem of justification since the restraints are mild ones.[44] Beauchamp offers no defense of such "weak paternalism" and next considers whether utilitarianism can provide "a justifying principle to limit voluntary risks that avoids paternalism."[45] In his view the utilitarian rationale (cf. his "economic argument") appeals to the costs to others imposed by voluntary risk-taking behavior, for example, the costs of emergency services, care of those who are public wards, impeding production, or even the cost of energy generated by the treatment of disease. In brief, Beauchamp finds this position untenable; he claims that

> To argue that we are not concerned with crippling diseases or early death per se but rather the avoidance of the burdens these misfortunes place on the rest of us would help to create a climate of callousness and disregard for the value of life and health.[46]

In passing, we note that utilitarians might well regard Beauchamp's worry as itself one which any sensitive utilitarian would take into account in determining whether limits or risks are justifiable. Nevertheless, for the reasons mentioned, Beauchamp considers what he takes to be a "third option," one which "disavows paternalism (even weak paternalism) and the economic argument"— the option being one "based on the tradition of social justice."[47] It is here that Beauchamp looks to Rawls' theory for guidance. He claims that participants in the original position would consent to restrict certain freedoms in order to provide everyone with those primary goods (liberty and opportunity, income and wealth, the bases of self-respect) that are a necessary means to the completion of anyone's life plan. This much seems reasonable, but Beauchamp further infers that participants in the original position would regard policies aimed at reducing or minimizing premature death, for example, prior to 65, as a primary good. In his view, then, they would consent to reasonable limits on freedom in order to secure this good. Also, they "would only refuse to eliminate the harm of early death when those restrictions on life-style risks incurred a more serious harm, such as a violation of fundamental liberty,

[44] Ibid., p. 443.
[45] Ibid., p. 444.
[46] Ibid.
[47] Ibid.

privacy, or autonomy."[48] Succinctly, in Beauchamp's view, even if there is a substantial component of voluntariness in most life-style risks, the demands of justice require their reasonable restriction.[49]

This brief summary of Beauchamp's suggestive explorations does not do full justice to the nuances he recognizes; still, I hope it is a fair sketch. With that proviso, let us examine the position. First, it may be observed that even if Beauchamp's proposed restrictive policies on voluntary risk taking are not motivated by paternalistic considerations, they are "paternalistic in result," and, indeed, involve restrictions like those sanctioned by "strong paternalism," namely, employment of presumptively wrongful means to interfere with the voluntary acts of competent persons to promote paternalistic ends. Second, if we ask for what reason such constraints are to be imposed, some of Beauchamp's own claims suggest that his concern is paternalistic; for example, in the prior (full) quote he implies that we should be concerned about "crippling diseases and early death per se" (I take this to mean: the welfare of persons subject to these). Elsewhere, he states "the issues of individual freedom and responsibility must be weighed against the harm of an early death."[50] These passages, and others, make it clear that his proposals, in part, are aimed at restricting the behavior of those who, voluntarily, risk harm to themselves. If such policies are to be carried out in order to prevent harm to those constrained, they are paternalistic in motivation. They are to be done *for the sake* of those constrained. This view of such restrictive policies—that they are paternalistic (in motivation or with reference to justifying grounds?)—is rejected by Beauchamp, although it is Rawls' view.[51] I shall not dwell on this point, but there is a serious question here as to whether an appeal to the "tradition of social justice," or Rawls' theory in particular, provides a "third option"—one *distinct* from the appeal to preventing harm to those not subjected to constraints (what Beauchamp calls the "utilitarian" argument) and the appeal to paternalistic considerations. In my view it does not, and a Rawls-like theory of justice itself seeks to delineate, broadly and in part, the domain of permissible paternalism (and, of course, much more).

A more interesting question, however, is whether Beauchamp

[48] Ibid., p. 447.
[49] Ibid., p. 450.
[50] Ibid., p. 448.
[51] John Rawls, *A Theory of Justice* (Cambridge, Mass.: Belknap Press of Harvard University, 1971), p. 249.

341

is correct in claiming that participants in the original position would agree to the sorts of mutual restraints he proposes. Both Beauchamp and Rawls may be correct in assuming that participants in the original position would agree to restraints of some sort. A key claim of Beauchamp's is that such participants "would only refuse to eliminate the harm of an early death when those restrictions on lifestyle risks incurred a more serious harm, such as a violation of fundamental liberty, privacy, or autonomy."[52] Unfortunately, Beauchamp provides no answer (nor does one seem to be in the offing) to the fundamental but difficult question: and precisely when do restrictions violate fundamental liberty, privacy, or autonomy? Without more specific criteria, the implied limit on restrictions is left indeterminate. With regard to reducing the incidence of premature death (cf. Beauchamp's more problematic talk of "minimizing"), it is clear that various ways of doing so are quite invasive, a point Beauchamp does not ignore. But a legal prohibition on hang gliding, boxing, mountain climbing, white water rafting, motorcycling, bicycling, and the use of ladders or chainsaws by uncertified persons, as well as taxes on cigarettes or alcoholic beverages can all be regarded as restrictions on liberty. Yet all might diminish premature death. It is not clear what principles could be used to decide, or would be used by participants in the original position to decide, *which* voluntary yet risky behaviors should be prohibited. A competing view, closer to Rawls', is that since participants in the original position do not know whether they will "later" be risk-aversive or not, or whether their peculiar purposes, hopes, and life plans involve risky activities, they would choose *not* to invasively restrict *voluntary* risky (to themselves) behavior (after all, their peculiar life plans might include mountain climbing, sky diving, or capping out-of-control fires at oil rigs) except under special conditions: for example, (1) they are incompetent to choose about risky behaviors, (2) they *evidently* have false beliefs which move them to make risky choices, (3) they, *after knowing* their own propensities for weakness of will or impulsive, imprudent, acts, consent to restrictions (cf. Odysseus), or (4) they would consent to the interference if apprized of relevant information. Such far more limited types of restriction, I conjecture, would seem reasonable to those self-interested rational participants who do not yet know their own particular interests, aims, and attitudes toward risks. This view of matters, of course, is closer to

[52] D. Beauchamp, "Public Health and Individual Liberty," p. 449.

the position we have defended here, but it is at odds with Beauchamp's inferences about what would be chosen in the original position. For the reasons mentioned, it seems more probable that participants would *not* choose mutual restrictions aimed at minimizing premature death *as such* but only restrictions aimed at deterring serious harms which might result from incompetent, involuntary, or grossly ill-considered choices (to put the matter in a crude but succinct way).

These conjectures about the interpretation and implications of employing Rawls' heuristic thought experiment for identifying basic principles of justice suggest that participants in the original position would distinguish between (what, independently, we have argued to be) legitimate and illegitimate paternalistic grounds for constraining the choices and behavior of persons. But a theory of justice must decide much more; it must provide a basis for determining the just distribution of other goods such as income and wealth. As such it must determine which possible social institutions are just and which are not. If the right theory of justice sanctions institutions such as courts, police, military defense, and systems of incarceration, citizens will have a duty to cooperate with such just institutions (those that are). Certain forms of voluntary behavior will generate risks to the existence or proper functioning of such just institutions.

As we have noted, those who voluntarily choose to engage in certain risk-laden activities may pass on significant costs to others, for example, by becoming public wards, or in other ways generating significant costs which they do not fully absorb themselves. Collectively, such activities can threaten the functioning of just institutions—by overwhelming their capacities or undermining their financial base. Although we may regard skate boarding, drinking alcohol and driving, recreational drug usage, drag racing, setting off fireworks, or motorcycling without a helmet as comparatively innocuous and nonmalicious activities when set against stealing, kidnapping, or protection rackets, the former activities can wrong others by passing on unconsented-to costs (as do the latter); hence, under certain conditions they can be regarded as a form of wrongful free riding and as contrary to a just distribution of social benefits and burdens. One need not accept the very strong claim that "society has a right to do *whatever* will serve to protect itself against subversion" in order to allow that certain sometimes innocuous and innocently undertaken activities pose too great a risk to the functioning of just institutions, and to perhaps unknown individuals, to go unconstrained. To take this view is to construe the "right to direct one's own life in ways not wronging others" in an appropriately broad manner—for we wrong others in not assuming our fair share of the burden of creating and/or perpetuating just institutions. Without elaborating in more detail, there are reasons for regarding unconsented-to costs to others (third parties) and paternalistic considerations as a *proper part* of any adequate theory of justice and not as three entirely distinct sorts of appeals on the basis of which one might attempt to justify constraints on individual choices and acts. Paternalistic grounds for constraint are distinguishable from nonpaternalistic grounds, but a theory of justice must attempt to identify both legitimate paternalistic and nonpaternalistic grounds for intervening in the lives of individuals.

SEVEN

OUR DEALINGS WITH INCOMPETENTS

The majority of mankind are *madmen at large*.
—Benjamin Rush

Physicians [are the] best judges of sanity.
—Benjamin Rush

Mankind considered as creatures made for immortality are worthy of all our cares. Let us view them as patients in a hospital. The more they resist our efforts to serve them, the more they need our services.   —Benjamin Rush

7.1 The Concept of Incompetence

Prior to turning to moral questions about our dealings with incompetent persons, some further clarification of the concept of general incompetence is in order. If we recognize the category of generally incompetent persons as a legitimate one, it is tempting to think that certain forms of paternalistic restriction toward them are permissible, which fail to be acceptable in dealings with competent persons. This general point I accept, but as soon as we begin to contemplate (as we do in 7.2) what principles are to guide us, perplexities arise. These in turn force us to return at later points to reconsider carefully what we mean by 'competence,' 'incompetence,' and what relevant distinctions must be made among incompetent persons. In our focus here, as in other cases (e.g., the abortion dispute), the conceptual and moral questions are closely interwoven.

We argued earlier (in Section 5.5) that there is an intelligible notion of general competence. Persons are generally competent if they normally possess a sufficiently broad set of *capacities* to take care of themselves prudently, given a reasonably propitious set of environmental circumstances. The fact that a particular person must rely in a crucial way on the assistance of others, for example for medical care, is not by itself a basis for attributing incompetence. That an individual cannot prudently function in certain hostile surroundings is no indication of incompetence. For example, the fact that a person cannot successfully escape from a plane crash is hardly a basis for attributing incompetence to that person. To call attention to these matters is to suggest that our conception of a generally competent person has as its core the features that a competent person has a sufficiently broad range of capacities primarily to reason and choose but also to act in ways likely to be prudent under a wide variety of circumstances. Such a conception of general competence is, as we have observed, fuzzy at the edges, but suffices to capture the basic criteria by virtue of which, except for certain "hard cases," we differentiate with little difficulty between the competent and the incompetent. On this basis most children must be deemed incompetent, but we need not forget or ignore the fact that most children are precompetent. Given their potential to be generally competent, they normally are not permanently incompetent; hence, the topic of children deserves separate treatment. They have "future interests" to be respected now which are not possessed by the permanently incompetent.

Even if this broadly-brushed distinction between generally competent and generally incompetent persons is acceptable, it does not suffice to mark all the morally significant distinctions we may wish to consider regarding our arguments about permissible or mandatory dealings with the competent or the incompetent. A few previously noted points are worth emphasis. One is that normal possession of general competence by an individual is compatible with "pockets of incompetence." A generally competent person may substantially lack capacities necessary for the performance of certain types of acts, for example, designing an airplane. Such incapacities may be "deep" and the explanation may be genetically based. Other incapacities may be rather fixed but remediable, for example, the inability to acquire non-basic mathematical skills. Such an inability may not be due to deep incapacity but to what is now referred to as "math anxiety" and the explanation may be found in socially inculcated attitudes. In any case, existing pockets of incompetence do not preclude the existence of general competence. Still, the recognition of particular incapacities provides a basis for allowing that generally competent persons may be "incompetent with respect to X" where X is replaceable with a description of some specific activity, such as disco dancing, doing

346

quadratic equations, typing, calculating income taxes, or driving a vehicle. Such pockets of incompetence might be distinguished from "episodes of incompetence" in generally competent persons. What I have in mind is that, in contrast to the permanent or the rather fixed disabilities noted before, generally competent persons may suffer from "temporary" losses of capacity, that is, lose normally possessed capacities for brief, or enduring, periods of time. The examples which come to mind include the diminished capacities resulting from disease, injury, fainting, drunkenness, drug usage, embarrassment, fear, and so on. Significantly diminished capacity is not always a corollary of such events or states, but it often is. In view of this fact we may dismiss the presumption that a person generally recognized as competent is competent on a particular occasion to decide or perform X. In such an event special questions arise regarding the treatment of the generally competent individual who is now incompetent with respect to X. This point, however, need not force us to regard such a generally competent person as not relevantly different from the generally incompetent person; the generally competent person who is in the midst of an episode of incompetence has a past, and quite likely a future, significantly different from that of the generally incompetent. I shall not explore this point here but it is worth noting the important differences among subjects who all may exhibit the feature that they are incompetent with respect to deciding to perform or performing some specific activity.

Analogously, the generally incompetent often exhibit pockets of competence. As we have observed, a retarded individual may have all the capacities required to perform certain tasks as safely and as well as the most gifted person, for example, scrambling eggs. Hence, from the fact that a generally incompetent person lacks the broad set of capacities to direct his own life, it does not follow that such a person must rely on others in all domains of activity, or that others may permissibly interfere in an invasive manner with the choices or activities of such persons *simply* on the ground that such persons are "incompetent"—or sick, injured, retarded, or immature.

Such distinctions should make us wary of accepting crude generalizations about those who are incompetent or façile inferences about what it is permissible or mandatory to do with regard to them.

If the core feature of incompetence is the lack of capacities of some sort, there is a basis for resisting one frequently proposed view about the competence of persons to make certain kinds of decisions. It is sometimes said, for example, that patients are not competent to make complex medical decisions which will significantly affect their own well-being. Such a claim is not normally an attribution of general incompetence; rather, it is that "S is not competent with respect to deciding about X." It is worth noting that the actual situation might be one of two different sorts. S may exhibit the deep and permanent incapacities which make reasonably prudent choosing an impossibility. On the other hand, S may be a generally competent person who, due to lack of training or explanation, cannot at the time make a reasonably prudent choice, although S is capable of making such a choice if given appropriate information. It seems better to say here that there is simply an "input deficiency" rather than to impute incompetence to S. To attribute incompetence to those lacking sufficient relevant information is to classify almost all of us as "incompetent" with respect to virtually all highly technical decisions. Such conceptual sleight-of-hand tricks go no way toward justifying the withholding of relevant information or justifying the reservation to "experts" of decision-making prerogatives which belong ultimately to competent, although allegedly "incompetent," subjects (who have not waived the right to make such decisions).

The key feature about generally incompetent persons (for they shall be our focus here) is not that they lack all capacities but that they lack capacities necessary to make reasonably prudent decisions regarding their own lives. Lacking such capacities, they may have the good fortune of not choosing means to ends where such choices have seriously self-harming results. The least able incompetents, of course, may lack the wherewithal to form goals or deliberately to choose except in the most lenient sense of 'choose.' Hence, if left to their own devices they unavoidably run serious risks. To stress the obvious, it *seems*, therefore, all right to intervene rigorously in their lives, or even a matter of duty, in order to prevent them from harming themselves. In this respect they are often like most young children. Still, questions arise concerning the limits of justifiable paternalism toward the generally incompetent (as well as the generally competent who are temporarily incompetent).

7.2 Should the Gifted Rule?

In the Platonic dialogues Socrates is confronted with the bold assertion of Thrasymachus that justice is (whatever promotes) the interest of the stronger. Such a claim may be tantamount to the view that whatever is in the interest of the stronger is what is just.[1] It bears a certain similarity to the familiar theme that "might makes right." It is not a great leap from there to the view that those who are superior, for example, intellectually, have a more comprehensive set of important rights than those who are intellectually inferior, perhaps including rights to direct or control the latter, but not conversely. Such notions are reminiscent of Aristotle's view that some are marked from birth to rule and others to be ruled. We associate such an outlook with elitism, authoritarianism, anti-egalitarian, and anti-democratic thought. From that standpoint it is surprising to read in John Stuart Mill's classic (and, I think, inspired) defense of individual liberty that "despotism is a legitimate mode of government toward barbarians."[2] It is not entirely clear what Mill meant by "barbarians." However, he may have had in mind highly primitive people and, possibly, those who, like young children, lack sufficient capacities to direct their own lives. Although we cannot be sure, it may have been Mill's view that quite invasive paternalistic restrictions on the liberty of the generally incompetent are morally permissible. The outline of a puzzle emerges here. How can one who values human liberty defend the view that severe restrictions on the liberties of incompetents are justified? One answer seems to be that the "bright have rights," or, similarly, that it is by virtue of the possession of superior capacities that some, thus, should "rule" over those who are inferior with respect to those capacities. But this response, were it to come from one who values liberty, sounds strikingly illiberal and too much like the mentioned views of Thrasymachus or Aristotle.

Daniel Wikler has posed the dilemma pointedly here, and shows how it arises in exploring the question of paternalism toward incompetents.[3] His focus, however, is on the mildly retarded, possibly a subset of our broad category of the generally incompetent. It is worth noting that the category of the retarded is often subdivided into those who are mildly, moderately, severely, or profoundly retarded. As Wikler observes, persons of *normal* intelligence often act in ways which pose or generate dangers to

---

[1] Thrasymachus, however, may have believed not that it is just that the strong prevail but that "justice" was only a fiction invented by those in power to encourage servility in the weaker. I am indebted to Richard Nunan for this point.

[2] J. S. Mill, *On Liberty* (New York: Liberal Arts Press, 1956), p. 14.

[3] Daniel Wikler, "Paternalism and the Mildly Retarded," *Philosophy & Public Affairs* 8, No. 4 (Summer, 1979), pp. 377–392. Further relevant discussion by Wikler and others is found in the useful volume edited by Ruth Macklin and Willard Gaylin, *Mental Retardation and Sterilization* (New York: Plenum Press, 1981).

themselves. They make bad choices regarding marriage, contracts, careers, and so on. Yet it is widely held that they have a right to make such choices for their own good or ill so long as they do not unfairly subvert the interests of others. Apart from whether such a view is widely held, such a view is similar to the one I have defended here. The general view is labeled by Wikler as "the liberal principle." One question is why an *exception* should be made to the liberal principle when we focus on our dealings with incompetent persons. One answer is that it is permissible for those of normal capacity to regulate the lives of those of inferior capacity. Wikler calls attention to the following problem. By comparison to the moderately retarded the mildly retarded are superior; further, "if the average, now deemed normal, are impaired from the point of view of those of greater intellectual ability, are persons of average intelligence, for this reason, rightly subject to a paternalistic denial of civil liberties?"[4] The apparent inconsistency is that, in Wikler's terms, normal persons are thought to have "a right to be free from constraint from any person whether of normal, subnormal, or high intelligence," yet "relative intellectual superiority" is frequently invoked as the rationale for regulation of the retarded.[5]

One response to this problem is to give up adherence to the aforementioned liberal principle, but, as Wikler observes, one need not do so, for the above argument rests on a questionable conception of competence, one he describes as "relativistic." On this latter view, mental capacity is an attribute which is a matter of degree, and judgments of impairment make sense *only* by comparison with, or relative to, the perspective of some other level. On this view, although we can distinguish different levels of ability, it is arbitrary to draw a line between the mentally impaired and the unimpaired. A similar point might be made about the distinction between those said to be competent and those said to be incompetent, or the "normal" and "subnormal." It is worth noting that this accusation of arbitrariness is not directed solely at those who employ a highly specific, theory-laden, and contested criterion for line drawing such as having an IQ below 100 or below 70, as the case may be.

On the relativist conception of competence and the assumption that the more gifted can permissibly regulate the less gifted, or the normal, the more gifted justifiably could impose on normal persons constraints as invasive as those we often place on the retarded, for

---

[4] Wikler, "Paternalism and the Mildly Retarded," p. 380.
[5] Ibid.

example, not allowing them to live alone, contract, marry, beget, or adopt children.[6] To avoid this unwelcome implication Wikler proposes an alternative conception of competence. Rather than understanding mental capacity in terms of "innate intellect," he suggests that the important consideration regarding competence is the ability to *perform* certain tasks. Two persons may vary in intellect but if both can adequately and fully perform a certain task, then they are *fully competent with respect to that task*. The more gifted person may have a surfeit of talent that simply goes unused with respect to that task. A case in point might be bicycle riding; both Genius and Marginal may be fully competent at this task even though their intellectual powers differ. Those who possess the capacities sufficient to perform the task are competent; those failing to possess such capacities are, in this respect, incompetent. Hence, there is a threshold point above which no one is "more competent" than another. Thus, the most intellectually gifted competent is not "superior" at this task than less gifted competents. Although Wikler does not pose the point in just this way, the suggestion seems to be that there is a plausible *performance-based* criterion of competence as opposed to one which seeks to rank all persons in terms of skills or powers, primarily "mental or intellectual" ones. His further suggestion seems to be that, regardless of intellectual ranking (supposing what is *not* obvious: that there are satisfactory criteria for employing such a notion and in practice making correlative assessments) and so long as persons are competent, there is no reason to regard intellectually superior competents as having special moral prerogatives to constrain less gifted competents. Hence, the defender of the liberal principle can avoid being committed to a troublesome "benevolent hierarchy of the gifted" since he need not rely on *relative intellectual superiority* as the basis for determining when, or under what conditions, paternalistic intrusions are permissible. Reliance, instead, on a *performance-based* conception of competence does not commit one to the view that those who are relatively superior in intellect are, for that reason, permitted to constrain the relatively less able.

This line of argument is, I believe, successful in handling the

[6] A similar perplexity exists regarding those justifications for the subordination of animals by humans which appeal to the superior capacities of most humans. On this, see Desmond Stewart, "The Limits of Trooghoft," in *Animal Rights and Human Obligations*, eds. Tom Regan and Peter Singer (Englewood Cliffs, N.J., Prentice-Hall, 1976), pp. 238–245; also, like Wikler, I stress threshold considerations in "Interspecific Justice," *Inquiry* 22, Nos. 1–2 (Summer, 1979), pp. 55–79.

difficulty noted. Further, it provides a good reason to reject the crude and unqualified assumption that in all cases generally competent persons with paternalistic aims may permissibly override the decisions, or constrain the actions, of generally incompetent persons. With respect to certain decisions and tasks, generally competent persons will not be more competent than generally incompetent persons. One implication of this view is that, for example, generally incompetent persons should not be restrained, across the board, from entering into contracts. With regard to *certain* contractual arrangements, generally incompetent persons will be no less competent than the more gifted. Hence, certain wholesale prohibitions are suspect. I leave open here the question of what other specific implications there are with regard to law and public policy once we reject resorting to the rationale which invokes mere relative intellectual superiority as a justificatory device.

7.3 What Is Competent Performance?

Thus far we have implied that in cases in which a person, S, is genuinely incompetent with respect to a certain task and another, A, is competent with respect to that task, it may be permissible, or possibly a duty, for A to constrain S. However, the analysis of competence as capacity to *perform successfully* leaves certain questions unanswered. What are the criteria by virtue of which we may judge that someone can successfully perform a given task? Various possibilities come to mind. Consider the example of bicycling once more. We might say that successful performance involves maintaining balance and keeping the vehicle in motion for some minimal period of time, doing so gracefully, deftly, quickly, stylishly, efficiently, or safely—or in such a way as to exhibit a set of such features. On the face of things, it would be quite arbitrary to insist that one who bicycles safely for considerable distances but does so without flair is incompetent with respect to the task of bicycle riding. On reflection it is clear that although we might adopt various standards for "successful performances," and hence "competent performances," what seems relevant to our primary concern with constraining or prohibiting others from engaging in certain activities is whether or not a participant *can* engage in the performance, or attempt it, in a manner unlikely to generate serious risks of harm to himself or to subvert the legitimate interests and rights of others.[7]

---

[7] To avoid a possible confusion, it is worth noting that the concept of competence on which I focus is a "minimalist" one—possession of capacities sufficient to allow the possessor prudently to decide whether to attempt a given activity or to perform

It is not obvious that there are any tempting grounds for invasive intervention with the activities of others, *competent or not*, unless their activities promise to result in such "harms" to themselves or others. However, we may wish to distinguish those cases in which persons may risk such harms from cases in which persons may simply fail to benefit themselves by pursuits they may undertake. The case for intervention by others is, however, strongest in those cases where individuals are likely to worsen significantly their own situation or that of others in the ways mentioned. Hence, a reasonable criterion for what counts as the capacity to perform successfully (and, hence, competence to perform) an act is that a person must have the *capacity* to engage in an act in such a manner as not to generate serious risks to self and not to subvert the legitimate interests or rights of others—or the capacity to choose to refrain from such risky acts.[8] Whether an individual is competent with respect to a task, then, will be an empirical question even though the standards of competence are in part normative. The view set forward here is, I maintain, the appropriate normative standard. Perhaps it is not surprising that the basic and relevant consideration underlying disputes about competence concerns whether in general, or with respect to specific tasks, individuals are, in familiar terms, "dangerous to themselves or others." In that respect there is nothing "special" about disease, injury, retardation, mental illness, or other types of disability except insofar as such conditions may contribute to the fact that an individual is not

---

it prudently (to put the matter succinctly). The concept involves the notion of being able to succeed in deciding or doing in a way which satisfies a standard of prudence. There is another, common, concept of competence (or perhaps we should say that other criteria of application are used for the same concept) which employs "maximal" standards of success. For example, we may say that a person is not a competent typist unless he can type correctly 80 words per minute. If he types only 40 words per minute, he is incompetent on the maximal standard, but competent on our minimalist notion.

[8] Thus, a child of three years is incompetent at using explosives. A normal adult may be competent at such a task; a drunk but otherwise normal adult may be incompetent in this regard. A psychopath may or may not be competent. If he is *capable* of using explosives in such a manner as to avoid serious self-harm or wronging others, he is competent in this respect; if not, he is incompetent at this task. If he is incompetent, we need not restrict ourselves to those forms of paternalistic intervention sanctioned by PARP. If he is competent, however, he may wrongfully threaten (or wrongfully harm) others even though he (by definition of 'competent') is *capable* of not doing so. Still, if he wrongs others, there are evidently reasonable nonpaternalistic grounds for invasive intervention. Similarly, if he is incompetent *and* wrongfully threatens or wrongfully harms others, again there will be nonpaternalistic grounds for invasive intervention. In the absence of adequate nonpaternalistic grounds for invasive interference, however, ascertaining competence is important since it is relevant to what sorts of paternalistic grounds can legitimately be invoked to justify intrusive measures.

capable of avoiding significant danger to himself or others. It is just the presence of that feature, of course, which creates some presumption in favor of the permissibility of interference—on paternalistic, nonpaternalistic grounds, or both.

So far we have explored the questions of how to understand the notions of competence and incompetence, the criterion for attributing incompetence, and the question of why incompetence is a morally relevant consideration in determining permissible or obligatory dealings with other persons. As with competent persons, there are, in principle, both paternalistic and nonpaternalistic grounds for constraint. Our focus throughout primarily has been on ascertaining the legitimate paternalistic grounds for intervention. Setting to one side the question of legitimate nonpaternalistic grounds for intervention with incompetents, we need to try to formulate a defensible answer to the question: what are the legitimate paternalistic grounds for invasive intervention (those employing presumptively wrongful means) with the choices and activities of incompetent persons.

7.4 Harm-Prevention Principles

A somewhat tempting principle which attempts to capture some of our intuitions regarding permissible paternalism toward generally incompetent persons is the following one; I shall call it the *Simple Harm-Prevention Principle* (SHPP, in short):

A's paternalistically doing X to S, where A is competent with respect to X and S is incompetent with respect to deciding about or doing Y, is permissible if

1. A's doing X wrongs no one other than S or A

and 2. A's doing X is quite likely to prevent S's causing significant harm (or risk of harm) on balance to S by S's doing Y

and 3. if A were to omit doing X it is certain or quite likely that S would cause significant harm (or risk of harm) on balance to S by S's doing Y.[9]

---

[9] It is worth noting that 3. requires some qualification to avoid difficulties with respect to overdetermination. That is, 3. may be false if B would intervene to prevent S's harming himself. Still, it seems permissible for A to intervene. How best to avoid this difficulty is not clear to me. Still, "A" can refer to any agent other than S and it is not contradictory to claim that it is permissible for any of various persons to intervene. Further, SHPP only purports to state a sufficient condition of per-

Such a principle has some virtues; it does not sanction invasive interferences with S in regard to acts at which S is competent even though S may be generally incompetent, for example, moderately retarded. For example, it does not sanction A's constraining or prohibiting S from making contractual arrangements S is competent to make (compare cases where A is an individual, a hospital staff, or a legislature), or constraining everyday activities at which S may be fully competent, such as choosing what to wear or which television program to watch. In this respect the sanctioning of wholesale, thoroughgoing, restrictions is avoided; those matters over which S is competent are left to S's discretion. Any principle with contrary implications would allow the arbitrary and capricious imposition of restrictions. Clauses 2. and 3. in obvious ways require that a prospective intervention be realistic and efficacious.

In spite of these virtues SHPP may sanction too much. Suppose S is moderately retarded and lives on a farm where highly toxic herbicides and pesticides are readily accessible. Suppose further that S is incompetent with respect to using such chemicals, for example, S is likely to cause significant harm to himself by using them. As it stands, SHPP would sanction cutting off S's hands to prevent S's harming himself. Not a welcome implication of our principle. To cope with this result we might revise SHPP to formulate the *Revised Harm-Prevention Principle* (RHPP). It is exactly like SHPP but adds:

> and 4. It is reasonable to believe that A's doing X will not render S worse off than S would have been had A omitted X, and it is reasonable to believe that A's doing X is one of the least harmful means of preventing S from doing Y.

RHPP embodies the firm intuitions that our intervention must not be a "cure worse than the disease" and that just because intervention to prevent harm is desirable interveners are not morally permitted to employ unnecessarily damaging means.

In addition to generating a revised principle, RHPP, which lacks the troublesome implications of SHPP, clause 4. has other significant implications. If it is correct that the generally incompetent lack the right to direct their own lives throughout the domain of

---

missibility (the truth of 1., 2., or 3.) and not a necessary condition. So, even if 3. is false because of overdetermination it does not follow that A's intervening is impermissible.

acts not wronging others, it does not follow that their interest in directing their own lives is morally without weight.

To note this point suggests the importance of making distinctions among those who may be classified under the broad rubric of "generally incompetent." Some, the profoundly retarded, may lack conscious goals and preferences. In that respect they may have no aims by virtue of which they could, if able, direct their lives along some paths as opposed to others. In an important way they are "directionless," even if sentient and, hence, possessing the morally relevant capacity to experience some satisfactions and dissatisfactions. But in such cases there seems no consent or dissent to take into account, no autonomy or incipient autonomy to consider. In contrast, the mildly retarded clearly have articulable, conscious goals and expressed preferences. In *some* cases competent persons may think the goals held by the mildly retarded are themselves irrational, possibly because they are impossible to achieve. For example, consider a case in which a mildly retarded person may wish to build a perpetual motion machine. Aside from reasons to dissuade, there is little ground for interfering with such an aim unless the incompetent person decides to take steps toward that end which he is incompetent to take, that is, cannot take without causing serious harms to himself or others. In other cases we may judge that the goals of the incompetent person are, in themselves, not patently unreasonable at all, for example, to contract, to marry, to have children, to achieve sexual satisfaction, or to go hunting. If a generally incompetent person, S, cannot hunt competently (I take this point to be nonredundant since generally incompetent persons may exhibit pockets of competence), RHPP may sanction interference to prevent S from hunting. Clause 4. in RHPP implies that the intervener must employ one of the least restrictive means of doing so, and must not cause a worse harm than he prevents. We have earlier argued that fair and open attempts to dissuade are not presumptively wrong and such an option would seem to be the morally first choice. If that fails, RHPP sanctions more invasive, including presumptively wrong, means. I shall not consider the various possibilities; however, it is important to observe that in this sort of case the subject has preferences or wants, and these may be intense ones. To that extent their nonsatisfaction may constitute a subversion of a not inconsiderable and legitimate interest of S. To frustrate these wants may constitute, in itself, a harming of S—even if we leave open the question of whether it is justifiably imposed harm. The central point is that RHPP, clause 4., requires employing means of constraint which it is reasonable to expect are among the least harmful to S; since the frustration of S's wants is a harm to S, S's wants must be taken into account and properly weighed. To disregard S's wants is to fail to assess adequately the harmfulness of the means of constraining S.

A general point which emerges here is that RHPP does require a reasonable weighting of the aims and preferences of persons who have them even if such persons fail to possess the broad range of competence for them to be "on their own" and to have the sort of right to direct their own lives which we have stressed. For this reason, we cannot ignore the wants and goals of generally incompetent persons even though, in the final analysis, it may be permissible to "substitute our judgment" for theirs on certain matters. Whether RHPP is a fully satisfactory principle has not been shown conclusively; however, it seems to be a reasonable view and one superior to SHPP and a number of imaginable alternatives.

Although we have denied that generally incompetent persons have a right to direct their own lives, our limited defense of RHPP allows that many or most incompetent persons have important convictions and intense desires such that thwarting their realization may be tantamount to harming them, that is, to subverting legitimate interests possessed by such persons. Hence, RHPP is an interest-respecting principle in a broad sense, that is, it does presume that, for example, we cannot legitimately ignore the preferences of incompetent persons and, somehow, respect or promote only their interests identified independently of their preferences and beliefs (e.g., nutritional, medical, or psychological "needs"). To pose a similar point, although RHPP focuses on harm prevention, it allows that thwarting basic dispositions is a kind of harm. To oversimplify, RHPP assigns some moral relevance to the viewpoint and preference schedule of the incompetent person; such psychological factors must be taken into account in determining what is permissible in our dealings with incompetents.

However, an important question arises as to whether RHPP gives due weight to such factors or whether (as we have complained about certain forms of utilitarianism) it tends to treat incompetents as mere utility containers. Crudely put, it is one thing, so it seems, for A to decide, from A's point of view, how an incompetent party, S (given his understanding of the incompetent's interests), may or ought to be treated, and another for A to decide, from S's point of view, how S may or ought to be treated. Perhaps this seeming difference is illusory. There are, however, reasons to think that it is not. So far we have avoided any discussion of a doctrine influential in the court decisions which suggests the importance of "donning the mantle of the incompetent" in deciding on his or her treatment, namely, the "doctrine of substituted judgment." The relation between RHPP and this doctrine involves a number of complications which I shall postpone to a later section (7.9). At that later point we shall reconsider the adequacy of RHPP. Prior to doing so it will be useful to explore other facets of the question of permissible dealings with incompetents. A more perspicuous view requires further attention to (1) who gets counted as incompetent and why, (2) the costs of alleviating the burdens of incompetence, and (3) whether current theories of justice provide a reasoned basis for deciding what are permissible or obligatory procedures for our dealings with incompetents. Such matters will be our focus in Sections 7.5 through 7.8.

7.5 The Social Component in Incompetence

There is a perplexity whose consideration I have so far delayed. It is one developed in Wikler's instructive investigation of paternalism toward the mildly retarded.[10] There are some activities at which neither generally competent nor generally incompetent persons are competent and in which the difficulty or impossibility of performing such tasks without harming oneself or others does not arise because society has "chosen" to structure the activity in a certain fashion, for example, swimming through shark-infested waters or fasting for months at a time. With regard to other activities, whether they can be performed competently is not only a function of native abilities and talents but also of a social component. For example, whether a child can play safely in her yard may depend in part on whether an expressway has been built adjacent to it and whether or not barriers between the yard and the expressway have been erected to render the yard a safe area. If there is no barrier and the child cannot play safely in the yard, we might rightly say that the child is not, in the sense previously defined, competent to play in the yard. To press our fantasy a bit further, consider the claim that the appropriate policy here is simply to prohibit, perhaps legally, children from playing in such yards; after all, for the reason mentioned they are, by assumption, incompetent with respect to such

---

[10] The basic idea is introduced and developed in Wikler's "Paternalism and the Mildly Retarded."

a task. This proposal may strike us as too glib, and it is instructive to ask why. The examples make it clear that there are some cases where (1) the risks associated with an activity are socially created (we build the expressway) and some where they are not (the sharks were not put there by people), and (2) in some cases reduction or elimination of the risks associated with a certain activity are socially remediable (the yard can be fenced in) and in other cases it is difficult or impossible to do so (in extensive waters we cannot readily fence in the sharks or persuade them to go elsewhere). In some cases, then, the fact that certain persons cannot competently perform certain tasks is a result of social arrangements. Some who could ride a horse competently cannot competently drive motor vehicles; such persons, therefore, may not be competent readily to get about in a technologically complex society. Apart from whether the risks associated with certain tasks are socially created, the more important fact may be that certain tasks, or certain types of tasks, can be made such that they can be competently performed by persons who, in the absence of such socially chosen risk reduction, could not competently engage in them. Compare again the example of the child and the expressway. A major point with respect to certain types of incompetences is that they are not engraved in stone, and the fact that certain persons are incompetent at certain tasks is not a fixed, unalterable, fact. Prohibiting such persons from the performance of such tasks is not the only means of preventing their risking serious harms to themselves or others.

As Wikler rightly notes, many of our social arrangements and practices are designed around the existing levels of ability and skill possessed by most people or at least the majority of adults. To that extent, it is not surprising that a significant minority of persons fail to be competent at the performance of a wide variety of tasks. A society many of whose practices are geared to the level of ability and skill possessed only by the most naturally gifted would result in counting a much larger number of persons as incompetent. Certain kinds of incompetence are in part, in the manner noted, social creations. It is also worth observing here that although much of the socially induced incompetence is in some sense inadvertent, we may reasonably classify some as deliberate or at least as foreseen consequences of social policies and laws that are avoidable. To the extent that invidious discrimination is, or has been, practiced against blacks, women, native Americans, and other groups, they have often been prevented from developing the skills, or acquiring the knowledge, necessary for the competent performance of certain tasks (e.g., careers as pilots, lawyers, dentists, physicians, or electricians) even though possessing the natural aptitudes and talents sufficient to succeed. Although the possession of a certain level of skill is necessary in order to be a competent surgeon and this is a comparatively objective matter (not just a byproduct of social preference), whether given individuals come to qualify as competent or incompetent in this respect depends in part on social practices, ones which affect access to skills sufficient for this type of competence. Invidious discrimination of the sort mentioned is the most visible type of socially induced incompetence. The social component in the "generation" of incompetence in the retarded is easier to overlook. A somewhat stronger point is worth making here: a social component is often involved in *who counts* as incompetent, retarded, or disabled. One way of seeing this more clearly is to imagine a primitive society, possibly a hunter-gatherer sort, in which the most demanding tasks are much simpler than the most demanding tasks in our own society. In such a case, given a similar distribution of innate talents as in our society, fewer persons would fail at the most complex tasks.[11] If so, it is less likely that certain groups of persons would be classified as generally incompetent or retarded. Much of the talent of the most gifted would go unnoticed and be a surplus rather than a prerequisite for competence. Correlatively, the limitations of the slower would be less likely to emerge as "incompetence at normal tasks."

If it is agreed that a social component enters into our classification of some as incompetent with respect to particular tasks or as gen-

[11] Who counts as generally competent, then, is partly a function of the prevailing, recognized, threshold for general competence in a particular cultural epoch. Thus, "relativism" seems to rear its head once more. However, the type of relativism that is recognized here is, I suggest, innocuous. If an Oxford philosopher, whom we may suppose to be a generally competent person, were left to survive in the wilds of New Guinea, he (or she) might well be regarded as generally incompetent by the natives; suppose, for example, he cannot effectively kill animals for food or otherwise take care of basic personal needs. He, no doubt, would remain competent at whatever he was previously competent at; still, he would not only be *regarded*, or counted, as incompetent by the natives (let us assume) but also *be* incompetent at certain important tasks in that locale. There is, then, no bald inconsistency here to the effect that "he is competent and he is not." Further, his possibly extensive range of incapacities may be the basis for legitimate but otherwise wrongful paternalistic interventions—a point similar to our earlier concession that persons generally competent in their normal habitat may undergo episodes of incompetence or, aside from actual loss of capacities, may confront particular situations which they cannot competently manage. The threshold for general competence may vary from context to context, and understandably so. Employing such a criterion, however, does not commit us to the view that recognized thresholds are arbitrary or purely a matter of private taste.

erally incompetent, the crucial questions remain. What follows regarding our dealings with those who turn out to be incompetent? Is there a justification for the sorts of restrictions we place on the incompetent? Again, if there is, is it grounded in paternalistic or nonpaternalistic considerations?

7.6 The Costs of a Safer World

Our revised principle, RHPP, is a principle of permissibility and not obligation. When certain conditions are satisfied, it permits placing on incompetents restrictions which are among the least harmful alternatives in order to prevent greater harms from accruing to the subjects. Our prior discussion makes it clear, however, that we often have a choice. We can (1) simply prohibit incompetents from engaging in certain activities (again, restrictions on voting, marrying, bearing children, adopting children, financially contracting, or other imposed disabilities), or (2) make efforts to arrange things so that otherwise incompetent parties can competently engage in certain activities. Certain analogies are useful here. We can prohibit those in wheelchairs from attempting to use buses or we can outfit buses with mechanical lifts. We can prohibit the visually impaired from driving or restrict their driving to daylight hours and/or doing so only with corrective lenses. We can prohibit the severely retarded from bearing children or require that such children be placed for adoption. We can prohibit the seriously handicapped from working in certain risk-laden environments or we can create safer working environments.

In some cases a means of preventing those impaired in some fashion from suffering serious harm or risk of harm would be to make the world safer for those incompetents who prefer to engage in activities which, as things may stand, are exceedingly risky. From the standpoint of the incompetents this may be the most welcome alternative, for it does not necessarily exclude them from certain desired practices or opportunities; rather it delimits the manner in which they may be performed. Analogously, the child might prefer being able to play in a yard where the risks are "fenced out" rather than being prohibited from playing in an otherwise risk-laden yard. RHPP is somewhat indeterminate concerning what to do about our general dilemma, one which we may refer to as the choice between "prohibiting or facilitating" otherwise risky activities.

An important problem here concerns the *costs* of facilitating.

Since RHPP is a principle of permissibility, it leaves open, as permissible, the choice by competent persons to go to expensive lengths to arrange the world so as to make it safer for otherwise incompetent parties to pursue certain activities. That is, interveners may bear the costs if they wish, so long as others are not thereby wronged. The harder question is whether any particular competent person, or society in general, has a *duty* to bear the costs of rendering certain avenues of endeavor safe for those who cannot otherwise competently pursue them. It is reasonable to think that there is no objection to voluntary efforts by individuals, individually or collectively, bearing the costs to make the world safer for themselves (in ways which wrong no others, e.g., members of a neighborhood fairly and jointly dividing the costs of setting up a crime-prevention program). It is quite likely, of course, that the costs of making the world safer for the incompetent will not be borne by them but by others. On the question which faces us, Wikler judiciously says:

> To change society so that mild mental retardation would be no handicap in any of the tasks in question might reduce the economic and social value of the relevant practices, thereby shifting hardships from the retarded onto those of normal and high intelligence. I have no way of estimating the degree of hardship at stake. If it is substantial enough to seriously impede economic and social functioning, perhaps the majority, which consists of normal persons, would have no obligation to change present practices so radically. *Some* redistribution of burdens, however, is undoubtedly in order.[12]

I will not attempt to explore in detail the extent to which society (or the normal and the gifted) has an obligation to make the world safer for incompetents. However, several considerations seem relevant here. First, in some cases it may be virtually impossible to make the world safer for some in a way that actually increases the liberty of incompetents on balance. For example, there may be no effective way of enabling incompetents (or some) to drive cars, fly planes, or deep-sea dive. In some cases activities can be made safe only at inordinate costs to others, for example, in providing constant human guides to the blind or personal monitors of the activities of those otherwise impaired.

Further, there is an additional complication which I have hitherto

[12] Wikler, "Paternalism and the Mildly Retarded," pp. 391–392.

ignored. The term 'incompetent' calls to mind those who are *in-voluntarily* impaired in some significant respect. However, given our analysis of incompetence in terms of inability to perform certain tasks, or sets of tasks, it not only covers the significantly retarded, the senile, and the special category of protocompetents (children); it also includes those who may suffer ongoing disabilities as a result of their own *voluntary* acts. Such persons may be generally or specifically incompetent even though they were, formerly, generally competent. For example, consider those paralyzed as a result of voluntary chosen, risk-laden, activities, for example, those seriously impaired by voluntarily pursued drug usage. Such persons may not have been dealt a weak hand by the natural lottery or even the social lottery. Special questions arise about responsible moral agents who have, by voluntary act (though not, in *one* sense, "intentionally") brought it about that they are generally incompetent or incompetent with respect to certain types of tasks. It is not obvious that any duty to alleviate, or make lighter, their burdens would be as stringent as any duty to those who exercised little or no influence over their current plight. In this regard it is important not to assume that apparently voluntary risk taking must be genuinely voluntary (consider the case of soldiers disabled because of fighting a war into which they were conscripted).

A further issue concerns whether the distribution (or more aptly: the redistribution) of the burdens of incompetence is solely a matter of distributive justice. Wikler concludes his explorations by suggesting that "the morality of paternalism reduces to a question about distributive justice."[13] This claim seems too strong; for even if there is a duty paternalistically to provide a safer world for incompetents derivative from considerations of social justice (a point to which we shall return), there is also a question about what sorts of paternalistic acts toward incompetents are *permissible* even if they are not *owed* to incompetents as a matter of justice. It is generally recognized that some acts benefitting others are normally beyond the call of duty (e.g., donating a kidney to a stranger). Further, not all duties toward others seem to be duties of justice, unless one dubiously equates 'duties toward others' with 'duties of justice.' Hence there are reasons to doubt that "the morality of paternalism *reduces* to a question about distributive justice" (my italics). Nevertheless, it is instructive to ask whether the leading

[13] Ibid., p. 392.

363

theories of social justice can help in our effort to determine what we owe the incompetent.

7.7 Justice Toward Incompetents: Three Theories

Given the reservations just noted it may remain that much that is owed generally incompetent persons *is* a matter of social justice, and this complex issue deserves our examination. We have characterized generally incompetent persons as lacking certain basic rational capacities and abilities, and these are understood to be rather global in nature even if persons in our broad category exhibit localized pockets of competence with respect to a number of particular tasks.[14] As such, the generally incompetent cannot control and direct their own lives—safely, without engendering serious danger to themselves or others. It is worth focusing briefly on the "dangerousness to others" feature. Establishing that a given individual is in fact likely to harm seriously, or otherwise wrong, others is no easy task, and there are empirical difficulties involved in doing so reliably. Let us suppose that doing so is possible in principle even if current approaches should be viewed with a healthy skepticism. Given that some incompetents may act so as to pose a serious danger to others, there is clearly a nonpaternalistic ground for coercively restricting the liberties of such persons. Indeed, the social duty to protect innocents from wrongful harm naturally is viewed as a duty of justice. If the incompetence of those who wrongfully harm others is sufficiently thoroughgoing, they may be viewed as "innocent threats" to innocent parties and, hence, not morally to blame for their acts. In the case in which the incompetent criminally wrongs others and is rightly judged mentally insane at the time of the act, the insanity exculpates the incompetent from criminal liability. Still, there are legitimate grounds for coercive restraint, that is, the protection of innocents against such threats. Hence, part of what justice requires with regard to incompetents is restraint of those who are serious threats to others. The more recalcitrant question regarding the linkage between justice and the treatment of incompetents concerns what *benefits* must be provided incompetents as a matter of justice. This is a question with implications for both incompetents who ought to be severely

[14] To emphasize a point, attribution of such incapacities is understood to be based on performance oriented criteria, and performance of normal tasks as opposed to performance on tests whose assessment relies on dubious theoretical assumptions, e.g., so-called "intelligence-quotient" tests.

364

restrained (e.g., are incompetents who are justly committed to an institution owed therapeutic treatment?) and those who justly cannot be severely restrained.

To answer the question of what benefits are owed the incompetent as a matter of justice requires that we are able to identify a satisfactory theory of justice. That is, we must know which of a number of competing theories of justice is the right, or the most defensible, one. Then and only then could we trace its implications for our dealings with incompetents and rightly rely on them. Properly adjudicating among the leading current theories of justice is an enormous task and far beyond my purview here. Nevertheless, it may be useful to strike a glancing blow or two at this problem. Indeed, there is reason to think that a number of leading theories fail to provide desirable guidance with respect to our perplexities about incompetents. Exhibiting such failings may bring us closer to a more reasonable view. I shall, with painful brevity, consider (1) extreme libertarianism, (2) utilitarianism, (3) perfectionism, and, in the next section, (4) Rawlsian approaches.[15]

One of the more sophisticated defenses of a rather *extreme libertarian view* is that found in Robert Nozick's influential book, *Anarchy, State, and Utopia*.[16] At the core of Nozick's position is the claim that all people have certain natural rights and, as a result, there are things no one else can justifiably do to them. Nozick does not exhaustively list the rights which he attributes to people, but central, in his view, is a right not to be coerced and, perhaps, a right not to be controlled by fraud. Such acts are unjustified, except as a means of defense against those who wrongfully transgress the rights of innocent others. This characterization involves certain simplifications, and Nozick instructively acknowledges difficulties which I here set aside. The mentioned rights are commonly classified as *negative* rights since other parties have, on this view, correlative duties to refrain from acts which would infringe such rights; there are things they must *not* do.

Nozick seems to deny the existence of any *positive* rights except those which may arise from voluntary agreements or gifts (the latter rights are often called "special" as opposed to "general," "natural," or "human" rights). A right is labeled a positive one if the duty to respect such a right involves the performance of a positive act or

---

[15] By 'Rawlsian' I mean the views of John Rawls in *A Theory of Justice* (Cambridge, Mass.: Belknap Press of Harvard University, 1971), and views inspired by Rawls' position.

[16] See Robert Nozick, *Anarchy, State, and Utopia* (New York: Basic Books, 1974).

a commission. Hence, if you mutually contract with Goodwrench to fix your car, you have a positive right that it be fixed, and Goodwrench a duty to provide certain services for you. Similarly, on Nozick's view, no one has a right against others that they provide benefits or services unless it arises from a prior voluntary act. Nozick's theory, vastly oversimplified here, has a number of plausible implications, for example, if I need a kidney transplant I cannot claim one of your kidneys as a matter of right, in the absence of your voluntary gift of it or your voluntarily contracting to provide it. Analogously, governments do not have a just claim on our bodily parts, our income, or our services in the absence of our voluntary choice to provide them.[17]

Nozick's theory, and libertarian theories in general, exude a certain attraction when one's gaze is fixed upon a variety of interactions involving competent adults. Their implications for our dealings with infants, children, and other incompetents seem more troublesome. Perhaps for that reason, such theories, as noted earlier, exhibit a tendency to promulgate doctrines which ignore pressing moral questions about our relations with those who are either incompetent or are not members of our species.[18] For our purposes the crucial point is that those who are not capable of acquiring positive rights against others by contracting, for example, children and other incompetents, are left only with natural negative rights or whatever positive rights they may have been granted by the voluntary choices of those capable of doing so, presumably: competent persons. One puzzle here concerns whether, on such a view, children have any positive rights, against their parents, to be cared for in positive ways, rights which are not contingent on the voluntary choice of parents to provide such care. Similarly, do incompetent persons have any positive rights against their parents or against society to be provided with benefits, rights which are not contingent on the voluntary choices of such parties to provide such benefits?

The seeming implication of Nozick's view is that neither children nor incompetents have such rights in the absence of others' voluntarily choosing to provide them. Nozick might well say that it

[17] It should be noted, however, that in Nozick's view, unlike anarchist views, the existence of a minimal state is morally justifiable and, hence, so are taxes necessary to pursue the legitimate, albeit limited, functions of such a state.
[18] There are important exceptions to this generalization; for example, Nozick takes seriously, and thoughtfully discusses, questions about the moral status of animals. See his *Anarchy, State, and Utopia*, Chapter 3.

is morally permissible or even praiseworthy to provide such benefits, but our question is whether it is impermissible *not* to provide certain benefits to such categories of persons. There are numerous complexities which arise here and various responses a libertarian might make, ones which I shall not explore, but, in brief, there is a strong presumption that on Nozick's theory there is no duty of justice to lighten the burdens of incompetence by rearranging society, when it is possible, in order to alleviate such burdens. The noted implication that even children may have no natural rights to be positively benefitted by their natural parents is, I think, radically counterintuitive and itself casts serious suspicion on the adequacy of libertarian ethical theories which tend to be oriented toward very competent, adult contractors. Although our duties toward those who cannot well fend for themselves, or cannot do so at all, may have important limits (compare current disputes over duties to animals or duties toward starving peoples), theories which imply no duties at all are not initially plausible, even if they exhibit a healthy antipaternalistic streak with regard to our dealings with competent persons and there rightly stress the importance of voluntary choice, consent, or dissent. Given these difficulties I shall, after one transitional step, turn to a consideration of utilitarianism.

Prior to examining utilitarian approaches to the question of justice toward incompetents, it is worth stressing some distinctions within the category of the generally incompetent. They are relevant to our later assessments. Within this category are those who are profoundly impaired. The main impairments I have in mind concern the inability to reason or the presence of a reasoning capacity which functions only in the most primitive way, and the absence of conscious preferences or, if they are minimally present, any barely stable ordering of them. Such a characterization is crude but it may serve to pick out those incompetents lacking a capacity for reasoned choice or a capacity for conscious satisfaction that is more than merely the absence of visceral discomfort. Such persons may include normal infants and toddlers, the profoundly retarded, some psychotics, the thoroughly senile, and the comatose. Given their potential for competence, *some* of these persons have a stake in the future, their future development toward competence, that others do not. That is a point worth keeping in mind, although I shall not dwell on it. The main focus is on those profoundly incompetent who shall remain so. By contrast, there are those incompetents who, to one degree or another, have a nontrivial capacity to reason, have conscious preferences, awareness of themselves as continuing entities and as agents who can affect their own lives and the lives of others. To some extent or another they can choose and be responsible for their choices. Although virtually all incompetents, except the comatose, are sentient (can experience pain), the most profoundly retarded substantially lack the capacity for felt satisfaction from fulfillment of conscious preferences. Further, given their lack of capacities they are not moral agents; that is, since they lack the wherewithal deliberately to choose and control their actions, there is no reasonable ground for imputing moral responsibility to them for their behavior. For example, it would be absurd to mete out criminal penalties to toddlers who start fires; similarly for the psychotic who does not know what she is doing. To say that such incompetents are not moral agents is not to deny them moral standing, for example, as lacking morally relevant interests or rights. Those incompetents who *are* moral agents may and do exhibit diminished capacity (at least for certain types of acts) and, hence, diminished responsibility (compare a normal eight-year-old who starts a fire). These differences among incompetents are relevant to assessing the implications of utilitarian, perfectionistic, and Rawlsian theories concerning what we owe them.

Let us, then, turn to *utilitarian approaches to justice*. A thorough examination of utilitarianism is a task demanding book-length treatment and hence is far beyond my purview here. The complexity of such a task is generated in substantial part by the fact that the classical utilitarian ethical theory has numerous descendants, versions of utilitarianism of various forms. Hence, our discussion will be succinct. As we earlier noted, the central principle of classical utilitarianism is that one ought to do whatever act will maximize total net utility or good.[19] Utility is typically identified with intrinsically good states of affairs, and the latter are understood to be felt satisfaction (or pleasure) on the classical view, or the existence of various states of affairs (e.g., friendship, beauty), including pleasure, on pluralistic views such as that of G. E. Moore, and preference fulfillment (as opposed to *felt* satisfaction from the fulfillment of preferences) on a more recent version. All of these

[19] An alternative formulation is that one ought to perform whatever act will bring about at least as much good, or utility, as any alternative act. Those unfamiliar with utilitarianism might consult the discussion in William Frankena, *Ethics* (Englewood Cliffs, N.J.: Prentice-Hall, 1963) or the introductory but most thorough discussion in Dan Brock's "Utilitarianism," in *And Justice for All*, eds. Tom Regan and Donald VanDeVeer (Totowa, N.J.: Rowman and Littlefield, 1982), pp. 217–240.

versions of utilitarianism share the feature that the criterion of right action is couched in terms of the production of certain types of consequences. Further, the classical utilitarian focus is an aggregative one; the total net utility of any possible act is to be determined by *summing* the distinct net utilities (or disutilities) of each of the individuals affected by the performance of a particular act. Hence, emphasis on production of the "greatest good for the greatest number" is not to be understood as "what the majority prefers." What will produce the greatest total net utility may or may not accord with what the majority prefers. There is no room here, nor is it my intention, to elaborate the attractions of this resilient and extremely influential ethical viewpoint (some who deploy it are often not fully aware of their reliance on the utilitarian principle; for example, some advocates of cost-benefit analysis and interest-balancing approaches seem to fall in this category). However, the theory holds out the "virtues" of: being comprehensive; not being inflexibly committed to specific rigid rules (such as "never break a promise"); avoiding perplexities about the meaning of rights claims, the grounds for attributing rights, and conflicts of rights; yielding, in principle, specific action-guiding implications in all cases; being sensitive to empirical facts; implying a *plausible* form of moral relativism (since the utilities of performing the "same type" of act may vary with cultural contexts), and so on.

One of the important criticisms of utilitarianism is the claim that it ignores considerations of distributive justice, or, if it does take into account considerations of how goods (benefits, opportunities, utilities, etc.) are to be distributed, it does so only to the extent that such matters are a *means* toward seeking the overriding goal of maximization of total net utility. Since only the total *amount* of utility is decisive, there is no *fundamental* role for distributive principles nor any non-instrumental reason for recognizing moral constraints on the way utility is distributed among a population; this is so in spite of an egalitarian element in utilitarian theory, namely, that, at the stage of calculating which act among options will maximize total net utility, each individual is to count for one and like amounts of utility, or disutility, are to be given equal weight no matter who is the prospective recipient of them (e.g., regardless of race, gender, nationality, creed, etc.).[20]

[20] The classic utilitarians, Bentham and Mill, allowed that the relevant individuals to be considered included not only members of our species but also sentient animals; hence, utilitarian theory seems to embody a significant degree of impartiality in contrast, for example, to perfectionist theories.

A standard sort of example proposed by critics, and troublesome for utilitarians, is the following. Suppose that there are various parties, A, B, C, D, and E, who will suffer a great deal or die in their prime unless an innocent party, S, is killed against his will and his bodily parts redistributed among A through E so that each, respectively, may receive a kidney transplant, liver tranplant, cornea transplant, another kidney transplant, and a heart transplant. Suppose further that these persons have no special claim on S arising from a unilateral promise or contractual agreements. It is conceivable that S might be spirited away and killed painlessly— to minimize disutilities to S. Further, it is conceivable that S may be without friends or relatives and the whole operation may be kept secret—and that those who do the job are such convinced utilitarians that they believe that this deed will maximize total net utility and is, therefore, right; hence, they are liable to suffer "guilt pangs" only if they *fail* to act in this manner. This is an unlikely and, for most of us, a gory tale. Such an act, as described, is unlikely to occur, but the description does not seem incoherent. Nor does it seem incoherent that it might maximize total net utility—given the moderate disutility caused to S (imagine, further, S has lived a full life, is now moderately unhappy, and will die soon anyway!) and the enormous sum of utility to be produced for A through E by proceeding as described. Yet if the act would maximize total utility we *must* conclude that it is right—*if* we accept the principle of utility.

At this juncture, defenders of utilitarianism have several possible replies. They can (1) surrender the principle of utility; (2) deny that such an act (or *any* other troublesome and analogous act) would in fact maximize utility and, hence, the critics somehow miscalculate or incoherently describe; or (3) accept the implication and insist, "intuitions" aside ("after all, are not intuitions parochial, moral prejudices"?) that it really is right to terminate S's life and dismember him. It is worth noting that utilitarians, logically, must make one of these sorts of responses. Very few utilitarians seem willing to give up utilitarianism (by choosing (1)) or bite the bullet (by choosing (3)). Hence, the tendency is to defend (2) and castigate critics for invoking "fantastic" cases. It seems to me that utilitarians are an endangered species because their proffered defenses of (2) are unconvincing even if shrewd.[21] In cases such as that mentioned

---

[21] As a result, staunch utilitarians are fewer in number, and there has been what Brian Barry has called a shift from consequentialism to absolutism (which Barry defines as: acts are right or wrong according to their nature) as a *starting point* (my

they are driven to claim that, in reality, initially hidden disutilities would manifest themselves such that, as a matter of *contingent* fact, acts such as the one mentioned would not maximize total net utility. Further, the burden on utilitarians is to show that in *every* actual or hypothetical, relevantly similar, case, the principle of utility does not sanction grotesquely sacrificing the interests of innocent parties against their will. There is little reason to think that such efforts can invariably succeed in the indefinitely large number of situations in which such troublesome questions can or do arise. To make this point is not to assume that there are *no* "emergency situations" in which it would be justifiable to kill unconsenting innocent persons, nor is it to assume that consequences of our acts which significantly affect the well-being or ill-being of others are morally irrelevant. In brief, however, there is a very strong presumption that utilitarianism, in its focus on the *sum* of net individual utilities, cannot give adequate recognition to questions concerning the fairness of the *distribution* of benefits and burdens among individuals. Although this brief statement of a much-disputed issue does not begin to consider the complexities of the dialogue between utilitarians and their critics, I shall largely rest my case here.

If it is correct that utilitarianism sanctions morally intolerable acts, then that is a sufficient reason not to explore its acceptability any further, except to filter out those features of utilitarian theory worth preserving in order to build them into a viable ethical theory. The case for rejecting utilitarianism is only strengthened by other obstacles to accepting classic, and/or certain other versions of, utilitarianism: (1) its assignment of moral weight to the satisfactions (or want fulfillment) of "deviant" wants (e.g., a desire to rape or torture)—or the assignment of excessive moral weight to such satisfactions, (2) its difficulty in distinguishing between what is a matter of duty and what is supererogatory, (3) its tendency to focus on sentient beings, especially persons, as only utility containers to be filled up or emptied by the acts of other parties, rather than viewing persons as entities with their own conception of the good, as centers of choosing whose choices must be respected and honored in many cases even when such decisions are or may be imprudent (in this respect utilitarianism at the very outset tends to nudge its devotees toward an unduly paternalistic posture in some respects, e.g., the agent should maximize what is good even if its

italics); see Brian Barry, "And Who Is My Neighbor?," *Yale Law Review* 88, No. 3 (January, 1979), pp. 630–631.

beneficiaries dissent). This list is by no means exhaustive and, so far, has omitted what economists generally, and many philosophers, have thought to be the most serious difficulty, namely, the question of whether (cardinally) measuring utility is logically coherent and, if so, practically feasible.[22]

Even if utilitarianism were a viable ethical viewpoint, and I now assume it is not, there is little reason to believe that it would require much lightening of the burdens of incompetence, at least for those profoundly incapacitated. Although many such persons can suffer, most lack the capacities necessary for experiencing certain types of satisfactions or contentment; hence it is not clear that nontrivial sacrifices (cf. foregone utilities) by others would be counterbalanced by a sufficient increase in the utility levels of the severely incapacitated so as to generate a net increase in aggregate utility. A similar point holds, with fewer qualifications, for those incompetents who cannot be said to have preferences at all. Important from a utilitarian standpoint, of course, would be the fact that the social costs of alleviating the burdens, or improving the lives, of the severely incapacitated are likely to be quite high. Oversimplifying somewhat, the utilitarian presumption for such cases is that we ought to place our dollars (and efforts) where we can get more of a utility bang for our bucks. If so, our current comparative neglect of the most incompetent is liable to be the right policy, or perhaps insufficiently neglectful, given the goal of maximizing the sum of individual net utilities. There is much more to be said here, on both sides, but I will leave it to those more tempted by the sirens of utilitarianism.

Understanding, as we have, a theory of justice to be a systematic reasoned attempt to answer the question "how ought benefits (and burdens) be distributed?," it is clear that extreme libertarians tend to respond by saying that persons are entitled to whatever they naturally have a right to or that which they can acquire short of infringing others' rights, and utilitarians claim that people are "entitled" to whatever distribution of goods would maximize total utility. *Perfectionist theories* maintain that we ought to maximize the

---

[22] Those interested in exploring utilitarian theory more thoroughly might consult the mentioned books or articles by Frankena and Brock, but see also Michael Bayles, ed., *Contemporary Utilitarianism* (Garden City, N.Y.: Doubleday, 1968); David Lyons, *Forms and Limits of Utilitarianism* (Oxford: Clarendon Press, 1967); Bernard Williams and J.J.C. Smart, *Utilitarianism: For and Against* (Cambridge: Cambridge University Press, 1973); and Richard Brandt, *Ethical Theory* (Englewood Cliffs, N.J.: Prentice-Hall, 1959). For criticism, see Nozick, *Anarchy, State, and Utopia*, and Rawls, *A Theory of Justice*.

realization of human excellence, typically defined in terms of intellectual and aesthetic talents.[23] These three theories can thus agree with the formal, or nonsubstantive, view that justice involves distributing benefits so as to give every person (or every sentient being) his due. The substantive criteria to be employed in order to determine what each is due is the source of contention. On perfectionist approaches those most deserving of benefits (e.g., wealth, income, services, opportunities, etc.) are the most talented in the respects mentioned; those less deserving are the less talented. On such an approach there is a natural aristocracy, assuming the distribution of these talents is not uniform, and a just distribution, hence, must be a notably unequal one. Elements of this view can be found in Aristotle (as noted, he viewed some persons as "natural slaves") and in Nietzsche. The implications of perfectionism for our question regarding just dealings with incompetents are straightforward. Barring exceptions like the "idiot savant," the generally incompetent are entitled to a lesser share of benefits, and the severely retarded, for example, to very little. Anomalously, a moderately retarded person possessing considerable musical or artistic ability might be entitled, in this view, to a greater share of manna than a normal person who lacked any notable intellectual or aesthetic talent. Generally, however, a perfectionistic theory of justice sanctions little or no significant improvement in the lot of the generally incompetent.

We may plausibly concede that certain deeds are meritorious and that certain character traits exhibit excellence. In some contexts these in turn may be a reasonable basis for concluding that a disproportionate share of benefits is deserved by those who exhibit such excellences. Such a view is most plausible when those whom we are comparing have had something like a fair and equal opportunity to develop or achieve such excellences, for example, fair competition in a sport. By contrast, it seems foolish to conclude that those who are involuntarily incapacitated or who, involuntarily, have not had the opportunity to develop skills are deserving of lesser shares of certain basic goods, for example, liberty, opportunity, or the bases of self-respect (to mention some of those goods John Rawls refers to as "primary goods," i.e., those things virtually all persons want whatever else they may want). Thus, those temporarily, or permanently, and involuntarily blocked from

---

[23] I follow David A. J. Richard's characterization in *The Moral Criticism of Law* (Encino, Cal.: Dickenson, 1977), p. 270.

developing excellence, for example, children or the retarded, may not deserve certain prizes or rewards, but it does not follow that they are less deserving of a fair share of basic goods, such as the basic liberties, rights, or opportunities distributed by a society's fundamental institutions.

Although these remarks do not suffice to rebut all forms of perfectionism, they call attention to a most troublesome feature of perfectionist theories, namely, their tendency to assume that excellence of character or achievement among those who have had a fair, or "more than fair," opportunity to pursue such is not only a basis for a disproportionately large share of benefits in circumscribed voluntary activities (e.g., sports, business, education, the arts, or military affairs) but that it is *also* a reasonable ground for disproportionately large shares of basic goods distributed by society's more fundamental institutions (primarily those resulting from constitution making, and the legal and political system). Such a claim is not at all obvious and is presumptively objectionable in view of the fact that many of those failing to show excellence never had or will have the opportunity to develop the relevant capacities. In short, perfectionist theories indirectly assign a moral weight to chance which is hard to defend. In an important sense the Tay-Sachs afflicted child lacks excellence of intellect and achievement but she did not *fail* to be excellent. Thus, there is no basis for saying that her non-excellence is a ground for no, or for meager, benefits or opportunities. If there is a reasonable basis for so concluding, it must be located elsewhere. Perfectionism is a view toward which few are tempted, given its rather *unqualified* assignment of moral importance to the fortuitous exigencies of the natural lottery—and, to an extent, the social lottery (aside from getting the "right genes," some are lucky to be born into families which can afford medical care likely to avoid brain damage at birth; others are not, even if they got the "right genes"). What seems most objectionable about perfectionism is not its sanctioning of inequality but its proposed *basis* or criterion of what counts as a just distribution. Although our discussion is hardly thorough, I shall presume that perfectionism is an unpromising view and, hence, I explore it no further.[24]

[24] If we agree that benefits should not be distributed among persons along some contour etched out by measuring natural talents, there is a not unimportant question concerning the acceptability of systems of distribution which tend to reward the most talented and fail to reward the least talented. The one point I note here, then, is simply that if perfectionism is an arbitrary view, *unrestrained* capitalism, insofar as it has the mentioned tendency, is subject to a similar criticism for, *in part*, it doles out benefits in proportion to certain kinds of raw talents.

7.8 Incompetents and Rawls' Theory of Justice

The most influential theory of justice developed in this century is that found in John Rawls' *A Theory of Justice*, a work that has altered, in fundamental ways, the thinking and viewpoint of a considerable number of professional moral and political philosophers and whose ideas have generated a fresh dialogue between philosophers and others who work in the fields of economics, jurisprudence, medical ethics, political theory, and public policy. Again, it is impossible to convey here the sophistication and complexity of Rawls' theory (as it also was with regard to Nozick's theory, or recent work in utilitarianism). Still, it will be useful to summarize more fully its central ideas. They are of interest for reasons quite separate from our primary focus here but also because of their bearing on questions about paternalism and our recent concern with appropriate dealings with the incompetent. First I shall briefly review the core of Rawls' theory.

Claims about what is a fair or just distribution of goods are often flawed in an obviously suspect way: they exhibit an arbitrary favoritism toward the interests of those making the claims, for example, defenders of slavery in the United States during the nineteenth century often defended existing black-white inequalities on the grounds that blacks were worse off in their native land and would be worse off if living freely under the difficult industrial conditions prevailing for workers in northern cities. To surmount the barriers of rationalization and arbitrary prejudice, Rawls asks us imaginatively to enter into a hypothetical contractual situation in which we are to negotiate what principles or rules will govern our mutual interaction, especially the constraints on basic social institutions which will structure our mutual dealings. Participants in this hypothetical situation, are, however, figuratively placed behind a "veil of ignorance." Such contractors in what he calls the "original position," thus, are to be rational, "self-interested" (in one sense) persons who, though seeking their own advantage, are ignorant of certain features about themselves which they might exploit to gain partisan advantage. More fully, such participants are to decide on principles to regulate and determine the basic structure of fundamental social institutions. These in turn will determine the basic forms of social cooperation and interaction among persons in society. The principles chosen would be, in Rawls' view, principles of justice and would identify, at least in part, the sort of just treatment owed to individuals in a just society. The participants are under a veil of ignorance: they do not know what their own position in such a society would be, nor their gender, their talents, their particular conception of the good, their race, or even to what generation they would belong. Hence, they would not be able to choose principles which might differentially favor the positions they are to occupy. Their ignorance is to guarantee impartiality in the consideration of which principles to adopt. If such rational choosers of principles knew they were going to be males, the principles they would choose would be different from those chosen under the Rawlsian veil of ignorance; for example, a modified Difference Principle might be chosen: inequalities are permissible only if they maximize the benefits of the least advantaged *males*.[25] Such a principle would be arbitrary (from our standpoint) and its implications need no further comment. The original position, then, is designed to prevent a disregarding of the interests of any person or set of persons or any arbitrary favoring of the interests of some over the interests of others.

A comment is in order about the characterization of the participants as "self-interested." The expression "self-interested" normally suggests a conscious interest in promoting benefits for oneself to the exclusion of, or to the detriment of, the interests of others. But a participant cannot be self-interested in this sense, for he does not know which position he "will" occupy in the society whose institutions he is designing, that is, which self he will be. Hence, the concern can only be to adopt principles which will maximally facilitate anyone's flourishing as a rational chooser of ends. As Stephen Darwall has noted, given the veil of ignorance, a completely self-interested or a completely altruistic chooser could seek only to adopt impartial principles, and in that way, not those which are especially self-regarding or other-regarding.[26] A participant is "self-interested" *only* in the special sense that his interest in the flourishing of selves will include a concern for whichever self he might be on a lifting of the veil.

[25] Rawls, by contrast, claims two basic principles would be chosen; one is called the Difference Principle; loosely stated here, it maintains that inequalities in the distribution of primary goods (income, wealth, liberty, opportunity, the basis of self-respect) are permissible only if they redound to the benefit of the least advantaged.

[26] Previously, I have misread Rawls on the above point. Darwall credits Arthur Kuflik and Terry Moore for this insight. See Stephen Darwall, "Is There a Kantian Foundation for Rawlsian Justice?," in *John Rawls' Theory of Social Justice*, eds. H. Gene Blocker and Elizabeth H. Smith (Athens, Ohio: Ohio University Press, 1980), p. 323; also Stephen Darwall, *Impartial Reason* (Ithaca, N.Y.: Cornell University Press, 1983), p. 247.

What basic principles would be chosen in the hypothetical contractual situation? Rawls' reasoning here is complex, but, in brief, it proceeds in this way. Given that all participants have so much at stake (for their opportunities and well-being will be affected greatly by which principles are to constrain and shape the basic institutions governing their lives as participants in the society being designed), Rawls claims that they would proceed conservatively by adopting the *maximin rule* of choice: choose that alternative whose *worst* outcome is better than the *worst* outcome of any other available alternative.[27] Hence they would be averse to gambling with their "future" well-being. For example, some might argue for a system of slavery. If they should turn out to be masters, after the veil of ignorance is removed and the chosen principles implemented, they would gain immensely. But if they turn out to be slaves, then they would lose immensely. However, since the veil of ignorance prevents them from knowing their actual positions in society, it would not be rational for them to endorse a principle that might condemn them to the worst possible social position. Without attempting to elaborate fully the reasoning of such participants in the original position, as Rawls projects it, he claims that two principles would be chosen (often labeled the *Liberty Principle* and the *Difference Principle*, respectively):

1. Each person is to have an equal right to the most extensive total system of equal basic liberties compatible with a similar system of liberty for all.
2. Social and economic inequalities are to be arranged so that they are both: (a) *to the greatest benefit of the least advantaged* . . . , and (b) attached to offices and positions open to all under conditions of fair equality of opportunity.[28] (my italics)

Rawls claims that such principles, chosen under conditions preventing anyone from arbitrarily pressing for special personal advantage, are the fundamental principles of justice. For reasons I shall not elaborate here, Rawls' theory is most attractive and seems

[27] This principle is also labeled the minimax principle. It contrasts with other principles such as the less conservative *maximax* principle: choose that alternative whose *best* outcome is better than the *best* outcome of any other available alternative. Both principles are candidates for being the principle or standard of rational choice under conditions of uncertainty, i.e., choosing when there is no firm basis for assigning probabilities to different outcomes.

[28] Strictly, the quoted principles are Rawls' "first formulation." Also, "the Difference Principle" is sometimes used to refer to 2. without the inclusion of (b). See Rawls, *A Theory of Justice*, p. 60.

to circumvent many of the serious objections confronting the theories of justice already discussed. A full assessment of the theory would require exploring a number of questions: (1) is the device of the original position adequate to justify the mentioned principles? (2) would participants in it actually choose the principles Rawls claims they would choose? (3) is the veil of ignorance designed so as to insure complete neutrality?, and (4) are the implications of the two principles independently reasonable?[29] Here our focus continues to be on what justice requires with regard to our dealings with the generally incompetent. Both of Rawls' principles seem to have implications for this matter. At a later point I shall explore these implications, but initially it is worth noting an anomalous aspect of Rawls' theory with regard to the severely incompetent, namely, those so incapacitated as to fail to count as moral agents and themselves to lack the capacities to have a sense of justice. Let us return to the viewpoint of those in the original position.

It does not seem contrary to the presuppositions of Rawls' heuristic device to think of the participants in the original position as yet-to-be embodied or yet-to-be-born souls at least temporarily having the sophisticated capacities rationally to consider alternatives (e.g., the subtleties of the maximax and maximin decision principles). If the participants knew they were going to *retain* this high degree of rational capacity on coming to function in the society whose basic design they are determining, they might, concerned to promote the flourishing of such beings, choose principles which would yield highly favorable treatment of more rational members of that society. So the continued retention of such rational capacities cannot be supposed by the participants. They should assume, I shall maintain, that they may turn out to be among the least advantaged, including the possibility of being among the least rational or the most incompetent. Indeed they may be victims of the natural lottery, for example, ugly, retarded, or deformed. At the same time they must suppose that they are going to interact with others in the society whose basic structure is under consideration. Were they to be transformed into rocks after their "moment of glory" as founders of a just society for humans, presumably they would have no concern about inequalities *among humans* in such a society. So,

---

[29] Those interested might consult, in addition to *A Theory of Justice*, Norman Daniels, ed., *Reading Rawls* (New York: Basic Books, 1980); Brian Barry, *The Liberal Theory of Justice* (Oxford: Clarendon Press, 1973); and Robert Paul Wolff, *Understanding Rawls* (Princeton: Princeton University Press, 1977).

our temporarily highly rational contractors should suppose, at most, that they will be humans, however disadvantaged in the society being designed.

This view, however, is in conflict with that of Rawls. Rawls claims that, strictly, not all persons are owed just treatment according to the principles the contractors would choose. Persons are owed such treatment, he claims, *if* and *only if* they are "moral persons" (not to be understood as "virtuous persons").[30] What is to be understood by 'moral person'? On Rawls' view a moral person is (1) a person with a capacity for a sense of justice, and (2) a person who has a conception of his good as expressed by a rational plan of life. There are humans who do not satisfy these conditions, but he believes that the "overwhelming majority of mankind" do and "therefore this question does not raise a serious practical problem."[31] Suppose that only one percent of humanity fail to be moral persons on Rawls' criteria. We would have, then, about forty million humans who are not, *strictly*, owed just treatment. Perhaps these include, for example, anencephalic infants, the seriously psychotic, Tay-Sachs children, the quite senile, the irreversibly comatose, and possibly a subset of Down's syndrome persons. There is no obvious reason to think that Rawls would deny that certain duties are owed to such human beings, though it is not entirely clear why, in his view, they are not owed just treatment even if *certain* requirements of justice on Rawls' view might be vacuous or pointless if provided for, say, the seriously retarded, for example, that all positions in the society are open to them. Rawls might have said that just treatment is owed these persons *insofar* as they are capable of enjoying its benefits or protections. However plausible such a view might be, Rawls does not take this position. He does say that "it would be unwise in practice" to withhold just treatment from these persons[32] who, on his view, do not satisfy the conditions sufficient for being owed just treatment. We are left without criteria for determining what is "unwise in practice" (except: whatever would cause too great a risk to just institutions) though not required by the principles of justice. He does maintain that the conditions specified, (1) and (2), are only "sufficient" for being owed just treatment and "not at all stringent." Still, to conclude that persons failing to satisfy these conditions are *not owed* just treatment seems to presuppose that satisfaction of (1) and (2) *is necessary*, in order

[30] See Section 77 of *A Theory of Justice*.
[31] Ibid.
[32] Ibid.

379

to be owed just treatment, in spite of Rawls's unwillingness to claim as much. It is therefore curious that at one point Rawls states that the "only contingency which is decisive is that of having or not having the capacity for a sense of justice." So we are left puzzled as to why we ought to extend just treatment to beings who are, in his view, not owed it, or, alternatively, why it is wise in practice to do so even when such beings are not owed such treatment.[33]

Among sources of inequality, the "accidents of birth" will result in the fact that some humans are born with serious defects and limited capacities; the genotype of others will lead to their being more attractive, in possession of superior skills and better health. Since no one *does* anything to deserve these traits they are, on Rawls' view, factors which are morally arbitrary. One would think that a just society would attempt to mitigate, if not nullify, the influence these factors would have on the unequal quality of people's lives.[34] Concerned participants in the original position, recognizing the possibility that *they* might be among those who would be seriously disadvantaged as a result of the natural lottery, then, would have good reason to choose principles which alleviate the plight of those so disadvantaged. Hence, in Rawls' view, the principle that inequalities are to be permitted only if they maximize the index of primary goods of the least advantaged would be chosen. Such a principle is, then, on Rawls' view, a principle of justice and identifies duties of just treatment owed to the least advantaged. This conclusion, however, seems inconsistent with the previously noted view of Rawls, that just treatment is *not* owed to those humans who fail to be moral persons (though it would, he claims, be wise to extend it to them in practice). The appearance of inconsistency exists, I think, for the following reasons. Participants in the original position are assumed to be concerned to promote the flourishing of selves and would recognize the possibility that they may occupy the position of beings who fail to have a capacity for a sense of justice and, hence, would fail to be moral persons (on

[33] In the preceding and following section I have relied substantially on remarks in my essay, "Of Beasts, Persons, and the Original Position," *The Monist* 62, No. 3 (July, 1979), pp. 368–377.

[34] There is a deeper problem here. Should we disfigure the more attractive in order to mitigate inequalities of attractiveness among persons or placate envious and unattractive parties? Should we coercively transplant organs to benefit the least advantaged? Nozick presses these points, rightly, I think, against Rawls' Difference Principle. Rawls, I believe, wants to answer negatively. Whether his theory yields a negative answer and whether it plausibly does so because of its assignment of priority to the Liberty Principle over the Difference Principle are further questions which I shall not explore.

Rawls' criterion). Given this rational concern they would choose a principle designed to secure certain benefits for the least advantaged. Surely, the category of the least advantaged would include not only badly off "moral persons" but those so seriously incapacitated as to be sentient yet not moral persons, for example, the severely retarded. As noted earlier, the participants cannot assume that they will "retain" their high degree of rationality or even their capacity for a sense of justice. For if they knew this they would choose principles favoring those with a modicum (or higher degree) of rationality. But the point of the veil of ignorance was to disallow the participants from choosing partial principles or "to be guided by their prejudices."[35]

It may be objected that Rawls is consistent, nevertheless, for the participants in Rawls' design of the original position do know, in spite of the veil of ignorance, that in the society whose basic principles they are determining, they will have a conception of the good. Further, this guarantees that they will be moral persons. So in choosing principles designed to benefit the least advantaged *moral persons*, they act rationally and with impartial concern. So, the resulting principles of justice do not require that just treatment is owed those who fail to be moral persons. So, no inconsistency obtains.

The objection, I believe, is correct; there need not be any inconsistency between (1) Rawls' insistence that those who are not moral persons are not owed just treatment and (2) his claim that one principle chosen (the Difference Principle) permits only those inequalities which benefit the least advantaged rational persons. Even if there is no inconsistency, there remains the difficulty at which I have hinted. It is simply this. Should not the veil of ignorance exclude the knowledge that all members of the society will have a concept of the good or of justice? Only if it is excluded can the participants succeed in adopting principles truly impartial between the least advantaged *moral* persons and those disadvantaged, yet sentient, members of the society who *fail* to be moral persons. The rationale of the veil of ignorance, on Rawls' own view, is to guarantee impartial consideration of principles. A veil of ignorance which achieves this end, then, must exclude such knowledge. Hence, a proper veil would result, conceding Rawlsian assumptions about rational choice here, in the choice of principles which would entail duties of justice to moral persons *and* those

---

[35] *A Theory of Justice*, p. 19.

humans who fail to be moral persons. If so, Rawls' claim that no duties of just treatment are owed the latter must be abandoned.

If the original position were designed in a more neutral way, it would not require that participants in the original position (let us call them 'participants OP') know that they shall have a concept of the good and a rational life plan on becoming participants in the resulting just society (let us call the latter 'participants JS'). Some participants JS will, as a result of the natural lottery, fail to have such capacities. Truly impartial participants OP, constrained by a proper veil of ignorance, will recognize this possibility. The participants OP should choose principles for all beings with nonderivative, morally relevant, interests, roughly for beings of whom one can sensibly speak of "their well-being or ill-being" even though *they* lack a conception of the good or their own good. The maximin rule requires choosing basic principles whose worst outcome (when applied) would make participants JS *better off* than the worst outcome of the application of any alternative principle. So, participants OP at least must assume that they are choosing principles to regulate interaction among beings who have morally significant interests, who could be better off or worse off. But this is true of *any sentient being whether or not it has the capacity for a sense of justice or a rational life plan*, and whether such a sentient creature is a moral person or not. For this reason the supposition that participants OP are deciding on principles to regulate interaction between moral persons is stronger than is necessary for participants OP to have a rational ground for preferring some principles over others; the weaker assumption that principles are to regulate interaction among sentient beings is strong enough to "motivate" *some* choice of principles in a choice situation somewhat like the original position, although not in the same fashion as Rawls suggests. I shall return to this important point shortly.

The assumption, by those in OP, that they will have a conception of the good and certain associated rational capacities as participants JS "motivates" members of OP to secure certain protections for themselves by adopting principles such as those Rawls proposes. This notion is perfectly intelligible. However, to emphasize a point, if the picture of human lives possessed by participants OP is not to be distorted unduly by a myopic veil of ignorance, they must, I maintain, both (1) recognize the *possibility* of "becoming" humans who are severely disabled or retarded and, thus, possibly lacking the capacities postulated as a characteristic of members OP, and (2) recognize that if they were to become such burdened humans they would still want certain guarantees that their lives could be decent ones—perhaps so long as the provision of such minima would not render the lives of others intolerable.[36]

However, participants OP *also* must look for the concerns of those who will be moral persons JS, those highly enabled agents with a developed conception of the good and a sense of justice. A focus only on the possibility of becoming merely sentient creatures, or incompetent humans, would also be myopic. Intuitively, a more neutral design of the original position would require consideration of all these possibilities. Rawls' design is too narrow for it disallows serious consideration of, and adoption of, principles of justice which would protect beings with moral standing though not moral persons. A contrary design which focused only on considerations concerning the protection of self-regarding interests (narrowly conceived) of interest possessors properly would include all beings with moral standing. However, it would fail to discriminate between the stringent standards required to respect (and promote the flourishing of) moral persons and the less demanding standards required to respect and promote the interests of the merely sentient or the permanently incompetent. A more neutral design would have participants OP consider the possibility of being in the position of any organism with moral standing; it would also motivate the participants to adopt principles to protect the diverse types of good and conceptions of the good which are associated (if they are) with beings of various relevant capacities. Such a more neutral design is less likely to lead to the counterintuitive implications of Rawls' current blueprint, one which is compatible with the view that, for example, it would not be *unjust* to perform highly risky, nontherapeutic, experiments only on the profoundly retarded. Rawls' own method of revising a theory so that it coheres with our considered moral judgments requires, I maintain, the noted revision of Rawls' fertile development of the concept that principles of justice are precisely those principles which rational choosers under impartial circumstances would adopt in order to adjudicate conflicting morally relevant goals and interests.

The revision I have proposed is grounded in part on the assumption that the concept of justice concerns the appropriate distribution of benefits and burdens (or opportunities for such) among all beings capable of having or lacking a morally relevant good of

[36] Once more, not wanting the lives of others to be intolerable is not a smuggling in of altruism; participants OP recognize that they may occupy the position of these "others."

their own, the class, it is sometimes labeled, of beings with moral standing. This class, I assume, includes but is larger than the class of all highly rational humans, all rational humans, or all rational beings. At least certain incompetent humans are included as well. I shall not pursue the point here, but possession of sentience seems sufficient and necessary for having moral standing and for being owed some duties of justice. However, this view need not assume that all such beings are capable of the same sort of good or primary good. For example, beings incapable of rationality cannot have self-respect; hence, they cannot be owed, as a matter of justice, the bases of self-respect. What they may be owed is a fair *opportunity* for the best life of which they are capable. What will count as such would depend on the array of capacities possessed. These matters are complex (hence, the disputes over permissible treatment of incompetent humans as well as sentient nonhuman animals). In brief, however, the view that justice is owed only to moral persons or rational humans is in tension with our considered judgments about just dealings.

Although participants in the original position, on any plausible version of it, must possess sophisticated rational capacities, they need not and ought not assume that the principles of just inter-action, which they are to consider and decide on, are to focus only on moral persons—any more than they are to be concerned only with the flourishing of males. Rather, a more neutrally conceived choice situation would be one in which principles would be chosen to adjudicate conflicts between any beings with moral standing— all moral patients whether or not they are also moral agents. The participants, so conceived, are trustees who are to look out for the diverse array of beings with a morally relevant good of their own (whether this includes an interest in rationally formulating and revising ends or the simpler interest of those I earlier labeled as mere wantons). Participants in Rawls' design are also like trustees (in some respects) in that even their thinner veil of ignorance drives them to adopt principles for fair treatment of persons other than the one a participant may be when he lifts the veil. My suggestion is that a thicker veil is needed to ensure neutrality; the trustees must concern themselves with a broader class of wards, that is, potential beneficiaries or maleficiaries of the principles to be adopted.[37]

[37] Darwall notes that Rawls himself thinks the term 'trustees' is fitting for partic-ipants in the original position. See Darwall, *Impartial Reason*, p. 248.

Since we have arrived at a possibly surprising result, some review may be in order. Due to the inequalities generated by the natural lottery, participants JS will not necessarily possess certain traits in common with participants OP, for example, a sense of justice, a conception of the good, or a significant degree of rational capacity. Since they may "become" any of the participants JS, they must adopt principles to secure protection of the diverse basic goods which beings with moral standing may enjoy, or need to pursue their conception of the good, and *not* assume that they will not be the participants JS with the least capacities (even though possessing interests). Participants OP function as rational, concerned, guardians for both moral persons and those who have moral standing but fail to be moral agents in the just society.

This version of the original position is not that of Rawls. Yet for the reasons mentioned, it is not clear why it ought not to be. In spite of the anomalous stance which Rawls' account implies for those who are severely incapacitated (given his intention of eliminating the possibility of bias in his design of the original position), one might take seriously the question of the implications of such a choice situation when revised along, what I have asserted to be, more neutral lines. Given such a revised view, we may question what bearing it has regarding those incompetents who fail to be moral persons as well as those general incompetents who do have the capacities for a sense of justice. At this point, focus on the Difference Principle is in order.

One might think that rational contractors in OP would choose a principle requiring strict equality in the distribution of benefits distinct from liberties—given their substantial ignorance of what sorts of position they would occupy in the society whose principles they are to design and, indeed, their ignorance about the sorts of persons they would be. Rawls argues, in brief, that allowing differences of wealth and income, for example, will result in a larger socioeconomic pie to be divided. There is a plausible presupposition here about the necessity of different levels of reward in order to draw persons into demanding or risky, and socially beneficial, roles. Further, a bigger pie makes it possible for the absolute size of the *smallest* shares of a large pie to be larger than the absolute size of *equal* shares in a smaller pie. Participants OP, then, would choose to permit departures from equal distribution, but only if such inequalities maximize the benefits of the least advantaged, that is, they would rightly adopt the Difference Principle. Our question is, if we accept Rawls' theoretical machinery so far: what implication does the Difference Principle have for those generally incompetent? Given our revised OP, which assumes that duties of justice are, at the least, owed to all persons, not just "moral persons," and that the Difference Principle is a principle of justice, what is owed to (sentient) incompetents? The answer remains non-obvious.

As Rawls suggests, it may be useful to imagine ourselves once more as participants in the original position. One of Rawls' examples helps bring out why the Difference Principle is attractive from such a standpoint. He suggests that some people should have certain privileges not possessed by others, for example, medical teams might have use of helicopters or other special means of transport not (publicly) provided for certain other people. Since this would allow quicker medical treatment for, say, the poor in remote areas, such an inequality would not just be a luxury for well-to-do physicians but one which would benefit the least advantaged. At the very least, it seems easier to defend inequalities which benefit the least advantaged as well—as opposed to those which do not. A serious worry about the Difference Principle, however, is whether or not it is unduly stringent. Although we can imagine ways of benefitting competent persons which also benefit the incompetent, it is not clear that all inequalities, or extensions of inequality, as a matter of justice, ought to be prohibited or foregone unless they benefit or maximally benefit the least advantaged. A competing view, one which participants in the original position would consider, is that a certain *minimal standard* of well-being ought to be sought ('guaranteed' is too strong, since it may be impossible to achieve) for persons, especially those (or perhaps only for those) who are involuntarily disadvantaged—and that once society has made those good-faith efforts within its grasp and which it can afford without great costs to its members or its morally acceptable institutions (costs to the Mafia need not count)—some further inequalities are morally permissible. Such a view (call it the *Decent Samaritan Principle*) plausibly suggests that there is *some* limit on what we owe the involuntarily disadvantaged and that it is all right for some to become even better off without having to satisfy the condition of making the least well-off better off. The rejection of this view threatens to undermine the plausible general distinction between what is a matter of duty and what is supererogatory, or what is decent Samaritanism and what is heroic-saintly.

I would press this point further by suggesting that it is reasonable to believe that participants in the original position impartially would draw this type of conclusion; its more precise formulation I leave open. Why think so? Participants OP would recognize that they might "become" profoundly retarded or that they might suffer from catastrophic diseases or serious defects which (1) are conditions impossible to remedy, or (2) are conditions whose treatment is extraordinarily costly. Further, beyond a certain point very costly treatment may exhibit diminishing returns for the one treated. Once treatment, for example, has achieved 95% of what it is possible to remedy it is not obvious that extremely high costs to progress toward 100% remediation are justified. The costs, in such cases, are typically borne by others, and it appears that, on the Difference Principle, such sums are not allowed to improve the lot of the better off *unless* doing so improves the lot of those least well-off whom we are now considering. Hence, the Difference Principle promises to place enormous costs on others who, to one degree or another, are better off; indeed, it forecloses *any* improvements in their lives which if foregone would allow benefitting the least well-off. Adoption of the Difference Principle would, on the face of it, *radically delimit* the prospects of those who are normal or those who would, otherwise, enjoy better than average prospects. If participants OP knew that they would become persons who are seriously and involuntarily disadvantaged, they, being rational and self-interested (recall: they, as participants, are to adopt mutually acceptable principles and do not come to the original position as advocates of strict equality, capitalism, the Golden Rule, and so on), would no doubt choose the Difference Principle. But since they are behind a veil of ignorance they know no such thing; they must choose principles not knowing whether they will be geniuses, normal, mildly retarded, profoundly retarded, or, at some point, comatose. And in our revised conception of the original position they will be concerned about the well-being of any such humans, not just those who will have the capacities for a sense of justice.

However, participants OP might recognize that there are important limits on what can be done to alleviate the plight of the severely disadvantaged without, at the same time, gutting the prospects of those who, as a matter of good luck, do better in the natural lottery. Hence, they might adopt something like the Decent Samaritan Principle, a principle requiring vigorous efforts to alleviate the plight of the seriously and involuntarily disadvantaged but only to a point. A crucial question, of course, is: to what point? An answer might develop as follows. The baseline for well-being, satisfactions, and meaningful life is set, to an important extent, by the natural lottery. Without supposing a sharp and precise dividing line between "nature" and "nurture," upper limits on potential, capacities, and satisfactions are comparatively fixed by one's genotype. Important boundaries are "laid down" depending on whether one "turns out" to be a Tay-Sachs, Down's syndrome, moderately, or mildly retarded, or whether one is born blind, deaf, or paralyzed. One might also consider the involuntary disadvantages which may be "bestowed" by disease, injury, or a family situation conducive to engendering schizophrenia. Such disabilities, of course, vary in severity, and are either not remediable at all or are so to differing limited extents. Some are preventable by human intervention and others not (short of destroying the potential victim). To what point should efforts be made to alleviate the plight of such persons? One proposal might focus on a *Life Preferability Standard* which would prohibit any treatment of such persons (except perhaps cases where their acts would, inadvertently or not, wrong others) which would make their lives, on balance, not worth living; further, it would require that positive efforts be made to render the lives of such persons worth living on balance. Further benefit-bestowing efforts might be left to voluntary individual discretion. My suggestion here is only a tentative and rough one, but it appears to avoid the seemingly riskier course (from the standpoint of participants OP) of adopting the Difference Principle. It realistically accepts the bounds set by bad luck and recognizes the heavy economic tradeoffs (broadly understood) involved in chaining the best prospects of the fortunate to the goal of making incremental improvements in the lot of the most unfortunate.

I am inclined to think that *the Maximin Principle* requires this type of choice as opposed to adoption of the Difference Principle, contrary to what one might initially expect. One might expect otherwise because maximin requires choosing that alternative whose worst outcome is better than the worst outcome of any available alternative; hence, it seems to sanction choosing a prohibition on any changes resulting in inequality unless they make better the plight of the least fortunate. But participants OP are confronted, rather, with choosing between the array of prospects permitted by some principles of social interaction as opposed to others (supposing, again, they could be appropriately implemented; our admittedly abstract discussion is here confined to ascertaining the basic design of a just society). Although the matter deserves far more discussion than I set out here, it seems reasonable to believe that participants OP would judge that the array of prospects to

which they would subject themselves on choosing the Life Preferability Standard, would be better than the array of prospects they
would confront on choosing the Difference Principle. In each situation there would be a worst-case scenario in which, for example,
one is born irremediably and profoundly retarded. Under either
principle one's resulting treatment would not significantly differ.
If the "floors" on the two arrangements are conquerable, why not
choose a principle which permits higher ceilings? Analogously,
suppose one is choosing between two investment funds, A and B.
The minimum yield on an investment in A is 5% and the maximum
is n% (and n far exceeds 5%). The minimum yield with B is 5%
and the maximum is m% where m is one half of n%. Since an
investment in B involves, at worst, at least a 5% yield *and* a *foregone*
opportunity to receive (n-m)% on one's investment, it seems a
worse result than the worst result of investing in A: at least a 5%
yield with the opportunity of receiving n%.

If the above argument is correct, the Difference Principle seems
too stringent and, for the reasons given, would be rejected by
participants in our modification of Rawls' original position. A case
has been made for acceptance of the less stringent Life Preferability
Standard. It may be too weak, and a case could be made for a
stronger standard which would require that more stringent efforts
be made on behalf of those seriously and involuntarily disadvantaged. I reach no firm conclusion. Still, any plausible principle
should take into account two factors. One is the cost to others of
benefitting those who cannot absorb the cost themselves. A second
is the extent to which the plight of the disadvantaged can be rem-
edied. Most obviously, there is no way of transforming the lives
of the profoundly retarded into ones which can involve the same
level of satisfaction or meaningfulness open to generally competent
persons. Alternatively, it is not obviously *fair* to sacrifice substantial
goods or utilities of the more fortunate to make small, incremental,
improvements in the lives of those less fortunate.[38]

Nevertheless, even though the Life Preferability Standard is less
demanding than the Difference Principle, satisfaction of the former
would require, as a matter of justice, a nontrivial redistribution of
goods in such a manner as to alleviate many of the burdens borne
by incompetents—especially perhaps by eliminating or lessening
those socially generated arrangements by virtue of which some are

---

[38] Although couched in terms of utility and supportable (perhaps) by the principle
of utility, such a sacrifice can be defended as unfair apart from any appeal to what
would maximize aggregate utility.

adjudged incompetent to perform activities which are actually or potentially fundamental sources of satisfaction for those deemed incompetent. These remarks are, of course, vague, sketchy, and need further elaboration and development. However, an example or two may be useful, if only to clarify the general position outlined here. Provisions for "special olympics" for handicapped persons and access to public buildings by those in wheelchairs are plausible examples of attempts to make possible decent lives for those who, in the absence of such provisions, have a significantly smaller chance of leading lives which are, at least, preferable all things considered.[39] That justice requires their public provision is not an uncontroversial notion, though it is perhaps less controversial now in the United States than in earlier decades. In the preceding discussion I have only attempted to sketch a plausible ground for thinking that some, albeit limited, social re-arrangement is in order—after attempting to show why certain influential theories fail to yield initially plausible answers regarding what we owe the (involuntarily) incompetent.

7.9 Principles of Substituted Judgment

Even if it is agreed that certain efforts are, as a matter of justice, owed to incompetents, residual questions remain regarding how to decide whether certain specific interventions are permissible either to prevent harm or to promote benefits. Which sorts of paternalistically motivated interventions with incompetents are legitimate? To that question we turn.

At an earlier point in this chapter, one principle, the Revised Harm-Prevention Principle (RHPP) was defended as a plausible principle of legitimate paternalistic intervention with incompetent persons (see Section 7.4). There is, as noted, a certain tension between RHPP and the much discussed (recently) doctrine of substituted judgment according to which, to put the matter loosely, it is permissible (or possibly obligatory) to do to (or for) an incompetent *what he would want if he were competent*.[40] What the latter doctrine requires is initially not clear; a further question (if we can obtain clarity on the prior one) is whether or not such a doctrine

[39] These examples focus on those incompetent at certain activities rather than generally incompetent persons who are subject to pervasive disabilities not only to act but prudently to decide for themselves.

[40] Historically, the doctrine was commonly invoked as a basis for determining the disposition of the real property of incompetents.

conflicts with RHPP. At a later point I shall suggest that there *is* a conflict and I shall sketch a way of resolving it. First, we will engage in some stage setting and attempt to clarify the doctrine of substituted judgment.

The legal doctrine of substituted judgment is one often invoked as a basis for deciding questions of treatment in clinical or institutional contexts.[41] A typical situation is that in which the incompetent party is institutionalized and there are substantive questions about how he shall be treated. Such questions may concern risky (and possibly painful) life-extending treatment, moderately painful therapy designed to restore competence, mood-altering drugs designed to dampen or eliminate impulsive, possibly dangerous, behavior, or whether to allow incompetents to be organ "donors." The main focus here is not on cases in which "treatment" designed to punish, pacify, or "domesticate" those dangerous to others is being considered. Rather, it is on those cases in which therapeutic and paternalistic aims obtain exclusively or are dominant. Hence, the central questions concern the bases of legitimate paternalistic intervention toward "innocent," generally incompetent, often institutionalized persons, and proposed interventions which are comparatively nonroutine in nature. The latter are usually characterizable in terms of involving a risk of harm to, or a presumptively wrong act toward, the subject—in the absence of valid consent by the latter.

And *there* is the rub; for generally incompetent persons, though they may have relevant preferences, cannot give valid consent. Nor, so it appears, is their dissent, if there is such, morally decisive in deciding on the permissibility of (nonroutine) treatment. For such reasons others must make important decisions regarding the incompetent.[42] One basis for decision is some form of a Good-

[41] For an excellent discussion, and an important critique of court decisions relevant to making decisions regarding treatment of incompetents, see Allen Buchanan, "The Limits of Proxy Decisionmaking for Incompetents," *UCLA Law Review* 29, No. 2 (December, 1981), pp. 386–408.

[42] *Who* should make decisions regarding treatment of incompetents is an important question. The leading contenders mentioned in the literature are (1) the courts (e.g., judges), (2) the health-care professional, (3) the incompetent's family or, if there is one, guardian, (4) an institutional ethics committee—or some combination of the above. It is crucial to observe, however, that even if there were a complete consensus on *who* should decide, that would not answer the more basic question of *how* the decision should be made, or more accurately, on the basis of which principles or grounds the decision should be made. The latter issue is our focus here. Indeed, how we answer the latter may well affect, and ought to influence, who would be authorized to make such decisions. The relevant "who question" is not just "who is most likely to decide on appropriate grounds?" The latter, prac-

Promotion (often called a "Best Interest" Principle) or, more likely, a Harm-Prevention Principle—an approach we have rejected when proposed as an acceptable basis for dealing *with competent parties*. As we noted earlier, a Good-Promotion, or a Harm-Prevention, Principle *can* take into account the existing preferences of an incompetent party since if the incompetent resists a proposed mode of treatment, or would resent it if carried out against his wishes, the long-term result of doing so may not promote the subject's good on balance (or, with regard to a Harm-Prevention Principle, may not prevent harm on balance). However, such principles are committed to ignoring or overriding the subject's preferences *when* that can be done in such a manner as to achieve the goal of overall benefit promotion or harm prevention. This point is of no small importance, a matter to which we return in later reassessing RHPP. Of course, in those special cases in which the incompetent subject is so impaired as not to have preferences and is such that he *will* not have preferences (cf. the permanently comatose individual), there are not actual or potential preferences to override or ignore.

In contrast to a highly outcome-oriented strategy (e.g., intervene to prevent the occurrence of harm on balance), one might think that the preferences—past, current, or future—of an incompetent subject (when such preferences did, do, or will exist) should have a very special weight, and a weight greater than Good-Promotion or Harm-Prevention principles seem to allow, in determining what is permissible treatment of the incompetent subject. Such a viewpoint is presupposed by the doctrine of substituted judgment, a doctrine according to which courts, in deciding on permissible treatment, must try to ascertain and act in accord with *what the incompetent subject would want or choose if he were competent*. There are close variants on this general theme. Sometimes the question is posed as one of identifying what the subject would want (1) if he were in his right mind, or (2) if he had retained his capacity to decide, or (3) if suddenly cured, or (4) if temporarily possessing rational capacities, or (5) what a rational person would choose if he had the preferences and, prospectively, would come to have the existing capacities of the incompetent subject.[43] These princi-

---

tically important, question is hardly settled; among the best discussions of it are those by Allen Buchanan in the previously cited essays in *The American Journal of Law and Medicine* and *The UCLA Law Review*.

[43] For legal references, see Gary Jones' instructive (currently unpublished) essay: "The Principle of Substituted Judgment and the Treatment of Mental Incompetents." Also see the probing essay by John A. Robertson, "Organ Donations by Incompetents and the Substituted Judgment Doctrine,"*Columbia Law Review* 76 (1976), pp. 48–78.

ples are by no means equivalent, and one can imagine cases in which they yield competing answers. For example, the principle (2), according to which one (or the courts) ought to decide treatment on the basis of what the subject would choose had he retained his rational capacities, simply lacks application in those cases in which the subject has never possessed such capacities—in contrast to those formulations which make no such presupposition [e.g., (1), (4), or (5)].

A basic point to be stressed about such principles is that they all seem "motivated" in substantial part by the notion that psychological individuating traits (whether wants or beliefs) of the particular subject are important or even decisive in reaching a final judgment about the treatment of that incompetent subject even though other parties must carry out the deliberations. In this fashion the distinctiveness of persons and their outlooks seems recognized and such individuals are not treated as mere utility, or disutility, containers. Decisions about treatment must be in accord with their particular psychological stance, their projects, preferences, or dispositions. In one sense such factors may be regarded as "stoppers" or "blockers," as strong reasons for not treating incompetent persons in some "beneficent" (e.g., harm-preventing) fashion even though their choices, if they can choose, may be viewed as neither necessary nor sufficient reasons, by themselves, in justifying proposed treatment. Assigning such weight to possibly idiosyncratic psychological traits of such subjects contrasts with viewing the subjects merely as homogeneous tokens of the type labeled 'incompetent person.' As such, this general approach is hospitable to the theoretical outlook developed and defended here. Still there is a puzzle. Much of the viewpoint defended earlier naturally is characterized as an *autonomy-respecting* theory of paternalism, but here we are faced with subjects who entirely lack autonomy or whose autonomy is radically impaired. In some cases there is just no fully autonomous person to be respected. However, it does not follow that there is no content to 'respect for persons' in all cases in which the subjects in question lack autonomy or even the capacity for becoming autonomous. What then is involved in respecting such persons? The idea that "customizing" judgments about treatment of incompetents to their individual dispositions or choice-affecting psychological traits seems a step in the right direction. Most of the principles alluded to as "principles of substituted judgment" share this roughly characterized feature. By contrast, it can be overlooked that a principle such as "do to S whatever you like or whatever promotes your own interest" also sanctions *substituting one's judgment* for that of S, but it utterly fails to adopt the *other-respecting* stance of the principles we have mentioned.

An assessment of proposed principles of substituted judgment must take into account the diverse types of persons that may be classified as generally incompetent. Let us briefly sort out cases. If we attend to the question of whether a person is, was, or will be competent, eight possible cases can be identified; however, only three or four of these are of interest here. For the sake of perspective and completeness, however, we note what they are. If we classify children as incompetents (as young children are legally classified), then we competent adults are all former incompetents. But let us henceforth restrict ourselves to adult phases of life. We are not immediately concerned with those *who are competent* "now" but who also (1) were competent, but will lose their competence, or (2) were competent and will remain competent, or (3) were incompetent and will later become incompetent. In short, we are here concerned only with those incompetent at the time intervention is being considered. Hence, questions center around (4) those who are *permanently incompetent* (were, are, and will remain incompetent), (5) those *protocompetents* (a rather special case) who were and are incompetent but who will come to be competent, (6) the *formerly competent* who were competent but are no longer and never will be again, and (7) the *temporarily* incompetent who were competent, no longer are, but will regain competence. Categories (4) through (7) all involve persons who, at the time of considering treatment of them are recognizably incompetent; evidently, they differ with respect to their histories and prospects (vis-à-vis competence). These simply are logically possible classifications. Usually there is no firm ground for assuming that a person now generally incompetent will come to be generally competent [i.e., that a person falls in category (5) as opposed to (6)].

From a slightly different angle it is worth noting that any attempt to conjecture or infer what an incompetent would choose if he were competent may be in an epistemological hard place. In cases of those who have always been comatose, the subject has exhibited no preferences or attitudes; indeed, he lacks them. Those permanently incompetent individuals who, although not comatose, are (substantially) mentally impaired may be so childlike that their expressed beliefs or preferences are not well developed, or are unrealistic (e.g., a subject believes he can fly without mechanical assistance), or are even in a bewildering, seemingly inconsistent, array. Hence, there *may* be good reasons to give little weight to the dispositions and attitudes of those who were and are incompetent. Much would seem to depend on whether the incompetent person has, at some point, a developed, integrated, personality such that it is possible to identify definite dispositions and ascertain how intense are his direct or obliquely expressed preferences. If one is to attempt to surmise what the incompetent person *would choose*, one must have at least a minimally firm grip on what sorts of personal traits would influence such a choice if it were to be made by the incompetent if he could. The problem is even more complex, but I here call attention to some initial difficulties. Hence, we must attend to the *history* of the incompetent. In some cases it will exhibit no expressed preferences. Less problematic (for purposes of invoking the substituted judgment doctrine) are the cases of the formerly competent (including the temporarily incompetent) for, as we have characterized them, there will be a history of presumably stable, expressed, dispositions and beliefs. Thus, in principle, there will be a firmer, and possibly adequate, epistemological basis for determining what the incompetent would choose if he were able.[44]

What an incompetent person would choose or what we should choose on his behalf would also seem to be a function of his prospects. In some cases there will be compelling reasons to assume that acquisition or reacquisition of competence is unlikely; in other cases the opposite may be true, and in many cases we will not have reason to wager one way or the other. However, in those cases where acquisition or reacquisition of competence is probable that fact seems relevant to deciding how the incompetent party should, or may, be treated. In such cases the incompetent party has a special interest to be considered, an interest, in part, in having certain choices substantially affecting his welfare *left undecided* so

---

[44] In brief, reconstructing what the incompetent would choose can exhibit various degrees of difficulty. At one extreme there may be a "living will," explicit instructions about preferred treatment provided by a person while competent concerning treatment if the subject becomes incompetent. Or there may have been explicit oral expression of such convictions relayed by trustworthy witnesses. In other cases no specific preferences will have been expressed, but the subject's relevant desires and convictions while competent may be beyond dispute, and, hence, the inference to specific preferred choice may be comparatively unproblematic. In yet other cases determining what the incompetent would choose is more conjectural. About here a shift may occur to a different standard, namely, to what "a reasonable person so situated would choose." That this is a different standard should not go unnoticed. This latter standard gives no serious weight to the possibly unique desires or convictions of the subject—independently of whatever merits the standard exhibits.

that he may make them himself on becoming competent. In passing, I note that this situation is mirrored in reverse by the situation of some victims of serious burns who remain competent to decide substantive questions of treatment during a number of hours after being burned (due to destruction of nerve endings they are initially not in intense pain); later, they may be in such pain as to be unable to employ their capacities reasonably to decide what is to be done.[45]

Returning to the question of incompetent parties who may acquire or reacquire competence, it is clear that not all decisions can be "put on hold" until the subject is competent since some decisions themselves may determine causally whether or not the incompetent subject will become competent. For example, suppose it were the case that an incompetent subject could be rendered competent by some more or less drastic, and more or less risky, procedure such as psychosurgery, electro-convulsive treatment, or the use of powerful psychotropic drugs. In such cases a decision about treatment must be made while the incompetent party is incompetent. Although we may recognize an interest on the part of the incompetent party in becoming competent to make certain decisions, a decision to bring about such a state of affairs is not one the incompetent can be said to have a satisfiable interest in deciding; at best, we can recognize that the subject has an interest in the decision's being made by others in a morally permissible and reasonable manner. It is just here, of course, that the proposal is put forth that the choice should be made in accord with (some version of) the doctrine of substituted judgment. So far we have not assessed the doctrine; rather, we have sought to classify relevantly different kinds of cases and identify some of the relevant considerations which are important in making decisions for incompetents and which should affect our appraisal of principles of substituted judgment.

Prior to an assessment of principles of substituted judgment, it is worth recognizing a rather special problem, largely to set it aside. Among those who are classifiable as permanently incompetent are not only those referred to as, for example, congenital idiots, and others less disabled, but also the "permanently comatose." This latter category, however, is ambiguous between 'those individuals comatose from birth on' and 'those individuals who were not but

---

[45] For an extremely sensitive and perceptive discussion of the problems regarding treatment of burn victims, see Sharon Imbus and Bruce Zawachi, "Autonomy for Burned Patients When Survival Is Unprecedented," *New England Journal of Medicine* (August 11, 1979), pp. 308–311.

are and will be comatose.' Karen Quinlan is a probable example of the latter. On either interpretation, there is a question which deserves mention here, namely, is such an individual a *person* at all? Expressions I have employed earlier, such as 'comatose person' or 'permanently comatose person,' tend to imply an affirmative answer to the question. However, that is a supposition whose truth is much in doubt.[46] It is worth noting that, if we do not assume that 'person' and 'human being' have the same meaning, it is not obvious that permanently comatose human beings are persons. On the views of some philosophers, for example, Michael Tooley and Mary Anne Warren, in order for something to be a person, it must possess certain psychological traits, such as an awareness of being a continuing self, have certain desires, or a capacity to make certain choices.[47] To be a person, on this view, one must exhibit the rudiments of personality. Hence, on *one* reading of 'comatose person' the expression is conceptually incoherent. More likely, such an accusation may be made regarding a "permanently comatose person." On the view noted, there are not, and logically cannot be, such entities; it would be a better bet that someone will find a flying pig. I simply want to recognize this dispute without taking sides in it. However, we should note that even if a view like that of Tooley and Warren is sound, the question of how permanently comatose individuals may or ought to be treated is not settled. That would be true only if certain further assumptions are established, for example, only persons have rights or only persons have moral standing. These claims I shall leave open. The relevance of these

[46] Throughout this investigation I have defended the view that competent persons have a strong right to direct their own lives. I have assumed and to a degree defended the view that only competent persons have this right, i.e., that beings lacking the relevant capacities of competent persons lack this right even though they may possess important rights or be owed important duties. I have not made much of this latter point, but elsewhere Allen Buchanan has, and rightly so for the following reason. There is a tendency in recent court cases to attribute a right of self-determination not only to competents but to incompetents as well. Such a presumption is, I think, radically misguided. Some incompetents do not have any sense of self or self-awareness. Some, e.g., the permanently comatose, lack any capacities to direct their own lives. Possession of such capacities seems a necessary condition of having a right to direct one's own life. Only some misguided egalitarianism seems to motivate the attribution of a right to self-determination to all incompetents. Further, as Buchanan observes, attribution of the right to all people threatens to undermine or obscure the point that relevantly different sorts of duties are owed to competents and incompetents. See Allen Buchanan, "The Limits of Proxy Decisionmaking," p. 391.

[47] See Michael Tooley, "Abortion and Infanticide," *Philosophy & Public Affairs* 1, No. 1 (Fall, 1972); pp. 37–65; Mary Anne Warren, "On the Moral and Legal Status of Abortion," *The Monist* 57, No. 1 (January, 1973), pp. 43–61.

contentions regarding the disputes over abortion and infanticide is well known at least in philosophical circles if not in congressional hearings. I shall set aside most of these difficulties and largely focus on treatment of those who were competent but are not now; further, we will focus on those who, although incompetent, are not comatose.[48] Such cases exhibit two important features: (1) the individual exhibits some history of preferences and beliefs, and (2) no serious claim can be made that such individuals are not persons or that they are lacking in moral standing.

Let us turn to the task of trying to understand what is meant by the claim that, in deciding on treatment of an incompetent, one may or must choose *what the incompetent subject, S, would choose if S were competent*. It is worth noticing some troublesome features of sentences of the form: if A were P, then A would choose X (where A stands for a person, P for a property, and X for an act type). First they are often obscure because it is not clear what is to be supposed or imagined by " 'if A were P.' For example, in saying, as we do, "if I were you I would marry Maria Theresa," what is meant by "if I were you"? I am not you; that is clear. But are we to imagine that I, with *my* preferences, beliefs and so on, am in your choice situation—*or* that if I had *your* preferences and most of your beliefs, but not all, I would choose to marry Maria Theresa. Analogously, what is meant by "if S were competent"? Suppose a decision must be made about treatment of S which holds out the hope of restoring competence to S, and someone proposed that if S were competent to make such a choice, he would decide in favor of the treatment. But it might be objected that if S *were* competent he would not need or benefit from competence-restoring treatment; so, he would certainly *not* choose to undergo it. Further, there are cases in which it would be silly to subject A to treatment X because it is true that "if A were P, A would choose X." It may be true that if A were radically disfigured, A would choose cosmetic surgery. That fact is hardly a good reason to subject nondisfigured A to the surgery.

These difficulties need not blind us to what I believe is an intelligible and reasonably determinate proposal implicit in, and ex-

[48] There is a sense in which we *cannot logically* substitute our judgment for that of the comatose individual, a fetus, or an infant; since the individual lacks the capacity for judgment, we cannot *substitute ours for his* (or hers). Thus, in spite of the comments of some—that we may substitute our judgment *for that of* such incompetents—such an "invocation of the doctrine of substituted judgment" is just incoherent.

tractable from, "the doctrine of substituted judgment." What we may reasonably do is perform a more or less complicated thought experiment in which the guiding features in deciding what S would choose are S's stable preferences, attitudes, and beliefs, those aspects (perhaps former aspects) of S which are most central to the personality S was and/or is. An adult person who is asleep is, in one sense, temporarily unable to choose; still we can rightly say that he *would* choose in a certain way if he were able to do so. Normally, if a decision must be made we wake him up; but suppose we cannot do so and that the sleep is like that of Rip Van Winkle and lasts for decades. Still, we may rightly say that Rip would choose a certain way if he could and if he were apprised of relevant information. In making such a judgment we may hypothesize or imagine that the subject has information he lacks and, of course, what he would decide even though he does not decide. Still, in doing so we need not imagine a decision process which turns on basic preferences, beliefs, or attitudes which S lacks or lacked. One image which captures the notion of an "accurate substituted judgment" is probably that of S's being temporarily empowered to decide a matter, given his historically most stable and basic preferences, attitudes, and beliefs, *with regard to* how S is to be treated *given S's actual state* of limited capacities. That is, an accurate substituted judgment is one identical with the decision such a hypothetical subject makes.

It is worth noticing the constraints on the process of ascertaining "S would choose if he could." The aim, then, is not to ascertain what a fully rational person, or a fully self-interested, a fully altruistic, a fully sadistic, or a fully masochistic person would choose, but rather *what S would choose* if able and, presumably, if given access to information about risks and benefits to himself or to others incompetent (which, in a clinical setting, would be owed to any competent person having to make an equally significant decision—compare the discussion in Chapter 4). These other criteria (e.g., deciding what a fully rational person or a reasonable person would choose for an incompetent party) are sometimes called *objective* interpretations of the doctrine of substituted judgment as opposed to *subjective* interpretations. Such terminology is misleading, at least to the extent that it suggests that there are no objective criteria for determining when a given substituted judgment accurately fits the description "what S, given his preferences, attitudes, and beliefs (those not definitive of his incompetence) and access to relevant information, would choose if temporarily empowered to do so."[49] Let us call this view, that the proper approach to arriving at a substituted judgment is to be carried out in this manner, the *Temporary Infusion Version of the Doctrine of Substituted Judgment*. (The relevant choice is whatever choice would be made by an incompetent imaginatively "infused" with his prior values, outlook, and capacities for reflection, and relevantly informed vis-à-vis choosing treatment for the incompetent as he actually is.) More than the other, problematic, construals noted, it seems to capture the moral conviction that, in brief, S's conception of the good while competent ought not to be ignored in deciding on the treatment of S while incompetent. Thus, we must, in some sense, "don the mantle of the incompetent." Later I shall suggest reasons for thinking that there is a more preferable, or less misleading, view to be articulated.

As our Rip Van Winkle analogy suggests, sometimes it may be possible to confirm the accuracy of a substituted judgment, for example, by getting confirmation from a subject who reacquires competence and agrees "yes, that is exactly the choice I would have made."[50] Similarly, we can be *mistaken* about what an incompetent would choose if competent. I am proposing that there are objective criteria (though not always adequate evidence) for determining, in principle, whether a substituted judgment made along the lines mentioned is accurate or not. For that reason the 'subjective' and 'objective' labels are misleading. The proposed "objective" interpretations are, preferably, classifiable as "non-individualized interpretations."

One possible point behind the subjective/objective distinction is that some proposed principles of intervention require ascertaining and highly weighting the *subject's* point of view and preference schedule, and some do not. If that is all that is involved, there is no serious conceptual quarrel. It may be worth observing here that some proposals *seem* to stress the individual's point of view (and, hence, seem "subjective"), but in reality do not. For example, in one case the Massachusetts Supreme Court flirted with the principle: decide what the subject "would choose if he were competent and *had normal desires*" (my italics).[51] However, consider the case of a previously competent Jehovah's Witness who exhibited the

---

[49] Also "objective interpretations" require thought experiments as well; on neither interpretation is S asked to choose. On both interpretations reasoned conjecture is essential.

[50] Or, even more reliably, on regaining competence, S *does* so choose.

[51] See Superintendent of Belchertown v. Saikewicz, Mass. 370 NE 2d, p. 417.

familiar opposition to blood transfusions. If a transfusion is being considered for the now incompetent Witness, the last-mentioned proposal and the Infusion Version of Substituted Judgment yield divergent, competing, guides (the latter prohibiting the transfusion and the former principle sanctioning it).

One conclusion to be drawn here is that if the (so far preferred version of) the Substituted Judgment Doctrine can be defended at all, it will certainly fail to be defensible in an important range of cases. In those situations in which the incompetent subject has never been competent (e.g., a fetus, an infant, an adult comatose from infancy), there cannot be an appeal to the preferences, beliefs, or concept of the good possessed by the subject. No such outlook has come into existence. In such cases the doctrine of substituted judgment has no relevance. Rather some sort of best interest or harm-prevention principle (perhaps, RHPP) may be defensible and applicable. In the cases which are our current focus, the formerly competent, it is *possible* to arrive, I have suggested, at a reasonable belief as to what S would choose if able. In a subset of these cases we may know what S would choose if able because we know what S *chose* when he was able, for example, S while competent explicitly expressed his preference or choice (perhaps in a "living will"). If so, the permissibility of according his choice (if doing so wrongs no others) is grounded in his prior valid consent (compare the Principle of Restricted Consent for competents). In this case epistemological perplexities about what S would choose if he could (at the time treatment is being decided) are unproblematic. In this case ascertaining the hypothetical choice is based on an explicit actual choice.

In other cases S, while competent, will not have made an explicit choice regarding the hypothetical situation of "current" incapacity, one which has been actualized. Still, enough may be known of S's beliefs, values, and commitments while S was competent to make it virtually certain that he would, or would not, choose a certain alternative for his incompetent self if (deus ex machina) he were temporarily empowered (infused with his prior capacities) to do so. A formerly competent atheist would not, if able, donate part of his estate to the Roman Catholic Church. A formerly competent black person would not, if able, leave his estate to the Ku Klux Klan. There are epistemological questions to be raised, but one ought not exaggerate the difficulties.

The considerations just noted suggest why the more or less tempting and defensible Temporary Infusion interpretation of the

Doctrine of Substituted Judgment is subject to improvement and revision. It still retains the overly perplexing suggestion that we must imagine what a "competent incompetent" would choose if situated in a certain manner. This bald way of putting the matter is just what lends force to the claim that the doctrine is incoherent, horrendously conjectural, or is totally indeterminate in its implications (and thus is a useless guide to decision making). What I wish to emphasize is that the core, plausible, element of the doctrine does not require mysterious flights of the imagination concerning what an incompetent, momentarily resurrected to competent status, would choose; rather, its central focus is on what S *chose* while competent or what choices S would have made *while competent* given his beliefs, desires, and concept of the good—if the opportunity arose. The focus is on historical matters: those more or less explicit actual choices, expressions of general or specific values and commitments evinced by S when he was competent. Such empirical matters are far less ethereal than some critics of, or even some defenders of, substituted judgment make out. Given this view, it is now clear why talk of "donning the mantle of the incompetent" functions like a magician's misdirection. What is plausible is that we, rather, *don the mantle of the competent* person who lost his competence. It is his outlook that, arguably, must be respected and must weigh in determining treatment of the incompetent. Thus, although we may substitute our judgment for that (if it is present) of the incompetent, the plausible goal is to *implement* the actual, or reasonably inferable, judgment of the competent.[52] For evident reasons it may be useful to think of this construal of the Doctrine of Substituted Judgment as the *Historical Version* of the doctrine. Perhaps what advocates of what I have labeled the Temporary Infusion Version have intended to defend the Historical Version, but the differences in how the central question is put, in how the images are evoked, and in articulation are reasons for contrasting the two as we have. Even if the Historical Version is not mystifying, it is controversial and we need to explore it further and consider objections to it.

People often make choices at a time t^n about what they would do or choose *if* in a situation at a later time t^{n+1}. However, even when competent Jones solemnly declares that "if I were in situation M, I would choose to do X," Jones may not choose X when in

---

[52] This way of putting matters suggests a parallel with two valid grounds for invasive intervention with competents, i.e., the Principle of Restricted Consent and the Principle of Hypothetical Individualized Consent.

situation M.[53] For example, people who declare that they would commit suicide if they became seriously impaired do not always do so. People who say they would divorce if a spouse were discovered to be unfaithful do not always do so. So, it may be claimed that even if S while competent states that he would choose treatment T if he were to become incompetent, we cannot be sure that S would so choose, if able. And we cannot "wake him" or temporarily empower him with competence to check out matters. True enough. Still, demanding "certainty" about what S would choose seems unnecessarily rigorous. In the case of competents, we respect their choices at t^n regarding their treatment at t^{n+1} even though what they would choose (or do choose) at t^{n+1}, if able, *may* not be the same thing. In this respect even a competent may be mistaken at t^n about what he would choose in some unactualized situation at t^{n+1}. But this provides no reason not to take S's preference or choice at t^n as decisive and deserving respect so long as S's choice was relevantly informed, was an expression of this reasoned reflection, and complying with it wrongs no others. The possible disparity, then, between what S chose at t^n and what S would choose at t^{n+1} seldom provides a reason for ignoring or discounting his choice or commitments at t^n.

Another source of objection to the application of the Historical Version of Substituted Judgment is generated by the fact that S's commitments and beliefs while competent may differ from those S exhibits as an incompetent. The Historical Version requires us to ascertain the choices or relevant choice-affecting features of S as a competent person—those which would determine the choice S would make if he were able at the time S is an incompetent. These features would be basic beliefs, preference ordering, and other dispositional traits (call all these factors 'D-traits'). Just here the problem arises. It is reasonable to think that the D-traits possessed by S when competent only (but at least) overlap with the D-traits possessed by S when incompetent.[54] Some of the divergence (imag-

[53] On this point and much else in this section, I have benefitted from discussions with Richard Wyatt.

[54] My focus is on cases in which an incompetent at t^2 is rightly describable as a later self of a competent person at t^1—as opposed to being a successor (see Section 3.10) of the competent person at t^1. In cases in which an incompetent at t^2 is the *successor* of a competent person at t^1, a principle I later label and defend, the Principle of Individualized Substituted Judgment (PISJ), is not a plausible guide to permissible treatment of the incompetent at t^2 since we do not respect the incompetent by invoking the outlook of the competent as a guide to treatment; after all, the competent was a numerically different person and not just an earlier competent stage of the incompetent person.

ine we have two lists of traits) may be due to "natural change," for example, learning, forgetting, maturation, and so on. However, some divergence, presumably, will be the result of the *onset* (whether slow or quick) of incompetence. Hence, some of the beliefs and desires of S will be definitive of, or a byproduct of, his incompetence.

Some preferences and beliefs of generally incompetent persons may also be bizarre, for example, the desire to fly (without mechanical assistance) or to walk on water (unfrozen) or beliefs that the subject is Napoleon or that he can divine the future. However, it is a mistake to focus only on the most bizarre beliefs and preferences and to take, for example, the paranoid schizophrenic as one's paradigm of an incompetent person. Whether we consider the mentally ill incompetent or, say, the seriously retarded, but not mentally ill, incompetent, it is reasonable to distinguish between desires/beliefs which are definitive of (or part of the criteria for attributing) incompetence and those which are not. How to do this is not crystal clear, and much depends on the proper explanation of why someone has a certain desire/belief. Since the core notion involved in incompetence is inability to direct one's own life in a reasonably prudent manner, it would be plausible to suspect that one who believes that an airplane is a type of bird is incompetent. Given that belief it is likely that the holder of it has a configuration of assumptions (e.g., about categories and causal connections) that render him unable prudently to direct his own life. However, this reasoning proceeds too hastily. Much depends on the grounds for holding the belief. A native of an isolated tribe may have good reasons to hold the belief in question; in such a case there may be no reason to assume that the native has some irremediable incapacity by virtue of which he is to be classified as generally incompetent. By contrast, the existence of such a belief in a typical, present-day, adult Parisian would be strong presumptive evidence of incompetence. These remarks only suggest the need to distinguish, and the occasional difficulty of distinguishing, desire/beliefs indicative of incompetence and those which are not. Making such distinctions forces us to recognize the desire/beliefs of incompetent persons which are not criterially associated with incompetence and draws attention to the question of why we should not give weight to, or facilitate, the satisfaction of such desires. It is one thing to constrain S's desire to fly off the top of the World Trade Center and another to constrain his desire to watch television. The set of desire/beliefs of an incompetent can be partitioned, and there is no obvious reason to dismiss as irrelevant every current desire or belief of an incompetent person. This conclusion is hardly a surprising one. Still, the argument provides a reason for taking some of the beliefs and preferences of incompetents seriously, a conclusion which, fortunately, is compatible with the view that incompetents are incapable of valid consent or dissent with respect to a certain range of substantive decisions about policies affecting them.

We are now in a better position to address the question of what it is permissible to do when an incompetent's current preferences are contrary to those he possessed when he was competent. Recall that our focus here is limited to those who were competent during an adult phase of life. For such an incompetent there was a most recent phase of competence when he was on his own with a full right to direct his own life. We presume further that during that phase he possessed a reasonably stable hierarchical structure of preferences and a stable cognitive viewpoint. To join the issues more sharply and to descend from a certain level of abstraction, let us suppose, once again, that S in his last phase of competence was a devout Jehovah's Witness and that on becoming incompetent (for whatever reason) S prefers to be a regular blood donor. Let us, rightly or not, assume that devout Jehovah's Witnesses do not collaborate in "tainting blood" by donating blood for purposes of transfusions. Imagine further a situation wherein a sibling of S needs blood and only S's blood will do.[55] S, as an incompetent, wishes to donate blood, but that is a procedure contrary to the preferences S possessed while a competent person. What is permissible according to PISJ? With persons who develop normally and never become incompetent during adult phases of life somewhat similar questions may arise to the extent that their most recent preferences may be contrary to those held earlier. In such cases we normally respect the current person by respecting his current outlook—in the absence of any compelling reason to assume that his current outlook is radically out of character, unstable, or a byproduct of temporary impairment. In a fashion, therefore, we recognize that people change and we respect them now by respecting their current leanings, ones which, for example, may be contrary to an earlier outlook. Compare the tension generated by parents who, by contrast, continue to treat their adult off-spring as the latter may have preferred at earlier stages of life. Thus, there

---

[55] One can imagine an analogous case involving organ donation by making similar suppositions.

seems to be a presumption in favor of respecting people by re-specting their current outlook. However, a difficulty arises here. We recognize that persons sometimes regress, or suffer "setbacks." Their most *recent* preferences are not always an expression of their most stable, most developed and integrated personality. In the type of case we are considering, the loss of competence seems just the sort of instance in which it is reasonable to construe 'respecting a person' as respecting his most stable, clearly ordered, and devel-oped outlook, that is, the one that prevailed during the last phase of competence. Hence, it is such an outlook that must be considered when we attempt to ascertain *what S would choose if he were competent*. Our answer must be determined by looking to those preferences and beliefs which prevailed when he was at the height of his power or, at least, competent.

I am proposing, then, this *Interpretive Proviso* to the Historical Version of the Substituted Judgment approach: we should respect the beliefs and preferences of the incompetent party insofar as they are in accord with those basic beliefs and preferences exhibited during the latest phase of competence and not do so to the extent that the existing outlook is definitive of, or a byproduct of, the onset of incompetence. In the example mentioned, the proviso implies that we should allow the incompetent to donate blood if the change of outlook is *not* explicable as a result of whatever induced incompetence; or, if it is so explicable, the proviso implies not allowing it. Suppose, in our example, the preference for blood donation arises because of mental illness and the incompetent pre-fers to donate because he believes that if he does so he will be made ruler of the world. The Interpretive Proviso requires that we should give precedence to the outlook prevailing during the last phase of competence. This seems an intuitively plausible result.

Still, consider the following objection. Suppose S* always pre-ferred chocolate ice cream and hated strawberry ice cream. On becoming senile, and to the point of incompetence, S* has the opposite preferences. In addition, S* now prefers strawberry be-cause he believes that if one eats a sufficient amount of it one will live forever (the belief is a facet of the senility). PISJ and Interpretive Proviso imply discounting the preference for strawberry and, say, withholding it—a bizarre result. This troublesome, and admittedly queer, example suggests the need for a second proviso regarding just when we may intervene, in presumptively wrongful ways, in the lives of incompetents. Let us call it the *Threshold Proviso*. On reflection, it is clear that there is no reason to intervene in presumptively wrongful ways in the lives of other persons, even incompetents, unless they are acting or will act in some manner likely to cause nontrivial self-harm (or wrong others). Hence, it is reasonable to insist that we need not, and ought not, consider such intervention unless the acts, or prospective acts, of incompetents involve one of the sorts of "threatening" aspects mentioned. An adequate theory of legitimate intervention in the lives of incompetents in a presumptively wrongful manner must, I conclude, include such a Threshold Proviso. In passing, I note that the Threshold Proviso supports a delimitation on invasive interventions in the lives of the formerly competent. For example, it is a reason in certain cases to favor "limited or partial guardianship," as opposed to "full guardianship" arrangements which tend to remove (potentially at least) all decision-making power from the formerly competent.

In addition, duties that incompetent persons have toward others or duties that we (as individuals or, collectively, as a society) have toward those other than the incompetent persons may prohibit the performance of certain interventions with incompetents. Hence, an extended statement of the fuller doctrine of individualized substituted judgment defended here requires a "no wrongs to others" (1. below)—as did those principles defended earlier as adequate guides to permissible paternalism toward competent persons.

Now we can state the plausible principle which seems extractable from the myriad of sometimes confused proposals which advocate a "substituted judgment" approach. I shall label this the *Principle of Individualized Substituted Judgment* (PISJ):

If S is incompetent with respect to doing Y(or choosing with regard to Y), then A's paternalistic intervention, X, with S is permissible if

  1. A's doing X wrongs no one other than S

and 2. A's doing X is quite likely to prevent S's causing significant harm (or risk of harm) on balance to S by S's doing Y (or choosing with regard to Y)

and 3. If A were to omit doing X it is certain or quite likely that S would cause significant harm (or risk of such harm) on balance to S by S's doing Y (or choosing with regard to Y)[56]

---

[56] Clauses 2. and 3. embody our Threshold Proviso.

and   4.   If S were competent to decide whether A should do X, S would choose that A do X (given our Interpretative Proviso to the Historical approach, the truth of 4. is to be determined by reference to the choices, or basic beliefs and preferences, of the incompetent party as these were exhibited during the latest phase of competence of that party).[57]

Earlier we noted that the Revised Harm-Prevention Principle is a tempting principle for determining permissible interventions with incompetents. We also observed, in passing, its apparent conflict with a substituted judgment approach. Now that the approach embodying PISJ has been stated and defended more fully, we are in a better position to both consider RHPP in further detail and to compare the two competing viewpoints. It will be useful to set out once more the Revised Harm-Prevention Principle (RHPP):

A's paternalistic intervention, X, with S is permissible if
1.   A's doing X wrongs no one other than S

and   2.   A's doing X is quite likely to prevent S's causing significant harm (or risk of harm) on balance to S by S's doing Y (or choosing with regard to Y)

and   3.   If A were to omit doing X it is certain or quite likely that S would cause significant harm (or risk of such harm) on balance to S by S's doing Y (or choosing with regard to Y)

and   4.   It is reasonable to believe that A's doing X will not render S worse off than S would have been had A omitted X, and it is reasonable to believe that A's doing X is one of the least harmful means of preventing S from doing Y (or according S's choice regarding Y).

To see one advantage of RHPP, it is worth noting a certain contrast between RHPP and the Principle of Utility-Maximization. From a

---

[57] It is worth emphasizing again that this doctrine is relevant only for decisions regarding the formerly competent. Also, it fails to address certain perplexities, e.g., the problem which exists if the beliefs or preferences of the formerly competent were inconsistent—a problem called to my attention by Scott Arnold. Still, inconsistency over time may not show gross irrationality (rather, a change of mind). Further, failure to recognize certain non-obvious inconsistencies hardly shows lack of rationality or absence of a reasonably coherent viewpoint. Complete consistency may be a necessary condition of full rationality, but, as noted in Chapter 3, *no* person may be "fully rational" so construed.

utilitarian standpoint it would not only be permissible but oblig-atory to treat an incompetent subject, S, in whatever manner would maximize net utility. It is worth emphasizing, though, that this principle does not require maximizing the *utility of the incompetent party*.[58] As noted earlier, the utilitarian outlook allows sacrificing the interests of particular individuals in order to maximize the sum of aggregate utilities. If an act sanctioned by utilitarianism happens to do well by an incompetent party, that result is not dictated by a principle which gives special weight to the interests of the in-competent. Rather, S will be treated respectfully or beneficently only in the event that so doing *happens* to fit in with the strategy of maximizing overall utility. For reasons already stated, and well developed outside this volume, such a viewpoint is difficult to defend.

By comparison, RHPP gives special weight to the interests of the incompetent subject in deciding on his own treatment. It also seems clear that RHPP can take into account, in *some* fashion, the existing preferences and beliefs of the incompetent subject. In this regard consider possible defenses of the decision made in Strunk vs. Strunk.[59] In this 1969 case in Kentucky, a 27-year-old incompetent was permitted to donate a kidney for transplantation to his 28-year-old brother. The incompetent, Jerry, was said to have the IQ of a six-year-old but could communicate well to those with whom he was best acquainted; he was also quite close to his brother, Tommy. In this case the court relied on the view that *if Jerry were competent he would choose to donate the organ*. It was also emphasized that if Jerry were not allowed to donate, he would feel guilty for not having done so. Further, it was agreed that, given Jerry's emo-tional dependence on Tommy, Jerry would be significantly worse off if Tommy were to die soon. Although the court ostensibly fo-cused on what Jerry would choose if he were competent, it is reasonable to believe that the same conclusion about facilitating Jerry's organ donation might be reached by invoking RHPP.[60] It is

---

[58] Or maximally advancing his (or her) interests.

[59] Strunk v. Strunk, 445 SW 2d (45 Kentucky Court of Appeals 1969).

[60] Since Jerry had never been competent, this case seems to be one in which talk of "donning the mantle of the incompetent" appears, but in fact there is no adequate basis for invoking the doctrine of substituted judgment. More likely, a judgment of what was in Jerry's best interest was made and, in the absence of facts about Jerry's values, preferences, and beliefs as a competent, it was simply "postulated" that if he were competent he would so choose. Since Jerry had never been competent it is not clear why one could not postulate an entirely different choice. Perhaps, a desire to rationalize the decision by something like hypothetical consent by the subject drove authorities to postulate it when there was no adequate, objective,

not surprising that in a variety of circumstances RHPP and PISJ may sanction the same sorts of dealings with incompetents. The harder question is: when the principles dictate divergent policies, which principle is the more defensible one?

Consider the following hypothetical case. Until his automobile accident at fifty years of age, Saul Mendelsohn has spent most of his life working for the Jewish Defense League and has deep anti-Nazi convictions and commitments. Due to the accident, Mendelsohn suffers brain damage and now has the mentality of a ten-year-old. He is then cared for by his daughter who can barely make ends meet for herself and Mendelsohn. Weissmann is a forty-year-old neo-Nazi who needs a kidney transplant and is willing to pay handsomely for a kidney (assume, then, that a market in organs exists and contravenes no legal prohibitions). Indeed, Weissmann offers Mendelsohn's daughter 100,000 dollars for one of Mendelsohn's kidneys. Assume further that if the transaction were carried out no one other than Weissmann or Mendelsohn would be treated in a presumptively wrong manner. Incompetent Mendelsohn is somewhat disinclined to donate the kidney. However, we may imagine that the acquisition of the 100,000 dollars would alleviate his rather deprived circumstances and prevent future similar, or worse, deprivations. It is conceivable, foregoing further elaboration, that requiring him to do so or "pressuring" him into agreement would prevent his becoming significantly worse off. In short, RHPP would imply, in this case, the permissibility of requiring Mendelsohn to submit to the organ treatment. By contrast, it is sufficiently clear that PISJ would dictate the impermissibility of such an intervention since, if Mendelsohn were competent—given his outlook when he was a competent person—he would, we can suppose, be firmly opposed to such a choice. Which principle should guide us?

My proposal is, simply, that the Principle of Individualized Sub-stitutive Judgment expresses the more defensible view. As noted earlier, unlike certain other principles, it genuinely seeks to give precedence to the competent subject's *outlook* (using 'outlook' tech-nically to cover cognitive and conative traits, mainly beliefs and

---

evidence for so doing. I have conjectured that something similar lies behind the tendency of some writers to try to justify certain experiments on young children by constructing "what the child would choose if he were able to do so" (e.g., if he were a competent, somewhat altruistic, adult!). On this, see my essay "Experimentation on Children and Proxy Consent," *The Journal of Medicine and Philosophy* 6 (August, 1981), pp. 281–293.

desires) during its most developed phase. Second, it reflects a plausible way of elucidating, in this perplexing context of decision making, the notion of recognizing the dignity of, and extending respect to, *individual persons*. To the extent that an incompetent's interests *qua* person are promoted (or not undermined), he may be respected as a possessor of interests—but not necessarily respected as the *distinct*, unique, person or individual that he is. PISJ seeks to respect the individual by giving important or decisive weight to that individual's most developed conception of the good, as a creature of choice and/or preference and not merely as one possessing interests. Such a stance exhibits a certain continuity with the position defended earlier with regard to our earlier conclusions about permissible paternalism toward competent persons. The thread of continuity consists, in large part, in viewing persons not just as entities that can be better or worse off depending on the machinations of others but as distinct individuals with unique outlooks, as persons wanting to achieve their own aims, and within limits having a right to do so or, at least, a strong claim that their outlook be given powerful weight in decisions significantly affecting their lives. To respect persons is not always to refrain from invasive intervention in their lives. Sometimes it is just that. Often it is to respect their choices and, hence, their preferences, even if we think they are foolish or shortsighted. Sometimes, as in the case of incompetents, we must decide in their behalf. Doing this, I have argued, requires more, and sometimes less, than promoting their interests.[61] A weighty and often overriding consideration in determining permissible treatment of others, in the sorts of contexts with which we have been concerned (roughly: nonpunitive dealings with adults choosing within the domain of acts not wrongful toward others) is what facilitates, or at least does not subvert, their settled conscious aims while they are competent persons. This last tortuous sentence does not recapitulate all the details of the view defended here. Still, it captures much of what is involved in the fundamental idea that, within limits, competent persons have a right to direct their own lives. If so, perhaps it places in sharper relief the important but difficult to elucidate notion of human dig-

[61] The appropriate final decision to be made in the case of Mendelsohn may be more complex than suggested above since nonpaternalistic considerations may support requiring a kidney transplant. The lessening of the burden on his daughter if there is a sale of the kidney may exert a certain pull toward that alternative. That is, her interests have weight; it is not obvious that the burden of caring for Mendelsohn should fall so heavily on his daughter.

nity and the question of what is involved in respecting it.[62] Given the vast diversity of desires, commitments, beliefs, attitudes, potentials, and capacities of the approximately four billion existing members of Homo sapiens, it is not surprising that the ongoing task of learning and saying what it is to respect persons is not as simple or as obvious as "good-hearted" people may be inclined to think. The wildly divergent views that have been and are defended about what is permissible paternalism seem a case in point.

Some further remarks in defense of PISJ against RHPP (or similar "Best Interest Principle") are in order. It is sometimes argued that, in dealing with the formerly competent, since their former values, desires, and beliefs are no longer present they are irrelevant; hence, we should simply do whatever is in their best, current, interests.[63] We have observed that such a divergence in outlook may not be so extreme. More importantly, in assessing the proposal that we disregard the former dominant outlook or conception of the good, we do well to consider our deeply entrenched convictions about analogous cases. Three types of cases come to mind. One is the situation in which we are strongly inclined to believe that competent persons, by (for example) employing a living will, rightfully determine whether they should be extended life-sustaining medical treatment when they become incapacitated or are in a condition of seriously diminished capacity to make rational decisions. Although, in one sense, such persons are "formerly competent" we usually view their prior commitment as decisive. This view seems to conflict in many cases with what RHPP dictates. Another case to consider is that of the use of written wills of competent persons to determine dispensation of their (nonbodily) property once they are deceased. Although not posing a question of how *they* are to be treated, in such cases we think it proper to follow their earlier directive. The key point is that we think that the earlier directive

---

[62] For this reason, the legal provision for "living wills" is desirable, and the failure of states to give such wills legally binding status cannot in general be defended on legitimate paternalistic grounds. The voluntary, knowing, directive of a competent person that he (or she) should not have his (or her) life prolonged by certain means ("ordinary" *or* "extraordinary") after losing competence should be decisive in deciding questions of treatment (barring some genuinely compelling nonpaternalistic ground for acting to the contrary). Thus, state statutes resembling the California Statute are in this respect defensible in a way that those granting final discretion to physicians are not (e.g., the North Carolina Statute). For relevant information, see the instructive brochure distributed by the Society for the Right to Die, *Handbook of Enacted Laws* (New York: Society for the Right to Die, 1981).

[63] John Robertson of the University of Wisconsin Law School has defended this point in a currently unpublished essay.

of a competent person is decisive (if no others are wronged) even though there no longer exists, at the time of dispensing property, a (that) competent person (with values, beliefs, and choices) who deserves our respect. Normally we think that the earlier outlook continues to be morally weighty even though the bearer of that outlook is no longer present. A third case concerns the dispensation of one's body after death. Again, we normally do not view the choices (e.g., burial, cremation, use of the body in medical schools, etc.) of competent persons with respect to such matters as irrelevant. Rather, it is thought dispositive, *ceteris paribus*. We need not, in such cases, indulge ourselves in talk of "harming the dead" if we act contrary to their earlier choices. Respect for living competent persons, and their conception of the good, is thought to require deference to their choices even though, once again, those choices, values, or beliefs are no longer incarnate in a living person. Reflection on these cases serves to undermine the attraction of a major consideration in support of relying on a "do whatever is in their best interest" approach, namely, the conviction held by some that if the person with preferences which reflect his conception of the good no longer exists, then those preferences or choices have no moral weight. For reasons mentioned this seems a dubious assumption.

Our questions here are, nevertheless, difficult ones and I emphasize that the view I have defended is hardly self-evident. Caution is in order, and the recent serious exploration of these matters deserves further reflection, a sorting, as well as a bringing together, of the issues. In cases of the permanently incompetent, RHPP seems the most reasonable principle to determine *permissible* treatment (questions of justice are especially important in determining *obligatory* treatment). In cases in which the epistemological difficulties are not horrendous (I do not think they always are), PISJ seems most defensible. When the epistemological difficulties in applying PISJ are most severe, then by default following RHPP seems the reasonable course.[64] But it is one thing to dismiss in principle the earlier, dominant, outlook and conception of the good of a formerly competent person (the wrong course, I have urged)

---

[64] RHPP is stated somewhat negatively in terms of harm prevention. It can be read so as to take into account benefit promotion (the "harm" of foregone benefits), and it is a variant of what some have called the Best Interest Principle. More needs to be said about what sorts of beings have morally relevant interests. If the irreversibly comatose human lacks morally relevant interests, RHPP, as I construe it, lacks application. Hence, it does not require sustaining the lives of such beings— quite aside from any relevant nonpaternalistic grounds for refusing to do so.

and another to ignore it because we can arrive at no justified belief concerning just what it was, or its application to the treatment decision which needs to be made.

If, as I have argued, we should not regard RHPP as a fully adequate principle for determining the permissibility of paternalistic interventions with formerly competent persons, the question may be raised as to whether it is an adequate guide with respect to permissible paternalistic interventions with those incompetents (though not the irreversibly comatose) who have never, as adults, achieved the capacities requisite for general competence. In short, I can think of no more plausible principle. However, I shall leave that question for others to examine.

7.10 Labeling, Testing, and Competence

With regard to our dealings with incompetents some cautionary remarks are in order—both with regard to the use of 'incompetent' and procedures for determining who is incompetent. As 'incompetent' has been used here, it is a descriptive term, even though society must make some normative judgment about how incompetents may or ought to be treated. Like other terms which suggest failure to "measure up" to some standard which we judge important for some reason, there is the risk that it will become an epithet of abuse; that is the history of similar terms perhaps introduced for neutral, classificatory purposes, for example, idiot, imbecile, moron, retarded—as elementary school children quickly learn. Any public policy directed at special treatment of the incompetent runs a number of risks. One risk which has received increased acknowledgement in the last decade or two is the effect of labeling persons by such terms. Persons publicly so labeled, especially at an early age, can be victims of "self-fulfilling prophecies" in two ways. First, if aware of being so labeled, they may unnecessarily suppress their own hopes and delimit their own aspirations. Second, others may, without good reason, encourage this process of self-denigration and, also, causally contribute to the failure of such persons to reach their potential. Such points are, perhaps, now obvious.

The basis on which reasonable judgments as to incompetence are to be made is a more serious matter. I have distinguished specific incompetence (incompetence with respect to particular tasks) and general incompetence. The latter here has been construed to mean, to oversimplify, the absence of an array of specific capacities sufficiently broad to take care of oneself and live one's

414

life without engendering serious risks of harm to oneself or others. This interpretation helps, I believe, to "demystify" incompetence and steer one away from another view which, historically and now, is both dangerous and ill-supported. The contrary view is that 'mental or psychological competence or incompetence' should be understood to refer to a one-dimensional property which each individual possesses to a greater or lesser degree—more commonly referred to as 'intelligence' or 'intellectual ability'—and measurable on a unilinear scale. Closely associated with this theory-laden assumption is the view that certain sorts of tests accurately succeed in measuring how much of this "stuff" an individual possesses, that is, "IQ tests." One early advocate of these views, Lewis Terman, suggestively characterized the alternatives between viewing general competence (intellectual ability) as we have here and what we may call the *Single Property View* when he queried, "Is intellectual ability a bank account, on which we can draw for any desired purpose, or is it rather a bundle of separate drafts, each drawn for a specific purpose and inconvertible?"[65] The hypotheses that 'intelligence' refers to a single property and that it can be accurately measured are not well confirmed, and the history of defenses of these views is ridden with dubious assumptions and even deliberate falsifications of data. Early twentieth-century biologists and eugenicists assumed that "feeblemindedness" was a property generated by a single gene—much like some of the traits of Mendel's peas, for example, color or size.[66] Recent work in genetics has shown that most isolable physical human traits are polygenic, that is, a byproduct, in part, of the influence of many genes. Further, the fact that people score differently on IQ tests does not provide a reason to accept the assumption that there is some unitary stuff or process, possessed in varying degrees, which is being measured by the tests. Closely associated with the mentioned assumptions is the view that what is in an individual's mental "bank account" is innate, and fixed at birth; hence "intellectual ability" was thought to be unalterable. If we do not assume the existence of undifferentiated Ability and allow for different abilities or capacities, we can concede that an individual's "bare potentials" are significantly affected by genetic factors. But that is a different matter and a far weaker claim than that advanced by advocates of the Single Property Theory. Further, genetic potential cannot be thought of as

[65] As quoted in Stephen Jay Gould's powerful critique of pseudoscience, *The Mismeasure of Man* (New York: W. W. Norton, 1981), p. 175.
[66] Ibid., p. 162.

some unilaterally functioning causal force operating independently of other biological factors and "social" ones, such as diet. The *array* of abilities which affect scores on IQ tests are a byproduct of bare potential, nutrition, variables such as receiving adequate oxygen to the brain at birth, training, motivation, and so on. Current evidence and theory provide no compelling reason to believe that we can filter out the influence of these factors, apart from the alleged bare potential, in order to measure "it." The facts, (1) that cultural factors very much influence scores in IQ tests and (2) that individuals, with training, significantly improve their scores, cast further suspicion on the use of such tests and the speculative assumptions commonly invoked to defend their usage.

The history of these pseudoscientific theories and practices is marked by what Stephen Gould has characterized as "the tenacity of unconscious bias and the surprising malleability of "objective" quantitative data in the interest of a preconceived idea."[67] H. H. Goddard brought the testing technique of Alfred Binet to America and, at Ellis Island in 1913, "tested" a number of immigrants. The results were startling since they "indicated" that 83% of the Jews, 80% of the Hungarians, 79% of the Italians, and 87% of the Russians were feebleminded. By tinkering with the results, Goddard managed to lower these anomalous figures to 40 to 50%. But rather than question the reliability of tests yielding such bizarre results, Goddard conjectured, later, that such immigrants, unlike earlier groups, were simply of lower quality, that is, they were from the bottom of the barrel.[68] In addition to exhibiting an unblinkered faith in the IQ theory, related racist-like biases were not uncommon among eugenicists, biologists, and psychologists of the period. For example, Lewis Terman, the vigorous marketer of the "Stanford-Binet" test in the United States, after testing twenty children in a California orphanage commented:

> They represent the level of intelligence which is very, very common among Spanish-Indian and Mexican families of the Southwest and also among negroes. Their dullness seems to be racial, or at least inherent in the family stocks from which they came.[69]

The tendency to ignore data and to distort it in order to support suspect and self-serving empirical and evaluative conceptions is a

[67] Ibid., p 175.
[68] Ibid., pp. 165–167.
[69] Ibid., p. 190.

persistent one and is by no means dead today. I have briefly reviewed such matters to emphasize the dangers of assuming that persons can be *readily* classified as incompetent, that deficiencies in ability are innate and inevitable, that such deficiencies are linked to membership in sexually, ethnically, or racially identifiable groups, that there exist unproblematic tests for measuring possession of some general property referred to as 'intelligence,' and that, therefore, it is reasonable to proceed with wholesale, invasively-restrictive, policies toward those selected out as generally incompetent. The mistakes and abuses mentioned add support to the view that great caution is in order in identifying, and setting policy, for, incompetents. Such appropriate wariness is compatible with recognition of the sorts of incompetence we have discussed and reasoned attempts to come to grips with the questions their existence poses for us.

Even if the biases and distortions just discussed are avoided, difficult questions remain concerning how, in particular cases, to ascertain whether or not a particular person, such as a patient, is competent to decide about some proposed treatment. We have noted reasons for being wary of IQ tests and of the inference that a person is incompetent to make certain decisions just because he lacks the broad array of capacities to be deemed generally competent. At least for adults, the law tends to presume competence. And in recent decades the presence of mental illness in a subject has not been regarded by the courts as sufficient automatically to qualify a subject as incompetent to decide matters affecting his welfare. The crucial question is often whether a subject is capable of prudently deciding whether to undergo some form of treatment. If he is, we have argued, his consent or dissent is a morally decisive consideration; if he is not so capable, the door is open morally to decide on treatment in a substantially different manner, for example, by appeal to what is in the subject's best interests or by appeal to some version of the "principle of substituted judgment."

Loren Roth, Alan Meisel, and Charles Lidz have usefully described and sorted some of the approaches commonly used to determine whether a subject is competent with respect to deciding about (and consenting or dissenting to) a proposed mode of treatment. Let us briefly examine such proposals.[70] The proposed criteria (in my terminology) are, respectively, (1) whether the subject

[70] Loren Roth, Alan Meisel, and Charles Lidz, "Tests of Competency to Consent to Treatment," *American Journal of Psychiatry* 134, No. 3 (March, 1977), pp. 279–289.

exhibits a preference regarding proposed treatment, (2) whether the prospective *outcome* of the subject's choice is deemed *reasonable*, (3) whether the subject's choice is based on adequate reasons or reasoning, (4) whether the subject exhibits the *ability to understand* factors relevant to deciding, and (5) whether the subject *actually understands* the factors relevant to deciding about treatment.[71] Which, if any, of these criteria is reasonable? I shall not fully examine this important and difficult question but, instead, offer some exploratory remarks. With regard to (1), there is an important question about what counts as "exhibiting a preference." In some cases nonresistance to an announced decision to treat is taken as showing a preference for treatment and, presumably, as indicative of competence to decide (and, presumably, of valid consent). This approach seems dubious in view of the fact that there are many explanations of why a subject might not resist. One is intimidation; another is incompetence. Further, even if the subject overtly states "that is what I want" or "fine," such overt expression is also compatible with lack of competence as we have understood it here. After all, a five-year-old child might say as much (suppose the decision is whether to donate an organ). Depending on how (2) is construed, there is a risk of unjustified paternalistic intervention. In one case mentioned by Roth, Meisel and Lidz, amputation of a leg was ordered against the subject's express prior dissent. If other indices of competence are present, then the mere fact that others deem the subject's choice unreasonable because its "outcome would be unreasonable" (equals conducive to deviation from species-normal functioning?) does not seem sufficient reason to override the patient's choice. The problem I am calling attention to is a type of "Catch-22" application of criterion (2), and the other criteria as well. The danger of undue paternalistic manipulation of the subject arises when a certain "game" is played. It goes like this. If the subject, S, prefers the treatment favored by the professional, employ a nonstringent standard of competence, such as (1) or (4). Result: the subject is deemed competent, he consents, his consent is counted as valid, and treatment may proceed. If S does not prefer the favored treatment, employ a stringent standard of competence, such as (2), or perhaps (5). Result: the subject is deemed incompetent, he dissents but his dissent is counted invalid; others can, therefore, act in the absence of the subject's consent and treatment may proceed. Hence, whether or not the subject

[71] Ibid., pp. 270–282.

consents, the favored treatment is deemed all right. That such a practice can occur, practically, is intolerable. It arises, in part, because of competing criteria for determining competence and the leeway professionals may have to shift from one to another. One conclusion that may be drawn from these considerations is that the criterion for determining competence ought, if at all possible, to be formulated in a manner which is *independent* of the subject's actual preference or choice regarding a proposed mode of treatment. That is, to avoid the wrong of invidious paternalistic manipulation of subjects, any test of competence should be employed, and a conclusion drawn, prior to, or at least independently of, ascertaining the subject's decision regarding treatment.

A similar worry confronts criterion (3), but some distinctions are in order here. An "inadequate reason" may be a false belief (e.g., "laetrile will cure cancer"), but, as noted earlier, the presence of *a* false belief is not sufficient to show incompetence. Much may depend on the nature of the false belief. In someone other than Napoleon, the belief that one is Napoleon is nontrivial evidence of incompetence. In short, some false beliefs are the sorts indicative of a "global" delusional system; others are not. "Inadequate reasons" may or may not show incompetence. The ultimately important issue, again, seems to be whether they are evidence of a lack of capacity to make prudent choice. Similarly, 'inadequate reasoning' may allude to an inability to make appropriate deductive or inductive inferences. But there is a great difference between one who cannot predict the course of the Dow-Jones average and one who infers that since he has never died he never will.

On one natural reading, (4) seems too weak for it seems important that S actually understand the factors relevant to proposed treatment in order to be able to make a prudent decision about it. However, intuitively a subject may have the ability to do so but simply not have access to the relevant information; if so, that is insufficient reason to deem him incompetent. On such reasoning, a person to whom procedures are not explained is incompetent and can be "kept incompetent" by withholding relevant information. Clearly, we must distinguish ability to understand and actual understanding. If a subject is able to understand, there is a presumption of competency. But it does not follow that the decision made by such a competent person will constitute valid consent or dissent (assuming that the latter requires voluntariness and some degree of knowledge or reasonable belief). If, however, our concern is only to ascertain competency, capacity to understand seems sufficient to infer competency on the part of the subject. There are simply two distinct questions. One is whether the subject possesses capacities sufficient for competent choosing. A second is whether an actual choice made by a competent person is sufficiently voluntary and informed for the choice to constitute valid consent or dissent.

These brief and exploratory remarks support, tentatively, several conclusions. Mere exhibition of a preference [criterion (1)] regarding treatment is insufficient for competence. Criteria (2) and (3) especially lend themselves to Catch-22 rationales for invidious paternalistic (or nonpaternalistic) manipulation. Hence, determination of competence should be made independently of the subject's actual choice regarding treatment. Criterion (5), if satisfied, shows that (4) is satisfied; hence, satisfaction of (4) or (5) is sufficient for competence. Determining whether a subject can or does understand factors relevant to deciding on treatment requires, however, some examination of the subject's beliefs and inferential capacities, factors mentioned in (3); reasonable assessment of these, I have observed, can be vitiated by imposing too stringent and arbitrary standards as to what counts as 'adequate reasons' and 'adequate reasoning.' There are, here, both theoretical and practical difficulties, ones which require much more extensive investigation. There is a presumption against employing nonuniform standards to ascertain competence just because how much is at stake on the subject's part will vary from case to case. However, when it comes to deciding whether the choices of a particular competent subject constitute valid consent or dissent, the reasonableness of the subject's choice may have to be decided, in part, by matters idiosyncratic to the subject. Less cryptically and for example, if we "respect" and take as given the belief-system of a Jehovah's Witness (that mixing blood is a grave wrong), then so long as that subject decides voluntarily not to undergo a transfusion and recognizes the possibility of personal death or disability, then her choice must be taken as valid dissent—even if we think certain of her underlying assumptions are false and irrational. We come back here to the slippery difficulty of how to weigh seemingly false or irrational beliefs, a problem discussed in Chapter 3. A guiding thread in the view roughly sketched here is that people can be competent to direct their own lives even if they hold certain false or unreasonable beliefs and that we cannot justifiably treat them in a presumptively wrong manner—"for their own good"—just because of such beliefs. In spite of the recalcitrant difficulties noted, I assume that the problem of determining competence is surmountable. Our primary focus in this chapter, by contrast, has been on the questions: what basic sorts of paternalistic intervention with incompetents are permissible and on what grounds?[72]

[72] To emphasize a point, even if it is clear that a subject S is generally competent, there may be certain domains of choice in which S may be incompetent, and the evidence regarding such may be most difficult to assess. A similar point may be made with regard to the generally incompetent who exhibit pockets of competence. General principles, our central focus, are of crucial importance, but no general principle carries with it a "mechanical decision procedure" for its sensitive, fair, and intelligent application to the nuances of particular cases. Moral casuistry does not settle disputes between competing basic principles, but settling on the latter leaves the task of resolving the epistemological and pragmatic difficulties in particular cases. An essay which instructively warns against oversimplications in these matters (especially concerning overly invasive restrictions on incompetents and public policy questions concerning who should decide for incompetents) is John Moskop's "Competence, Paternalism, and Public Policy for Mentally Retarded People." See also Richard Momeyer's helpful "Medical Decisions Concerning Noncompetent Patients"; both essays are in an issue of *Theoretical Medicine* 4, No. 3 (October, 1983) devoted to Diminished Competence and Paternalism, pp. 291–302 and 275–290, respectively.

EIGHT

OVERVIEW, RESERVATIONS,
AND IMPLICATIONS

> . . . mankind are greater gainers by suffering each other to
> live as seem good to themselves, than by compelling each
> to live as seems good to the rest.   —John Stuart Mill

Our examination of the moral permissibility of paternalistic intervention is largely complete. In this last chapter some basic
themes will be reviewed, some lingering reservations and antici-
pated objections addressed, and a limited effort made to sketch
some of the implications of the theory defended here for some
broader questions.

8.1 Overview

Many of our efforts, both privately and in concert with others
(through government and other social institutions), are aimed at
warding off threats to the welfare-interests of persons, for example,
death, disease, poverty, injury, and alienation. As such we are
often concerned to avoid or prevent the harms associated with bad
luck or natural disasters as well as those promised by the wrongful
acts of moral agents. Achieving a certain modicum of protection
of welfare-interests is generally a prerequisite to achieving whatever other goals we may adopt. Hence, the aim of securing benefits
for, or preventing harm from befalling, others, is attractive and
seems an important advance over situations in which persons ego-
tistically ignore the well-being of others, for example, the situation
of some members of the Ik tribe who, when faced with extreme
scarcity, pulled food from the mouths of their own parents.[1] As
we have observed, the path to intervention with others, to protect
or secure their own good, seems morally smooth and inviting, one

[1] Colin Turnbull, *The Mountain People* (New York: Simon & Schuster, 1972).

less likely to receive moral scrutiny. Paternalistic intervention proceeds from "good intentions," a good and not an ill-will toward others. Paternalistic intervention seems proper and fitting when we consider one most basic and intimate common task, namely, raising and caring for our children.

However, competent persons do not merely have welfare-interests. They are not mere passive experiencers of pleasure and pain. They possess the capacities prudently to direct their own lives. Further, they can reasonably form, assess, and revise their own conception of the good, including both a conception of what is for their own good as well as a conception of morally appropriate or desirable tradeoffs between their own good and that of others. As such they are not mere utility locations or mere recipients of harm or benefit. They are assessors of the desirability of pursuing or foregoing either, in the light of reason as applied to their own unique circumstances, dispositions, and preferences. In this fashion they are (at least) the moral equals of those who contemplate invasive intervention with their choices and acts. Thus, there is a striking asymmetry between (1) those cases in which competent persons consider intervention with their moral equals—and (2) those cases in which competent persons consider intervention with incompetents, for example, newborns, young children, the seriously retarded, or the seriously mentally ill.

I have argued that competent persons have a right to direct their own lives according to their own conception of the good by virtue of their capacities reasonably to form and revise such a conception and pursue it in ways which wrong no others. This limited attribution of a basic autonomy right is, then, not a right to do as one pleases. Nor is it a right possessed by all sentient creatures or even all human beings. In principle, it is a right which could be possessed by beings of other species. In this respect the theory defended here is a part of a theory of respect for (competent) persons. Thus, it rejects the assumption of much (if not all) natural law theory that all humans and only humans have a special moral standing by virtue of membership in our species. To the extent that natural law theory tends to discount individual autonomy and fails to urge respect for competent persons when they fail to pursue their own good or fail to fulfill their "natural function," the Principle of Autonomy-Respecting Paternalism also parts ways. Although persons may not legitimately pursue goals which, on balance, wrong others, they have no determinate fixed ends which they must pursue. Thus, we cannot, in the absence of their valid consent, foist our conception of their good or the good on our moral equals when they choose and act in ways wronging no others. Morally we cannot invasively intervene to see that they achieve "natural ends," "what is for their own good," "their own moral good," or what would "respect humanity in oneself." To do otherwise is to view and treat other competents as our moral inferiors, as welfare receptacles, or as moral-good containers to be filled. For reasons set out earlier in some detail, the special respect owed to competent persons prohibits invasive paternalistic intervention toward them in ways that fail to respect their autonomy. It permits, of course, intervention that respects autonomy, namely, fair and open attempts to dissuade, constraints sanctioned by the prior valid consent of competent persons, least-invasive interventions to ascertain competence, and invasive paternalistic interventions in special cases in which it is reasonable to believe that competents are acting (or omitting acts) in a seriously encumbered manner and that it is highly probable that they would give valid consent to the intervention if the opportunity were available. The guiding general conception behind these derivative principles of permissible and impermissible paternalistic intervention concerns what would respect competent persons as independent centers of will and choice possessing a reasoned conception of the good. This view of the special respect owed to competent persons is, for reasons discussed earlier, at odds with fundamental assumptions embodied in natural law, perfectionist, utilitarian, and at least certain strains in Kant's ethical theory. At the same time the theory defended here has antecedents in, or is compatible with, aspects of natural rights theory, J. S. Mill's conclusions in *On Liberty*, Kant's emphasis on respect for autonomy, and Rawls' defense of the principle that "each person is to have an equal right to the most extensive basic liberty compatible with a similar liberty for others."

I have argued that any adequate ethical theory must base its conception of legitimate duties and/or rights on a view of the sorts of beings who possess rights or are owed duties. Further, given the diverse sorts of beings toward whom moral agents have direct duties, a plausible theory must discriminate among the types of duties owed, or rights possessed, according to the unique sets of empirical capacities exhibited by the type of being in question. A theory urging that we have the same types of duties toward all living creatures, or all living humans, is unacceptable. Especially stringent duties are owed to competent persons by virtue of their capacities to form, revise, and act on a conception of their good.

424

Other duties, sometimes also stringent, are owed to incompetents. In the latter case, however, intentional interveners (moral agents) are not in a symmetrical moral relation since recipients of intervention are not their moral equals; duties to respect others' conception of the good are absent. I have not here, of course, sought to set out a theory of duties toward those lacking rational autonomy (in the sense explicated earlier) except to sketch some prerequisites for a theory of legitimate dealings with incompetent persons (primarily, the formerly competent). On the view defended here traditional ethical theories often go awry by their misconception of the morally unique features of competent persons—in failing to recognize the moral equality that obtains between interveners and subjects, in failing to distinguish or give due weight to the relevant differences between competent persons and beings possessing only welfare-interests or wants unguided by a reasoned conception of the good, or by viewing persons as organisms with determinate fixed ends which can be "read" from their "essential nature" or are laid down by their status as God's creation (to serve only "His ends" and not to adopt their own). Such theories often tend to conclude further that, given their more fundamental assumptions, it is all right, not just to try to dissuade but, invasively to intervene in the absence of valid consent with the reasoned choices of competents—solely to prevent harm to (or promote) welfare-interests, to preserve or enhance moral goodness, promote net aggregate utility, or preserve autonomous capacities on balance (even though doing so may totally subvert important autonomous choices of competents effectively to pursue their own concept of the good in ways wronging no others).

As a result we find such theories countenancing (relying on our prior arguments) illegitimate paternalistic intervention in a wide variety of public and private acts, for example, meddlesome dealings with competent persons in health-care settings and laws unduly restricting certain risky activities. That such acts or practices sometimes prevent harm or promote certain welfare-interests of subjects tends to blind us to the morally significant cost of such policies, namely, the failure to respect competent persons with unique conceptions of the good. In some cases such intervention not only blocks competent persons from acting on cherished moral principles, from pursuing their central life plans, or from avoiding the degradation of being treated as an inferior; it also imposes useless pain, for example, when voluntary euthanasia by competents is disallowed and a miserable existence is perpetuated. In other cases harms are prevented but only at the cost of making a mockery of another's life, as, for example, when a person dying of cancer is deceived against his will and he is allowed foolishly to dream dreams or pursue goals impossible to realize, and others "guiltily" cooperate in preserving the delusion. Harm prevention and benefit promotion are desirable goals, in the absence of other morally relevant considerations to the contrary. On the theory defended here, however, there are often other relevant considerations, ones which legitimately limit what acts we may perform in order to prevent harm or promote good. There are moral bounds on benevolence, and these bounds are, in part, set by what must be done in order to respect our moral equals. Hence, unless principles purporting to identify good-samaritan duties, duties to preserve or promote good, or principles of mercy incorporate the provisos of autonomy-respecting paternalism, they are morally suspect.

It may be that most of the egregious wrongs which persons commit stem not from benevolent impulses but from malevolence, prejudice, or callousness. Nothing I have argued is meant to deny that. Nevertheless, if the argumentation here is sound, such a fact should not blind us to the illegitimate constraints placed on persons "for their own good"—with the invitation to comfortable self-righteousness implicit in such an expression. Given our strong desire to believe that we are "reasonable persons of good will" we, as parents, as friends, as professional care-givers, or as legislators, are less likely to avoid the self-deceptions associated with acts which are seemingly innocent instances of "doing good."

8.2 Lingering Reservations

Having briefly reviewed the general features of the theory defended here and emphasized how it differs from competing theories, I consider some criticisms which will arise. One concerns the frequently expressed doubts regarding any "rights theory," for example, that they are in vogue, individualistic, and encourage contentiousness. A second sort of objection worries that the theory here justifies "too little," that is, that surely a number of substantive restrictions on the behavior of competents are justifiable which are contrary to, or fail to be justified on, the principles defended here; hence, the theory is seriously counterintuitive. A third type of objection concerns a certain inegalitarian dimension of the view proposed. I turn to the series of general reservations about rights theories; some are more serious than others but all have been expressed.

Rights, What is Fashionable, and Contentiousness. One criticism of the recent emphasis on rights, and by implication the right to direct one's own life, is that "rights talk" or "appeals to rights" are fashionable. Perhaps any matter which receives great attention during a given period is, therefore, fashionable. However, not all fashionable matters are *merely* fashionable or in vogue.

The simple fact that appeals to rights are more common in recent decades is not, in itself, a serious objection to claims of rights. One might just as well complain that protests about abuses of blacks were fashionable just prior to, and during, the Civil War in the United States; that protests about Nazi treatment of Jews was "in vogue" during World War II, or that heightened outcries concerning rape in the last decade are "all the rage." The recent tendency to dismiss appeals to rights as "fashionable" is itself fashionable, but nothing of interest follows from such a tendency. More important questions are whether appeals to rights are defensible or whether they are somehow invidious.

Some writers, of course, press the matter further by suggesting that today we not only encounter talk of civil rights and women's rights, but chimpanzee rights or even attributions of rights to redwood trees, snail darters, or ecosystems. The frequent implication is that "rights talk" is somehow arbitrary and misguided. It is surprising, perhaps, that otherwise intelligent persons take such "arguments" seriously. There is no reason to assume that *all* appeals to rights are rationally defensible. Further, there is no reason to assume, in the absence of explicit argument to the contrary, that all attributions of rights stand or fall together. This point is too obvious to deserve elaboration.

Critics of rights stand on somewhat less shaky ground when they suggest that appeals to rights are otiose, that they "have a commercial flavor," or that they are "appropriate only when loving and trusting relationships break down."[2] The suggestion, in part, is that the invocation of rights reflects some non-optimal relation between persons or that invocations of rights may generate distrust, alienation between persons, or a more contentious society. Indeed the recent legal and social emphasis on patient and con-

[2] Compare Robert Young, "Dispensing With Moral Rights," *Political Theory* 6, No. 1 (February, 1978), pp. 63–74.

sumer rights has resulted in an increasing number of actions at law and a heightened wariness on the part of large groups of citizens. Distrust, readiness to take offense, and bleeding those who can pay do seem unfortunate results (if they are such) of the recent emphasis on rights.

However, we do well to ask what follows from such (alleged) facts. In particular, do they provide a reason for denying that people have moral rights? Is it wrong to exercise moral rights? More generally, do such facts cast serious doubt on the possibility of developing a fully adequate theory of moral rights? We must, I believe, answer these questions in the negative.

It may be conceded that charitable persons do not readily complain about infringements of their comparatively unimportant rights. To do otherwise may be to lack a certain virtue. In that way it is reasonable to say that *some* appeals to rights are "otiose." This point, however, cuts very little ice. In general, we ought to distinguish (1) *taking into account* that someone's rights are affected by an act, from (2) *calling attention* to the fact that someone has a right relevant to some decision or act (which may be done by one party on behalf of another), (3) *asserting one's own rights* or complaining of a rights infringement, and (4) *seeking to gain compensation* for an infringement. That it is sometimes unkind or unforgiving to do (3) or (4) may be conceded; that hardly commits one to the view that (3) or (4) should never be done or that there are never good reasons to do (1) or (2).

If it is true that people have moral rights, it is not inevitable that any particular right holder will in an "otiose" manner do (1), (2), (3), or (4). It may be objected that so doing is, however, inevitable in the aggregate—reasonable point. Still, it should not go unnoticed (though it does) that a similar complaint may be made about a theory of *duties*. It is difficult to see why the complaint "you violated your duty to me" cannot be as otiose as a complaint that "you infringed my rights." In either case the complaint may be uncharitable, shrill, contentious, and indicative of an unbecoming readiness to take offense. If so, it is puzzling as to why there is any *specially* contentious dimension to an ethics of rights as opposed to an ethics couched solely in terms of duties. In addition, it is worth noticing that even if some "appeals to rights" are otiose or inappropriate, it is reasonable to think that some *failures* to appeal to rights by right holders are also otiose, for example, when a serious right is infringed and the bearer is too servile to insist on decent treatment. In some cases failure to "stand on" or affirm

428

one's rights is *not* a virtue but a byproduct of a lack of self-respect and, perhaps, in Kantian terms, an acquiescence to letting oneself be used as a mere means.[3] It is surprising that critics of appeals to rights tend to ignore the point.

A further claim made by some critics, as noted earlier, is that appeals to rights are appropriate only when loving relationships break down—or are inappropriate in relations betweens friends or family. This claim is, at worst, false or, at best, misleading. First, some infringements of rights are unintentional, for example, I absentmindedly walk off with a friend's tennis racket. There need be no breakdown in a loving or affectionate relationship here, and it is hardly otiose for the friend to say "that's my racket." Second, persons who trust and care for each other may simply be attempting to *figure out* how to deal fairly with each other. A may say to B "I have a right to decide where we vacation this year; remember, last year we agreed to take turns deciding." Or A may say to B "*you* have a right to decide this year; remember, last year we agreed to take turns deciding." In either case, such an interchange may *express* caring and respect and not be indicative of a breakdown in trust. Again, recognition of rights or "appeals to rights" are not inherently otiose, reflective of failure, or "commercial in flavor." Appeals to rights may occur more often in relations of unequal power and/or relations in which there is limited or little trust, but this is understandable and predictable since in such situations one party is less likely to respect the other's rights. A similar point may be made regarding contexts in which appeals to violation of duties are likely to occur.

In short, the arguments just discussed leave unanswered *all* the important questions which must be answered by any adequate theory of rights. They do not advance the case against rights theories; the replies I have made also leave such questions open, but, if correct, such replies may help subvert the deflection of our attention from the substantive issues.

Another source of objection to the principles, and limitations on intervention, is that if the Theory of Autonomy-Respecting Paternalism were accepted, it would force us to conclude that much governmental activity (for example) cannot be justified—much that, so it seems, is right and proper. To an extent, of course, one upshot of our inquiry is that much such constraint cannot be jus-

---

[3] Similarly, a failure to protest when the rights of *others* are unjustifiably infringed may be otiose in the sense of being cowardly or indifferent.

tified and that, even if we have traditionally thought it acceptable, we should not—for the reasons set forward. If the conclusions are resisted, the arguments need to be joined. However, it is important to recall that our focus has been on the question of when invasive intervention toward competent persons can be justified, and when not, on paternalistic grounds. Thus, little has been proposed with regard to our dealings with incompetent adult persons, and much less with regard to fetuses, children, the comatose, or animals. More importantly, we have frequently noted and sometimes explored nonpaternalistic grounds for intervention (in Chapters 4, 5, and 6). If our inquiry is sound, then in certain cases no invasive intervention can be justified on paternalistic grounds. Thus, the moral burden shifts to determining whether there are legitimate nonpaternalistic grounds for constraint—considerations, roughly, concerning the effects on other parties of constraining a given subject. It is here that comparative judgments are crucial, namely, ones concerning the distribution of benefits and burdens among different parties (parties often with claims of unequal strength). Here, at least, we need a theory of distributive (or redistributive) justice. That is altogether obvious. I would stress the point that nonpaternalistic grounds (including those concerning cases in which some persons wrong others) may justify more extensive constraints than may initially be obvious—at least when a suitably sophisticated and defensible construal of "wrongs to others" is employed. I shall return shortly to this particular point.

Prior to doing so, I wish to suggest that the prohibitory implications of autonomy-respecting paternalism may not be as extensive as they initially seem. Consider the policy of fluoridating public water reservoirs. Such a policy seems (1) intended to benefit people, (2) is an instance of invasive intervention by government (cf. coercive taxation), and (3) is not a policy to which all consent. Thus the policy seems paternalistic. Further, it is no doubt false that all would consent if duly apprised of relevant facts. On the theory here, in short, it *seems* to be a case of unjustified paternalistic intervention—at least with regard to the probable minority who neither actually nor hypothetically consents. Appearances, of course, can be deceptive.

We should note that in so acting a government need not be aiming coercively to benefit the dissenters. Hence, it need not have paternalistic aims. Rather, it may be aiming to provide a good for the vast majority who (let us suppose) do consent. Strictly, nevertheless, there is a presumption that it ought to refrain from imposing a benefit on our dissenters by not taxing them for this purpose and by allowing them an affordable alternative. However, there is a range of not so easily identifiable cases in which it is very costly to provide a good for any one without providing it for all (or for large groups). Further, it would sometimes be very costly to exempt some from sharing the burden of providing it. I leave open which cases are in this category, but one might reflect on government provision of, or assistance in, communications networks, highways, national parks, organ transplants, education, disaster relief on the oceans, and the national defense. The issues are complex but, in brief, it is plausible to believe that certain governmental provisions of benefits, or opportunities for benefits, are required or permitted as a matter of justice, that citizens should bear their fair share of the burden of such provisions, and that insistence on an exemption from doing so is an insistence on being allowed to occupy, unjustly, a free-rider role.

It is sometimes impossible or too costly to develop laws and public policies tailor-made for individual cases.[4] In some cases, policies which seem "paternalistic in result" (although possibly not paternalistic in motivation) are defensible on nonpaternalistic grounds, for example, the just provision of opportunities for social benefits—a provision with which all citizens have a duty to co-operate. In the fluoridation example, dissenting competent citizens are not *compelled* to drink fluoridated water. With regard to the small tax burden falling on them because of the public policy of provision, justice may require their cooperation. In general, such a policy is not necessarily paternalistic toward them; further, it is one defensible on nonpaternalistic grounds. I do not wish to suggest that matters are so simple or that any public policy benefitting some is readily so justifiable. Case by case examination is essential, but the general line of justification noted should not go ignored. It is not necessary to assume that such a policy, if justified, must be justified on paternalistic grounds and that, hence, there are legitimate paternalistic grounds beyond those defended here. Actual consent to public policy by a citizen is *not* in all cases necessary for the policy to be justified. In some cases ideal policy avoids imposing benefits on those who do not consent; in others, considerations of efficient justice may require it. The cases of national

---

[4] 'Too costly' wanders between (1) lack the resources to do and (2) it would be unjust to do.

defense and domestic police protection seem clear examples of the latter.

Earlier, I suggested that an appropriate understanding of the range of acts which wrong others may serve as an adequate ground for certain constraints and perhaps a broader range of constraints than one initially might surmise. Formulating a satisfactory theory of wrongs to others, including a theory of justice, is a complex matter and beyond my purview here. Still, a few remarks are in order. Consider a case similar to the fluoridation example. It has been claimed that keeping household temperatures closer to 65° may be healthier for its occupants than the 72° to 75° range. Could a governmental policy coercively prohibiting the higher temperature level be justified? It is doubtful, for reasons discussed, that such a policy could be justified on paternalistic grounds. Suppose, however, that energy for home-heating is extremely scarce (and not as a result of unjust acts). In such a case justice may require that all share in the burden of conserving energy and no one may be allowed to free ride by using as much as he wishes. We have, in this situation, another instance in which an invasive constraint may in fact benefit those constrained. Still, there may be a nonpaternalistic justification for the implementation of such a policy. Similarly, a policy of required vaccination may benefit those constrained and may be defensible on nonpaternalistic grounds, for example, to protect innocents from an epidemic. To emphasize a point, whether this is so needs to be determined on a case by case basis.

The paradigm of an act wronging another is, perhaps, the case in which one party deliberately causes serious harm to an innocent without the valid consent of the latter and the harm is a rather "direct," foreseen, upshot of the agent's act. Compare ordinary homicide or rape, for example. However, not all acts wronging others seem to embody all these features. Some acts are ones which, unless others act similarly, impose no significant burden on innocents—as in our example of the energy free-rider. Hence, unlike the paradigm case, the wrongful act has a "contributory, cumulative" quality and is not one of the sort which wrongs others in a way virtually independently of what others do (contrast, again, rape). Rather, it is a refusal to cooperate fairly in sharing the burdens of social coordination to achieve a just distribution of goods. In the paradigm case of wrongful harm to others, we tend to find (1) an agent directly, by positive act, causing "direct," (2) significant harm to (3) innocent, (4) unconsenting, and (5) assignable or iden-

432

tifiable persons (or other beings with moral standing). In our energy use example the way in which (5) is satisfied is far less obvious, to say the least, than in a case of rape or child abuse.

A basic point is that the range of wrongs to others is often understood too narrowly; there are numerous wrongs to others aside from those which can readily be seen to conform to the paradigm case—especially with regard to features (1) and (5). Consider a further example. Suppose I were to plant a time bomb underneath the library at my university; it, let us suppose, will go off in a month. This is a clear wrong to others no doubt. Consider a variant case: the bomb will go off in 100 years. Again, this seems a clear wrong to others, but we may not have the slightest evidence as to which persons will be injured. Indeed, the probability of bodily injury is lower. After all, perhaps the library will cease to exist before then; perhaps only a vacant parking lot will be there. Indeed, people who may be injured then may not now exist. Or suppose I randomly leave time bombs of an unreliable sort at various locations which will go off, if at all, at times between 25 and 500 years hence. Again, such an act seems a clear wrong (in the absence of other moral considerations to the contrary). One upshot of these reflections is that when we impose a risk of serious harm, even if the probability of its occurrence is not high, such an act may be wrong, a form of recklessness not unlike that of an automobile driver who drives at 110 mph on a sparsely populated road. Suppose that, in our last bomb example, you know where the bombs have been left. Assuming some duty to be a minimally decent samaritan, would not your refusal to warn anyone normally be wrongful, a type of blameful negligence?

In short, I am proposing that the range of our positive and negative duties toward others supports the recognition of a wider range of acts (or omissions) wrongful to others than is suggested by a myopic focus on paradigm cases. The relevance of such a conclusion, for our purposes here, is just that what initially may appear as meddlesome paternalism, by governments in particular, *may* be defensible on nonpaternalistic grounds when due reflection is given to the range of ways we may wrong others—especially considering duties to cooperate with the burdens of maintaining just institutions (and not free ride), other duties to avoid imposing certain risks of harm on innocents, and "minimal samaritan" duties to prevent or alleviate harms to others. Giving due weight to these matters (1) may make us more cautious in concluding that subject-constraining policies are paternalistically *motivated*, and (2) may make us assess more carefully the question of whether such policies can be defended on *nonpaternalistic grounds*.

These observations go some way, I believe, toward subverting the accusation that if the theory proposed here were accepted, seemingly clear cases of justifiable intervention are wrongful or groundless (hence, better to reject the theory). It remains to be shown, I believe, that the theory posed "proves too little." Further, as emphasized, certain *ostensibly* paternalistically motivated constraints may not be so motivated, and they *may* be defensible on nonpaternalistic grounds, for example, other aspects of justice— whose implications are not always self-evident.

8.3 Persons, Perfectionism, and Protopersons

I have emphasized the importance of the unique capacities of competent persons and urged that the especially stringent duties owed them constrain invasive intervention in their lives. Recall some contrasts we have noted. We may intelligibly speak of what is in the interest of a plant, that is, conducive to its well-being, but its well-being is constituted by what is normal for its species (or its relevant subgroup within that species). Nonhuman animals may have wants as well as biological needs. Unlike plants their good consists not only in satisfaction of biological needs but, in some cases, in want satisfaction. I have supposed that the interests of plants are not in themselves morally relevant, but that the interests of many animals at least are relevant.[5] We have direct duties to certain animals but that is not an issue explored here. Some humans, like many animals, have morally relevant interests, and are owed duties, but lack the capacities to form, revise, and pursue a conception of the good. By contrast, competent persons possess such operative capacities. Human infants and young children, although perhaps appropriately "wired" to develop such operative capacities, have not developed them. Moral agents, as competent persons, in contemplating permissible dealings with plants, animals, children, some of the mentally retarded, and some of the seriously (mentally) ill are contemplating how to treat those who lack a conscious, reasoned, conception of their good or, more in-

[5] This assumption is both more radical than anthropocentrists would accept, and not radical enough for some who would view it as expressing an "elitist sentientism." On these matters, and related debates in environmental ethics, see Donald VanDeVeer and Christine Pierce, eds., *People, Penguins, and Plastic Trees: Basic Issues in Environmental Ethics* (Belmont, Cal.: Wadsworth, 1986).

clusively, the good. The relation is asymmetrical. It is not one between moral equals; the duty to respect moral equals, not to usurp or bypass their judgment, not invasively to disrupt its pursuit (when they wrong no others), does not obtain—even if other important duties are owed or such beings possess certain important rights.

This view of matters may be accused of being *invidiously perfectionist* in that it supposes that those beings which populate our world which are not competent persons are not all regarded as having moral standing, or equal moral standing (in the sense of all possessing the same rights or owed the same duties). In *one* sense the larger theory supposed here does recognize a "moral hierarchy of being." However, none of this, I believe, shows that the broad picture here is unreasonable or invidious. That special duties are owed to competent persons, and not to those who are not, is not a view which appeals in any way to some alleged divine ordering of things (as assumed in certain religious doctrines and in many versions of natural law theory). Further, it does not suppose that race, gender, or membership in a given species—*as such*—is a source of special rights or high moral standing. The view here also does not suppose that successful performances (e.g., creation of meritorious intellectual, scientific, or artistic works) are a basis for some right to rule those who do not exhibit such excellence. Nor is exhibition of moral excellence or virtues (e.g., courage, honesty, humility, graciousness, etc.) assumed to be a necessary condition for attribution of a right to direct one's own life. In these latter respects there is no similarity to the suspect sort of perfectionism associated with Aristotle or Nietzsche. Such views recognize the permissibility of *some* competent persons "lording it over" *other competent persons* without their consent, and, hence, failing to respect them as moral equals. All leading ethical theories recognize some distinctions among living creatures as to which sorts of rights or duties are owed to whom. This sort of "discrimination" (mere differentiation) can be innocuous; the crucial questions are *how* the lines are drawn and *why*. The view defended here is, of course, incompatible with some forms of egalitarianism (a concept too often thought to be less elusive, or to be more straightforward, than it is). It seems altogether obvious that claims such as "everything has the same value" or " all beings deserve equal treatment" (including cancer viruses) are silly. That some intellectually superior creatures (e.g., competent persons) can use other entities (e.g., carrots) as a mere means is hardly controversial. It remains to be shown why

435

the theory set out here should be thought, in any way, *invidiously* inegalitarian or *invidiously* perfectionist.

As noted earlier, since our focus is on competent persons, we have not explored an important topic: permissible paternalistic dealings with children. We have implied that they (or most) are generally incompetent and lack the already specified right to direct their own lives (even if competent to direct parts of their lives). Most children (excepting, say, anencephalic ones) are "wired" to be able to develop into competent persons. Hence, they have a morally weighty interest in not being treated in any ways which would thwart, or seriously impair, their prospective status as competent persons with a right to direct their own lives. Arguably, they have a right, as protocompetents, to be treated accordingly.[6] This right is one important starting point for consideration of just dealings with children. The nest of important questions here is beyond my purview. It may be noted, however, that included in a typical child's interests is an opportunity to be able to develop into a strongly autonomous person, one capable of reflectively and critically formulating and revising a conception of the good. Respecting this interest, and facilitating it, requires among other things not stifling the capacity to reason, not foreclosing access to competing views, and not engendering attitudes and views in a manner which subverts the capacity to reflect critically and impartially on those conceptions of the good which vie for our commitment and allegiance. A long story needs telling here, but one suggestion is that proper dealings with children require promoting the capacity of a child critically to review and revise his (or her) allegiances and ideals as those develop on the path to becoming competent and autonomous.

By contrast, engendering attitudes and convictions by emotional manipulation, subliminal guilt trips, or insulating the child from reasoned competing viewpoints are elements of invidious indoctrination, and subvert the development of strong autonomy. They render the child vulnerable to the attractions of an unexamined,

---

[6] I am much influenced here by Joel Feinberg's "A Child's Right to an Open Future," in *Whose Child*, eds. William Aiken and Hugh LaFollette (Totowa, N.J.: Rowman and Littlefield, 1980), pp. 124–154. A similar point was made by Jeffrey Murphy in "Rights and Borderline Cases," *Arizona Law Review*, 19, No. 1, (1977), pp. 228–241 (the essay is reprinted in his *Retribution, Justice, and Therapy* [Dordrecht, Holland: D. Reidel, 1979], pp. 26–39). Special qualifications need to be added with regard to radically defective newborn children. I defend one view in "Whither Baby Doe?," in Tom Regan, ed., *Matters of Life and Death*, 2nd edn. (New York: Random House, 1986).

heteronomous, life, one in which major goals, ideals, or directions are adopted but not consciously and rationally appraised: as a result "macro-decisions" are seen as settled (e.g., viewpoint regarding religion, ethical and political outlook, vocation, "a man's place," "a woman's place," and so on) and only "micro-decisions" are "seen" as matters up for individual reflection and choice. In some cases the resulting adult, analogous to those dependent on pacemakers, is like a sentient computing machine implanted with a "pathmaker," a being so programmed as to be barred access to certain paths. This possibly gradual shutting down of circuits, paths to truth or to self-realization, may be more or less deliberate, and is often thought perfectly innocuous since it is "for the child's own good." This suspect sort of sculpting of the "child material" has received too little scrutiny, perhaps because of the incremental manner in which it occurs and our too-ready refusal to be critical of cultural stereotypes, "proper parental prerogatives," "legitimate authorities," or "compelling state interests." In brief, these merely sketched points characterize some important avenues for reflection concerning permissible and impermissible paternalism toward children—avenues compatible with the theory defended here, but ones left unexplored. These remarks also hint at matters left incompletely explored in our inquiry: "structural" or institutional sources of the subversion of respect for persons, in particular how certain institutions and culturally dominant views give "social sanction" to invidious dealings with competent persons and others.

8.4 Paternalism and Other Isms

To trace the connections between the theory of paternalism defended here and the leading political philosophies would be an enormous task. In lieu of attempting that, I shall set out, succinctly, some conjectures—without attempting any serious defense of them. I shall suggest some connections regarding the inculcation of comprehensive views and some tensions between the theory here and certain traditional political viewpoints.

At a minimum, a political philosophy or an "ideology" (understood nonpejoratively) is a set of claims—some empirical in nature and some normative. The set of claims will, more or less explicitly, conceptualize the world, its population, and embody more or less explicitly a range of ideals concerning the good society, a good life, and proper dealings between persons, institutions, and nations. Its vision of the good, or the good of persons, may derive from its vision of the good society, or will go in the reverse direction. Its concept of the good of persons will contain both ideals of the morally best life and of a satisfying life. Its assumptions in this regard may be highly general or, alternatively, quite determinate in nature. Even if quite detailed or determinate, it will advocate principles requiring, or allowing, quite invasive means of promoting good lives, or the good society—or it will advocate principles delimiting the things of legitimate intervention. Succinctly, it will allow a wider or a narrow sphere of discretion for individuals, a range of choices in which others and governments may not intervene legitimately. The range of such a sphere will depend on which paternalistic and nonpaternalistic grounds it articulates, supposes to be acceptable, and defends by argument. Some "isms," of course, so barely and vaguely articulate ideals, and proffer argument in their defense, that they hardly merit the labels 'theory' or 'doctrine.' Still, they may be highly influential—surrounded and infused with myth, symbol, tradition, espoused by the committed, embodied in powerful institutions, passed on from parent to child, and viewed as so evidently true as to be questioned only by the disloyal, the eccentric, "foolish young people," or those who would "corrupt the youth."

Important here is the concept of a discretionary sphere and paternalistic grounds for delimiting its range. A number of general points emerge from the theory developed here, ones which should affect one's appraisal of influential moral, political, and religiously based isms. Respect for the right of competent persons to form, revise, and pursue their concept of the good in ways which wrong no others requires deference to their choices—except in the special cases of ascertaining competence or when there is prior valid consent to invasive intervention, or it is *reasonable* to believe that *they, given their basic outlook and values*, would consent to the intervention *when* there is *no* viable opportunity or means to ascertain whether or not they actually and validly consent to such intervention. This principle, defended at length here, partly determines the boundaries of the discretionary sphere. If our account is correct, certain interventions must be deemed immoral and not the proper business of the state, institutions, or of persons in their private relations with others.

We may roughly distinguish four modes of influencing others, means of affecting their behavior—a path tempting for various reasons, one of which, of course, is that we think it for their own good. They are (1) directly shaping their initial and developing preferences (mainly by shaping their beliefs), (2) directly altering their existing preferences and beliefs, (3) blocking certain behavior, for example, by erecting barriers to their performance or using brute force on their bodies, or (4) attaching certain incentives or disincentives to certain types of performances, for example, inducements or threats. As we have noted, use of fair, open, rational discussion is normally not a presumptively wrong means of doing (1) or (2). Use of deception, misdirection, distortion of facts or arguments, and blocking access to information, criticism, or counterargument—are some of the presumptively wrong means of attempting (1) or (2). Similarly there is a presumption against the use of force [as in (3)] and coercive threat [as in (4)]. These latter modes of influence, when employed for paternalistic reasons but violating the Principle of Autonomy-Respecting Paternalism, are unjustified. They fail to give due respect to competent persons.

Some forms of indoctrination of children (though not our central focus), I note, undermine a child's developing capacity rationally to form and critically revise his (or her) conception of the good. Some doctrines not only espouse a conception of the good of persons, or the good society, but sanction the use of wrongful means of inculcating that vision, one aspect of which is subverting the capacities of the young as well as adults critically to appraise it for themselves. To the extent that "true believers" think they have the truth or know the way, they often assume, erroneously, that it is morally innocent to bypass the cognitive capacities of potential recruits, or to use illicit means of engaging such capacities (placing a phony "stamp of reason" on doctrines which, even if reasonable or true, may be "accepted" *but not* for good reasons). Nonbelievers are thought to exhibit "false consciousness," to be victims of this or that ideology (capitalist, religious or irreligious, sexist, racist, fascist—or even feminist) and in need of liberation. That is, it is thought to be "for their own good" to be converted or deprogrammed. I do not wish to deny that there are false ideologies or that there are those who are victims. Indeed, that is one point I am making. But one can be victimized by those who hold true beliefs as well as by those who hold false ones. The prohibitions noted, on the means of seeking to shape or alter the beliefs and preferences of competent persons, apply to all who wish to disseminate what they take to be the Good, or the Right, or the True.[7]

---

[7] I will not explore the point, but those who *really* have been victimized by invidious forms of indoctrination (if the forms are approved, we tend to call them "education") may not be competent in certain respects. An important point here,

Given this point, institutions which use *the illicit means* noted to inculcate a conception of the good, must be condemned—whether they be camouflaged as "re-education," "teaching values," "religious instruction," "parental guidance," or "promoting patriotism." States, churches, parents, and others do not do well when they insulate their citizens, members, or children from competing views and arguments, or subvert the capacities of such persons autonomously and critically to make up their own minds. The means of such subversion are myriad. Censorship in certain contexts, loyalty oaths, card-stacking presentation of doctrines, social ostracism for questioning or dissent, and incarceration in mental institutions are only a few such means. Encouragement of passive, unquestioning trust in, or respect for, "authorities," "parents," "elders," "doctors' orders," "professional" or "expert" opinion, or "duly elected representatives" tends to encourage servility, passive acceptance, and an uncritical appraisal, or no assessment, of views about what is good or right.

Marxist and fascist countries, notably, have been willing to employ illicit means of rectifying and shaping the preferences of their citizens. The Soviet Union, in particular, stands out as a nation whose psychiatrists label dissent as a sign of mental illness, and as a ground for incarceration. Whether this policy is a logical implication of, or only causally related to, the Marxist doctrine of ideology, and false consciousness, I leave open.

What is called "conservatism" in the United States includes what may be labeled (1) *Theoretically Skeptical Conservatism* (TSC), and (2) *Theoretically Bold Conservatism* (TBC). TSC is, roughly, the view that we should rely on the wisdom embodied in traditional practices and be cautious in accepting new and innovative moral

however, is that we should not judge that someone has been so victimized *just* because we think their views false or foolish.

It is of some interest to note that, on one interpretation of Christianity, unless people make certain choices they will endlessly suffer after death (on this view, "death" does not involve permanent cessation of consciousness). However, on the interpretation in question, God does not paternalistically intervene by invasive means, contrary to the consent of persons, to see to it that this horrendous harm is prevented. Is God (if there is one) committed to PARP? If so, why do some religious institutions which accept such a view of "neocidal" prospects employ invidious means to prevent the harm—and, thereby, fail to emulate the divine model, one which seems considerably more laissez-faire in respect of dealings with persons? On another view, God *brings about* eternal suffering for those who do not choose to believe and follow. On this conception, the divine model is that of a coercer who demands compliance or delivers on the promise to make noncompliers worse off; this god indeed seems "no respecter of persons." Perhaps, however, being omnipotent is an exculpatory condition.

and social conceptions. Such a view seems to embody a certain skepticism about ascertaining, or defending, a position about what is the good or the ideal society.[8] Better to stick with "proven ways." This vague, sketchy, timid outlook does not deserve further elaboration here. By contrast, TBC, a more robust and influential outlook, is too complex for full analysis here. Suffice it to say to characterize it (partly), such conservatives (at least the nonlibertarian segment) tend to support a wide sphere of individual discretion in the marketplace but a narrow sphere of discretion in other domains. For example, some views approximate "legal moralism" (that if an act is morally wrong it should be prohibited by law). If the "wrong" is thought to be a violation of a "duty to one's self" (cf. dueling, gambling, or prostitution), the view in question may rely on what I have called the Appeal to Moral-Good Preservation, and have previously argued to be indefensible. To the extent that such conservatism seeks to repress for paternalistic reasons consenting acts between competent persons, which wrong no others—it must be judged unacceptable. When conservatives defend such repression on nonpaternalistic grounds (e.g., certain such sexual acts seriously offend others) and yet reject the persuasiveness of at least equally strong nonpaternalistic reasons for regulating private gun ownership (for example), there is a serious question of whether such bold conservatism is a byproduct of any articulate, logically consistent, set of moral principles.[9] At its worst, it may be "moralizing

[8] The skeptical, sometimes subjectivist, attitude toward moral claims results in curious anomalies. For example, Milton Friedman has claimed that " 'fairness' is not an objectively determined concept," like 'needs' it is "in the eye of the beholder." Yet on the next page, he argues that a certain policy "is not fair." One wonders why Friedman goes to such great length in defending his vision of how society ought to be structured, or why government ought not to intervene in certain matters, if he takes himself only to be expressing what is "in his own eye." If that is all there is to it, why should we care—any more than we might care about his preferences in music, carpeting, or bowties? See Milton Friedman, *Freedom to Choose* (New York: Avon Books, 1980) pp. 126–127.

[9] His espoused claims favoring tolerance aside, Jerry Falwell, leader of the Moral Majority in the United States, maintains "This is still a nation of majority rule. Although we do and should protect minority rights, we should not do so in a way that renders the majority impotent." See "The Maligned Moral Majority," *Newsweek* (September 21, 1981). If one held the bizarre view that people have a right to do whatever they wish, one could not gainsay Falwell's remark. The worry is that it seems to maintain that we should not ever protect minority rights if it renders the majority impotent. This principle would seem to put no right beyond the grasp of majorities. If protection of a right to form one's own religious opinion precludes a majority's desire to undermine the process, then the majority is rendered impotent *in that respect*. That is precisely the *point* of constitutional protection of certain rights, i.e., to render majorities impotent with respect to certain matters. If competent persons, as I have argued, have a right to direct their own lives in ways which

without a moral theory." To be fair, these points are not conclusive, and they only criticize one identifiable tendency of conservative thought. The apparent lack of coherence, however, goes some way toward explaining why "neoconservative" libertarians emerged from the bosom of traditional conservative thought—seeking, I take it, a purer, principled, commitment to respect for individual liberty and autonomy.

As with other "isms," a clear, systematic, canonical articulation of liberalism is not anywhere engraved in stone. One must be cautious in appraising the tradition. In general, liberalism has been committed to greater protection of individual liberties outside the marketplace and has assigned greater weight to certain egalitarian ideals—than has conservatism. Succinctly, the view defended here is more congenial to a traditional liberal stance. It may be of greater interest to identify a few points of divergence. The relevant class of beings possessing a right to direct their own lives (as elaborated earlier) is the class of competent persons. Liberals, at least in practice, and perhaps in doctrine (if we regard Locke, Rousseau, and Kant as important progenitors of liberalism), have tended to take both a too narrow and a too broad view of the class of bearers of this right. Perhaps it is fair to judge that some defenders of "equal rights" for children and for incompetents are expressing a liberal view or tendency in maintaining that whatever basic moral rights are possessed by any humans are possessed by all. This view, for reasons elaborated, deserves rejection. Indeed it can lead to, or support, *undue non-intervention* (of a paternalistic sort) with children and certain incompetents. Conversely, traditional liberalism has also tended to exclude certain competent persons from having a recognized equal right to direct their own lives, namely, female persons—mainly due to the view that they are quasicompetent at best, and their husbands or fathers will choose for them whatever is for their own good.[10] This assumption conjoined to an assump-

---

wrong no others, then constitutional limitations on majority preferences should protect it. But the Moral Majority (or anyone else) cannot have it both ways; if the religious have a right to form and pursue their own conception of the good in ways wronging no others, then so do others—be they homosexual or heterosexual, God-fearing or God-denying, capitalist or socialist, American or Russian. This lesson has not been learned by many moralistic conservatives (and others). Too many, as John Stuart Mill notes, still subscribe to the logic of persecutors: that repression is all right because *we* are right and *they* are wrong. The "Moral Majority's" talk of being "pro-morality" (are others "anti-morality"?) only encourages this way of thinking; this ploy is, I judge, itself morally perverse.

[10] That many of the great philosophers assigned some diminished moral place to women is well documented by Susan Miller Okin, *Women in Western Political Thought* (Princeton: Princeton University Press, 1979).

tion that invasive paternalistic intervention is all right if it promotes the good (see Chapter 3) seems to have caused liberals (and virtually everyone else!) to avoid moral scrutiny of the ancient and venerated (the "wisdom" of our forefathers) practice of subordinating about half the human species—in all the direct and subtle ways "mankind" has been so clever to devise.

The otherwise commendable aim of liberalism to help the helpless, to render aid to the victimized, to remedy the plight of the poor or starving has sometimes led to a kind of aggressive benevolence and related disregard for the conception of the good possessed by those whom liberals have been bent on helping. In the United States in the last half-century, liberal doctrine has tended to support urban renewal projects, rent control, minimum wage laws domestically—and technology development and agricultural reform in "less developed" countries. These are complex matters, but in some cases the effects seem laudable and, in other cases, not so. In some instances the main benefits, arguably, have gone to those other than the intended beneficiaries. Considerations of cost-effectiveness have often received too little attention. In some instances, and of greater interest here, the outlook, values, and preferences of the proposed beneficiaries have been overlooked in the effort to "meet the needs" of the needy. Most striking are cases in which neighborhoods, cultural traditions, ethnic allegiances, and community bonds are eroded or destroyed by urban renewal projects—or similar effects are generated by projects which thrust peoples of other nations into an urban, capital-intensive, high technology mode of living in ways contrary to their own choices and commitments. Unscrutinized assumptions about "primitive people" and "noblesse oblige" tend to pave the way for conceptualizing poor people as incompetents and, thus, for believing that the more invasive modes of paternalistic intervention permissible with incompetents or children are justifiable in dealings with the third or fourth world. As we noted, however, it is myopic to focus only on what is "for the good" of competent persons; in doing so we are likely to fail to respect their conception of the good, one which may diverge considerably from our own.

This point is related to the fact that various theories of justice tend to assume that justice requires equality of some sort, especially equality (or limits on inequality) in the distribution of certain outcomes, often the more easily measured ones (e.g., income). Liberal, and other, doctrines in their insistences on equality (or limited inequality) of measurable outcomes as a matter of justice, are liable

443

to overlook the fact that those whose incomes (or wealth) are low (or contribute to the actual distribution's deviation from some ideal matrix of distribution) in fact may be pursuing their own conception of the good. This point is not new, and I do not wish to overemphasize it, but some prefer, for example, to seek their own good in the form of leisure time as opposed to the more popular package of little leisure and a higher income. Others pursue their conception of the good by foregoing income or wealth in order to help others, for example, Mother Theresa. Such instances of "falling below the poverty line" are not obviously moral tragedies. The point is modest, but any full blown political philosophy seeking to work out the appropriate tradeoffs between "liberty and equality" must be sensitive to the fact that efforts to achieve a just distribution of goods, wherein 'goods' gets explicated ultimately by some theory of the good (hedonic, species-normal functioning, and so on), may thwart the efforts of persons to pursue their conception of the good in ways wronging no others. In some cases normally bad events or states such as premature death, ill health, poverty, or vulnerability to risks can be mitigated or prevented only at the cost of invasive intervention in the lives of competent persons, against their will, who are pursuing their plan of life in ways wronging no others. This point is not an invitation to ignore egregious involuntary inequalities, genuine tragedies, or important injustices. It suggests only that certain more or less egalitarian, outcome-fixated, conceptions of the just society, be they liberal, socialist, or other "ism," may well fail to respect persons by treating them as good containers in some preferred, allegedly "just" distributional matrix.[11]

8.5 The Concept of the Tragic

If we respect the reasoned, autonomous, choices of competent persons, in a variety of cases they will "come to a bad end." That is, they will die prematurely, suffer pain, impairment, or deprivation. In one sense they will suffer harm and certain goods will be foregone. As noted before, this in itself is no cause for celebration, and is commonly an occasion for a certain sadness. Here we tend to speak of disaster, downfall, and tragic results. One thesis I have defended is that certain means of preventing harms are

[11] Without here endorsing much in Nozick's theory, I find his criticism of patterned principles of justice an important one; see Robert Nozick, *Anarchy, State, and Utopia* (New York: Basic Books, 1974), Chapter 7.

impermissible. Certain invasive paternalistic interventions are prohibited, and prohibited because we must respect competent persons who possess a right to direct their own lives in ways which
wrong no others. If we simply focus on *outcomes* (such as premature
death, or injury) we are tempted to think that such outcomes ought
to be prevented. But given the view defended here, there is a sense
in which "tragedies are permissible." Indeed, there is a sense in
which some tragedies (outcome-wise) are not "purely tragic" but,
in one respect, abstractly desirable. A hard saying it seems, but let
us reflect.

Often the possibility of achieving normal goods is intimately
associated with the possibility of being subjected to normal harms
or "evils." In some cases the relation is logical and in some cases
contingent; I shall try not to sort out which is which. To care for
others is to risk pain and loss. To commit oneself to a way of life
or to a cause is to risk disillusionment or defeat. Sexual intercourse
carries the potential for pleasure and expression of affection but
also for unwanted pregnancy or a stillborn child. For a zygote not
to develop is to avoid pain; for it to develop into a living person
is to be subject to pain. Substantially to avoid risks is to avoid much
that is meaningful and satisfying. To be insulated from loss is to
be insulated from gain. Not all bad ends, of course, are inevitable,
and some are rather purely tragic. Although some harms are avoidable, the substantial risking of some is part of an active, choice-
filled, autonomous, and reflective life. Hence, some instances of
pain, impairment, and premature death are a byproduct of the
expression and pursuit of important values and deeply held commitments. The costs of avoiding some harms or the serious risk of
such can be enormous; it can involve the surrender of what makes
one's life meaningful, indeed, foregoing the pursuit of one's fundamental conception of the good. Pain, impairment, or premature
death as a result of a person's reasoned pursuit of the good is, I
suggest, not tragic in the way that it is in other circumstances. To
be struck by lightning or to become afflicted by Alzheimer's disease
is one thing. To lay down one's life (to save a friend), to die or to
become diseased (in an effort to cure diseases) are in themselves
serious harms, indeed avoidable harms; still, to pursue one's conception of the good may require assumption of serious risks. The
occurrence of certain great and avoidable harms can be a byproduct
of persons living meaningful lives, lives which command our respect and perhaps our admiration. Some avoidable harms are not
in vain—either from the standpoint of the subject or from that of

445

others. Thus, it is myopic to focus solely on harmful outcomes, or their prevention, apart from the web of beliefs, choices, and aims of those persons who risk them. Competent persons, as our moral equals, deserve our respect. Invasive intervention in their lives, when they wrong no others, treats them, in the absence of their valid consent, as inferiors, disregarding or discounting their conception of the good, for the sake of preventing harmful outcomes or promoting beneficial ones. If my argument here is sound, the unrestricted pursuit of these latter aims is misguided. Neither is there an unqualified duty to do so nor is it unqualifiedly permissible to do so. With competent persons we must respect their right to choose and not just "right choices."

Given the specially stringent duty to respect competent persons and not invasively to intervene in their efforts to pursue their conception of the good, those who are allowed to be arbiters of their own lives will act in more or less rational ways, with more or less true beliefs, will choose more or less risky endeavors, and may or may not pursue a concept of the good with which we agree or approve. If we respect them, however, and if they have reasonably propitious circumstances, they will play their own hand, pursue the good as they see it, and will enjoy the dignity of being our moral equals—as others, like us, who are centers of will, purpose, originators of ultimate ends, and responsible for their choices. They will not be degraded as inferiors, treated without respect, or viewed only as utility locations—to be deceived, forced, coercively threatened, or otherwise wrongfully manipulated so as to prevent their "coming to a bad end."[12] Rather, they will be afforded the opportunity to live their own unique lives as comparatively free and reasoned beings. From this standpoint, not all "bad ends" in such lives should be viewed as "senseless tragedies." A gravestone of a competent person which truly read "he never took a (nontrivial) risk" or "he was never allowed to take a (nontrivial) risk" is a more sure mark of a tragic life. We need not encourage or permit all forms of risk taking, or rejoice over the purely tragic, when we recognize and respect the prerogative of competent persons to direct their own lives along, more or less, risky paths some of which inevitably (from an aggregative viewpoint) will lead to a bad end. As I have maintained, it is one permissible mode of intervention fairly, openly, and reasonably to attempt to dissuade competent

---

[12] Or to maximize the total or average utility of the population which is subject to utility or disutility.

persons to avoid paths which we believe will be purely tragic. When we genuinely *care* for competent persons, we will do *more* than *respect* them, but our caring for them provides no moral license for doing *less* than that which respects them as our moral equals.

John Stuart Mill claimed that ". . . mankind are greater gainers by suffering each other to live as seem good to themselves, than by compelling each to live as seems good to the rest." On the view defended here, two qualifications to Mill's remark are in order. One, which Mill surely would accept, is that there often are legitimate nonpaternalistic grounds for not letting "each other to live as seem good to themselves." The other is that, in the absence of such grounds, we may intervene paternalistically in the lives of other competent persons only in ways which respect their conception of the good *even if* mankind are not greater gainers. This point is not the whole of an adequate ethical theory concerning our proper dealings with competent persons; but it is, I believe, an essential part.

INDEX

449

Library of Congress Cataloging-in-Publication Data

VanDeVeer, Donald, 1939-
Paternalistic intervention.

(Studies in moral, political, and legal philosophy)
Includes index.
1. Respect for persons.   2. Paternalism—Moral and ethical
aspects.   I. Title.   II. Series.
BJ1533.R42V36   1986   170   85-43320
ISBN 0-691-07306-6 (alk. paper)